A History of Germany
From the Medieval Empire to the Present

A History of Germany
From the Medieval Empire to
the Present

DIETHER RAFF

Translated from the German by
BRUCE LITTLE

BERG
Oxford / Hamburg / New York
Distributed exclusively in the US and Canada by
St. Martin's Press New York

English edition first published in 1988 by
Berg Publishers Limited
77 Morrell Avenue, Oxford OX4 1NQ, UK
175 Fifth Avenue/Room 400, New York, NY 10010, USA
Nordalbingerweg 14 2000 Hamburg 61, FRG
Originally published as *Deutsche Geschichte vom alten Reich zur Zweiten Republik* © Max Hueber Verlag 1985
English edition © Berg Publishers 1988

British Library Cataloguing in Publication Data

Raff, Diether
  A History of Germany: from the Medieval Empire
  to the Present.
  1. German 1750–1987
  I. Title II. Deutsche Geschlichte vom
  alten Reich zur Zweiten Republik. *English*
  943
  ISBN 0–85496–235–2
  ISBN 0–85496–236–0 Pbk

Library of Congress Cataloging-in-Publication Data

Raff, Diether
  [Deutsche Geschichte. English]
  A History of Germany : from the Medieval Empire to the Present
Diether Raff : translated by Bruce Little.
    p. cm.
  Translation of: *Deutsche Geschichte . . .*
  Bibliography
  Index.
  ISBN 0–85496–235–2
      0–85496–236–0 (pbk.):
  1. Germany—History—1780–1900. 2. Germany—History—20th century. I.
  Title.
  DD175.R3313 1988
  943—dc 19   88–86–13

Printed in Great Britain by Billings of Worcester

61,890

Contents

Preface

The impetus to write this book came from the First Foreign Language University of Peking, where in the spring and summer of 1981 I had the pleasure of lecturing and holding seminars in modern and contemporary history for the university's students and for German teachers from nine universities in the People's Republic of China. The lively interest that I encountered among academic colleagues and students alike encouraged me to respond to the requests of the Peking University and endeavour to set forth recent German history in all its diversity.

I have attempted to place the facts in the context of the entire sweep of German history, to evaluate them with the requisite prudence, and finally to capture something of the atmosphere of each era by working original sources into the text. The introductory survey of German history till the late eighteenth century is intended to highlight the political and social factors that are essential to the comprehension of modern German history. For this reason, emphasis is placed on the division of the German people into various tribes, German dualism, developments in the German states that promoted a highly diversified cultural life, the cultivation of particularist traditions and, at the same time, the craving for national power and glory. Events beyond the frontiers of Germany which impinged directly on her development are included to the extent that this is necessary for an adequate understanding of modern and contemporary German history.

To delineate this history in some detail struck me as all the more important in that only an analysis which highlights the competing political forces of the nineteenth and twentieth centuries will be able to explain the deep cæsura in German history brought about by the catastrophe of the two world wars. The Third Reich and the frightful crimes committed by the National Socialists demand an explanation while at the same time they trivialise by their very enormity any attempt to come to terms with them. By the same token, they tend to overshadow the development of democracy in Germany. I therefore felt that an attempt should be made to promote an understanding of German history and to inform interested readers about the life of the German people in their European context.

In planning this book I have allowed myself to be guided by more than twenty years of experience in lecturing and giving seminars to foreign students both at the Studienkolleg of the University of Heidelberg and at the Institute for German as a Foreign Language of the Department of Modern Languages and Literatures. Accordingly, a chronological overview is included at the beginning of each chapter and an annotated name index appears at the back of the book to help students find their bearings. This book is not intended to replace the various textbooks in use. My aim has been to relate the various historical eras to one another in a comprehensible language and in such a way that a sense of flow is maintained, the reader does not weary of his task and interest is fostered in further, more detailed studies. The Select Bibliography is intended to further this aim and contains a selection of the most important works reflecting the present stage of research.

As Richard von Weizsäcker has said, our history 'never belonged to us alone' and was always interrelated with that of our neighbours. I am well aware of the enormous challenge posed by any attempt to present, in a single volume, all German history in an informative, understandable way, tracing both the causes of events and international influences. I owe a debt of gratitude to Berg Publishers who have assumed part of that challenge by undertaking a translation into English in response to the strong interest among English-speakers in a work of this kind.

I am deeply indebted as well to Dr Eike Wolgast, Professor of Modern History at the Ruprecht-Karls-Universität in Heidelberg. Professor Wolgast took an interest in the writing of the entire volume, pointed out numerous valuable references and always encouraged me in my task. Thanks are due as well both to my friend and predecessor Dr Günther Rögler and to Dr Oda von Gal for all their help. I owe in conclusion a special debt to my wife, without whose understanding and collaboration this volume could never have been completed.

Diether Raff

Translator's Note

There is a coherence to German history and an interconnectedness evident in the progression from the medieval *Deutsches Reich* presided over by a *Reichstag* and a *Kaiser* to the nineteenth century *Deustscher Bund* with its institutions of the *Bundestag* and *Bundesrat*, to Bismarck's *Deutsches Reich* governed by a *Reichstag*, a *Reichskanzler* and a *Kaiser*, to the *Weimarer Republik* governed by a *Reichstag*, a *Reichskanzler* and a *Reichspräsident*, to Hitler's *Drittes Reich* and finally to the *Bundesrepublik Deutschland* with its major federal institutions of the *Bundestag*, *Bundesrat*, *Bundeskanzler* and *Bundespräsident*.

Unfortunately, this continuity is largely lost in the usual English terminology of a medieval German Empire presided over by an Imperial Diet and an emperor giving way to the nineteenth-century German Confederation with its Diet and Federal Council, to Bismarck's German Empire governed by a *Reichstag*, a *Kaiser* and a chancellor, to Hitler's Third Reich and finally to the Federal Republic of Germany with its major institutions of the *Bundestag*, *Bundesrat*, federal chancellor and federal president.

Wanting neither to ignore the established English terminology nor sacrifice the continuity so evident in the German terms, I opted to employ both, in the belief that the reader would soon realise that the German Empire and the *Reich*, the German Confederation and the *Deutsche Bund* etc., were simply English and German terms for the same thing.

Another problem I faced was whether to translate *Land* as state or province. State has the inherent disadvantage of the confusion it sows over whether the entire country is meant (*Staat*) or the subdivisions within a federal system. In view of all the current discussion in Germany about the national state in the nineteenth century and again after 1945, I opted to reduce the confusion by referring to *Länder* as provinces rather than states. As a Canadian I found this notice both natural and clear; I can only hope that those more influenced by American or Australian usage find it equally so.

Bruce Little
Toronto, July 1988

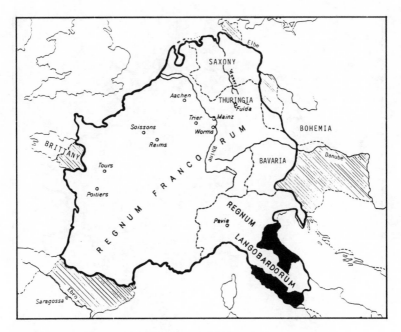

Map 1   The Empire of Charlemagne (768 – 814)

Map 2 The Mediaeval German Empire under the
Hohenstaufen dynasty (1138 – 1254)

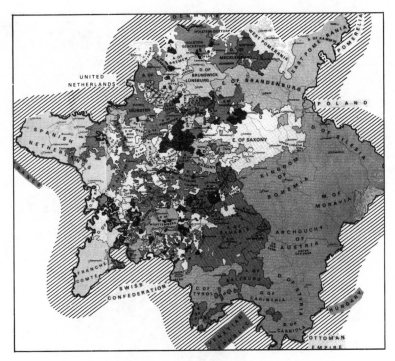

Map 3 Germany in 1648

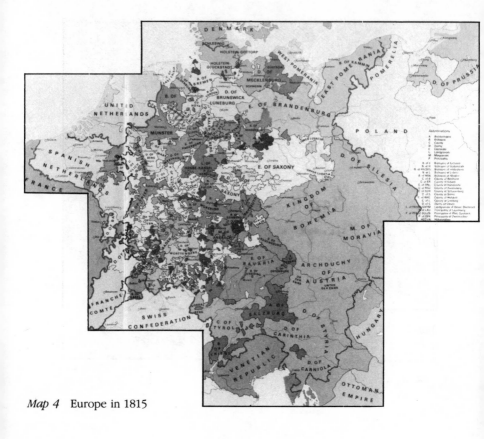

Map 4 Europe in 1815

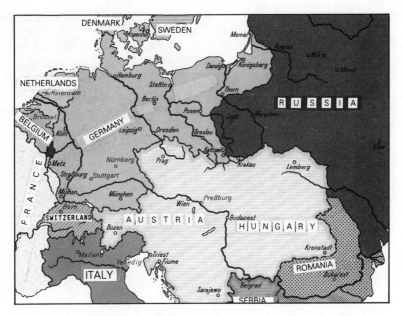

Map 5 Europe on the eve of the First World War

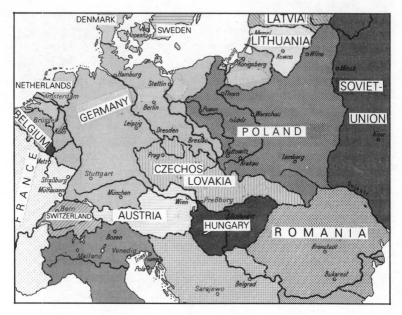

Map 6   Europe after the First World War

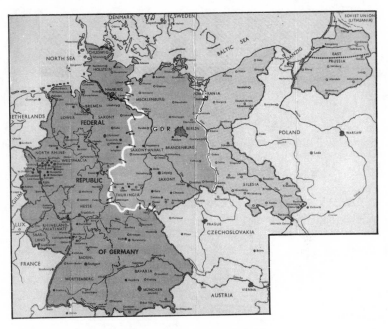

Map 7   Germany after the Second World War

1

Introduction

It is impossible to comprehend the present without a knowledge of the past.

(Leopold von Ranke, 'On the Similarity and Difference between History and Politics')

History endeavours to set down man's past 'so that its memory might never be lost'.[1] Mankind is therefore the subject of history within the context of social, political, cultural, legal and economic life.

Time and space provide the coordinates by which we describe this life. Also necessary, however, are subjective criteria which spring from individual experience and affect each individual's point of view.

By 'history' we mean not only events themselves, but knowledge of these events and the way in which they are recounted. The historian accordingly draws a distinction between real events and the telling of these events. The tension created by this distinction helps to explain the active nature of historical research and the heavy responsibility the historian bears when setting forth the results of his or her research. The following episode related by Sir Walter Raleigh illustrates the problem that can arise when real events are described. Condemned to death in 1603 by James I on account of treason and awaiting execution in the Tower of London, Raleigh resolved to pass the time by writing a history of the world. A quarrel, which he could not help observing, erupted one day between two guards on the floor below. Shortly thereafter a friend, who had also been witness to the quarrel, visited Raleigh and reported what he had seen. Raleigh was struck by the strong discrepancies in their observations but most of all by the differences

1

in the ways in which the two of them related these events. In a fit of depression he scanned his manuscript of world history and observed that truth could only be served by burning it for if he was incapable of reporting, objectively and accurately, an event which he had just witnessed in person, how could he possibly claim to write a true history of the world? This anecdote helps to clarify the limitations on any historian's claim to write the 'truth'.

Historians and philosophers alike have endeavoured to define the precise content and scope of 'history'. According to Georg Friedrich Hegel, history comprises both the subjective and objective aspect of events, 'both the *historiam rerum gestarum* (the recounting of events) and the *res gesta* (the events per se)'.[2] Karl Marx wrote that 'the history of all previous human society is the history of class warfare',[3] Jakob and Wilhelm Grimm saw it as the 'essence of all that has happened in the world'[4] and Johan Huizinga understood it as 'the intellectual form which a culture gives to its past'.[5] What interests the historian, according to Karl Georg Faber, is all past human action and suffering;[6] Golo Mann wrote that the historian's interest focuses on what is new: 'how it emerges from the past and was shaped there, but after emerging has a definite character all its own; how it mingles with world conditions which could not be foreseen, with the fortuitous appearance of various personalities and with the accomplishments of their individual wills.'[7] These definitions round one another off and define as 'history' events which expose fundamental relationships in society and reveal the changing conditions under which people live. Change moreover seems to be the essence of history, which never comes to an abrupt end.[8]

It is the task of historians to attempt to comprehend this process of change. They endeavour to explain 'how it really was',[9] to reconstruct the past and in so doing to foster an historical view of the world.

To do their work historians rely on vestiges of the past—sources which, when logically sorted, yield the requisite information. Among these sources historians distinguish between physical artefacts, abstract artefacts and traditions.[10] Physical artefacts are buildings, tools and the products of all manner of skill and occupation. Abstract artefacts include institutions which survive or are remembered, the legal and constitutional systems, language and manners and morals. Written artefacts comprise all that was produced in a certain period for public or private consumption. Traditions refer to sources which were created for the purpose of historical instruction: tales and legends, annals and memoirs.

The historian selects those sources that are pertinent to his or her interests and specialization, attempts to piece together a version of the facts, and adds a critical explanation—always adhering to Ernst Troeltsch's dictum that every age needs to be 'judged by its own spirit and ideals no matter how puzzling'.[11] The more the historian assesses the past according to the criteria of the present, the more subjective is the resulting account. Only those able to detach themselves sufficiently from the present in order to enter the spirit of the past will understand 'how it really was'. Only then will they live up to their tasks as historians.

In order to schematise the past historians commonly divide it into large, cohesive units. Since the seventeenth century world history has generally been split into pre-recorded history, ancient history, medieval history and modern history. Since 1945 the term 'contemporary history' has been added. A schematic rendering of Western history looks as follows:

Pre-recorded history
The very earliest history of mankind and of particular peoples from their origins to the beginnings of recorded history.

Ancient history: 3000 BC to AD c. 500
The period from the first historical records (cuneiform script and hieroglyphics before 3000 BC, Chinese script *c.* 2000 BC and the Greek alphabet *c.* 900 BC) to the end of Greco-Roman antiquity.

Medieval history: the fifth to the fifteenth centuries
The middle ages, or *medium aevum*: the period between antiquity and the modern age; a term coined by the humanists to describe the era between the collapse of the ancient world and its rebirth (renaissance), that is the period from AD 476 to the end of the fifteenth century.

Modern history: sixteenth to eighteenth centuries
The period from approximately 1500 to the French Revolution.

Recent history: nineteenth to twentieth centuries
The period between the French Revolution and the end of the First or Second World War.

Contemporary history: after 1945
The most recent past.

Each of the suggested cæsuras marks a point at which something new appeared, a new impetus was felt or an event changed the course of history. These events are called epochal, and the ensuing period that is conditioned by their impact is called an era or epoch.[12] It should be remembered, though, that these historical segments are always somewhat arbitrary, especially since they are contingent on the intellectual and cultural outlook of those who draw them up.

These cæsuras do, however, reflect the essential content of an historical view of events.

The same considerations hold true for what are thought to be the essential features of each epoch. To select particular facts from an infinite number of possibilities, to examine them as 'the key to the understanding of the present',[13] and to portray them in full awareness of one's obligation to the historical truth is the inescapable duty of the historian with a sincere interest in the events of the past and the present. The question of why the past and the present have evolved in one direction and not in another fills the historian with the same sense of salutary discomfort as queries about his or her own hopes and fears. It satisfies the curiosity and helps to foster a feeling of identification with the political and social environment. This feeling becomes especially intense when, in the lives of peoples and countries, catastrophes rock the very foundations of communal existence. The survivors surmount their terror and search for the reasons for their catastrophe, trusting that detailed and painstaking research will reveal the multiple causes of events and help to provide an answer to the burning questions of humanity. They endeavour to salvage from their experience, from the essence of history, solutions to the problems of the present and of the life to come.

2

A Survey of German History to the Late Eighteenth Century

The Ancient Germans

c.2000 BC:	The Beginning of the Bronze Age; development of a farming culture in central and northern Europe; emergence of distinct Indo-Germanic peoples
1800 BC:	The Germanic settlement of southern Scandinavia, Jutland and the North German Lowland
c.600 BC:	The Germanic tribes push as far southward as the Lower Rhine and the Vistula
c.50 BC:	The Germans expand in the area between the North Sea and the Central Uplands as far as the *limes*, the Roman frontier wall
50 BC–AD 400:	The Roman Empire consolidates itself on the left bank of the Rhine, in the provinces of Upper and Lower Germania and in the area between the Rhine, Danube and Neckar rivers
Post AD 200:	The emergence of the West Germanic tribes: the Alemans, Franks and Saxons
AD 250:	The Alemans and Franks press across the Rhine and the *limes*
c.AD 375:	The beginning of the great migrations.
AD 400:	The Romans withdraw from ancient Britain and Germany
476 BC:	The collapse of the Roman Empire in the West

Germany lies at the heart of Europe, between the Alps and the Baltic and North Sea. This geographic location, in the midst of many neighbours, combined with numerous rivers flowing from south to north and from east to west, fostered the development of

5

international trade routes, stimulated commercial and intellectual activity and helped shape the political face of Germany. Deprived of natural boundaries to the east and west, its inhabitants struggled to create a national state, with which they have had the chance to identify over only short periods of time.

A moderate climate, a well-defined topography (Alps, Central Uplands, and Lowlands) and broad stretches of fertile soil combined to form an attractive land in which life could flourish. Germany became home in the third century BC to a large proportion of the tribes speaking Indo-Germanic—tribes from which the ancient Germans, Celts, Italics and Greeks eventually derived.

The Germanic element of these tribes settled first in southern Scandinavia, Jutland and the North German Lowland between the Weser and the Oder. Around 600 BC Germanic tribes moved farther south, reaching the Lower Rhine in the west and the Vistula in the east. The northern tribes slowly extended their tracts in Denmark, Norway and Sweden. To the east, the Goths and Burgundians seized lands in the area of the Vistula; to the west, the Germanic tribes had driven the Celts into the Black Forest by the middle of the first century AD and settled the district between the North Sea and the Central Uplands. In the first century AD the Romans conquered the region west of the Rhine and south of the Danube and defended it by constructing a border wall, the *limes*. The Germanic tribes beyond this wall in the zone between the Rhine, the Elbe and the *limes* and the tribes in the region of the Oder and Vistula, were almost totally untouched by Roman rule.

In AD 375 the Huns burst into the kingdom of the Goths. The East Germanic tribes—Vandals, Burgundians and Goths—thereupon fled their traditional homes and moved westward and southward while Slavic peoples advanced into formerly Germanic areas, reaching the Elbe and Saale in places. Meanwhile the West Germanic tribes succeeded in strengthening their hold over the region between the North Sea and the Alps. Six large tribal groups lived here: the Frisians along the North Sea coast and on the off-shore islands; the Saxons between the North Sea and the Central Uplands, the Elbe and the Central Ems; the Franks along the Main and the Central and Lower Rhine; the Thuringians along the Saale; the Alemans on the Upper Danube, the Neckar and the Upper Rhine; and the Bavarians on the approaches to the Alps and the northern slopes.

The Kingdom of the Franks

481–511: Clovis (Chlodwig), King of the Franks
486: The Frankish Kingdom founded by Clovis
496: The conversion of the Franks to Christianity
768–814: Charlemagne (see Map 1)
800: The coronation of Charlemagne
843: The Treaty of Verdun: Charlemagne's empire partitioned into three kingdoms, the West and East Frankish kingdoms and a middle kingdom of Burgundy, Provence and Italy.
911: The end of Carolingian rule in the East Frankish Kingdom, and the full separation of the Germanic tribes from the Frankish Empire

After approximately AD 250, the Franks began to extend their traditional domain between the Lower Rhine and northern Gaul. In approximately 500 BC King Clovis of the Merovingian family succeeded in unifying the Franks, defeating the last Roman governor of Gaul, subduing the Alemans and uniting most of the remaining West Germanic tribes in one mighty empire. Reckoned according to present frontiers, this realm incorporated almost all of France, the Rhineland and the region between the Alps and the Central German Uplands. The conciliation of the Germanic peoples and the conquered Roman population was facilitated by Clovis's conversion to Christianity. In the end the Christian faith spread the length and breadth of the Frankish Empire, firmly implanting itself here at the very time when Islam was conquering the formerly Christian provinces of the Roman Empire in Africa and Asia, advancing as far westward as Spain and menacing the West.

The most important of the Frankish kings was Charlemagne (Karl der Grosse), whom the pope crowned Roman Emperor in the year 800. He ruled over the temporal vestiges of the old Roman Empire and was considered chief protector of the Christian faith.

Charlemagne's empire comprised almost all of present-day France and Italy and the region of central Europe bordered by the Eider, Elbe, Saale, Danube and Drava rivers. When this enormous empire was partitioned among Charlemagne's successors, its unity crumbled and each segment went its own way. Within a century the mighty Carolingian Empire had split into the West Frankish Kingdom, the East Frankish Kingdom and the kingdoms of Burgundy, Provence and Italy. The face of Europe had changed forever and the stage was set for the states of the medieval and modern eras to emerge.

In order to consolidate his hold on power, Charlemagne divided the empire into counties, each ruled by a *Gaugraf*, or count. The count dispensed justice in the name of the king, administered the crown lands, collected taxes and led his troops in battle. The marches created along the borders of Charlemagne's empire protected it against external assault. These margraviates were far more extensive than the counties, and the ruling margraves more independent of the central authority than the counts, even issuing arrière-bans on their own authority when danger loomed. Charlemagne's emissaries roamed the counties, reviewing the administration of justice and tax receipts, listening to grievances and promulgating imperial laws. They represented the central authority and ensured the unity of the empire. The economy rested of course on the barter system.

The bureaucracy of Roman times was replaced by a nobility sworn to serve the king. In return for this service the nobles were endowed with a fief and certain sovereign rights. As the king's vassals they were required to swear an oath of allegiance to him and to provide military support. The emergence of this feudal system was encouraged by the existence of a class of nobles in all the Germanic peoples.

The power and influence of the feudal lords was magnified after fiefdoms became hereditary in the ninth century. The might of these local potentates *vis-à-vis* the central authority increased further when Charlemagne's weak successors partitioned the empire and proved unable to defend it against invasions of Arabs, Normans, Slavs and Magyars.

The imperial borders were especially endangered in Austria as a consequence of its geographic location. In their peril, the Saxons, Lorrains, Franks, Swabians and Bavarians looked to their military leaders, the dukes. In view of the weakness of the central authority these dukes sought to augment and consolidate their own power and to ensure peace and security throughout their own domains.

When the last of the Carolingian monarchs died in 911 the dukes of the eastern kingdom elected one of their own as the new king. This election of the Frankish Duke Conrad marks the split of the Eastern Kingdom from the Frankish Empire as a whole and the beginning of German history.

The German Empire: The Foremost Power in the Western World

911–18:   Conrad I
919–1024: The Saxon emperors

919–36:   Henry I
936–73:   Otto I, the Great
973–83:   Otto II
983–1002: Otto III
1002–24:   Henry II

In the western half of the Frankish Empire the common folk spoke largely Old French, while in the eastern half they spoke *deutsch*, or German. The word *deutsch* stems from the Old High German *diot* meaning 'people' and was originally an erudite term denoting the dialect spoken by the ancient tribes of the east. After the middle of the tenth century this term was customarily applied as well to the land where these people lived: the 'Deutsches Reich', or German Empire. The English word 'German' is derived from the Latin 'Germanus'.

Conrad I proved unable to establish an effective central authority over the other dukes, but he did succeed in persuading them to elect as his successor the Saxon Duke Henry. Henry and his son Otto subsequently met with far greater success in their attempts to consolidate the young German Empire in the teeth of both internal and external threats. Like Charlemagne before him, Otto I relied on the unifying effect of the Christian Church and on the bishops who were loyal to him. In another step which recalls Charlemagne Otto betook himself to Rome to be crowned emperor, 162 years after Charlemagne's journey in the year 800. Otto then reigned over the eastern portion of Charlemagne's empire and over most of Italy as the temporal leader of Christianity and defender of the western church. The restoration of the Roman Empire in the year 800 had raised high hopes for an era of peace, and this second restoration had a similar effect. Fated to endure for eight centuries, this empire later came to be known as the 'Holy Roman Empire of the German Nation'.

Otto I and his Saxon successors did their utmost to expand the might of the empire at the cost of the tribal dukes. No longer content with mere *pro forma* recognition of supreme royal authority, Otto and his successors demanded actual submission. Efforts to reinforce the authority of the king resulted in the transformation of hereditary tribal duchies into non-hereditary duchies and the accordance of temporal powers to ecclesiastics. Bishops and abbots were endowed with such sovereign rights as supreme judicial authority and the power to raise taxes and armies as well as a royal prerogative to establish market towns, collect custom duties and issue coinage. The prelates, their estates and the cities on them were freed from the suzerainty of the dukes or counts. Endowments of land from the royal domains and the transfer of whole counties to ecclesiastical rule placed the German Reich on an entirely new footing.

The empire was no longer administered by feudal lords, eager to expand their hereditary fiefs and maximise their autonomy, but by bishops bereft of legal heirs. Since the right to invest bishops fell to the king, the danger that royal sovereignty would continue to erode seemed dispelled for the moment. By ensuring that each successive regent of the church domains received his lands and sovereign rights directly from the king, the Saxon rulers made loyal supporters of the bishops and offset the might of the dukes. The secular lords of course had exploited the hereditary system of land tenure in order to gain a large degree of independence from the crown and were always endeavouring to extend their autonomy. The prelates had the further advantage of literacy over most of the secular lords and were therefore better administrators. The taut organisation of the church from one end of the empire to the other helped them in this task.

So long as the king remained competent and able to assert himself against the church, this system proved successful and the unity of the *Reich* was assured. This unity was to be imperilled, however, when the secular overlord, the king, clashed with the spiritual overlord, the pope. Compelled to choose between their oath of fealty to the emperor and the obedience they owed to the pope, the ecclesiastical princes would opt for the spiritual benefits which the church alone could provide.

For the present, however, the empire continued to expand in glory and might under its Salian and Frankish rulers. After the death of Henry II, the last of the Saxon line of emperors, the dukes selected the Frankish duke Conrad, a great-grandson of Otto I, as the new monarch. In contrast to his predecessors, Conrad II viewed his election not as a gift bestowed indirectly by God but as a public mandate requiring that he subordinate his own interests to those of the empire. Conrad II was similar to his predecessors, however, in that he too was forced to contend with dukes eager to increase their autonomy.

In order to bolster the central authority, Conrad awarded the duchies of Bavaria and Swabia to his son, Henry, thus extending the royal domain and strengthening those subvassals whose fiefs were rendered hereditary. In return, this lower level of the gentry entered his service, fulfilling military and administrative functions. Even under Conrad's Saxon successors, literate imperial ministers from this class continued to be the mainstays of the empire.

Not content merely to rein in the dukes, Conrad set out to

re-establish the primacy of the empire over the pope and the Church. When he subsequently inherited Romanic Burgundy and incorporated it into the *Reich*, German rule was secured in Italy and the borders of the empire were thrust far to the west.

The Empire and the Papacy Struggle for Ascendancy in Europe

1024–52:	The Salian emperors
1024–39:	Conrad II
1033:	The acquisition of Burgundy
1039–56:	Henry III
1056–06:	Henry IV and the growing conflict over lay investiture
1054:	Partition of the church into eastern and western entities
1059:	Nicholas II's decree governing papal elections
1077:	Henry IV goes to Canossa
1095–1291:	The Crusades
1106–25:	Henry V
1122:	Concordat of Worms—temporary settlement of the quarrel over investiture
1125–1350:	German colonisation of the east
1138–1254:	The Hohenstaufen dynasty (see Map 2)
1138–52:	Conrad III
1152–90:	Frederick Barbarossa
1190–7:	Henry VI
1215–50:	Frederick II
1220:	Alliance of Frederick II with the prelate-princes
1232:	Statute of Princely Prerogatives
1250–4:	Conrad IV
1254:	Rhenish League
1358:	Hanseatic League
1376:	Swabian–Rhenish League

Under Conrad's successors, the ascendancy of the emperor was jeopardised by an ecclesiastical reform movement, the original function of which was to combat the mounting secular influence within the monasteries. This reform movement spread quickly through France, Italy and Germany and soon turned its attention to other offences within the church. Celibacy was re-emphasised and simony was discouraged. In addition, lay investiture came under attack, even though the emperor's right to appoint bishops had become an essential pillar of imperial authority. If he lost this prerogative, he would lose control not only of the church but of much of the empire since the bishops also functioned as territorial lords.

Henry III died young, and under his six-year-old son and further successors, royal authority crumbled. As the power of the empire shrank, the papacy sought to escape its authority by promulgating a new decree which transferred the right to select the pope to a College of Cardinals, thus nullifying the influence of the emperor over the selection.

The church reformers aimed as well to abolish all secular authority over ecclesiastical officials and to establish the precedence of the spiritual realm (*sacerdotium*) over the secular realm (*imperium*). The church, not the empire, was to be the principal supranational authority preordained to lead the concert of nations. In 1075 the pope forbade lay investiture throughout the church and instituted stiff sanctions for any transgressions. This ignited a quarrel that endured almost fifty years before the issue was settled by the Concordat of Worms. Henceforth church functions, imperial domains and the secular justice system were disentangled. The German bishops were elected by ecclesiastics in the presence of the emperor, then invested by him with temporal fiefs and rights and finally consecrated by the church. Thus the bishops retained their worldly possessions and remained secular lords nominally in the service of the monarch, though he lacked all power to control their appointment.

Thus the Ottonic system expired. The emperor's dominion over the church was extinguished and the pope became the recognised overlord of the universal church. The German church was deprived of its unique position and became merely another branch of supranational Christianity as in England or France. At the same time, royal authority within the empire was gravely damaged.

The temporal and spiritual princes of Germany exploited the quarrel between the pope and the emperor to advance their own interests, to expand their possessions and prerogatives at royal expense and to reinstitute an elective monarchy. This increase in the power of the princes had fateful historical consequences, as a dualism of king and princes emerged and eventually the princes established unchallenged dominion. The resultant particularism was to remain the bane of Germany for many centuries to come.

The Hohenstaufen dynasty succeeded temporarily in strengthening the position of the German emperor through the acquisition of new royal domains, close attention to the courts and strict enforcement of the *Landfriede*, or land peace. The Hohenstaufens restored the glory and power of the empire and presided over a flowering of Gothic architecture, *Minnesang* and the cultural life of the knighthood. After the decline of the Hohenstaufen line, the supranational empire collapsed and was supplanted by a new order of states. The last of the Hohenstaufen kings in Germany was the gifted Frederick II, a multilingual patron of science and the arts. In order to win the support of the lay and prelate princes in his attempts to subordinate the papacy and restore the might of his empire, Frederick transferred to them many royal powers and prerogatives. However, the princes only exploited these powers to further entrench the new order in their domains.

In the remainder of Europe national states were arising, reflecting the spirit of their native peoples. In Germany the title of 'emperor' had accrued to the king many centuries earlier as a sign of particular distinction; but by now his power had eroded away and he became merely the most prestigious of innumerable territorial princes. Thus the popes triumphed over the German emperors, leaving Rome as the sole supranational power in the Christian world. Thereafter it was the spiritual authority of the church which held the West together and shaped its intellectual life.

In its campaign to liberate itself from temporal authorities, the church had to contend not only with the emperor but also with the rising tide of Islam. The Arabs conquered part of Spain, while the Seljuq Turks subdued Palestine in 1070, threatened Byzantium and appeared ready to invade Europe from the south-east. In 1095 Pope Urban II summoned Christendom to a great crusade against Islam. From across Europe, emperors, kings, princes, knights, clerics, townsmen and peasants threw themselves into seven different crusades over a span of two centuries in order 'to do God's will' and liberate the Holy Land.

After meeting with initial success the crusaders began to flounder. Discord and disunity spread, religious zeal dwindled and high spiritual aims degenerated into secular, political squabbling; meanwhile, the Moslem foe united under capable leadership. In the end, Christendom failed to achieve its aims in the Holy Land, but succeeded in liberating Spain, southern Italy and the islands of the western Mediterranean from Islamic rule.

In their wake the crusades left an enduring cultural and economic imprint on the face of Europe. The sophisticated Islamic countries enriched the West with their knowledge of geography, science and philosophy. Arabic numbers were adopted; Western poetry, architecture and handicrafts were stimulated; and Eastern goods flowed onto the markets of the West. Meanwhile, economic life was transformed by the transition from a barter economy to a money economy, and the merchants in the great cities of Italy, France and Germany gained power and prestige. The leadership which the papacy provided during the crusades magnified the supranational authority of the church, and the popes reigned supreme till the early fourteenth century.

In Germany itself, a movement to colonise the east and south-east of Europe sprang up early in the twelfth century and persisted for over 200 years. This German colonisation substantially altered the political, economic and social life of Germany and Eastern Europe alike.

A series of battles east of the Elbe led to the subjugation of a number of Slavic tribes. The Duke of Poland was compelled to recognise the sovereignty of the German emperor, and the rule of German princes over the Slavic peoples of the Havel and Prignitz was extended. Christian missionary work was initiated in these regions. In continuation of Otto's eastern policies, new bishoprics were established and the Polish church was subordinated to the archbishopric of Magdeburg, which did much to organise the eastern missions. To the south-east, the Hohenstaufen emperor Frederick Barbarossa divided what is now Austria from Bavaria in 1156, establishing it as an independent duchy, and added Styria and Carinthia to the German Empire.

This period of primarily violent conquest was followed after approximately 1210 by an era of peaceful settlement of Mecklenburg, east Brandenburg, Pomerania, Silesia, northern Moravia and Poland. All social classes of the old *Reich*—princes, knights, bishops, monks, peasants and townsmen—participated in the colonisation of these areas and of Prussia, which had been vanquished by the Order of Teutonic Knights between 1226 and 1283. The brunt of eastern colonisation was borne however by peasants invited by Slavic princes to settle in their domains primarily in order to cultivate marshlands or other wastelands. These peasants stemmed for the most part from Flanders and Holland but hailed as well from central Franconia, Thuringia and upper Saxony. They hoped to find both better economic conditions in the thinly settled colonies and a degree of personal freedom unknown in their overpopulated homelands where the legal status of the peasantry was often very poor. In the east the peasants received hereditary, freely alienable leasehold estates which had moderate rents and were unencumbered by further obligations to the overlord. Cistercian and Premonstratensian monks proselytised the Slavs from newly erected churches and monasteries, while young German knights defended the region in return for larger fiefs.

Once Slavic peasants adopted Christianity, they were granted the same personal freedoms and economic rights as the German settlers. The long-term inhabitants and the newcomers soon intermingled, and the German language gradually began to prevail in the lands between the Elbe and the Oder. The region which had been settled by Germanic peoples before the Great Migrations was thus recovered and absorbed into Christian, Western culture.

The movement to colonise the east spawned not only new villages but a string of cities such as Lübeck, Rostock, Danzig, Thorn, Marienburg and Riga. These emerging municipalities organised themselves similarly to cities in the western part of the *Reich*. Many of these western cities—Xanten, Cologne, Bonn, Coblenz, Mainz, Worms, Trier, Strasbourg, Augsburg, Regensburg, Passau, Vienna, Zurich and Basle for instance—had arisen on the ruins of Roman border towns destroyed by Germanic tribes during the Great Migrations; others such as Fulda, Hildesheim, Paderborn, Bremen, Bamberg and Würzburg developed around cloisters, churches and bishops' palaces; still others, such as Aachen, Frankfurt am Main, Goslar, Brunswick and Lüneburg, were spawned by nearby imperial palaces and castles.

From the ninth century, more and more strongholds were erected in order to defend the river crossings and passes through which international commerce flowed. Many of these strongholds were subsequently awarded a market charter by the emperor. Armed with such a charter (which after the eleventh century could also be granted by liege lords and lords of the manor), the emerging cities began to escape the orbit of their overlord and to govern themselves according to their own law. The city council and the chief magistrate whom it elected were responsible for defence, the collection of taxes and fees, the protection of crafts and trade, the administration of justice and the care of the sick and the poor. City dwellers were not considered vassals and could freely dispose of their own property. Anyone could win personal freedom by dwelling in a town for a year and a day without raising objection.

The autonomy of the towns fostered the emergence of a new middle class comprising both urban merchants and artisans. The nobility played a role as well in the development and administration of the cities, especially in Italy, Switzerland and the northern and southern sections of the empire. The first city councils were populated by nobles in cooperation with merchants. After 1300 some artisans grew wealthier, organised themselves into guilds and participated as well in town government. The free imperial cities in particular became great centres of wealth thanks to their crafts, commerce and art. The cities gradually expanded by purchasing the surrounding land and, as they waxed in power and autonomy, inevitably came into conflict with territorial princes eager to extend their authority.

In the absence of a strong central government the German cities joined leagues to protect their commercial interests and to defend themselves against attack by the surrounding princes. In this way the city leagues of Switzerland, Swabia and the Rhineland were born in the mid-fourteenth century. While the Swiss League repulsed the claims of the Habsburgs, the Swabian League and Rhenish League were not so successful. Loyal only to their commercial interests, they eventually succumbed to the military superiority of the princes.

Only the international Hanseatic League had economic bonds strong enough to withstand all outside attack over an extended period of time. The league was originally formed in the thirteenth century by the seafaring cities rimming the Baltic. It reached its zenith in the fourteenth century under the leadership of Lübeck, when it included almost 150 cities from Cologne to Cracow, from Nijmegen to Visby and Reval (Tallinn) as well as trading stations from London to Stockholm and from Bruges to Novgorod on Lake Ilmen. The Hanse afforded its members protection in their far-flung trading depots; mediated disputes between member cities; regulated strand and staple rights; established a system of coinage and weights; and attempted to impede the foreign trade of nonmembers while preserving and augmenting its own privileges and monopolies, if necessary through the use of military force. The downfall of the Hanse was sealed towards the end of the fourteenth century when the Nordic states consolidated themselves and world commerce was sent off in a new direction by the Age of Discovery. As the bulk of world trade shifted from the Baltic and North Sea to the Atlantic, the Hanseatic League declined. Weakened commercially and still lacking the protection of a strong central authority, the Hanseatic cities—like all other municipalities in the empire— grew vulnerable to the aspirations of territorial princes lurking in the surrounding countryside.

The End of the Universal Empire and the Development of Independent German States

1254–74:	The Interregnum
after 1257:	Prince-electors gain the right to elect the emperor
1278–91:	Rudolf von Habsburg
1309–78:	The Babylonian captivity of the pope in Avignon
1338:	The electors' union of Rense establishes the validity of imperial elections lacking papal approval

1347–78:	Charles IV
1356:	The Golden Bull legally establishes the right of the prince-electors to select the emperor
1400–68:	Johann Gutenberg
1493–1519:	Maximilian I
1492:	Christopher Columbus discovers America
1495:	The Diet of Worms—Maximilian I reforms the empire
1498:	A sea route to the East Indies is discovered by Vasco da Gama
1519–22:	Ferdinand Magellan first circumnavigates the world

The territorial princes vastly increased their autonomy during the quarrel over investiture and under the reign of Frederick II, the last of the Hohenstaufens. The princes succeeded in appropriating unto themselves the most meaningful of the royal prerogatives: the administration of justice and the right to approve fortifications, grant market charters, issue coinage and impose duties. Thus the feudal lords strengthened their hold over their fiefs at the expense of the emperor and the townsfolk. Around the middle of the thirteenth century they attempted virtually to eliminate the power of the central government by selecting as German kings foreign princes who were too weak to assert their new authority. The outcome was anarchy as the state slithered into lawlessness and private warfare.

This 'frightful time without an emperor'[1] came to an end in 1273 with the election of Count Rudolf von Habsburg. The right to select the king had been transferred in the interim to an electoral college composed of three ecclesiastical princes (the archbishops of Mainz, Cologne and Trier) and four secular princes (the King of Bohemia, the Duke of Saxony, the Margrave of Brandenburg and the Count Palatine of the Rhine). The Archbishop of Mainz presided over the meetings. At first this procedure lacked any legal basis, but was eventually authorised by Emperor Charles IV in the Golden Bull of 1356. Moreover, the electoral principalities were declared henceforward indivisible and inheritable according to the rule of primogeniture. The sovereign rights of the prince-electors were also vested, and royal judicial authority over their territories virtually eliminated. This gave the princes well-nigh absolute authority over their own principalities.

The various principalities thus acquired full legal status, obviating the possibility that a strong central authority would once more impose itself. Before the Golden Bull was promulgated, the prince-electors even defended their right to select the emperor against no less a claimant than the pope. The king they elected would no longer require the approval of the Holy See and would be endowed directly upon election with the title and powers of the Roman emperor. With that the pope's traditional right to crown the emperor lost all legal significance.

Henceforth a German emperor would have to rely on the wealth and might of his own house if he hoped to command respect and occupy a powerful position within the empire. The king-emperor's authority over nobles and commoners alike would be rooted in the power of his own family and not in the institutions of the empire, which could no longer confer might and prestige.

The empire of the late middle ages was therefore composed of an emperor struggling to extend the power of his own house, and electors clinging tenaciously to their vested privileges. Legions of prelate princes—archbishops, bishops and abbots—also wielded temporal power. Dukes governed to the east in Silesia, Pomerania and Mecklenburg, though the old tribal duchies in the west had largely shrivelled into counties. Scattered among these larger domains lay over fifty 'free imperial cities' and a host of politically autonomous pigmy states, puny in population but great in 'imperial lords and *Stifter*'. Together they comprised the *Reichsstände*, the various states of the empire. Since the early fifteenth century they had shared with their king and emperor in governing the realm and claimed a voice in the *Reichstag*, or Imperial Diet.

This Imperial Diet evolved from court sessions which the emperor convened in various locations and at irregular intervals during the high middle ages. By the late middle ages the *Reichstag* could be convoked by the princes who were now full-fledged members and no longer liege lords participating at the emperor's pleasure. After 1495 the members of the *Reichstag* met in three separate colleges—the College of Electors, the College of Princes and the College of Cities—before gathering to arrive at a joint decision. When a resolution was adopted by a majority vote, it was ratified by the emperor and became an imperial decree. The *Reichstag* was charged with discussing and deciding upon imperial taxes, laws, wars and military expeditions.

The finances of the empire were in a shambles and local wars never ceased, lord against lord, town against prince and knight against town. All aspired not merely to defend their lands and privileges but to augment them. Towards the end of the fifteenth century efforts were undertaken to reform the empire and create a more stable environment. The *Reichskammergericht*, a national court of justice independent of the emperor, was instituted and perpetual land peace proclaimed. States and individuals alike were forbidden to engage in private warfare. Early in the sixteenth century the *Reichstag* divided the empire into ten districts, each ruled by a prince. Attempts to establish a sound financial footing by introducing a head tax, the 'common penny', failed, as did efforts to establish an executive council to oversee imperial policies.

The imperial estates with their array of local interests proved powerful enough to block all reforms of no direct and immediate benefit to them. As the countries of Western Europe grew more capable of united political action, Germany lost her pre-eminent position in Europe and remained till the second half of the nineteenth century a loose collection of individual states which took note of European affairs only in so far as they impinged directly on their own interests.

The decline of the Reich into a welter of principalities meant that one of the pillars of the medieval world—the temporal power of the German king and emperor of the Holy Roman Empire—had disintegrated. As a result, the second pillar of medieval society—the church and the papacy—was deprived of the reinforcement it sorely needed in order to maintain its sway over the West.

The popes had striven to establish the ascendancy of the Church over the empire, and their victory brought the church to the zenith of its spiritual and temporal power at the culmination of the high middle ages. By the second half of the thirteenth century, however, the church was discovering that it did not possess enough material power to maintain its spell over the national states that emerged after the disintegration of the empire. Instead of tending to its religious duties, the church became consumed with worldly pursuits while its spiritual foundations, on which its authority was based, crumbled away.

As the papacy was drawn more deeply into temporal affairs in the second half of the thirteenth century, it was forced to rely increasingly on the power of the King of France. Eventually the French king compelled the popes to move their seat to Avignon. Here, in 'Babylonian captivity', the pontiffs lived in lavish splendour between 1305 and 1377. In order to augment their earthly wealth, the popes devised schemes to put spiritual power to monetary advantage. Vacant church offices were often filled in return for large bribes. In this way hundreds of German bishoprics and benefices were awarded to Italian prelates who transferred the income to their homeland. Not only were ecclesiastical offices turned to profit but papal authority as well. Encroachment on the temporal interests of the Holy See was punished with excommunication—a clear misuse of spiritual authority. As the curia's involvement in earthly pursuits increased, the lower clergy followed suit, further discrediting the spiritual authority of the church. The humanist writer Petrarch claimed that for the papacy, 'all hope of a future life is an empty fable; all stories of hell pure invention. . . Unbridled sin is considered the height of munificence and a good name is worth less than dirt'.[2]

In 1378 two popes were elected, one in Rome and the other in Avignon, and Western Christianity split into warring camps. The schism in the church drew latent national antagonisms to the fore: Italy and most of Germany recognised the Roman pope, while France remained loyal to Avignon. Increasingly calls echoed across western Christendom for the 'reform of the church from head to toe'. In England, France and Bohemia reformers lashed out at the secularised church and urged that it return to its biblical roots. With the church beset by a weak, divided papacy and mounting religious discontent across all strata of Western society, reform councils were organised with the help of Christian lay members, who thus participated for the first time in church government.

Efforts to rectify the situation failed, however, to live up to expectations. Church reform was rather unsuccessful for the most part, and requests that lay members be allowed to participate in the decision-making process were rejected. Only the schism was overcome and unity restored. However, this period of trial and tribulation for the church produced in many believers a deep sense of spiritual autonomy which could never be eradicated. Their ideas would revolutionise the world-view of medieval man.

There began to emerge late in the middle ages a new appreciation of the value of a human being and a sense of awe at human potential. Man, it was thought, had been placed by God 'at the centre of the world'. Endowed by his creator with a proclivity for purposeful action, man 'can be whatever he wills'.[3] This was a virtue which had to be cultivated if man was to prevail over *fortuna* and achieve his potential.

As the might of the German emperors shrivelled to a mere shadow of its former self, the educated classes in Italy began to dream of a return to the glory and grandeur of ancient Rome. Classical values were rediscovered. Renewed appreciation for the works of the ancients opened the door to a fresh vision of God, nature and art. Men took greater pleasure in their surroundings and sought the harmonious cultivation of all human powers. They opened themselves to the temporal world in a way which medieval man never had, and aspired to emancipate themselves from all confinement and constraint—especially that of the church. Knowledge should be freely sought, they felt, and mankind thus served.

'O new century! O knowledge!' rejoiced the humanist Ulrich von

Hutten in 1518. Life was joyful, he proclaimed, for the human mind had reawakened, a vast programme of study was underway and barbarism had been banned.[4] Convinced of the high value of ancient life and science, the humanists studied ancient languages and renewed man's knowledge of the fountainhead of Western culture. Thus they hoped to improve the world and human life. After Johann Gutenberg's invention of movable metal letters and the printing press, novel ideas spread like wildfire in books and pamphlets.

The urge to discover was not confined to intellectural explorations of the ancient world. Western man set sail for new and unknown lands. Nicholas Copernicus's declaration that the earth is round and the invention of the compass and gunpowder made it possible to voyage to distant continents, to conquer them and return with their treasures. Statesmen and merchants alike learnt to think in distances never before imagined.

The routes plied by world commerce shifted to the Atlantic coast, while the ports of the Mediterranean, Baltic and North Sea stagnated. New foodstuffs and luxury goods—coffee, tea, tobacco, maize and cocoa—transfigured European life-styles. Economies of barter and exchange were eradicated by the money economy. Gold and silver flowed from the new world to the old, and the bourgeoning demand for metals stimulated the development of mining. In Italy the first banks appeared, and in Germany numerous lords and princes grew dependent on the great banking families of Augsburg: the Fuggers and the Welsers.

The wealth that accumulated from the expansion of world trade benefited only a very few, economically powerful families and those states and cities whose revenues increased. The broad mass of the population suffered as goods became more expensive and money lost its value due to increasing amounts of precious metal in circulation. Social unrest spread in the towns and the countryside. Salary disputes between master craftsmen and apprentices, strikes and lengthy lock-outs disturbed the peace of the cities and spawned a proletarian class, bitterly poor but for the present still politically insignificant. When urban middlemen set prices without regard for the devaluation of money, peasants too became impoverished as their yields no longer sufficed to cover costs. The value of estates sank. The nobility, excluded from the cultural progress of the bourgeoisie, withdrew village allowances in order to counteract the declining value of its lands. The misery of the peasants intensified and riots erupted.

The church did nothing to alleviate the social tension; indeed, it sought to profit from the political and economic trends. Missions were established in recently conquered regions, and their riches helped to slake the papacy's mounting thirst for capital. Deeply enmeshed in secular affairs, the church was no longer able to minister to a widespread yearning for a direct experience of the divine. Corrupt in its theology and ministrations, the church could no longer light the way for those who sought salvation.

Unrest was rife in this era—intellectual, political, social and spiritual. The humanists, with their flair for critical and rational thought, censured the abuses they saw all sides, and eventually Martin Luther emerged to challenge the church from the bedrock of his Christian faith.

Reformation and Counter-Reformation

1483–1546:	Martin Luther
1484–1531:	Ulrich Zwingli
1491–1556:	Ignatius of Loyola
1509–64:	John Calvin
1517:	Luther's 95 theses
1519:	The disputation at Leipzig between Luther and Eck
1519–56:	Charles V
1520:	Luther's pamphlets
1521:	The Diet and Edict of Worms
1522:	Luther's translation of the Bible
1525:	The Peasants' War
1526:	Spread of the Reformation; the First Diet of Speyer
1529:	The Turks threaten Vienna, the Second Diet of Speyer
1540:	Foundation of the Jesuit Order, the principal upholder of the Counter-Reformation
1545–65:	The Council of Trent
1549:	The followers of Calvin and Zwingli unite
1555:	The religious peace of Augsburg
1556–98:	Philip II of Spain
1558–1603:	Elizabeth I of England
1588:	The Spanish armada is defeated by England
1562–98:	The Huguenot Wars
1567–1648:	Wars of liberation in the Netherlands
1608:	Foundation of the Protestant Union
1609:	Foundation of the Catholic League

Martin Luther took little comfort from the doctrine of salvation propounded by the church. His study of St Augustine and, more specifically, of St Paul's Epistle to the Romans led him to conclude that the God of vengeance was also the God of mercy. Luther found the foundation for his belief in the New Testament, particularly in Romans III : 28 which reveals how man is to be justified before God: not by good works but by faith in the grace of God. The sole source of this faith was the Bible, to which the individual believer should have access, Luther believed, without the mediation of the priesthood. The path to salvation lay in divine grace and faith, and the keepers and interpreters of this route were not lofty ecclesiastics but the community of believers. The priest is summoned merely to serve his parishioners through his preaching and tending of souls. Luther thus denied the princes of the church their august role as the conduit through which God's mercy flows, and he cast doubt on the foundations of the Roman Church, its dogma, structure and rituals.

At first Luther confined his views on reform to theological lectures delivered at the University of Wittenberg. The widespread abuse of indulgences, however, eventually propelled him to take a public stand. In ninety-five theses Luther protested against the sale of indulgences in order to meet the pecuniary needs of the pope and the Archbishop of Mainz. Ordered by the authorities to recant, Luther denied in a disputation with Professor John Eck of Ingolstadt the biblical justification for the supremacy of the pope and the infallibility of ecumenical councils. Rome responded by condemning Luther's teachings and by excommunicating him.

Luther's ninety-five theses and three great pamphlets of 1520—*Address to the Christian Nobility of the German Nation, On the Babylonian Captivity of the Church* and *On the Liberty of a Christian*[5]—made him the chief advocate of the widespread desire in Germany for a renewed church independent of Rome.

In England, France and Spain royal authority had vanquished the universal church well before Luther's time, and religion had entered the service of the state. In Germany, however, a national church could not emerge where no national state existed. Indeed, the medieval idea of an international state seemed to be reviving with the election as emperor of Charles V of the house of Habsburg, who ruled the German Empire, the Netherlands, part of Italy, and Spain with its overseas colonies. Throughout his reign Charles never abandoned his claim to rule Christendom as well. This claim combined with the traditional coronation oath to defend the church and all its belongings only reinforced his insistence on a universal church and culture. He accordingly failed to comprehend the mounting desire for independence in Western Europe and felt no sympathy for the forces of renewal as propagated by Martin Luther. Luther's contention that 'faith and love . . . flow freely through the

ranks composing all troubles, for they allow each, to live according
to his conviction'[6] inevitably eroded not only absolute papal authority over spiritual questions but imperial rule over temporal
affairs. Charles V therefore did not hesitate to support Rome in its
battle with Luther.

The *Reichstag* which convened in Worms in 1521 failed to resolve
the conflict. Luther had already been excommunicated by the
church, and the Edict of Worms now declared him and his followers
under the ban of the empire as well. Furthermore, all Luther's
writings were ordered to be destroyed. Even such stringent measures as these, however, could not prevent many cities and territorial princes from supporting the Reformation.

Protected by many local princes, Protestant beliefs quickly
spread across Germany and northern Europe. On all sides Protestant communities clustered around Luther's translation of the Bible.
Circulating the length and breadth of the empire, it not only
provided direct access to the word of God but created a written
standard for the German language that became universally accepted
despite numerous differences in the spoken dialects.

Luther's battle against the authority of the Catholic Church
sowed the seeds of a social revolution of which he himself did not
approve. When the terms of the Edict of Worms became known in
Erfurt and Wittenberg, a revolt broke out against the church. Places
of worship were stormed, altars and treasuries plundered and
paintings destroyed. In Thuringia Thomas Münzer proclaimed the
advent of a new *Reich*, unencumbered by church or state.

Peasants demanded equality in the name of the holy gospel and
resisted the efforts of feudal landlords to abolish traditional rights
such as the freedom to hunt and cut wood. Many lords began to
increase the services owed by peasants and to raise rents and court
fees with the result that numerous peasants could no longer afford
them. As overpopulation and the custom of partitioning estates
caused agricultural production to decline, feudal lords were increasingly tempted to intervene. Finally, they succeeded in having
the old German law replaced in many regions of Germany by
Roman law, which failed to recognise existing popular rights. This
goaded the peasants into creating secret societies directed 'against all
injurious innovations'. Early uprisings flared between 1513 and
1515, and a major insurrection erupted in central and south-western
Germany in 1525. The rebellious peasants formulated twelve articles in which they demanded the abolition of serfdom, the right to
elect their own priests and administer church dues, the freedom to
hunt, fish and cut wood, the retention of old German law, a

limitation on services to 'those which our parents provided', and the right, as granted by the Bible, to be free.[7]

These demands met with a sympathetic response from the smaller imperial states, some knights and the petty bourgeoisie of the free cities of Franconia. However, most princes rejected out of hand the idea of negotiations with the peasantry. Armed conflict broke out in spite of Luther's admonition to keep the peace. The peasant revolt spread quickly from Swabia into Alsace, the Alpine regions, Franconia, Thuringia and as far as the Harz. The peasants organised themselves in 'Christian associations' to force the lords to accede to their demands. At first Luther attempted to mediate between the peasants and the princes, but dismayed by the peasants' excesses and their misinterpretation of Christian freedom, he later turned passionately against them in his pamphlet *Against the Murderous and Rapacious Hordes of the Peasants* and admonished the princes to 'beat, stab and throttle' the rebels mercilessly.[8] Faced with an attempt on the part of the peasantry and elements of the petty bourgeoisie to transform ecclesiastical reform into social and political revolution, Luther seemed prepared to sanction any measure that would help to restore order.

The peasants lost the war and with it their remaining rights. They were no longer allowed to bear arms or congregate, and though they managed in the second half of the sixteenth century to restore a measure of their material well-being, they remained politically inert for centuries to come, subsisting as a down-trodden mass while the princes successfully quashed any democratic stirrings.

During this period the imperial knights also lost their political significance. Supplanted militarily by mercenary foot-soldiers, the knights fell increasingly under the control of the lords of the manor. These princes viewed the independence of the imperial knights and the free cities as a challenge to their own authority and strove to subdue them and incorporate them into a unified realm.

The Diet of Speyer (1526) allowed the individual states to devise their own solution to the religious issue in accordance with their responsibility to God and the emperor. As a result, Lutheran territories emerged, and the princes, already the highest secular authority in their principalities, became the highest spiritual authority as well. Soon the common Lutheran believer became a perfect subject, expected to honour without complaint the authorities supposedly appointed by God.

In the end the emperor too was compelled to accept these developments. The judicial equality of the Lutheran and Catholic faiths was legally established in 1555 by the religious peace of

Augsburg. The empire was to allow the individual states to establish their own religion. The princes and imperial cities were therefore free to choose their own faith, further enhancing their sovereignty. The princes' subjects, however, were constrained to adopt the religion of their overlord in accordance with the principle *cuius regio, eius religio* ('whoever's kingdom, his religion'). This summarisation of the basic thrust of the Peace of Augsburg characterises the authority granted to the states in 1555 to determine the religion of their subjects. The only alternative was to emigrate. Only in the free cities were religious minorities tolerated. Thus the empire was further divided, this time along confessional lines. The religious settlement excluded, however, the Reformed Protestants—the followers of Ulrich Zwingli in Zurich and John Calvin in Geneva.

Zwingli and Calvin resembled Luther in their insistence on the Bible as the sole source of a Christian life. But they differed from him in their desire to harness the power of the state in order to effect the triumph of God's will and not to rely on divine inspiration alone. To this end Calvin and Zwingli sought to reorganise both state and spiritual life. Harsh ecclesiastical discipline was instituted without regard for the individual, and transgressors were subjected to severe earthly punishment. The reformed Protestant churches functioned democratically and involved the laity much more intensively than the Lutheran Church. Calvin was convinced that every Christian state had a moral obligation to assist in establishing divine rule on earth and that every Christian soul was duty-bound to resist any secular power which flouted the will of God and failed to fulfill its spiritual mission. Calvinism therefore recognised the people's right to resist higher authority and helped to prepare the way for the development of modern democracy.

Calvinists developed an internal cohesion and a spirit of initiative lacking among Lutherans by dint of stiff discipline, tightly organised communities, a fierce determination to defend their secular and spiritual realm against any lay or ecclesiastical power which threatened it, and a strong messianic conviction that they had been selected to prepare the Kingdom of God. A zealous though often superficial sense of morality evolved into a work ethic which tended to view achievement and material success as visible signs of God's pleasure. Hence Calvinists brought a religious sanction to capitalism, and their communities flourished. Calvin's followers expanded the Reformation into a world-wide movement and became highly influential in Switzerland, France, the Netherlands, various parts of Germany (especially the Palatinate), England, Scotland and later North America.

The success of the Reformation aroused forces of reform within Catholicism eager to revitalise the church and recover lost territories. The Council of Trent was instituted and convened from 1545 to 1565, though with long interruptions. Such abuses as the accumulation of benefices, the sale of indulgences and wanton lack of discipline were eradicated while the training and supervision of the clergy, the education of Catholic youth and care for the poor were reorganised. In matters of faith, however, no concessions were made. Church traditions were reaffirmed as valid sources of faith alongside the Bible, and the sacramental nature of the church and its priests was confirmed. The Inquisition was renewed and intensified. Together with censorship and the Index of Forbidden Books, it served to uphold the purity of Catholic dogma. The Counter-Reformation aimed to steer the church away from earthly affairs and to restore its essentially religious function. With a restored emphasis on centralism, missionary work and the care of souls, Roman Catholicism, differentiated itself clearly from Protestantism and set out to recover lost territories. The papacy emerged from the conciliar movement with renewed vigour, and added a powerful new weapon to its arsenal when Ignatius of Loyola founded the Society of Jesus in 1534.

This highly centralised order became the chief agent of the Counter-Reformation. Pledged to complete obedience, the Jesuits played an active role in the community, devoting their attentions primarily to the education of the upper classes and to Catholic missions in Africa, America and East Asia. The Jesuits erected churches, founded magnificent schools, opened missions, assumed university posts and functioned as teachers and father confessors in the courts of princes. The broad masses of the population were favourably impressed by the accessibility of Jesuit preaching and by the efforts of the order to alleviate poverty. Within the Holy Roman Empire the Society of Jesus strove to unite the Catholic states against the Lutherans and Reformed Protestants. Their efforts were crowned with success when much of southern Germany returned to the Catholic fold.

The religious strife of the sixteenth and seventeenth centuries was also fuelled by political struggles: in Germany the attempt to uphold the sovereignty of the emperor *vis-à-vis* the particularist ambitions of the princes; in England and France the desire to establish a strong national government; and in the Netherlands the yearning for political autonomy. At the same time, the challenge posed by Turkish Moslems to all of Europe had to be met.

Charles V represented the last glimmer of the medieval ideal of a universal Roman empire, but he failed to resolve either the spiritual or the political conflicts in his realm. While enormously successful at extending the might of the Habsburgs and conquering vast new territories in America, Charles's attempts to restore religious and political unity in Europe floundered. His successor, Philip II, moved the court to Spain and made the affirmation of royal authority his overriding objective. Utter obedience to king and church were demanded throughout the realm. But the existing rifts in society only widened. After a period of unchallenged dominion over both the north of Europe and the Mediterranean, Philip's grip weakened and what remained of medieval Europe finally disintegrated. England evolved during the course of its wars with Philip's Spain into a mighty sea-power brimming with confidence. Across the channel, a portion of the Spanish Netherlands—later termed Holland—struggled for freedom and independence, eventually escaping the orbit of Habsburg rule. The political independence of both countries reinforced religious liberty so that attempts to restore Catholicism were doomed to failure. France, too, not only successfully resisted Spanish power but even began to surpass her rival during the first half of the seventeenth century. The Spanish Habsburgs succeeded, however, in persuading the French government to eradicate Calvinism, which flourished mainly in the south and west of France, and to reintroduce Catholicism. The Huguenots were crushed in a bloody civil war around the mid sixteenth century.

In Germany the Austrian branch of the family likewise tied its star to the traditional church and refused to honour the Augsburg compromise of 1555. Early in the seventeenth century the Austrian Habsburgs joined the Catholic League, which had been formed under Bavarian leadership, in order to confront the Protestant states in the empire which had united in the Protestant Union. Thereafter both bodies engaged in political manoeuvring and signed treaties with outside powers, the League with Spain and the pope; the Union with France, England and States General of the Netherlands.

The Empire Prostrated

16128–48: The Thirty Years' War (see Map 3)
1629: The Edict of Restitution
1630–5: Gustavus Adolphus of Sweden intervenes in the war
1635: Peace of Prague and the beginning struggle for supremacy in Europe
1648: Treaty of Westphalia

The great war to arrest the further spread of Protestantism was ignited by an apparently insignificant incident in Prague. At first the conflict was primarily a contest between the Catholic League and the Protestant states of the empire, and it inflicted great cruelty and suffering on the civilian population. Eventually the Habsburg Emperor Ferdinand II gained the upper hand, with the able assistance of Albrecht von Wallenstein, who had been elevated to Duke of Friedland in 1625 and had raised an army at his own expense. In his peace terms, the emperor demanded the restitution to the Catholic Church of all ecclesiastical lands that had been ceded to the Protestants since 1552, seriously threatening the independence not only of the Protestant princes of the empire but of the Catholic princes as well. This brought Gustavus Adolphus of Sweden into the fray to save German Protestantism from annihilation. After his death the Peace of Prague was negotiated in 1635. Its terms virtually annulled the Edict of Restitution and halted the wars of religion, but it ignited a great struggle among the European powers, especially France and Sweden against the Habsburgs. The German Empire was devastated. This war marked the beginning of a new era in European history, an era in which the political interests of the rising national states would replace religion as the dominant factor.

The Thirty Years' War ended in 1648 in the Treaty of Westphalia, which confirmed the emergence of a new order in Europe. The hegemony of the Habsburgs was broken, and central Europe was neutralised. France and Sweden emerged as great powers, thrusting their borders forward into the soft flanks of the German Empire. Switzerland and the Netherlands gained their independence and parted from the empire, which became a confederation of small sovereign states each empowered to conclude treaties with foreign powers so long as they were not directed against the emperor. Of the more than 360 particular states, only Austria, Brandenburg-Prussia, Saxony, Bavaria and Hanover carried any weight. The remainder were tiny shreds of the once mighty German *Reich* over which the emperor himself had finally lost all authority. His prerogative to sign alliances and make war or peace in the name of the empire was made conditional on the approval of the *Reichstag*. The *Reichstag* became a permanent representative assembly in 1663, but was stripped of all effectiveness by the requirement of unanimity. So far as religion is concerned, the Treaty of Westphalia reaffirmed the religious peace of Augsburg and extended it to include the Calvinists. Northern Germany remained predominantly Protestant while Catholicism prevailed in the south, in Austria, Bohemia, Moravia, Bavaria and the Upper Palatinate.

The political woes of the German people were aggravated by the ravaged state of the economy. The population, decimated by war, eked out a living in shattered towns and cities. Industry, trade and agriculture were devastated. Economic recovery was impeded by enormous debts and by hordes of beggars and discharged soldiers who roamed about pillaging the land. The peasants had already been deprived of their rights and politically paralysed by the outcome of the Peasants' War; now the burghers in the cities discovered that their political influence declined sharply as their economic power dwindled. In consequence, the aristocracy largely determined the Germans' political fate until the nineteenth century and Germany remained subjected to foreign domination.

After the termination of the Thirty Years' War Germany's real masters became France and Sweden. Together they were guarantors of the Treaty of Westphalia, and as chief arbiters of the peace, they gained the right to intervene at any moment in Germany's internal affairs. They proved more than willing of course to protect the 'liberty' of hosts of German princes. In the end Sweden was only able to assert its dominion over Germany for a short period before losing control over the Baltic to Russia; France, however, succeeded in establishing paramountcy in Europe, which lasted into the nineteenth century, deeply influencing the course of German history.

The shift in the constellation of great powers reflected the mutation that had occurred in the social and political structure of most of the states of Europe during the seventeenth century. Absolutism had come to predominate, especially in France, in the German states and in Russia, which was opening to the West under Peter the Great (1688–1725). Absolutism implied that the full power of the state was vested in the personage of the king or prince to whom all other concerns were subordinate, even religion and morals. As the sole source of all law and authority—*princeps legibus solutus* (the prince stands above the law)—the ruler was responsible to God alone and had no need to concern himself with legality. The feudal society that had evolved during the middle ages lost its vested rights and privileges and became wholly subservient to the will of the ruler.

While the political representatives of the various estates were deprived of all influence in most of the continental Europe, the English Parliament asserted its right to represent the sovereign people and succeeded in protecting and extending the rights ensured by the Magna Carta of 1215. Although the King of England attempted to institute absolutism, he was compelled in 1689 to relinquish legislative powers and the concomitant supervisory function and to confine himself to an executive role.

The Emergence of German Dualism

1640–88: Frederick William, the Great Elector
1683–99: The Turkish Wars
1713–40: Frederick William I
1740–80: Maria Theresa
1740–86: Frederick the Great
1740–8:   The War of Austrian Succession
1756–63: The Seven Years' War

Among the many absolutist rulers of Germany, the Habsburgs in Austria and the Hohenzollerns in Brandenburg-Prussia rose to particular power and brillance.

In 1683 the Turks in alliance with France laid siege to Vienna. With the assistance of Poland, Venice and numerous German states, Austria managed to repel the Turks and in so doing to consolidate its position in the south-east of Europe. Austria had traditionally focused her foreign policy on the German Empire, but henceforth she developed strong interests to the east and south-east. As a result, Austria encountered resistance not only from her traditional rival, France, but also from Russia, which was expanding to the west.

During this same period, the Hohenzollerns were constructing a powerful state in Brandenburg-Prussia relying on military prowess and an effective civil service. All social classes were bent to the task: the nobility became officers and senior civil servants; the burghers oversaw trade and manufacturing; and the peasants, still deprived of all rights, supplied cheap food and recruits for the army. Chiefly concerned at first with internal colonisation, the Hohenzollerns offered sanctuary to religious refugees from France and Salzburg, stimulated trade, industry and agriculture, and improved land and water routes. The highly centralised civil service oversaw the financial affairs of a state which aimed to do 'everything for the people but nothing through the people'.[9]

Frederick the Great, one of the 'enlightened despots' of the age, styled himself the first servant of the state. He practised religious tolerance and encouraged an independent judiciary. Under Frederick's guidance Prussia seized the Austrian province of Silesia and ascended to the level of a great European power. Though severely threatened, she maintained this status during the Seven Years' War and managed, in league with England, to fend off the allied armies of Austria, France and Russia. At the same time England defeated France in North America and India, thereby laying the foundations of a world-wide empire.

These events set the stage for a new period in German history: the era of dualism, or a power struggle between Austria and Prussia. This dualism weighed heavily on Germany's fate till the second half of the nineteenth century, when Bismarck resolved the issue in Prussia's favour.

Political affairs in Europe largely revolved around the interests of the various sovereign states which struggled for power in accordance with *raison d'état*. Early in the seventeenth century the effects of the intellectual movement of the Enlightenment began to be felt. This movement was rooted in unequivocal reliance on reason and the optimistic conviction that rational insights could eventuate in concrete social change. All the time-honoured notions of religion, the state, society and economics were subjected to rational study, and society was urged to adopt the philosophers' conclusions. The Enlightenment seized the imagination of the educated classes across Europe and spawned a political movement which finally overthrew absolutism through the French Revolution and created entirely new social structures.

While the ideas of the Enlightenment were largely implemented in North America and the states of Western Europe, intellectual and political life in Germany remained hopelessly divided, Torn into countless liliputian states ruled by despots living beyond their means, the empire lacked a political centre which could have organised broad economic and political reforms. In contrast to France, for instance, a strong, confident bourgeoisie did not exist in Germany, save in the free cities. Since the German nation could not hope to achieve broad economic and political reform under these conditions, the hopes and dreams of the educated classes tended to revolve around either the grand empire of the past or imaginary future utopias.

On the eve of French Revolution, the *Sturm und Drang* movement in Germany awakened the historical and national consciousness of many Germans, though it did not affect the princes. Freedom as postulated by the Enlightenment remained the dream of Germans like Immanuel Kant, who chafed at their subjugation and longed to throw off outside rulers.

Foreign ascendancy remained a political reality both for the population in general and for the myriad of tiny potentates consumed with their petty rivalries; eventually the old empire collapsed completely under its effects. This final disintegration had the positive effect of clearing the way for reform along more modern lines. The whirlwind of the French Revolution and the Napoleonic campaigns awakened the Germans from their deep slumber and set the stage for the eventual appearance of a unified nation, equal in stature to its neighbours.

3

Germany and the French Revolution

The Enlightenment and its Aftermath

The Enlightenment

1583–1645:	Hugo Grotius
1588–1679:	Thomas Hobbes
1632–1704:	John Locke
1689–1755:	Charles de Montesquieu
1694–1778:	Voltaire
1712–78:	Jean-Jacques Rousseau
1729–81:	Gotthold Ephraim Lessing

German Idealism

1724–1804:	Immanuel Kant
1762–1814:	Johann Gottlieb Fichte
1770–1831:	Georg Wilhelm Friedrich Hegel

Classicism

1749–1832:	Johann Wolfgang von Goethe
1759–1805:	Friedrich Schiller
1732–1809:	Joseph Haydn
1756–91:	Wolfgang Amadeus Mozart
1770–1827:	Ludwig van Beethoven

Romanticism

1767–1845:	August Wilhelm Schlegel
1772–1829:	Friedrich Schlegel
1773–1853:	Ludwig Tieck
1776–1848:	Joseph von Görres
1778–1842:	Clemens Brentano
1781–1831:	Achim von Arnim
1785–1863:	Jacob Grimm
1786–1859:	Wilhelm Grimm

1768–1834:   Friedrich Daniel Ernst Schleiermacher
1779–1861:   Friedrich Carl von Savigny
1776–1831:   Barthold Niebuhr
1795–1886:   Leopold von Ranke

The new era in world history which dawned towards the end of the eighteenth century was characterised by an effort to base the legitimacy of the state on natural law alone. This law was thought to be rooted in human nature itself and hence independent of time or place or traditional jurisprudence. It was immutable, in contrast with positive law, which responds to human experience and is therefore subject to incessant modification. 'Natural law is so immutable that God himself can no more alter it than he can alter the fact that two times two is four.'[1] God's will, however, is manifested in the law of nature as discovered by reason. The relations between individuals and peoples should therefore be based, according to the philosophers of the Enlightenment, on reason alone.

No longer was the state thought to embody, as in the medieval period, a grand design originated by God and safeguarded by the emperor and the church; no longer was the state considered, as under absolutism, an instrument for bending subjects to the unfettered will of the ruler. Instead, the state became a 'judicial organisation representing a plurality of the interests of the people inhabiting a certain region'.[2] It was created through the voluntary association of free people and was to benefit the entire community while ensuring the freedom and happiness of its citizens.

According to the English philosopher John Locke, the state is a union of people created for the sole purpose of representing, asserting and developing their civil interest.[3] These interests consist, Locke says, in the preservation of the natural right to life, liberty and property. In order to safeguard these rights, Locke developed the principles of representative government and the division of powers. Absolutism was clearly on the demise, in theory at least.

The French writer and political theorist Charles de Montesquieu also singled out the division of powers as essential for the freedom of the individual. According to *The Spirit of Laws*, which appeared in 1748:

Every state holds three powers: the power to legislate, the power to carry out what has been legislated, and the power to enforce the law. The second power is called the executive function and the third power, which enables the prince or ruler to punish transgressions or settle disputes between citizens, is called the judicial function.

If the legislative and executive functions are fused, then freedom is endangered because one individual could pass tyrannical laws and then enforce them. Freedom is also endangered if the judicial function is not separated from the legislative and executive functions. If the judicial function is combined with the power to legislate, the judge makes the laws; if the judicial function is combined with the executive function, the judge can also become an oppressor.

All would be lost if a single man or authority, whether noble or commoner, should succeed in combining all three powers. In a free state, every rational individual would ideally rule himself, and hence the people as a whole would exercise the judicial function. Since this is impracticable in large states and very difficult even in small ones, the people must decide through the agency of their representatives all that which cannot be decided directly.[4]

To the philosophers of the Enlightenment, liberty meant the freedom to do what the law requires and not to be compelled to do what arbitrary or outside authorities demanded. All men, they declared are created equal and are equal before the law.

Thomas Jefferson, a delegate to the Virginia constitutional convention, summarised these ideas when he wrote:

We hold these Truths to be self-evident, that all men are created equal, that they are endowed by their Creator with certain unalienable Rights, that among these are life, Liberty, and the Pursuit of Happiness— That to secure these Rights, Governments are instituted among men, deriving their just Powers from the Consent of the Governed, that whenever any Form of Government becomes destructive of these Ends, it is the Right of the People to alter or to abolish it, and to institute new Government, laying its Foundation on such Principles, and organising its Powers in such Form, as to them shall seem most likely to effect their Safety and Happiness.[5]

On 26 August 1789 the French National Assembly declared:

Men are born and remain free and equal in respect of rights. Social distinctions shall be based solely upon public utility.

The purpose of all civil associations is the preservation of the natural and imprescriptible rights of man. These rights are liberty, property, security, and resistance to oppression.

The nation is essentially the source of all sovereignty; nor shall any body of men or any individual exercise authority which is not expressly derived from it.

Liberty consists in the power of doing whatever does not injure another. Accordingly, the exercise of the natural rights of every man has no other limits than those which are necessary to secure to every other man the free exercise of the same rights; and these limits are determinable only by the law.[6]

Many of these ideals were realised in the United States of America. With the Declaration of Independence on 4 July 1776 the increasingly self-assured colonists created a constitution which placed the future state squarely on the foundation of human rights. The colonists were clearly determined to defend those rights against all internal or external foes. Under George Washington, commander of the American army and impending first president of the United States, the colonies overthrew British rule and won their freedom. Similarly, the French bourgeoisie overcame absolutism in 1789 and eradicated feudal privileges. The French Constitution of 1791 embodied the revolutionary demand for liberty and equality, and the monarchy acknowledged human rights and the division of power. Although the stormy course of the revolution later strayed far from its original goals, the French bourgeoisie had seized the initiative and would henceforward consider the affairs of state to be its own concern.

In contrast to the United States and France, 'Germany experienced an intellectual movement rather than an actual political movement'.[7] No powerful state existed or strong, confident bourgeoisie to revolt against the impositions of that state. Attempts by stout-hearted individuals to free themselves from any one of the myriad of petty princes remained isolated incidents without further ramifications. Unlike the case in France, no political centre existed to inspire emulation in the rest of the empire. Any revolt against absolutism had immediately to contend with the local prince and was not seen as a threat to the entire system. With Germans too divided to unite around common political and economic goals, the ideas of the Enlightenment failed to rally a large following and radically change the political shape of the empire.

This failure explains the curious schism in German political and cultural life in the second half of the eighteenth and the early nineteenth century. Politics became the preserve of Prussia and Austria, the various principalities, aristocrats and senior bureaucrats, while culture and intellectual life were reserved for the subjugated middle class.

German intellectual life in the first half of the eighteenth century was deeply influenced by Protestant Pietism and the intense religiosity of Catholic Germany. Pietism replaced the old religious forms with an intensely personal religion. Inimical to rationalism and thought, it appealed directly to the emotions. Pietists informed their Christian belief with reverence and a love of virtue, sought the salvation of individual souls and spread the word of God among the youth. The ardent emotion and sincere religious faith of the Pietists were manifested in heartfelt poetry and song. On a social level, Pietism exerted its greatest influence through the works of theologian and professor August Hermann Francke. Based in Halle, Francke sought to make Christian charity the cornerstone of practical evangelical education.

The intense emotionalism of Pietism provided the spawning grounds for the music of Johann Sebastian Bach (1685–1750) and Georg Friedrich Händel (1685–1759). The profound religious sensitivity of Friedrich Gottlieb Klopstock (1724–1803) found expression in the *Messiah*, a verse epic generally taken to mark the beginning of the grand revival in German letters. The revival of emotion in Germany was deeply influenced as well by authors in England and France. In scaling the heights and sounding the depths of human experience, William Skakespeare (1564–1616) revealed a vast range of feeling, while Jean-Jacques Rousseau's call for an immersion in nature fostered an entirely new temper in educated circles.

Gotthold Ephraim Lessing (1729–81) inaugurated 'middle-class tragedy' in Germany and set the stage for a national German literature. His striking dramas focus on reason and tolerance, the ideals of the Enlightenment. In the second half of the eighteenth century, Johann Gottfried Herder (1744–1803) became the prime catalyst of intellectual and artistic endeavour in Germany and pointed out the role of history in human development. His stimulus ignited the creative potential in Johann Wolfgang von Goethe (1749–1832), whose first poetry and dramas burst the bonds imposed by the rigid rules of French models, marking a new departure in German literature. His work encompasses all literary genres as well as philosophy, art criticism and natural science. During his lifetime Goethe gave comprehensive expression to the vast remoulding of the German spirit during this period. The ancient and medieval worlds, the Christian belief in redemption, and the self-fulfilment of the writer enter into a unified vision of humanity—a vision which sees the key to life and the world in the development of the human personality.[8] Friedrich Schiller (1759–1805) was a great dramatist and writer of philosophical poetry and, after Goethe, the most renowned figure in German letters. He elaborated an ethical approach to life patterned after the philosophy of Immanuel Kant, a political and national understanding of history and an educational programme rooted in aesthetics. In his efforts to come to terms with the events of the French Revolution, he became a proponent of human freedom within man's natural and social limitations.

At the same time Immanuel Kant (1724–1804) was at work in Königsberg. To him the dawning of the modern age and the intellectual movement of the Enlightenment represented the 'Ausgang des Menschen aus seiner selbstverschuldeten Unmündigkeit' (emergence of man from self-imposed subjugation). He enjoined his contemporaries to use reason and to liberate themselves from outside domination in order to develop freely and responsibly the capacities with which they were endowed. According to Kant, man should always act in such a way that the precepts of his 'will could at any time be taken as the basis of universal law'.[9] In this way Kant established the fundamental principle of morality and ethics: the categorical imperative of moral reason or of a reasonable morality.

Christoph Willibald Gluck, Joseph Haydn, Wolfgang Amadeus Mozart and Ludwig van Beethoven brought Western music to its apogee. Gluck (1714–87) placed German opera on an equal footing with its Italian counterpart, while Haydn (1732–1809) gave symphonic music its classical form. The genius and catholic musical talent of Mozart (1756–91) created a treasury of concertos, religious music and chamber music and raised symphonic music and opera to the brink of perfection. The deeply emotional music of Beethoven (1770–1827) influenced the entire culture of his own and the following age. His music pointed far beyond classicism itself and has become an enduring component of the history of ideas.

At the end of the century German Romanticism emerged as a counterpoise to the Enlightenment and Classicism. Inspired by Rousseau, Herder and the young Goethe, the Romantics first considered themselves citizens of the world. They gloried in freedom and nature and were convinced of the value of organic growth. When the Romantics focused their attention on law and politics they concluded that the state and jurisprudence had evolved organically from the innermost nature of the people and were therefore part of its essence. Accordingly, they drew attention to the culture, the individuality and the history of various peoples.

This resulted in a sense of national self-awareness which solidified under the pressure of the Napoleonic occupation. The inner life of a people was defined in depth, and the German national spirit was sought out in the *Volkslied* (for example *Des Knaben Wunderhorn* by Achim von Arnim and Clemens Brentano, 1805), in fairy tales such as those of the Brothers Grimm, in popular books (e.g. Görres) and customs (e.g. Turnvater Jahn), in language (Jakob Grimm), law (Savigny) and religion (Schleiermacher). Historians turned to original sources in their efforts to understand the past as the product of intrinsic creative impulses. This approach to historiography, initiated by Barthold Georg Niebuhr (1776–1831), was later perfected by Leopold von Ranke (1795–1886). So far as practical results are concerned, the intelligentsia examined the principle of liberty as defined by the Enlightenment, German Classicism and Romanticism, and sought a method of translating it into political reality within the context of the French Revolution and the Napoleonic Wars. Apolitical at heart, the German intelligentsia resorted primarily to the liberating power of the mind. It would overcome the humiliations of the past and present and assist Germany towards a humane and independent future moulded by freely associated individuals responsible to their own consciences.

The Revolutionary Wars, the Collapse of the Holy Roman Empire and the Emergence of German Nationalism

1789:	The outbreak of the French Revolution
1791:	The first constitution
1792:	The beginning of the revolutionary wars— overthrow of the monarchy and creation of the French Republic
1793:	The execution of Louis XVI—dictatorship of the Jacobins
1793–7:	The First Coalition
1795:	The Peace of Basle
1795–9:	The Directory
1797:	The Treaty of Campo Formio
1798–9:	The Egyptian campaign
1798–1801:	The Second Coalition
1799:	Napoleon Bonaparte, First Consul of France
1801:	The Treaty of Lunéville
1803:	The Principal Decree of the Imperial Deputation (*Reichsdeputationshauptschluss*)
1805:	The Third Coalition
1805:	The Peace of Pressburg
1806:	The Confederation of the Rhine
1806:	The defeat of Prussia at Jena and Auerstedt
1807:	The Peace of Tilsit—Continental Blockade

The revolutionary war in North America and the French Revolution were at first welcomed in Germany as harbingers of the new era. The enlightened middle class in the various German states largely supported the elimination of all feudal dues and privileges; the Declaration of the Rights of Man and Citizen; the expropriation of church property; the dissolution of monasteries and religious orders; the secularisation of schools; the introduction of civil marriage; the emancipation of Jews from the ghetto; and the constitutional limitations which French National Assembly imposed on absolute monarchy. The original wave of sympathy, however, began to give way to a mounting tide of criticism in Germany as the

French Revolution became radicalised and apparently deviated from its original ideals. East of the Rhine, liberty was not thought worth the heavy price and a desire for order became paramount even among the educated classes. The various German governments, led by Austria and Prussia, never hesitated to do their utmost in support of 'order'. Driven by fear that the revolutionary movement might spill across national frontiers, they propounded the solidarity of thrones against the common enemy. At the same time the French revolutionaries believed that France was destined to endow the other peoples of Europe with the new ideas. War between the old and the new was virtually inevitable.

War was declared by the Legislative Assembly in Paris in April 1792. The combined forces of Prussia and Austria scored some initial successes but were thrown back by the revolutionary armies which occupied Savoy, Nice and the cities of Basle, Speyer, Worms, Mainz and Frankfurt.

The leader of the allied Prussian and Austrian forces, Duke Karl William Ferdinand of Brunswick, had issued a manifesto which utterly misinterpreted the mood in France. The duke urged the French to disavow the revolution and 'to revert without delay to reason, justice, order and peace'. He threatened that

if the Château of the Tuilleries is stormed or attacked, or if any harm or abuse befalls His Majesty the King, the Queen and the entire royal family, and if their life, safety and liberty are not immediately assured ... [the Allies] shall extract a vengeance that will live in memory for ever by delivering the city of Paris to military execution and complete destruction and the revolutionaries themselves, who are responsible for these deeds, to their deserved death.[10]

Paris was outraged and a wave of revolutionary passion swept the city. The monarchy was overthrown and the Jacobins established their dictatorship.

The war intensified in 1793 as first England and then Spain, the Papal States, Naples, Tuscany, Venice, Sardinia and Portugal joined the Austro-Prussian coalition. France lost the territories she had recently conquered in the Netherlands; Mainz and the left bank of the Rhine were reoccupied by Prussia and Austria; and Toulon was besieged by the English. In France itself Royalists and Girondists revolted against the Jacobin terror. In this apparently hopeless situation, the former engineering officer Count Lazare Nicolas Carnot organised a *levée en masse*, an army law passed by the *National* Convention on 23 August 1793. It bound all Frenchmen to perpetual military service 'till the day the enemy is driven from the soil of the French Republic'. For the first time in human history an entire people was required without condition or restriction to serve the cause of national defence.

Young men go off to battle; married men forge arms and haul provisions; women make clothing and tents or serve in hospitals; children shred used linen, while old men are conveyed to the public squares to fire the courage of youthful warriors and to fill them with hate for the monarchy and love for a united republic.[11]

With total mobilisation a new element began to appear: the cosmopolitan ideals on which the French Revolution had originally been founded succumbed to nationalism— which would grow to become a major influence in the nascent nineteenth century. A fanatical minority stoked the fires of nationalism in the struggle against the *ancien régime*, and those fires soon found fresh fuel in France's traditional rivalry with England and Austria. Like the monarchy of old, the Jacobins sought to advance French frontiers to their 'natural' limits of the ocean, the Rhine and the Alps. A fierce determination arose not only to maintain traditional French prestige vis-à-vis England and Austria but to advance it beyond anything previously imagined.

By 1795 Prussia, Russia and Austria had partitioned Poland, and Berlin was increasingly preoccupied with its eastern interests. Hence Prussia abandoned her erstwhile allies and concluded a separate peace with France in which she agreed to vacate her German holdings on the west bank of the Rhine. This afforded France an opportunity not only to consolidate her sway over Alsace and the reconquered territories in the Netherlands but also to establish French pre-eminence in Europe. But in return northern and central Germany experienced ten years of peace—years which produced the cultural zenith of German Classicism.

Meanwhile, the coalition fought on. After an unparalleled string of victories, Napoleon Bonaparte compelled the Austrians in upper Italy to sue for peace and to vacate the left bank of the Rhine, the Austrian Netherlands and northern Italy. An attempt seriously to damage England through attacks in Egypt proved unsuccessful, however.

On the continent of Europe Napoleon reigned supreme and by dint of the *coup d'état* of 1799 was proclaimed First Consul of the French. A second coalition was formed by England, Austria and Russia in order to resist French ambitions, but Austria was compelled in 1801 to accept a peace which sealed her withdrawal from the left bank of the Rhine and isolated England. Consonant with the traditional anti-Habsburg policies of the French monarchs, Napoleon now attempted to organise the empire in such a way that French hegemony would be assured. Austria, already weakened by the previous treaties, would be confronted with a second powerful German state in the guise of an enlargened Prussia. Moreover, the smaller German states traditionally friendly to Austria would be replaced by independent, medium-sized states whose political interests would lead them to look more towards an alliance with France than with one of the twin German powers. In order to compensate the secular princes who had lost territories to France west of the Rhine, the church lands were secularised in accordance with the French model by the Principal Decree of the Imperial Deputation of 1803. Forty-five free cities and the lands of 1,500 Imperial Knights were also absorbed into the surrounding states ('mediatised') and subordinated to various princes. With the exception of Bavaria and Austria, most of the proceeds from the secularisation of Catholic property fell to Protestant princes, especially the Prussian Hohenzollerns. The Hanseatic cities of Hamburg, Bremen and Lübeck retained their independence, as did the free imperial cities of Nuremberg, Augsburg and Frankfurt on the Main. To the south, Baden, Württemberg and Bavaria became well-entrenched states of medium size. Although the new order was initiated solely in the French national interest, it did serve to eliminate the hopeless mosaic of tiny jurisdictions which had paralysed Germany ever since the Hohenstaufens. Without the reorganisation inspired by Napoleon, a modern state could never have arisen.

The Holy Roman Empire suffered its final mortal blow in 1806 when sixteen small medium-sized states in the south and west withdrew at Napoleon's behest and united to form the Confederation of the Rhine. Emperor Francis II, having already violated the Imperial Constitution in 1804 by uniting the hereditary Habsburg domains with the Austrian Empire, set aside the crown on 6 August 1806. The Holy Roman Empire of the German Nation ceased to exist. The collapse of the German empire was thus sealed, *de jure* as well as *de facto*, and an avenue was opened to create a new country that would correspond more closely to the desires of many Germans.

For the moment, though, Napoleon's hold over the continent was unassailable. England alone remained unvanquished and able to challenge the little Corsican. The English victory over the French fleet in the Battle of Trafalgar had thwarted Napoleon's ambitious plans to attack Albion directly; but Napoleon did triumph over

England's allies, the Austrians and Russians, at Austerlitz, and in the Peace of Pressburg compelled Vienna to vacate more territory in southern Germany and Italy. Prussia had gained ten years of peace but was now completely isolated. Napoleon attacked in 1806 and inflicted a devastating defeat that brought about the collapse of the Prussian state.

The French Empire now stretched to the banks of the Elbe. Napoleon, at the height of his glory, dictated a peace intended permanently to insure his position. Russia resigned from the anti-French alliance and joined Napoleon's continental blockade against England in return for concessions in Turkey and Finland. Prussia survived, thanks to the Tsar's mediation, but was compelled to resign all territories west of the Elbe to the Kingdom of Westphalia, newly established under Napoleon's brother Jerome. Prussian acquisitions in the second and third partitions of Poland were transferred to the Grand Duchy of Warsaw, over which Napoleon placed the King of Saxony. Danzig became a free city garrisoned by French troops. In addition, the French seized all Prussian fortifications, demanded an indemnity of an unspecified amount and set the maximum strength of the Prussian army at 42,000 men.

In the regions under Napoleonic rule, the administrative system, jurisprudence, social life and economics were thoroughly reformed in conformity with the legal, social and economic ideas of the French Revolution. Serfdom, the system of social estates and the privileges of aristocrats and the clergy were all abolished. They were replaced by civic equality, religious liberty and a free economic life untrammelled by the traditional restrictions, some of which had roots in medieval times. Jurisprudence was reformed and unified by the adoption of the French *code civil*. The administration was centralised and modern ministries wiped out the compartmentalisation of the state that had resulted from grants of feudal privileges. The German states under French rule also began to consolidate their sovereignty over schools and the church. All these reforms aroused great admiration for the brilliant young emperor.

Later, bitter opposition to Napoleon began to develop, largely in response to the ruthlessness with which the little Corsican, ever more prone to megalomania, compelled allied and conquered lands to serve his ambitions. Though the Continental Blockade against England provided some benefits by generating new industries and products, in the long run it damaged economic life on the continent. The conscription of Germans into the French army and Napoleon's financial demands on Germany were increasingly viewed as unjust harassment. The Germans were irked as well by the imposition of a foreign culture, which after the introduction of the French language into the occupied territories, seemed about to submerge the indigenous way of life.

It is therefore not surprising that gathering forces in the occupied countries were determined to throw off the yoke of foreign rule. In Germany the ideas of the French Revolution were widely revered as the basis for a renewal of political life, but messianic French nationalism was increasingly rejected in favour of allowing Germans themselves to shape their political life. This aspiration could only be fulfilled if the various German states agreed to unite against Napoleon and French domination of Germany.

The pursuit of these ends fostered a new sense of national identity which profoundly altered the Germans' perception of themselves. Previously, Germans had looked upon their local area as their homeland. Now they began to sense a common bond and a moral duty to concern themselves with pan-German life and a pan-German fatherland. Thus foreign pressure stimulated a German national consciousness which would send the political struggle off in a new direction.

Reform in Prussia and Austria

1807–8:   Reforms of Baron Karl vom Stein
1810:   Wilhelm von Humboldt founds the University of Berlin
1811–12: Reforms of Prince Karl August von Hardenberg

Napoleon's victories over Prussia and Austria convinced both great German powers that their traditional political systems were to blame for the defeat and collapse. These rigid systems, based on 'strict controls' to prevent the populace from participating in political life, were overwhelmed by the tidal wave of the French Revolution which succeeded marvellously in 'marshalling the strength of the entire French people'.[12] The reformers, especially in Prussia, drew the consequences of defeat and sought the means to propel the state into the modern age. In so doing, they were fully prepared to learn from the enemy and to 'appropriate the results of the revolution'.[13] Inspired by the intellectual rebirth that had been gaining ground in Germany ever since the Enlightenment, they hoped to create a social order which reflected the new mentality and the new political realities forged by Napoleon. None of the important leaders of this movement—Baron Karl vom Stein, Karl August von Hardenberg, Barthold Niebuhr, Gerhard von Scharnhorst and August Neidhardt von Gneisenau—were native Prussians and they tended to take a broad view which extended to all Germans. As Baron vom Stein said in St Petersburg on 20 November 1812:

I have but one fatherland and that is Germany; and since I have long felt that I belonged to it and not to any particular part, I am devoted to Germany, and not to any part of it, with all my heart. In this moment of great opportunity, dynasties are of no interest to me, they are mere instruments; it is my wish that Germany grow great and strong in order to recover her independence, self-reliance and nationhood. Germany must assert herself in her geographic location between France and Russia. This is in the interests of the nation and of all Europe, but it cannot be achieved through the decayed and mouldering structures of the past: . . . I believe in unity.[14]

In the interests of the nation, the citizenry would have to be encouraged to participate in national affairs. The state would have to create opportunities for citizens 'to provide for their happiness to the extent and in the way which they see fit'.[15]

It was a question of creating a legal opportunity for all the people to develop freely their human potential in a moral direction. In this way the people would be induced to love their king and fatherland to such an extent that they would gladly sacrifice both goods and lives for their sake.[16]

Every individual who 'worked and contributed in his own way'[17] was urged to enlist in the struggle against the enemy and to contribute to the common weal.

By taking up the spirit of German idealism, Stein sought through his reforms to foster a sense of responsibility and civic duty, of nationalism and love for the fatherland. But the people had to be allowed sufficient freedom to cultivate these virtues. Self-government would be slowly extended, first in the municipalities, then in the districts and provinces. Finally national organs of representative government would be created, affording the citizenry an opportunity to participate in the nation's business. Furthermore, serfdom would be abolished and legal restrictions on the right to exercise various occupations would disappear.

When Stein became a minister of the Prussian king, he succeeded in realising part of his great design. The Reform Edict of October 1807 provided for the free possession and utilisation of landed property and the elimination of serfdom and all domestic service to the overlord. All Prussians would be free as of St. Martin's Day, 1810. The peasantry gained personal freedom and freedom of movement, though field labour obligations remained in force, while the nobility was permitted to practise middle-class occupations.

Stein's Municipal Ordinance of 1808 introduced self-government in the cities. Burghers were henceforth permitted to elect representatives who then selected the town council. Cities also gained sole authority over their budgets, the school system and the poor, and were permitted to manage police affairs in the name of the state. Finally, Stein reorganised the bureaucracy, modernised the administration and severed its ties with the judiciary. At Napoleon's behest, however, the King of Prussia dismissed Stein in November 1808. His reforms were nevertheless continued by Karl von Hardenberg. Church property was secularised and in 1811 full freedom of occupation was proclaimed. Agrarian laws were reformed so that peasants could henceforth acquit the dues, rents and field-labour they owed in the form of money and could own the land they tilled. The Jews were emancipated in 1812 and became full citizens. However, Hardenberg abandoned Stein's emphasis on self-government and centralised the administration by replacing elected district councils with a director appointed by the king.

These social reforms were seconded by reorganisation of the army carried out by Gerhard von Scharnhorst, Neidhardt von Gneisenau and Hermann von Boyen. Parallel with the French model, universal military service was introduced in Prussia, and the recruitment system and the corporal punishments customary in the old mercenary armies of Frederick the Great were eradicated. Traditional exemptions from military service were discontinued, and officers were selected according to education and merit, not social class. Thus the military reforms also embodied an underlying ethical impulse which saw 'the essence of the new concept of the nation in the dignity and freedom of the individual'.[18] In the view of the reformers the renewed army should be composed of a standing army, a *Landwehr*, or militia, comprising all able-bodied men not on active service who would form the heart of the citizen soldiery, and a *Landsturm*, or home defense force, comprising older able-bodied people and those unfit for regular duty. Though Napoleon disallowed the *Landwehr* and though the nobility vehemently objected to a restructured military, the reformers succeeded in laying the foundations of an army whose foremost goal was to harness the spirit of self-sacrifice which free men brought to the service of their country.

For reform of the state and the army to be fully effective, education had to be reformed as well. Under the supervision of Wilhelm von Humboldt, the *Volksschule*, or elementary school, was reorganised in accordance with the educational theories of Johann Heinrich Pestalozzi, who advocated the natural development of the innate strengths and capacities of each individual. Humboldt bestowed a structure and content on the secondary schools which they have largely preserved to this day, and the Berlin university he founded became a model for other German universities. These universities came to view freedom of research and instruction 'across the full spectrum of science and the humanities' as crucial to their success.[19]

Austria too sought to revitalise the state under Count Johann Philipp von Stadion-Warthausen and to encourage the people to participate responsibly in political life. However, the internal strains of a multinational empire, financial constraints, the disorganised administration and the political indifference of much of the population proved insurmountable. The reformers' main attention was therefore soon diverted to the immediate goal of a war of liberation against Napoleon. In consequence, universal conscription was introduced and the Austrian army was reorganised by the popular Archduke Charles. After Stadion's dismissal in 1809, his successor, Count Klemens von Metternich, reverted to absolutist policies. Only absolutism, he thought, could counter the threat posed to the Habsburg Empire by the rising tide of nationalism.

Liberation from Napoleonic Rule

1808–9:   Revolt in Spain and Austria
1812:   The 'Grand Army' in Russia
1813–14: The Wars of Liberation
1815:   The Hundred Days; Waterloo

The war of liberation against Napoleon commenced in 1809. After an early victory, Austrian hopes were eventually crushed near Wagram. With defeat came Stadion's dismissal and an abrupt end to reform in the lands of the Habsburgs. The reorganised Austrian army with its companies of volunteers had managed to shake the myth of Napoleonic invincibility, and Austria had stood alone against the mighty French Empire, but her victories were fleeting. A multinational state such as Austria could not mount the kind of national war of independence which the Spanish had been waging since 1808 with the help of British arms. The ensuing peace treaty, signed in Vienna, compelled Austria to cede broad stretches of Bavaria to the French and .o renounce any and all attempts to lead a revolt of the German states against Napoleonic rule.

Of all the countries that sought to resist French domination, only Great Britain remained defiant. The Continental Blockade, which was intended to force the island kingdom to her knees, failed to achieve its political ends and indeed inflicted mounting damage on its instigators. Britain ruled the seas and could not be vanquished by an economic boycott; however, continental Europe could not long sustain the economic dislocation it was suffering. Moreover, if the blockade was to succeed, the French had continuously to redouble their efforts and further extend their sway. Sweden was constrained to enter the boycott, and Denmark joined the Tilsit scheme, though the British retaliated by destroying her fleet and bombarding Copenhagen.

Napoleon's rule over the Continent itself was threatened when Britain seized the opportunity afforded by the Spanish revolt and landed troops in Iberia. When later reviewing his life as a prisoner of the British on the island of St Helena, Napoleon commented, 'This hapless war was a calamity, the first cause of France's misfortune.' It 'ruined me'.[20]

The turning-point in Napoleon's career was reached when Russia withdrew from the Treaty of Tilsit and sought a rapproachement with Britain. Napoleon quickly responded to Alexander I's diplomatic manoeuvres with an invasion in June 1812. A huge French army supplemented by German, Italian, Dutch and Polish troops was expected to surprise the Russians, break their resistance and enter Moscow before the onset of winter. This strategy reflected the constraints of Napoleon's own position: hermetic control had to be maintained over the Continent if Britain—the only power that dared to defy French hegemony and Napoleonic dreams of world empire—was to be brought to heel. The emperor of the French therefore attacked Russia with a gargantuan army of 700,000 men. But all was in vain. This marvellous army was defeated in the end by the enormous expanses of Russia, the severity of the winter, and the passionate resistance of the conquered peoples of Europe.

At first though the Grand Army knew nothing but success and swept into Moscow in the middle of September 1812. But it did not find the expected refuge in which to pass the winter: as the Russians withdrew, they sent the city up in flames. Napoleon was thus deprived of the quick peace he expected in order to consolidate his grip on the Continent. The Grand Army, insufficiently supplied with food and equipment, was compelled to withdraw. It dragged its way across the interminable wastes of the Russian winter, continuously menaced and harassed by Cossack attack. As it finally thrashed across the Berezina River it was completely chewed up by Russian onslaughts.

On 30 December 1812 the commander of a Prussian auxiliary

corps, General Ludwig von Yorck, decided on his own initiative to withdraw from Prussia's forced alliance with France and to conclude a neutality pact with Russia. Napoleon's skilfully contrived web was beginning to unravel. Yorck had acted without the authorisation of the Prussian king, but as he explained in a letter to Frederick William on 3 January 1813, he believed his actions were warranted by the change in circumstances:

So long as everything proceeded normally, a loyal servant was bound to heed the constraints of the times; this was his duty. Circumstances have however created an entirely new situation and it is likewise the servant's duty to take advantage of a situation which may never arise again. I speak as an old and faithful servant and what I say expresses the feelings of well-nigh the entire nation.[21]

Eventually, the Prussian reformers managed to force the hand of the irresolute king, whose 'personal dislike of the war' had been 'immeasurably magnified'[22] by a peace party of conservatives hostile to reform. For a time Frederick William III hesitated to declare himself openly, concerned only that he act in concert with Austria which was cautiously awaiting developments. Then Baron vom Stein engineered the proclamation of general conscription in East Prussia. Finally convinced of which way the wind was blowing, Frederick William decided to ally himself with Russia in a final attempt to overthrow Napoleon. A call was issued to the Prussian people:

Neither My loyal subjects nor Germans require any explanation of the war that now begins. The Peace [of Tilsit], which deprived Me of half My subjects, inflicted deeper wounds than the war itself. We realised all too clearly that the emperor's treaties would slowly ruin us more surely than wars. Brandenburgers, Prussians, Silesians, Pomeranians, Lithuanians! remember why our forefathers fought and died: for honour, independence! Great sacrifices will be needed; we know you will willingly endure them for the sake of the fatherland and your native king. There is no other way but an honourable peace or glorious defeat. Even this you would face with good cheer for honour's sake.[23]

Following East Prussia's lead, a general uprising now began. Volunteers from across Germany streamed into Breslau—the temporary seat of the Prussian king—and mobilised for the war which, they hoped, would free them from Napoleon and revive the German Empire. 'Germany is arising and the bold beating of the wings of the Prussian eagle awakens in all true hearts the great hope of German or at least north German freedom. My heart sighs for the fatherland'[24]—so effused one of the young volunteers, the poet Theodor Körner who gave voice to the passion and enthusiasm of the rebels. The danger was great, but the rewards of peace and freedom in a pan-Germanic empire seemed worth the risk. But again Napoleon outwitted his enemies, defeating the combined Prussian and Russian forces near Grossgörschen and Bautzen. However, the heavy losses suffered by the French in this engagement convinced Napoleon that he should agree to an armistice mediated by Austria. This allowed the prostrated Prussians and Russians time to recover. In the ensuing negotiations, Austria demanded the return of Illyria and the dissolution of the Confederation of the Rhine and the Grand Duchy of Warsaw in return for recognising the Rhine as the French frontier. When Napoleon refused this abridgement of his power, Austria joined the grand coalition of Britain, Russia and Prussia. The Corsican's fate was sealed.

Bonaparte finally succumbed to his enemies at the battle of Leipzig in 1813 and was forced to withdraw with the remnants of his battered forces to France wither the allies pursued him. At home in Fontainebleau he agreed to vacate the throne. The victors restored the Bourbon dynasty to its ancestral privileges and permitted France to retain her borders of 1792. Napoleon was granted asylum in Elba and sovereign rights over the island.

The first Peace of Paris (1814) did not last. The discord among the allies over the new order in Europe and discontent within France over the restored Bourbon kings fed Napoleon's dreams of a return to power. In a surprise landing, he reappeared in the south of France where he was welcomed by the populace and French troops. But in his final battle at Waterloo, the little general again tasted defeat at the hands of Prussia and Britain. Once more he was compelled to abdicate and this time was banished to St Helena where he died in 1821.

The Napoleonic Empire was no more. Ultimately, Napoleon's attempt to exploit the forces unleashed by the French Revolution in order to extend French hegemony across the Continent was foiled. Napoleonic dominion over the occupied countries stirred up a tidal wave of nationalism which eventually engulfed the mighty general. A sense of nationhood and the struggle for freedom triumphed over the Napoleonic ideal of a rationally organised universal state.

The Reorganisation of Germany and Europe

1814–15: The Congress of Vienna
1815:   The Final Acts of Vienna; Second Peace of Paris (see Map 7)

The allies' ultimate victory over Napoleon spelled the end of more than twenty years of virtually uninterrupted warfare. But the upheaval of the French Revolution and the Napoleonic Wars had indelibly changed the face of Europe. New borders had been drawn, ancient dynasties had been overthrown and new monarchies had emerged. Time-honoured kingdoms had been replaced by regimes favourable to the emperor of the French. Vast stretches of the Continent were impoverished by war and financial exactions. Over three million men had died in battle. The general population longed for peace, security and governments that would recognise the new-found self-respect of their citizenry. All those who had worked to defeat Napoleon, patriots and statesmen alike, were preoccupied by the question of how a permanent peace could now be arranged in the wake of incessant turmoil.

The patriots hoped to overcome the quiltwork of German states and to found a united empire which, Johann Gottlieb Fichte proclaimed, it was now their duty to postulate.[25] But the princes, with Metternich in the vanguard, decried national unity as a serious threat to the peace of Europe. The great ideas of the century— freedom, the people and the fatherland—had struck a chord in German public opinion, but political realities seemed to shroud them in hopelessness and to defer far-reaching change to the distant future.

Summarising the spirit of the times, Goethe wrote in December 1813:

Do not believe for a moment that I am indifferent to the great ideas of freedom, the *Volk* and fatherland. No, these ideas are in us; they are part of our essence, and no one can ignore them. I too have a warm place in my heart for Germany. Often have I felt a deep pang when I think of the German people, who are so estimable individually and so wretched as a whole. To compare the German people with others arouses in us a feeling of anguish which I only attempt to overcome in any way which I can. Science and art provide the wings to carry one away. But the consolation they offer is cold and cannot replace the proud sense that one belongs to a people that is great, feared and respected. Comfort can only spring from faith in Germany's future.[26]

The great powers of Europe did certainly not consider that their best interests lay in the creation of a strong, feared and respected German empire in the heart of Europe. During the struggle against Napoleon, Britain, Austria, Prussia and Russia agreed that after the war the balance of power would be restored and guaranteed through a system of treaties. It was with this in mind that the statesmen gathered in Vienna sought to solve Europe's problems.

Relations between the powers would be set on a solid legal foundation guided by the principles of legitimacy, restoration and the solidarity of princes. Legitimate governments were those who could claim a historic right to govern. If a government had been overthrown by Napoleon, it was restored. Territorial integrity was guaranteed by treaties and defended by the concert of nations against any interloper. The 'legitimate' Bourbon kings were restored to their throne in France, and under these conditions the French were allowed to participate in Vienna as the fifth of the great powers of Europe.

Britain undoubtedly emerged as the great beneficiary of the struggle to end French dominance of Europe. Alongside Metternich, the British emissary, Lord Castlereagh, carried most weight at the congress. Britain drew further advantage from the fact that British and Austrian interests tended to run parallel: both powers were eager to halt French and Russian expansionism and to consolidate their own position. London considered the security of the coast facing England as a key to the restoration of the balance of power and to the consolidation of its own maritime superiority. English dominion over the seas was now unquestionable thanks to the acquisition of Gibraltar, Cyprus, Malta, Heligoland, Ceylon and the Cape of Good Hope, and in London's view, none of the five great powers should be allowed to dominate the continental coast. Since Vienna no longer wished to assume responsibility for protecting Germany's western flank against French encroachment (prefering instead to focus attention on Austrian interests in southeastern Europe), it willingly forsook the Austrian Netherlands. They were united with Holland to form the Kingdom of the United Netherlands. To the north, Sweden was to provide a bulwark against Russia which had expanded into Finland. Sweden was weakened by the cession of Upper Pomerania to Prussia, but received Norway as generous compensation.

Castlereagh, Metternich and the French foreign minister, Charles Maurice de Talleyrand, formed a united front against further Russian annexations in Poland. So the Grand Duchy of Warsaw, which Napoleon had concocted in 1807 from former Prussian and Austrian holdings, was given a new lease on life as the Kingdom of Poland with its own constitution, administration and army. However, Tsar Alexander I did manage to have Poland linked with Russia through the personal union of a Russian vice-regent. And at the end of the negotiations, Russia was confirmed as the mightiest land power in Europe.

Austria lost not only the Netherlands but also her south German possessions, the *Sundgau* in upper Alsace and the *Breisgau* in Baden. But she recovered Tyrol and Carinthia, annexed Carniola, Trieste, Galicia and Lombardy and emerged as a great eastern European power.

Thanks to Talleyrand's superior diplomatic skills, France recovered her status as a great power and retained Alsace, much to the sorrow of German patriots. It was with considerable pride that Talleyrand reported to Louis XVIII:

No longer is France isolated in Europe. . . . Your Majesty now possesses a system of alliances which could not have been devised in fifty years of negotiations. Today you may act in concert with two of the greatest powers and with three powers of the second rank; soon you will be allied with all states whose principles and political goals are not subversive. One can only assume that providence, which was so conspicuously present in Your Majesty's ascension to the throne, had a hand in such a great and fortunate reversal.[27]

The territorial restructuring of Germany was far-reaching, creating a completely new balance of power in Central Europe. But the German question itself remained unresolved.

The Germans were in a unique position, quite unlike that of any of the other nations with whom they joined to gain the victory. Russia and England, Sweden, Prussia and Austria emerged in their well-known configurations and needed only to gather the fruits of victory and incorporate them into the existing whole. Poland and Italy, long deprived of independence and only deluded by Napoleon with illusions of such, bowed to the hazards of war though they did not seem to suffer considerable loss. Spain, Portugal and Denmark, though shaken, remained in command of their ancestral domains. The Netherlands were pleased to have added territory and Switzerland to have renewed itself and received universal guarantees. But in Germany everything was torn asunder, the fragments partly reattached and partly surrendered.[28]

As Austria withdrew from Germany, Prussia consolidated her position within the empire. By acquiring the Rhineland and Westphalia, Prussia became France's immediate neighbour in the west while elsewhere it added northern Saxony and, with the annexation of Posen, Thorn and Danzig, cemented ties to its eastern territories. The lands conferred upon Prussia at the Congress of Vienna deeply involved her in the affairs of Western Europe; at the same time, the continued bifurcation of Prussia into separate parts meant that she would pursue an expansionist course.

As the great German power in the north, Prussia faced to the south three states of medium-size: Baden, Württemberg and Bavaria. As in central Germany, local pride and local loyalties in the south had intensified when Napoleon elevated petty princes to new glory. Hence the region was now little inclined to renounce its sovereignty in favour of a unified German state. South Germans cherished 'no other interest than the preservation and prosperity of their dear homeland. What sort of a disaster would it be if their dear homeland should not survive, if it should be replaced by another?'[29] In regard to Germany, the statesmen assembled in Vienna were largely moti-vated by dynastic egotism, multinational Austria's distrust of the forces of nationalism and liberalism and finally the fear in Britain, France and Russia of the incalculable consequences 'if a mass of people as in Germany become aggressive when mingled'.[30] The ultimate result of all these considerations was the formation of the *Deutsche Bund*, or German Confederation.

The *Bund* was conceived as a loose federation comprising thirty-five sovereign states and the four free cities of Frankfurt on the Main, Bremen, Hamburg and Lübeck. Its avowed purpose was to 'maintain Germany's external and internal security and the inde-pendence and integrity of the several German states'.[31] Its political heart was the *Bundestag*, a federal diet of delegates which met permanently in Frankfurt on the Main under the presidency of Austria. Decisions required at least a two-thirds majority and in many cases unanimity. As a result, the Diet was seldom capable of action. Its deliberations were further complicated by the fact that three foreign princes were members of the Confederation: the British king in his role as King of Hanover, the Danish king as Duke of Holstein, and the King of the Netherlands as Grand Duke of Luxembourg.

As sole concession to the intellectual climate of the times, the Act of Confederation contained assurances that the several states con-stituting the *Bund* would enact constitutions and guarantee freedom of the press. At the outset, however, this provision remained a dead letter with the exception of several small states and the medium-sized states in the south which were eager to reiterate in constitu-tional form their annexation of new regions.

The restoration of the old system of states was sealed by the signing of the second Treaty of Paris on 20 November 1815. The prudent self-restraint evidenced by all the statesmen at the congress doubtless went a long way towards bestowing a lengthy period of peace upon the Continent. The five great states had devised a balance of power, carefully tended by Britain, which would deter-mine the outward shape of Europe for four decades. France reverted to its boundaries of 1790, and the Russian drive to the west was halted at the Vistula. Relieved of her concern that one of these powers might come to dominate the Continent, Britain felt free to consolidate her dominion over the seas and the colonies. Austria strengthened her hand in south-east Europe and Prussia established an impregnable position in northern Germany.

The problem of German dualism remained however unresolved. Eventually, the system so carefully elaborated in Vienna would be destroyed by this failure together with the refusal of the traditional states to recognise the spirit of the times and to accommodate the national and liberal movement in Germany. The political and intellectual history of the nineteenth century would be dominated by the struggle which soon resumed between national and constitutional ideals on the one hand and the traditional social and political order personified by Metternich on the other.

4

The Restoration

1815:   The Holy Alliance, Foundation of the German *Burschenschaft* in Jena
1816:   Haller's *Restoration of Political Economy*; the end of reform in Prussia
1817:   Wartburg Festival of the *Burschenschaft*
1819:   Karl Ludwig Sand assassinates August von Kotzebue; Karlsbad Decrees
1821–3: Greek War of Independence
1823:   Monroe Doctrine
1830:   July Revolution in France; rebellion in Belgium, Spain, Switzerland and Poland; uprisings in Germany
1832:   Hambach Festival
1834:   Foundation of the German Customs Union
1837:   The Göttingen Seven
1840–61: Frederick William IV
1840–1: The Rhenish question; France joins Egypt against the great powers of Europe; Turkey saved by the Treaty of the Dardanelles

Europe under the Holy Alliance

Time hurtles forward; it would be vain to attempt to arrest its stormy course. All that the friends and protectors of order can do is to mitigate its destructiveness through firmness, moderation and wisdom, through unanimity and wise appraisal of the strengths which unanimity confers. . . . Our aim is very simple to delineate: nothing more or less than the preservation of the world as we know it. All that exists can be saved and part of what has been lost can be recovered. To this end must be bent all individual efforts and all public undertakings by those who share similar interests and a similar outlook. In times such as these, transition from old structures to new structures is more fraught with danger than retreat from new structures to the crumbling old structures.[1]

Prince Klemens von Metternich penned these lines after the Congress of Vienna in a letter to Wilhelm von Berstett, a government minister in Baden. They unveil what would be the guiding principles behind state policy for the next thirty-three years. This tranquil era seems generally void of striking political events, if understood in terms of wars, revolutions and grand struggles.[2] It seems much more remarkable, however, if we consider that the political order drawn up by the Congress of Vienna—including the restructuring of Germany in the German Confederation—largely contradicted the spirit of the times. Moreover, beneath the placid exterior, the national and constitutional ideas that prepared the political reality of the middle of the century were quietly maturing. As the century progressed, resistance to aristocratic rule slowly waxed, eventually bursting into open opposition. The developing antagonisms gave rise to a new social order and sparked the wars which once again reshaped the face of Europe in the second half of the nineteenth century.

For the present, though, the princes of Europe stood united in their attempts to achieve the goals outlined by Metternich and to protect the social order which they had created after 1815. Their claims to the obedience of their subjects and to the territories ascribed to them by the Congress of Vienna were based on theories of legitimism akin to those advanced by the Swiss patrician Carl Ludwig von Haller in his six-volume opus, *The Restoration of Political Economy*. This work, which lent its name to the era whose guiding ideology it defined, assailed all notions of the sovereignty of the people and all contract theories of government in order to advance the case of legitimism:

Princes . . . are not entrusted with the right to rule but possess it innately. Power is not delegated to them by the people . . . for they already possess that power and the higher freedom which it confers. They are not created by the people; on the contrary, it is they who have slowly gathered the people around them, taken them into their service. Princes are not the first servants of the state . . . not high-ranking bureaucrats, not even heads of state (as the faulty principles of the civil contract, the sovereignty of the people and delegated authority would imply); princes are . . . independent lords . . . with dominion over their own affairs.[3]

The rulers of Europe were determined to defend the status quo in international relations and within each state to restore absolute monarchy based on the grace of God. This firm intention was embodied after 1815 in a series of reactionary internal and external measures. At the instigation of Tsar Alexander I, the rulers of

Russia, Austria and Prussia formed the Holy Alliance, swearing to uphold patriarchial authority over their subjects, 'to defend justice, peace and religion' and 'to provide help and support in any place'[4] against all revolutionary activities. The five great powers of Europe agreed to settle any disputes among them by way of negotiation at international congresses and conferences. If rebellion or revolution were to rear its ugly head, a joint resolution would be passed offering military assistance in defending the divine rights of the ruler.

By 1820 this declaration had already been put into effect. At the Congress of Laibach the eastern powers agreed, despite British opposition, to dispatch Austrian troops to help quash a rebellion in Italy. Two years later these powers resolved at the Congress of Verona to request that French troops put down disturbances in Spain.

Germany formed a 'Congress Europe in miniature', as one wit observed.[5] Austria assumed the leadership of the German states while the new confederation stood watch over the interests of the sundry rulers. The princes of Germany had welcomed the national movement during the dark days of the Napoleonic Wars, but now the Bund acted 'as an opponent rather than a proponent' of nationalism.[6] The strength and love of freedom inherent in the national movement were now seen as dire threats. Almost without exception, censorship and police powers were heavily utilised.

The rulers and their ministers observed with distrust the 'demagogic agitation' of students who had grown politically aware during the struggle against Napoleon and who now rejected the intellectual world of their fathers—men, in their view , who were indifferent to 'great thoughts and deeds, enamoured only of never-ending quietude'. The older generation wished only to 'leave everything as it is'[7] and to conform to the social conditions imposed by the Congress of Vienna. Buoyed by the cameraderie of the Wars of Liberation and by pride in the victory over Napoleon, some of these students joined together in Jena in 1815 to form the German *Burschenschaft*. They swore 'to recapture, at least within the life of the university, the unity which went astray in the larger world'[8] and to seek a 'German national state founded in freedom and unity'.[9] As the outward and visible sign of their movement they choose the colours red, black and gold. These subsequently came to symbolise the struggle for German unity. Red, black and gold fleetingly became the national colours in 1848 and once more in 1919 before they were adopted by the Federal Republic of Germany in 1949 as a sign of the free and democratic order to which the students had aspired so many years before.

Heinrich von Gagern, a law student and later President of the German National Assembly in Frankfurt, formulated the aims of the students in a letter to his father:

we wish to see among the several states of Germany a stronger sense of community, greater unity of policy and of state precepts, not particularism but close federative cooperation. In summary, we wish Germany to be viewed as one country and the German people as one people. We strongly hope that this will be possible in concrete terms and we demonstrate it in the life of our *Burschenschaft*. Regional cliques are banned for we live in a German *Burschenschaft*, one people in spirit as we should like to be in reality across the length and breadth of Germany. We have enacted the freest of constitutions, since we hope to have in Germany the freest possible constitution that suits the German people. We want a constitution for the people that is enlightened and reflects the spirit of the age; each ruler should not merely concede to his subjects what pleases him and serves his interests. In general, we want the rulers to be convinced and to believe that they exist for the country, not the country for them. Most of us are of the opinion that the constitution should not be the work of the individual states but that the basic principles of the German constitution should be universally valid and enacted by the Diet of the German Confederation.[10]

With these aims in mind, the Jena *Burschenschaft* invited students from all the German lands to a celebration to be held in October 1817 at Wartburg Castle in Thuringia. The immediate occasion was the third centenary of the Reformation and the fourth anniversary of the Battle of Leipzig on 16–18 October 1813, though the students' advocacy of a united Germany and democratic political rights were much in evidence. Ludwig Rödiger, a nineteen-year-old philosophy and theology student, rose to demand the 'just and united fatherland'[11] which the princes had promised during the dark days of the Wars of Liberation and proclaimed that 'He who has bled for the fatherland has earned the right to say how he best can serve it in times of peace'.[12]

Two years later a student close to the *Burschenschaft* movement, Karl Ludwig Sand, assassinated the writer and alleged Russian agent August von Kotzebue. Metternich seized the opportunity to promulgate the Karlsbad Decrees with the help of the German Confederation. These decrees provided for government officials to supervise German universities, banned the *Burschenschaften*, tightened censorship and established a Central Office of Investigation 'to enquire more deeply into the revolutionary intrigues uncovered in several German states'.[13] A new execution ordinance was introduced as well. Originally Metternich had opposed the concession of any universal competences to the Diet of the German Confederation, but now he relented in the interest of enforcing peace and tranquility in Germany.

Frederick William III exploited the same events to extend the full severity of the Karlsbad Decrees to Prussia. He ordered the arrest of Friedrich Ludwig Jahn, founder of the gymnastics movement and a co-founder of the *Burschenschaften* and suspended from his professorship in Bonn Ernst Moritz Arndt, a well-known and ardent advocate of German unity. Even such stalwart figures as Stein, Gneisenau and Schleiermacher were suspected of 'demagogy', and the reforms that had been initiated were postponed or cancelled. Self-government was not instituted in the countryside, and the liberation of the peasantry in the end benefited the latifundia, simply creating a kind of rural proletariat.

The King of Prussia also took measures to reduce the independence of the Lutheran and reformed churches. He proclaimed the Prussian Union between Lutherans and reformed Christians, thus founding the Prussian Evangelical Church. State control of the church, which had almost completely disappeared under the old absolutistic state, was resurrected, and the church returned to the purview of the king. In this way Frederick William created a specifically Prussian brand of Protestantism with strong political overtones (similar to the brand of Catholicism restored by Pius VII after 1815 with emphasis on the unquestioned authority of the pope). Thus the union of throne and altar, which became emblematic of the period after 1815, was institutionalised in Prussia.

The heads of the several Prussian bureaucracies were invited to sit on a newly created State Council (*Staatsrat*), and the heavy-handed bureaucrats so deplored by Stein returned to power and influence. Not a word was breathed of joint responsibility and participation, so much in vogue under Stein; the order of the day was now virtually absolute monarchy reinforced by phalanxes of 'hired academics—disinterested bureaucrats without property of their own' who carried out the commands of the king 'unnoticed, unknown and unrecognised'.[14]

The bourgeoisie, once again excluded from politics, withdrew into its inner sphere of family life, business interests and the rich spirituality which typified the culture of the Biedermeier period with its neo-Gothic architecture, home music and skilful craftsmanship. Ever since the late middle ages the German bourgeoisie had assumed economic power and had developed great enthusiasm for education, but it failed to gain political power. Though total abstention from the political arena proved of short duration, withdrawal from politics remained typical of the German people as their nation gradually took shape.[15]

This was probably the most influential legacy of the philosopher Georg Wilhelm Friedrich Hegel who conceived of the state as an all-embracing absolute:

Only through the state does man's existence become reasonable. Man owes all that he is to the state and in this is his essence. Man derives his value and spiritual reality from the state. . . . The state does not exist for the burgher; instead, the state is the goal, and the burgher is the means.[16]

Political Liberalism and the Effects of the July Revolution in France

The Hegelian view of the state stood in stark contrast to that of the liberals. Liberal political and economic interests demanded the dismantling of the all-powerful state and the liberal conception of freedom required that the state merely serve to defend its citizens in accordance with the provisions of a written constitution.

Elsewhere in Europe, liberals in Spain and Italy had already revolted in 1820 against the restoration of the old regime. Though these revolts were shattered by dint of French and Austrian arms, the Holy Alliance failed to extend its sway to Latin America, where Spanish and Portuguese colonists were fighting for their independence under the leadership of Simon Bolivar. Here the Holy Alliance was confounded by British opposition and strong objections from the United States President James Monroe declared:

The political system of the [European] powers is essentially different . . . from that of America. . . . We owe it, therefore, to candor and to the amicable relations existing between the United States and those powers to declare that we should consider any attempt on their part to extend their system to any portion of this hemisphere as dangerous to our peace and safety. We could not view any interposition [in this hemisphere] by any European power in any other light than as the manifestation of an unfriendly disposition toward the United States.[17]

Thus, for the first time, the United States laid claim to a sphere of influence in both American continents. The Monroe Doctrine, named after the president who promulgated it, established the principle of 'America for Americans' and served notice on the Europeans that intervention in the Americas would be a *casus belli*.

Britain, aware that her commercial interests would suffer from European intervention, also opposed intervention by the Holy Alliance. In so doing, the British government artfully contrived to leave the impression that it wished to champion freedom and the

interests of the developing countries of the Americas against interference from the reactionary states of the old world. Propaganda
about freedom subsequently came to play a major role in the British
presence around the world.

At the same time, Greece rose in revolt against its Turkish
oppressor. Once again Britain took the side of the freedom fighters,
as did Prussia and Bavaria. The Bavarian king even went so far as to
dispatch an army corps. Many European intellectuals became warm
supporters of the Greek cause, and even Goethe declared himself
'moderately' pro-Hellenist.

The Russian tsar, still the chief standard-bearer of orthodoxy and
the initiator of the Holy Alliance, was torn by the thorny connun-
drum of whether a Christian ruler ought to recognise legitimate
Islamic rule. Metternich, on the other hand, did not hesitate to
decry the uprising in Greece as a highly dangerous example to the
multinational Austrian Empire. Fearing a shift in the balance of
power in the Balkans, he threw Austria's support behind the Turkish cause. The resulting wrangle tore the Holy Alliance to shreds. In
1825 Russia declared war on the Turks while Britain and France also
interceded against them. Ultimately Prussia mediated in 1829 the
Peace of Adrianople, which made Greece an independent monarchy. The eastern question precipitated by these events, however,
would long haunt relations between Austria, Russia and Britain
over pre-eminence in the Balkans and the Turkish straits.

The tranquillity of Europe was shattered in July 1830 when a
revolution broke out in France. Liberal and national ideals welled to
the surface and played an ever-increasing role in public affairs,
eventuating in the great mid-century crisis, the revolution of 1848.
In France the Bourbons had been restored to power in the personage of Louis XVIII, brother of the hapless Louis XVI, who had been
executed in 1793. The constitution proclaimed by the king in 1814
was derived from the British model and fashioned a French constitutional monarchy. The crown constituted the executive while a
bicameral parliament assumed legislative powers. The members of
the first chamber were selected by the king, and the deputies in the
second were elected by a relatively restricted circle of French
citizens who held enough property to qualify as voters. The nobility, returning from exile, insisted on the restoration of the *ancien
régime* with full restitution of their privileges and properties. This
objective was bitterly opposed by the French bourgeoisie, which
was equally determined to preserve what it had gained in the
revolution. In the summer of 1830 Louis' successor, Charles X,
decided to limit further the right to vote and to extend press

censorship. Workers and students in Paris reacted violently and forced Charles to abdicate. The deputies then named Duke Louis Philippe d'Orléans 'King of the French'. He ruled in accordance with the principles of parliamentary monarchy, while the nobility, which had regained its pre-eminence under the Bourbon restoration, was once again displaced by a bourgeoisie determined 'to uphold the rule of law and to defend the nation'.[18]

In the same year an insurrection broke out in the United Netherlands. The Congress of Vienna had fused the Catholic, artisan south, which had been pro-French and democratically minded ever since the French Revolution, with the largely Protestant north, the economy of which turned more on trade. In 1830 the Catholic south rose in revolt against Dutch rule and demanded union with France. Britain, however, opposed any such extension of French territory. Ultimately the Kingdom of Belgium was created as a compromise. According to a resolution passed in 1831 at the London conference of the great powers, she would be a neutral state guaranteed by all five powers. London thus successfully upheld the principle enunciated in 1815 that none of the great powers of Europe should occupy the coastline facing England.

Not only in Western Europe did the revolution in France trigger further changes in the political status quo. Central, southern and eastern Europe were also shaken by insurrection and revolt. Civil war erupted anew on the Iberian Peninsula, and Italy was swept by a wave of revolution. In Switzerland the bourgeoisie pushed through a liberalisation of the constitution of the cantons, and in those stretches of Polish territory which the Congress of Vienna had handed over to Russia, a revolution broke out. After a year of heroic struggle, the Polish patriots were crushed by massed Russian power with assistance from Prussia. The last vestiges of Poland's modest autonomy disappeared.

In Germany the Polish cause fired the imagination of the liberal bourgeoisie. After the disillusionment of the restoration era, ever more German burghers supported the time-honoured demands of the patriots for political rights set down in a constitution, constitutional guarantees, freedom of the press, jury trials, a people's militia and closely cooperating individual states within a single federal system. The tension between these demands and the reactionary mood of the various local governments prompted a great radicalisation of the liberal movement in virtually all the German states. The Duke of Brunswick was compelled to yield, and here as well as in Saxony, Hesse-Kassel and Hannover constitutions were granted after serious outbreaks of violence in the major cities. The provincial Diet of Baden took steps in 1831 to reinstate the constitution, which the reaction had emasculated, and turned its attention once again to the problems of federal reform, freedom of the press, elimination of the tithe system and jury trial.

Writers of the late Romantic period, styling themselves the Young Germany movement (*Das Junge Deutschland*), threw themselves into the struggle against the autocratic state. The two most prominent representatives of this literary vanguard were Heinrich Heine and Ludwig Börne. The Young Germany movement stood for civil emancipation, the equality of men and women, full civil rights for Jews and freedom of the press, literature and the theatre. These writers demanded constitutional limitations on the absolute power of the princes and extolled the sovereignty of the people, which would eventually culminate in a republic. Autocracy, meanwhile, received strong support from the forces of reaction within the Protestant and Catholic churches.

The demands of the Young Germany movement dominated the first large political demonstration in Germany organised by the Radical Liberals Philipp Jakob Siebenpfeiffer and Johann Georg August Wirth. On 27 May 1832 approximately 30,000 students and citizens gathered at Hambach Castle near Neustadt on the Hardt. Standing beneath a flag of red, black and gold, the symbol of German freedom, Siebenpfeiffer prophesied, 'The day will surely come when a common German fatherland arises'; in this hope and expectation, cheers were offered to a free and united Germany and to 'every nation that bursts its chains and pays hommage with us to the league of freedom. . . . Cheers to the fatherland, freedom, the league of peoples!'[19]

If the Hambach Festival had alarmed the various German governments, the 'storming of the Frankfurt guard-house' on 3 April 1833 unnerved them completely. Students from the *Burschenschaft* and some citizens stormed the main Frankfurt guard-house and rang the alarm-bell till soldiers appeared. Even before the Hambach Festival, Metternich had been urging the monarchies of the German Bund to adopt suitable measures in their joint defence. Now the *Bundestag* hastened to act, quickly approving regulations similar to the earlier 'Karlsbad Decrees'. The rights of the deputies from the German states were curtailed, freedom of speech and assembly were abrogated, and censorship tightened. Again a Central Office of Investigation was constituted, this time in Frankfurt on the Main, and it adopted even severer measures against 'demagogues'. Hundreds of the regime's opponents disappeared for long stretches in prison. The liberal national movement fell silent for the time being, and another wave of emigrants fled into neighbouring countries and the United States. Many of these emigrants—persecuted intellectuals, students, radical artisans and journeymen—published pamphlets and newspapers and smuggled them across the border into Germany in an attempt to continue influencing political developments in their homeland. In Paris a group of radical republicans founded the league of the Outcast (*Bund der Geächteten*) in 1834, from which a socialist branch soon broke off calling itself the League of the Righteous (*Bund der Gerechten*). The latter stood for an idealistic socialist conception of shared property and it was this group which Karl Marx contacted upon his arrival in Paris in 1844.

In 1837 the King of Hanover took steps to suspend the constitution, but German society had become so politicised that autocratic measures were no longer greeted with quiet acquiesence. The storm of popular protest was led by seven professors at the University of Göttingen. 'This concerns all of Germany', declared one of the 'Göttingen Seven', the historian Friedrich Christoph Dahlmann. 'If a state constitution can be smashed like a toy before the very eyes of the Confederation ... then Germany's immediate future has already been determined.'[20]

The German Customs Union

Despite the radicalisation of the liberal movement and surging popular support for nationalism and liberalism, no concrete political success had yet been achieved. Suddenly, from an entirely different quarter, came a highly significant step in the direction of national unification.

The German Confederation had tried but failed to eliminate the tariffs between the various German states. This economic division endured despite the determined attempts of the Swabian Friedrich List—professor, deputy and later consul of the United States of America—to call attention to the benefits of a unified German economy. Only when Prussia decided to pursue economic treaties with most of the states of the German Bund did List's concept of a German customs union reach fruition.

The Prussian economy was particularly vulnerable to all the tariffs hampering commerce in the German lands. Prussia's Rhenish provinces were separated from the rest of the country by a string of small states, and she lacked both direct access to the North Sea and control over the mouths of the Elbe, Weser or Rhine. By the tariff law of May 1818 Prussia united her territories in a single customs block and introduced the principle of moderate free trade. But the other German states proved loath to adopt the Prussian system and continued to suffer from the adverse economic conditions which Friedrich List so eloquently condemned:

Thirty-eight different tariff and customs barriers in Germany hobble internal commerce and have approximately the same effect as if each limb of a human body were so trussed that the blood could not flow from one to the other. For Hamburg to do business with Austria or Berlin with Switzerland, ten different states have to be crossed, ten tariff and customs schedules studied, ten transit tariffs paid. Those who have the misfortune of dwelling in a border region where three or four states converge spend their entire lives dealing with hostile customs-officers and tariff agents; they have no real homeland. Their plight becomes hopeless if they should like to engage in trade and industry. Such men cast envious glances across the Rhine where a single great people lives, from the English Channel to the Mediterranean Sea, from the Rhine to the Pyrenees, from the Dutch frontier to Italy, engaging in commerce on free rivers and open roads, with never a customs officer to be seen.[21]

The German Customs Union of 1834 finally created a cohesive economic zone comprising 23 million people. In this unified market the steadily expanding production of the German states could be bought and sold in accordance with one set of rules. So far as foreign trade is concerned, the Customs Union pursued a policy of moderate free trade and allowed nearly all imported goods to enter tax-free. The advantages this conferred on nascent German industry were immediately evident.

From a political point of view, the Customs Union divided the German Bund into two blocs. However, the distinctive political, economic and geographic dualism of Germany was overcome for the first time in the economic sphere through Austria's self-isolation. Contemporaries were doubtless aware of the impact that economic union would have on the Metternich system. Prussia's minister of finance, Friedrich von Motz, who deserves much of the credit for the customs arrangement, summarised its probable consequences in a memorandum to the king:

If it is an axiom of political economy that import, export and transit taxes are due solely to political divisions between states, the converse must also be true, namely the unification of these states in a customs and trade union will eventually induce union within one and the same political system.[22]

Frederick William IV, the new Prussian king who had ascended the throne in 1840, basked in the glory of the ensuing upswing in his nation's prestige and became the darling of the German national movement which expected much of him. Only too soon did it become obvious, however, that these hopes were misplaced. To the bitter disappointment of those patriots who expected Prussia to drive Germany towards national unity, Frederick proved to be a late Romantic at heart yearning for a return to the old order. He commenced his reign with a series of liberal edicts which liberated political prisoners, loosened censorship, rehabilitated patriots such as Friedrich Ludwig Jahn and Ernst Moritz Arndt, who had been persecuted under his father, and reinstated some of the Göttingen professors; but he proved unwilling to enact a modern constitution, a mere 'sheet of paper'. Like his father before him, Frederick refused to redeem the long-standing pledge—announced in the dark days of the Napoleonic Wars—to grant a constitution. Eventually the Diet had to be convened since its approval was required to take out the financial loans necessitated by the expanding railway system. Only then in 1847 did Frederick William summon the Estates to Berlin, though he spelled out in an opening address that the convocation of the United Diet by no means implied that constitutional changes should be expected:

I feel it is imperative solemnly to declare that no power on earth shall ever succeed in impelling me to transform into a constitutional convention the natural relationship between the ruler and his people, a relationship whose inner truth is a source of great strength, especially to us. I shall never allow a written sheet of paper to intervene like a second Providence between this land and God in Heaven, to rule us with its paragraphs and to raise them above the sacred fidelity of old. Let us speak bluntly and openly. I know I am free of one vice: I do not seek vainly to curry popular favour. . . . My only wish is to do my duty to the best of my ability and in accordance with my conscience and to earn the gratitude of my people even though it might never be forthcoming.[23]

There could be no doubt that cooperative change in the authoritarian regime was out of the question.

In the meantime, the sense of German nationhood had been reinforced by the French threat. In order to further her policy of conquest and colonisation in Africa, France supported the Egyptian viceroy, Mehmed Ali, in his hegemonic claims over Turkey. Paris immediately found itself on a collision course with Britain, Russia and Austria, which refused to accept a further weakening of Turkey's position in the Mediterranean. Ultimately, France felt compelled to recognise the Treaty of the Dardanelles between Turkey and the great powers by which Turkey's territorial integrity was guaranteed and all non-Turkish ships of war were excluded from the Straits. Isolated and eager to make amends for her diplomatic defeat, France once more turned a covetous gaze to the Rhine.

The gathering threat set off a wave of indignation in Germany. The old enmity towards France flared anew, and a feeling of nationalism rooted in Francophobia pulled Germans closer together despite all the territorial divisions. Those who yearned for a free and united Germany, which observed the rights of her citizens and commanded the respect of her neighbours, succumbed to the spell of new patriotic songs: Nikolaus Becker's 'Sie sollen ihn nicht haben, den freien deutschen Rhein' (You shall not have it, the free German Rhine), Max Schneckenburger's 'Die Wacht am Rhein' (The Watch on the Rhine) and, one year later, Hoffmann von Fallersleben's 'Deutschlandlied' with its programmatic conclusion, 'unity, justice and freedom for our German fatherland'. Whether young patriots in the *Burschenschaften* or older, liberal burghers concerned about economic progress, many Germans felt that the Metternich system was cracking and would no longer be able to contain the momentum in the direction of social and national emancipation.

The Revolution of 1848

1847: War of the *Sonderbund* in Switzerland
1848: February Revolution in France; March Revolution in Germany; Independence struggles in Italy, Bohemia and Hungary; National Assembly in Frankfurt am Main; Formation of a provisional central government; war against Denmark; Truce of Malmö; the old established powers recover their strength
1849: The national constitution is passed; the King of Prussia is elected German emperor; the German National Assembly is dissolved; the people rebel
1850: The Prussian Constitution; the failure of Prussian plans for a union

War of the *Sonderbund* in Switzerland and the Outbreak of Revolution in France

On the eve of the fateful events of 1848 discontent with the prevailing conditions had become widespread. From the English Channel to the borders of the Russian Empire a public debate was beginning to assert its authority and press for the realisation of its political and social demands. In Italy and Germany these demands were intensified by a frustrated longing for national unity and independence which united almost all sections of the population. At a time when the population of almost all countries was increasing sharply, economic difficulties, unemployment, failed harvests, food shortages and rising prices did nothing to reduce the political unrest. Governments which resorted to force met with no success. On the contrary, this only added to the widespread discontent of societies in the throes of political turmoil and strengthened the repressed peoples in their will to resist.

The first impulse which prompted the violent and bloody struggle about to take place between the conservative systems wrought by Metternich and the liberal and progressive new order passionately desired by all classes of society came from Switzerland. The Congress of Vienna had replaced the United Helvetic Republic with a loose confederation of states consisting of twenty-two cantons of varying political and religious orientations. In 1831 those cantons which were of a primarily Protestant persuasion had succeeded in abolishing the aristrocracy from their own territory and extending their constitutions along democratic lines. The conservative Catholic cantons, fearing that they would be overruled by a majority vote, joined together in a special federation, known as the *Sonderbund*, which opposed the efforts of the democrats to unite the cantons in a federal state.

In 1847 Geneva and St Gallen joined the side of the radical democratic cantons, and a majority of them demanded the dissolution of the *Sonderbund*. This led to a civil war which ended in victory for the supporters of the federal idea. In place of the confederation of states there arose a strong unitary federal state with a democratic constitution, which centralised the military, the post, the mint, weights, measures, and customs and excise, and guaranteed the people important fundamental rights, but also recognised the basic sovereignty of the individual cantons.

This victory for the popular democratic movement caused immediate reactions in the rest of Europe. In addition to this, the forces intent on change were encouraged by events in Italy, where a wave of political, liberal and national unrest had swept the country after the election of the reformist Pope Pius IX in 1846, to be rekindled in January 1848 with the Sicilian uprising, which, with Britain's assistance, resulted in the setting up of both a liberal government and a constitution.

The real revolutionary spark which suddenly caused the pent up energies to explode was once again however, kindled in France. After the July Revolution of 1830 the policies of the French king Louis Philippe, which favoured the middle classes, had enabled the bourgeoisie to become the dominant political and economic force in France. The petite bourgeoisie and the workers, who felt cheated of the fruits of the July Revolution, reacted against this. They demanded equal political rights, and universal and secret franchise instead of the property qualification, which favoured the wealthy. Moreover, in the face of rapidly spreading unemployment—a consequence of the economic crisis which was shaking the whole of Europe—they demanded the statutory right to work. Demonstrations for electoral reform held by students and workers led to the battle on the barricades from 22 to 24 February 1848, to the abdication of the king and to the proclamation of the republic.

The provisional government of the poet Alphonse de Lamartine promised to guarantee the right to employment demanded by the workers. National workshops were set up to combat unemployment, guaranteeing the workers a minimum wage, and the right of universal franchise was proclaimed. The crisis began when the petite bourgeoisie, afraid of the increasingly radical proletarian movement, and the peasants, whose taxes had been increased in order to finance the national workshops, took the side of the wealthy bourgeoisie, giving them a clear majority in the National Assembly after the election. In spite of this electoral defeat, the radical minority hoped that mass demonstrations would force a new government to be formed. Finally the critical finances of the state and the radicalisation of the workers in the totally uneconomical national workshops caused the government to order their closure, and open conflict ensued.

In the June battle, the working-class masses in Paris were subdued by military force, and Prince Louis Napoleon, Bonaparte's nephew, was elected president for a period of ten years in a national referendum. Thus the peasants, the petite bourgeoisie and the upper-middle classes gained victory over the proletariat, who had for the first time intervened in the course of events from a position of class consciousness and had challenged bourgeois society by raising the social question. The result was that, from then onwards, the fear of a proletarian revolution, the spectre of which first appeared in 1848, was to determine the social and domestic struggles of all industrialised European countries.

The Revolution in Germany

The news of the events of February in Paris hit Germany like a thunderbolt. Though many had expected, hoped for and feared them, the startling pace of the events which now overtook Germany was greater than most people had bargained for; everything for which they had been fighting so determinedly since 1815 seemed to have become reality overnight. Carl Schurz, who took part in the events of March 1848 while still a student, and later emigrated to America, where he became a distinguished figure, remembered in his old age that, 'The word "democracy" was on all tongues and many thought it a matter of course that, if the princes should try to withhold from the people the rights and liberties demanded, force would take the place of mere petition'.[1] Nevertheless, the members of the bourgeoisie who strove for and demanded progress had not really wanted the revolution. 'A revolution with the most desirable outcome is still a difficult crisis, which confuses consciences, disrupts internal security and not least, endangers all international treaties',[2] wrote Friedrich Christoph Dahlmann, the leader of the Göttingen Seven in his *Politik* and thus expressed what many liberals thought: 'They wanted national and liberal reform without the rupture of a revolution, which would endanger property and education, and they used every available opportunity to come to an agreement with princes and governments. In the last instance, the revolution was thrust upon them by force of circumstances rather than by their own decision.'[3]

As in France, the focus of political life in Germany had shifted in the wake of the process of social emancipation. The expansion of the national movement across society had given rise to new, sometimes convergent aims. The liberal *Bürger*, the radical democrats, the peasants and the workers all hoped for the fulfilment of their demands.

General economic hardship, a lack of staple foods, rising prices, unemployment and frequent epidemics, which affected the German states as much as the rest of Europe, endangered people's existence, especially that of the workers and peasants. However, the skilled craftsmen and artisans (*Handwerker*) were also hit hard by the economic crisis at the middle of the century which spread fast in all directions. They suffered unemployment and hunger as many small and medium-sized firms went bankrupt. Georg Büchner, who like Heinrich Heine had to emigrate from Germany, made it very clear that this material hardship was as burning a problem as the loss of intellectual freedom: 'The material oppression from which a large part of Germany suffers is as sad and as reprehensible as the spiritual kind: in my eyes it is far less depressing that some liberal or other is not allowed to print his thoughts, than that many thousand families are not able to get dripping for their potatoes.'[4]

However, the decisive force behind the revolutionary uprising in Germany was not, as in France, the lower classes caught up in a struggle for existence, but the bourgeoisie, which had been taken unaware by the revolutionary events in France and forced into action. Even before the outbreak of the February Revolution in France, the German bourgeoisie had come together to form a unified political movement which transcended all particularist state boundaries, combined liberal and nationalist elements, and was led by learned men. The National Conferences of Professors of German (*Germanistentage*) in 1846 and 1847 in Frankfurt on the Main and in Lübeck, the assemblies of democratic politicians in Offenburg and of liberal parliamentarians in Heppenheim an der Bergstrasse, turned into meetings calling for a unified Germany and demanding the formation of an all-German constitutional state.

In a similar vein, the liberal deputy, Friedrich Daniel Bassermann, in a motion presented to the second chamber of Baden even before the outbreak of the February Revolution in France, proposed that 'the chamber address a petition to his royal highness, that he exert his influence to ensure the representation of the German chambers of estates in the Federal Diet, thus creating a sure means of achieving common legislation and common national institutions.'[5]

Bassermanns moderate proposal, which had caused a stir and been applauded throughout Germany, was not to take effect. It was now the turn of the radicals, moved by the events in Paris, to take the floor. At a mass meeting near Mannheim on 27 February they demanded freedom of the press, trial by jury, the right of free association, the formation of a people's militia and the summoning of a German parliament. These demands were adopted everywhere in the German states and were made known by means of broadsheets.

Formation of a people's militia and free election of its officers. A German parliament freely elected by the people. Every German man over the age of 21 is entitled to vote and is himself eligible as a delegate. A delegate will be nominated for every 1000 souls, a parliamentary representative for every 100,000. Every German, regardless of rank, estate, wealth or religion may become a member of this parliament as soon as he has reached the age of 25. The parliament will meet in Frankfurt and conduct its own business. Unconditional freedom of the press, complete freedom in matters of religion, conscience, and teaching. An administration of justice accessible to the common people with trial by jury. Civil rights for all Germans. Just taxation proportionate to income. Prosperity, education and teaching for all. Protection and guarantee of employment. Redress of the imbalance between capital and labour. Cheap public administration which is accessible to the common people. The responsibility of all ministers and officials. The abolition of all privileges.[6]

Riotous assemblies in the towns and in the country, where the peasants hoped to achieve the commutation of feudal obligations and the regulation of land distribution, gave support to the widespread popular demands, and princes hastened to concede what they had withheld for decades—constitutions and long-overdue reforms. In Baden, Württemberg, Hesse-Darmstadt, Bavaria, Saxony and Hanover, moderate liberals were appointed to government office. The permanent conference of member states of the German Confederation, the Federal Diet in Frankfurt, now proclaimed as the German standard the same black-red-gold flag that it had banned in 1832 after the Hambach Festival. Furthermore it gave its consent to the convening of a 'pre-parliament', whose task Gustav Struwe, a politician from Baden, described as follows:

A long period of the deepest humiliation weighs upon Germany. It can be characterized by these words: the tyranny, stultification and sucking dry of the people. . . . The people's distress has become intolerable. In Upper Silesia it has reached the point of famine. Thus the ties that bound the German people to the previous, so-called order of things have been dissolved. The task of the assembly of German men, which has come together on the 31 March of this year in Frankfurt is to prepare new ties which will bind all German people together in a free and great whole.[7]

When this speech was made the revolution had already spread to the two great German powers, and likewise forced their governments into making concessions. However, unlike the central states in southern Germany, where liberalism had created a political platform in the provincial assemblies at a much earlier date, Austria was still caught up in a feudal way of life and had remained completely in the sway of Metternich's tactics of obstruction until March 1848. Furthermore, the awakening of national consciousness in the non-German population of the multi-nation state of the Habsburgs, the very thing Metternich had feared and suppressed, meant that its non-German subjects were now making passionate demands for freedom and a constitution, pushing the revolutionary situation further to a head.

Petitions to the government and the court of the emperor, urging long-overdue reforms in the administration and the economy, the lifting of censorship, less-severe police surveillance and an assembly of the estates, remained unanswered. This reactionary attitude, the refusal of even the most minor concessions—incomprehensible in face of the events in Paris and the central German states—finally led, on 13 March, to a popular uprising in Vienna. The students, citizens and workers of the city formed a mob and demanded freedom of the press, trial by jury, control over the national budget, a constitution and, above all, the fall of the loathed Metternich.

The emperor yielded and dropped Metternich, who fled to London and thus prepared the way, temporarily, for the revolution. The previous ministers resigned, the emperor's court withdrew to Innsbruck, and the armed masses and students seized power.

In northern Italy there was a simultaneous uprising against Austrian rule, in Prague a Slav congress debated secession from Austria, the Croats strove for a southern Slav state, and the Hungarians, who had managed to beat the Austrian troops, proclaimed the republic under the leadership of Lajos Kossuth. The Habsburg Empire was on the verge of collapse.

These events, which put the great German state in the south-east through its first test of strength, pulled its counterpart in the north-east into the vortex of revolutionary upheaval. While the events of March were still fresh in everyone's mind, it seemed as though Frederick William IV of Prussia, who had long refused the liberals a regular assembly of the united estates, was about to give in, especially as there was now a threat of demonstrations in Berlin. A patent issued on 18 March conceded the freedom of the press, the formation of a people's militia and the withdrawal of troops, and Friedrich William also agreed to grant a constitution and declared himself in favour of federal reform and federal representation. On the very same day a crowd gathered before the palace in Berlin to thank the king. Angered by the troops, who remained in the palace courtyard in spite of the king's promise to withdraw them, it rebelled. Enthusiasm suddenly turned into resentment. Frederick William, alarmed by the threats against the palace guard, ordered the palace square to be cleared. Suddenly two shots were heard. Although they had been fired by accident, they shocked and enraged the crowd. An eye-witness reported the ensuing panic:

Crowds fled down Königsstrasse. People surged by stirred to a frenzy, grinding their teeth, pale, out of breath. They cried 'They've just been shooting at us in the Palace Square'. All along Königsstrasse, all over the city, cries of anger and screams of revenge could be heard. There was a roar throughout the city as though the earth had opened. Flagstones were torn up, arms stores were plundered, people stormed houses and fetched hatchets and axes; in Königsstrasse twelve barricades were erected in no time at all, built from carriages, omnibus coaches, woolsacks, wooden beams, and coverings ripped off wells; all this was turned into expertly constructed barricades.[8]

Bloody street battles followed. Shaken by the bloodshed, the king surrendered that same night; in an appeal to his 'beloved citizens of Berlin' he declared himself willing to withdraw the soldiers into the palace if the barricades were removed. However, contrary to this royal command, the troops now withdrew from the whole town, which thus fell into the hands of the revolutionaries. In the palace courtyard the rebels forced the royal couple to salute those who had fallen on the barricades. Two days later the king rode through the streets of his capital and announced:

Germany is in the grip of inner unrest and may be threatened from without, on more than one border. Only the closest unity of the German princes and people under the leadership of one man can save us from this dual and imminent danger. Today we shall assume this leadership for as long as the danger threatens. Our people, which does not flinch in face of danger, will not desert us, and Germany will put its trust in us, and join us. Today we have adopted the ancient German colours, and placed ourself and our people under the sacred banner of the German Empire. From now on, Prussia is a part of Germany.[9]

This meant that the revolution had succeeded in Prussia, too. The aristocratic Officers' Corps felt betrayed by the king's weakness and withdrew in resentment. Frederick William IV, whose romantic ideal of a relationship of loyalty between prince and people had been destroyed, appointed the liberal opposition to the government, and summoned a Prussian National Assembly to Berlin to draft a liberal-democratic constitution.

The fall of Metternich and the victory of the revolutionary forces in Vienna and Berlin prevented the two largest German powers from becoming a determining force in solving the German question. Likewise neither the Federal Diet nor the governments were in a position to produce any federal reform.

The decision now lay completely in the hands of the German people. The pre-parliament was convened in Frankfurt; all former and present members of legislative assemblies had been invited, with 574 assembling. It had arisen out of the popular movement and, as such, was of revolutionary origin. With the consent of the Federal Diet it moved that a national assembly should be convened to determine a constitution for the whole of Germany. A committee of fifty, elected by the pre-parliament and acting for a transitional period as a representative body for the whole of Germany was to prepare the election to the constitutive National Assembly and cooperate with the governments in carrying it out. However, the radical delegates in the pre-paliament, who supported the proposal that the pre-parliament, which had arisen from a directly revolutionary act, should assume governmental responsibility for the whole of Germany on a permanent basis, left Frankfurt as soon as this decision was made. They organised a republican uprising in the Black Forest which was quickly crushed by federal troops. Thus the election of deputies to the National Assembly was able to take place, in accordance with the motion carried by the moderate majority.

On 18 May 1848 the elected deputies walked in procession into the Paulskirche (St Paul's Church) in Frankfurt. The participants were mostly men with a legal education: judges, public prosecutors, administrative officers, lawyers, a few professors, writers, representatives of the agricultural community, merchants and a few middle-ranking officials and skilled craftsmen and artisans. There was not a single worker present; it was an assembly of educated and respected citizens with noble aims, filled with high ideals and great expectations.

The Parliament's elected president, the former liberal minister of Hesse, Heinrich von Gagern, formulated its supreme task as follows: 'We are to create a constitution for Germany, for all German people. It is the sovereignty of our nation which calls us and empowers us to fulfil this task.'[10] But before the National Assembly commenced its debate on the Constitution, it tried to create a provisional central government. Von Gagern solved the question of whether or not Parliament should consider individual governments and their right of consultation in this matter in accordance with the majority opinion in Parliament. He announced, 'I shall make a bold assertion and say to you: we must create the provisional central government on our own.'[11]

With an eye to the presidial power of Austria, the National Assembly elected the liberal Archduke Johann, a member of the House of Habsburg, as the provisional administrator of the Reich (the *Reichsverweser*). He, in his turn, appointed a national ministry. Prince Karl zu Leiningen, a supporter of Prussia, the second great power, was made its political leader.

While the German Federal Diet transferred its powers to the *Reichsverweser*, who was also recognized by the individual governments, he, and the executive he formed, remained without any real power. Neither the central states nor the great powers were willing to allow their armies to swear oaths of allegiance to the *Reichsverweser* and thus place them under the command of central government. In addition, the newly formed central government had neither a fixed income to dispose of nor an adequate administrative bureaucracy.

The complete impotence of the Frankfurt National Assembly and the new provisional government became further evident in the Schleswig-Holstein question, a matter of great importance to the progress of the revolution with regard to both national and foreign affairs. The two duchies, which according to an ancient treaty were to remain eternally undivided, had been attached to the Danish crown in personal union for centuries. However, Holstein simultaneously belonged to the German *Bund*. In 1848 the Danes granted themselves a new constitution, which they imposed, against its will, on Schleswig, a state inhabited mostly by Germans. Upon this, the German population declared secession from Danish rule and proclaimed a native prince the lawful heir of both duchies. In the hostilities which ensued, the Prussian troops, summoned to the aid of the National Assembly, gained a victory but were then forced by pressure from England and Russia to agree to an armistice with Denmark, renouncing all German claims to the two duchies. In spite of the wave of national outrage which swept through Germany, circumstances forced the Frankfurt National Assembly to approve the treaty.

The unfortunate end to the Schleswig Holstein affair forced the National Assembly to recognise that its programme of national unity could not be put into practice without the consent of the major powers in Europe. Thus, at long last, they attempted to produce a constitution. To begin with the delegates agreed on the Basic Rights of the German people. They were to form the preamble to a later constitution and form the guarantee of constitutionality in the future German state. It was decreed law on 27 December 1848 and was adopted into the National Constitution (*Reichsverfassung*) of 28 March 1849. As in the Federal Republic of Germany today, these rights were to be upheld in law. Personal freedom and equality before the law, freedom in economic affairs and in trade, freedom of movement, protection from arbitrary arrest (the right of habeas corpus), protection against improper treatment by judges or by the police, the freedom of the press, religious freedom, freedom of association and the right of assembly, academic freedom and free choice of profession; these were the basic principles which Germany formulated for the first time in a written constitution, on a basis of general consent. Thus the delegates in the Pauls Kirche founded a tradition, which would be upheld in the National Constitution of the Weimar Republic in 1919, and in the Basic Law (*Grundgesetz*) of the Federal Republic of Germany in 1949. However, the question of social reform was not taken into consideration by the 1848 formulation of Basic Rights.

The debate on the German Constitution as such was more difficult than that on Basic Rights. There were fundamental problems to be solved: the national, the federal and the constitutional. On these questions the parties' opinions were divided.

The first question alone, that of the borders of the nation-state, split the assembly into those in favour of a *Grossdeutschland* and those in favour of a *Kleindeutschland*. The latter argued for a Germany which would form a closer federation under the leadership of Prussia with the Prussian king as hereditary emperor, while the former wanted Germany to include the German speaking parts of Austria, or even the states governed by the Habsburg monarchy in their entirety.

The question of how federal relations were to be structured saw a majority of those advocating the *Kleindeutschland* solution favour a unitary structure, that is a strong national government, as independent as possible of individual states, to be represented by a national parliament (*Reichstag*) and a national ministry. Those in favour of a *Grossdeutschland*, on the other hand, argued for a federalist state, which gave individual states a large measure of independence, enabling not only the formation of an empire containing two major powers but also leaving the political and cultural decentralisation characteristic of Germany untouched.

So far as the decision regarding the form of government was concerned, the moderate delegates favoured a constitutional monarchy, the small radical minority supported the setting up of a republic.

To begin with these was a *Grossdeutschland* majority in the Paulskirche, but its plan to include German-speaking Austria failed on account of the veto of the revived Habsburg Empire, whose chief minister, Prince Felix von Schwarzenberg, made the following statement to the Austrian Parliament in November 1848: 'The continued existence of Austria as a united state is necessary both for Germany and for Europe. ... Only when a regenerated Austria and a regenerated Germany have acquired a new, more stable form, will it be possible to determine their mutual relations at state level.'[12] In accordance with this general policy and after the imposition of a state constitution for the whole Habsburg Empire, Schwarzenberg demanded in a note of 9 March 1849 the admission of Austria in its entirety with the exception of the Italian provinces, into a German state.

This caused many in favour of the *Grossdeutschland* solution to withdraw from their previous position. Karl Theodor Welcker, a liberal politician and lecturer on constitutional law who had supported a greater Germany, now moved that 'the hereditary powers of the emperor entrenched in the Constitution',[13] be transferred to the King of Prussia. Finally, on 27 March 1849 the National Assembly voted (267 votes to 263) for the *Kleindeutschland* solution.

The next day the Assembly elected Frederick William IV of Prussia German emperor with 290 votes in favour and 248 abstentions. A few days later a delegation of thirty-two men from the National Assembly under the leadership of its president, Eduard

Simson, offered the Prussian king the office of emperor.

Frederick William, for his part, declined and declared he would only be able to accept this high office if the crowned heads, the princes, and the free cities of Germany gave their free consent. He had already given the real reason for his refusal, however, in a letter to the Prussian ambassador in London, Josias von Bunsen:

In the first place, the crown is not really a crown. A crown which a Hohenzollern might take when circumstances made it possible is not one created by an assembly grown from revolutionary seed, albeit one which has met with princely consent, but one which carries the seal of divine approval, one which, after the holy annointing, makes its bearer king 'by the grace of God'. This one, however, dishonours thee, and unfortunately, us, ... reeking of the whoredom of the 1848 revolution. ... Should a legitimate king, by the grace of God, and a king of Prussia at that, bear an imaginary little crown like this, baked from dirt and clay ...? We say to you quite openly: if the thousand-year-old crown of the German nation, which has rested for forty-two years now, is to be worn again, then it is we and our peers who will decide who wears it.[14]

Frederick William's rejection of the crown marked the final death knell of the work of the Paulskirche. The more powerful German states recalled their delegates from Frankfurt. A remainder, the so-called 'rump parliament' appointed an imperial regency consisting of five left-wing delegates, which repaired to Stuttgart, where the government of Württemberg forcibly dissolved it on 18 June 1849 in accordance with the demand of Prussia.

The Victory of Reaction

Frederick William's attitude arose from the real balance of power which had developed in the intervening period. The Frankfurt Parliament, which had been totally absorbed by the constitutional debate, was fast overtaken by events moving in the opposite direction. The decisions had been too long in coming, and so it had failed to take advantage of the favourable moment when the great powers were preoccupied with their internal struggles and paralysed by them. Furthermore, those in the Paulskirche had underestimated the loyalty princes could command from their armies and even their subjects. Both in Austria and Prussia the old authorities had regained their self-confidence and re-established their rule with the aid of their armies and civil servants. The monarchy on the Danube, which had been on the verge of disintegration, had been saved by military victories in Italy, Bohemia and Hungary; in Vienna itself a second wave of revolutionary activity had been successfully put down.

In Prussia, too, the affairs of the conservative forces had taken a turn for the better. Frederick William IV had dismissed the liberal ministry he set up at the beginning of the revolution and replaced it with a military one. Berlin, which had once been cleared of troops, had been reoccupied. The National Assembly, which had met after free general elections, had been dissolved, and a constitution of the king's making was imposed upon the people. Though much of its contents were based on liberal ideals, it maintained the principle of monarchical power and put the executive in the hands of the king, who appointed ministers without parliamentary consultation and had the final word in questions of war and peace. The victory of reactionary forces in Austria and Prussia produced a quick response in the other German states, where the old authorities soon re-established a peace and order of their own choosing.

In a last desperate rebellion, the left-wing democrats in Dresden, in the Palatinate, and in Baden tried to wrest recognition of the Constitution from their governments by the use of force. Without ever having had any prospect of success, the rebellions were put down by the overwhelming strength of the Prussian troops, under the command of Prince William, the brother of Frederick William IV. That was the final defeat of the Frankfurt Parliament's efforts to form a united Germany.

This revolution had lasted scarcely more than a year, a revolution which had been prompted from outside and which developed its greatest strength during the events of March 1848, only to loose its *élan*, and finally peter out in June 1849. At the moment of its greatest impetus it had seemed to fulfil the Germans' long-held desire for freedom and unity. A freely elected German parliament had met in Frankfurt to turn these same hopes into reality and create freedom and unity. As Carl Schurz was later to remember, this task was beyond the capability of the men who had met in the Paulskirche:

The Parliament suffered from an excess of intellect, scholarliness and virtue, and a lack of the kind of political experience and insight which recognises that a true statesmen will be careful not to squander a favourable moment, and endanger the achievement of more important aims by obstinately insisting on dealing with less essential matters. I suppose the world has never seen a political assembly which contained a greater number of noble, learned, conscientious and patriotic men, and there is possibly no comparable book that is deeper in knowledge and richer in examples of great oratory than the stenographic reports of the Frankfurt Parliament. But it lacked the genius to recognise its hour of opportunity and grasp it. It forgot that in times of violent change, world history does not wait for philosophers. And thus it was to fail on every count.[15]

But that was not the only reason for the Parliament's failure to succeed. The German dynasties' will to assert themselves and their continued vitality was not to be broken without some kind of military, financial and administrative power. Furthermore, the revolutionary movement was itself not united. The liberal bourgeoisie feared the radicals who united with the proletarian elements suddenly appearing in the large cities. And, as in France, it tried to defend itself, and was willing to throw its weight behind the forces of order rather than allow its own world to be destroyed; in so doing it supported, albeit unwillingly, the old powers. Last and not least, the German question was lodged between the forces and tensions of the great European powers, who were all fearful of disturbing the balance of power so laboriously re-established.

The French foreign minister, Jules Bastide, commented in July 1848, 'I am of the opinion that the unification of Germany by this people 40 million strong will lead to the emergence of a power which will cause its neighbours greater uneasiness than Germany does today. From this moment on, I do not know what interest we have in even wishing this unification, let alone encouraging it.'[16]

And at the same time as the Frankfurt Parliament was discussing the shape of the future empire, the Russian ambassador in Berlin, Baron Peter von Meyendorff, was heard to say:

Prussia's proposal to form a federal state in Germany as the core of the unification is aimed at mediatising the kings and excluding Austria. In order to prevent the worst happening, every party must reject the idea of a more or less concealed mediatisation and return to the forms of organisation of the old German Confederation, with the proviso that Prussia again be allowed to assume the leadership in economic affairs and the legislative power in foreign policy, matters for which Austria is not yet ready. . . . But there is another stumbling block. It is said that Austria, with its great multitude of non-German states, will either become part of Germany or withdraw from it entirely. Now, that would be a much more significant change, and a different one from that suggested by Prussia. The European balance of power would without doubt be endangered by the creation of a central power at the head of a united Germany, but it would be even more threatened if 25 million Austrian subjects were united with 45 million Germans, and this great mass of people was brought together in one state. We cannot in all seriousness agree to this merger.[17]

After the Paulskirche failed in its efforts to form a German state, Frederick William tried to negotiate with the German princes to create a *kleindeutsch* union, with a *Reichstag* and a constitution, and the Prussian king as head of state. Austria used its right of veto, and Russia hastened to support this move. In Olmütz the Prussian king yielded to the united will of Austria and Russia, and abandoned his plans for a union.

The French ambassador in London, Drouyn de l'Huys, confided to the privacy of his diary the relief Prussia's western neighbour felt at this:

It has always been France's aim to encourage the formation of independent states in Germany, or to secure their preservation, and to prevent the unification into one body of all the elements that make up the German people. ... The superiority of France lies in its national unity. Its main interest is to prevent the formation of European bodies which become mightier than France itself by uniting together in a single state people who today are ruled by different heads of state. Everything which counteracts these efforts for unity, everything which maintains the division of large peoples, is to our advantage.[18]

Despite the resistance of surrounding countries, the fact that this striving for German unity had taken hold at all levels of society, and was to remain a living force, gave the revolution an overall importance which transcended the merely ephemeral. Moreover, the 'German question' had been thought over thoroughly, and there was widespread awareness of the obstacle which Austria's multinational empire posed to any solution to this question. Fundamental human rights had been formulated for the first time, and were adopted into the constitutions of individual German states, above all in the National Constitution of 1919 and in the Basic Law of the Federal Republic of Germany on 23 May 1949. The idea of freedom had been absorbed by the German people, and had politicised society—a process which could not be halted even by the period of political reaction which was now beginning. In addition, the liberal bourgeoisie had learnt that if the desire to build a German state founded on liberal ideals was to become reality, it needed real power to support it. Moreover, this state would not only have to settle the national question but also the social one. Without this learning process set in motion by the revolution, the unification of Germany, which came about later, would have been inconceivable. In the new order of political and social life which now began in Germany, the idealism which had inspired the men in Paulskirche would be foresaken, and there would be a move towards a 'strong realism and materialism'.[19] In future, politics would be understood to mean *Realpolitik*, that is the combination of idealism and power.

Shortly before 1848 the Prussian writer and diplomat Varnhagen von Ense jotted down in his diary the following, rather strange remark of an acquaintance: 'In the capital it isn't as noticeable yet, but in commercial centres and provincial towns a generation is growing up, which, forgetful of all idealism, or even hostile to it, is charging boldly and without refinement into starkest reality, and which will soon acknowledge nothing that does not concern its outward needs and pleasures.' In 1848 this generation had not yet had its chance. Its turn came in the 1850s and 1860s; it made Germany into an industrial state: The empire was founded for it and to meet its needs, and the essence of this empire therefore differed substantially from the ideals of the best men of 1848.[20]

6

Industrialisation and the Social Question

1769: James Watt patents the steam engine
1775: The spinning-machine is invented in England
1786: The power-loom is invented in England
1814: George Stephenson builds the first locomotive
1818: Prussia eliminates internal tariffs
1824: Repeal of the Combination Acts in England
1825: The first German polytechnical institute (*technische Hochschule*) opens in Karlsruhe
1826: Gas lighting introduced in Berlin
1833: The electromagnetic telegraph is invented by Carl Friedrich Gauss and Wilhelm Eduard Weber; the first Factory Act is passed in England; *Rauhes Haus* is founded
1834: Creation of the German Customs Union
1835: The first German passenger railway between Nuremberg and Fürth
1836: Spinning and weaving mills established in Esslingen and Augsburg: the industrialisation of southern Germany begins
1837: The first German goods railway between Leipzig and Dresden; founding of a training centre for Protestant nurses in Kaiserswerth; Samuel Morse develops the first practical telegraph
1839: First Prussian legislation to protect industrial workers
1840: Justus von Liebig founds agricultural chemistry
1841: Friedrich List publishes *The National System of Political Economy*; August Borsig and Joseph Anton von Maffei begin production of locomotives
1842: Steamship travel commences between Bremen and New York
1845: The physician and physicist Julius Robert von Mayer publishes the law of the preservation of energy; completion of the railway between Berlin and Hamburg
1847: Founding of the Siemens and Halske companies; the Ham-

burg–America Line is established; Karl Marx and Friedrich Engels
write the *Communist Manifesto*

1853: Foundation of the Darmstädter Bank, the first large bank for
commerce and industry

1863: Ferdinand Lassalle establishes the General Association of German
Workers (*Allgemeiner Deutscher Arbeiterverein*)

1867: First World Exhibition in Paris; Werner von Siemens invents the
dynamo machine; Nikolaus Otto concludes the development of his
atmospheric gas engine

The Origins of Industrialism in England

Many Germans were deeply disappointed by the collapse of the
revolution of 1848 and the concomitant failure to overcome German particularism and to create a unified state embodying their
sense of nationhood. The era which now dawned was characterised
by the renunciation of grand ideals and a profound reorientation of
all strata of society. Pragmatism became the order of the day as
workers, farmers, burghers and the various German governments
all turned their attention to practical concerns.

Their attention focused largely on industrialisation, which now
struck root in Germany as well. The ensuing period of explosive
growth and economic prosperity propelled the German states out of
their sleepy backwardness and insignificance, while the swelling
volume of commercial trade reinforced the sense of German unity.
An industrial and technological life-style increasingly displaced the
old order as the foundation of daily life, as Germany gathered
strength for a revolutionary 'leap into modernity'.[1]

As previously in England and France, it was the bourgeoisie
which led the way into the new era. Largely excluded from active
participation in politics after 1849, the German middle classes
focused the bulk of their abundant energies on the bourgeoning
sphere of commerce and industry which would soon revolutionise
German society, culture and standards of living.

This profound mutation, commonly termed the 'Industrial Revolution' because of the enormity of the changes it wrought at all
levels of society, originated in Britain in the last third of the
eighteenth century. Here innovative methods of production sparked
social, political and cultural upheavals so sweeping in their effects
that contemporaries experienced them as revolutionary and compared them with the great political upheavals of the late eighteenth
century in America and France.[2]

Around the middle of the eighteenth century, the English population began to rise sharply as a result of improved sanitation and medical techniques, an escalating marriage rate with an accompanying increase in the birth rate, mounting agricultural production and the cultivation of the potato, a new crop imported from America. When the demand for merchandise rose proportionately, it could only be met by supplementing traditional handicraft production through machine production. The demand for suitable machines triggered the invention of a number of devices that generated mechanical power in order to augment the energy traditionally provided by men, animals, wind and water. The Industrial Revolution had begun.

James Watt's steam engine, the blast furnace, the power-loom and the spinning-machine revolutionised the mining, iron and textile industries. Mass production became possible, and with it an enormous increase in the goods available to cover the needs of a rapidly expanding population. Machine production was widely viewed as necessary, beneficial and profitable.

Factory wares were manufactured by a swelling army of workers easily recruited from the bourgeoning population. The poorer strata of the rural population were driven off the land by the agrarian reform and the redistribution of farmland which followed the liberation of the peasantry. Large estates absorbed numerous small and medium-sized peasant holdings leaving jobless cottagers and peasants to seek new means of subsistence in the emerging factories.

Fallow land disappeared and the three-field system was introduced. In addition, peasants attached great importance to their choice of seed and began regularly to fertilise, irrigate and loosen the soil. Farm labour was facilitated and rationalised through the introduction of sowing machines, the triangular plough, a kind of threshing machine and other farming equipment. At the same time animal husbandry was developed into an independent and highly profitable branch of agriculture. Finally, strong pressure developed after 1760 to unite disconnected parcels of land with the result that members of the lower middle class largely lost their holdings.

Thus industrialisation, technological innovation, the modernisation of agriculture and the population explosion supported and reinforced one another. A successful factory, however, required other factors as well: purposefulness, industriousness, a readiness to assume risk, a head for business, and most importantly, pools of capital large enough to build a great industrial enterprise.

The victories of English arms over Spain, the Netherlands and France helped the island kingdom to become the world's leading commercial power in the course of the seventeenth and eighteenth centuries. England possessed the world's largest merchant marine and, after the victory over Napoleon, a position of unchallenged political and commercial pre-eminence. Foreign trade greatly enhanced English living standards and generated a flood of capital which needed to be invested and often found profitable placement in the mushrooming factories. The English economy surged ahead thanks to the large pool of available capital, the Calvinist and Puritanical work ethic of the English middle classes, their search for ever more rational means of production, their readiness to assume risk, their desire to increase profits as commended by their religion, and the modesty of their personal needs.

Complete economic freedom was needed if technology was to reach its full potential and if factory owners were to maximise their profits. No longer could the state be allowed to impede the citizen's desire to employ his commercial skills to the utmost. The demand for economic liberty ran deep in the followers of John Calvin, who saw economic success as a visible sign of God's grace. The Puritan theologian Richard Baxter commented in 1665:

If God shows ye a path by way of which ye can legally earn more, without harm to your soul, than you can by another path, and if ye turn back and take the less profitable way, then ye thwart one side of your calling. Ye refuse to be God's steward and to accept his gifts so that that ye might use them on His behalf when He so commands. Ye may work to be rich, not for purposes of lust or sin, but for God's own sake.[3]

The spirit of these words lived on 100 years later in the work of Adam Smith when he sought to vindicate the new means of production in his epochal *Wealth of Nations* published in 1776:

Since profit is the purpose of the accumulation of capital, capital naturally seeks the most beneficial investments, that is, those which produce the greatest profits. This best fosters, though indirectly, the productivity of the entire economy. Each man believes he is serving only his own interest, but in so doing he indirectly serves the best interests of the entire economy. . . . The individual is a better judge than the state of which investment is the most beneficial. The natural propensity of each individual to better his position is such a mighty principle when allowed free rein that it will not only lead the entire society to riches and prosperity but will also overcome the hundreds of shameful barriers by means of which foolish human laws all too often seek to frustrate it.[4]

Like the Calvinists and Puritans, Adam Smith saw hard work and thrift as the fountainhead of wealth. Economic activity was driven by the enlightened self-interest of the individual who should be granted free rein within certain fundamental parameters. Smith therefore championed individual economic freedom as the sole source of social progress. The improvement of society as a whole, in Smith's view, corresponded to the sum total of individual betterment. Individual progress was based on enlightened self-interest and would redound to the benefit of the entire community so long as the individual possessed sufficient freedom to act in accordance with his own interest: 'Every man, as long as he does not violate the laws of justice, is left perfectly free to pursue his own interest his own way, and to bring both his industry and capital into competition with those of any other man, or order of men.' It was self-evident for Smith that this recommendation of a free economy applied as well to international trade:

Between whatever places foreign trade is carried on, they all of them derive two distinct benefits from it. It carries out that surplus part of the produce of their land and labour for which there is no demand among them, and brings back in return for it something else for which there is a demand. . . . These great and important services foreign trade is continually occupied in performing, to all the different countries between which it is carried on.[5]

According to Adam Smith, free trade would also foster economic peace among the nations of Europe. The prosperity of a neighbouring people, though possibly dangerous from a political viewpoint, could only be beneficial from a commercial perspective. Any nation which hoped to grow wealthy through foreign trade required neighbours which were rich and commercially active.

It was in this spirit that the entrepreneur Matthew Boulton wrote to James Watt as early as 1769 about a lucrative project in which they might both engage. A factory would be built near Boulton's other enterprises and would furnish the entire world with machines of every shape and size. To satisfy the demand solely of the surrounding counties would not be profitable, but to sell to the entire world would be tremendously lucrative.[6]

According to Adam Smith, a hallmark of effective management was the division of labour, so typical of capitalist firms:

The great increase of the quality of work which, in consequence of the division of labour, the same number of people are capable of performing is owing to three different circumstances; first to the increase of dexterity in every particular workman; secondly, to the saving of the time which is commonly lost in passing from one species of work to another; and lastly to the invention of a great number of machines which facilitate and abridge labour, and enable one man to do the work of many.[7]

The value of the labour and of the final product would be determined by the forces of supply and demand.

Adam Smith's economic theories marked a clear break with the earlier philosophy of mercantilism. Under mercantilism the state oversaw capital investment and sought to maintain a positive balance of trade by means of export premiums and the exclusion of finished foreign goods. Only raw materials could be imported. The national state itself was regarded as a closed, economically self-sufficient entity to be protected by steep tariffs.

Smith and his successors (most notably David Ricardo, who did much to flesh out the new philosophy) urged that traditional mercantilism be replaced by economic liberalism with its emphasis on complete equality before the law, free trade and freedom of movement and occupation. The transition was first made in England, especially in the cotton industry in Manchester. Under the name of the 'Manchester School' of economics, liberalism profoundly influenced the growth and development of English industry. The new technologies were exploited to the hilt. Production, capital and personal wealth were allowed to grow free of feudal hindrances or government restrictions while adverse social effects were largely ignored.

Those with little economic strength in the early capitalist era were utterly devastated, in England and later in Belgium, France and Germany. The resulting social conditions posed a serious challenge to these rapidly evolving societies. In his *Notes of a Voyage to England* Alexis de Tocqueville eloquently described the glory and the pity of this period, using Manchester as an example:

A rippling plain or rather a group of small hills. At the foot of these runs a narrow river . . . two brooks . . . three man-made canals. Across this landscape, so well-watered by nature and man's hand, are strewn palaces and huts alike. Everything in the appearance of the city points to the power of the individual; nothing to the ordering hand of society as a whole. On all sides, the wilful creativity of individual liberty is manifest. Nowhere is the slow, steady hand of government in evidence. . . . On the hills described above rise thirty or forty factories. Six stories high, they soar into the sky. Their endless expanse proclaims what is known as an industrial agglomeration. Strewn randomly around them are the miserable hovels of the poor; a maze of paths leads to them. . . . The roads that link the poorly integrated parts of the city disclose, like all else, a hasty and incomplete appearance: the hurried creations of an avaricious people who seek to amass money so that they might instantly attain all they want from life while in the meantime dismissing all pleasure. Some of these roads are paved, but most are bumpy or muddy so that pedestrians or waggons sink into them. Puddles, building debris and piles of refuse lie scattered before the dwellings of the local inhabitants or on the public squares. Here and there in this foul-smelling labyrinth, in the midst of this dreary brick desert, arise beautiful stone palaces whose fluted columns astonish the eye of the traveller. . . . But who can describe the bowels of those unobstrusive districts, those haunts of misery and vice, which wind their smothering coils around the mighty palaces of the wealthy? A swampland lies beneath the level of the river, dominated on all sides by colossal factories. . . . Here end the narrow twisting lanes lined by low houses. Their poor construction and broken windows betray even from afar their role as the final asylum of people lingering between misery and death. Beneath these wretched shacks lie a series of cellars to which entrance ways have been dug in the mud. Into each of these dank, vile chambers are crammed twelve to fifteen human beings selected at random. . . . A thick layer of black smoke lies over the city. Through it the sun appears a pale disk. Three hundred thousand creatures move incessantly about in the dim daylight. A never-ending clatter and clamour arises from the damp, dark labyrinth. . . , the steps of the scurrying crowds, the screach of wheels rubbing against one another, the hiss of steam escaping from boilers, the regular pounding of spinning-wheels, the heavy grinding of carts. . . . The city is overflowing with crowds of people, but their steps are heavy, their eyes apathetic, their countenances grim and churlish.[8]

Since liberal economic theory rejected any state regulation of the employer–employee relationship, the factory owners became the absolute masters of their workers and subjected them to unconscionable exploitation. Low wages forced them to work twelve to fourteen and more hours a day with very little time to eat and no rest periods. Sunday labour and the employment of even cheaper female and child workers became widespread. Families disintegrated and the youth was neglected; alcoholism proliferated and in the slums hunger and disease were rampant.[9]

In these dire straits the working class sought means to help itself. The Combination Acts were repealed in 1824 and trade unions founded. They fought inhuman living and working conditions, collected funds to support needy workers and created self-help groups. Thus the organised struggle for social reforms and political equality began. During this same period, the first Factory Act was passed, limiting daily working hours to twelve hours for youths and eight hours for children and forbidding them to work at night. The second Factory Act of 1850 introduced the ten-hour working day and provided for factory inspectors whose reports were published semi-annually by Parliament. By the end of the century these measures were gradually improving the lot of the industrial proletariat in England.

By the middle of the nineteenth century, Britain had become an industrial nation furnishing most of the world with the manufactured products it required. Britain's rise to the 'workshop of the world' was the result of its liberal economic credo but also of its favourable geographic location, its reserves of coal and ore, its roads, coastal waters, navigable rivers, canal system and far-flung railway network. Not to be forgotten are the equilibrium of its state finances and the stability of the British pound resting on the solid foundation of the colonial gold reserves. In the rest of Europe, the changes associated with the Industrial Revolution appeared substantially later.

The Industrialisation of Western Europe and Germany

The first continental economy to feel the full impact of industrialisation was that of Belgium. By the turn of the century British entrepreneurs and capital were already engaged in the construction of factories across the English Channel. After the foundation of the new state of Belgium in 1830, the government immediately took steps to create a national railway network modelled after plans by George Stephenson. Belgium subsequently grew into the most densely populated country in Europe, an industrial state capable of competing with Britain on equal terms.

In France industrialism proceeded at a slower pace. Impeded in her development by a mass of free peasants groaning under high taxation, by a national debt that grew extremely onerous towards the end of the eighteenth century, and by the turmoil of the French Revolution and the numerous wars which followed, France did not begin to industrialise in earnest until after the July Revolution of 1830. The Continental Blockade decreed by Napoleon had encouraged the development of industry in France, but the government's dogged insistence on the mercantilist policies of the seventeenth and eighteenth centuries impeded its growth. Production was largely confined to luxury items and finished goods for the upper end of the market. In addition, the retooling of French factories was hampered by the British prohibition on machine exports which was not lifted until 1825. However, France too began to industrialise rapidly under the reformist and pro-bourgeois policies of Louis Philippe. Production was mechanised, trade and commerce blossomed and construction was begun on a railway network.

The advent of the machine age was marked by the founding of a number of mighty concerns, notably around Paris, Lille and Rouen as well as in some regions of Alsace and Lorraine. Industrialisation also bred an army of workmen compelled to live and toil in miserable conditions comparable to the early days of English industrialism. Deprived of all recourse in regard to both pay and hours of work, these workers lived at the mercy of a bourgeoisie which had already organised highly influential political parties to defend its interests. The continuing division of farmland into tiny parcels drove many rural youths into the cities where they joined the ranks of a proletariat which soon began to view itself as a distinct social class. Intermittent periods of economic downturn, unemployment, inflation and famine created a tense social climate which by 1847 had grown explosive. Countless industries and workshops closed their doors. In the cities there was neither work nor bread.

Food riots broke out among artisans and industrial workmen, eventually culminating in the bitter revolutionary year of 1848. Under the socialist leadership of Louis Auguste Blanqui and Jean Joseph Louis Blanc, the workers demanded that the new government vindicate its promise to guarantee the right to work—a right proclaimed by Blanc as early as 1840 and which the government had upheld for a time through the National Workshop programme.

However, the election of Louis Napoleon as President of the French Republic signalled a return to the old ways, and the deep social stresses of the times were once more ignored. Industrialisation proceeded apace, the railways were completed and France reaffirmed her status as the mightiest industrial state and the strongest military power on the continent of Europe.

Eventually Germany too was seized by the Industrial Revolution, though her evolution into a modern industrial society was far slower and more tentative than that of other countries, and was not really apparent before mid-century. The reasons for this tardiness lie in the peculiar nature of Central European society, which contrasted sharply with England and France both politically and demographically.

By the end of the eighteenth century, Germany's western neighbours had developed into strong, united countries comprising a confident and politically influential bourgeoisie. But in the divided feudal quiltwork of the 'Holy Roman Empire of the German Nation', the rigid old caste system continued to survive due to the existence of over 300 princes and prince-bishops and more than a thousand free cities, knights of the Holy Roman Empire and imperial abbeys. Here the social tone was clearly set by the feudal nobility that had preserved its paramountcy over the educated middle classes engaged in commerce and industry.

Of the 20 million people living in the empire in around 1800, some 17 million dwelled in the countryside under the sway of lay

and ecclesiastical landlords. Approximately 4000 cities were scattered across the land, but only a few such as Berlin (172,000
inhabitants) Hamburg (130,000 inhabitants) and Frankfurt on the
Main (48,000 inhabitants) possessed a population surpassing 1500.
In the relatively small cities and towns of Germany, craft guilds
thwarted the development of a free economy by throttling all
competition. In each town the guilds established a monopoly and
passed strict rules to prevent outsiders from entering the market.
Thus the master craftsmen secured their incomes, while municipal
governments stood by helplessly. Early in the nineteenth century a
contemporary observer vividly described the effects of this rigid
economy in his diary:

Frankfurt is virtually devoid of factories. The reason, according to the
locals, is the compulsion to join a guild. A manufacturer cannot hire
workers without bargaining with virtually every guild. The . . . wagon
manufacturer from Offenbach would be compelled here to have his manifold   needs   met   by   local   smiths,   mechanics,   carpenters. . . .
harness-makers . . . varnishers, etc. In so doing he would forgo . . . countless advantages. [A strong desire exists to check] the local guilds, but this
would be a very thorny task [for the municipal government].[10]

Even the impetus emitted by the Enlightenment, whose core had
wandered after 1750 from England to France and thence to Germany, proved unable to overcome the political, social and economic
inertia of Central Europe. In his conversations with Eckermann,
Goethe lamented the inability of the Germans to put theory into
practice: 'If only the Germans like the English would learn less
philosophy and more action, less theory and more practice.'[11] In
this environment it seemed only natural that German Romanticism,
which began to pervade intellectual life after 1790, tended to flee the
modern world with its factories, technology, bureaucracy and material calculations in order to seek refuge in the idealised middle ages
and a lopsided fascination with the cultural heritage of the common
people.

The turning-point for 'poor, exhausted, cloven Germany'[12] was
reached when her neighbour France began to expand under Napoleon and occupied her. The slow dissolution of the feudal economy
and the spread of capitalism and industrialism were encouraged by
the Principal Decree of the Imperial Deputation of 1803 and the
subsequent political restructuring of Central Europe, the collapse of
the Holy Roman Empire and the reforms undertaken in the liber-
tarian spirit of the French Revolution. Serfdom and compulsory
guild membership were first abolished in the Confederation of the
Rhine and the provinces of western Prussia that had been occupied

by the French, before gradually withering away in almost all of Germany during the following decades. The renewal of the German economy was further stimulated by Prussia's introduction of free-dom of occupation in 1807 and 1811, her municipal ordinance of 1808, the emancipation of the Jews in 1810, and the spread of primary, secondary and vocational schools.[13]

Another factor which cannot be ignored was the population explosion in Germany after the turn of the century. By 1850 the number of people living in the territories of the old German Reich had increased by approximately 10 million. This spurt in the popu-lation was prompted by conditions similar to those experienced in England fifty years earlier and was encouraged by freedom of occupation, the liberation of the serfs and the accompanying agri-cultural reforms. Since the liberated serfs no longer required the permission of their overlord in order to wed after 1807, the number of marriages soared and the birth rate rose accordingly.

The mounting birth-rate and the crumbling of the traditional social order due to freedom of occupation and the liberation of the serfs spawned a steadily rising surplus population in the country-side. Many souls sought relief in emigration while others flocked into urban centres, even though the underdeveloped economies of the cities could not support such an influx. The result was mass poverty which could only be cured by industrialisation. 'Penury is quite different now from what it used to be', wrote the Swiss author Jeremias Gotthelf in 1841, 'it has developed into a rampant weed with a life of its own. It is hereditary and contagious, a tumour on the life of the people and the plague of our time.'[14]

In England the emergence of a strong surplus in the rural popu-lation coincided with a great leap in agricultural productivity which generated the purchasing power needed in order to soak up indus-trial products. In Germany, however, agricultural productivity remained static because of backward technology, and rural pur-chasing power failed to strengthen. When a surge in demand even-tually did trigger industrialisation, the new purchasing power came from an entirely different sector: from railway construction and hence from industry itself.

Napoleon's imposition of the Continental Blockade had helped to foster industrialism in Germany, especially in Saxony, Silesia and the valleys of the Rhine and the Wupper. However, even though German industries introduced modern production techniques, no-tably in the manufacture and processing of textiles, many of these industries proved unable to compete once the collapse of Napo-leonic rule opened the floodgates to a tide of English goods.

Furthermore, German trade and commerce had been severely damaged by the war years, and the general misery was rendered even more acute by the famine caused by a series of poor harvests after the advent of peace. Industrialisation was further delayed by the inability of the German Confederation, which had been cobbled together by the Congress of Vienna, to build a unified economy.

In 1818 Prussia passed tariff legislation which brought economic unity to its own fractured domain and created the first, relatively strong German market. Despite the resistance of most central and south German governments (most notably of Austria), this market was extended in 1834 to include another eighteen states through the creation of the German Customs Union under Prussian leadership. The Union eliminated the sundry tariff barriers which were the economic ruination of the *Bund* and were vehemently decried by Friedrich List and most central and south German manufacturers and business people.

The Customs Union subsequently expanded to include most German states in a unified market. This in turn induced manufacturers and government bureaucrats to undertake the investments necessary to endow the Union with a modern transportation system. As a result the Customs Union formed Germany's first modern economic market, able to absorb and generate capital. 'The Customs Union (*Zollverein*) and the railway system are Siamese twins; born at the same time . . . of a single intent and purpose, they support and reinforce one another',[15] wrote Friedrich List in 1841 after years of endeavouring to point out the benefits of an effective transportation system. 'The rapid, safe, regular and inexpensive conveyance of people and goods is one of the mightiest stimulants of national wealth and civilisation in all its manifestations.'[16] Like List the economist, so Friedrich Harkort, the Ruhr steel and machine magnate, saw railways as a source of national wealth and the harbinger of a sense of common purpose which would overcome German particularism in the interests of the whole.[17] In fact, railways did prove to be the main impetus behind German industrialisation. The first German passenger service between Nuremberg and Fürth was inaugurated on 7 July 1835, and the first long-distance line between Leipzig and Dresden opened in 1837. Other stretches followed, and by 1850 Germany possessed 6000 km of railways binding the country from east to west, from north to south, and linking it to the rest of the industrialised world.

In order to service the railway, new industries emerged. Rails, locomotives and carriages had to be built, tracks laid, tunnels dug and bridges raised. The demand for coal and iron leapt ahead, and an industrial heartland took shape in the Ruhr valley. Here immense coal reserves had been mined since the 1850s with the help of steam-driven conveyers. The smelting industry prospered mightily, and the new machine-building factories of Berlin and Saxony were soon supplying not only the internal market with their wares but also France and even Britain.

The first Krupp foundry—one of Germany's original cast steel manufacturers—had been forced to close in 1816 due to heavy debts. It was reopened by its founder, Friedrich Krupp, in 1818 and still besieged by creditors, was inherited by Friedrich's son Alfred in 1826. Forced to work as a labourer in his own factory, Alfred barely kept his head above water until 1834 when the railways first began to purchase cast-iron wheels and the Krupp foundry landed an important contract. The foundry expanded and the number of employees rose from eleven in 1831 to sixty-two. By 1846 the firm had 122 employees, and this number soared to 683 employees in 1849 and 1700 around mid-century. Besides weldless cast-steel wheels, Alfred Krupp also entered the munitions business, shipping over half his production to foreign countries.

Meanwhile, the steam engines, power-looms, ovens and hydraulic presses of Friedrich Harkort were sweeping the Ruhr. Germany's first steamship, constructed by Harkort, traversed the mouth of the Rhine and the North Sea in the winter of 1836 and sailed into the Weser. Just six years later, the city of Bremen inaugurated regular steamship traffic between Bremerhaven and New York. In 1841 August Borsig began production of locomotives in Berlin and a decade later had already constructed 500. Karl Anton Henschel in Kassel and Joseph Anton von Maffei in Munich followed hard on his heels.

Railways and heavy industry had finally achieved a signal breakthrough in Germany. The impoverished surplus population found jobs and a source of income in coal-mining, iron-working, machine-building and railway construction. This further stimulated demand for consumer durables, especially textiles, and more factories sprang up to supply the demand.

As transportation improved, better means of communication appeared. The electromagnetic telegraph was invented by the Göttingen professors Carl Friedrich Gauss and Wilhelm Eduard Weber, and was put into practical use by Werner von Siemens and the American Samuel Morse. Siemens also insulated electrical wires with gutta-percha and laid the first underground cable in 1848. Only a few years later, submarine cable linked Europe with the other continents, providing governments, merchants and newspapers with the latest information. The news was quickly disseminated far and wide thanks to the invention of the rotary press by the American William Bullock.

Though the Ruhr became the economic and industrial heart of Germany, industry developed as well along the Saar and in Prussia, Silesia, Saxony and the south German states. Modern means of transportation and communication fostered a great deal of interaction among the infrastructures of these states and the ultimate emergence of one large economic unit. The cities expanded, and after 1850 their traditional physiognomies began to change. Ever more capital was invested in industry and the first large private banks appeared. The gloom that enveloped the land in the early 1830s was dissipated by a euphoric belief in the power of progress. The liberal bourgeoisie had seen its political dreams shattered in 1849, but now it discovered new interests and new goals towards which to direct its energy: the creation of an industrial state and hopefully of a new era, in which economic power might eventually spawn political independence.

The newly founded polytechnical institutes (*technische Hochschulen*), first established in Karlsruhe in 1825 and then in Darmstadt, Munich, Dresden and Stuttgart, churned out technicians with a mind for the real world. In the classical universities empirical and experimental science triumphed over holistic and idealist natural philosophy, and Germany gained world-wide respect for the quality of her scientific research. Theodor Schwann, born in Neuss am Rhein and engaged as a researcher at the universities of Louvain and Liège, demonstrated that both plants and animals are composed of cells. Julius Robert von Mayer, a medical doctor and physicist in Heilbronn calculated the mechanical equivalent of heat. Hermann Ludwig Ferdinand von Helmholtz, a physicist and physiologist at the universities of Bonn, Heidelberg and Berlin developed physiological optics and acoustics, the scientific theory of sound and colour sensation and the modern conception of electricity. The physicist Gustav Robert Kirchhoff and the chemist Robert Bunsen, collaborating in Heidelberg, invented spectral analysis and opened new paths into the future. As an Augustinian monk teaching natural history and physics at upper school (*Oberrealschule*) in Brünn, Gregor Mendel studied the laws of heredity in plants. Justus von Liebig, a professor of chemistry in Giessen and Munich, pioneered the great advance in German chemistry and in particular revolutionised agriculture with his discoveries in the sphere of agricultural chemistry. A former artillery officer, Werner von Siemens, discovered the dynamoelectric motor which inaugurated heavy-current engineering and opened new industrial vistas.

At the same time Friedrich List continued his crusade to inspire Germans with a passion for industry and to protect emerging German industries with high tariffs, a policy quite opposed to the prevailing free-trade theories of Adam Smith and the Manchester school of economics. These tariffs should not be removed, according to List, until German industry had fully taken root and become competitive with English industry. Freedom and enduring world peace could only be attained through nationalist economic policies, which one day would make the union of all nations feasible. List was convinced that the emerging age of science and technology had the power to elevate humanity to a higher plane and to make men better, happier, freer and more contented.

At the time when List set these ideas down in *The National System of Political Economy*, published in 1841, the bulk of the German population was anything but free and happy. The bourgeoisie, the 'locomotive of the modern, capitalist economy', 'the sole productive, i.e. inventive and creative force',[18] had overcome feudalism from an economic point of view but had achieved very few political reforms. The power of the state still rested in the hands of the princes and it was they and their entourage who set the social tone. The bourgeoisie had seized the economic initiative, thanks to its pioneering spirit, creativity and commercial accomplishments, but this only deepened the penury of broad strata of the population. As industrialisation progressed, the capitalist entrepreneurs were confronted by the ever-swelling ranks of dispossessed workers.

In the early nineteenth century, agricultural yields began to rise in Germany, as elsewhere, as a result of crop rotation, introduced by Albrecht Thaer, improved agricultural techniques and most notably the use of artificial fertilisers as advocated by Justus von Liebig. However, improved productivity created surplus labour, as evidenced earlier in England, and migrants from rural areas poured into the cities. Here small farmers, who had lost the struggle for survival, joined cottage workers and craftsmen, deprived of their livelihood by machines, in the search for a better future. Craftsmen in particular waged a desperate battle against the encroachments of the machine age during the entire first half of the nineteenth century. In England and France, workmen had already been spurred to open revolt by their fear of the omnipresent machine, bearing down on them like a thunderstorm, in Goethe's words,[19] or like a slithering monster with heads 'growing and gaping on all sides', in the words of Jeremias Gotthelf.[20]

Fierce competition erupted in the textile trade between Silesian products and cheap English imports. Traditional cottage weavers were caught in the middle of the conflict, driven to the brink of starvation and then into open revolt. Out of the depths of their misery and despair arose a song which spread throughout the textile districts in 1844 and was later incorporated into Gerhard Hauptmann's play *Die Weber* (The Weavers) (1893). It recounts in haunting terms the terrible events of those years:

> Hier wird der Mensch langsam gequält,
> Hier ist die Folterkammer,
> Hier werden Seufzer viel gezählt
> Als Zeugen von dem Jammer.
> Ihr seid die Quelle aller Not,
> Die hier den Armen drücket,
> Ihr seid's die ihm das trockene Brot
> Noch von dem Munde rücket.
> Ihr fangt stets an zu jeder Zeit,
> Den Lohn herabzubringen,
> Und andre Schurken sind bereit,
> Dem Beispiel nachzuringen.[21]

(This is where people are slowly racked, / this is the torture chamber, / this is where countless groans / evidence the depth of our pain. / You are the source of the misery / that here afflicts the wretched, / It is you who steal dry bread / out of the mouths of the poor. / You who are always prompt / to reduce our wage still further / While other scoundrels wait / to follow your dread example.)

The Social Question and the Social Movement in Germany

By mid-century the industrialisation of Germany was in full swing. But even as capitalism and technology celebrated their final triumph, the vast army of job-seekers had swollen to such an extent that the social question became increasingly urgent, as beforehand in England. The growth of communications and heavy industry created new jobs, but German manufacturers remained locked in bitter competition with foreign producers. Factory owners sought to gain the upper hand by vigorously depressing wages, which soon sank below the minimum needed for survival. Countless women and children were compelled to seek work, aggravating unemployment and depressing wages still further. The cycle of despair seemed endless.

Manufacturers increasingly demanded that employees accept their meagre earnings in the form of goods drawn from company shops. Thus wages were transformed into 'rotten potatoes, tainted bacon, rancid lard'.[22] This practice was not prohibited until 1849, when Prussia passed legislation requiring employers to compensate their workforce in cash.

Working conditions were harsh and often inhuman. Workers, bereft of virtually all legal protection, found themselves at the mercy of their employers. Brutal discipline, lack of insurance and short notice of dismissal made human life an ordeal to be endured. By the end of the 1840s the working day had 'reached fifteen, sixteen, seventeen and more hours';[23] not until a quarter-century later was it reduced to a legal limit of twelve hours. While the cities expanded, the working-class districts degenerated into frightful slums. The plight of the poor was vividly depicted in 1843 by the Romantic poetess Bettina von Arnim in a report prepared for Frederick William IV:

The bulk of the proletariat can be found in inconspicuous streets and quarters of the city, the so-called slums. . . . To the left and right of the *Hamburger Tor* vast numbers of dilapidated shacks stretch into the distance. Here can be found the supposed family homes. . . . In the midst of the miserable hovels stand large, isolated houses, seven in all, where 2500 people are crammed into 400 rooms. This is a sequel of private speculation, as neither the state nor the municipality has decided that great numbers of the poor should inhabit these large asylums in preference to their stinking caves. . . . The chambers are generally small and uniform, as their numbers would indicate. Nevertheless, two families are often squeezed into a single room, separated only by a rope. . . . Large families being expressly forbidden, these homes are generally inhabited by poor, helpless individuals and occasionally by small families of three or four. The rent is usually two *Taler* per month.[24]

Child labour was a social evil of a singular kind. In some cases, children barely four years old were torn 'struggling and screaming from their mothers' sides' and dragged off to work 'at five in the morning through the cold and the wet'.[25] As a rule, child labour began at the age of eight and the working day lasted as long as fourteen hours, including Sundays and holidays. The health of these children suffered accordingly, and opportunities for education were out of the question. An official factory inspector in Prussia wrote the following report on their plight:

These unfortunate creatures hardly ever smell fresh air, are badly clothed, poorly fed and spend their youth in sorrow and deprivation. Pale faces, dull and swollen eyes, bloated bodies, puffy cheeks, inflamed lips and noses, tumid throat glands, loathsome skin eruptions and asthmatic attacks differentiate their health from that of other children of the same social class who do not work in factories. No less disturbing is their moral and intellectual state.[26]

The Prussian state, concerned about the devastating effect on the supply of recruits for the army, promulgated its first labour legislation in 1839. Children were forbidden to work at night and on Sundays and holidays, child workers under nine years of age were not allowed in mines and factories, and youths under sixteen were limited to a daily maximum of ten hours of work. At the fifth Rhenish diet, a delegate declared during a debate in 1837 on legislation to protect minors that 'human beings who begin to work like slaves as children pass their entire lives in privation'; a worker like this has 'to contend with all manner of hardship' is 'exposed with his family to great suffering and hunger' and is happy 'finally at his grave's edge to be freed of this life'.[27] The industrialist Friedrich Harkort warned: 'These offshoots of industrialism, often without a real dwelling and without hope or faith in the future . . . pose through their rising numbers a serious threat to the welfare of civil society.'[28]

Marx and Engels pointed out in the *Communist Manifesto* that the bourgeoisie had successfully bent the forces of nature to man's will: it had invented machinery, applied chemistry to industry and agriculture, built steamships, railways and the electric telegraph, and cleared whole continents for cultivation;[29] but at the same time this bourgeoisie destroyed an ancient way of life and created a highly insecure economy for the bulk of the population and for mounting numbers of workers dependent on wages for their existence. Powerless, bound to impersonal factory jobs, stripped of all property or position in society, these workers coalesced into an industrial proletariat sharply distinguished from the bourgeoisie. As in England beforehand, two classes arose in Germany

between whom there is no intercourse and no sympathy; who are as ignorant of each other's habits, thoughts, and feelings, as if they were dwellers in different zones, or inhabitants of different planets; who are formed by different breeding, are fed by a different food, are ordered by different manners, and are not governed by the same laws.[30]

The first measures to bring comfort and succour to the underprivileged classes of Germany were initiated by individuals within both large Christian confessions whose sympathies were stirred by the depths of the deprivation they saw around them. In a speech before the National Assembly in August 1848, Karl Zittel, the evangelical pastor for Heidelberg, called on all Christians 'to seize the times and to shape them in a Christian spirit' in order to solve the social question 'which permeates all aspects of our existence'.[31] In October of the same year Wilhelm von Kettler, the future

Catholic Bishop of Mainz, declared: 'The most compelling problem that has yet to be solved, despite all attempts at legislation and all forms of political organisation, is the social problem.'[32] The solution, he thought, fell within the preserve of the church: a Christian disposition and an activist love for one's fellow man would solve the plight of the downtrodden. Acting in this spirit, Johann Hinrich Wichern had already established 'Tough House' (*Rauhe Haus*) in 1833, a Protestant educational asylum in Hamburg which sheltered orphaned and abandoned children. Fifteen years later Wichern founded the home missions' (*Innere Mission*), which fulfilled their Christian duty by caring for the poor, the sick and the suffering. In 1839 Pastor Theodor Fliedner established a *Diakonissenhaus* in Kaiserswerth for the purpose of training Protestant nurses who then fanned out across Germany to care for the sick in a spirit of Christian love. The charitable institutions founded in Bethel by Pastor Friedrich von Bodelschwingh also brought much relief. Asylums for homeless journeymen were opened by the Catholic chaplain Adolf Kolping. Together with Wilhelm von Ketteler, he developed them in 1846 into the first Catholic journeymen's unions (*Gesellenvereine*) which combined a Christian-inspired education with material provisions for sickness and old age.

The struggle to improve the workingman's lot was also taken up by the practical labour movement, which constituted itself in 1848 as the German Workers' Association (*Allgemeine Deutsche Arbeiterverbrüderung*). Under the leadership of Stephan Born (a typesetter and later professor of modern literature and publisher of the *Baseler Nachrichten*), the Workers' Association championed higher wages, shorter hours of work, welfare payments for sick or injured workers, the establishment of credit banks for the construction of dwellings, the elimination of indirect taxes, a progressive income tax, free education, free movement of labour and freedom of association. The Workers' Association hoped to achieve all its goals through the institution of universal and equal suffrage.

After 1849 the spreading reaction briefly suppressed the activities of various local chapters of the national association, but organised labour could not be stopped. It increased in strength and launched in the middle 1850s one of the largest strikes ever seen in Germany at the time.

The period of fiercest reaction ended in 1858, when Prince William became Regent of Prussia and the so-called New Era of moderate liberalism began. The labour movement returned to the charge, and in May 1863 the General Union of German Workers (*Allgemeiner Deutsche Arbeiterverein*) was founded under the leadership of Ferdinand Lassalle, a merchant's son from Breslau. Lassalle gave workers their first politically effective representation. He hoped to work within the system in order to gain universal, equal and direct suffrage and then to exploit the political power this conferred in order to democratise the state and gain supreme authority for the workers. The vocation of the new, democratic state would be 'to foster and promote the great cause of the free association of individual workers'[33] and to allocate the necessary funds to establish worker-controlled corporations which would eliminate the need for factory owners and profits. In sharp contrast to the liberals, Lassalle sought state control over the economy in order to ensure a fairer distribution of income. 'Guided by the ideas of the working class', the state would bring into effect 'with great determination and enthusiasm a level of health, education, freedom and happiness . . . unparalleled in human history.'[34] A socially minded monarchy could even assist in restructuring the state so that it served the interests of the masses, an eventuality which Lassalle kindly outlined in conversations with the Prussian minister Otto von Bismarck.

The liberals too were not wanting for a reform programme. Beginning in the early 1840s a few far-sighted industrialists, notably Harkort and Krupp, established factory funds through which their workers could provide mutual support in case of sickness or injury. They further encouraged the construction of dwellings and schools for employees. Early in the 1860s worker education associations supported by the liberal bourgeoisie sprang up 'in order to uplift the worker through education and to improve his lot through self-help'.[35]

These efforts were largely inspired by Hermann Schulze-Delitzsch, a democratic representative in the Prussian national assembly, who promoted the idea of worker self-help and assisted as early as 1849 in establishing savings and loan associations and consumers' cooperatives. These associations, backed by liberals, also attempted to fix the legal relationship between employer and employee, between capital and labour, and to settle their differences through joint action. All this could be achieved, the liberals hoped, 'unimpeded by political wrangling and the caste spirit, freely stretching out a hand in order to work together in harmony'.[36] The liberals were eager to stifle a politicised and independent working-class movement, while at the same fostering social mobility on an individual basis in order to discourage any thinking in terms of the class struggle.

According to Karl Marx and Friedrich Engels, however, class

struggle was the very heart of the problem. Marx was born into a family of Jewish academics in Trier in the year 1818, and he came to interpret all of human history as a fundamental struggle between social classes. Marx was convinced that the 'Fourth Estate' (the oppressed working class) would one day fulfil the same historical mission towards the 'Third Estate' (the affluent bourgeoisie) which this Third Estate had once fulfilled towards the feudal aristocracy. This would be the case because 'the modern bourgeois society, that has sprouted on the ruins of feudal society, has failed to eliminate class antagonisms'.[37] In contrast to Stephan Born, Ferdinand Lassalle and all other reformers who sought to resolve the social question within the framework of the existing social system, Marx aimed at nothing less than a political revolution that would overthrow the existing order. He accordingly denounced all cooperation with bourgeois elements as a 'betrayal of principle'.

The older French and German socialism of François Noel Babeuf, Louis Auguste Blanqui, Etienne Cabet, Wilhelm Weitling and Moses Hess was based on a feeling of moral revulsion before the vast economic disparities in society. It demanded legal and economic equality for the fourth estate and the just distribution of material goods. Marx's brand of socialism, however, was founded on what he considered to be an objective historical process which would eventually destroy the capitalist system through the agency of the forces inherent within it. On the basis of his historical studies and methodical analysis of the contemporary economy, Marx developed the theory of historical materialism in collaboration with Friedrich Engels (born in 1820 as the son of an Elberfeld manufacturer). Thereafter Marx never ceased to defend the precise, scientific nature of this theory, first expounded in *The Communist Manifesto* of 1847 and in *Wage-Labour and Capital*, published in 1848. Marx and Engels further amplified and developed their sweeping social, historical and political theory in *Das Kapital*, the essential first volume of which appeared in 1867.

Marx and Engels arrived at their conviction that 'the history of all hitherto existing society is the history of class struggles' as a result of their reading of Hegel's philosophical history. Hegel conceived human civilisation as a dialectical progression, that is as a struggle of opposites (thesis and antithesis) that eventually achieve resolution in a higher synthesis. This synthesis reconciles the opposites and elevates humanity to a higher stage of civilisation. Where Hegel saw contending ideas as the motive force in human history, Marx and Engels saw the method of production and the resulting social stratification and social tensions, that is the class struggle, as the creative force behind all political and intellectual institutions.

According to Marx and Engels in *The Communist Manifesto* the class struggle which drives the historical process is rooted in the 'basis', or economic structure, of a given society, and not in its 'superstructure', or dominant intellectual, religious and political beliefs. 'What else does the history of ideas prove than that intellectual production changes . . . in proportion as material production is changed?' According to the Hegelian dialectic, changes in the relations of production are both a cause and a result of the class struggle, for every relation of production creates in the exploited class its own antithesis with which it must eventually be reconciled in the higher sythesis of a new relation of production.

In their analysis of specifically capitalist relations of production and hence of capitalist society in general, Marx and Engels adopted David Ricardo's theory of prices and wages and applied it to the worker engaged in industry. Unlike the medieval artisan, they reasoned, the industrial worker does not own the means of production, that is the tools and materials of his trade. Instead, he disposes solely over his labour which—if he wishes to survive—he must sell in the market-place. Marx and Engels argued that the value of this labour is determined, similar to all other wares, by the value of the time required to produce it. In the case of labour, this value is determined by the 'cost of survival and reproduction', which varies according to the cultural circumstances. If the worker labours longer than this 'socially necessary timespan', he produces a greater value than is required for his survival and that of his children. All this surplus value accrues to the capitalist, who thus disposing over the unpaid labour of others increases his capital holdings.

The greater the stock of capital, the more production can be rationalised, mechanised and thereby increased. Labour costs can be reduced, and the number of those forced to rely on wage-labour rises, creating an 'industrial reserve army' the existence of which further depresses wages. In consequence, runs *The Communist Manifesto*, 'the modern labourer . . ., instead of rising with the progress of industry, sinks deeper and deeper below the conditions of existence of his own class. He becomes a pauper, and pauperism develops more rapidly than population and wealth'.

The surplus value so acquired is then reinvested by the capitalist in additional means of production. This further concentrates the number of capitalists as smaller entrepreneurs are driven out of business and fall back into the proletariat. The surviving companies grow steadily in size, continually increasing the total volume of production. Since the ability of the exploited masses to consume this production is diminished, excess goods go unpurchased, the markets become saturated and sales stagnate. The cycle of recurrent economic crises grows more and more severe as industrial output outstrips the purchasing power of a monied class that is continually diminishing in numbers.

Great wealth arises in the midst of ever-expanding pauperism. Eventually, runs *The Communist Manifesto*, the division of society into decreasing numbers of wealthy capitalists and teeming masses of desitute proletarians leads to the collapse of the capitalist system. 'The weapons with which the bourgeoisie felled feudalism to the ground are now turned against the bourgeoisie itself. But not only has the bourgeoisie forged the weapons that bring death to itself; it has also called into existence the men who are to wield those weapons—the modern working-class.' When the climactic hour is reached, capitalist firms are taken over by a class-conscious proletariat, and 'the whole superincumbent strata of official society' is 'sprung into the air'.

The revolution is followed by the dictatorship of the proletariat, the proletarian class state, a lynch-pin of *The Communist Manifesto*.

The proletariat will use its political supremacy to wrest, by degrees, all capital from the bourgeoisie, to centralise all instruments of production in the hands of the State, that is of the proletariat organised as a ruling class; and to increase the total productive forces as rapidly as possible.

Of course, in the beginning, this cannot be effected except by means of despotic inroads on the rights of property, and on the conditions of bourgeois production; by means of measures, therefore, which appear economically insufficient and untenable, but which in the course of the movement outstrip themselves ... and are unavoidable as a means of entirely revolutionising the mode of production. ...

When, in the course of development, class distinctions have disappeared, and all production has been concentrated in the hands of a vast association of the whole nation, the public power will lose its political character. Political power, properly so called, is merely the organised power of one class for oppressing another. If the proletariat during its contest with the bourgeoisie is compelled, by the force of circumstances, to organise itself as a class, if, by means of a revolution, it makes itself the ruling class, and, as such, sweeps away by force the old conditions of production, then it will, along with these conditions, have swept away the conditions for the existence of class antagonism, and of classes generally, and will thereby have abolished its own supremacy as a class.

In place of the old bourgeois society, with its classes and class antagonisms, we shall have an association in which the free development of each is the condition for the free development of all.

Once this state has been reached, the alienation of mankind will be overcome, according to Marx. Labour will cease to be a purchasable commodity and will again become the hallmark of human nature. Humans, freed of dependence on their own products, will once again learn to dominate their appetites. Once the struggle between private property and the proletariat is resolved, the overproduction of goods will cease and with it the incessant creation of new needs encouraged by overproduction and by the covetousness and the undesirable impulses which it fosters such as greed, deceitfulness, exploitation and a lust for power. Mankind, alienated from his own nature, will recover and in recovering itself will recover the world. Accumulated labour will serve to nurture, broaden and enrich the workers' lives and not only, as in bourgeois society, to augment the comforts of a narrow élite.

The utopianism and doubtful validity of this attempt to explain the past and light the way into the future did not escape the notice of Marx's and Engels' contemporaries. It is perfectly true that economic interests and forces are among the most influential of all historical impulses; however, to reduce all history to a series of class struggles based on economic interests is to deform and debase actual events. The utopian element in the thought of Marx and Engels cannot be denied. The positive anthropology of the French Enlightenment and primeval desire to return to the paradise whence the first humans were evicted, animate their yearning for the day when freedom, fairness and joy will prevail and men will live together in harmony.

None the less, the longing for redemption from the evils of this world, dressed up in the form of Marx's socio-economic theory, proved able to mobilise generations of workers. The ardent final appeal of *The Communist Manifesto* to the proletarians of all nations to unite, throw off their chains and win the world gave hope to the masses and appealed to their need for irrational belief. It has survived all misguided social theories, dogmatic distortions, economic disasters and social injustices. The fascination of Marxist theory doubtless rests on its ambivalence: it is mystical prophecy dressed in scientific clothing and as such appeals to both the irrationality and strong belief in science which together typify the industrial age.

When Marx and Engels published *The Communist Manifesto* in 1847, they believed that their expectations would soon be consummated. Later events in France encouraged the notion that violent revolution was at hand. By 1871, however, the founders of 'scientific socialism' had resigned themselves to a longer evolution during which capitalist society would slowly grow ripe for destruction.

From a political standpoint, *The Communist Manifesto* and *Das Kapital* endowed the European working class with a coherent strategy which greatly influenced trade unions and Social Democratic parties alike in their struggle towards political and social equality for the Fourth Estate. The work of Marx and Engels thereby continued to exert a major influence over the Continent despite the erroneousness of certain prognostications and fundamental assumptions, as pointed out even by labour leaders themselves.

The further course of German history in the nineteenth century was, however, determined more by nationalism than by social issues—despite all Marxist predictions and appeals to the international solidarity of the working class and despite the desire of the liberals to maintain free trade. The failed attempt at national unity in 1848 only magnified the yearning of the middle and lower-middle classes for a political *tour de force* that would finally fulfil their age-old dream. In the second half of the nineteenth century the drive for national unity became increasingly enmeshed in the struggle for economic expansion. Such expansion required a large national state able to stand on an equal footing with the other great industrial nations of Europe. In contrast to the expectations of Marx and Engels, the social question was posed far more in a national than in an international context, and the first steps towards a solution resulted from conditions and pressures within the nation-state.

7

Bismarck and German Unification

1850:   The Prussian Constitution is revised and recognised by Frede-
         rick William IV
1851:   The reinstitution of the German Confederation, Otto von Bis-
         marck is appointed Prussian envoy to the Federal Diet (*Bundes-
         tag*), the crisis over the Customs Union begins, Louis
         Napoleon's *coup d'état* in France, the Austrian Constitution is
         abolished
1852:   The death of Prince Schwarzenberg
1853:   Napoleon III is crowned Emperor of the French, the treaties
         creating the Customs Union (*Zollverein*) are renewed
1854–6: The Crimean War
1858:   The Prussian government passes under the regency of Prince
         William and the 'New Era' in Prussia begins
1859:   The German National Association (*Nationalverein*) is estab-
         lished
1859–61: The War of Italian Unification
1861:   Victor Emmanuel of Piedmont-Sardinia is proclaimed King of
         Italy, Camillo Cavour dies
1861–5: The Civil War in the United States
1861:   William I is crowned King of Prussia
1862:   Conflict over the Army Bill in Prussia, Bismarck is named prime
         minister of Prussia, constitutional conflict in Prussia;
1863:   The Diet of German princes in Frankfurt, the Alvensleben
         convention
1864:   War between Germany and Denmark
1865:   The Convention of Gastein
1866:   The Prusso-Austrian War
1867:   The foundation of the North German Confederation, the Aus-
         trian Empire becomes the dual monarchy of Austria-Hungary
1868:   The opening of the Customs Parliament (*Zollparlament*)

1870:   The Vatican Council, Prince Leopold von Hohenzollern-
          Sigmaringen becomes a candidate for the Spanish throne
1870–1:   The Franco-Prussian War
1871:   The foundation of the German Empire

The Struggle of the Old and the New

The industrialisation of Germany proceeded at a very rapid pace in the second half of the nineteenth century, but the political structure survived the failed revolution of 1848 largely intact and failed to reflect the new economic reality. Conservative, pre-industrial social strata continued to deny the bourgeoisie a political role even remotely consistent with the economic leadership it provided. Conservatives could not, however, close their ears to the mounting demands that Germany be endowed with a political structure more in keeping with her modern economy.

The economic upsurge overflowed the narrow bounds of particularistic German states and created a degree of prosperity which these individual states could not help but welcome. Politically, however, the German patchwork remained, though 'everything is on the point of collapse, immeasurably decayed and rotten; everything old is worn out, falsified, worm-eaten and beyond redemption', as the Prussian historian Johann Gustav Droyssen lamented in 1854.[1] The dynastic interests of the various kings and princes and the suspicions of foreign governments conspired to stymie Germany's political development and to deny the nation the satisfaction of unification. The pride of the German bourgeoisie in the constitution it had framed and in its efforts to erect a state on the foundation of liberalism had suffered a fateful blow, and its confidence in its own political capacities sank to a low ebb.

'Whosoever wishes to rule Germany must conquer it; proceeding à la Gagern will get nowhere', Prince William of Prussia remarked in 1849 after the last desperate attempts to achieve unity—by force if necessary—had been crushed.[2] Thus the future Prussian king and German emperor evaluated the existing array of forces and the only possible solution to the national dilemma.

The prince was a firm believer in the divine right of kings and was convinced that the historical process of unification would prove irresistible once it had been initiated: 'Whether the time for unity has come, God only knows! But that Prussia is destined to ascend to the summit of Germany is manifest in our entire history—all that remains to be determined is when and how.'[3] Much of *how* this would come to pass was already clear, at least in William's mind: Germany would have to be conquered under Prussian aegis, as had already occurred in the economic sphere thanks to the Customs Union (*Zollverein*). The politically feasible would have to be distinguished from the politically desirable, and a policy developed that took account of the existing powers and that assessed their strengths in order to bend them to the final goal. Contemporaries termed this kind of policy *Realpolitik*, in reference to the primacy of action over reflection and conjecture. *When* all of this would occur, still lay hidden in the mists of time, especially since William had just played a major role in foiling the first attempt at unification. These mists were rendered all the heavier by the period of political reaction that now set in and the subsequent reinforcement of traditional political divisions. For the moment it was the forces of the old that had triumphed—in Germany and in Europe alike.

There had been two failed attempts at German unification—the popular movement stemming from the Paulskirche and the *démarches* undertaken in Erfurt by the German princes under Prussian initiative and leadership. The various German states then met in December 1850 at a conference in Dresden to debate the reform of the German Confederation, and in May 1851 the *Bund* resumed its work in Frankfurt on the Main.

The discussions in Dresden revealed that after the humiliation of Olmütz, Prussia would not be able to make good its claims to parity with Austria within the German Confederation and to be named alternating president of the *Bundestag*. Further events confirmed that Austria and its prime minister Prince Schwarzenberg were not going to share Vienna's traditional position of primacy within the Confederation. In contrast to the pre-revolutionary era of Metternich, however, the experience of the revolution had awakened the various German states to the extent of their power and had made them far more willing to employ it. This tended to reinforce the Prusso-Austrian dualism within the Confederation and in the end to frustrate its primary goal: to regain the thread of pre-revolutionary times. The envoys assembled in Frankfurt were, however, united in their desire to roll back liberalism within their own borders.

In December 1851 Prince Schwarzenberg annulled the March Constitution in Austria and re-established an absolutist and centralist government rooted in the army and the church. Local self-government was abolished, stringent police measures were initiated to maintain internal security, and a tightly organised bureaucracy was introduced to unify the administration. Austria and Hungary were to be firmly bound together by a modern economic policy devised by Karl Ludwig von Bruck, a Calvinist originally from Elberfeld. Bruck abolished the tariff barriers between Austria and Hungary, attempted to link the Austrian economic zone to the German Customs Union and expanded the postal service and the network of roads and railways. Trade and commerce were placed on a modern footing with commercial courts and chambers of commerce, and a central oceanic authority was established in Trieste.

Although the bureaucratic police state re-emerged in Austria, the constitution survived in Prussia. King Frederick William IV, however, fell under the influence of a camarilla of conservative cronies and sought to suppress any freedom of political expression. The public, the press and civil servants once more came under the close scrutiny of the police and the reactionary bureaucracy. Schools were supervised by the re-emergent Evangelical High Council (*Evangelischer Oberkirchenrat*), and political unions, labour organisations and strikes were forbidden. Totally disillusioned, the bourgeoisie retreated—partly because it was intimidated by the renewed vigour of the old order and partly because it feared the consequences of a proletarian revolution. Henceforth the middle classes would concentrate their attention on commerce, education and scientific research, or the spheres of *Besitz und Bildung* (property and education) which Max Weber later characterised as the quintessence of the nineteenth-century German bourgeoisie.

The constitution to which Frederick William had agreed in December 1848 was largely deprived of its liberal content and remoulded to suit the reaction. When finally signed by the king on 31 January 1851, equal suffrage had been replaced by a system of three-class suffrage, which was to persist in Prussia till 1918. The population was divided into three equal classes according to their tax-paying capacity so that 'one thousand rich people' counted as much 'as one hundred thousand poor'.[4] In an indirect and open election, the three classes each selected an equal number of electors, who subsequently elected the deputies who would represent the people in the second chamber of the Prussian Diet. Conservative influence was further strengthened when the first chamber was transformed into an unelected 'House of Lords'. It thus became a chamber composed of the high nobility, country squires appointed hereditary members at the discretion of the king, and envoys from approximately thirty larger cities and the six universities of Prussia. Since legislation required the approval of the Chamber of Deputies, the House of Lords and the crown, the forces of reaction seemed secure. This effect was intensified when the squirarchy, deprived of its economic clout but all the more determined to maintain its political and social prestige, succeeded brilliantly in re-establishing its influence at the royal court and within the army and the civil service.

In the rest of Germany, the Fundamental Rights were formally abolished in August 1851 in conformity with a joint proposal of Austria and Prussia. Henceforth the various state constitutions were to be revised in a reactionary direction. However, the friction between Austria and Prussia intensified, effectively precluding the kind of cooperation that had prevailed in Metternich's day and dispelling the unity of purpose which the governments represented in the *Bundestag* required in order to interfere jointly in the internal political affairs of the small and medium-sized states. The discussions in the *Bundestag* in Frankfurt therefore tended to revolve more and more around the political role of the various German states and especially the role of the two largest German powers within the Confederation and within Europe as a whole.

The dispute about the relative stature of Austria and Prussia within the German Confederation arose largely as a result of Prince Schwarzenberg's persistent attempts to reinforce Austrian primacy in Central Europe. The issue came to a head when Schwarzenberg attempted to compel the admission of Austria to the Customs Union through a vote of the *Bundestag*. In accordance with the commercial and economic plans of Bruck, the new minister of trade, Schwarzenberg hoped to undermine Prussia's economic leadership in Germany and thus to deprive her of the firm foundations of her influence in the rest of Germany. At first the medium-sized states hesitated between the material advantages they enjoyed as members of the Prussian *Customs Union* and their qualms over Prussia's strength within the Confederation. But in the end they rejected the Austrian scheme and voted for a continuation of the Customs Union treaty. This Prussian victory (in which Berlin's envoy to the Federal Diet, Otto von Bismarck, played a prominent role) not only saved the second greatest power in Germany from economic isolation but also ensured a continuing economic upswing in the other states adhering to the *Customs Union*. These smaller states gradually adopted Prussia's liberal economic legislation, boosting the ascendancy of free trade over the system of protective tariffs favoured by Austria.

The Customs Union, newly consolidated under Prussian leadership, concluded commercial treaties with France and Britain, thereby finally ensuring German access to the markets of Western Europe and through them to the world. The real advantages which accrued to Prussia by dint of her vigorous reaction to competition from Austria-Hungary further enhanced her prestige. During the series of European crises which now loomed on the horizon, Prussia would have need of all the prestige she could muster if she was to advance her interests at the cost of the smaller German states and an Austrian empire that continued to insist on primacy in Central Europe. This task was facilitated by two events: the sudden death on 5 April 1852 of Prince Schwarzenberg, the most persistent and able champion of the Austrian cause, and the debut of a highly efficacious Prussian envoy to the *Bundestag* in Frankfurt, Prince Otto von Bismarck-Schönhausen.

Born on 1 April 1815 Bismarck represented the twin pillars of the Prussian state: the aristocracy and the bureaucracy. His father was a Brandenburg Junker from east of the Elbe and his mother a middle-class woman whose family had connections to academe and the upper echelons of the bureaucracy. After an early childhood on the family estates in Pomerania, Bismarck was sent to school in Berlin at an early age, at the urging of his highly ambitious mother. After completing the *Gymnasium*, he studied law at the University of Göttingen for one year before moving to Berlin, where he eventually took his examinations. He entered government service, spent one year in training as a junior assistant in Aachen and then three and a half months in Potsdam. Soon wearying of the civil service routine, Bismarck volunteered for the Potsdam rifle battalion, was sent to Greifswald in 1836 to finish his military service and attended the agricultural institute in neighbouring Eldena.

It was at this time that the twenty-three-year-old made up his mind not to return to government service. He revealed his feelings in a letter to his cousin, Countess Bismarck-Bohlen, who had appealed to his patriotism in an attempt to reverse his decision.

That the status and the nature of the work of our government officials do not appeal to me; that I do not consider it an unalloyed blessing to be a civil servant or even a minister; that I find raising corn as respectable as writing administrative decrees and possibly more worthwhile; that I am more attracted by not having to obey than by commanding; these are facts for which I can find no justification other than personal taste. . . . Individual government officials, even the highest, enjoy little independence and the work of the others is largely confined to nudging the administrative machinery down its predetermined path. The Prussian civil servant is like the individual musician in an orchestra: whether he plays first violin or the triangle, he is confined to his own part which he plays without influence or overview, as it is written, whether he likes it or not. I, however, want to make my own music in my own way or none at all.[5]

This self-description was only confirmed when Bismarck later re-entered government service as a highly singular outsider.

Back home once again on the family estates, Bismarck remained restless and uneasy, vaguely dissatisfied with his place in life. He delved into Shakespeare, Byron, Louis Blanc, Voltaire, Spinoza and Schiller, but not finding the solace he sought, set out on travels through England, France and Switzerland. He was even considering volunteering to serve in the British army in India when his father bid him to return home 'in a tear-stained letter that spoke of lonely old age, death and reunion'.[6]

Once more living the life of a country squire, Bismarck was introduced by his friend Moritz von Blankenburg into a circle of Pomeranian Pietists, a Christian sect that believed in a literal interpretation of the Bible and combined strict religious orthodoxy with unbending political conservatism. Many highly influential noblemen adhered to this circle, including Leopold Gerlach, the later aide to Frederick William IV who did most to sponsor Bismarck at the royal court.

It was there that Bismarck met Johanna von Puttkamer, whom he later married. Under her influence he abandoned his virulent scepticism and established a relationship with God which helped him to transcend the disturbing transitoriness of human existence. Later he would write, 'I am God's soldier and whither he sends me I must go. I believe that he dispatches me and shapes my life as suits His purposes.'[7] A new determination replaced the restlessness, rebelliousness and biting saracasm of the young man. After his father's death, Bismarck moved in 1845 from Kniephof to Schönhausen, another family estate on the Lower Elbe, where he became dikegrave and was then nominated by the local squirarchy as parliamentary vice-deputy. When the deputy fell ill, Bismarck was elected in his place to a seat in the United Diet. The political career of Otto von Bismarck had commenced. He quickly acquired the reputation of an archconservative junker who, to the astonishment and awe of his reactionary friends, spoke out with impressive boldness, clarity and sarcasm in defence of the power and prestige of the Prussian crown and state. When they were threatened by the revolution of March 1848 he fought passionately on their behalf, convinced that only Prussia and its monarchy could solve the German question.

During this phase of his career Bismarck considered that postrevolutionary Germany could be restructured peacefully and harmoniously only in cooperation with Austria. Frederick William was of the same mind after the failure of his attempt at union caused him to forsake all grandiose national ambitions, and Bismarck struck him as the right man to become Prussian envoy to the Federal Diet in Frankfurt.

In a speech before the Second Chamber of the Prussian Diet vehemently defending the capitulation of Olmütz, Bismarck had declared that 'national egotism is the only healthy basis of a great state—quite unlike the situation of a smaller state'.[8] Consistent with these views, he now took up in Frankfurt his country's categorical insistence on equal status with Austria. His approach to the Habsburgs was amicable and conciliatory until he realised that Austria was not prepared to make any concessions to Prussian pride and was even doing her utmost to block Prussia's natural interests and to subordinate them to Austria's own ambitious plans to extend her empire in Germany. As dispassionate as ever, Bismarck soon concluded:

In order to succeed in its internal policy of centralisation and Germanisation, Austria needs to strengthen its ties to Germany; expressed in Viennese this means rigid hegemony over the *Bund*. We can only get in the way. No matter how we flatten ourselves to the wall, a Germanic Prussia with 17 million inhabitants will always bulk too large to allow Austria the latitude it desires. Our policies have no other natural outlet than Germany, if only because we are so interwoven geographically. But Austria requires this stage for itself. Austrian intentions leave no room for both of us, and we cannot possibly co-exist in the long term. We breathe one another's air. One of us must withdraw or 'be withdrawn'; till then we shall remain enemies. This I consider a fact that cannot be ignored, regardless of how unwelcome it is.[9]

Just as the pre-revolutionary condominium of the two German powers could not be revived, so the entire concert of European states could not find its way back to the peaceful days before 1848. In France Louis Napoleon Bonaparte had been elected President of the Republic in December 1848 with an overwhelming majority. A successful *coup d'état* led to a plebiscitary dictatorship and the resurrection of a Bonapartist empire which, if it was to survive, needed to score quick successes in internal and foreign affairs. Like his uncle before him, Napoleon III enacted a constitution which through legal slight of hand transferred all power to the emperor. The success of this measure was ensured by a programme of strict centralisation. In order to master the strong class conflict within France, Napoleon endeavoured to secure the favour of the bourgeoisie through a generous plan to promote industrialism; the favour of the peasantry through agricultural improvements; and finally the favour of the working class through welfare programmes.

Furthermore, he allied himself closely with the church in order to sweep strong Catholics into his fold. Success was not long in coming. The transportation system expanded at a rapid clip, the big cities were modernised and cleaned up, and Paris was endowed with its modern physignomy, once again becoming the social centre of Europe.

The energy which Napoleon III devoted to domestic affairs was also evident on the international scene. Here he sought to revamp the political structure of Europe in order to release France from the isolation in which she had been maintained since 1815. In keeping with this plan, the French attempted to ally themselves with the forces of nationalism within Europe, even though this deepened the enmity of the conservative and legitimist camp, which regarded the Second Empire, like the First, as a creature of revolution to be rejected a priori.

Bismarck believed that this conservative attitude could not long succeed in frustrating the French desire to play a major role in European affairs. Rejecting conservative repudiations of France and its 'illegitimate' government, he declared: 'France is only of interest to me in so far as it reacts to the situation of my fatherland. We must deal with France as it is and not attempt to exclude it from the constellation of powers.'[10]

In fact, this constellation was on the verge of being scrambled by the rash activities of the Russian tsar, Nicholas I, the most reactionary ruler in Europe and the standard-bearer of legitimacy. Nicholas had played a decisive role in the defeat of revolution in Central and Southern Europe, thanks to the assistance he had lent Austria in crushing the Hungarian uprising, and he believed that the time had come for Russia to reap her reward in the form of the remnants of the disintegrating Ottoman Empire in the Balkans. Constantinopole would be taken and the free passage of Russian ships between the Black Sea and the Mediterranean henceforth assured.

The tsar's first step was to demand that he be awarded a protectorate over the orthodox Christians living within the Ottoman Empire. When the Turkish government refused, Nicholas occupied the Danubian principalities of Moldavia and Wallachia (modern Romania), and sparked a war 'destined to burst once and for all the bonds which still managed to hold the concert of powers in place'.[11]

British concern over the free passage of ships to India and fear that Russia might enclose Europe in a ring of steel,[12] thus upsetting the balance of power, induced London to come to Turkey's aid and declare war on Russia. Napoleon III quickly joined forces with Britain discerning in the conflict between Britain and Russia an opportunity to destroy the old constellation of powers, free France from her isolation and set the stage for French hegemony over the Continent. Austrian interests in the Balkans were directly affected by the Russian attack, and Vienna had every reason to fear both the prospect of independent Balkan states under Russian protection and the encouragement which Napoleon III was offering to national states. In the hope that a show of support for the Western powers would dissuade France from seeking to change the status quo in Italy, Vienna massed its troops menacingly along the Balkan border but did not intervene actively in the fighting. This did serve, however, to distract the Russians and to weaken their war effort in the Crimea. When the tsar withdrew from the Danubian principalities in July 1854, Austrian troops marched in together with the Turks. A subsequent treaty with Britain and France confirmed the about-face in Austrian foreign policy. Henceforth St Petersburg and Vienna would be deadly foes.

Of the great powers, only Prussia remained neutral because the king could not make up his mind between the contending pro-Russian and anti-Russian factions in Berlin. This won for him the gratitude of the tsar—gratitude which stood Prussia in good stead during its impending forays on the international stage.

Defeated in the Crimea by the British and French, the Russians had perforce to accept the terms of the Western powers. These were delivered in Paris, where the peace conference was held under the presidency of a renewed France, liberated from her international isolation and restored to her former glory and power. According to the terms of the Treaty of Paris, Wallachia and Moldavia received their independence, and the warships of all nations were banned from both the Bosporus and the Black Sea, which was declared a neutral zone. Even more significant for the future of the Continent was the fact that this war completed the destruction of the elaborate framework which Metternich had designed in 1815 for the governance of Europe.

Russia and Austria were henceforth hostile powers. The enmity stemming from the whole oriental question would prove to be a source of perennial conflict in Europe till the final collapse of the Habsburg monarchy in 1918. Austria, moreover, had alienated both Britain and France by her indecisive attitude towards the war, and had prompted the smaller German states to move closer to Prussia in reaction to Vienna's bootless attempts to activate the German Confederation against Russia on behalf of Austria's own interests in the Balkans.

Great Britain emerged as the prime beneficiary of the war. Not only was Turkey saved from Russia's clutches, but Britain's own position in the Mediterranean was greatly strengthened—a region of overriding importance now that the construction of the Suez Canal was imminent. Moreover, the victory over Russia helped to consolidate Britain's hold over India, Afghanistan, Persia and China.

The mutual hostility that had arisen among the great powers of Europe had the further effect of releasing the German states, most notably Prussia, from the constraints previously imposed by Vienna and St Petersburg. Bismarck's prediction that 'great crises would generate an atmosphere in which Prussia's cause could prosper was thus borne out. Russia had expected no more from Berlin than benevolent neutrality, and by complying the Prussian king succeeded simultaneously in reinforcing his friendship with the tsar and enhancing his prestige within the German *Bund* many of whose members felt displeased and alienated by Austria. In a memorandum written in March 1858 Bismarck noted that 'in Germany's eyes, Prussia is beginning to regain her natural magnitude and importance'.[13]

The defeat of Russia dealt a crushing blow to the forces of reaction all across Europe. The land of the tsars had been a wellspring of conservatism where absolutism ruled unchecked and uncompromising, where censorship and the secret police still repressed any basic criticism of the traditional order, and where serfdom, aristocratic rule and the Russian Orthodox Church still survived fully intact. The desire of the liberals for a shift in the political winds thus came to pass, and Europe gained 'scope for new movement'.[14]

The reaction that set in after 1848 had cast a chill over the national movement in Germany, largely rooted in the liberal bourgeoisie. But under the new political circumstances it now grew stronger and more articulate than ever. Public opinion became a factor which could no longer be ignored and to which Bismarck admonished the government to pay heed in his March memorandum of 1858. Nationalism grew especially virulent among those peoples of Europe whose desire to give political expression to their sense of nationhood had long been frustrated. Nationalist sentiments also mounted, however, in countries such as Britain and France, which had long enjoyed political unity. Their peoples took a strong interest in the glory of the nation and demanded increased participation in legislating and governing. At the same time, public opinion in Western Europe was sensitised to the hopes and dreams of those peoples who were still struggling to establish national unity.

Napoleon III discerned in these changing circumstances an opportunity to exploit the forces of nationalism in his quest to shatter the status quo, to strengthen the French position on the Continent and to gather allies in a campaign to redraw the national frontiers agreed upon in 1815.

The first major opportunity appeared three years after the end of the Crimean War, when an international crisis centred in Italy, again set the political pot boiling. The Italian unification movement, like the German, had been soundly defeated during the revolutions of 1848. Now however, it resurfaced under the leadership of King Victor Emmanuel of Piedmont-Sardinia and his able prime minister, Count Camillo Cavour. Directed primarily against Austria and the alien dynasties ruling over the particularistic Italian states, the unification movement aimed to free Italy from Austrian domination and to forge a united state.

While most of the Italian duchies took advantage of the reaction to rescind the liberal reforms and constitutions promised during the rebellions of 1848, Victor Emmanuel proceeded to grant his kingdom a constitution. This afforded Cavour an opportunity to develop Piedmont-Sardinia into a model liberal state, which was warmly supported by the bourgeoisie and even won the loyalty of republican-minded patriots. Having identified the 'state with the common cause',[15] Cavour set out to forge an alliance with a foreign power capable of helping him to expel Austrian forces from Italy and to advance towards his ultimate goal of Italian unification.

Napoleon III proved more than willing to cooperate, and a treaty was drawn up which guaranteed French assistance in case of an Austrian attack on Piedmont. In return, Napoleon expected the Italians to cede Savoy and Nice to France. Evincing the political talents with which he was so richly endowed, Cavour began to arm Piedmont-Sardinia for the inevitable confrontation with Austria— but in such a way, as he himself said, that 'on the day when the struggle commences . . . the entire world will say: Piedmont is in the right'.[16] The great powers took steps to preserve the peace, but on 19 April 1859 Vienna issued an ultimatum to the government of Piedmont demanding that it immediately cease its rearmament programme. When the ultimatum was rejected, Austria declared war.

The ensuing Austrian onslaught immediately triggered the secret agreement with Napoleon. Suddenly confronted by the combined forces of France and Italy, the Austrians went down to defeat in the bloody battles of Magenta and Solferino, the murderous horror of which launched the young Swiss Henri Dunant on his passionate crusade to found the Red Cross. However, Prussia, unwilling to see

Austria driven out of Italy from Piedmont to the Adriatic, began to mobilise her troops.

In an attempt to forestall intervention by the great powers, Napoleon abruptly dropped his Italian allies and concluded the Treaty of Villafranca with the Austrians. The Austrian emperor agreed to relinquish Lombardy to Napoleon, who then bestowed his booty on Victor Emmanuel. Although the rewards of the war fell short of Italian expectations, the drive for full national unity could no longer be contained. In Toscana, Parma and Modena the populace rose in open revolt and drove out the old rulers. Subsequent elections disclosed (as later in Romagna, the largest of the church states) an overwhelming majority in favour of annexation to Piedmont. Cavour mollified French opposition to such a step by renouncing Savoy and Nice. When Giuseppe Garibaldi and his followers succeeded in driving the Bourbon kings from Sicily and lower Italy, Cavour ostensibly threw his support behind the celebrated national hero, while cleverly managing to foil Garibaldi's plan for an Italian republic. Cavour finally completed the drive for Italian unification with the help of royalist Piedmont troops.

On 17 March 1861 delegates from across the land proclaimed Victor Emmanuel King of Italy. Unity, though incomplete, was accomplished. Venetia, to be sure, was still a Habsburg possession which would not revert to Italy till 1866 after the Prusso-Austrian War, and Rome remained in the hands of the pope, whom Napoleon protected in return for the domestic support of the French clergy. Casting about for a capital, Victor Emmanuel chose first Turin and then Florence. Italy did not recover its natural capital of Rome until 1870, when Napoleon went down to defeat at the hands of the Prussians.

The peoples of Europe were deeply impressed by Cavour's *tour de force*, accomplished with French intervention, Russian backing and the sympathy of Britain. A liberal national movement had triumphed over both extreme nationalism and resistance from other European powers. In spite of all the obstacles, a national, constitutional state had been born. The Italian experience seemed to prove that national unification could only be achieved through force of arms, and the public became more and more obsessed in the second half of the century with the amassing of a military power. Rulers grew increasingly concerned with the economic, technical and military might of the nations they ruled. These considerations would soon occupy centre stage in both the American Civil War and the founding of a great German state by Otto von Bismarck. It was thanks to the might of the Prussian army that the German

Empire again arose, overcoming a welter of opposing forces within Europe and within the German lands themselves.

The Resolution of the German Question

The Italian war galvanised public opinion in Germany and reinforced the craving for a national state. The greatest obstacle on the road to national unification was posed of course by the old German question.

Bismarck (and with him only a handful of other national figures such as the liberal politician Ludwig Bamberger, the socialist Ferdinand Lassalle and Constantin Rössler, a professor of philosophy in Jena) insisted that Prussia should take action. On 5 May 1859 Bismarck, then Prussian ambassador to Russia, wrote to the aide-de-camp of the prince regent, General Gustav von Alvensleben:

The present circumstances once more afford us an opportunity to seize the grand prize. If we simply wait for Austria and France to become heavily engaged in the war, we can send all our forces south, taking along the border posts in their rucksacks and replanting them at Lake Constance or along the line where Protestantism ceases to predominate. Where else is there a European state with 18 million people (or 14 million if I subtract the Catholics of Upper Bavaria and Swabia) living between its disjointed regions and demanding nothing more than to be admitted? Twenty-four hours after we annex these people, they will fight harder for us than for their previous rulers, especially if the prince regent does them the favour of renaming the Kingdom of Prussia as the new Kingdom of Germany.[17]

With a benevolently neutral Russia in the rear, Bismarck evidently believed that Prussia should march against Austria at the same time as France and Piedmont in order to expel her from the *Bund* and to solve the German question once and for all by force of arms. However, the new Prussian government and public opinion as expressed in newspapers and countless pamphlets, adopted a far different stance: they rallied in virtual unanimity to the cause of their fellow member of the German Confederation in her struggle against the French. Prussian troops mobilised for war—but failed to intervene on Austria's behalf partly due to the pretensions of the prince regent, who claimed supreme command over all the contingents of the *Bund* and partly due to Napoleon's swift peace initiative aimed at pre-empting a Prussian attack.

All that remained was a sense of annoyance and discontent both in foreign lands and in Prussia and the smaller German states. Again it had been clearly demonstrated that the interests of the two great

German powers were far too divergent to ever be reconciled and that the German Confederation itself was so weakened by these contending interests that it could never vigorously pursue a policy of its own. As a result, new life was breathed into the solution to the German question most favoured in the Paulskirche: a federal state led by Prussia.

The desire for unity and the inspiration provided by the Italian example led in the autumn of 1859 to the creation of the German National Association (*Nationalverein*) in Frankfurt on the Main. Here liberal and moderate democrats from the various German states met 'in order to bring about the unification and free development of the German fatherland'.[18] The vast majority of these nationalists placed their hopes in Prussia. The drive for national unity also gave rise, as during the Metternich reaction, to a number of festivals of German singers, archers, gymnasts and traditional costume makers. The centenary of Schiller's birth on 10 November 1859 was also taken as an opportunity to stage a large demonstration of unflagging national will. A number of historians came forward to champion modern political demands, and their writings about the past were often influenced by the partisan political enthusiasms of the present.

The optimistic spirit of the age and the belief in progress reinforced the conviction that 'the natural course of events' would inevitably lead to 'what is rational and modern',[19] to wit, a national state under Prussian leadership of which liberals could approve. Liberal elements were all the more convinced of the likelihood of this scenario by the accession of a new Prussian king. When Frederick William IV sank into incurable mental illness, his brother Prince William was proclaimed regent in 1858. As regent he appointed moderately liberal ministers and declared in a speech on 8 November 1858, 'Prussia must make ethical conquests within Germany by her wise internal legislation, by her commitment to morality, and by taking hold of the forces of unity, as exemplified by the Customs Union—which moreover, should be reformed.'[20]

Such a programme sent liberal hopes soaring and induced Grand Duke Frederick of Baden, son-in-law of the prince regent, to pen enthusiastic congratulations: 'The present—thanks to your paternal solicitude—is more beautiful than ever.'[21] Most of those who were carried away with adulation for the new ruler simply closed their ears to his comments that the government must not 'continually allow itself to be driven into liberal policies'[22] or to his remarks about 'urgent though costly improvements to the army'.[23] The first elections to be held under the prince regent produced a triumphant victory for the liberals—a result not without impact on the rest of Germany.

Soon, however, the gap between the prince regent's real aims and the hopes which the liberals had invested in him grew all too apparent. More pragmatic and resolute than his brother, William was actuated by Prussian appreciation for power. The army's deficiencies were underlined by the mobilisation of troops during the crisis of 1859, and William grew all the more determined to embark upon a programme of military reform.

The responsibility for conducting the reform fell to the new minister of war, Albrecht von Roon, who introduced a corresponding bill before the Chamber of Deputies in February 1860. The army would be enlargened by extending the annual draft to take in 63,000 recruits instead of 40,000—a provision which actually only reflected the increase in the Prussian population from roughly 11 million to 18 million. In addition, the regular army would be strengthened at the cost of the reserves, most notably of the militia. The length of service, having fallen to two years, would revert to three years as originally planned in 1852 in accordance with in the original decree of 1814.

Most of the deputies were prepared to accept the bill in principle, but they dug in their heels over the return to three years of military service and the consignment of younger members of the militia to the regular army. The militia symbolised 'the people at arms' as encouraged by the old reformers at the time of the Wars of Liberation. In the questions of the militia and the duration of compulsory service the deputies perceived crucial liberal gains whose final disposition would determine whether the army was a creature of Parliament or the king.

The crown had traditionally viewed the army as the mainstay of its foreign and domestic power. William, now King of Prussia after the death of his brother on 2 January 1861, was determined to defend the traditional prerogatives of the crown against the inroads of a constitution which none the less he had sworn to uphold. Army reform therefore became much more than a purely technical and military question and emerged as the criterion by which the liberalism of the New Era would be measured. Leopold von Gerlach, a traditional conservative himself, recognised the full import of the debate. William, 'who initiated the era of liberalism, is now attacking the most thoroughly liberal institution of the Prussian monarchy, in order to eradicate it. . . . If the liberals allow this to succeed, they have no real power.'[24]

Indeed, in order to avoid an outright break in relations, the

Chamber of Deputies approved increased appropriations for the army in two successive years. Thus it sought to delay the final decision in the hope that an eventual understanding could be reached with the king.

William, however, was in no mood to concede to Parliament the right to intervene in military matters and continued to insist that soldiers must serve for three years. The newly elected *Landtag* of December 1861 was no more disposed to capitulate when the new Progressive Party, formed from the radical wing of the old liberals, swept 100 seats while the Conservatives took merely twenty-four. Under these circumstances, the struggle over army reform could only intensify. The new deputies eliminated appropriations for army reform from the budget for 1862, and were promptly condemned by the House of Lords. The king then moved in March 1862 to dissolve Parliament and to call new elections on 6 May. However, the Progressives returned triumphant with an even greater plurality of seats and the Chamber refused once and for all to appropriate funds for army reform. The government was deprived of all legal means to continue its programme and, unwilling to jeopardise its constitutional legitimacy, prepared to resign. In July 1862 Bismarck opined in a letter to the minister of war, Roon: 'The longer this affair drags on, the lower the Chamber sinks in public esteem. . . . It will grow tired of waiting for the government to exhaust itself.'[25] By September, however, the opposite seemed to have come to pass. The Prussian king had not forsworn army reform and the three years of military service he considered essential, but was now pondering abdication in favour of his liberal-minded son in preference to acceptance of a compromise solution.

William was all the more obdurate in that the row over the army had developed into a constitutional conflict. The Constitution assumed that the crown and Parliament would eventually arrive at an agreement in legislative and budgetary matters and did not provide for irreconcilable conflict. The Conservatives therefore developed the 'gap' theory of the Constitution, according to which the government had the right to bridge the gap and raise sufficient funds to carry on the affairs of state until a final budget could be agreed upon. The king and his contemporaries were fully aware that this interpretation was untenable from the standpoint of constitutional law, that it struck 'at the heart of the liberal sense of legality and constitutional government',[26] and that it denied the most important right of any parliament, the right to raise taxes.

If William had abdicated, the conflict would have been decided in Parliament's favour—indeed, the power of the crown would have been appreciably weakened, Parliament would have assumed essential responsibility for all affairs of state, and the rest of German history would have gone off in a different direction.

However, the times were not ripe for such a turn of events. As Lassalle had written to Marx, the people were both 'overwhelmingly loyal to the king'[27] and favourably disposed to a powerful state. Only a strong state, they thought, would be able to forge the mighty, unified nation which they so ardently desired. And whoever might realise this collective ambition 'will be rewarded', as the writer Julius Fröbel forecast in 1859, 'with greater adulation than can possibly be imagined'.[28]

So it was that William summoned Bismarck as his prime minister. He feared that Bismarck 'would turn everything upside down'[29] after Bismarck informed him in a long interview in Babelsberg Castle that he was prepared not only to fiercely defend the prerogatives of the crown and to see through the army reform but also to rule against the wishes of the majority of the Chamber and without a constitutional budget. For Bismarck personally, this royal summons marked his hotly desired debut on the grand political stage and the assumption of a role for which he had thoroughly trained himself during his long years as Prussian envoy to the *Bundestag* in Frankfurt and as ambassador to St. Petersburg and Paris.

Bismarck was a man of brilliant intellect, with a passionate and forceful will, and a high-handed thirst for power. He combined an unfettered imagination with sure political judgement and an unerring instinct for what was politically possible. Feeling that courage should inevitably be rewarded, he apprehended political defeat as a personal humiliation. He bitterly hated his political opponents and poured scorn on them in attacks that at times became unethical and completely unjustified. He was loyal only to his duty, his country and his king. He had a rich but contradictory nature and, despite his arrogance, could humbly submit to what he called God's will. He was at once a conservative and a revolutionary, though with a profound appreciation for the moderation that underlay the relations between the great powers. Free of all hubris, he could be modest when the circumstances called for it. Though a man of deep passions, he was extremely realistic in his evaluation of the contending political forces and therefore able to exploit them for his own advantage and that of the state which he served. As an individual he was both magnanimous and petty; as a statesman he achieved greatness in his own time. He had no rival in the extent to which he was both honoured and loathed by his own contemporaries. He set his people on a fateful path, for better or worse, and always seems to elude historians' attempts to take his full measure.

Like the man himself, Bismarck's political legacy remains a subject of controversy. As the achievement of an inveterate monarchist, Bismarck's Germany was always viewed in Western Europe as anachronistic and menacing. Internally, the Germany he created was rent by division, and the excessive admiration for power which his methods fostered only aggravated these antagonisms.

In his new position as prime minister Bismarck faced two major problems: how to resolve the impasse over army reform and how to resolve the German question in a way which advanced Prussia's own interests. To the liberals he seemed highly unsuited to both tasks and they passionately denounced him as the reaction incarnate. Though the substance of army reform was of little interest to him, he was eager to win the confidence of the king and thus secure his own power base. Prepared to adopt the king's will as his own, he took up the struggle with a parliament that rebuffed his every approach.

At first Bismarck attempted to play down the conflict and to appeal to the nationalism of the deputies. However, the words and phrases in which he couched his belief that their national goals could not be achieved without the backing of a strong army were not well-calculated to win over the members of the budget committee. In fact his approach outraged them and the public, and entrenched for many years the liberal view of Bismarck as an unprincipled and Machiavellian advocate of brute force. 'Germany does not look to Prussia's liberalism but to her might. . . . Prussia must gather her strength for the decisive moment, which has been missed in the past more than once. . . . The great issues of the day will be settled not by speeches and majority votes—this was the great mistake of 1848 and 1849—but by blood and iron.'[30]

The liberals and European public opinion in general interpreted these words as heralding a policy of war and conquest. Although they were convinced (at least since recent events in Italy and the United States) that German unity could only be achieved through war, the context of Bismarck's remarks would have had to be substantially different in order to gain their support. Heinrich von Treitschke wrote to a fellow liberal, 'You are aware how passionately I love Prussia. But when I hear a shallow Junker like this Bismarck boasting of the blood and iron with which he intends to subjugate Germany, I feel that his vulgarity is surpassed only by his foolishness.'[31]

The ensuing wave of outrage startled even the king and Bismarck's friends such as Roon, who worried that the clever vilifications in which the prime minister loved to indulge only served to aggravate the social conflict.

The confrontation between the government and Parliament proved utterly intractable. The Chamber of Deputies again reduced funds for army reform; the House of Lords refused to approve such a reduction, and Prussia was left once more without a valid budget. In this situation Bismarck resorted to the legally untenable 'gap' theory. He announced that the affairs of state could not stand still and that the goverment must therefore spend the necessary funds with or without a constitutional budget. This implied that Parliament's right to approve the budget could easily be overridden. The conflict over the Army Bill therefore widened into a full-blown constitutional conflict.

After the Chamber was again dissolved, the Progressive Party called upon the people to withhold taxes. Bismarck responded with escalating repression: public officials sympathetic to the opposition were disciplined, attempts were made to tamper with the elections, and the freedom of the press was curbed. Even the crown prince protested publicly against these measures, reminiscent of Metternich's Karlsbad Decrees, but to no effect. Despite the repression, the Opposition emerged from the subsequent elections with an increased majority. However, the Constitution had assigned a preponderance of power to the government, and Parliament looked on helplessly as Bismarck ruled for four years without a legal budget and carried out army reform in accordance with the wishes of the king.

While the internal conflict over the Army Bill and related constitutional and political questions intensified, external events were compelling the government to take a number of momentous decisions in the realm of foreign policy as well.

In January 1863 the Poles rose in revolt against Russian rule. As in 1830, the sympathies of German and European liberals clearly lay on the side of the Poles, and the British, French and Austrian governments strongly urged St Petersburg to grant Poles the freedom they so long had craved. Alexander II seemed prepared to make concessions so long as Poland remained bound to the Russian Empire through personal union. But Bismarck adopted a strong anti-Polish stance. General Gustav von Alvensleben was dispatched to St Petersburg, where he proposed a convention to clear the way for Prussian and Russian troops to assist one another in putting down the rebellion and to cross one another's frontier in pursuit of Polish rebels. By this policy, Bismarck not only deterred the re-emergence of a Polish state, which he regarded as a threat to

Germany's eastern provinces, but also forestalled the danger of a Franco-Russian alliance and secured Russian neutrality during his subsequent attempts to unify Germany. Friendly relations with Russia were essential to Bismarck's ultimate purpose of establishing Prussian hegemony in Germany, and he never lost sight of his aim, though standing 'rather alone in a world of hate and anger'.[32]

Austria took advantage of Bismarck's damaged reputation and the universal outrage of European liberals to attempt to solve the German question in accordance with her own interests. According to the plan unveiled by the prime minister, Anton Ritter von Schmerling, in August 1863, the role of the German Confederation as a federal, 'large German' institution would be enhanced. A five-member Directory would be established and a Chamber of Delegates taken from the state assemblies. In addition, a Council of Princes would be formed and would meet periodically. Bismarck vehemently objected to this plan, which would have reduced Prussia to only one seat among five on the Directory, thereby leaving her dependent on the other German states. In its place he suggested that Austria and Prussia should be accorded equal status as the leaders of the *Bund* and that in place of an appointed Chamber of Delegates direct elections should be held to a federal parliament. In embracing the demand of the revolutionaries of 1848 for a directly elected national parliament, Bismarck revealed the outlines of his future strategy: he would integrate crucial liberal demands into his solution to the German question in order to increase support for a 'little Germany' in which Prussia would be the dominant power.

In order to advance the Austrian design, Emperor Francis Joseph I invited the German princes to a conference in Frankfurt on the Main. All the German princes attended the illustrious assembly—with the exception of William I of Prussia, whom Bismarck managed to restrain. This effectively torpedoed the conference, since the various German princes were reluctant to join in a federation with Austria which excluded Prussia.

Prussian influence within the Confederation seemed, however, to have been weakened seriously and perhaps permanently by Bismarck's outright rejection of a 'large Germany'. But suddenly the situation was saved by events in Schleswig-Holstein. After the failure of the princes' conference, Austria was eager in any case for a reconciliation with Prussia, and the crisis to the north provided Bismarck with a welcome opportunity to join hands with Austria, approach the German question from a different angle and finally solve it in accordance with Prussian interests.

The question of whether the duchies of Schleswig and Holstein should adhere to Germany or to Denmark was highly complex. In 1848 the Danes attempted to enact a constitution which included Schleswig and thereby sparked a political row in which the German Confederation and eventually the great powers of Europe intervened. The duchies had been linked to Denmark in 1460 through a personal union and, according to a charter granted by the king, were forever to be united with one another. Although they were governed by a joint Diet, Holstein became a member of the German Confederation. A crisis erupted when the Danes began to dispute the union of Schleswig-Holstein while the national movement in Germany insisted on it. With the exception of northern Schleswig, the duchies themselves were populated by German-speakers who opposed annexation to Denmark and looked with favour towards Germany.

During the revolution of 1848 Schleswig-Holstein managed to sever its ties with Denmark, but the great powers intervened and in the London Protocol of 1852 re-established the personal union with the Danish crown. The conflict continued to smoulder, however, with neither party satisfied by the solution that had been imposed. In 1863 King Frederick of Denmark died, and the new king agreed to a constitution whose provisions applied expressly to Schleswig as well as to the rest of the country.

This incorporation of Schleswig into Denmark, in clear violation of the London Protocol, provoked a storm of nationalist protest in Germany. The public insisted that the duchies be immediately liberated from Danish rule and turned over to the next legitimate Duke of Schleswig-Holstein, Friedrich von Augustenburg. Avoiding the temptation to leap onto the bandwagon of nationalist emotion, Bismarck adopted a policy that clearly conformed with the London Protocol in order to establish a strong justification for any further action. He was confident that the great powers would not cave in to such flagrant disregard of the London Protocol and thus ensured their benevolent neutrality during a future war while he sought active support from Austria. The Danish Constitution, Bismarck modestly asserted, would have to be withdrawn. Though cleverly dissembling the fact, he never lost sight of his ultimate goal—Prussian annexation of Schleswig-Holstein—as can be seen in a New Year's conversation he held with his brother-in-law Otto von Arnim in 1864:

They [the people of Schleswig-Holstein] must become Prussians. This is the goal for which I strive, though whether I shall be successful or not rests in God's hand. I do not wish to be held responsible, however, for spilling

Prussian blood solely in order to create another minor state which would join the others in the Confederation in always voting against us.[33]

The multinational Austrian Empire was itself very reliant on continued respect for the legal status quo in Europe. It therefore felt compelled to join Prussia in denying support to the nationalist, pro-German movement in Schleswig-Holstein (as it had already done in 1848) and in insisting on observance of the London Protocol. Austria's stance therefore seemed to mirror the Prussian position, and Bismarck could declare with some satisfaction, 'never before has Berlin guided Austrian policies to this extent—*en gros et en détail*'.[34]

In order to protect Holstein from Danish claims, the two great German powers proposed in the *Bundestag* that federal troops be sent to the duchy. The Danes promptly retreated across the Eider without firing a shot, but continued to stand by their constitution. When they failed to respond to the Prussian and Austrian ultimatum of 16 January 1864 demanding that this constitution be rescinded, Prussian and Austrian troops crossed the Eider and occupied all of Jutland. This forced the Danish king to sign the Peace of Vienna ceding Schleswig and Holstein to Prussia and Austria (not, it should be noted, to the German Confederation). As previously in Italy, the principle of nationality was thus vindicated.

At first the duchies were placed under joint Prusso-Austrian administration, with Prussia well-located geographically to play the dominant role. Since Austria had little to gain from the joint condominium, she offered to cede to Prussia her share of the northern spoils in exchange for concessions in Silesia. When Bismarck and the king refused this offer, Austria adopted a new tack and threw her support behind the public demand that Augustenburg be installed as Duke of Schleswig-Holstein. A motion to this effect was even introduced before the *Bundestag* in Frankfurt.

The tensions between Prussia and Austria were relieved for a time by the Treaty of Gastein, which dissolved the system of joint administration. Austria was henceforth to administer Holstein, and Prussia to administer Schleswig with the port of Kiel. Prussia also gained permission to build the Kiel Canal across Holstein. Despite this agreement, it was growing clear that Bismarck intended to establish Prussian hegemony over northern Germany and that the alliance of convenience with Austria would last only so long as it served his purposes. The entire German question, which had been pushed into the background by the events of the war, once again dominated political life and cried out more loudly than ever for an ultimate solution.

Humiliated in Italy, detested by Russia and spurned by the Western powers, Austria found that her actions in Schleswig-Holstein only earned her disfavour in Germany. Isolated and cornered by Bismarck, Vienna sought to regain lost ground and to resist all further Prussian advances. It was obvious that a permanent understanding with Prussia was impossible to achieve and that joint Prusso-Austrian leadership of Germany was equally improbable. Both powers therefore rushed to make diplomatic preparations for the final violent solution to the German question. Berlin and Vienna could only go to war, however, if France and Russia remained neutral.

It was the policy of Napoleon III to claim that the struggles for national unity were inevitable and to seek to exploit the resulting upheaval in order to rearrange the national boundaries established in 1815. Paris favoured moderate Prussian expansion in northern Germany in the hope that a protracted war would provide France with an opportunity to mediate a settlement. In this situation, Bismarck intimated to Napoleon that Prussia might be willing to support French territorial expansion in Luxembourg or Belgium in return for French acceptance of Prussian gains in northern Germany. His appetite whetted, Napoleon even encouraged an alliance between Prussia and Italy. Such an alliance was duly concluded on 8 April 1866 for a space of all of three months 'in case negotiations in respect to reforming the *Bund* should fail and Prussia should be compelled to take up arms'.[35]

The time had come for Bismarck to push for a rapid solution. Prussia presented another motion in the *Bundestag* calling for a national parliament, to be elected by direct, general suffrage, which would debate reforming the Constitution of the German Confederation. Bismarck hoped till the last minute that Austria would yield to Prussian demands and recognise her as the dominant power in northern Germany in order to avoid a war. However, Vienna countered by calling upon the *Bundestag* to take up the whole question of Schleswig-Holstein. Prussia thereupon declared the Treaty of Gastein nul and void and sent troops over the border into Austrian-administered Holstein. Austria responded by moving in the *Bundestag* that federal troops be mobilised against Prussia. When this motion was adopted in modified form, Prussia resigned from the German Confederation. The partial mobilisation of federal forces against Prussia and Berlin's declaration that this violated the Constitution of the Confederation spelled the outbreak of general war.

In the end the lengthy struggle for primacy in Germany was decided on a battlefield in Bohemia. After overrunning almost all of central Germany in only one week, the Prussian forces met the united Saxon and Austrian armies near Königgrätz and dealt them a resounding defeat. This victory proved decisive, even though at the same time Austria defeated the Italian troops that had marched into Venetia at Custozza.

The day after the crucial battle of Königgrätz, Napoleon intervened and demanded that Prussia and Italy immediately conclude a truce with Austria. The Italians refused Napoleon's mediation and crossed the Po—having discovered that Vienna had ceded Venetia to the French and wishing to conquer it for themselves rather than accept it as a gift from Napoleon. Prussia, on the other hand, was ready to agree to a truce so long as it guaranteed that her essential war aims would be satisfied in the ultimate peace treaty. These aims included the dissolution of the German Confederation, the exclusion of Austria from German affairs, the recognition of a North German Confederation under Prussian leadership, the union of the south German states in a similar confederation, and Prussian annexation of Schleswig-Holstein and of certain stretches of northern Germany which would provide a physical link between Prussia's western provinces and the old heartland in the east.

When Napoleon agreed to these stipulations (on condition that Prussia accept the Main as her southern boundary), Bismarck urged King William to negotiate a peace treaty at once. He wished to avoid any humiliation of Austria and above all refused to annex any Austrian or Saxon territory or old Hohenzollern lands in Bavaria. The king, however, blamed Austria and Saxony for the war and, like his victorious generals, was not satisfied by Bismarck's demands. While Bismarck advised moderation, they longed to march triumphantly into Vienna and to punish the defeated Austrians and Saxons with reparations and annexations. Bismarck only prevailed with the help of the crown prince after a series of stormy interviews in Berlin. In the course of these interviews he impressed upon the king that it was Prussia's task 'to govern Germany and not to administer justice. Austria's rivalry with us is no more culpable than ours with her. Our task is the creation and/or preparation of German national unity under the leadership of the King of Prussia'.[36]

The ensuing negotiations with Austria soon drew to a satisfactory conclusion. A preliminry truce concluded in Nikolsburg on 26 July 1866 was followed one month later by the final Treaty of Prague. Austria lost Venetia, which was transferred to Italy through Napoleon, but suffered no further territorial dismemberment. In return

Vienna consented to the dissolution of the German Confederation
and the establishment of the North German Confederation, renounced its rights in Schleswig-Holstein and acquiesced in the
Prussian annexation of Hanover, Hesse-Kassel, Nassau and Frankfurt. At Napoleon's insistence Baden, Württemberg and Bavaria
were guaranteed their national independence, though Bismarck
managed to extract a secret agreement from these states according to
which their armies would come under the supreme command of the
Prussian king in case of war.

The Prussian victory at Königgrätz shocked all Germans into
sudden awareness of a profound shift in the political landscape of
Europe. Celebrated as the cornerstone of German political unity,
Königgrätz transformed overnight liberal opinion about Bismarck
and his policies. Before the battle, Bismarck's liberal opponents had
loudly condemned his 'violation of all principles of justice and
morality' and the 'shameful, cruel carelessness'[37] with which he had
provoked this war; after the victory of Königgrätz they bowed
before 'the genius of Bismarck, the German Cavour and Garibaldi'.
A contemporary enthused:

How wonderfully this man spun all the strands of his magnificent web, so
firm and secure that not one of them broke. With what precision he
recognised and exploited all ways and means: his king, Napoleon, the
army, the bureaucracy, Austria and his own capacities. In short, a *Meister-
stück* of calculation! . . . What appeared to the uninitiated as criminal
arrogance later turned out to be an essential step towards the ultimate
goal. . . . For such a man of action I would give a hundred liberals with
their impotent principles.[38]

Even the historian Heinrich von Treitschke, who had condemned
Bismarck prior to 1866, suddenly perceived in him the presence of
reason in history. The liberal historian and politician Hermann
Baumgarten proclaimed that he now wished 'to begin a new life of
modest devotion and true faithfulness, of genuine submission before the great revelations which we this year have witnessed'.[39]

Having shown forbearance towards his vanquished foreign foes,
Bismarck now reached out in the full flush of victory to his internal
enemies. The newly elected Chamber of Deputies was asked to
grant an indemnity covering all the expenses which the government
had illegally incurred since 1862—and by implication to approve the
measures which the government had taken during the constitutional
conflict. In return Bismarck tacitly recognised Parliament's right to
control the purse strings, though he simultaneously emphasised the
constitutional rights of the crown and made absolutely no con-

cessions in the question of who held supreme command over the army. The target of this policy was the liberals, whose goodwill and support Bismarck urgently needed in order to frame a constitution for the North German Confederation.

Bismarck's tactics triggered a great realignment of political parties, with the left-wing liberals and right-wing conservatives splitting from their parties in order to refuse the reconciliation which Bismarck offered. The extreme conservatives refused to forgo any of Prussia's individuality and clung to their conviction that the government had acted properly during the constitutional conflict; similarly, the extreme liberals in the Progressive Party refused to compromise on their principles and continued to oppose the government. So the Act of Indemnity undid both the Progressive Party—from which the moderate liberals seceded in order to form the National Liberal Party—and the Conservative Party, from which the minority that supported Bismarck seceded in order to found the Free Conservative Party. Throughout the twelve years that followed, Bismarck relied on the support of both these new groups.

This resolution of the internal political conflict was critically important to the development of the national state, but no less significant for the evolution of the political structure within that national state. The ideals of freedom and legality had been overshadowed by national ambitions. In Italy liberalism and nationalism advanced hand in hand; but in Germany liberalism was weakened by nationalism. Some liberals hoped that democratic institutions could be introduced after unity had been achieved, but this plan was foiled by the crown which clung to supreme authority, despite slowly spreading constitutionalism, till the end of the First World War.

After forging a compliant majority in Parliament, Bismarck concluded a treaty with the states north of the Main only five days after the Treaty of Prague had been signed. The parties agreed to found a federal state with a constitution drawn up in cooperation with a parliament to be chosen through universal, equal and direct elections. The resulting North German Confederation consisted of the various north German states, Saxony and a greater Prussia which had annexed Hanover, Hesse-Kassel, Nassau and the imperial city of Frankfurt. Powers were divided between the federal government and the individual states in a manner which would ensure the necessary cohesion both internally and externally. In contrast to the Constitution of the Paulskirche, that of the North German Confederation contained no statement of fundamental rights and was framed in such a way that the basic outline of the state constitutions remained unchanged.

Executive powers were invested in the presidium, an office retained by the Prussian King. He represented the Confederation internationally, had the right to declare war and make peace, commanded the federal armed forces, drafted and promulgated the laws that were enacted, and nominated the federal chancellor. Legislative powers were shared by two bodies: a *Reichstag* selected in universal, free and equal elections, and a *Bundesrat*, or Federal Council, to which the Constitution assigned most real power. The latter was composed of delegates from the individual states under the presidency of the federal chancellor. It passed the bills to be placed before the *Reichstag* and the resolutions passed by it. Prussia's ascendancy within the Confederation was ensured by the fact that she controlled the federal presidium and fourteen of the twenty-six votes in the *Bundesrat*. Bismarck attempted to assuage the particularistic sensibilities of the smaller states, primarily by permitting great diversity in cultural legislation.

The Opposition was unimpressed, maintaining in the words of August Bebel:

The Constitution of the North German Confederation was a document which failed to include the rights necessary for constitutional representation of the people: no statement of fundamental rights, no power to approve taxes, no ministerial responsibility, no parliaments. Instead an iron-clad military budget and far-ranging powers for the chancellor.[40]

Indeed, the new federal state was based not on the sovereignty of the people but on the power of the Prussian monarchy, and its constitution was moulded to suit one man, Bismarck. This was the constitution which the new German Empire soon adopted with but few changes.

For the time being most liberals, and along with them the bulk of the German people, were content to glory in a wave of national pride. They hoped for swift fulfilment of the promising phrase with which Bismarck had concluded his speech during the general debate of the constituent *Reichstag* of the North German Confederation: 'Let us put Germany into the saddle. It doubtless already knows how to ride.'[41]

The path to German unification was still blocked in 1867 by imposing foreign obstacles. Königgrätz not only awakened Germans to a rapidly changing world but also sowed fear and distrust among the great powers of Europe. 'The world is collapsing', exclaimed the papal secretary of state, Giacomo Antonelli, when news reached him of the Prussian victory; and in England *The Spectator* commented: 'Thirty(!) dynasties have been swept aside. The fate of twenty million people has changed irrevocably. The world has a new political face.... It took Prussia but a moment to leap into the position of the leading continental power in Europe.'[42]

The French politician and historian Adolphe Thiers concluded that for 400 years no greater misfortune had befallen France than the birth of the North German *Bund*,[43] Austria, the vanquished second power of Germany, found herself excluded from the emerging nation. Vienna sought to overcome the internal paralysis by focusing attention henceforth on the south-east of Europe and the ethnic problems within the Austrian Empire. Its political structure was loosened in order to create a federal system, and an attempt was made to accommodate nationalist sentiment in Hungary. In a compromise agreement with the Magyars immediately following the great defeat of Königgrätz, the Austrian Empire was restructured as the Dual Monarchy of Austria-Hungary. Hungary plus Croatia and Transylvania became largely autonomous regions. Foreign affairs and the army remained, however, under a joint ministry directly responsible to the monarch, who reigned as Emperor of Austria and King of Hungary.

The Founding of the German Empire

Though appeals for the completion of national unity grew ever more strident, Bismarck abided by his gradualist approach to the southern states. He was somewhat concerned that precipitate action would ruffle their particularist sensibilities, but his greatest problem was the French reaction. Aware that the nationalist fires in Germany could not long be contained, Bismarck nevertheless attempted to dampen the mounting public frenzy with which 'people not involved in this matter [seek] the stone of wisdom which would instantly bring about German unity.... We can set our clocks ahead, but that does not make time go any faster. The ability to wait while the situation ripens is essential to practical politics'.[44] So Bismarck firmly resisted all further modifications of the political status quo, most notably Baden's desire to enter the North German Confederation. His resolve in this respect was much stiffened by warnings from France that any attempt to expand beyond the Main river would be taken as a *casus belli*.

Napoleon's prestige in France had sunk to a dangerously low level: he had failed in 1866 to thwart Prussia's rise to the status of a great power, and his imperialist adventures in Mexico were going badly. France was buffeted by a series of internal crises and the economy was in decline. The working class was becoming restive, the state was deeply indebted, and ever more citizens rejected the emperor's autocratic style of government and demanded a more liberal regime. In an effort to save the situation through a signal success in foreign affairs, Napoleon attempted in 1867 to purchase the Grand Duchy of Luxembourg—a land which had contained a federal fortress until the dissolution of the German Confederation and in which Prussian troops were still garrisoned.

Bismarck was prepared to see the French absorb Luxembourg, and the King of Holland, who was also the Grand Duke of Luxembourg, was willing to sell. However, the prospective deal so aroused public passions in Germany that Bismarck was compelled to seek a compromise in order to avoid war. At a conference organised by the British government, Luxembourg was declared a neutral state and the Prussian garrison was removed, though the Grand Duchy remained a member of the Customs Union.

The peace of Europe was saved. Bismarck had been urged by his military advisers to exploit the favourable political situation in order to wage a preventive war, but now as at other times he flatly refused on moral and religious grounds. As he declared to Robert von Keudell, one of his diplomatic aides: 'One must not wage war if it can be avoided with honour; the possibility of success is not sufficient justification for unleashing a great war.'[45]

None the less, Bismarck feared that such a war could not be averted if Germany was to be united, and he commented to Karl Schurz in 1868:

I shall never agree to a war that can possibly be avoided, let alone provoke such a war. But war with France is inevitable, the French emperor will force it upon us. Louis Napoleon has lost much of his prestige for two reasons: firstly his adventure in Mexico, which was extremely foolish and an awful mistake, and secondly the fact that he allowed Prussia to become so powerful without exacting any 'compensation' for France, any territorial gains that could be presented to the French people as the reward of his brilliant diplomacy. It was widely known that he sought this sort of 'compensation' and that I manoeuvred it away before he realised what had happened. He knows that he has lost much of his prestige, far more than can be measured, and that this loss, if not quickly made up, could threaten his reign. Since he can assume that his army is once again fit and ready for war, he will take steps to recover the esteem which has become a matter of life or death for him. For this reason he will find some pretext to begin a conflict with us. I do not believe that he personally desires war, I even believe that he would rather avoid it; but his precarious internal position will drive him to it. We of course must be prepared—and that we are. We shall emerge victorious, and the outcome will be the exact opposite of what Napoleon seeks: the complete unification of Germany and probably Napoleon's own downfall.[46]

The crisis foreseen by Bismarck materialised when Queen Isabella II of Spain was overthrown in the autumn of 1868 by a military coup, and the Cortes offered the vacant throne to Prince Leopold of Hohenzollern-Sigmaringen. Leopold was a scion of the Roman Catholic branch of the Hohenzollerns and had married a sister of the King of Portugal. The Hohenzollerns were inclined to refuse the Spanish offer, but Bismarck encourged them to accept in the belief that close relations between Spain and Germany would help to deter French aggression. Eventually both Leopold and King William agreed that they would accept the Spanish offer. But before the Spanish parliament could officially elect Prince Leopold, word of the negotiations reached France, where a storm of protest erupted. In a highly emotional speech before the Chamber, the French foreign minister, Duke Antoine-Agénor-Alfred de Gramont, declared:

[The government cannot stand idly by while] a foreign power places one of its princes on the throne of Charles V, disturbs the current balance of power in Europe to our detriment, and imperils the interests and the honour of France. If this should occur, we will do our duty resolutely and without hesitation, fortified by the knowledge, gentlemen, of your support and that of the nation.[47]

French public opinion, inflamed by the Parisian press, demanded that Prussia either withdraw its candidate for the Spanish throne or prepare for battle. Prince Leopold, not wishing to be the immediate cause of a great war, thereupon relented and withdrew his candidacy with the agreement of King William. Bismarck had not envisaged a war with the French until after the death of the French emperor, who was severely ill. Bismarck had hoped that the presence of Leopold on the Spanish throne would strengthen Napoleon's hand against the French ultra-nationalists and militarists. With his plans in ruins, Bismarck seemed ready to swallow a diplomatic defeat—when suddenly the French government bowed to a demand from the Chamber that 'Prussia not be allowed to escape so cheaply',[48] and that France require special guarantees. The French ambassador in Berlin, Count Vincent Benedetti, was instructed to exact a declaration from King William that he concurred with Leopold's renunciation of the Spanish throne and would not permit a Hohenzollern candidacy in the future.

Benedetti delivered this message in Bad Ems where King William was taking the waters. William politely refused the French demand, pointing out that he could not give firm guarantees about an uncertain future. When Prince Leopold then officially announced his resignation, William regarded a second audience that had been arranged with the French ambassador as superfluous. An aide was dispatched to apprise Benedetti of the king's decision and to inform him that the matter was closed so far as William was concerned and need not be discussed any further. William advised Bismarck of these events by telegraph and left it to his minister's discretion whether the Prussian ambassadors and the press should be informed. Bismarck perceived a glowing opportunity to parry the French thrust and to strike a blow of his own. He shortened the royal dispatch and had the following version published:

After the Royal Spanish Government officially informed the Imperial French Government that the candidacy of the Prince of Hohenzollern had been withdrawn, the French ambassador demanded of HM the King in Ems that he be authorised to inform Paris that HM the King pledged never again to lend his approval if the Hohenzollerns should once more revive their candidacy. HM the King declined to receive the French ambassador once again and informed him through a military aide that HM the King had nothing further to add.[49]

Bismarck foresaw that this 'far more caustic version' would 'be like a red cloth to the Gallic bull'.[50] With one stroke the rôles had been reversed. Now France was compelled either to swallow a diplomatic defeat or to declare war on Germany, which would appear to all the world as the offended party. Bismarck's response to the French challenge ignited a sense of jubilation and delight across the land. In the south as well as in the north, the nation gathered itself to complete the task of unification. Napoleon, isolated internationally because of his adventurism and seriously weakened internally, declared war on 19 July 1870.

The Germans mobilised their numerically superior army with lightening speed and pushed quickly into France. A series of battles along the border carried them as far as Metz, where they encircled the French Army of the Rhine. The Second French Army, under Marshall MacMahon, sought to lift the siege but was thrown back to the north. Surrounded by two German armies, it took refuge in the fortress at Sedan, where it was forced to capitulate. Among the 90,000 men taken prisoner was Napoleon himself, who was accompanying MacMahon's army.

Two days later, the French Republic was proclaimed in Paris

under a provisional government headed by Jules Favre and Léon Gambetta. The new republican government resolved to continue the war when Bismarck rejected its demand that 'not one inch of territory and not one stone of French fortresses will be surrendered'.[51] While German troops marched on Paris and besieged it, Léon Gambetta organised a *levée en masse* modelled on the great French Revolution and guided the people's war first from Tours and then from Bordeaux. Newly raised French armies marched on Paris but were thrown back in heavy fighting. The French capital, besieged and finally bombarded at Bismarck's insistence, was eventually compelled to capitulate by the ravages of starvation and civil war.

A general truce was quickly arranged. A newly elected French national assembly convened in Bordeaux to form a government and to open peace negotiations. On 1 March 1871 the prime minister, Adolphe Tiers, signed the preliminary Peace of Versailles, which was followed on 10 May by the final Treaty of Frankfurt.

The terms of this treaty required France to pay a war indemnity of 5000 million francs and to cede Alsace and most of Lorraine to Germany. From the German point of view, this was simply a case of amending an historic injustice. The recovery of lands that had been part of Germany until 1648 and their incorporation into the restored German Empire were the logical fruits of victory. Bismarck was convinced that 'lasting hostility between Paris and Berlin'[52] was inescapable and was therefore not inclined, as he had been in 1866, to moderate Prussian demands. Instead, he made 'every attempt to weaken France, especially from a geostrategic viewpoint, so that a rational calculation of the probabilities of success would inhibit future French policy-makers from attempting to revise unilaterally the results of the war in Central Europe'.[53] The future would show that the annexation of Alsace and Lorraine heaped an enduring burden on the new German Empire and earned it the relentless and inexorable hostility of France.

With the joy and jubilation of the victory of Sedan still ringing in his ears, Bismarck turned to complete the political unification of Germany. In contrast to the liberals and the crown prince who envisaged a centralised state with responsible government, Bismarck hoped to found a *Kaiserreich* which would be a mere extension of the North German Confederation. He contrived to deal tactfully with the traditional local loyalties of the southern states and to avoid any impression of direct compulsion. A sense of voluntary accession to the existing Confederation would go a long way, he thought, towards scotching any nationalist movements and ensuring southern support in case of a French war of revenge. A wave of pan-German nationalism swept the land, providing Bismarck with a welcome ally in his laborious negotiations with the southern states, especially Württemberg and Bavaria, where particularist feelings ran high. Bismarck accommodated their desire for special statues within the federation by agreeing to certain concessions in the fields of taxation, the postal system and the army. This smoothed the way for Württemberg and Bavaria to acquiesce to an accord which extended throughout Germany the presidential powers which the King of Prussia had assumed within the North German Confederation.

Bismarck considered it advantageous for national unity that the president and the *Bund* be renamed the emperor and the *Reich*— concepts which the nationalists had held in the highest esteem ever since the turn of the century. He succeeded in convincing the Prussian king of the usefulness of this step despite William's well-founded belief that the new appellation would detract from the glory of the ancient title of King of Prussia. In return King Ludwig II of Bavaria was persuaded personally to offer the emperorship to William in a proclamation composed by Bismarck. Although the title 'German Emperor' was the only possible one from a constitutional viewpoint, William insisted that he be named 'emperor of Germany' in order to highlight the glorious heights to which the house of Hohenzollern had risen. The ensuing dispute only served to aggravate German particularism and to cast a shadow over the grand proclamation of the empire and the emperor in the Hall of Mirrors in Versailles. The Grand Duke of Baden cleverly evaded the whole controversy by offering his toast to 'Emperor William'. These festivities on 18 January 1871 brought to a triumphant close the long struggle for German unity.

In a congratulatory address composed by liberals, one could read that Bismarck had achieved through war what the bourgeoisie had hoped to achieve through peace and under the banner of freedom. 'The law of battle has led to a decision, in a manner which differs from ours but which is quite in keeping with our wishes. . . . We believe in unity.'[54] This desire had not abated in the slightest ever since the first attempts by the National Assembly to extract from the ruling princes a German *Reich* based on the sovereignty of the people. In fact it had only grown in intensity the more the princes sought to reinforce their rule against the rising tide of democracy.

Ultimately, though, the German Empire was a creation of the aristocracy, guided by the genius of Bismarck. The new emperor capped a militaristic monarchy, and the princes toasted his health in military ceremonies conducted in the most splendid castle of a conquered neighbour. The general public was uninvited. A delegation of citizens headed by Eduard Simson (formerly president of the National Assembly in Frankfurt and later president of the *Reichstag* of the North German Confederation) came to Versailles in order to request William to accept the laurels of emperor, though he looked rather insignificant in the midst of this august assembly of princes and generals. But at least some reference was made to the tradition of 1848–9.

For the vast majority of Germans, the age-old dream of a restored German empire and emperor was achieved in full on 18 January 1871. The *Reich* satisfied their ancient yearnings and endowed them with a grand and powerful state equal to any of the other great nations of Europe. They identified themselves with the new Germany without reservation.

Grateful and profoundly moved, the liberal historian Heinrich von Sybel summarised the temper of the times in a letter to his colleague, Hermann Baumgarten: 'Why are we so favoured by God to be allowed to witness such stupenduous events? That which was the object of all our hopes and struggles for twenty long years has finally been so gloriously achieved! Where at my age shall I find a new meaning to the rest of my life?'[55]

In its relatively authoritarian and martial character, the new empire differed appreciably to be sure from what many Germans had desired. Yet despite all the problems inherent in its manner of creation, its internal structure and external borders, a unified German state finally did exist. In the hour of its birth, no one doubted that these manifold difficulties could be resolved, least of all the middle class. Fortified by its faith in progress, the middle class looked to the future with confidence and faith that freedom would soon be achieved as well. The liberal leader in Baden, Carl Eckhard, voiced these sentiments when he said before the state assembly in Karlsruhe:

We must now continue to work on our great achievement and to promote the healthy evolution of the entire constitutional life of the German state—this would be the final and highest consecration of our work of unification. As our German warriors hastened from victory to victory, making possible the unification of Germany, so, with God's help and with equal bravery on the part of our political warriors, will freedom hold its triumphant entry into the new *Reich*.[56]

8

The German Empire under Bismarck's Leadership

1870: First Vatican Council
1871: German Constitution
1872: Three Emperors' League
1873: May Laws
1878: Tariffs enacted; anti-socialist law; Congress of Berlin
1879: Dual alliance of Germany and Austria-Hungary
1882: Triple Alliance: Germany, Austria-Hungary and Italy
1883–4: Enactment of health and accident insurance legislation
1884–5: Establishment of German colonies
1887: Mediterranean Entente; Reinsurance Treaty with Russia; Triple Alliance
1888: Death of Emperor William I; death of Frederick III; crowning of Emperor William II
1889: Enactment of disability and old-age insurance legislation
1890: Dismissal of Bismarck

The New Constitution

The German Empire had re-emerged much more abruptly than anyone had expected, especially its founder. In the late 1840s and early 1850s the European powers had warily observed the attempts to unify Germany undertaken by the National Assembly and the Prussian crown and had expressed their concern that the balance of power might be disturbed. In the late 1860s, however, the great powers did not seriously attempt to block the national movement in Germany, and in the case of France even assisted it, first by hesitation and prevarication and then by careless overreaction. German nationalism, skilfully manipulated by Bismarck, triumphed

145

amidst an immense sense of pride that Germans had finally created the sort of unified state which other European peoples had long enjoyed. The wave of national enthusiasm that swept the land on the eve of the war with France astonished even the Prussian king, imbuing him with 'great fear'.[1] After the founding of the empire, nationalism took on an almost sacred cast. Gerhart Hauptmann later recalled:

> The coronation of the emperor in Versailles was for Germany an act of creation. Our people was seized by a new sense of self-awareness. This was the merit of a number of great men, led by Bismarck, whom the rest of the world viewed with surprise and trepidation, but most of all with great esteem. Everyone, even a little boy like me, felt immense pride in them, in their victories and the victories of the German people. I did not hesitate to claim on the basis of my blood a share in these successes.[2]

Along with the feeling that the German people itself had triumphed came the conviction that the empire marked a new beginning in German history—a beginning whose practical effects would soon be felt.

The foundations of the new state were laid on 16 April 1871 when the Constitution was proclaimed. It was primarily the work of Bismarck and for the most part simply transferred the Constitution of the North German Confederation to the new German Empire.

The new *Reich* was a federal state, freely created by the various princes and free cities, to which twenty-five local states and the imperial territories of Alsace-Lorraine adhered. Sovereignty over the empire lay in the hands of these individual states, the twenty-two princes and the senates of the free cities, whose total of fifty-eight representatives convened in the *Bundesrat*, or Federal Council. This was the most important institution in the empire and the main locus of power according to the Constitution. It prepared legislation for the *Reichstag* and debated its resolutions. The *Bundesrat* also held executive authority. The chancellor, named by the emperor, presided over the *Bundesrat* and set its agenda.

The King of Prussia became the hereditary president of the *Bundesrat* and in this capacity assumed the title of 'German Emperor'. He represented the new state internationally, decided questions of war and peace in consultation with the *Bundesrat*, concluded alliances and treaties with foreign powers, accredited ambassadors, held the post of Supreme Commander of the Armed Forces, and promulgated the laws, which he was responsible for drawing up and which were passed by a majority of the *Bundesrat* and the *Reichstag*. He was also entitled to nominate and dismiss the

Imperial Chancellor.

The chancellor managed federal affairs, and all regulations and decrees issued by the emperor required his counter-signature. Since the emperor did not answer to the people, the chancellor was deemed to be responsible, morally if not legally, for what he had signed and he felt compelled to defend it before the *Reichstag*. The state secretaries who headed the ministries in the gradually evolving federal administration reported directly to the chancellor. As chairman of the *Bundesrat* the chancellor also represented the 'imperial territory' of Alsace-Lorraine, which sent delegates to the *Reichstag* but not to the *Bundesrat*.

The populace was represented in the *Reichstag*, which was elected by universal, equal, direct and secret suffrage according to the system of majority representation. The *Reichstag* convened in public and embodied the will of the nation as against the particularism of the individual states. The deputies of the various parties enjoyed immunity, were not bound by instructions and directions, and were unpaid till 1906. They participated in the legislative process, were empowered to initiate legislation, and could block the budget. Legislation required a majority of both the *Reichstag* and the *Bundesrat* in order to be enacted. The *Reichstag* had no influence over appointments to the office of chancellor, the formation of governments or the carrying out of executive powers. The emperor summoned, opened and dissolved it, though premature dissolution had to be approved by the *Bundesrat*.[3]

Whereas the proposed constitution of the National Assembly had provided for the sovereignty of the people and a strong central government, Bismarck's constitution was federative and monarchist. Liberals complained that national unity had been compromised by excessive pandering to particularism, but in actual practice the federative structure furthered national unity rather than impeded it. Federalism eased the entry of the various states into the empire, especially the southern states with their strong historical distinctiveness. Prussia, by far the largest of the states, controlled seventeen of the fifty-eight votes in the *Bundesrat* and was thereby able to dominate the political and military life of the *Reich*. This preponderance of power was heightened by the fact that Prussian officials usually filled the high offices of the empire and the president held a veto in military, financial and constitutional affairs. The German emperor was also the Prussian king, the chancellor was also the prime minister of Prussia, and the imperial secretaries of state were usually members of the Prussian Ministry of State.

The disparate parts of the empire was cemented together primarily by the *Reichstag* and by the widespread feeling of satisfaction and delight with the new Germany. The *Reich* soon became the focal point of German nationalism, and pride in being German eclipsed all local loyalties.

The source of much future dispute could be found in the fact that the executive branch of government was independent of the *Reichstag*. Though the composition of the *Reichstag* was thoroughly modern and democratic, it lacked the powers of a genuinely democratic assembly. The government was not legally responsible to the *Reichstag* and did answer to it only for vague moral and historical reasons. The discrepancy between modern appearances and reactionary reality largely set the tone of domestic politics and of the relations between the chancellor and the parties in the *Reichstag*.

Domestic Policies

Bismarck had made very successful use of the middle-class national movement in creating the empire, and he now set out to complete the task in alliance with these liberals. Their self-confidence and optimistic faith in progress had been immeasurably strengthened by the fulfilment of their national ambitions, and it was easy for them to believe that the state could gradually be set on a liberal, constitutional footing consistent with the dynamic, modern industrial society which Germany had become.

However, modern industrial society with its liberalism, parliamentarism and incipient economic democracy was alien to Bismarck. He aimed to 'subdue' liberalism and 'to fulfil or not to fulfil liberal demands in accordance with the reasons of state'.[4] It was on this basis that Bismarck prepared to cooperate with the National Liberals. They had become the strongest party in the *Reichstag* in 1871, winning 118 of 382 seats, and they seemed willing to assist the Iron Chancellor out of respect for immense accomplishments in the practical world. Though this alliance was limited and purely tactical from Bismarck's point of view, it did produce a number of measures which satisfied liberal demands, especially in the spheres of the economy and the law. In return, the liberals were prepared to make extensive concessions in areas of paramount concern to Bismarck: royal prerogatives and national defence.

The unified commercial code had been drawn up by the old North German *Bundestag* and introduced by 1865 into all the German states. In 1872 a federal penal code was added. One year later, work was begun on a federal civil code. This code was finally enacted in 1896, came into effect on 1 January 1900 and remains valid to the present day. In 1879 the judicial systems and codes of procedure were unified. Legislation governing the constitution of the courts eliminated the last remnants of manorial judicial power, separated the administration of justice from the government bureaucracy, established the successive stages of appeal from county courts all the way to the Supreme Court of the empire, and clarified the competence of the various courts and the basic rules of procedure. In 1879 the Supreme Court of the German Empire was established in Leipzig, manifesting to all the supreme judicial authority of the federal government.

The liberal majority in the *Reichstag* also enacted unifying legislation in the realm of transportation. A currency reform replaced the previous silver standard by the gold standard and introduced the mark as the new monetary unit, replacing the provincial coins in legal tender until 1878. The *Reichsbank* was established in 1875 and it controlled the circulation of bank-notes. The unity of the empire was further enhanced by unified standards of weights and measure. Metres, litres and kilograms replaced all the various measures previously in use in the individual states. Freedom of occupation and free movement of labour, introduced in the North German Confederation in 1869, were extended throughout the realm. The postal service was modernised to conform to contemporary economic standards and placed under a central post office headed by the state secretary, Heinrich Stephan. Stephan launched the idea of a postal union, founded in Bern Switzerland in 1874, and developed an exemplary telegraph and telephone system.

Bismarck attempted to gain federal control over the railways in order to secure a source of revenue independent of the *Reichstag*. This attempt was resisted, however, by the various states which were eager to retain these monies for themselves. In the end the federal railway was confined to Alsace-Lorraine and Bismarck had to content himself with nationalising the Prussian railway.

Various measures were adopted within Prussia to reflect the liberal legislation at the federal level. District regulations issued in 1872 deprived landlords in the six eastern provinces of their control over the police and the village administrations. This measure together with the provincial regulations taking effect in 1875 tended to strengthen self-government at the local and provincial levels.

The government and the liberal majority in the *Reichstag* worked smoothly together in all this legislation, and Bismarck did his utmost to accommodate economic liberalism by avoiding governmental controls and interference in the economy. However, the relationship grew much more contentious as soon as the partners left the realm of economics and general legal questions and approached the question of political power. This was evidenced during the debate about the press law and even more clearly during the struggle over the military budget. In both these instances agreement could only be reached when the liberals either abandoned a fundamental principle for fear of damaging their relationship with the chancellor—as in the case of the press law—or heavily compromised their principles, as in the case of the army budget. The latter compromise proved to be of considerable importance for it diminished the power of the *Reichstag* and greatly inhibited the gradual democratisation of the political system.

In 1867 the *Reichstag* of the North German Confederation had agreed to approve army budgets for four-year periods and in 1871 this agreement was extended for three more years. In 1874 Bismarck and the chief of general staff, Count Helmuth von Moltke, proposed that the peacetime strength of the army be established at a constant figure. The liberals refused to renounce Parliament's right to approve the budget each and every year because the loss of this right would have deprived Parliament of much of its leverage and real power. However, the National Liberals and Progressives were very sensitive to widespread popular nationalism and to the high esteem in which the army was generally held as the author of German unity. They therefore agreed to seek a compromise with the Iron Chancellor, fixing the peacetime strength of the army for seven-year periods. This of course deprived the *Reichstag* of much of its control over the budget. Bismarck for his part was well pleased: the compromise freed him for long periods from parliamentary interference and at the same time avoided the political danger of freeing the army completely from Parliament's will.

The willingness of the National Liberals to compromise on so fundamental a principle as Parliament's ability to approve the budget was due to more than just the pro-government attitude of the German public. In an entirely unrelated question, the government was facing the most troublesome dispute in the short history of the *Kaiserreich*, and the National Liberals were eager to support Bismarck in this matter for reasons of their social background and aspirations.

The quarrel originated in the tension between the Catholic Church and the modern state. A power struggle between these institutions had been underway since the middle of the century, not only in Germany but also in France, Austria, Italy and Switzerland. The public life of these states was consumed by this quarrel after

1869, when the Vatican Council summoned to Rome by Pope Pius IX promulgated the dogma of papal infallibility in questions of faith and morals despite the objections of the French and German bishops.

European liberals perceived this declaration as an attack on the modern belief in progress and as a reversion to a medieval mentality which seriously threatened freedom of conscience. Pope Pius IX had been the object of much liberal distrust ever since 1864 when he first published the *Syllabus of Errors*,[5] denouncing a multitude of current ideas and beliefs and categorically refusing to 'reconcile and align himself with progress, liberalism and modern civilisation'.[5] The declaration of papal infallibility only fortified liberals in their determination to resist any further attack on their principles.

German Catholics founded their own political party, the Centrists, first in Prussia in the autumn of 1870 and then throughout the empire in 1871. However, Catholics were in a minority in Germany, unlike Austria, Italy and France, and the ensuing conflict was exceptionally intense.

While the liberals were largely concerned with preserving fundamental freedoms and combating the forces of the restoration, their ally Bismarck viewed the conflict primarily as a power struggle between the state and the Roman curia. In his view the curia represented an independent political force 'eternally caught up by the same desire to expand'[6] that animates every great power. The declarations of the Vatican Council were only of interest to him to the extent that they overflowed the strictly religious realm and began to encroach on state interests. In May 1869 he telegraphed Count Harry von Arnim, the Prussian ambassador to the Holy See: 'Both constitutionally and politically Prussia has but a single policy: the complete freedom of the Church in religious affairs and the total rejection of any ecclesiastical interference in the affairs of state.'[7]

The principle of ecclesiastical freedom had already been enunciated in Prussia in 1848 and entrenched in the Constitution. The church had gained important powers such as the right to appoint the clergy, ecclesiastical supervision of the schools, the liberty of ecclesiastical orders and associations and an independent church administration. Bismarck later endeavoured to preserve these liberties for both confessions and avoided any religious quarrels which might disturb the peace. When the Italian government approached Prussia in 1867 with requests for support against the pope, Bismarck bluntly refused, explaining: 'The Catholic population of Germany has the same right as the Evangelical population to see its religious convictions respected. This respect implies that a state with a mixed population cannot proceed against the supreme head of the Catholic church in any way which would wound the hearts of devout Catholics.' Carrying on to remark on attempts to integrate the remnants of the papal states into the Kingdom of Italy, Bismarck forthrightly stated: 'It is a prerequisite of Prussian relations with Italy that the papacy retain a status which German Catholics regard as worthy.'[8]

However, certain events now induced Bismarck to cast off his neutrality towards the Vatican Council. German Catholics opposed to the principle of papal infallibility banded together in 'Old Catholic' congregations and requested state protection. The smouldering dispute broke into the open when some theologians with state appointments joined Old Catholic congregations and were thereupon dismissed by church authorities. The theologians resisted, pointing to their status as civil servants. This reopened the ancient question of ecclesiastical versus state sovereignty, and Bismarck felt compelled to assert state interests.

Other factors also played a role. The Centre Party, cemented together by its Catholic faith, emerged unexpectedly from the elections of 1871 as the second strongest party in the *Reichstag*. It demanded that the German chancellor help the pope to recover the temporal powers of which he has been deprived by the Italian government after the withdrawal of the French garrison from the papal states. Under the leadership of Ludwig Windthorst, a former royal minister in Hanover, the Centrists further requested that the articles in the Prussian Constitution guaranteeing the freedom of the church from state interference be taken over into the Federal Constitution. These requests were denied by both Bismarck and a majority in the *Reichstag*, the first because it would have required German interference in the internal affairs of a sovereign people and the second because it would have infringed on the cultural sovereignty of the individual states in the empire and violated its federal structure.

The Polish question also became a factor. The Catholic Church was highly sympathetic towards the Poles living in the outlying districts of Prussia. It supported the Polish national movement and promoted use of the Polish language. In a polemical letter to the Russian tsar, Bismarck wrote:

The Poles find their mainstay in the Catholic Church. It is their most effective means of gaining the sympathy of both the internal population and foreign powers. The Church for its part will never turn its back on the highly devout Poles, and in order to preserve such a strong hold will continue do all it can to support the Polish cause.[9]

All these factors led Bismarck to embark on a crusade to reorganise the relationship between church and state. At first the Iron Chancellor endeavoured to win the support of the curia and the German episcopate against the Centre Party, which he falsely accused of declaring war on the state.[10] This party had been organised in 1870 in order 'to represent Catholic interests in the parliaments'[11] and it tended to attract those who opposed Bismarck's rule: Hanoverians, Alsacians and Poles. These people were hostile to Germany, in the chancellor's view, and he prepared to launch a great struggle—all the more since the Roman curia refused to exercise a moderating influence on the Centrists. The result was a rapidly escalating conflict waged with mounting vehemence first in Prussia and then throughout the empire. The contemporary historian, physician and liberal deputy Rudolf Virchow dubbed it a 'great *Kulturkampf*' (struggle of civilisations).[12] To Bismarck it represented the age-old 'contest between the king and the priesthood',[13] though he only injured himself through this exaggerated view of the situation.

The first measures which were adopted in order to clearly separate church from state were the abolition of church supervision of the schools and the elimination of the Catholic Department of the Prussian Ministry of Culture and Education. 'The Catholic Department of the Ministry of Culture, originally intended as an institution through which Catholic Prussians could give voice to the rights of their state in its relations with Rome', had become in Bismarck's view, 'an organisation at the very centre of the Prussian bureaucracy which advanced Roman and Polish interests against Prussia'.[14] The Catholic section was then combined with the Evangelical section in a new department of religious affairs. Furthermore, a school law was enacted to replace church supervision of the schools with state supervision. Since both confessions were affected, Bismarck came into conflict with Evangelical old conservatives who broke with him over this issue and thereafter refused him their support.

These measures in Prussia to strengthen the state at the expense of the church were reflected at the federal level by the addition of the 'pulpit paragraph' to the criminal code—at the request of the government of Bavaria. This section made it a crime for clerics to discuss 'matters of state in a manner dangerous to the public peace'[15] during the accomplishment of their religious duties. Virtually any discussion of political issues from the pulpit was thus outlawed. Six months later in July 1872 a 'Law Concerning the Order of the Society of Jesus' was enacted, again at the instigation of Bavaria. It outlawed the creation of Jesuit centres in Germany and limited the length of time individual members of the order could remain in the country.

The *Kulturkampf* reached its height with the promulgation of the 'May Laws' in Prussia in 1873. The articles guaranteeing the independence of the Catholic Church were struck from the Prussian Constitution, and the state began to require candidates for Church offices to pass a prescribed series of examinations at state schools and universities. In addition, a state court for church affairs was established. In 1874 the May Laws were extended to make civil marriage mandatory. Henceforth only marriages conducted before civil registrars had legal force, and the keeping of vital statistics became a purely civil matter. Both these laws were adopted at the federal level in 1875. The Prussian government also withdrew all financial support for the Catholic Church and intervened in the administration of the bishoprics.

Pope Pius IX declared all this legislation invalid and threatened those who obeyed it, laymen and ecclesiastics alike, with excommunication. 'Meet persecution from your fatherland with prayer and steadfastness', he urged. 'Have recourse to the press and public speeches. Be as cautious as you are determined.'[16] The Catholic population and clergy responded. They defied the strong-arm measures of the state and, making great use of their civil rights of free speech and freedom of association, built up newspapers and Catholic associations. By 1878 half of all German bishops had been deposed, but neither they nor most priests could be coerced into abandoning their opposition—neither by fines, nor by arrest, nor by imprisonment, nor by expatriation. By 1878 many parishes were without a priest, but Catholics clung to their Church, and the Centre Party nearly doubled its membership over a very short period. In the elections to the Prussian *Landtag* in 1873 the party's strength increased from fifty-two seats to ninety, and in the *Reichstag* elections of 1874 the party's seats rose from sixty-three to ninety-one.

Bismarck had failed to reckon with such fierce resistance from the clergy and the Catholic population. Realising that the state had been placed in a hopeless position, he called off the struggle. First he moderated enforcement of the legislation, and eventually abrogated all of it apart from the 'pulpit paragraph', state supervision of the schools, civil marriage and the anti-Jesuit laws. The latter legislation was eventually rescinded in 1917. Bismarck's retreat was made easier by the conciliatory stance of the new pope, Leo XIII, who set out after his election to restore peace to relations with Prussia and Germany.

The winding down of the *Kulturkampf* marked the end of Bismarck's cooperation with the National Liberals. Even at the height of the struggle he had striven, though often in vain, to limit governmental concessions to the liberals in order to preserve flexibility in his management of the conflict. In a speech to the Prussian House of Lords in 1873 he emphasised that the struggle between 'the pope and the German emperor' should be judged like any other struggle that necessarily has its lulls, ceasefires and peace treaties.[17] In contrast to the liberals, he was therefore inclined to wage the struggle through easily reversible administrative measures rather than through legislation which was difficult to undo. The opposition of the Centrists to the *Kulturkampf* and the hostility of the Conservatives left the chancellor increasingly dependent on the liberals. But when the failure of these policies became evident, Bismarck sought to restore the political balance.

Not only the religious situation induced Bismarck to loosen his ties with the National Liberals and to draw closer to the Conservatives and the Centrists. The year 1878 brought a great reversal in the chancellor's commercial and social policies. Immediately following the establishment of the *Reich*, a wave of prosperity had swept the land, magnified by the war reparations flooding in from France. The liberal economic policy introduced by the Customs Union (*Zollverein*) helped new companies to take root throughout the empire, and the general standard of living rose rapidly. The prestige of the Manchester school of economics, with its emphasis on a market economy and free trade, was so great that even the Conservatives embraced free trade on behalf of Prussian grain exports.

However, the economic depression beginning in 1873–4 and lasting till the end of the decade provoked a reversal in the general mood. The slump was sparked by the collapse of the Viennese stock exchange in 1873. Close economic ties with Austria pushed German shares into rapid decline as well, wiping out countless businesses, depriving thousands of their livelihood and severely depressing the economy. Fear and uncertainty spread throughout the land. The Association of German Manufacturers, formed in 1876, joined forces with the large landowners to demand state protection and the introduction of high tariffs in order to save at least the internal market. Iron manufacturers and the owners of cotton mills were particularly hard hit by cheap British imports and faced ruin if nothing was done. Large landowners also found it impossible to compete with the cheap grain imported from America, India and Eastern Europe thanks to the new technology of steamers and a rapidly expanding railway network.

All these factors convinced Bismarck to reverse his economic policy. Playing down German exports and appealing to patriotic sentiment, the Iron Chancellor claimed that Germany had become 'a dumping ground for foreign overproduction' and that he must attempt 'to lend German work and production in the fields and in the cities, in industry and in agriculture all the protection we can, without doing harm to important national interests'.[18] The introduction of tariffs on iron, wood, grain and livestock had the happy effect of not only defending the national market but also of increasing the revenues of the central government which previously had been almost totally dependent on the various states. Federal expenses were covered by fees levied annually on the states in proportion to their population, placing the imperial government in Bismarck's words in the role of an irksome creditor and boarder. The chancellor planned to reform the tax system by introducing indirect taxes or federal government monopolies on tobacco, coffee, tea, sugar, spirits, beer and wine. This was intended to help free the federal government from its dependence not only on the individual states but also on the financial prerogatives of the *Reichstag*.

Most National Liberals refused to support the new policy of protective tariffs and revenue-raising duties. Since Bismarck was already suspicious of the liberals' attempts to democratise the empire, he turned to Windthorst, whose party together with the Conservatives supported him in the tariff question. A minority of the National Liberals remained loyal to the chancellor, but most joined forces with the Progressive Party to form the German Liberal Party (*Deutsch-Freisinnige Partei*). It along with the Social Democrats formed the Opposition to the government in the *Reichstag*.

The introduction of protective tariffs marked the end of government refusal to intervene in the economy. An activist social policy also began to emerge as a fundamental characteristic of the *Reich* as it entered a period of considerable economic and social transformation. Bismarck ascribed great importance to this policy as an antidote to the bourgeoning working-class movement in which he saw a serious threat to the empire and the continuation of monarchical rule.

The rapid spread of industrialism in the second half of the nineteenth century had a considerable effect on the distribution of population. The overwhelmingly agrarian population of the old Germany began to move in rising numbers (thanks to freedom of occupation and movement) into the rapidly expanding cities. Here the moderately wealthy middle class and the capitalist grand bourgeoisie were confronted with an ever-increasing army of workers to whom economic liberalism only seemed to bring hardship. As society grew increasingly differentiated, the workers were left defenceless and without legal recourse in the face of entrepreneurial whim and the vagaries of sickness, injury and unemployment.

The workers attempted to remedy their plight by joining labour unions and political associations. After freedom of association was restored in Saxony in 1861 and across the North German Confederation in 1867, unions and working-class parties were organised. The most important was the German Workers' Union founded in 1863 by Ferdinand Lassalle, with its support for a 'small Germany' and agitation on behalf of a universal, equal franchise. Lassalle's early death and the achievement of much of his political agenda caused his followers to lose interest in the German Workers' Union and to transfer their allegiance to the Social Democratic Workers' Party, founded in 1869 by Wilhelm Liebknecht and August Bebel. In contrast to Lassalle's party, which supported a strong state and sought to work within the system, the Social Democrats insisted on Marxist class war and condemned the existing state as the instrument of bourgeois class rule. Karl Liebknecht declared:

Social Democracy cannot negotiate with its foes in any area, under any circumstances. Negotiations are possible when some common ground exists, but to negotiate with people to whom one is essentially opposed can only mean the sacrifice of one's principles. Whosoever parleys with the enemy, plays the parliamentary game; and whosoever plays the parliamentary game winds up entering into pacts and alliances.[19]

Consistent with this declaration, the Eisenach Programme approved by the Social Democratic Workers' Party on 8 August 1869[20] contained a series of revolutionary, Marxist-socialist demands, though some pragmatic aims achievable within the existing system were added out of deference to the *Lassalleaner* in attendance.

This sort of agitation convinced Bismarck of the need to improve the social conditions of the working class. As early as November 1871 he declared: 'Only action by the existing government authority can arrest the confusion sown by the socialist movement. It should achieve what is justifiable in the socialist demands and integrate it into the existing state and social order.'[21] However, the Iron Chancellor was determined to fight with every means at his disposal those socialists who opposed the state in principle.

Bismarck's fear of what he considered to be unpredictible revolutionaries was shared by most of the bourgeoisie. Having witnessed the revolt of the Paris Commune in March 1871 and the bitter street battles which ensued, it vastly overestimated the 'red menace' and for a long time refused to countenance any social demands of the working class no matter how justified.

The chancellor's initial attempts to combat Social Democracy by dint of emergency laws floundered on the opposition of the liberals, who feared that it would damage the fundamental freedoms guaranteed by the Constitution, but two assassination attempts on the emperor in May and June of 1878 provided the impetus Bismarck needed in order to force the repressive legislation through the *Reichstag*. On 28 October 1878 a 'Law against Social Democratic Activities Dangerous to the Public Welfare' was enacted.[22] It outlawed all organisations serving Social Democratic, socialist or communist purposes, provided penalties for those who disregarded the provisions of the law and made party functionaries subject to arrest. The law, enacted for three years, was regularly renewed until 1890—but still failed to achieve Bismarck's purposes. Far from being destroyed, Social Democracy grew in strength and increased the number of its representatives in the *Reichstag* from nine in 1878 to thirty-five in 1890. Anti-socialist legislation made most of the working-class feel unjustly treated and excluded from national life. The longer the repression lasted, the more the working class tended to turn its back on the state and develop its own separate culture through trade unions, party schools, sporting clubs and numerous glee clubs with their own publications.

At the same time that he was enforcing the anti-socialist legislation, Bismarck encouraged 'all efforts which aim to improve the condition of the workers'.[23] By responding through 'legislation and administrative means' to the needs of the working class, the Iron Chancellor hoped to cut off 'the roots of Social Democracy'.[24] If the German state provided some security for its workers, he hoped, the causes of social tension would be eliminated.

A message from the emperor in 1881, initiated by Bismarck and read before the *Reichstag* by the chancellor himself, proclaimed the advent of a state-sponsored system of social security. This was to be the core of Bismarck's effort to establish internal peace:

We consider it our royal duty once more to enjoin the *Reichstag* to take up this task. We would take even greater satisfaction from all the successes with which God has clearly blessed our government if We could be assured of leaving the fatherland a new and lasting covenant of inner peace which would grant to those in need greater security and more bounteous assistance.[25]

This task in Bismarck's view was incumbent upon the state alone:

'The state must take this matter in hand. Not as charity but as a right to sustentation when the will to work no longer suffices. Why should those who were disabled by war or those civil servants disabled by old age have a pension while the soldiers of labour have none?'[26]

Bismarck's plan found concrete expression in the social legislation of the next few years. The health insurance law of 1883 formed public corporations endowed with funds to pay sickness costs and benefits. An accident insurance law was passed in 1884 to cover the costs of treatment and of a pension till the patient was once more able to work. Finally, a disability and old-age insurance law was passed in 1889. The cost of all three schemes was shared by employers and employees, and the empire contributed solely to disability and old-age insurance.

This social legislation and its further extension in subsequent years were doubtless a great boon to the German people. Bismarck's plan to improve the lot of the working masses—despite the opposition of liberals and Social Democrats—laid the foundations of state intercession in social problems, an intercession which to this day remains an essential feature of German society.

Yet Bismarck's fundamental plan of reconciling the working class to the ruling regime did not succeed. The Social Democrats condemned the social legislation, fearing that it would deepen the workers' dependence on the existing state. The chancellor for his part refused to go beyond these insurance schemes, and thus failed to satisfy the workers' demand for legislation dealing with maximum hours of work, female and child labour, and labour arbitration. Nevertheless, the chancellor had initiated a social programme to serve the purposes of state—to which he counted aid to the needy alongside national defence and communications.[27]

The limits of Bismarck's political art were clearly defined by his social policy. The contradiction between anti-socialist laws and welfare legislation henceforth set the tone of the internal political debate until his final demise. This debate was typified less by well-founded liberal and democratic objections to the chancellor's policy than by a bitter reaction against his imperious manner. Many liberal deputies in the *Reichstag* simply marked time till the anticipated accession of the new emperor brought a climate more favourable to their cause.

The *Reichstag* elected in 1878 immediately after the assassination attempts on the emperor had a very conservative bent with 115 seats controlled by the Conservative Party and the *Reich* Party (*Reichspartei*). But even it did not always see eye to eye with the chancellor, let alone the *Reichstag* of 1881–6, which vacillated according to its shifting majorities. The government did not gain a reliable majority until 1887, when the Conservatives, National Liberals and *Reichspartei* formed an electoral 'cartel' and agreed to assist the one candidate of the three parties who was strongest in each constituency. With the backing of this conservative majority, Bismarck reinforced the army and again fixed its appropriations over seven-year periods. Federal revenues were also increased by raising the tax on sugar and spirits. However, the Iron Chancellor did not succeed in setting the level of tax he thought necessary in order to consolidate the empire internally and to free him from parliamentary control of the purse strings. His repeated attempts to this same end to bring the railways under Federal control also miscarried. He failed as well to pacify the Alsatians and Poles within the empire who felt mistreated by imposed government regulations and responded with a renewed sense of national purpose.

Foreign Policy

Though Bismarck's internal policy was calculated first and foremost to bring all the divergent forces of modern Germany under the thumb of the central government, his foreign policy was directed primarily at preserving all that had been gained in 1871. By evincing great moderation in all his actions, the Iron Chancellor hoped to restore the international balance that had been severely shaken by the sudden emergence of strong central powers.

Germany's victory over France compelled all five of the great powers of Europe to reconsider their foreign policy. For the first time in centuries Germany had overcome her internal fragmentation, had stepped out from under the shadow of her neighbours and had acquired sufficient strength to send a shiver of fear down the spines of the rest of Europe. A few weeks after the proclamation of the German Empire, Benjamin Disraeli, the leader of the Opposition in the British House of Commons, remarked:

This war represents the German revolution, a greater political event than the French revolution of the last century. . . . You have a new world . . ., new and unknown objects and dangers with which to cope. . . . We used to have discussions in this House about the balance of power. . . . But what has really come to pass? The balance of power has been entirely destroyed, and the country which suffers most, and feels the effect of this great change most, is England.[28]

Bismarck directed all his energies towards shaping this 'new world' in peaceful cooperation with the other powers. Only through a balance of power, he thought, could Germany's new-found position in the world be safeguarded. This was to remain the guiding principle of Bismarck's foreign policy—for unlike most of his contemporaries, he was highly aware of Germany's narrow leeway. He commented:

We lie at the centre of Europe, and therefore have at least three exposed flanks. France has only an eastern border and Russia a western border where they are vulnerable to attack. We are also more vulnerable than any other people to the danger of hostile coalitions for reason of our geographical position, the entire evolution of world history, and the lack of internal cohesion which till recently characterised the German nation in comparison with others.[29]

Strong, consistent support for the status quo appeared to Bismarck to be the best method of safeguarding Germany against the pressures of the surrounding states, which would only come to accept a vastly strengthened *Reich* if their own independence was not threatened. He therefore emphasised immediately upon the founding of the empire that Germany was satiated, that she had no further territorial ambitions and wished for nothing more than 'to be left to herself in peace in order serenely to pursue her future development'.[30] The chancellor went to great lengths lest it appear that Berlin entertained any intention other than peace. For these reasons it was not until the last years of his tenure as chancellor that Bismarck reluctantly began to engage in colonialism.

Bismarck's policy towards France also aimed at the preservation of the status quo. The French never reconciled themselves to their defeat in battle, the Treaty of Frankfurt or the loss of Alsace-Lorraine, and Bismarck anticipated unrelenting hostility. He therefore strove for as long as possible to keep France weak and unattractive as a coalition partner. This task could be eased, in Bismarck's view, by the internal rivalry in France between monarchists and republicans. He hoped for an eventual victory of the republican forces in the belief that a democratic republic would find coalition partners more difficult to come by in the rest of largely monarchical Europe. A restored monarchy would also be much more dependent on foreign successes in order to whip up public support and would accordingly pose a far greater threat to Germany. Late in 1872 Bismarck wrote to Count Harry von Arnim, the German ambassador in Paris:

What we require is to be left in peace by France and to prevent her from finding allies if she should not wish to keep the peace. So long as France has no allies, she does not present a danger to us and so long as the great monarchies of Europe band together, no republic can endanger them.[31]

Two years later Bismarck instructed Arnim's successor, Prince Chlodwig von Hohenlohe, that Germany's primary concern was 'that France not become internally so strong and externally so respected that she is able to gather allies'.[32] During the well-nigh two decades of his tenure as chancellor, Bismarck endeavoured first and foremost to engineer a political 'situation in which all the powers apart from France need us and so far as possible are deterred from joining coalitions against us by their relations with one another'.[33] The guiding principle behind Bismarck's entire foreign policy, whatever the means and whatever the eventual success, was to link the great powers of Europe in such a way that they would be dissuaded from joining forces with France. Thus Paris would be prevented from declaring war in order to achieve its ends.

Since Britain clung to its policy of splendid isolation, only Russia and Austria remained as the objects of special German attention. Bismarck's pre-1871 successes were due not least to the friendly relations between Berlin and St Petersburg, and now under changed circumstances he sought to cement these relations. While avoiding any sense of dependence on the Russians, Bismarck made good relations with St Petersburg the keystone of his foreign policy. Reconciliation with Austria was relatively easy to achieve due to the moderation Bismarck had shown in his negotiations with her in 1866 and also to the fact that Vienna now had no real alternative to the renunciation of its plans for a 'Greater Germany'.

Despite the Russo-Austrian rivalry in the Near East, Bismarck succeeded in 1872 in arranging an accord among the emperors of Germany, Russia and Austria. This loose agreement was reinforced on 22 October 1873 when the emperors issued a written declaration proclaiming their intention 'to strengthen the prevailing peace in Europe and to obviate the possibility of a war which could disturb that peace'. If the peace were threatened by another power, the emperors pledged 'to arrive at an understanding among themselves in order to agree upon a joint course of action without seeking or concluding alternative alliances'.[34]

The weaknesses in this defensive alliance rooted in monarchic rule soon became apparent. France embarked upon a rearmament programme in 1875 and Bismarck countered by attempting to exert political pressure. An article entitled 'Is War in View' was placed in the Berlin press as a warning to the French against militarism. However, not only Great Britain but Russia as well sought reassurances from Berlin that Germany intended to keep the peace. Although no immediate danger of war actually existed, the crisis was highly significant for what it revealed: the governments of Britain and Russia and public opinion in those countries were unwilling to accept a further increase in German power at the expense of France and would likely side with the French in case of a German attack. Like a flash of lightning, the crisis cast into bold relief a coalition of powers that would one day be the bane of the empire. Bismarck himself felt confirmed in his view that Germany would only be weakened by any threat to the peace and that the *Reich* should move with supreme caution in foreign affairs.

If the 'War in View' controversy shook the Three Emperors' League to its very foundations, the Eastern crisis of the following year completely destroyed it. Bosnia and Herzegovina had risen in revolt against Turkish rule in 1875, and the entire Balkans were soon in turmoil. Russia felt immediately concerned as an adjacent great power harbouring a powerful pan-Slavic party. Under heavy pressure from these circles, which longed to unite all Slavs in a mighty empire under Russian leadership, St Petersburg sought permission to intervene from the other powers and requested that Germany hold a conference for this purpose. Bismarck was unwilling fully to endorse Russian claims in the Balkans, and he refused this proposal. However, Bismarck did request of William I that he write to the tsar in order to assure the Russians of German neutrality in case of conflict with Turkey as recompense for the benevolence which the tsar had demonstrated towards Germany in 1870.

The Turks had again pacified the Balkans by the autumn of 1876 when the tsar proposed to the Austrian emperor that they undertake joint military action against the Porte. This was coupled with a threat to invade Austria herself if she did not consent. The Austrians none the less refused, and Bismarck stepped in to make it known in the name of the German *Reich* and the European balance of power that a severe weakening of either Russia or Austria would not be acceptable. Obliged to give ground, the tsar once again came to terms with the Austrian emperor over their respective spheres of interest in the European portion of the Turkish Empire.

Russia alone then declared war on Turkey in the summer of 1877, soon emerging victorious. In the subsequent Treaty of San Stefano, the Porte was deprived of almost all its European possessions. Serbia, Bulgaria, Montenegro and Romania became independent (though Bulgaria still owed tribute to the Turks), while Russia retained Bessarabia in the Balkans and a vast expanse in Asia.

London and Vienna, however, refused to countenance such an

extension of Russian power to the detriment of Turkey, and the outbreak of a great war seemed inevitable. Bismarck strove to avoid the conflict and took up position between the fronts. On 19 February 1878 he declared before the *Reichstag* that Berlin harboured no further ambitions than to play the role 'of the honest broker who only wishes to effect a deal'. Germany, in his view, could 'mediate just as well between England and Russia, if needed, . . . as between Austria and Russia'.[35]

In the summer of 1878 the Iron Chancellor succeeded in gathering all the powers interested in the Eastern question for a conference in Berlin—a sure sign of his international prestige and the trust which other nations placed in him. The suspicion and fear that met the German Empire upon its creation had been supplanted by confidence in Bismarck's moral authority and a willingness to take seriously his efforts on behalf of peace.

After a month of strenuous negotiations, Bismarck succeeded in arranging a compromise, although the crux of the Balkan question, with all the tensions emanating from it, remained unresolved. The Mediterranean was an area of vital concern to Britain and she insisted on propping up the Turkish Empire while Austria opposed any appreciable strengthening of Russia's position in the Balkans. St Petersburg was therefore obliged to acquiesce once again and to abandon some of the positions she had recently acquired. The tsar renounced his project of a Greater Bulgaria, accepted the re-establishment of a Turkish foothold in the Balkans and agreed that Britain should become the guarantor of Turkish possessions in Asia. England was to receive Cyprus as compensation for the expansion of Russian power into formerly Turkish lands in the Balkans and Asia. Austria meanwhile was allowed to occupy and administer Bosnia and Herzegovina as a buffer against Serbia and in exchange for the other changes in the region.

So far as Germany was concerned, the Berlin Congress only resulted in a considerable cooling of relations with Russia. Embittered by a belief that they had been robbed of the fruits of victory, the Russians blamed the diplomatic reverses they had suffered on Bismarck, largely overlooking the fact that he had saved them from a great war which they had few chances of winning given the exhausted state of their military and material resources. Germany had failed, in the Russian view, to redeem her debt of 1870 and a mounting malevolence towards her began to spread throughout public opinion, spurred on by the pan-Slavic movement.

The Three Emperors' League had become a dead letter for all practical purposes, and the German Empire found itself further than ever from its political goals as outlined by Bismarck in the Kissinger *Diktat*. The chancellor, to whom, so his *Memoirs* tell us, 'the thought of coalitions gives nightmares', began to cast about for other alliances.

We had defeated two of the great powers of Europe. Now we had to induce at least one of the powers with which we had struggled in the field of battle to resist the temptation to seek revenge in combination with others. That this power could not be France was evident, for reasons obvious to anyone familiar with history and the Gallic temperament.[36]

Since England was not about to forswear its policy of 'splendid isolation' (despite a certain rapprochement with Germany during the Berlin Congress), the only available power was Austria-Hungary. Negotiations between Bismarck and the Austro-Hungarian foreign minister, Gyula Andrassy, opened immediately following the Congress of Berlin, and by October 1879 agreement had been reached on a secret defensive alliance. The deal was almost scuttled by the German emperor, who refused to ratify it on account of a sentimental dynastic attachment to the Russian Romanovs till Bismarck finally forced his hand by threatening to resign. The resulting 'Dual Alliance' bound Germany and Austria to assist one another in case of a Russian attack; to remain neutral in case of an attack by another power; and again to provide assistance if this attacking power was supported by Russia. Vienna refused to provide military support if the *Reich* were attacked by France, but Bismarck accepted this condition in view of the fact that unassisted French aggression seemed highly unlikely. Bismarck did not consider this alliance to be an alternative to friendly relations with Russia (although it did strengthen Germany's position vis-à-vis her eastern neighbour). He hoped to employ the alliance in order to exert a moderating influence on Austrian policy and expected eventually to engineer a Russo-German entente.

Thus Bismarck never lost sight of the need to keep open his 'wire to St Petersburg' lest the tsar be tempted to look to France for support. He skillfully exploited Anglo-Russian tensions in Asia in order to draw St Petersburg closer to Germany, and eventually succeeded in 1881 in negotiating a reaffirmation of the Three Emperors' League and a neutrality agreement between Russia, Germany and Austria-Hungary. The three powers pledged to adhere to a policy of benevolent neutrality in case one was attacked by a fourth party, promised to respect the interests of the other signatories and promised to agree on their war aims if conflict with Turkey should break out. The treaty was limited to three years, but was extended in 1884. Although it had to be secret because of the strong opposition it would have aroused from the pan-Slavic movement, its terms bound the tsar and the Russian government. The three emperors' pact secured the peace in Eastern Europe and protected Germany from the danger of a two-front war, but could only endure so long as Russo-Austrian relations were not completely envenomed by developments in the Near East.

Bismarck was well aware of this soft spot in the alliance. He therefore welcomed the mounting tensions in the Mediterranean between Britain, France and Italy—tensions which promised for a time to keep the gaze of these powers firmly fixed on Africa. The tensions centred primarily on Egypt and Tunisia, territories nominally under Turkish suzerainty but dominated economically by France and Britain and of concern for geographic reasons to all three European powers. Britain and France had agreed at the Berlin Congress on the demarcation of their respective spheres of interest: Britain was to acquire Egypt with the vital link which the Suez Canal provided to British India, while France took control of Tunisia. Italy, however, was left empty-handed, and when the French occupied Tunisia in 1880, assuming control over 10,000 Italians who lived there, Italy abruptly reversed her pro-French policy. She turned to the central powers, and the Dual Alliance was enlarged to form a Triple Alliance. According to the terms of this treaty, signed in 1882, all three parties could call on the alliance if attacked by both France and Russia. Germany and Austria were to come to Italy's aid if she were attacked by France alone, and Italy (but not Austria) was to support Germany if she came under French attack. If another power attacked, the signatories agreed to maintain their neutrality. The terms of the pact did not pertain to Britain, because Italy with her long coasts was dependent on English seapower. The Triple Alliance was again enlarged in 1883 by the secret admission of Romania. Bismarck thus succeeded in uniting the central powers in a security system that excluded France and reduced the danger of anti-German coalitions to a minimum.

However, the Triple Alliance had its weaknesses. The antagonism between Italy and Austria had only been papered over, and Rome had not renounced its claims to Trieste and south Tyrol. Furthermore, the alliance could only exist so long as it was favourably viewed by Britain. If the British were to become hostile to the central powers, Italy would have to withdraw. In Eastern Europe, security depended heavily on the ability of the German government to moderate Austrian and Russian ambitions in the Balkans and to preserve scope for manoeuvre.

That Bismarck was determined to maintain a free hand shortly became apparent. A war erupted between Serbia and Bulgaria in 1885, exacerbating the antagonism between Vienna and St Petersburg and threatening to draw much of Europe into a great conflict. Russia was intent upon using her influence in Bulgaria in order finally to arrange matters there to her own satisfaction, but Austrian intervention on behalf of Serbia severely limited St Petersburg's options. One year earlier, the Three Emperors' League had been renewed for a space of three years, and Vienna had agreed to recognise a Russian sphere of influence in Bulgaria and to confer with her allies before resorting to arms. Bismarck was firmly resolved that the whole Eastern question not become a *casus belli*, and in reaction to Vienna's intervention he quickly proclaimed that he would not allow 'a leash to be thrown around my neck on account of this question in order to drag me into a dispute with Russia'.[37] There were certain Austrian interests, he declared, which Germany could not support.

The situation was all the more dangerous in that the crisis in the Balkans coincided with a recrudesence of the revenge movement in France. It had found two able spokesmen in Georges Boulanger, the minister of war, and Paul Déroulède, president of the League of French Patriots. Faced with a dual threat to Germany from east and west, Bismarck sought additional security by endeavouring to draw closer to Britain and by attempting to replace the lapsed Three Emperors' League with a Russo-German alliance.

After the Triple Alliance was renewed in early 1887, Bismarck promoted a pact which did not include Germany but which nevertheless tied her more closely to Britain through her association with Austria and Italy. In this pact—the so-called Mediterranean Entente—Britain, Italy and Austria-Hungary pledged to preserve the status quo in the Mediterranean, Adriatic, Aegean and Black seas. Italy also promised Britain her support in Egypt in return for British backing of Italian ambitions in Tripoli and Cyrenaica. The threat to Germany from the west seemed banned by May of 1887 when Spain signed an agreement with Italy that bound her as well to maintain the status quo in the Mediterranean and to refrain from joining any alliance with France directed against Italy of her allies in the Triple Alliance. Vienna and Berlin were soon admitted to this pact. Finally, Britain, Italy and Austria-Hungary reached an agreement by the end of 1887 which bound them to uphold Turkish independence and the status quo in the East. The parties further agreed that Russia should be the only power allowed to step in if Turkey abandoned sovereignty over Bulgaria.

On the eastern front Bismarck also managed to arrive at an understanding with the tsar. By the terms of the secret Reinsurance Treaty, Russia and Germany promised to observe benevolent neutrality if one of them were attacked by a third nation. The treaty recognised and encouraged a Russian sphere of interest in Bulgaria. Germany also promised in a 'top secret supplement' to maintain neutrality coupled with moral and diplomatic support in case Russia should find herself compelled to occupy the approaches to the Black Sea. By virtue of this treaty Bismarck warded off a possible Franco-Russian alliance while the tsar gained support in the event of an English attack on Russia.

The Reinsurance Treaty, like all of Bismarck's alliances, was designed to protect Germany against hostile coalitions, to prevent war and to preserve the peace. He remarked to Emperor William:

At least one bond remains of the tsar's treaty with your majesty. It increases the possibilities that Russia will follow a peaceful path and cleave to her monarchistic policies. If Russia were to be without a treaty with us or Austria in the immediate future, we would loose all control over the political path which she might choose to follow.[38]

Bismarck realised that the Reinsurance Treaty could not obviate a Franco-Russian rapprochement, but it seemed likely to discourage such a development. The treaty appeared all the more essential in that Bismarck's inquiries about a defensive alliance with Britain were rebuffed by the British prime minister, Robert Salisbury.

The intricate system of alliances which the chancellor forged after 1879 reflected the increasingly tortuous political conditions in Europe. Each individual treaty was intended 'in the end to help create a political situation in which actual application of the terms of the alliances would become unnecessary'.[39] Weights and counterweights were artfully distributed so as to leave Bismarck some scope for manoeuvre in his efforts to avoid war. 'We have no military aims', the chancellor never tired of repeating, 'we belong to those states which old Prince Metternich called saturated. We have no desires which could be fulfilled by the sword'.[40] He was utterly opposed to any suggestion of preventive war and always emphasised that he would 'never recommend that war be declared simply because it might have to be waged later'; so far as France was concerned, he stated many times: 'We shall never seek a deal, we shall never attack France.'[41]

The rapprochement between St Petersburg and Paris in the critical year of 1887 was a matter of enormous concern to Bismarck. Indeed, his successors would later fail to recognise the key position which the Russo-German alliance occupied in Bismarck's artful scheme and would cancel the Reinsurance Treaty. Thus Bismarck's worst fears were eventually realised, to Germany's great detriment. The chancellor himself always viewed Germany's military might solely as a means of frightening off her potential enemies and increasing her value as an ally. He was careful that the army always felt firmly subordinate to the political leadership. He also conceived of Germany solely as a European power and he abstained from world-wide ambitions. Previous historical developments and the interests of other nations had to be respected in his view. He declared before the *Reichstag* in 1888:

Every great power that goes beyond its legitimate sphere of interest to attempt to pressure and impose on other nations and to guide their affairs in its own interests is straying dangerously far outside the realm which God has given it. It is pursuing power and prestige rather than legitimate interests. This we shall not do.[42]

In Bismarck's view, the string of treaties he had negotiated safeguarded Germany's legitimate interests, promoted a salutary internal situation and thereby helped to protect the international peace. Germany's alliances seemed secure and long-lasting in that they 'did not make one signatory more dependent on the others than is compatible with its own interests'.[43]

This political approach characterised Bismarck's years in office. It, together with his ability to maintain a sense of moderation even in the flush of victory, earned him and Germany a recognised and respected place in Europe.

German Colonial Policy

So far as Bismarck was concerned, German colonial endeavours had to be viewed first and foremost in the European context. For many years he was not only sceptical of colonialism but repudiated it in view of Germany's exposed international position. Only in the 1880s, when Britain's relations with France and Russia were deteriorating on account of colonial rivalries in Afghanistan and the Sudan, did Bismarck agree to protect the overseas establishments of the Hanseatic merchants. In 1883 the Bremen merchant Adolf Lüderitz had acquired from the natives some territory on the Bay of Angra Pequena in south-western Africa, and it was taken under the protection of the *Reich* in 1884. In the same year the imperial counsellor for West Africa, Gustav Nachtigal, hoisted the German banner in Togoland and the Cameroons. One year later, Karl Peters procured some lands along the East African coast from the local chieftains, and they too became a German colony. Footholds were established as well in the western Pacific, where the New Guinea Company, founded in 1884 under the leadership of the banker Adolf von Hansemann, had acquired territory. Dubbed Kaiser-Wilhelm-Land, it was taken under the wing of the *Reich* together with the islands lying off the coast, the so-called Bismarck Archipelago and Marshall Islands.

However, these remained isolated incidents for the time being. Bismarck rejected any suggestion that Germany should become a world power, as proposed by the historian Heinrich von Treitschke and the German Colonial Association founded in December 1882. The chancellor also strongly opposed German emigration to the colonies. So far as he was concerned, they should remain mere commercial bases, necessary in order to assist German merchants in their competition with traders from the other European powers. In creating colonies, Bismarck assured the *Reichstag* in June 1884: 'I have made every effort to determine that we were not encroaching unjustifiably on the well-established rights of other nations.'[44]

In the Anglo-French tiff over Egypt and the Congo, the chancellor sided with France in the hope that the satisfaction of her colonial ambitions would reconcile her to the loss of Alsace-Lorraine. He cooperated closely with the French at the Congo Conference in Berlin over which he presided from December 1884 to February 1885. Britain found herself completely isolated at this conference and was obliged to accept the creation of a neutral Congo under King Leopold II of Belgium. The conference also introduced free trade and free navigation on the rivers of Central Africa, a provision which wiped out Britain's commercial monopoly in the region. Despite his collaboration with France, Bismarck managed to avoid an open rupture with Britain, and even drew closer to London after March 1885, when the ministry of Jules Ferry, with its strong colonial interests, was defeated in France.

Germany's colonial endeavours were doubtless influenced by internal considerations as well. Bismarck wished to divert the energies of the German bourgeoisie into a broad new sphere of activity and to suggest another focus of national attention. This did not, however, change Bismarck's fundamental conviction that Germany stood to gain very little from colonialism and had no vital interests outside Europe. The empire's location at the centre of Europe compelled her to concern herself primarily with European affairs. However, Europe as a whole had entered the age of imperialism and the post-Bismarckian generation longed to burst the narrow bonds of the Continent in order to tackle world affairs. Only the future would tell what success this generation would have at manoeuvring through the shoals of world affairs without overstepping the limitations imposed on Germany by her place in Europe. This would necessitate great sensitivity to what Bismarck liked to call the 'imponderables': the moral and psychological effects of various policies. It would also require a responsible and cautious approach to political power, the moral constraints on which Bismarck always recognised and respected.

Bismarck's Dismissal

Emperor William I died on 9 March 1888, shortly before his ninety-first birthday. Barely nine months beforehand, Bismarck had achieved his ultimate triumph on behalf of European peace by allying Germany with Russia for a period of three years. Four weeks before the demise of the emperor, the chancellor enjoined the nation in one of his last great speeches before the *Reichstag* to love and nurture peace and to manifest true strength and leadership by mastering its own emotions and coming to terms with whatever situation it had to face. At the same time, he reviewed the Prusso-German foreign policy, which he had done so much to shape in the service of the dying king and emperor. The support he had received from William I was essential to his success. He could count on the loyalty and constancy of the monarch even when their opinions diverged and William only accepted his advice reluctantly and grudgingly. It was one of William's great virtues that he freely acknowledged Bismarck's genius, and the chancellor thanked him by vigorously defending the throne and by anchoring the prerogatives of the monarchy in the Prussian and German constitutions.

In the 1880s Bismarck grew very apprehensive of the liberal regime which Crown Prince Frederick would allegedly establish one day to the delight of many Germans. However, Frederick was severely ill by the time he succeeded to the throne and in the end had no influence on political life. He died after reigning for a mere ninety-nine days and was succeeded by his twenty-nine-year-old son, William II. With Frederick's death came crashing down all the hopes of that generation 'which as heir to the intellectual and political movement of 1848 had waited in vain to see liberalism triumph in Prussia and in Germany'.[45]

The young emperor demonstrated a bumptiousness and a hunger

for prestige which Bismarck was unable to moderate. Soon after his succession, William II proclaimed with the enthusiasm of youth that it was his 'most heartfelt desire' that Bismarck continue 'for many years to uphold the banner of the *Reich*'.[46] William's admiration for the aged statesman turned to fury, however, the moment Bismarck criticised the political inexperience, immaturity and brash overconfidence of his public statements. Although the *Reich* was a constitutional monarchy, the power-hungry monarch ached to assume at least some of his chancellor's functions. According to court chaplain Adolf Stoecker, William commented in August 1888, 'I'll just let the old man catch his breath for six months, then I'll rule by myself'.[47] As the minister of state Robert Lucius von Bellhausen noted, this was William's retribution for 'Bismarck's numerous warnings to the young boy that he should be certain to make full use of his sovereign rights and to treat with the greatest disdain the wishes and resolutions of parliaments and government ministries'.[48]

William II was eager not to commence his reign in an atmosphere of bitter confrontation with Social Democracy, and it was over a question of social policy that the latent conflict between Bismarck and the young monarch came to a head. A violent miners' strike had erupted in the Ruhr district and quickly spread to all other mining areas of Germany. William intervened personally in May 1889 in order to end the strike by requiring employers to increase wages. He further planned to ensure the social peace by enacting legislation to provide adequate protection for the working class. Bismarck on the other hand announced his intention to hold firmly to his previous policies, to extend the anti-socialist legislation and to intensify the struggle against the Social Democrats, in his eyes the sole source of social unrest.

Soon Bismarck found himself at odds with the *Reichstag* as well. The widespread dissatisfaction with Bismarck's internal policy crystallised in the elections of 1890. The former Opposition parties emerged with a majority of the seats, and the Social Democratic vote leapt ahead.

Unable to find a majority in Parliament to support his policies, Bismarck cast about for a means of reinforcing his position. He considered both a compromise with the new parliament and a *coup d'état* to free himself from the constitutional prerogatives of the *Reichstag*. However, a step of this import would have required the unreserved support of the emperor, support which William was all the less likely to give in that it would have made him utterly dependent on his chancellor. Bismarck therefore had recourse to a cabinet order of 1852 which stipulated that the king could only deal with government bureaucrats through the responsible minister. In this way he hoped to gain control over the myriad influences on William and to escape the mounting isolation in which he found himself. However, this tactic only sealed the breach between the monarch and his chancellor. In a final dramatic statement, the emperor demanded that the cabinet order be rescinded because it allegedly infringed on his sovereign rights. He further announced that the understanding he had already reached with Bismarck on military funding would be curtailed and that he had reservations about their plan to dissolve the *Reichstag*. William also criticised Bismarck for having received Windthorst, the leader of the Centre Party, the previous day without his knowledge. The chancellor, so far as William was concerned, was not authorised to treat with any parliamentarians without prior permission.

It was clearly disagreement over internal policies which were primarily responsible for the split between the politically experienced though imperious chancellor and his energetic though insecure and immature emperor, who yearned one day to take over the reins of government. However, Bismarck's authority was also called into question at this time in a crucial area of foreign policy. The tsar instructed his ambassador, Count Paul Shuvalov, to open negotiations with Bismarck or his son Herbert in regard to a prolongation of the Reinsurance Treaty. As it turned out, Bismarck resigned in the meantime and the treaty was therefore not renewed. With the intention of making his letter of resignation public, Bismarck cleverly dissembled the internal issues, in which he enjoyed very little public support, and emphasised external affairs as the crux of his differences with the emperor. He would find it impossible, he complained, to carry on a foreign policy which reflected the young monarch's wishes:

I would thereby endanger all the important successes which the foreign policy of the German Empire has accomplished for decades in our relations with Russia during the rule of Your Majesty's two blessed predecessors. These successes were achieved under very difficult circumstances and Shuvalov assured me after his return from St Petersburg of the importance, exceeding all our hopes, which Russia now attaches to these relations.[49]

Bismarck's retirement meant more than the loss of an extraordinary personality. Even contemporaries recognised that an era had ended and a new age bristling with fateful questions had commenced. Bismarck's dismissal was met with both relief and fear for the future, in Germany and Europe alike. The novelist Theodor Fontane wrote to a friend on 1 May 1890 shortly after Bismarck's dismissal:

Bismarck had no greater admirer than me; whenever my wife read me one of his speeches, letters or pronouncements I felt a tingle of delight. The world has rarely seen a greater genius, rarely a man of greater courage and character, and rarely a greater humorist. But he did lack one thing: generosity. The contrasting quality, which by the end reached the pettiest sort of vindictiveness and spitefulness, runs throughout his life. If it had not been for his infernal humour he would have become insufferable far sooner. This lack of generosity . . . is the root cause of the relative indifference with which even his admirers watched him go. . . . In the end nothing but nasty episodes, so nasty that one feels happy to be finished with this era, which ended with such clamorous Bismarck-worship that all spontaneous admiration for the man was submerged. We are fortunate to be rid of him, and many, many questions will now be answered better, more honestly and more clearly. He only ruled in the end by force of habit, doing what he wished, letting everything else slide and demanding adulation. His great days lay behind him. They will live on in the hearts of the German people and as an important part of history; but what he did in the last three years does not amount to much.[50]

The Berlin historian Friedrich Meinecke reminisced:

Only once did I, for a very short time, place my hopes in William II. That was when he dismissed Bismarck—even though most people's confidence in him was rather shaken by this. I was not sufficiently apprised of foreign affairs to discern the dangers that now loomed. But the social decrees of the emperor and Bismarck's opposition to extensive social reform seemed to me to have engendered a moment of historical necessity when the heavy blow of Bismarck's departure had become inevitable. An extremely grave air hung over Bismarck's birthday meal . . . on 1 April 1890. . . . I drove home with Koser, he deeply saddened and depressed while I suggested that 'the emperor is taking out an immense mortgage on the future. If he can redeem it, history will vindicate what he has done. . . .' He proved unable to redeem it.[51]

After the intransigent domestic policy of Bismarck's last years, many Germans such as Fontane and Meinecke looked to William II with high hopes that the *Reich* could be reformed and the class conflict diminished. Outside Germany, the departure of a man who had striven to keep the peace aroused fear of an uncertain and menacing future. The German chargé d'affaires in Paris, Baron Wilhelm von Schoen, reported:

The extraordinarily serious and with few exceptions respectful language in which the French press has commented on the retirement of Prince Bismarck illustrates the profound impression this occasion has left here. For years the French press sought to defame German policy, to impute aggressive intentions, to discover a conniving Prince Bismarck behind every political occurrence and to exhaust itself in personal insults; but now it is not in the least disposed to celebrate his departure. It is almost unanimous in viewing this event as far from a joyous occasion for France, and even offers belated recognition, sometimes covert and reluctant and sometimes open and without hesitation, of the peaceful policies of our former chancellor. The press now views the future with some concern. There is an obvious fear that German policy will seek out or be driven towards armed clashes, that European controversies could develop into insoluble conflicts, now that the skilful master is no longer at hand.[52]

The impression which Bismarck's dismissal left in St Petersburg was summarised by the German military attaché:

The suspicion and hostility which the Russians had demonstrated towards Prince Bismarck ever since the Berlin Congress were suddenly forgotten. They realised they had lost not an enemy of Russia but a friend. They mourned the man who for almost three decades was the greatest assurance of good relations between the adjacent empires and to a certain extent guaranteed the peace between the two of them. The Russians finally realised that they have him to thank for the fact that they have been able to live in peace and quiet since the last Turkish war, to improve their finances and to complete their rearmament. And so triumph was replaced by honest regret at his departure. . . . Now this element of stability has disappeared from their future calculations and been replaced by 'uncertainty' and 'the mystery of the new era' as they like to call it. The Russians peer into the mists of the future with great unease. The self-confidence and the conviction that they were in control of Europe's fate have receded. The Russians look with a certain fear on the great upheavals and profound changes which they predict with absolute certainty as a result of Bismarck's departure. People here engage in hypothetical speculation about the course of these changes and especially about future German policies.[53]

The visibly relieved emperor declared rather exaggeratedly in a telegram to Emperor Francis Joseph: 'As God is my witness, I spent many a night praying and begging that the heart of this man would be softened and that I would be spared the frightful fate of seeing him leave my side.'[54] William apprised the King of Saxony that, 'I am as sad as if I had again lost my grandfather. But certain acts of God must be borne, even if they are one's downfall. I am now the officer of the watch on the ship of state. The course remains the same. Full steam ahead!'[55] The English weekly *Punch* published a famous cartoon of Bismarck as the pilot leaving the ship.[56] William II is depicted as the ship's captain, fairly bursting with satisfaction and pleasure now that he is lord and master and able to chart the course. Shortly thereafter, however, William revealed his true thoughts on the matter: 'It was a question of whether the Hohenzollern dynasty or the Bismarck dynasty would reign.'[57] After Bismarck's death in 1898 he noted, 'Bismarck, master of the situation and of the empire; the House of Hohenzollern of no importance. I recognised my fearful duty to save the crown from the overpowering shadow of the minister. When he hatched his malevolent plots against me and did not even shrink from high treason, I cut him down.'[58]

The shadow of the grand old man was indeed heavy and weighed upon the *Reich*. It had been his creation and was tailored to accommodate him. 'Everything depends on Bismarck alone',[59] judged the staunchly conservative ambassador General Hans Lothar von Schweinitz; the National Liberal politician Ludwig Bamberger declared that Bismarck's enormous authority 'set the paths along which the institutions, the laws, and what is more, men's minds would move'.[60] It escaped Bismarck's notice, as Max Weber noted in his inaugural address at the University of Freiburg in 1895, that 'the work of his hands, the nation to which he had given unity, slowly and inexorably changed its economic structure and became something different, a people which required other structures than those he had given it and into which he could fit his imperious nature'.[61]

The new era was increasingly marked by science and industry and indeed did require new initiatives. Initiatives which would have made allowances for economic expansion and would have reduced the traditional privileges of the nobility in order to foster democracy and parliamentarism. Bismarck failed to understand this new age. During a visit to the Hamburg harbour in 1896, he noted with a shiver the hustle and the bustle, the cranes and the ships. 'It is a new and different world', he said, 'a new age'.[62]

Despite his failings, Germany owes its unification to him. This was the paramount historical achievement of the second half of the nineteenth century, regardless of all the justified criticism of the manner in which he achieved unity and fleshed out the empire. Bismarck's untiring efforts to preserve the peace after the founding of the empire were doubtless the supreme accomplishment of policies which aimed to foster international cooperation.

9

Wilhelmine Germany

1890:	'New course' commences; failure to renew the Reinsurance Treaty with Russia
1892–4:	Dual Alliance between France and Russia; military convention followed by a formal alliance
1898:	Spanish–American War; Germany acquires Kiaochow; Fashoda crisis
1899–1902:	Boer War
1900:	German Navy Bill
1901:	Last British offer of an alliance with Germany
1902:	Baghdad railway; the Anglo-Japanese Alliance
1904:	Anglo-French Entente
1904–5:	Russo-Japanese War
1905–6:	First Russian revolution
1906:	Morocco Conference
1907:	Anglo-Russian Entente
1908:	Austria annexes Bosnia
1911:	Morocco crisis
1912–13:	Balkan Wars; the Haldane mission
1913–14:	Armaments race among the great powers
1914:	Opening of the Panama Canal; Crown Prince of Austria is assassinated

Rapid Social Evolution within the Reich

At the time of Bismarck's dismissal Germany was swiftly becoming the leading industrial and economic power of Europe. As new markets opened, Germany's share of world commerce surged ahead. By the turn of the century the *Reich* almost equalled Great Britain in industrial production and surpassed her in total output, making the German economy the second largest in the world after the United States.[1]

When the empire was founded most Germans lived in the countryside or in small towns and villages. But the rapid emergence of huge industrial centres along the Ruhr, in the brown-coal fields of central Germany, in Saxony, Silesia, Berlin and southern Germany, reversed this situation almost overnight. Of a total population of more than 50 million in 1900 (compared with 41 million in 1871), 54 per cent lived in industrial cities. The urbanisation of Germany was accompanied by changes in the economic and social structure as well. Though some 50 per cent of the labour force was employed in forestry and agriculture in 1871, this figure declined to less than 35 per cent in 1900. Industry, mining, commerce and the public service absorbed vast numbers of new employees and soon provided more employment than the agricultural sector. The strong demand for labour, combined with the fact that free land was no longer available in the United States, prompted an abrupt decline in the high emigration rate. By 1900 the number of emigrants was matched by the number of immigrants moving into the *Reich* from Austria-Hungary, the Russian region of Poland, Italy and south-eastern Europe.

Not only industry prospered but agriculture as well. Production rose in response to continually rising prices and increasingly rational and scientific husbandry. The grain and potato harvest more than doubled during the last thirty years of the nineteenth century. Nevertheless, the mounting population could not be fed without steady increases in exports of industrial goods, especially since improvements in the standard of living spurred demand for highly nutritious foods such as flour and meat. Exports also had to earn enough foreign exchange to pay for enormous imports of raw materials such as cotton, ores and rubber demanded by German industry. Thus the empire grew increasingly reliant on exports of German products and imports of foreign goods.

The dominant place of industry in the national economy was described in the early 1880s using Berlin as an example:

If we quickly glance at commerce and industry in Berlin, we are struck by the gigantic size of most enterprises. A few particular industries will illustrate the point. Beer production has risen to previously unimaginable levels, and Berlin now surpasses any other German city with fifty-six breweries consuming an annual total of some 850,000 hundredweights of malt. Iron foundries and machine-building have lost none of their traditional renown. These 'workshops of the modern Cyclopes' supply a large portion of the demand both in Germany and abroad. From the day the Borsig works was founded by the 'machine king' in 1841, it has manufactured far more than 3000 locomotives. They carry Berlin's reputation for iron to the far corners of the earth. Besides these behemoths, hundreds of thousands of sewing machines are exported annually from approximately one hundred factories to be found in Berlin alone. Twenty thousand people work in some 300 machine shops and iron foundries. The last decades have witnessed the blossoming of the garment industry which has settled on Berlin as its German centre. Ladies' coats have enjoyed particular success, and annual revenues from coats sold only in Berlin are estimated at 50 million marks. This industry employs about 60,000 workers and its exports are substantial, reaching 12 million marks in 1883 in both England and America.[2]

Not only heavy industry and textiles flourished but also modern economic sectors highly dependent on scientific innovation—electronics, pharmaceutics, and the chemical industry with its emphasis on artificial dyes and chemical fertilizers.

At the same time, more and more Germans found employment in the mining industry. Bituminous coal was mined at ever-increasing depths and the production of brown coal from open-cast pits reached startling levels in response to rising demand from the electrical and chemical industries. A potash deposit discovered in Alsace at the turn of the century gave Germany a world monopoly on this product.

Hand in hand with intensifying industrialisation went an enormous expansion of the transportation system. The Kiel Canal between the North Sea and the Baltic was inaugurated in 1895 and construction began on the *Mittelland* canal. An ever more extensive railway system opened up every corner of the *Reich*. By 1900 more goods were shipped through Hamburg than through London, Liverpool or Marseilles and the German port took over third place in the world behind New York and Antwerp. Meanwhile, the Hamburg—America Line developed into the world's largest shipping company. The label 'Made in Germany', required by a British law of 1887 on all goods exported from the *Reich*, was increasingly viewed in the world as a sign of high quality.

The technological achievements of the age invaded everyday life, altering the habits of virtually everyone. Notwithstanding the enthusiastic popular response to the marvels of the modern era, the benefits of modern medicine, and the alleviation of many tasks in the home and on the job, a sense of foreboding was widespread. The following passage appeared in a contemporary novel:

The emerging wonders were bright, hard and sharp. With lightning-speed they mowed down the manners and customs of the ages. They rearranged the physiognomy of the city and burst asunder a way of life that had endured for centuries. It was the age when the automobile first appeared, puffing and shaking its way over sentimental attachments and pensive dreams. It transformed with an abruptness never previously imagined the face of the city—like a visible symbol of the rapidity of technological change. In comparison with this despotic intruder, how much quieter and inconspicuous the telephone had seemed! Tramways too had emerged slowly, almost imperceptibly, from horse-drawn carriages running on rails to full electrification. But the automobile simply raced into view one day, without sign or warning. It just appeared, screeching out 'I shall overtake you' to passers-by. And it did—especially those who dared to climb in and to imagine that they were steering the automobile when in reality its spirit was guiding and shaping them.[3]

Just a few years after Gottlieb Daimler and Karl Benz conquered the road with their automobile, Count Ferdinand von Zeppelin began work on his airship, and Otto Lilienthal built the first aircraft.

The rise of the machine, the emphasis on technological innovation and Germany's extraordinary economic advancement created a myriad of competing economic interests. As society evolved, groups sought to exert political pressure in order preserve and advance their own cause. Social and economic associations began to exert a mounting influence over political parties, and the internal policies of the government succeeded in severely curtailing traditional economic liberalism.

Trade unionism developed into a mass movement in the 1990s. Besides their traditional concern for social issues, the unions took a strong interest in working conditions and strove to improve the workers' standard of living. The labour movement split into social-ist, liberal and Christian camps, reflecting philosophical and politi-cal differences. The socialist unions, first founded in 1860, united under the leadership of Carl Legiens in 1890 to form the 'General Commission of Free German Trade Unions', the largest union on the continent of Europe. The 'Free Unions' were closely affiliated with the Social Democratic Party, despite many tensions between them, and they encouraged an increasingly revisionist tendency within the party. In comparison with the Free Unions, the liberal Hirsch-Duncker unions, with their nationalist bent, were quite small.

Somewhat larger and more influential were the Christian unions founded in 1894–5. They supported the Centrist Party and, like the Free Unions, sought to advance the concrete interests of the work-ers through customary trade-union means. However, they rejected all notions of class warfare as irreconcilable with Christian ethics, though they acknowledged that society did have a class structure.

Consistent with the social teachings of the Catholic Church as elaborated by Pope Leo XIII in his encyclical *Rerum Novarum* (1891), the Christian unions believed that the common weal was the highest priority of the political order and that it could only be fostered through legislation and the authority of the state.[4]

Among Protestants, the National Social League founded by Pastor Friedrich Naumann in 1896 sought to integrate the working class into the *Reich* by promoting trade-union rights and a democratic government.

The working class was not the only segment of German society to form clubs and organisations. Business associations had been established as early as the 1870s to promote a protective tariff and to defend industrial interests. In the 1890s employers' associations were formed to represent industrial interests in their dealings with government and the trade unions. In 1893 agrarian interests founded a league to agitate for lower taxes on German agriculture, high tariffs on foreign agricultural products and the creation of chambers of agriculture. The Agrarian League had its own candidates stand for election to the *Reichstag* and thereby acquired considerable political influence. Since the Agrarian League represented primarily large landowners, it had many sympathisers in the government bureaucracy and ministries, and its political clout quickly eclipsed that of the trade unions and business organisations.

While all of these groups pursued predominantly social and economic aims, other associations with a more political agenda also emerged. Many of them promoted a vigorous brand of nationalism and imperialism. Typical of this type of association, recruited largely from the middle class, were the Pan-German League (*Alldeutscher Verband*), the German Colonial Association (*Deutscher Kolonialverein*) and the German Navy League (*Deutscher Flottenverein*). All three were created in the 1890s to agitate for an aggressive colonial, naval and foreign policy. They hoped to see the establishment of German hegemony over the Continent as the springboard to a grand world policy rivaling that of Britain.

These social, economic and political pressure groups had a strong and immediate influence on political parties. The introduction of equal, universal suffrage and the social transformation engendered by industrialism caused the political parties to evolve from loose associations of local notables with similar views into tightly-knit organisations. The various interest groups provided financial assistance to sympathetic political parties, especially at election time, thus assisting candidates who previously had to finance their own campaigns. This gave the interest groups influence over the list of candidates and thereby over the entire *Reichstag*.

As a result of this phenomenon, trade unions gained increasing leverage within the Social Democratic Party after the turn of the century. Influenced by generally favourable economic conditions and rising real wages, they used their clout to strengthen the revisionist tendencies within the party. Despite resistance from the party leadership, the drift away from revolutionary Marxism could no longer be stemmed. Everyday involvement in the legal political process also tended to shift the party's emphasis away from revolutionary Marxism and towards reform. Yet even though they relinquished most of their Marxist ideology, in fact if not in theory, the Social Democrats remained the pariahs of the political system.

Middle-class liberalism had already lost its mass appeal in Bismarck's era and only survived as a small movement limited to largely Protestant intellectuals and segments of the upper bourgeoisie. It promoted restorative and nationalist policies through the National Liberal Party.

Left-wing liberalism split into several parties which drew support primarily from professionals and some strata of merchants and artisans. These liberals advocated a parliamentary monarchy along British lines, and their growing sensitivity to social problems induced them to cooperate with the Social Democrats on some issues, especially in the last years of the *Reich*.

The tightly organised Centre Party appealed to the Roman Catholic minority within the predominantly Prussian and Protestant empire. Drawing support from all social strata, the Centrists avoided overidentification with any particular interest group. They pursued a policy of social equity and attempted to balance the interests of entrepreneurs, peasants and workers. Strongly nationalist like the liberals and conservatives, the Centre Party used its influence in the *Reichstag* to support colonial and imperialist endeavours.

The conservative parties drew their strength not from sheer numbers but from their intimate relationship with the traditional social élite of landed nobility, military officers, government bureaucrats and Protestant clergymen. They strove to preserve the social privileges of their supporters, venerated the monarch 'by the grace of God', and championed a role for Germany as an imperialist world power. The German Conservative Party acted in close cooperation with the most powerful rural interest group, the Agrarian League, and thereby acquired a broad base of support for its socially reactionary policies. The 'Free Conservatives' campaigning under the name of the *Deutsche Reichspartei* derived the lion's share of their support from industrial interests.

The numerous conflicts between these associations and parties reflected the deep antagonism which still prevailed between social groups and classes and which failed to dissipate after Bismarck's departure. This antagonism had its roots in the tensions of a modern industrial society governed by a traditional feudal élite. The deeply engrained rigidities and hostilities made it impossible for the political structure to adapt to the modern era.

The aristocracy formed the greatest obstacle to harmonious relations by standing on its traditional right to rule. It clung tenaciously to ancestral privileges and sought to isolate itself from other social classes. The nobility's privileged position in the army, the diplomatic corps and the upper echelons of the civil service remained unabbreviated and in Prussia was reinforced by the three-class franchise. The middle class, drawing on its economic power, rose to prominence in many aspects of social, civic and cultural life, but was still largely excluded from political power by the existing constitution.

The extent to which the nobility and bourgeoisie were isolated from one another was best described in a letter by Theodor Fontane:

You know as well as I or better, that there are establishments in our fair land of Prussia (as in every other land) to which one must submit. These establishments are of various kinds: the wealthy, the nobility, army officers, civil servants, professors. The trick is to have life and your special gifts deposit you in the right place. For if you don't wind up in the right place, misery will ensue. Bankers' sons are scorned by army officers or professors while officers are held to be no better than beggars in banking circles.[5]

At the bottom of the social pyramid came peasants and workers, though each of these classes was further subdivided. Small farmers, artisans and labourers lived a modest, at times scanty existence, even though living and working conditions steadily improved after the turn of the century. Real penury still existed among large working-class families, widows with small children and the handicapped. Women's work was underpaid and women were generally denied the same chances for advancement which men enjoyed. The first women were admitted to the university merely as auditors in 1891.

At the end of the nineteenth century the youth movement arose in opposition to rigid convention and the strict separation of social classes. Rebelling against life in the big cities, youths set out on country hikes to discover nature and a new relationship with the common people. They sought to unite Germans of all social strata and classes and looked for inspiration to the social philosophy produced by the Wars of Liberation. Rejecting the narrow rigidity of the German home and school, they demanded greater personal freedom—a freedom which they hoped to transmit to society and the state in order to forge a nation based on true community.

Economic and social life in Germany were revolutionised in the second half of the nineteenth century, but the intellectual and cultural spheres failed to undergo the same tumultuous change till much later. Late romanticism and various revivalist movements remained the dominant tendencies in the arts until 1910, when expressionism began to take hold. The rapidly improving standard of living often prompted an exaggerated interest in material possessions. Never before had Germany witnessed such a scramble for property, success, power and prestige. The broad masses trusted unquestioningly in rationalism and science, though the belief in progress as propagated by positivism was being increasingly undermined by the spread of cultural pessimism emanating from the works of Arthur Schopenhauer. Relativism rooted in greater historical awareness also grew more popular and was expressed in Friedrich Nietzsche's *Vom Nutzen und Nachteil der Historie für das Leben* (Of the Use and Abuse of History for Life) and later in Ernst Troeltsch's treatise, *Historismus und seine Probleme* (Historicism and Its Problems).

The sciences flowered and grew more and more specialised. Stunning discoveries in science and medicine were matched by great technological advances. Sigmund Freud's concept of psychoanalysis and his book *The Interpretation of Dreams* (1900) proved extremely influential throughout the coming century. The humanities, and especially history, also underwent increasing differentiation.

Science and technology expanded mightily in the universities and *technische Hochschulen*, and in 1911 the 'Kaiser William Society for the Advancement of Science' was established.[6] It freed outstanding scholars from their teaching duties in the universities in order to devote themselves fully to research. The quality of the research done in these various institutions long assured Germany of a leading role in the natural sciences. At the same time schools were modernised and grammar-school graduates were admitted to academic studies and thence to senior positions in the civil service.

Notwithstanding all the signs of progress and scientific accomplishment, a sense of cultural malaise, rooted in Schopenhauer and historicism, began to emerge, especially among the intellectual élite. The pessimistic outlook elaborated by Schopenhauer in his principal work, *Die Welt als Wille und Vorstellung* (The World as Will and Mental Representation) was widely embraced. Friedrich Nietzsche revived Schopenhauer's influence and importance for the second half of the nineteenth century in the third of his *Unzeitgemässe Betrachtungen*, characteristically entitled *Schopenhauer als Erzieher* (Schopenhauer, the Educator). The intellectual impact of Nietzche's own writings was described by a contemporary observer in the following terms:

Scarcely has an era ever been so revisionist-minded as that of Nietzsche, so recklessly determined to 're-evaluate all values'. But would Nietzsche's work have been so epoch-making at another time? Whether consciously or not, the spirit of the times penetrates far deeper than is commonly realised. But was this spirit created by Nietzsche? or did he simply flourish in it and give it philosophical expression? Never would Nietzsche have created such a sensation, never would he have elicited such an enthusiastic response, if the ground had not been so fertile. He appeared to his acolytes as the messiah 'for the time was come'. He lent—in his magnificent way!—the speechless eloquence and the blind sight. Covert anti-Christianity, the unconscious religious and ethical nihilism to which no one previously dared to admit though it was smouldering in many, suddenly found its 'master', its 'scientific expression'.[7]

Nietzsche's ideas met with such resonance because of a profound sense of disquiet and discontent. Industry and technology had brought enormous material advancement, but the social and spiritual problems they generated were far from resolved. The result was a reaction against the bourgeois world and the ideals it proclaimed. 'Progress' became suspect. The state and society had imposed an all-enveloping order and discipline on the individual in the name of progress, and in many cases the intellectual youth reacted by discarding all traditional rules and fleeing into irrationalism. This social phenomenon was analysed by the Berlin philosopher Friedrich Paulsen:

Intellectual anarchy is the individual's reaction to the incessant admonishment and censure he suffers at school and in church, at the hands of society and the state. The 'proper' attitude towards all things—whether historical and political, religious and moral, or literary and linguistic—is pounded into us through years of schooling and examinations, public censure and private rebuke, and the tedious, verbose rhetoric of patriotic celebrations. The effect of all this discipline is to make what it advocates appear insufferable, insipid and jejune. Therefore we tear everything down and throw it away—the proper views and old truths, the conventional standards and the spent icons, finally even logic and morality. We throw ourselves into a Saturnalia of paradox celebrating the re-evaluation of all values.[8]

Contemporary literature bore witness to the declining faith in progress and to the trend away from the rationalism and positivism at the heart of the naturalist movement. Literary realism which had coexisted with naturalism continued to prosper with such writers as Theodor Fontane and Thomas Mann. In reaction to naturalism, the Romantic sensibility experienced a revival in Viennese Neo-Romanticism with its refined sensitivity and search for beautiful forms. The mounting wealth of the German bourgeoisie rendered a new bohemian life-style possible and supported an avant-garde of aesthetes.

On the stage, the naturalist plays of Gerhart Hauptmann in particular were produced alongside traditional classical works. The operetta reached new heights with Johann Strauss, Franz Léhar and Karl Zeller, and the new medium of film began to develop.

Music around 1900 was dominated by Richard Wagner. His art influenced the young Gustav Mahler and lingers in the work of Richard Strauss, especially in the symphonic poems. Late Romantic strains can be heard in the music of Max Reger and Hans Pfitzner, while Anton Bruckner and the later Mahler escaped Wagner's thrall and developed a style of their own. However, music did not set off in an entirely new direction until the second Viennese school with Arnold Schönberg and his pupils.

Painting and sculpture were strongly influenced at first by a type of official art advocated by William II. This style found expression in Anton von Werner's colossal paintings of battles and uniformed men and in the statues of princes adorning the *Siegesallee* which the emperor had constructed in Berlin. The view of the German past was heavily influenced not only by Werner but also by Adolph von Menzel, who depicted the age of Frederick the Great. This official, academic art was countered by styles derived from French Impressionism, which began to reach their high-water mark in Germany in the early 1890s in the work of such painters as Max Liebermann and Lovis Corinth. Art Nouveau carried on the rejection of historical subjects and furthered the trend towards aestheticism and symbolism. The early German Expressionists then spurned both historicism and aestheticism in order to portray elemental, primordial experience.

Architecture passed through a period of indiscriminate imitation of traditional styles before taking up Art Nouveau between 1900 and 1910. Thereafter architecture settled into a clean, simple, functional style making use of concrete and iron.

The popular sport movement developed such momentum that it burst all social and class barriers and spread throughout society.

Sports of all kinds joined the gymnastics movement spawned by the Wars of Liberation as favourite pastimes.

The turn of the century thus witnessed an array of trends and movements in which broad strata of the population participated through popular science, public libraries, evening courses and worker education. Yet all this frenetic activity could not resolve the cultural crisis, especially virulent in educated circles, and German society failed to develop the stability that comes from a firm foundation of clear convictions and principles.

Internal Policy after 1890

The young emperor, William II, initiated a 'new course' in response to the gathering pressures within the empire. The numbing immo-bility of the last decades of Bismarck's chancellorship was to be overcome by thorough-going reform. Anxious 'to reign and rule'[9] in person, William was determined to subvert the channels of authority set out in the Constitution and to reduce the chancellor's role to that of a mere executor of the emperor's will. In a speech before the Provincial Assembly of Brandenburg in 1891, William stated, 'I hold that my position and duties have been conferred upon me by Heaven above and that I have been summoned to serve a higher authority to which I shall one day have to answer.'[10] Con-sistent with this conception, he aimed to restore a semi-absolutist regime incompatible with the form of government anchored in the Constitution. The contradiction between William's reformist pro-clivities and fondness for old-fashioned absolutism was recognised even by his contemporaries as the supreme obstacle to the evolution of a modern political system. Theodor Fontane commented in 1897:

What I like about the emperor is his clean break with the past; and what I dislike about him is his desire to revive the ancient past. . . . He believes he can serve the present with antiquated means, he wants to build a modern state with tools from the junkheap. He offers new wine, and because he no longer trusts the old wine-skins he binds them with ever thicker thread and thinks: now they will hold. But they will not hold.[11]

Gifted with a quick mind, high intelligence, a remarkable memory and a rich imagination, William had a flair for all that was new and modern. His passionate rhetoric could be impressive. But his con-genitally crippled arm, his poor relationship with his parents and the harshness of his upbringing left him sadly lacking in self-confidence. Restless and unsettled, he was without the steadfastness of his grandfather and the bent for steady, serious work which government affairs demand. Erratic and unsure of himself, always craving popular acclaim, he proved incapable of defining and resolutely pursuing a particular policy. His impulsiveness and vulnerability to flattery and cajolery exasperated the political authorities. Lacking political sensitivity and all sense of proportion, he vacillated between boundless optimism and defeatist fits of depression. In his pride and vanity he was 'a figure not without tragedy, but limited in stature'.[12] In a malicious moment his uncle King Edward VII of England once called him history's most brilliant failure.[13] Concealing his self-doubt beneath a dashing and forceful exterior, William struggled to overcome the ever-broadening gulf between the great responsibilities that he had assumed and his own inability to meet those responsibilities. In this he epitomised the deficiency of his entire generation in Germany.

Almost pathologically afraid of men of strong and independent mind who might tend to dominate him, the young emperor turned to General Leo von Caprivi as Bismarck's successor. William expected that Caprivi, a soldier accustomed to military discipline, would defer to his conception of personal rule. The new leadership tandem set about implementing those social designs to which Bismarck had been so adamantly opposed. The socialist laws were not extended and protective legislation for workers was introduced. Sunday labour was banned, child labourers under the age of thirteen were no longer allowed in factories, youths under sixteen were limited to a ten-hour working day and women to eleven hours. Industrial courts were instituted to resolve disputes between employers and employees and to ensure greater social security for the working masses. According to the leader of the Bavarian Social Democrats, Georg von Vollmar, these reforms did much to alleviate 'the greatest curse afflicting the empire'; 'The first steps towards an improvement were taken'.[14]

The tense social situation in Prussia was mitigated by tax reforms which introduced progressive income and wealth taxes, restructured inheritance and commercial taxes, and directed commercial and property taxes to local governments. The three-class franchise in Prussia was reformed to create small electoral groups within the classes.

At Caprivi's initiative, trade agreements were reached primarily with other European states in order to open foreign markets to German industry. This ensured more stable demand for German products and greater security of employment. In return, Germany partially reformed her policy of high protective tariffs and reduced import duties on livestock, lumber, wheat and rye. The price of bread in Germany declined as a result, and the standard of living of the working class rose perceptibly.

The Social Democrats supported these treaties in the *Reichstag* and for the first time voted in favour of a government bill; but the Conservatives were outraged. Heavily influenced by the Agrarian League and voicing the concerns of large landowning interests, the Conservatives henceforth opposed Caprivi's economic policy. The governments of Prussia and the *Reich* slowly swung back to a more conservative course, and progressive social policies came under increased attack. William II expected Social Democrats to support his government out of gratitude for the social initiatives it had taken, but the Social Democrats continued their opposition. Bitterly disappointed, William abruptly reversed his field and reverted to Bismarck's hardline tactics. The Social Democrats were again decried as 'the party of revolution' and William demanded the enactment of another emergency law against them. When Caprivi firmly opposed this course, his days as chancellor were numbered.

Caprivi's attempt 'to lead the nation back to normalcy after an era of great men and deeds'[15] required the achievement of a broad social compromise. He experienced some initial success in this direction, but foundered in the end on William's inability to stear a steady course.

Caprivi was succeeded as chancellor by seventy-five-year-old Prince Chlodwig zu Hohenlohe-Schillingsfürst, who had been foreign minister and prime minister of Bavaria from 1866 to 1870, German ambassador in Paris for a short period after the founding of the *Reich*, and then governor of Alsace-Lorraine after 1885. Hohenlohe's appointment as chancellor greatly surprised contemporary observers, and even William considered it merely a stop-gap measure. The aged Hohenlohe could no longer summon the energy to carry out the functions of his office and to contend with the complex problems facing the empire—a task that was further complicated by the indecisiveness and capriciousness of the emperor. Lacking any insight into the salient issue of the times—the social question—he gave full rein to the forces of reaction. He inherited from his predecessor the so-called Revolution Bill proposing severe punishments for political offenders; but when he introduced it in the *Reichstag* in December 1894 it was soundly defeated.

Despite this setback, the government continued the attack, moving to limit the right of combination which had legalised union activities. In September 1898 William even threatened to imprison anyone who encouraged strikes or impeded strike-breakers.[16]

However, this policy raised the ire not only of deputies in the *Reichstag* but of the population at large, which felt outrage to its sense of fairness and justice. When the Prison Bill was defeated in Parliament, the government reverted after the turn of the century to attempts to alleviate the most serious social abuses. But by now the atmosphere was so poisoned by the previous attempts to ride roughshod over basic principles of justice that the relationship between the state and the working class could not be repaired.

William II proved as capricious and unreliable as ever in implementing this second phase of the 'new course', and mounting tensions with the chancellor were inevitable. In 1897 William dismissed Hohenlohe's closest collaborators, and the chancellor grew increasingly isolated. Finally he asked to be relieved of his duties. The reasons he adduced provide an excellent illustration of William's behaviour:

Everything related to foreign policy is discussed and decided by HM and Bülow. Internal policy is formulated by ministers who do consult with me because they know that HM does not take my advice. I am held accountable by the press and called to answer before the *Reichstag* for matters of which I have no knowledge. All appointments and promotions are decided without seeking my advice and without even informing me.[17]

After Prince Hohenlohe's retirement in October 1900, the task of reconciling the emperor's contradictory whims and wishes with the prevailing sentiment in the *Reichstag* fell to the new chancellor, Bernhard von Bülow. Bülow was a flexible, intelligent and highly educated diplomat who had led the Foreign Office since 1897. In this skilful political tactician William believed he had finally found the right man to implement his instructions dutifully and diligently. Bülow continued even as chancellor to concentrate most of his attention on foreign affairs, leaving the secretary of state for internal affairs, Count Arthur von Posadowsky-Wehner, with a virtual free hand in domestic matters.

Posadowsky was eager to reduce social tensions. He eschewed the repression of Social Democracy and revived the reform policies pursued under Caprivi. The sickness and accident insurance schemes were substantially improved and the industrial courts, formerly optional, were made mandatory in communities of over 20,000 inhabitants. The laws governing child labour were extended to cottage industries, and state grants were offered to encourage the construction of working-class apartments. The restrictive combination laws, which prevented unions from joining forces with one another, had already been repealed under Hohenlohe's chancellorship. In sum, many of the essential demands of the labour unions and of the Social Democratic Party were met. Moreover, Posadowsky succeeded in effecting a compromise between industry and agriculture during negotiation of a renewal of the trade agreements originally concluded by Caprivi. A modest increase in tariff rates appeased agrarian interests without seriously damaging industrial exports. However, higher tariffs sparked an increase in the general cost of living, and the new duties with their increased levies on grain remained a source of great controversy. The federal government also failed to overcome its financial dependence on the states. An inheritance tax—the first direct federal assessment—was levied in 1906, but it did not suffice to prevent steep increases in the federal debt.

Bülow's government had found its most reliable parliamentary ally in the Centre Party, but the 1904 rebellion of Hereros and Hottentots against German rule in South-West Africa precipitated a rupture. This occurred when the Centrists joined forces with the Social Democrats to defeat a supplementary budget which the government introduced in order to strengthen German forces in the colony. Bülow dissolved the *Reichstag*, and after the ensuing election sought support from the liberals and conservatives who formed the new majority. However, the conservatives disliked Posadowsky because of the social reforms he had introduced and the liberals distrusted him because of his record of cooperation with the Centrists. Posadowsky clearly could not continue and was forced to resign in favour of the former Prussian minister of interior, Theobald von Bethmann Hollweg. The liberals wished to see the prerogatives of the *Reichstag* extended and the three-class franchise in Prussia abolished, while the conservatives adamantly opposed these reforms. The political system was however evolving. The *Reichstag* grew steadily more important and its influence was on the increase relative to that of the *Bundesrat*, especially as a result of the financial reforms undertaken by Chancellor Bülow. Nevertheless, the three-class franchise in Prussia continued to result in extremely conservative political policies in what was by far the largest state in the empire, and the conflicts that arose because of the discrepancy between the imperial and Prussian electoral laws dogged the empire until its eventual demise in 1918.

The problem of electoral reform eventually destroyed the alliance between liberals and conservatives. At the same time, William II initiated the '*Daily Telegraph* affair' by his offensive and politically foolish remarks in an interview with the English newspaper. The mounting crisis was resolved by Bülow's departure and an end to the emperor's experiment with 'personal rule'. His remarks had offended Englishmen and Germans alike and had done irreparable damage to his prestige. The German government, the public and the deputies of all parties were united in their outrage over his irresponsible deportment and in their desire for an end to personal rule. The National-Liberal deputy Bassermann commented:

Political interest in all segments of the population has been awakened as never before and a feeling has arisen that things cannot go on as they are. . . . People are asking, what should be done? We can only say one thing: the public demands firm guarantees that there will be no return to personal rule.[18]

The establishment of parliamentary government would doubtless have afforded the best guarantee of this, but most of the parties in the *Reichstag* were not ready for such a radical step. The left liberals hoped to cooperate with the Social Democrats in order to create eventually a parliamentary monarchy in which the ministers would be responsible to the *Reichstag*. But even the left liberals preferred gradual reform to radical transformation. In the meantime Germany remained undemocratic and politically backward compared to the other modern states of Europe.

Even the antiquated electoral system in Prussia could not be reformed. A continuation of the reform policies pursued under Chancellor Bülow and his secretary of state for internal affairs, Posadowsky, was impracticable because of strong conservative opposition. (The government now had to rely on the parliamentary support of the conservatives together with National Liberals and Centrists if it wished to avoid dependence on the left.) If the conservative resistance was to be overcome, Bülow's successor, Bethmann Hollweg, would have to prevail over strong conservative influence in the officer corps, in the higher echelons of the civil service and in pressure groups such as the Agrarian League, the Pan-German Association and the Colonial and Navy Leagues. Bethmann Hollweg, a 'grind'—'ein schwerer Pflüger'[19]—in contrast with his slick and urbane predecessor, simply lacked the will and the finesse to confront such a powerful array of forces. Only in Alsace-Lorraine did he effect constitutional reform—a reform which brought self-government to the *Reichsland* and made it an equal partner in the empire.

On the eve of the Great War, Germany was still strongly divided into hostile groups and classes and was burdened by a government which failed to reflect the social reality. Neither the *Reichstag* nor the various chancellors who succeeded Bismarck were able to effect the social compromise essential to the emergence of a modern political system. The political vacuum created by Bismarck's departure remained unfilled and the art of governing declined into mere bureaucratic administration. 'When the world war began', a contemporary was later to remark, 'Germany was the economically strongest, the best-administered but the worst-governed country in Europe.'[20] While the political leaders failed to resolve the stresses in the social fabric, the bureaucracy amassed ever greater power. Eventually it developed a momentum of its own which successive governments found difficult to control. And yet—despite powerful domestic tensions and the disproportion between socio-economic power and political power, despite an emperor eager for personal rule though unfitted for such responsibilities and a strong conservative heritage at odds with the driving forces of the era—none of the contending forces cast doubt on the validity of the German Empire as the national home of the German people.

Imperialism and Colonialism

While the structure of the German Empire slowly evolved and the internal political struggle carried on, the outlook of all the great powers of Europe was being transformed by profound changes in traditional intellectual and political views. New strains of political thought, with ramifications far beyond the nation-state, emerged in Britain and quickly spread to the Continent. A generation of Germans was inspired by the British example to see the consummation of their nationalist sentiments in 'the spread of German influence around the world'.[21]

This desire, known as imperialism, fostered an atmosphere of crisis and confrontation. 'Imperialism' originally implied 'the personal dominion of a great ruler over a number of different territories whether in Europe or overseas'; in the late nineteenth century it 'shed its restriction to a system typified by the existence of a single great ruler and came to be generally understood as a means of extending the power of the nation-state beyond its own borders in an effort to acquire independent territories overseas and to weld these territories, if possible, into a world empire.'[22] Thus imperialism came to connote 'the violent extension of national rule to generally underdeveloped territories, regardless of the desires of the local population, for the purpose of creating a colonial empire likely to enhance the prestige of the mother country in the circle of great powers. The crowning glory was to achieve the status of a world power'.[23] Imperialism was often seen as the inevitable consequence of the rise of nation-states. 'Relentless expansion of the nation-state, if necessary by violent means, and the creation of an overseas empire seemed desirable first, for the preservation and advancement of one's own nationality and, second, as a wellspring of renewed vitality.'[24]

The imperialist endeavours of the great powers were also actuated of course by strong economic motives. Marxist and non-Marxist historians alike have emphasised this aspect of modern imperialism and have often interpreted imperialism as an inevitable consequence of the economic and social system of the industrial states. The essence of imperialism is seen in high levels of capital exports and the merging of financial and industrial capital or else in the aggressiveness of traditional political élites eager to preserve their power.[25]

The origins of imperialism were however much more varied. It derived intellectually from a mingling of nationalist ideology with popular Darwinism proclaiming the natural right of the strong over the weak. The original moral justification of the nation-state—that each people possesses the inherent right of self-determination—was entirely disregarded. The great powers justified their complete reversal of attitude by claiming that they embodied human progress. The relations between the peoples of the world were conceived as a power struggle, whether overt or covert, and the will of the industrial nations to win this struggle was fired by a strong belief in the superiority of their own race, religion and civilisation. The English, in accordance with their Puritan heritage, believed that they had a divine mission to educate and civilise the rest of the world. Accordingly the Enlightenment and England's proud parliamentary tradition became distorted into a crude brand of political moralism. Cecil Rhodes, the most successful advocate of British expansion in Africa and later prime minister of Cape Colony, wrote in his last will and testament, 'I contend that we are the first race in the world and that the more of the world we inhabit, the better it is for the human race.' Since God has evidently forged the English race into his chosen instrument, Rhodes continued, through which he intends to build a community based on peace, justice and freedom, he obviously wishes Englishmen to do all they are able to gain for their race as much power and territory as possible and to paint British red as much of the map of Africa as they can.[26]

The French were equally convinced of the superiority of their nation rooted in the traditions of the Enlightenment and the French Revolution. They commonly believed, as Jules Ferry phrased it, that 'the higher races have rights because they have duties. It is their duty to civilise the lesser races.'[27]

The Russians pointed to Moscow's place at the heart of the Orthodox Church and deduced therefrom a claim to lead the Slavic world. Feodor Mikhailovich Dostoevsky openly envisaged in his *Diary of a Writer* the expansion of Russian civilisation across the length and breadth of Asia:

As we push into Asia our intellectual powers will revive. . . . In Europe we were nothing but slaves and beggars but in Asia we are masters. In Europe we were Tatars, but in Asia we are Europeans. Our civilising mission in Asia will enchant our spirit as soon as the movement begins.[28]

The young German Empire with its fledgling national pride aspired as well to the glory of a colonial empire. 'The days', said Chancellor Bülow, 'when Germany renounced the earth in favour of one of her neighbours and the seas in favour of another, reserving for herself only the skies above, . . . those days have passed. We do not wish to overshadow anyone, but we want our place in the sun.'[29]

The Americans, heirs to the heritage of their pilgrim forefathers, were equally convinced that the United States was a great nation and could ill-afford to abstain from the crusade to spread civilisation around the world and advance the cause of the white race.[30]

All the great nation-states sought to extend their political rule far beyond the limits of their own borders, convinced that failure to keep pace in the struggle for colonies would eternally condemn them to second-rate status in the councils of the world. Political hegemony seemed the only way to satisfy their thirst for prestige. In a passionate speech to the nation in 1872, Disraeli demanded to know whether Englishmen wished to content themselves with the comfortable but subordinate role of a merely continental power or whether they were prepared to become a truly great nation, 'an imperial country, a country where your sons, when they rise, rise to paramount positions and obtain not merely the esteem of their countrymen but command the respect of the world'.[31]

From an economic viewpoint, imperialism appears to be a logical outgrowth of the Industrial Revolution. Relentless industrialisation created large pools of capital which were reinvested in immense new means of production till local markets were finally saturated and an overseas demand was required. At the same time, the population of the industrialised countries was rising rapidly and new sources of raw materials had to be made available. Mounting imports of foodstuffs and raw materials and the compulsion to export surplus industrial goods created a sense of economic dependence and a concomitant desire to gain political control over regions of primary economic importance. This in turn exacerbated the political tensions between the great powers.

The people heeded the imperialist message of their political élites and in many cases provided enthusiastic support—with the exception of autocratic Russia, where the bulk of the population was not allowed any voice in national affairs. Their ardour was all the more intense in that all strata of the population were said to benefit from imperialist expansion. The working class was no exception to the rule and placed great stock in the civilising mission of the imperial powers. Furthermore, as the Social Democrat Eduard Bernstein pointed out, the proletariat considered itself the historical heir of the bourgeoisie and as such had a direct interest in the rational geographic expansion of the nation. 'The colonies are there', Bernstein said, 'one ought to occupy them.'[32]

The concept of imperialism first took hold in England. As a result of her early industrialisation, the need for new markets and for new sources of raw materials were felt at a relatively early date. England, moreover, had a surplus population and Puritanism had imbued her people with a strong belief in their divine mission to spread their purportedly superior religion and civilisation. These factors taken together resulted in the establishment of an enormous empire. It was Britain's second empire—arising after the defection of the American colonies—and it expanded steadily throughout the second half of the nineteenth century, sometimes through peaceful penetration and sometimes through violent conquest.

This second stage of British colonialism was sparked by a great revolt that broke out in India in 1857 against abusive administration of the country by the East India Company. The British government put down the Indian revolt, though with great difficulty, and one year later decided to dissolve the East India Company and to transform its holdings into a crown colony. British foreign policy was henceforth largely determined by the need to defend this greatest 'jewel in the British crown' and to protect the sea lanes that linked it to the motherland.

A strong military presence was established in the Mediterranean Sea, the Persian Gulf and the Indian Ocean, especially between 1874 and 1880 under the prime-ministership of Benjamin Disraeli, the first consistent exponent of modern imperialism. In 1875 Britain purchased 51 per cent of the shares in the Suez Canal, which the Frenchman Ferdinand de Lesseps had finished constructing in 1869. For more than seventy years Britain retained sovereignty over this strategic passageway which shortened the journey to India by 10,000 km. Two years later Disraeli persuaded Queen Victoria to accept the title of 'Empress of India'. At the same time the British conquered Baluchistan and in 1878 signed a treaty granting them a naval base in Cyprus in addition to those they already possessed in Gibraltar, Malta, and Aden, which had been occupied in 1838. The Russian advance into Turkey was halted and a war was waged to bring Afghanistan into the British orbit. In 1882 Egypt was seized and East Africa occupied, thereby securing the western rim of the Indian Ocean. India was then protected to the east by the occupation of Burma and by checking the French thrust into Indo-China. In 1884 the French had acquired Tongking and Annam from the Chinese and occupied Laos, Cambodia and Cochin China; but when they moved up the Mekong River towards Bangkok, Britain imposed a treaty that defined the British and French spheres of interest and recognised the sovereignty of the Kingdom of Siam.

The advance into the African interior, initiated by such explorers as David Livingstone and Henry Morton Stanley, continued. In the hope of herding all of Southern Africa into the British fold, Cecil Rhodes founded the enormous colony of Rhodesia, surrounding the white Boer republics of the Transvaal and the Orange Free State. Rhodes also planned a 9000 km railway and telegraph line from Cairo to Cape Town. The Boers refused, however, to submit to British rule, and a bitter war erupted which was waged with extreme cruelty on both sides. Eventually the Boers submitted to British rule, though they were soon granted full self-administration. Cape Colony, Natal, the Transvaal and the Orange Free State united to form the South African Union, which achieved dominion status after Canada, Australia and New Zealand. Rhodes' great dream of a contiguous world empire around the Indian Ocean from Cape Town through Cairo and the Near East to Calcutta was eventually realised, but not until after the First World War and then only temporarily.

When Jules Ferry assumed the reins of government in France the enthusiasm for colonies reached a fever pitch, penetrating all strata of society. Though never losing sight of the priority of European affairs, Paris embarked upon a campaign to add to the territory it had already acquired in North Africa through the conquest of Algeria in 1830. French troops overran Tunisia in 1881 and surged south and south-east as far as Lake Chad. At the same time, the settlements that France had established around 1850 along the west coast of Africa in Senegal, the Ivory Coast and Guinea, were merged into a huge West African empire. To the east, Djibouti was founded on the Red Sea in 1888, and a railway was planned to Abyssinia. As the French unfurled across Africa from west to east, they inevitably collided with the British who were expanding their influence along a north–south axis. Particularly coveted were the Sudan and the source of the Nile. When British and French expeditionary forces met at Fashoda in Upper Egypt, the clouds of war gathered. But France gave way and negotiated a settlement whereby she agreed to withdraw from the Upper Nile in return for further expansion in equatorial Africa. France along with Belgium thus became the dominant power of West and Central Africa.

Germany did not propose to stand idly by while her neighbours painted the world in their colours. As the mightiest industrial nation in Europe, alongside Britain, and the strongest military power on the Continent, the young *Reich* clamoured to make its influence felt around the world. Plans were drawn up to expand the colonial empire initiated under Bismarck and to build a powerful fleet in order to protect German merchantmen and to underscore the high ambitions of the imperial government. However, this 'world policy' fell far short of expectations, and German colonialism was not even as successful as it had been under Bismarck. A few territories were acquired in China and in the Pacific Ocean, but in some cases they were virtually worthless and could not compare with the British, French or Russian acquisitions of the period. The *Reich* moved into Kiaochow in 1897 and the city of Tsingtao soon flourished. The islands of Caroline, Marian and Palau were purchased from Spain the following year, and in 1899 some of the Samoan islands were acquired by means of a treaty with Britain and the United States. But the only German advance of world significance was the construction of the Baghdad railway. In Germany it raised high hopes of new regions of economic activity and political influence in the Near East; but Britain and Russia perceived the railway as a threat to their interests in the area. German participation in the railway soon became a heavy political and economic millstone, and turned the distrust the other powers felt for Germany's imperial pretensions into open hostility.

Russia's expansion to the east and west was crowned with far greater success, even though her western interests conflicted with those of Turkey, Austria and Great Britain. After attempts at expansion into the Balkans were frustrated by the Congress of Berlin, Russia redirected her efforts towards East Asia, the Persian Gulf and the Turkish Straits. The Congress invited Russia to expand south of the Caucasus towards Kars and the Persian border. The tsar occupied Turkestan in 1873 and advanced into Afghanistan in 1888, posing a threat to British interests in India. In the Far East the Russians had seized the province of Amur from China in 1858 and founded Vladivostok on the Sea of Japan two years later. Sakhalin Island was occupied in 1875 and Port Arthur was leased from China. The 7000-km long Trans-Siberian Railway was built between 1891 and 1904 after permission to traverse Manchuria had been obtained from the Chinese government, thus linking the new territories to the distant capital. However, when Russia set out to expand further into Manchuria and Korea, she encountered resistance from the rising power of the East, Japan.

In 1854 an American fleet had compelled Japan to end her 200 years of isolation and to open her ports to foreign commerce. The Japanese swiftly adopted the achievements of Western civilization. Railways were laid and modern factories erected. An army was organised and a fleet was modelled after the British and German examples. Schools and universities were built, and the state was reorganised through the adoption of a constitution, akin to that of Prussia, which entrusted the government to ministers responsible solely to the crown. These reforms helped Japan to maintain her independence, and by the 1890s she was ready to adopt Western-style imperialism in order to cope with a rising surplus population and a severe lack of natural resources. The main thrust of Japanese expansionism was directed against the adjacent mainland in Korea, Manchuria and northern China. The Japanese successfully invaded China in 1894, but were forced to withdraw by the combined intervention of the European powers and the United States. When expansion into Korea caused tensions with Russia, Tokyo reinforced its position by signing a treaty with Britain in 1902. Thus fortified, the Japanese attacked Port Arthur in 1904 and ventured into the Russian sphere of interest in Manchuria. In the resulting war, Japan soundly defeated the tsar's forces on the land and at sea. The ensuing Treaty of Portsmouth, mediated by the president of the United States in 1905, gave Japan possession of Korea, Port Arthur and the southern half of Sakhalin Island, while Russia was compelled to return Manchuria to Chinese rule.

The tsar's defeat in the hands of Japan, a recent and little-noticed power, sparked a revolution in Russia that severely tested the tsar's hold on political power and forced him to grant a constitution. With her expansionary policies in Asia reduced to a shambles, Russia quickly turned her gaze southward and westward to Persia, the Near East and the Balkans.

Like Japan, the United States became a world power after 1890. By the end of the nineteenth century the continent had been opened, the unsettled lands of fifty years earlier had been populated, and the United States had surged ahead to become the largest industrial power in the world. A contemporary writer captured the spirit of the times when he proclaimed to his fellow Americans:

Whether they will or no, Americans must now begin to look outward. The growing production of the country demands it. An increasing volume of public sentiment demands it. The position of the United States, between the two Old Worlds and two great oceans, makes the same claim.[33]

In the course of a triumphant war with Spain, the Philippines were conquered, Cuba was taken over and Hawaii and Guam were annexed. The Monroe Doctrine, enunciated in 1823 by President James Monroe in order to prevent the European powers from intervening in the Americas, now became the prime justification of American intervention and of the imperialist policies pursued by President Theodore Roosevelt. Roosevelt announced:

It is not true that the United States feels any land hunger. . . . Any country whose people conduct themselves well can count upon our hearty friendship. . . . Chronic wrongdoing or an impotence which results in general loosening of the ties of civilized society may in America, as elsewhere, ultimately require intervention by some civilized nation, and in the Western Hemisphere the adherence of the United States to the Monroe Doctrine may force the United States. . . . in flagrant cases of such wrongdoing or impotence to the exercise of an international police power.[34]

The acquisition of Hawaii and the Philippines rendered the construction of the Panama Canal a commercial and strategic necessity. Its completion in 1914 ensured American domination of the seas to the south and helped the United States to become a major power in the Far East. While the European powers tended to expand through conquest and the creation of protectorates, the United States relied chiefly on loans in order to extend her influence. In return for these loans the debtor nations were obliged to accord certain economic privileges which rendered them both economically and politically dependent on Washington. America's economic interests in China were advanced by means of the 'open door' policy.

Until the beginning of the nineteenth century, China had little contact with Europe. Marco Polo first brought the Middle Kingdom to Europe's attention around 1300, and Jesuits delved into the 4000 years of Chinese history and culture during the seventeenth and eighteenth centuries. The first political contacts with China were established in 1727 and 1793 when Russia founded a trading settlement and Britain dispatched an ambassador to Peking. The Middle Kingdom soon became a prime trading partner, especially for Britain, which wished to export opium, which generated high profits, in order to pay for Chinese goods. When Peking imposed a tariff on the incoming drug, the so-called Opium War resulted. This conflict, lasting from 1840 to 1842, fully exposed China's weakness to the outside world. She was compelled to open Shanghai and four other ports to foreign 'trade, to cede Hong Kong to Britain and to grant special privileges to European merchants and missionaries. Thus began the era of forced grants of land and extraterritorial concessions to the European powers. Grave internal difficulties coupled with repeated humiliation of China by the foreign powers sparked the Tai-ping rebellion, which was tinged with Christian and socialist ideas. The government in Peking crushed the revolt with European help, but the conflict undermined the economy and destroyed the financial system. The ruling Ch'ing dynasty was stripped of most of its powers and by the turn of the century China had became a semi-colony. Russia, Britain, France, Germany and Japan seized broad swaths of territory partly by force of arms and partly by arranging leases and outlining 'spheres of interest'. The Chinese hatred of the foreign interlopers exploded into open revolt in 1900, but a joint expeditionary force of European troops defeated the insurgents and inflicted a heavy indemnity upon the country. The Chinese monarchy slowly succumbed to this series of blows and was finally overwhelmed in the 1911 revolution led by the offshore Chinese Dr Sun Yat-sen.

The imperialism of the great powers devastated the social and political structures of Africa and Asia and subjected their peoples to economic and political domination by foreigners. In daily contact with a civilization that was technically and economically superior to their own, the conquered nations began to adapt to a European life-style. Meanwhile, the intense imperial rivalries throughout the world aggravated the friction between the great powers. In the Far East and the islands of the Pacific Ocean, Russia, Britain, Japan and the United States competed to extend their influence. Britain, France and Germany struggled for ascendance in Africa; Germany, Britain and Russia for supremacy in the Near East; and Russia and Britain for dominance of the Middle East. The rival colonial claims of the great powers touched of a series of crises which exacerbated the antagonisms already existing within Europe and provoked a diplomatic revolution in the system of alliances.

German Foreign Policy after 1890

The sea-change in the system of alliances began immediately after Bismarck's dismissal. The authors of the 'new course' in German policy abandoned Bismarck's painstaking efforts to ensure European stability in favour of an attempt to thrust Germany forward on the international stage. In so doing they forsook the former chancellor's complicated system of alliances without establishing suitable replacements. This enabled France to escape her isolation while Germany found herself increasingly alone in a time of mounting tensions and heightened danger.

The first step in the gradual erosion of Germany's diplomatic position occurred when Berlin failed to renew the secret Reinsurance Treaty with Russia. Caprivi was incapable of continuing the policies of his great predecessor. He explained to the German ambassador to Russia, 'that the greatest dilemma which he faced was whether to renew the Russian treaty, for he could juggle only two balls at a time, not five as Prince Bismarck had done'.[35] In the end Caprivi steadfastly refused to renew the treaty even when St Petersburg offered far-reaching concessions in second and third attempts to arrive at an understanding with its western neighbour. Caprivi was not well versed in foreign affairs, and his rejection of the Russian entreaties was largely prompted by the assistant undersecretary in the Foreign Office, Friedrich von Holstein. Owing to his experience and expertise in foreign affairs, Holstein virtually 'ruled over the Foreign Office' (in the words of Count Alfred von Waldersee),[36] heavily influencing German foreign policy during the next decades under a parade of different chancellors and foreign ministers. Holstein's analysis of the international situation rested on three fundamental assumptions: first, a long-term coalition between France and Russia was impossible; second, 'the bear and the whale' (i.e. Russia and Britain) would never see eye to eye; and third, Britain would eventually seek an alliance with Germany because of British rivalry with France in North Africa and with Russia in the Near East, Persia, Afghanistan and East Asia. Germany therefore enjoyed a 'free hand' and could afford to wait. But these underpinnings of German policy fatefully disintegrated one after the other, while the opportunity to ally Germany with Britain, which presented itself repeatedly between 1898 and 1901, was not seized.

The failure to renew the Reinsurance Treaty had no immediate serious consequences such as a severing of relations, but it did arouse Russian suspicions of a shift in German policy. This impression was reinforced when Germany concluded that same year the Heligoland–Zanzibar treaty with Britain. This agreement settled the boundary dispute between German and British colonies in East Africa, and the island of Zanzibar off German East Africa was exchanged for Heligoland off Germany's North Sea coast. However, the Heligoland–Zanzibar treaty prompted the Russians to suspect that an Anglo-German alliance might be in the making which would inevitably pose a strong and immediate danger to Russian interests.

In her isolation Russia resolved to take the step which Bismarck had so dreaded after 1871: she took up the offers which Paris had been proffering since the late 1880s. A squadron of the French fleet visited Kronstadt in 1891 and received an enthusiastic welcome. In August of 1892 the Russian and French chiefs of general staff signed a military convention which bound each power to help the other in case Russia was attacked by Germany and Austria or in case France was attacked by Italy or by Germany or by both in concert. After much hesitation on the part of St Petersburg, the French and Russian foreign ministers confirmed this defensive arrangement and translated it into a formal treaty in January 1894. The abiding strength of this accord disproved the first of Holstein's fundamental assumptions.

With the signing of the Dual Alliance, two hostile coalitions suddenly faced one another in Europe, and Germany was confronted with the danger of a two-front war. Still the government in Berlin hesitated to draw the necessary consequences. The chancellor hoped that the Heligoland–Zanzibar treaty would introduce an era of closer relations with Britain, but he abandoned all efforts in this direction when the Liberal government of William Ewart Gladstone refused to enter into a formal agreement with the Triple Alliance.

In fact, Anglo-German relations cooled somewhat as a result of Germany's bumptious search for colonies and world-power status and her efforts to build a powerful battle-fleet. Yet despite the enthusiasm displayed by William, the public and the naval command for a strong German battle-fleet, no insurmountable obstacle existed to warm relations between Germany and Britain. In the spring of 1898 Joseph Chamberlain informed the German ambassador in London, Count Paul von Hatzfeld, that Britain was increasingly inclined to reverse her policy of 'splendid isolation' and actively seek out allies. Britain was prepared to negotiate a settlement of her outstanding differences with Germany, according to Chamberlain, and to enter into an informal arrangement which would be tantamount to partnership in the Triple Alliance. Still the German government insisted on a formal alliance ratified by the British parliament. When London refused to undertake so firm a commitment, the German government broke off negotiations after more than three years of talks. The government's concern was that an alliance with Britain might result in Germany becoming subservient to Britain's global interests. Now that the Trans-Siberian Railway was in place and the Russians were taking a greater interest in China, relations between London and St Petersburg were worsening and Germany did not wish to appear to be spearheading British interests on the Continent. Furthermore, William II and the secretary of state for the navy, Grand Admiral Tirpitz, were concerned that closer ties with Britain would lead to the imposition of restrictions on the German battle-fleet. London intimated that it might seek closer relations with France and Russia if negotiations with Germany failed, but Bülow and Holstein took this as an idle threat.

Under the influence of the Fashoda crisis and some instances of Russo-German cooperation in the Far East, the government in Berlin completely misread the political situation. It clung to the conviction that Germany had a free hand in the selection of her alliance partners and for a time even considered uniting the Triple Alliance and the Dual Alliance in a grand continental block directed against Britain. But Britain was soon to demonstrate that it was she, not Germany, who had a free hand. In January 1902 Britain emerged from her self-imposed isolation and entered into an alliance with Japan directed against Russia. This treaty bound both parties to observe benevolent neutrality if one of them was attacked by a single power and to offer military assistance if one of them was attacked by two or more powers. In this way London and Tokyo hoped to dispel the threat of Russian hegemony over East Asia.

At the same time Britain drew closer to France. The French foreign minister, Théophile Delcassé, believed that France should strive above all to strengthen her position on the Continent and he was much more interested in recovering Alsace-Lorraine than in far-away colonies. He therefore looked to Britain as a likely ally and, already at the time of the Fashoda crisis, had begun to prepare a future reconciliation with France's greatest colonial rival. After the failure of the Anglo-German negotiations, Delcassé approached London about the possibilities of an Anglo-French rapprochement and was favourably received. The ensuing negotiations proceeded all the more smoothly in that Delcassé—unlike Bülow and Holstein—did not insist on a formal treaty. He was content to reach an understanding about contentious colonial issues and to arrive at a comprehensive settlement. In April 1904 the Entente cordiale was signed. Britain accepted French intervention in Morocco and the likelihood of a French protectorate, while France recognised Britain's position in Egypt. The powers further agreed that if the sultan of Morocco was forced to relinquish sovereignty to France, Spain would be appeased with a slice of northern Morroco.

The German government, following Holstein's lead, believed that the Anglo-French understanding could not last. The Russo-Japanese War had erupted in February 1904 over Korea and Manchuria, and Berlin was convinced that the Entente would collapse when Britain sided with her ally, Japan, while France supported Russia. However, the friendly relations between Britain and France were not disturbed in the least by the conflict between their allies. Britain's obligations to Japan required only that she observe benevolent neutrality in case of war against a single foe, and France was required to take up arms on Russia's behalf only in case of a European war against the Triple Alliance.

Berlin's analysis of the probable effects of the Russo-Japanese War turned out to be a monumental miscalculation in more ways than one. Russia, defeated in war and weakened by the consequent internal troubles, her eastward expansion blocked by the rising power of Japan, renewed her interest in the Balkans. Britain in the meantime lost interest in protecting the weak Ottoman Empire. Thus the way was cleared for an Anglo-Russian accord over spheres of interest in Asia. In accordance with the pattern set by the Entente cordiale and with the eager backing of Paris, Britain and Russia reached a friendly understanding about the contentious issues dividing them. Britain agreed to refrain from interfering in Tibet, while Afghanistan was to remain a neutral buffer zone in the British sphere of interest. Persia's basic independence was recognised, though the country was divided into a northern Russian sphere of interest, a southern British sphere of interest, and a neutral central zone including the coast along the Persian Gulf. Thus the second of Holstein's fundamental assumptions came crashing down.

Germany's position was further weakened by the fact that Italy, though an essential partner in the Triple Alliance, signed a secret treaty with France in 1902. By the terms of this agreement, Rome agreed to respect French interests in Morocco in return for French recognition of Italian interests in Tripoli, while both powers agreed to observe strict neutrality if one of them was attacked by a third power. This secret deal caste severe doubt on the strength of the Triple Alliance. Indeed, as Anglo-German relations worsened, Italy increasingly distanced herself from her alliance partners, leaving them isolated in the centre of Europe.

The constellation of powers in Europe thus shifted enormously after 1900, to the great disadvantage of Germany. Great Britain abjured 'splendid isolation' and sided with France and Russia to create the Triple Entente. Italy was formally allied with Germany and Austria-Hungary in the Triple Alliance, but she sought every opportunity to strengthen her relations with the Triple Entente powers. Russia, defeated in East Asia and restrained in Central Asia by her treaty with Britain, turned her attentions to the Balkans, where conflict with Austria seemed probable. Germany and Austria-Hungary therefore found themselves increasingly isolated in Europe. To add to the misery of German foreign policy, German efforts to forge a far-flung colonial empire had failed as miserably as those of Italy. This caste doubt on the logic of Berlin's entire *Weltpolitik*. German 'world policies' and continental policies both lacked cohesion and a clear sense of purpose.

The Path to the First World War.

In the years after 1890 several opportunities to secure Germany's position in Europe had been missed while William II's brash behaviour increasingly irritated Germany's neighbours. These neighbours sought closer ties with one another and began to distance themselves from the young *Reich*. The European balance of power, a key element in the preservation of peace on the Continent, began to shift. Meanwhile the general sense of stability and security was eradicated by a series of crises. All attempts to moderate the mounting hostilities were doomed to failure by fear of the other camp—a fear which only deepened as Europe stumbled from one crisis to another. Germany believed herself encircled by a hostile phalanx of jealous neighbours eager to deny the *Reich* what they accorded themselves. In reality, Berlin had done much to provoke the enmity of the other powers, and Britain, France and Russia all had sound reasons to fear German military and naval power. The governments of all the great powers were edgy and belligerent, spurred on by the intense nationalism of the public. Press propaganda was effectively used for the first time to raise national animosities to an hysterical pitch.

Despite the explosive atmosphere, responsible statesmen sought repeatedly to defuse the situation. However, their margin of manoeuvre was severely limited by the arms race, by the system of alliances to which both sides anxiously adhered, and by the enormous influence of military planners and commanders. Foreign policy was increasingly influenced by military commitments within the respective alliances.

The Moroccan crises of 1905 and 1911 set the stage for the final confrontation which triggered the great war. The Entente cordiale between Britain and France had cleared the way for the French to undertake the 'peaceful penetration' of Morocco. In so doing, France endeavoured not only to concentrate Morocco's entire national debt in her hands but also to gain control of Morocco's tariffs and armed forces. At first Germany acquiesced in these policies, but then announced in the spring of 1905 that she wished to have her commercial rights in Morocco observed—rights which an earlier treaty had accorded all European powers. In order to underscore this demand and the German desire for an international conference to settle the Moroccan question, Bülow urged William II to visit Tangiers. William dutifully called on the sultan and voiced the German support for Moroccan independence. Berlin had reverted to its earlier plans for an alliance of the continental powers and hoped to drive a wedge between Britain and France. The tsar had already expressed his willingness to enter a defensive alliance with Germany provided that France would later be admitted. However, the tsar insisted on first informing the French of this plan, and the German government was convinced that Paris was most unlikely to agree. Bülow and Holstein therefore decided to exert political pressure in Morocco in order to drive the French into seeking an accommodation with Germany.

Paris reacted with outrage. Foreign Minister Delcaseé, fortified by promises of British assistance, was prepared to risk all-out war in order to stonewall German demands in Morocco. However, Prime Minister Maurice Rouvier insisted on negotiations in view of Russia's weakness after her defeat by Japan and the attempted revolution. Rouvier therefore suggested to his German counterparts that France and Germany compose their colonial differences along the lines of the Entente cordiale. But Bülow and Holstein planned to humiliate France and insisted on an international conference. Rouvier eventually agreed, though Delcaseé resigned in disgust, and a conference was convened in January 1906 in the southern Spanish town of Algeciras. Germany's satisfaction of having forced the French to yield soon turned to dismay when she discovered that all the other powers were aligned against her. Even Austria-Hungary urged Berlin to seek a compromise. In the end Moroccan independence was recognised, at least formally, and German commercial demands were partially met by the appointment of an international team of French, British, Spanish and German officials to oversee the Bank of Morocco. But France, together with Spain, was left in control of the Moroccan police, and remained the dominant power in Morocco. On the whole, the conference marked a clear diplomatic defeat for Germany.

The Moroccan crisis reignited hostilities in France and Germany alike. William II was convinced that the French take-over of Morocco could only be halted by war and therefore agreed at first to recognise French pre-eminence there in the hope of reducing Franco-German hostilities. The primary source of the friction between the two countries seemed to be eliminated when an accord was signed in 1909 recognising the fundamental sovereignty of the sultan and granting German commercial interests free access to Morocco. But in April and May of 1911 French troops occupied Fez and Rabat in the wake of popular disorders. Berlin was willing to allow France a free hand in Morocco but demanded the French Congo as compensation. The seriousness of the German claim was underscored when Alfred von Kiderlen-Wächter, the newly appointed secretary of state in the Foreign Office, dispatched the gunboat *Panther* to the west Moroccan port of Agadir. But France, supported by Britain adamantly refused to submit to the new German demands and together they compelled Berlin to content itself with some sections of the French Congo, access to the Congo river and a narrow strip of coastline.

Again the *Reich* had been forced to retreat, while Britain and France drew closer together. The British chancellor of the exchequer, David Lloyd George, warned ominously that Britain could never be compelled to foresake vital interests even at the threat of war.[37]

While Germany's relations with her western neighbours deteriorated, the Austro-Russian tensions in the Balkans took a decided turn for the worse when Vienna annexed Bosnia in 1908. The German Empire, increasingly driven into the arms of the Habsburg monarchy, thus found herself facing increased hostility along her eastern flank as well.

The revolution of the Young Turks in the summer of 1908 caused the historic rift between Austria and Russia to widen once more. The overthrow of the despotic sultan and the establishment of a constitutional Turkish state orientated towards Western liberalism seemed to presage a more effective administration of the Turkish Empire and an energetic assertion of Turkish rights. Bulgaria, which had been self-governing since the Congress of Berlin but under Turkish suzerainty, seized the opportunity to declare herself independent. Meanwhile Vienna annexed outright the Turkish provinces of Bosnia and Herzegovina, previously under Austrian administration. At first Russia acquiesced in Austria's unilateral action because the Austrian government agreed to support the opening of the Dardanelles to Russian ships of war. But Russia's ally Serbia was infuriated by the threat which the Austrian annexation posed to her long-term ambition of gathering all the southern Slavs in a unified state, and she prevailed upon St Petersburg to lodge vehement protests. When the Russians demanded that a conference be called of all the participants in the 1878 Congress of Berlin, Germany insisted that St Petersburg first recognise the Austrian annexation of Bosnia and Herzegovina. Since Russia could not rely on French support at this juncture and Britain was playing the role of mediator, the Russians reluctantly yielded and advised Serbia that nothing could be done for the time being. Thus the crisis ended—an apparent victory for the Central powers. But the price was high. Russia felt deeply humiliated, the Western powers distrusted Austria, and the partners in the Triple Entente drew closer together.

Emboldened by the success of the Central powers in the Balkans and by the French penetration of Morocco, the Italian government decided to make its move by seizing Tripoli, nominally a part of the Ottoman Empire. Italy quickly won the ensuing war with Turkey, once more calling Turkish power into question and emboldening Serbia, Bulgaria, Greece and Montenegro to rise in revolt in the hope of driving Turkey from the European continent. Russia had helped to forge the Balkan League and now she backed the war aims of the Balkan states. Turkey, defeated militarily, appealed to the European powers to mediate a peace. The ensuing negotiations once again pushed Europe to the brink of war when Austria threatened to resort to arms if necessary in order to thwart Serbian expansion to the Adriatic. In the end Britain and Germany saved the peace. Berlin restrained the Austrians while London convinced the Russians not to offer Serbia armed assistance. The great powers then agreed to create the new and independent state of Albania between Serbia and the Adriatic.

In June 1913 a second Balkan war flared up, provoked by dissension over the division of Macedonia with its Bulgarian, Serbian and Greek population. Bulgaria, with Austrian encouragement, attacked Serbia and Greece, which were supported in turn by Turkey and Romania. Germany intervened once again to discourage Austria from actually extending the direct military assistance she had implied would be forthcoming. Bulgaria, suddenly isolated, was quickly overwhelmed by her enemies, and all hope of establishing Bulgarian hegemony over the Balkans with Austrian assistance were dashed. Austria's diplomatic defeat in this affair and the triumph of the Russians and Serbs lent new impetus to the pan-Slav movement in the Balkans and increased the difficulties Vienna was experiencing in containing the conflicts in the area. The danger associated with the swelling pan-Slav movement had been apparent to Karl Marx as early as 1853:

If Russia ever flanks the protective states around Austria to the north, east and south, Austria herself will inevitably become a Russian vassal. And then the long, rolling borders of western Russia will reach out in search of completion and security in the conviction that Russia's natural western border runs for instance from Danzig or even Stettin to Trieste. And just as inevitably as one victory and one annexation leads to the next, the annexation of the Turkish Balkans would only be a step towards the annexation of Hungary, Galicia and Prussia. And then that mighty Russian Slavic empire would arise, of which fanatic pan-Slavs dream.[38]

While this series of crises was pushing Europe to the brink of war, the international peace movement, which had been particularly active in Western Europe since the end of the nineteenth century, redoubled its efforts. Its efforts were reinforced by peace proposals of the Russian tsar which culminated in peace conferences in The Hague in 1899 and 1907. However, the fledgling peace movement could achieve very little against traditional power politics. None of the participating states was willing to discuss arms limitations, which they all considered an unacceptable infringement on their national sovereignty. General disarmament was therefore not even discussed at the conferences. All that was accomplished was the creation of an international tribunal, whose competence did not include political matters, and various agreements on the ways in which war ought to be waged.

Several attempts to arrive at a comprehensive Anglo-German settlement likewise failed. None the less, there were periods of relative harmony and individual conflicts were resolved. For instance, the old dispute over the Baghdad railway was settled in June 1914, just before the onset of war. Britain was allowed to build the final leg of the railway from Baghdad to the Persian Gulf, and Germany was promised the remnants of the Portuguese empire in Africa. However, the fundamental suspicion and distrust between the two countries could not be dispelled, especially as the German fleet had become a matter of personal prestige to William II, who would not brook any curtailment of the fleet no matter how heavily it weighed on relations with Britain. Egged on by Grand Admiral Tirpitz and many of his enthusiastic countrymen, the emperor no longer saw the fleet as serving the needs of politics, but rather politics as serving the needs of the fleet, In such an atmosphere it is hardly surprising that all of Bülow's and Bethmann Hollweg's attempts to reach a settlement with the British met with failure. Any British suggestions of a negotiated limit on the size of German fleet were frostily received by the emperor:

We shall never allow anyone to prescribe to us the nature of our armaments.... France and Russia could then with equal justification demand a limitation on our land forces. As soon as one allows a foreign state to intervene in armaments policy, for whatever reason, one has abdicated one's responsibility[39]

This attitude robbed responsible German statesmen of the leeway they needed in order to reach an agreement with Britain. Meanwhile Anglo-German relations sank into a baffling dilemma as the quest for prestige and national security continued: Germany, the greatest land-based power in Europe, sought to build a battle-fleet equal to that of Britain in order to raise the hazards of war to such a level that it would never break out. Meanwhile Britain redoubled her armament efforts so that she would be prepared just in case war did break out.

Hence the failure of the last great attempt at a settlement under-taken by the British secretary of war, Richard Burdone Haldane, during a visit to Berlin in February 1912. By then the politicians who wished to moderate the mounting hostility between the peoples of Europe had seen their margin of manoeuvre reduced to almost nothing by the feverish arms race and by military obligations to allies within the context of two great alliances.

Never was a great European war so likely for so many reasons as in the final years before 1914. Of this the public had no doubt. Every citizen knew it, though most did not really believe it. Reason told them that war was imminent, when they chose to use it, but somehow the imagination could not grasp it. This was because they had lived so long in peace, had grown so accustomed to a solid international order, to banknotes that could be exchanged for gold, to travelling without documents.[40]

Commercial and industrial interests were not at all enthused by the prospects of war. Germany's prodigious economic advance had resulted in strong commercial ties, not only with industrial nations like Britain and France but with Russia as well. However, the danger that war might break out, as it had between Russia and Japan in 1904, could never be forgotten. August Bebel, leader of the Social Democrats, warned of the impending horror in 1911 in his last speech on foreign policy before the *Reichstag*:

Some fine day one side may say: Things cannot go on this way. It may also say: If we wait any longer, we will lose, we will be the weaker party instead of the stronger. Then the catastrophe will unfurl. The general call to arms will resound across Europe, and 16 to 18 million men, the flower of their nations, armed with the most murderous of weapons, will march out to face one another on the field of battle. But I am convinced that behind the general call to arms lies the great collapse—yes, you have laughed often about that; but it is coming, it is only deferred. It is not we who will bring it about but you yourselves . . . . It is you who are pushing things to the breaking point . . . . It is you who are undermining your own political and social system . . . . What will be the result? Behind this war stands mass bankruptcy, mass misery, mass unemployment and mass starvation.[41]

10

The First World War

1914: Assassination of the heir apparent to the Austrian throne in Sarajevo (28 June); Russia orders full mobilisation (30 July); Germany
mobilises and declares war on Russia (1 August); Germany declares
war on France (3 August); Britain declares war on Germany (4
August); Japan declares war on Germany (23 August); war of
movement on the eastern and western fronts (Battle of the Marne
and Battle of Tannenberg); war of position in the west from the
autumn of 1914 till March 1918 and in the east from December 1914
till the autumn of 1917; Turkey enters the war (October)

1915: Italy declares war on Austria (May); Bulgaria joins the central
powers (October); Serbia is conquered (November); the slaughter
of Verdun

1916: Romania enters the war on the side of the Entente (August); the
U-boat question; German peace overtures and mediation by the
president of the United States

1917: The United States declares war (6 April); internal crises within the
warring states of Europe and attempts at a negotiated peace; the
February and October revolutions in Russia

1918: The Peace of Brest-Litovsk (3 March); major German offensives in
France; Allied counter-offensive; Turkey, Bulgaria and Austria-
Hungary collapse; revolution in Germany; Scheidemann proclaims
the German Republic (9 November); William II flees to the neutral
Netherlands (10 November); the Armistice of Compiègne (11
November); the Council of People's Commissars is constituted (12
November); William II abdicates (28 November)

The Causes and the Outbreak of the War

Ever since the onset of the string of crises to the south-east and
south-west, the peoples of Europe had lived under the threat of

213

imminent war. Finally one crisis pitched most of Continent into a bloody confrontation, just as Bebel had forseen. The fateful sequence of events was initiated on 28 June 1914 when the heir to the Austrian throne, Archduke Francis Ferdinand, was assassinated together with his wife in the Bosnian capital of Sarajevo. The assassin was a Slav nationalist, assisted by Serbian officers and officials with the knowledge of their government. Slav nationalists wished to murder the Austrian archduke because of his plan to save the Habsburg Empire by endowing it with a federal structure which would have conferred considerable local autonomy on the various peoples within its borders. The nationalists feared that this plan would rob the pan-Slav movement of much of its momentum and would cripple dreams of a great Serbian empire.

After the assassination the Austrian government sought to exploit the revulsion felt across Europe 'in order to eliminate Serbia as a political force'[1] and thus alleviate the problem posed by this advance post of Russian interests in the Balkans. In Berlin William II and Chancellor Bethmann Hollweg gave their unconditional blessing to the Austrian plan for military action, and informed Emperor Francis Joseph through the German ambassador that William 'would stand loyally by Austria-Hungary's side, in accordance with his treaty commitments and time-honoured friendship'.[2] Germany was reluctant to restrain Austria once again, partly because she feared losing her last ally and partly because she felt that the assassination of the Austrian archduke provided Vienna with a final opportunity to prove through a small war that Austria was still a great power. Hence a blank cheque was issued authorising Vienna to do as it saw fit. The German emperor and his chancellor were willing to run the risk of a great war (from which, they were convinced, Britain would stand aloof) because they believed that Russia and France were not yet prepared for conflict and that it would therefore be likely to remain confined to Austria and Serbia.

On 23 July 1914 Vienna issued a short-term ultimatum, demanding that Serbia suppress all anti-Austrian propaganda and allow Austrian officials to participate in the investigation of the assassination. In response the Serbian government ordered general mobilisation, but at the same time agreed to most of Austria's demands while suggesting that points still in dispute be submitted to the international tribunal at The Hague or to a conference of the great powers. Vienna, however, was not about to be deterred and declared war on 28 July. William II had expressed his belief that Serbia's cleverly worded response to the Austrian ultimatium would satisfy Vienna and prevent war, but he rejected London's suggestion that the conflict be submitted to a European conference. Germany insisted instead that direct negotiations be opened between Austria and Russia. The German government also twice warned Austria on 29 and 30 July not to provoke a world conflagration through her carelessness.

The British and German attempts to confine the crisis to a limited area were doomed by the Russian decision on 29 July to mobilise her army. William II immediately implored the tsar to rescind this order, but succeeded only in delaying it till the following day. Berlin responded with an ultimatum demanding that Russia desist from all warlike preparations within the space of twelve hours. When her demands were ignored, Germany declared war against Russia. The date was 1 August 1914.

With the outbreak of war, military strategy assumed a fatal precedence over politics. The German plan for a two-front war, devised in 1905 by the chief of the general staff, Count Alfred von Schlieffen, required the army to concentrate on defeating France swiftly before the ponderous Russian army could fully mobilise. The declaration of war against Russia therefore implied that France would have to be invaded very soon. Berlin urgently inquired of the French government if it would remain neutral in case of a Russo-German conflict, and when no clear answer was received, declared war against France two days later on 3 August. Thus Germany appeared in the guise of aggressor in both East and West.

In London the government waited till German troops invaded neutral Belgium in an attempt to circumvent the heavily fortified Maginot Line and quickly attack the French army from the rear, in accordance with the Schlieffen plan. This gave the war party in the British cabinet the impetus it needed to win over the government and public opinion to the war. On 4 August Britain too declared war, though not legally bound to do so by her military agreements with Paris. As to the further consequences of this decision, Edward Grey, the British foreign minister, had little doubt: 'The lamps are going out all over Europe; we shall not see them lit again in our life-time.'[3]

Germany's alliance partners of Italy and Romania claimed that this war was not covered by the terms of their treaty and they remained provisionally neutral. In the last days of August, Japan sided with the Entente while Turkey threw its weight behind the Central powers out of fear of Russian ambitions in the east.

Thus the assassination in Sarajevo touched off a great explosion of the tensions that had accumulated between the great powers. The cataclysm that followed had numerous causes: Austria's determi-

nation to vanquish the Serbs; Russia's decision to support a greater
Serbia and to pursue her own expansionist dreams despite Austrian
resistance in the Balkans and German resistance in the Orient;
France's abiding desire for revenge; Germany's determination to
carve out a place for herself as a world power; and finally Britain's
decision to ally herself with France out of fear of both German
power in Central Europe and Russian expansionism in Asia.

Though no government actively sought a great war, they all
preferred to run the risk rather than make concessions to their foes.
Germany too did not desire a European war, nor even a preventive
war calculated to catapult her to the rank of a world power.
However, Berlin wittingly ran the risk of provoking a great war by
firmly backing its only ally, Austria-Hungary in the assassination
crisis and by issuing her a 'blank cheque' to respond as she saw fit.
William's attempts to exert a moderating influence on Austria came
too late, and his efforts were undermined in any case by the German
military command which had begun to supplant the diplomats in
the final days of the crisis. On 30 July the chief of the German
general staff, Helmuth von Moltke, sent the Austrians a telegram,
without the knowledge of the emperor or chancellor, urging them
to order the general mobilisation and assuring them of full German
support. Thus military strategy interfered with political attempts at
appeasement and helped to initiate the chain of events that burdened
Germany with the stigma of aggressor. The peace which all had
wanted—and yet not so very much[4]—was submerged by the mutual
hostility of the two armed camps that had arisen after 1907. Europe
plunged into a war from which it would never recover.

In Germany as elsewhere, 'liberation' from the oppressive atmosphere of threat and confrontation united the people in an outburst
of patriotic enthusiasm. The masses trusted in their leaders, convinced of Germany's moral right to defend herself against a jealous,
avaricious and megalomaniacal foe. A wave of popular enthusiasm
swept the land. 'Such sentiments as at the outbreak of war in 1914
will never be seen again', reminisced Carl Zuckmayer,[5] while Max
Weber celebrated this 'great and awesome war'[6] and marvelled at his
good fortune to live long enough to experience such an event. '*Es
geht los*' was the joyful cry.

You feel it in your bones . . . and before you are aware of what is happening
a parade is formed. No one knows the others, but all share a wondrous
feeling: War, War and we are all one. . . . And then a song floats up the
evening sky, grave and majestic: 'a cry is heard like a clap of thunder, like
crashing waves and clanging swords, to the Rhine, the German Rhine!'[7]

The emperor, often bitterly criticised in former times, was thrust forward as the living symbol of the new-found unity of the German people. Buoyed by the wave of popular acclaim, William was moved to proclaim, 'I no longer recognise parties or confessions; today we are all German brothers, nothing but German brothers.'[8] Even the Social Democrats, long denounced by their emperor as *vaterlandslose Gesellen*, spoke of a fateful moment and an event of earth-shaking importance in which they would prove, as they had always claimed, that they would 'not forsake the fatherland in its hour of danger',[9] in the words of Hugo Haase, the leader of the radical wing. At one with 'the whole German nation without political or religious distinction', the Social Democrats were now prepared 'to take up this conflict forced upon us by Russian barbarism and to fight to the last drop of our blood for Germany's fame, independence and grandeur'.[10] A contemporary enthused: 'It was wonderful at the outbreak of the war how the great storm that had broken upon us not only cleared the stuffy political atmosphere but uplifted the people and restored their old ideals.'[11]

This wave of enthusiasm and unanimity was doubtless a product of ignorance. No one could imagine what the war would be like. Germans believed in the sanctity of their cause and that they would gain a quick victory in a war that did not differ substantially from the conflicts of the 1860s. Only too soon would sentiments change. Exaltation turned to hate, and the sense of community and comradeship was blotted out by a re-emergence of profound social divisions as the war grew more and more horrible.

The Course of the War Before the Entry of the United States

In contrast to all previous wars, the First World War touched almost all peoples of the world. It was waged by armies several million strong along fronts thousands of kilometres in length. Battles lasted whole days, weeks and even months. Armaments and war matériel had become so technically perfected that men were helpless adjuncts. The war, moreover, was not confined to the front but increasingly invaded every aspect of daily life. Vast, fanatic propaganda campaigns spurred the passions of the warring peoples and poisoned relations between the nations of Europe for many years to come. In Germany the supreme command of the army intervened in all aspects of civilian and political life till finally the original unity and enthusiasm of the nation was crushed. The emperor, who should have interceded to moderate the army's grip of the nation, made no such attempt and even opined that 'politics emperor, who should have interceded to moderate the army's grip on the nation, made no such attempt and even opined that 'politics must be silent till strategy once more permits it to speak'.[12] The chancellor, Bethmann-Hollweg, and his two successors, Georg Michaelis and Count Georg von Hertling, proved too weak to control all competing forces and to assert the primacy of the political leadership. The vacuum at the top was filled by military men, primarily generals Paul von Hindenburg and Erich Ludendorff, who became the power behind the throne, though they lacked all political expertise. Thus the war gradually seeped into every corner of German life. The growing influence of the military ended only with the victory of the Entente powers, due largely to their superior economic capacity, especially after the United States joined the fray.

At first the war seemed to unfold in favour of the Central powers. Germany and Austria-Hungary had to face the threat of invasion on three fronts—to the west, the east and the south-east. When international political tensions began to mount after the turn of the century, Germany's military commanders elaborated a plan to cope with a war on several fronts. This plan called for a concentration of all possible forces in the west in order to force a quick decision with France while thin German forces fought a rearguard action in the east and Austrian forces held the south-east.

In August 1914 German forces successfully overran Belgium (in violation of her neutrality and international law), and stormed through northern France to the outskirts of Paris. However, they failed to encircle the enemy army and bring about a quick end to the war. The supreme commander of the French forces, General Joseph Joffre, mounted a counter-offensive, and after three days of fighting brought the German advance to a halt along the banks of the Marne. The Germans then raced towards the sea in an alternative attempt to turn the enemy line and surround him while taking control of the Channel ports. After a series of extraordinarily bloody battles in which three corps of volunteers, the flower of German youth, were wiped out, this offensive likewise failed. The war of rapid movement froze into a war of position as the opposing armies dug themselves into a continuous front stretching from the North Sea to Verdun and on to the Swiss border. All attempts by either side to break through this front failed until just before the end of the war, though hundreds of thousands of lives were lost in vain attempts to do so. After 1916 the German soldier suffered more 'than those of any ally or opponent. . . . Poorly fed, rarely allowed to any leave, with little hope of escaping the horror of the frontline while on all sides his comrades fell or were wounded',[13] he endured for four long years, 'four years that devastated the soul'.[14]

On the eastern front, strong Russian forces first pushed forward to the south and west, contrary to Germany's strategic hopes, conquering Galicia and part of northern Hungary. Two Russian armies advanced on East Prussia, driving back the thin German forces. The Russian advance was finally halted at Tannenberg and the Masurian lakes by the supreme commander of the Eighth Army, Paul von Hindenburg, and his chief of general staff, Erich Ludendorff. In order to relieve her Austrian ally, Germany then mounted an offensive, recovering Galicia, conquering Warsaw and occupying Lithuania and Courland. However, these successes did not bring final victory on the eastern front either, though the front remained fluid as late as October 1915. Thereafter a rigid continuous front stretched from Riga in the north to Romania in the south.

Responsibility for the southern front fell to Austria-Hungary. At first her forces advanced eastward past Belgrade, but were then driven back out of Serbia. In May 1915 Italy declared war on Austria in order to gain Trieste and the Tyrol. Though Italy did not pose a serious military threat to the Central powers, she did succeed in tying down strong divisions which were urgently required on other fronts.

The hopes of the Central powers were boosted by the entry of Turkey into the war. The Turks successfully blockaded the Dardanelles, cutting Russia off from her Western allies and interdicting the flow of essential arms from the more heavily industrialised West. Winston Churchill, first lord of the admiralty at that time, urged that an Anglo-French fleet be dispatched to open the straits. However, the Allied fleet floundered under heavy fire from Turkish forts and in the mines of the Bosporus. When army units were sent ashore, they too suffered heavy casualties.

In October 1915 Bulgaria threw in her lot with the Central powers, and Serbia was again overrun. By the autumn of 1915 a swath had been cleared from Berlin to Constantinople and on to Baghdad, and German armies operated from the North Sea to central and south-east Europe and the Near East. As a result, the lines of communication between the Entente powers were cut in the Sound and the Turkish Straits. In August 1916 Romania declared war on Austria but was quickly defeated and occupied. Her grain fields and oil reserves proved a windfall to the hard-pressed economies of the Central powers.

Striking successes in the field notwithstanding, the overall position of Germany and Austria-Hungary steadily worsened. Their

armies successfully defended the homelands and occupied broad
stretches of enemy territory, but Britain ruled the seas. German
colonies were not allowed to provide any assistance and were
quickly overrun. Meanwhile, the British blockade of the North Sea
between Scotland and southern Norway took a toll far more severe
than any army campaign. Immediately upon the outbreak of war,
London declared this to be a prohibited zone, in violation of
international law. German ships were excluded and neutral ships
heading for German ports were boarded and their cargoes seized.
Britain justified her blockade by contending that enemy strength in
a modern war depended not only on arms but also on industry and
agriculture. The interception of all German imports, whether raw
materials or foodstuffs, was therefore warranted and necessary.

In response to the British action, Germany decided upon a
counter-blockade enforced by submarines. According to the principles of international law, ships could only be sunk if demonstrably
transporting war matériel. The German campaign of unrestricted
submarine warfare ignored this injunction and neutral ships were
torpedoed without warning beginning in 1915. The U-boats were
later called off in response to vigorous protests from the United
States, but the campaign was renewed on 1 February 1917.

The German battle-fleet, the pride of the emperor and the most
important obstacle to a rapprochement with Britain before the war,
lay uselessly at anchor. It contacted the enemy only once, in the
Battle of Jutland in May 1916, and though it inflicted heavy losses,
never threatened to break the British blockade of Germany or
jeopardise Britannia's command of the seas.

As the blockade continued, the penury of raw materials grew so
severe that the German government was compelled in late 1916 to
order much more vigorous enforcement of the rationing system. At
the outset of the war the industrialist Walther Rathenau urged that
all strategic raw materials be rationed and he harnessed existing
production to serve the war effort. However, sufficient substitutes
could not be found for all the interdicted foreign imports, despite
the many ersatz materials developed for the civilian economy and
the invention of new methods of producing essential war matériel,
such as the Haber-Bosch process for recovering nitrogen from the
air for use in the munitions industry. Agricultural production
declined steadily due to the shortage of fertiliser and fodder and the
lack of vigorous, young farm hands. The amount of bread and
potatoes allotted through the food-rationing system introduced in
1915 declined from year to year. When the potato crop failed in
1916, producing a harvest less than half the amounts of the previous

year, turnips had to be substituted. The food shortage grew more and more unbearable, and a sense of hopelessness swept the home front.

Meanwhile the demand for war matériel continued to climb. Ludendorff responded late in 1916 by instituting the 'Hindenburg Programme' and the *Reichstag* passed a law requiring 'auxiliary patriotic service'. The Hindenburg Programme provided for the subordination of the entire economy to military procurement and for service in the war economy by all German males unfit for active duty and between the ages of seventeen and sixty. The nation was mobilised for total war.

However, the political unity of 1914 crumbled and internal division spread. Passionate political disputes erupted over the question of Germany's war aims and her ultimate peace terms, endangering national solidarity. Germany's successes in the first two years of the war encouraged broad strata of the population, especially conservatives and National Liberals, to overestimate their nation's strength. They accordingly insisted on a *Siegfrieden* (peace on German terms) which would compensate Germany for her suffering. Vast tracts of land would be annexed to ensure German security: in the West the ore deposits of Briey and Longwy would be seized, the German frontier would be extended to the Meuse, and Belgium would be integrated politically and economically into the *Reich* with German administrative rights over her coasts and the fortress of Liège. In the East, Poland and the Baltic states would be annexed. On the other hand, the Social Democrats, the Centre Party and the Progressive Party (*Fortschrittspartei*) campaigned for a 'peace of reconciliation' without annexations or reparations.

Despite internal differences of opinion, a majority of the Social Democrats continued to vote for the war credits demanded by the government, encouraged the trade unions to ensure the smooth operation of the armaments industry and thus supported the war effort. However, the suffering and material deprivation occasioned by the war induced the left wing of the party to secede and to found the Independent Social Democratic Party in the spring of 1917. The Independent Socialists then openly opposed the continuance of the war. The mounting internal tensions in Germany were underscored by a strike of munitions workers outraged by their meagre food rations in the spring of 1917 and by a naval mutiny in the summer.

In response to the internal threat, the chancellor attempted to allay social tensions by reforming the three-class franchise in Prussia. William II set the stage for social change in his Easter message, announcing that after all the 'momentous accomplishments in this frightful war' by every segment of the population, 'no more room exists for the class franchise in Prussia'.[15] The conservatives reacted bitterly while the majority faction in the *Reichstag*, composed of Centrists, liberals and Majority Social Democrats closed ranks under the leadership of the Centrist deputy Matthias Erzberger. Convinced that victory was no longer possible, despite the recourse to unrestricted submarine warfare, the majority declared in a joint peace resolution that it henceforth sought 'a peace of understanding and permanent reconciliation among the peoples'.[16] Bethmann Hollweg had agreed to unrestricted submarine warfare against his own better judgement, and in the question of the Prussian franchise he was again outmanoeuvred. His political credibility shattered, he was shunned by the parties in the *Reichstag*, though William II continued to support the chancellor. But eventually William bowed to pressure from Hindenburg and Ludendorff, and Bethmann Hollweg was dismissed. With Bethmann Hollweg's departure, all civilian influence in the government was lost. Henceforth, Ludendorff directed government policy and determined military and political strategy in Hindenburg's name. Bethmann Hollweg's successors as chancellor served simply as willing tools.

In the meantime, the military situation had seriously deteriorated from the viewpoint of the Central powers. The strain of the war had provoked severe internal crises in Britain and France, but David Lloyd George and Georges Clemenceau managed to crush all domestic resistance and to focus the energies of their nations on final victory. Their most effective weapon on the domestic front was the mounting hope that the United States would enter the fray. These hopes reached fruition in the spring of 1917, when Washington declared war on the Central powers, dramatically tipping the scales in favour of the Entente powers. The American decision was largely provoked by Germany's campaign of unrestricted submarine warfare, a strategy urged upon Berlin by Admiral Tirpitz. Since the High Command saw no possibility of successfully concluding the war without 'the full utilisation of all possible weapons',[17] Ludendorff took up the demand for unrestricted submarine warfare, oblivious to all political ramifications and despite Bethmann Hollweg's objections. However, the expected military advantages failed to materialise, and the political catastrophe of the United States' entry into the war helped to speed the final collapse.

In addition, Germany's Austrian ally was experiencing great difficulties in controlling her ethnic minorities after the death of Emperor Francis Joseph in November 1916. As their demands for autonomy and independent states grew more vociferous, Vienna made secret inquiries behind Berlin's back about the possibilities of concluding a peace with the Allied powers.

Before the United States entered the conflict Germany and her allies made their first peace overtures. After another of many secret attempts to negotiate a separate peace with Russia had failed, the *Reich* proposed in December 1916 on behalf of all the Central powers that a comprehensive peace treaty be negotiated. However, this suggestion was rejected by the Entente powers because it failed to specify any concrete conditions (Germany still hoped to change the political status quo especially at Belgium's expense) and spoke only of peace and reconciliation. The American president, Woodrow Wilson, intervened to urge all the warring nations to make known the precise conditions under which they would be prepared to conclude a truce and declared in a speech before the Senate that peace without victory was the goal for which all should strive. However, neither side was ready to accede to such a proposal.

Shortly after the peace resolution of the *Reichstag* was published, Pope Benedict XV's peace proposals were also rejected by the Entente powers on 1 August. Berlin reacted evasively to the papal note because it required Germany to restore full independence to Belgium, a condition strongly opposed by the High Command and those parties on the right who still believed in final victory. Since the Entente powers were equally determined to recover Alsace-Lorraine for France, the papal initiative failed.

The fateful year of 1917 dragged to a close with the drained and debilitated nations of Europe still locked in bitter conflict. France had managed to reassert herself in grinding trench warfare, and Britain's mastery of the seas remained unchallenged. When the United States and almost all the nations of Central and South America entered the conflict, Germany found herself at war with twenty-eight states, including six great powers, at a time when the strength of her own allies was ebbing. Despite the odds, the High Command clung to the hope that the German army could achieve a great breakthrough before the Americans reached Europe and could thereby compel the Allies to accept a peace favourable to the Central powers. A highly successful offensive in Italy at the end of October and the impact of the Russian Revolution seemed as if by providence to free enough forces for Germany to strike a quick, overwhelming blow on the western front. But this window of opportunity turned out to be a mirage.

The Bolshevik Revolution and Russia's
Withdrawal from the War

At the outset of the war Russia scored swift victories over Austrian forces in Galicia and thin German forces in East Prussia. But a counter-offensive mounted by Hindenburg and Ludendorff in August 1914 put the tsar on the defensive. In 1916 and 1917 the Russian army launched various attacks in an effort to break through the fronts established in 1915, but these attempts were sapped by the deepening exhaustion and demoralisation of the Russian troops. Morale and the will to fight were undermined by inadequate planning and coordination of military actions and by supply problems resulting from the fact that the Central powers had cut Russia's connections with the West. The huge losses at the front, the lack of labour in the homeland and the consequent famine in the large cities eventually drove the people into open revolt against the tsarist regime. Early in 1917 the British attempted to land in the Near East and to re-establish a bridge over which foodstuffs and war matériel could flow into Russia. But this attempt, like the tsar's belated efforts to suppress the insurrection, came too late to be effective.

After Russia's defeat in the war against Japan in 1904–5, the tsar had managed to control revolutionary forces by promulgating a constitution, creating a representative assembly or Duma, and pledging extensive land reform. But in 1917 the regime was overwhelmed. After an initial uprising of soldiers, peasants and workers, the Duma burst the pseudo-constitutional role it was supposed to fulfil and took charge of events despite the tsar's order to dissolve. A provisional government was formed, and Tsar Nicholas II was forced to abdicate in the middle of March. The new government, consisting mainly of progressive middle-class politicians, hoped to harness the revolution and institute a bourgeois-democratic republic. Freedom of the press, of assembly and association were guaranteed, a constituent assembly was promised, and all those persecuted or exiled for political reasons were allowed to return home.

However, the new government failed to respond to the chief demand of the common people: land and peace. In insisting on continuing the war and in failing to undertake long-overdue land reforms, the provisional government lost support to the soviets of soldiers, peasants and workers which sprang up in factories, the army and the countryside. These soviets increasingly viewed themselves as the sole legitimate voice of the people. The most powerful of the soviets, that in St Petersburg, began to function as an alternative government, severely undermining the authority of the provisional government. The crisis came to a head when the exhausted Russian army gathered its forces for a final offensive in Galicia under the new minister of war appointed by the provisional government, the Social Revolutionary Alexander Kerensky. Soldiers deserted the Russian colours in large numbers and fled homeward in order to be present when the land was redistributed. Revolting army units and sailors attempted to seize the capital in July, but the putsch was quashed by the government and the still-moderate majority in the soviets. In September Kerensky, who had assumed control of the provisional government, succeeded in crushing a counter-revolution launched by army units under General Lavr Kornilov. However, 'the transition from the first phase of the revolution, . . . which gave power to the bourgeoisie, to the second phase, which will put power in the hands of the proletariat and the poorest peasants',[18] could no longer be stopped.

The leader of the Bolsheviks, Vladimir Ilyitsh Lenin, was determined that he alone would decide when the time was ripe for this transition. He had arrived in St Petersburg in the middle of April by way of Switzerland and Sweden with the assistance of the German High Command, which hoped 'to sow revolution in Russia and thereby shatter the Allied coalition'.[19] Lenin immediately set out to undermine the provisional government with the appeal, 'All power to the soviets'. However, Lenin's Bolshevik followers were in a minority in the soviets compared to the Social Revolutionaries and the Mensheviks (moderate Russian social democrats) as late as the summer of 1917. Yet the inaction of the Kerensky government in the burning question of land and peace, the dynamism and discipline of the revolutionaries and their skilful use of propaganda propelled the Bolsheviks into a majority position between August and October 1917. The party swung into action. In November the Revolutionary Military Committee of the St Petersburg soviet under the direction of Leo Trotsky (the later organiser of the Red Army) urged the army regiments stationed in the capital to rise in revolt against the government. After quickly occupying all public buildings according to a carefully elaborated plan—especially telegraph and postal offices and train stations—the Bolsheviks took over St Petersburg and compelled the government to resign on 7 November. The All-Russian Congress of Workers' Soviets ratified the Bolshevik coup the next day after the less radical majority of Social Revolutionaries and Mensheviks had walked out of the Congress in protest against the use of violence. The first soviet government was constituted on 8 November with the creation of the Council of People's Commissars presided over by Lenin. This council immediately issued a 'peace decree' proposing a general armistice in the war and a second 'land decree' announcing the redistribution of land and the institution of worker control over production. The revolution spread like wildfire to Moscow and other centres. Soon a secret police force was organised, the 'Extraordinary All-Russian Commission of Struggle against Counter-Revolution, Speculation and Sabotage', better known as the 'Cheka' from its Russian initials. This force systematically eliminated all those opposed to Bolshevism.

The last obstacle to be overcome was the Constituent Assembly, whose delegates had been legally elected in an process supported by the Bolsheviks and which finally convened on 5 January 1918. A majority of the assembly advocated a socialist democracy in preference to a Bolshevik dictatorship, and after tumultuous disorders, Lenin had the assembly dissolved following its first day of meetings. He thereby brought about, in his own words, 'the complete and open liquidation of democracy in favour of the dictatorship of the proletariat'.[20] The Soviet Socialist Republic was born.

The Bolsheviks renamed themselves the Russian Communist Party and declared Moscow to be the seat of government. The first constitution of the Russian Soviet Federated Socialist Republic, promulgated on 10 July 1918, proclaimed the dictatorship of the proletariat and paid only lip-service to the sovereignty of the people. Soviets were retained from the revolution, but peasants, workers, party functionaries and soldiers in the new Red Army were only allowed to elect local councillors. All other soviets—the regional and provincial soviets and finally the All-Russian Congress of Soviets—were composed of deputies recruited from soviets one step lower in the hierarchy. Democratic elections to these bodies were out of the question. Moreover, all soviets exercised both legislative and executive powers in their sphere of competence. The thousand delegates to the Congress of Soviets elected a Central Executive Committee as the highest legislative, administrative and supervisory body in the land. The task of controlling the Executive Committee and managing daily affairs fell to the Council of People's Commissars comprising the eighteen heads of department. Alongside this system of soviets and the bureaucracy stood the party, taking its direction from its political heart, the Politburo. The party's organisational wing, the Orgburo, was responsible for appointments to the highest positions in the land. Opposition was not allowed, either in the party or the state, and those suspected of harbouring contrary opinions were arrested and executed. Supreme power fell to the general secretary of the Communist Party, who used this key post to rule over the state.

Resistance to the new government mounted in many segments of the Russian population in reaction to the total restructuring of society, the murder of the tsar and his family, the dispossession and liquidation of political opponents and the former ruling classes, and the ban on all religious manifestations outside churches. These grievances, aggravated by famine and internal chaos, sparked a fierce civil war. In a bloody struggle lasting three years, Lenin and Trotsky triumphed over the White Russian forces, supported by the Entente powers, and firmly entrenched Bolshevik rule.

Final victory, however, came at a high price. In order to 'gain some leeway during a certain period to further and consolidate the socialist revolution',[21] Lenin concluded a ceasefire with the Central powers on 15 December 1917, followed by the Treaty of Brest-Litovsk on 3 March 1918. The German High Command exploited to the hilt the weakness of the budding Bolshevik government, despite the protestations of the secretary of state in the Foreign Office, Richard von Kühlmann. Though the Russians insisted on peace without annexations or reparations and on the self-determination of peoples, the German military leadership domi-nated by Ludendorff eventually imposed a treaty which deprived Russia of the Baltic states, Finland, Poland and the Ukraine. The Russian Empire lost much of its population, three-quarters of its iron and steel industry and almost one-quarter of its textile indus-try. The peoples liberated from Russian rule were delighted to receive their freedom and independence, but as German occupation of the areas vacated by the Russians dragged on, their original sympathy for Germany began to dissipate. The harsh conditions imposed on Russia in the Treaty of Brest-Litovsk also hardened the resolve of the Western powers to fight to the finish, lest they fall victim to the same fate.

The Treaty of Brest-Litovsk greatly eased the military pressure on the Central powers. This effect was reinforced in May by the Treaty of Bucharest, which conceded control over the Romanian economy to Germany. Even though some troops were still required on the eastern front to hold the occupied territories, the bulk of these armies could be transferred to the west. Thus rough numerical equality was re-established in the western theatre, at least until large numbers of American soldiers arrived.

Military Defeat and the Flight of the German Emperor

The departure of Russia from the ranks of Germany's foes raised hopes in the High Command that the war could still be won by launching an enormous offensive in the west which would pierce enemy lines before US reinforcements could arrive. Between March and July 1918 Ludendorff led four great assaults on the Allied trenches—at the Somme, Ypres, the Chemin des Dames and the Marne. The Germans dented the Allied lines but failed to break through. By July the German army was exhausted, reserves were spent, and supplies were depleted. On 18 July the Allies launched a counter-offensive under the supreme command of Marshal Ferdinand Foch. Strong contingents of French, British and American troops soon drove the Germans from all the land they had gained since May. An attack spearheaded by tanks on 8 August near Amiens finally compelled the Germans to retreat. Exhausted, the army barely managed to prevent the better equipped and numerically superior enemy forces from achieving a major breakthrough.

However, military defeat could no longer be averted in the long run. The army sensed it, from the highest ranks to the lowest, though still outwardly denying it. 'Victory is impossible',[22] was the consensus of soldiers' letters after September. The chief of staff of the Seventh Army, General Walther Reinhardt, wrote to his wife in early October:

We must admit reality. Over a million men have sacrificed their lives for the sake of the fatherland, and those prepared to die are no longer so numerous. To carry on a highly disadvantageous struggle solely for the sake of honour can probably be demanded of a good army unit, but it cannot be demanded of an entire people.[23]

Imminent collapse loomed on other fronts as well. On 15 September the Entente powers launched a successful offensive against Bulgaria. Already by the end of September the Bulgarians had been forced to conclude a truce that opened their ports and railways to the Allies. The whole southern flank of the Central powers was torn asunder. Romania could no longer be held, communications between Turkey and Germany were interrupted and the Allies were free to advance on Constantinople. At the same time the British army broke through Turkish lines in Palestine, taking Damascus, Beirut, Aleppo and Mosul. By the end of October Turkey had capitulated. In mid-September the Austrian emperor proposed peace parleys when his soldiers of many nationalities simply deserted the front. He hoped as well to save the Austrian Empire through a number of concessions to the various national groups, but these measures came too late. The Allies could sense final victory, and mindful of the dimensions of their victories in France and Belgium and of the demise of Germany's allies in the east, they pressed for capitulation not negotiation. The Entente powers officially recognised the Czechs as co-belligerents, and they together with the Poles and the Croats insisted all the more vehemently on their national independence. The signs of dissolution in the Austro-Hungarian Empire and the demise of Bulgaria and Turkey suddenly prompted Ludendorff to lose his nerve at the end of September. Together with Hindenburg he insisted that the government 'seek without delay an armistice from President Wilson of America with a view to obtaining a peace on the basis of his fourteen points'.[24]

Wilson had elaborated his Fourteen Points early in 1918 before the Congress of the United States as a response to the peace proposals of the Russian revolutionaries and the negotiations of Brest-Litovsk. Wilson hoped to minimise the possibility of such terrible wars in the future by bringing about a 'just peace' on the basis of the democratic self-determination of peoples. In place of the traditional international system based on secret understandings, national interests and power politics, the American president hoped to see 'A general association of nations . . . formed under specific covenants for the purpose of affording mutual guarantees of political independence and territorial integrity to great and small states alike'.[25] The voluntary cooperation of the nations of the world in such a league required states that were democratic in nature rather than autocratic or totalitarian. The American war aims outlined in this programme included the full restitution of Belgium; the return of Alsace-Lorraine to France; Italian borders that observed the nationality of the local population; an independent Poland with access to the sea; the liberation of foreign peoples under Turkish domination; the internal autonomy of the various nationalities in the Austro-Hungarian Empire; a settlement of colonial claims that considered the interests of the natives; public peace treaties; and the freedom of the seas.

In the meantime, on 3 October, a parliamentary government was established in Germany, also at the urging of the High Command, in the hope that a 'revolution from above' would help to prevent the collapse of the political and social order. The new government was formed by the majority parties in the *Reichstag* under the leadership of Prince Max von Baden, a well-known liberal and proponent of peace without annexations.

In his capacity as chancellor, Prince Max at first resisted the High Command's demand that Germany sue immediately for peace. He pointed out the harmful consequences, both internal and external, of overly precipitous action: it would inevitably produce internal disorder, which parliamentary government had been instituted in order to prevent, and would apprise Germany's enemies of the full extent of her military collapse. But Prince Max soon yielded to the High Command, and in the night between 3 and 4 October a request was sent out for 'the immediate conclusion of a truce'.[26] After a lengthy exchange of notes with the American government, a reply was received on 23 October. It demanded that Germany immediately withdraw from the occupied territories and cease submarine warfare. Wilson further indicated that 'the government of the United States cannot deal with any but veritable representatives of the German people'[27] thereby signalling the demise of the monarchy.

Ludendorff's immediate response was to oppose capitulation and to appeal to the troops to carry on the struggle; but then he disclaimed all responsibility and asked to be relieved of his command. The *Reichstag* altered the Constitution to prepare the transition to a parliamentary government, and Prussia finally abolished the three-class franchise. However, these long overdue reforms came too late to ensure stability and were easily overlooked in the ensuing maelstrom of events. By the end of October, sailors had mutinied in Wilhelmshafen and refused to put out to sea in order to engage the enemy. In just a few days the revolt spread to the other German ports as well. The abdication of the emperor was just a matter of time. William was blamed by much of the population for continuing the war and had become the object of their anger and despair. On 7 November a revolution broke out in Munich and quickly spread to Berlin, where striking workers joined forces with disaffected soldiers.

The revolution swept through the other cities and states of the *Reich*, toppling not only the Hohenzollerns but all the ruling dynasties. Completely isolated, William II fled into exile in Holland. In Berlin Philipp Scheidemann of the Social Democrats proclaimed the German Republic, and Prince Max von Baden resigned his position as chancellor in favour of Friedrich Ebert.

The new government, known as the Council of People's Representatives, had to confront the painful duty of concluding a peace treaty. Ludendorff cynically remarked before the chiefs of the High Command that in so doing it would be forced 'to swallow the soup that it prepared for us'.[28] Ludendorff thus sought to shift responsibility for the final catastrophe to those very political parties which had urged the government to seek a conciliatory peace at a time when this may still have been possible and when Ludendorff was still demanding a peace favourable to Germany, before finally admitting military defeat and insisting on an immediate truce. While responsible politicians from the governing parties shouldered the burdens of defeat, conservative politicians and military leaders strove to deny their own failure by claiming that the army had not been defeated in the field but rather stabbed in the back by socialists, anti-war agitators and the November revolutionaries. Though this interpretation was clearly at odds with the facts, it was encouraged by Hindenburg and Ludendorff and was passionately embraced by much of the German public, which had been totally unprepared for the suddenness of the military collapse. This stab-in-the-back theory would weigh heavily on the political atmosphere in Germany throughout the Weimar Republic.

The primary responsibility for the ultimate catastrophe was further clouded by the High Command's insistence that Germany's delegation to the peace parleys be headed not by a military man but by the Centrist politician Matthias Erzberger. The irony of this situation was compounded by the fact that Erzberger had been one of the first politicians in Germany to call for an end to the war and a conciliatory peace. In this way the generals who had insisted on an immediate truce were spared the humiliation of admitting defeat, while foisting off on politicians the odium and shame which many Germans attached to the military collapse and capitulation.

The Allied peace terms turned out to be extremely severe, far exceeding the worst fears of the German government. Alsace-Lorraine and all the occupied territories in France, Belgium and Luxembourg were to be evacuated; the Allies would occupy the left bank of the Rhine; all German submarines and large quantities of guns, ammunition and trucks had to be relinquished; the German fleet was to be disbanded, and all Allied prisoners-of-war were to be freed immediately. The peace treaties of Brest-Litovsk and Bucharest were declared invalid and the food blockade around Germany was to continue. When asked for instructions, Hindenburg replied that the treaty had to be accepted even if no alleviation of its terms could be achieved. With the words, 'a people numbering 70 million suffers but does not perish',[29] Erzberger thereupon signed the document prepared by Marshal Foch, the supreme commander of the Allied forces. Thus Germany's capitulation was accomplished and an end set to four years of enormous bloodshed.

The *Kaiserreich*, which Germans believed had been attacked in the first days of August 1914 and to whose defence they had valiantly rallied, existed no more.

Two million had perished and the people were in a state of shock. The foe, over which victory was confidently expected in 1914, had emerged triumphant. . . . The world seemed out of joint. Citizens wandered the streets poorly fed and barely clothed. They had sacrificed their gold for the fatherland, their sons were dead or in prison camps and those who did return were cruelly changed.[30]

The values to which the vast majority of Germans had cleaved in 1914 'were shattered and—if one may speak of the confidence of an entire nation—that confidence was shaken'.[31]

The world had changed, though not only for Germans. All Europe had suffered terribly. The war had exacted terrible sacrifices of blood and property: almost 10 million dead, towns and villages in ruin, nations weighed down by debts, shaky currencies, stagnant world commerce, and hunger and poverty across broad stretches of what once had been a flourishing continent. The passions of war had loosed a paroxysm of nationalism which made reconciliation virtually impossible. The lights of Old Europe had gone out; only the future would tell whether they would ever shine again—a future to be largely shaped by Germany's foes. The heirs to Wilhelminian Germany suddenly found themselves in a fledgling republic, unburdened by responsibility for the collapse of the *Reich* but heavily handicapped by its legacy.

11

The Weimar Republic

1919:   Elections to the Constituent Assembly; the Weimar Coalition;
        the Weimar Constitution; Germany signs the Treaty of Versailles
        (see Maps 5 and 6)
1920:   Kapp putsch; communist uprisings in the Ruhr district and
        central Germany; Weimar Coalition loses its parliamentary
        majority in elections to the *Reichstag*
1922:   Treaty of Rapallo
1923:   The year of crisis: struggle in the Ruhr district; inflation reaches
        its peak; uprisings of the radical right and left in Hamburg,
        central Germany, eastern Germany and Bavaria; stabilisation of
        the currency and the fall of Gustav Stresemann
1924:   Dawes Plan; Friedrich Ebert dies
1925:   Hindenburg elected *Reichspräsident*; Locarno
1926:   Germany admitted to the League of Nations
1928:   Kellogg Pact
1929:   Great Depression; Young Plan
1930–2: Heinrich Brüning becomes chancellor and Hindenburg
        is re-elected president
1933:   Adolf Hitler named chancellor

The Origins of the Republic

After the collapse of the old regime, confusion and uncertainty
reigned. 'The word "freedom" took on a bitter meaning'[1] in
Germany—a consequence of the deep animosity between the peoples of Europe encouraged by their national governments—and
many Germans shared the hope or fear of the writer and front-line
officer Ernst Jünger that 'this war will not mark the end but the
beginning of violence'.[2] Yet the vast majority of the German people,
long accustomed to obedience, simply resigned themselves with a
feeling of despondency and alienation to what seemed the inevitable

233

consequences of military defeat. Few Germans desired and none had fought for the republican form of government which now befell them. Hence they tended to view it as a consequence of defeat. Even Philipp Scheidemann had only proclaimed the republic in order to steal a march on a determined minority eager to exploit the social collapse in order to create a soviet republic akin to Russia.

The maintenance of the Allied food blockade greatly magnified the general distress. Hunger and disease were widespread. Women, children and the aged dreaded the onset of winter, whose icy blasts they could not hope to escape for want of fuel. Fathers and sons, whose help was so badly needed in the home, were still immobilised on the front—in so far as they had survived at all.

The political situation was anything but encouraging after the revolution at the end of October. To be sure, the revolution and the armistice had helped at first to heal the rift between the Majority Social Democrats and their Independent brethren, enabling Friedrich Ebert of the Majority Social Democrats to take over the office of chancellor from Prince Max von Baden and to form a government, the Council of People's Representatives, with three representatives from each of the two parties. Soon, however, the accord between the parties dissipated and the old quarrels erupted again. The Majority Socialists advocated the immediate convocation of a national assembly, chosen through universal, direct, secret and equal election, in order to form a democratic, parliamentary state based on the rule of law. The Independent Social Democrats wanted a period of time to consolidate the power they had acquired through the revolution before summoning a national assembly which would proclaim a socialist republic. Both Social Democratic parties were opposed by the Spartacus League, founded in 1917 by Karl Liebknecht, the son of one of the co-founders of the German Social Democratic Party, and Rosa Luxemburg, a Polish socialist. The Spartacus League worked to establish the dictatorship of the proletariat.

In the course of the ensuing power struggle, Friedrich Ebert succeeded as chairman of the Council of People's Representatives in consolidating his authority. He was a firm opponent of violence and a 'true statesman'[3] who had risen from a journeyman harness-maker through the trade-union movement to the leadership of the Social Democratic Party. Cautious and moderate, Ebert rightly believed that there were severe restrictions on the lengths to which the German revolution of 1918–19 could be carried, given the weakness of the revolutionary forces in Germany. Eduard Bernstein, the chief proponent before the war of a revisionist course in the Social

Democratic Party, later commented:

The republic could take up the struggle against some bourgeois parties and classes, but not against all of them without placing itself in an untenable position. The republic could only support the great burden it bore if substantial portions of the bourgeoisie were committed to its survival and prosperity. . . . It was essential as a matter of self-preservation to lure bourgeois republican parties into the government. This was necessary as well if Germany was to survive as a nation.[4]

Even the trade unions, which deemed themselves the 'legitimate representative of the working class',[5] thought that the socialisation of large industry in Germany was impossible because of the difficult social conditions at the end of the war. So long as the unions' concrete objectives in regard to wages, hours and working conditions were met, they were content to leave industry in the hands of the traditional industrial élite. This conclusion on the part of the trade unions rendered any radical political transformation utterly impossible. It also set the stage for a compromise between the two great social adversaries: employers and workers. This new social phenomenon found tangible expression in the Central Cooperative Union, founded on 15 November 1918 thanks not least to the friendly personal relationship between Carl Legien, the chairman of the Central Commission of Trade Unions and the Ruhr industrialist Hugo Stinnes.

Radical political change was also stymied by the fact that industrial workers represented only about one-third of the entire population. In contrast with Russia, there was little chance that they would join forces with the peasantry, which had never shown the slightest inclination to join the socialist movement, even in areas where it was largely composed of easily exploited farm-hands.

Ebert's final victory over the radical left was assured not only by the cooperation between industrialists and workers but also by the decision of the Majority Socialists to seek the support of the army, the officer corps and the old bureaucracy. With their help Ebert was able to limit the impact of the German revolution on the economic and social spheres. However, this tactic resulted in the admission into the body politic of traditionally minded groups who were indifferent or even hostile to the republic. The Majority Socialists were apparently willing to run this risk as the lesser of two evils— probably in the expectation that right-wing opposition could be gradually overcome.

The revolutionary socialists clung to their original goals, from which they could not be diverted even by majority resolutions of the Workers' and Soldiers' Councils. The three Independent Socialists in the government resigned their positions and were replaced by deputies from the Social Democratic Party. The working-class movement suffered a further schism at the congress of the Spartacus League when radicals led by Karl Liebknecht, Rosa Luxemburg and Lenin's representative in Germany, Karl Radek, founded the Communist Party on 30 December 1918. It immediately announced that the Ebert government had been deposed and on 6 January 1919 launched a hopeless uprising in Berlin known as the Spartacus Revolt. This revolt, together with the later uprising in Hamburg, was crushed in bloody street battles by the 'free corps'—armed bands formed from remnants of the German army under the command of Gustav Noske, a Majority Socialist and member of the Council of People's Representatives. The same fate befell the short-lived soviet republics created in Munich, Brunswick and Bremen.

Besides all the internal disturbances, the government had to cope on the international front with Polish incursions across Germany's eastern frontier. Two days after the Spartacus Revolt the government issued an appeal for the creation of a voluntary border patrol to fend off these attacks.

Despite all the perils, elections to the Constituent Assembly were duly held on 19 January 1919, as advocated by the General Congress of Workers' and Soldiers' Councils. Participating in the electoral campaign were the Social Democrats, the Independent Social Democrats, the Centre Party, the Bavarian People's Party, the German Democratic Party (formed from the old Progressive Party), the German People's Party (formed from the monarchist wing of the defunct National Liberal Party), and the German National People's Party, which had emerged from conservative, nationalistic circles. The Communists however refused to take part.

With the exception of the Independent Socialists, all the parties advocated 'the only possible form of government, the parliamentary system'.[6] The new parliament would delegate the necessary authority to a central organ resting 'on the firm foundation of the will of the people' and would put an end to 'the disorder to which Germany is unfortunately subjected'.[7] Most of the parties hoped that the new Germany would 'not take the form of a socialist republic'[8] but would become instead a democratic republic. The majority actively opposed the German Nationals, who planned to restore the monarchy, and the Independent Socialists, who hoped to experiment with socialisation.

Eighty-three per cent of eligible voters participated in the election and the Majority Social Democrats, the German Democrats and the Centre Party collected almost four-fifths of the votes. These parties had been advocating parliamentary government ever since their deputies in the *Reichstag* had established a joint committee in 1917. The Social Democrats formed the strongest fraction, as in the parliament of 1912, but they failed to achieve an absolute majority despite a substantial increase in their popular support to 37.9 per cent of the votes cast. They therefore continued to rely on the Centre Party and the German Democratic Party. These parties banded together in Parliament to form the so-called Weimar Coalition, backed by 76.2 per cent of the electorate. The German people, hard pressed by internal and external dangers, had clearly rejected both monarchism and soviet-style socialism. This unequivocal verdict was made possible by the strongly pro-democratic stance of the Social Democratic Party, which in alliance with the trade unions, rallied the support of most of the working class.

The danger of disturbances in Berlin led the National Assembly to meet in the town of Weimar, the symbol of the humanist legacy of German classicism. Friedrich Ebert transferred to the National Assembly the governmental authority he had exercised in the name of the Council of People's Representatives. The deputies then elected him to the office of *Reichspräsident* and empowered his party, the Social Democrats, to form a new cabinet. In his acceptance speech, Ebert promised 'to act as a representative of the entire German people, not as the spokesman of a single party', and he described the common objective of all German parliamentarians in the following terms:

to secure a peace treaty that will bestow self-determination on the German people; to advance and defend the Constitution, which guarantees political equality to all German men and women; to create work and provide food for the German people; and to develop the economy in such a way that 'freedom' does not continue to mean the freedom to beg but rather freedom to develop a rich cultural life.[9]

In this programmatic declaration Ebert put his finger on the twin tasks which the government would have to fulfil if the stability and longevity of the German republic was to be assured.

On 16 February 1919 the cabinet was formed from Social Democratic, German Democratic and Centrist deputies, and Philipp Scheidemann was named chancellor. The National Assembly then began to debate the future constitution of the republic, which was finally approved on 31 July 1919 in a roll-call vote of the deputies and promulgated by the *Reichspräsident* on 11 August.[10] Conceived in the depths of the worst crisis the nation had ever faced, the Constitution drew heavily on the ideas of 1848 and strove to entrench democracy at both the federal and provincial levels. The new republic, based on the fundamental principle of the sovereignty of the people, was again styled the German *Reich*. Its flag of red, black and gold alluded to the ideals of the revolution of 1848 rather than to Bismarck's empire symbolised by red, black and white.

The framers of the Constitution originally planned to restructure the *Reich* in order to create *Länder*, or provinces, of equal size, which meant that Prussia would have to be dissolved. In the end, though, the traditional structure of Bismarck's Germany was retained. The federal government, as the supreme legislative authority, was endowed with far greater authority over the *Länder* than had been the case in the Bismarckian constitution, as a result of the perceived threat at the time to German unity. The special rights of the south German states were extinguished and the central government was strengthened, especially by provisions which allowed the *Reich* to levy direct taxes.

The universal, secret and equal franchise was extended to include women, and proportional representation replaced the system of majority representation hitherto in force. Provisions for plebiscites and referenda strengthened the democratic nature of the Constitution. Like the framers of the old constitution of Paulskirche, the authors of the Weimar Constitution included a separate bill of rights to safeguard freedom, personal liberties, and rights of churches and social groups. The bill of rights also guaranteed the right of assembly and of coalition, the right to petition, freedom of faith and conscience, free scientific inquiry and the independence of the judiciary. The bill of rights contained further provisions related to labour and the social and economic interests of blue- and white-collar workers; it protected marriage and the family and it detailed rights and obligations concerning property and the distribution and use of land. However, the bill of rights was not legally effective by itself and had to be expressed in laws.

Among the key institutions of the republic—the *Reichspräsident*, the *Reichstag* and the government—supreme authority fell to the *Reichstag* as the voice of all the people. It was empowered to pass legislation, and the government was responsible to it. It alone could vote a lack of confidence in the chancellor or his ministers and demand their resignation.

Not only the *Reichstag* was directly elected by the people but also the *Reichspräsident*, whose term covered seven years. He represented the government, appointed and dismissed civil servants and army officers, and possessed wide-ranging emergency powers in order to safeguard public order. Although Article 48 of the Constitution limited these emergency powers by subjecting them to endorsement by the *Reichstag*, this check was later virtually nullified when the *Reichstag* proved unable to fulfil its responsibilities. This was primarily the result of the very fair but politically impractical scheme of proportional representation. Numerous splinter parties gained representation in the *Reichstag*, and strong majorities could not be formed. The resultant political vacuum was filled more and more by the *Reichspräsident* having recourse to his emergency powers. This unhappy situation eventually led to the collapse of the parliamentary system and the end of the Weimar Republic.

While attempting to fashion a new political system, Germans also had to contend with the final provisions of the peace treaty with the Allies. These provisions turned out to be extremely harsh and varied substantially from the Fourteen Points of President Wilson on which the imperial government had relied when suing for an armistice. What had been offered in the spring of 1918 turned out to be no longer valid by the autumn. In order to gain European acceptance of a League of Nations, President Wilson had to relinquish nearly all his ideals—though in the end even the League failed to fulfil the purpose which Wilson had intended. The peace negotiations were heavily influenced instead by the desire of the victorious European powers to seek revenge and to ensure their own security. Germany was not even allowed to be present at the discussions, lest direct negotiations foster divisions between the Allied powers. The leading statesmen of Europe, especially the French prime minister, commonly known as 'Tiger' Clemenceau, lacked the moderation and cool rationalism that had typified delegates to the Congress of Vienna in 1815. Like their peoples, the statesmen were animated by blind hatred and a thirst for revenge, and their efforts were destined to have baleful results. Germany had to expect harsh terms as an inevitable consequence of defeat, and she probably would have accepted with equanimity a rather painful peace treaty, especially since the German annexationists would hardly have proved any more lenient if the outcome of the war had been different. What deeply embittered the Germans, however, was the victors' determination to so weaken Germany in every possible way that the much heralded 'freedom' in which they believed betokened nothing more than the freedom to be destitute. The Allied demand that the Germans acknowledge their sole responsibility for the war and extradite so-called war criminals were felt to be outrages which only added fuel to the fire. In insisting on these demands, the Allies did much to assist the cause of extremists in Germany who rejected the Weimar Republic out of hand, and sought to destroy it with the help of deep-seated resentment of the Treaty of Versailles.

The Allied peace terms deprived Germany of a good eighth of her territory, with losses in the north, south, east and west. Germany lost six and a half million inhabitants, one-quarter of her coal production, three-quarters of her ore deposits and almost half her pig-iron- and steel-producing facilities. The left bank of the Rhine was occupied for a period ranging from five to fifteen years and thereafter would be permanently demilitarised. The army was reduced to 100,000 men and the navy to 15,000. All merchant ships over 1600 register tonnes and half of all ships between 1000 and 1600 register tonnes were confiscated. Large quantities of railway equipment, submarine cables, wood livestock, and so on, were likewise seized. Monetary reparations of an amount and over a period as yet to be determined were also exacted. The Saar region was placed under the administration of the League of Nations for fifteen years while France exploited its mines. At Clemenceau's insistence, Austria was prevented from uniting with Germany, which would have been the culmination of an ancient dream. Claiming that Germany had administered her colonies incompetently, Britain appropriated most of them in addition to the Arab lands seized from the Turks, and ruled them through a mandate from the League of Nations. Germany and the states allied with her during the war were at first barred from the League, which took up its deliberations in Geneva on 20 January 1920. Germans inevitably gained the impression that this association of Allied and affiliated powers existed solely in order to secure the war booty of the victorious powers. Germany's allies—Austria, Hungary, Bulgaria and Turkey—were forced to accept equally punitive terms and all suffered large losses of territory to the victors or to the newly emerging states of Eastern and South-Eastern Europe.

When the German delegation, led by foreign minister Count Ulrich von Brockdorff-Rantzau, was finally presented to the victors in Versailles, it faced a *fait accompli*. All it could do was to sign the treaty on 7 May 1919. As Clemenceau handed over the text, he informed the German delegates:

This is neither the time nor the place for superfluous words. . . . The hour of reckoning has come. You have asked us for a peace and we are disposed to grant [it] to you. But it has been purchased far too dearly by all the peoples represented here for us not to be unanimous in our determination to employ all methods at our disposal to achieve every satisfaction to which we are entitled.[11]

When the terms of the Treaty of Versailles became known in Germany, a passionate debate arose over whether such a treaty should be refused. All the parties in the *Reichstag* were at first inclined to reject it. The government majority was loath to put its signature to the treaty, sharing Scheidemann's view that the hand 'which lays itself and us in such shackles' would surely wither.[12] The cabinet consequently resigned. On 16 June the Allies delivered an ultimatum demanding that Germany sign the treaty within a week and threatened to resume the war, continue the blockade and invade the *Reich*. The High Command, recognising the hopelessness of the situation, declared a resumption of hostilities to be utterly futile, and the National Assembly authorised the new government, composed of Social Democrats and Centrists, to sign the treaty without conditions. The Opposition parties affirmed the patriotic motives of those who voted to sign the treaty, since they too saw no alternative if the nation was to be saved. In the decisive session of the National Assembly on 22 June 1919, the Social Democrat Paul Löbe directed the following appeal to the victors:

When we vote to accept the peace treaty, we are prepared to do all we can to fulfill its terms to the limits of our endurance. This is the inexorable consequence of the outcome of the war. But what is impossible remains so even after our signature. A crushed and hungry people is not able to work; an abused and violated people is not only deprived of its own pleasure but deprives its violator as well. What is impossible in the peace terms will therefore have to be removed through peaceful negotiations conducted in a spirit of understanding and cooperation.[13]

The treaty was signed on 28 June 1919 by Hermann Müller and Johannes Bell—in the very Hall of Mirrors of the Palace of Versailles where a united German empire had been proclaimed almost fifty years earlier. It was to take effect on 10 January 1920. By deeply humiliating the German nation the Treaty of Versailles added appreciably to the stresses which the Weimar Republic had to bear as it sought to consolidate itself while besieged by enemies from within and without.

In the end it was not the Kaiser but the Weimar Republic which had signed the Treaty of Versailles and now sought to fulfil its provisions. This was a source of great strength to internal enemies of the republic. Compelled by the treaty to reduce the army to 100,000 officers and men, the government had immediately to confront soldiers banded together in the free corps, who naturally resisted the dissolution of their units. They openly revolted and attempted to seize power, occupying Berlin and proclaiming the installation of a new government under the East Prussian official Wolfgang Kapp. The bulk of former soldiers in northern Germany joined the putsch, and the republican government was forced to flee to Dresden and then to Stuttgart. The Army High Command under General Hans von Seeckt refused to take an active role in putting down the revolt, though it did disapprove of it. The putsch was overcome after only four days by a general strike of industrial workers and by the refusal of senior civil servants to cooperate with Kapp. But the prestige of the German republic had suffered a stinging blow, and the communists were emboldened to undertake a putsch of their own. A series of communist uprisings broke out in Berlin, Münster and the Ruhr district—only to be crushed with the assistance of the army and troops who had participated in the Kapp putsch. Despite the government's success in meeting the challenges from the left and the right, the confidence of the citizenry in the new government and in the parties responsible for the new constitution was permanently damaged. In the elections of 6 June 1920 the Weimar Coalition lost its parliamentary majority while the parties of the extreme right and left gained seats. The *Reichswehr* also consolidated its position as a 'state within the state' as a result of the government's serious error in judgement in summoning it to help put down the communist uprisings.

Immediately after the great military collapse of 1918, Germans had come together in hope of a new beginning and in a broad commitment to democracy. But this consensus was fleeting. Enthusiasm for democracy and for the new republic was quickly undermined by the humiliation of Versailles and Germany's economic woes. While the parties which supported the republic should have been agreeing on a joint programme, they remained fixated on their clashing fundamental ideologies and short-term goals. Never having had an opportunity to participate in government under the emperor, these parties had not learnt the art of compromise. This quality was sorely missed when they suddenly assumed responsibility for the republic and were called upon to build coalitions able to command a solid majority in the *Reichstag*. Instead, all that emerged in Parliament were relatively homogeneous minority governments, dependent on the toleration of the majority.

The campaign against the democratic state and its leaders began in earnest early in 1920 when the Treaty of Versailles came into effect and the government took steps to comply with its political and economic provisions. The Kapp putsch, the communist revolts and the ongoing vituperation against the democratic government unleashed a wave of lawlessness and disorder. In the odious political atmosphere of this time, the radical right resorted with mounting frequency to political assassination. As early as 1919 it had murdered the communist leaders Karl Liebknecht and Rosa Luxemburg and the prime minister of the revolutionary government of Bavaria, Kurt Eisner. Rightists then assassinated Matthias Erzberger and Walther Rathenau, two politicians who had done much to help Germany recover from her greatest defeat but who were often defamed as 'November criminals' and 'appeasement politicians'. They paid with their lives for their valiant attempts to cope with a difficult situation, which those who presumed to judge them had done much to bring about. Broad segments of the public, and most importantly many officials in the judicial system, came to detest the new republic and sympathised with the right-wing fanatics organised in secret assassination squads.

Fanatical nationalism reached new heights when the Allies finally set Germany's total reparations bill at 132,000 million gold marks. The right-wing press had formerly denounced democratic politicians for having 'botched the victory', 'extended the war' or 'mangled the peace'; now they decried them for 'selling out Germany'.[14] In actual fact, the German government had only caved in to the demands of the Allies when French troops advanced to the gates to the Ruhr district in Düsseldorf, Duisburg and Ruhrort and threatened to occupy the entire region if payment was not forthcoming.

The government's attempts to meet the Allied demands for reparations hastened the collapse of the German currency. The inflationary process, initiated by huge state loans taken out during the war, suddenly leapt ahead. The savings of the German people—accumulated during the war and immediately thereafter because of the shortage of consumer goods—rapidly lost all value. Vast numbers of people, and the middle class in particular, forfeited their life savings. As war bonds lost their value, the public lost confidence in the financial stability of the state. The government did not dare to stanch the flow of reparations to the West, lest the threatened sanctions be imposed; but at the same time it feared internal uprisings and a revolution if it sought to increase its revenues by adopting a sharply deflationary policy accompanied by rising taxes, diminished social programmes and a wage and price freeze. It therefore allowed inflation to run its course. Between 1919 and mid-1921 the mark fell on international money markets from 8.9 per dollar to 56; between July 1929 and the end of the year it tumbled further from 76 per dollar to over 191. By January 1923 the mark had collapsed to 17,972 to the dollar and by the peak of the inflation on 15 November the astronomical figure of 4.2 billion marks to the dollar was reached. As the value of the currency sank, prices shot upwards and the supply of goods dwindled. In August 1922 the insolvent *Reich* was granted a moritorium on its cash payments to the Allies, but large quantities of goods and materials continued to be delivered. When these deliveries finally fell behind schedule, the Allied Reparations Commission officially declared on 9 January 1923 that the *Reich* had failed to meet its commitments and had intentionally contravened the Treaty of Versailles.

Raymond Poincaré, the prime minister of France and an implacable Germanophobe, was determined to see the stipulations of the treaty fulfilled. Over British objections but with the backing of Italy and Belgium, he arranged to dispatch a Franco-Belgian commission of engineers to Germany in order to ensure the regular flow of cash payments and to enforce strict adherence to the delivery schedule drawn up by the Reparations Commission. In order to protect this civilian commission, French and Belgian troops occupied the entire Ruhr district.

The German government thereupon halted all reparations payments to France and Belgium. (This government had consisted since November 1922 of representatives of the German People's Party, the German Democratic Party, the Centre Party and the Bavarian People's Party as well as some figures without party affiliation. The office of chancellor was held by Wilhelm Cuno, who had risen through the financial bureaucracy and was not affiliated with any party.) The German ambassadors to Paris and Brussels were recalled and a campaign of passive resistance was initiated throughout the occupied territories. Clerks and railway workers were instructed to refuse to assist the French in their economic exploitation of the Ruhr. Poincaré reacted by deporting German railway workers from the occupied territories, expropriating factories, and laying criminal charges against leading industrialists.

National antagonisms deepened. Germans were convinced that the occupation of the Ruhr district was not only financially motivated but was also the first step towards French annexation of the left bank of the Rhine in order to realise Poincaré's failed ambition of 1918. The French, for their part, believed that Germany was maliciously attempting to circumvent her obligations under the Treaty of Versailles. Eventually radical nationalist groups in Germany began to engage in acts of violent sabotage, despite government instructions to the contrary, and tensions rose to the breaking point. The German economy crumbled and the mark lost all its remaining value.

In order to prevent the complete political and social collapse of the nation, the Weimar Republic capitulated to the French on 26 September 1923 and ordered that the campaign of passive resistance be discontinued. A new cabinet had been formed in August by Gustav Stresemann, the chairman of the German People's Party, on the basis of a grand coalition of Social Democrats, German Democrats, Centrists and representatives of the German People's Party, and it issued the following appeal to the German people:

On 11 January French and Belgian troops occupied the German Ruhr district unlawfully and in violation of the Treaty of Versailles. Since this time, the Ruhr and Rhine region has suffered enormously. Over 180,000 German men, women, children and old folk have been driven from their homes and their farms. For millions of Germans, personal freedom no longer exists. Innumerable acts of violence have accompanied the foreign occupation, and more than one hundred of our brethren have laid down their lives. Hundreds more are languishing in prison. The illegality of this invasion has outraged our sense of justice and our patriotic sensibilities. The population refuses to work under the threat of foreign bayonets. The entire German people offers its gratitude 'for the loyalty and steadfast devotion to the German *Reich* demonstrated in this most difficult of times.

The government undertook to assist our suffering compatriots to the best of its ability. Steadily increasing resources were devoted to this end. Last week support payments to the Rhine and Ruhr reached the sum of 3500 billion marks; this week at least twice as much can be expected. Production has ceased in the Rhine and Ruhr district. The economy of occupied and unoccupied Germany lies in ruin. If present policies are continued, we run the terrible risk of being unable to create a stable currency, maintain a functioning economy and ensure the naked survival of our people. This danger must be averted in the interests of both the Rhine and Ruhr region and all of Germany. In order to ensure the survival of our people and our country, we find ourselves faced with the bitter necessity of calling a halt to the struggle.[15]

The German people looked on helplessly as the chaos spread. The sense of despair was palpable. The working class and much of the middle class were impoverished by inflation, while speculators, exporters and some large manufacturers profited enormously. Demagogues on the left and the right exploited the crisis to provoke the deepest crisis in Germany since the collapse of 1918. The Social Democrats and Communists had achieved a majority in Saxony and Thuringia in the provincial elections of 1923 and once in government distributed arms to proletarian centuries. The socialisation measures they envisaged endangered the unity of the *Reich* and the dominant position of the Social Democratic Party in Prussia, which was dependent on a great coalition with middle-class parties. The

Reichswehr was sent into Saxony and Thuringia by means of a Federal Execution ordered by Streseman and endorsed by Ebert. The government of Saxony was deposed and the Communist ministers in Thuringia were expelled from the cabinet. A communist uprising in Hamburg was quashed by police under Social Democratic direction.

In the west, separatists supported by the French proclaimed the establishment of a Rhenish republic in several cities between Aachen and Koblenz and sought to found a Palatine republic as well. However, these separatist movements were rebuffed by the mass of the population which remained loyal to the *Reich*.

The Bavarian government had proven sympathetic to extreme nationalists, and Bavaria had become the favourite refuge of right-wing groups. After resistance in the Ruhr district ended, the Bavarian government declared a state of emergency, and the president of Upper Bavaria, Gustav von Kahr, was named commissar general with dictatorial powers. Under Kahr particularist elements anxious to restore the Bavarian monarchy threatened to join forces with revolutionary National Socialism, despite the latter's belief in a unitary state. Much impressed by Benito Mussolini's march on Rome but with little understanding of the political climate in Germany, National Socialists under Adolf Hitler planned a march on Berlin to be undertaken in conjunction with Erich Ludendorff and other nationalist organisations. As the negotiations reached their climax, Hitler attempted to use a mass meeting on 8 November 1923 in order to compel the Bavarian government to support this scheme. Finally Hitler declared the Bavarian government, the federal government and the federal president deposed and proclaimed himself the next chancellor and president. After some initial hesitation, the Bavarian government took action to oppose Hitler, and the first National Socialist attempt to seize power failed miserably on 9 November in a short but bloody confrontation with the police. Ludendorff turned himself in to the police and Hitler, who had fled, was captured two days later. He was later sentenced to a minimal prison term in a trial scandalously biased in his favour. The federal government in Berlin outlawed the two most extreme parties—the National Socialists on the right and the Communists on the left—thus ending the acute threat. However, both the National Socialists and the Communists managed to continue their attacks on the republic.

The dangerously charged atmosphere did not really begin to moderate until 15 November 1923, when Stresemann took steps to reform the currency and stabilise the mark. The new monetary issue was limited to 3200 million marks backed by gold and mortgages on property, commerce, industry and banks. This ended the inflation and restored confidence in the German currency both at home and abroad. The currency reform was planned by Karl Helfferich, a prewar secretary of the Imperial Treasury and present member of the German National People's Party, and by Rudolf Hilferding, the leading Social Democratic expert in financial affairs. Their plan was executed by Hjalmar Schacht, the federal currency commissar and later president of the *Reichsbank*, and by Hans Luther, the minister of finance. However, the currency reform was not carried out without severe repercussions: 300,000 civil servants, office employees and workers lost their livelihoods, and the social fabric was severely strained as state expenditures were cut to the absolute minimum. Those who benefited most from currency reform were industry, the peasantry, property owners and above all the state. They were all relieved at a single stroke of their entire debt. The war debts of the German government to its own people fell from 150,000 million gold marks to 15.4 pfennigs. Those citizens who had subscribed to war bonds saw their hard-earned savings reduced to nothing. Stresemann himself commented that the greatest injustice of the war was that 'the intellectual and commercial middle classes, the traditional backbone of the state, paid for their loyalty to Germany with proletarianisation and the loss of all their wealth'.[16]

But the republic and German unity were saved. The dimension of the danger that had been warded off in this 'most fateful year in German history'[17] was underlined by the British ambassador in Berlin, Viscount Edgar d'Abernon, in his diary entry for 31 December 1923:

Thus ends a year of crisis. The dangers from without and within have been such as to threaten the whole future of Germany. . . . Looking back, one sees more clearly how near to the precipice this country has been. In the twelve months from January till now, Germany has lived through the following dangers: the Ruhr invasion, the Communist rising in Saxony and Thuringia, the Hitler *Putsch* in Bavaria, an unprecedented financial crisis, the separatist movement in the Rhineland. Any one of these, if not overcome, would have brought about fundamental change, either in internal conditions or external relations. If successful, each and any would have wrecked all hope of general pacification. Political leaders in Germany are not accustomed to receive much public laudation; those who have seen the country through these perils deserve more credit than is likely to be their portion.[18]

The Return to Normality

The Weimar Republic never adequately thanked Stresemann—like Erzberger, Rathenau, Ebert and Müller before him—for all he had done on its behalf. As a National Liberal before the war, Stresemann had supported Germany's naval ambitions and annexationist peace plans as late as 1917; but after the war he reconciled himself to reality, underwent a political conversion, and recognized the republic as the legitimate government of Germany. He helped the fledgling republic immeasurably at the height of the crisis by his courageous decisions to abandon the struggle in the Ruhr and to end the inflation. In return, he was overthrown the following November by Social Democrats in league with the German Nationalists and the Communists. The former never forgave Stresemann for having taken far firmer action against the extreme left-wing governments of central Germany than against the extreme right-wing government of Bavaria because of his concern over the reaction of the army. The German Nationals resented the fact he had called off the struggle in the Ruhr, and the Communists opposed him because he had vigorously suppressed their various uprisings. Stresemann would never again lead the government but assumed the portfolio of foreign minister in every cabinet till his death in October 1929.

The stabilisation of the currency had an immediate calming effect on the economy and politics, which was already felt in late 1923. D'Abernon noted on 25 December:

The most salient characteristic of the new situation is the astonishing appeasement and relief brought about by a touch of the magical wand of 'Currency Stability'. . . . Food has become abundant in the great towns; potatoes and cereals are brought to market in large quantities. . . . Animals crowd the abbatoirs and queues have disappeared from before the shops of butchers and provision merchants. The economic détente has brought in its train political pacification—dictatorships and putsches are no longer discussed, and even the extreme parties have ceased, for the moment, from troubling.[19]

The next spring, the internal situation quietened further. When French policy in the Ruhr failed to produce the expected results, Poincaré agreed in late 1923 to the establishment of an international committee of experts, including Americans, which would examine Germany's ability to meet her reparations payments. The American banker Charles G. Dawes was appointed chairman of the committee, which convened in London. Its work was greatly facilitated by the election in Britain and France of left-wing governments willing to compromise with Germany and to place reparations on a sound economic footing.

The new reparations plan, or Dawes Plan, was based on the assumption that Germany required a balanced budget and a positive balance of payments. It therefore provided for annual payments gradually rising from 1,000 million to 2,500 million marks. In order to ease the initial payment, an international loan of 800 million marks was arranged, drawing primarily on American coffers. However, the international supervision of Germany's financial affairs represented an intrusion on her national sovereignty and she was forced as security for the loan to introduce a transportation tax and to accept liens on her industry and the national railway.

In spite of these disadvantages, the German government declared its willingness to accept the Dawes Plan, and even some members of the German National Party voted for it. Soon foreign, especially American, capital was streaming into Germany. The reparations schedule could once again be met and the modernisation of industry, so urgently required after the years of war and inflation, was begun. The flood of capital greatly benefited the provinces and local governments, though in many cases they invested short-term credits in long-term projects. Production rose markedly and unemployment declined. The general debt load increased and a sudden recession caused many bankruptcies, but on the whole the German economy began to prosper again. The loss of many of Germany's sources of raw materials, as a result of the Treaty of Versailles, was soon offset by the substitution of light metals for heavy metals and of brown coal for bituminous coal and by the increased use of electricity. Giant companies such as I.G. Farben and United Steel Works again enabled Germany to compete effectively in world trade with the other industrial nations. The merchant fleet, decimated by the Allies, was quickly built up, and an integrated air transportation network emerged. The German *Reich* once again began to achieve technical firsts with the record-setting crossing to New York of the luxury liner *Bremen*, Hermann Köhl's flight across the Atlantic from east to west, and the flight around the world of the airship *Graf Zeppelin* in 1929.

The provinces and districts were also engaged in the economy, building roads, schools, playgrounds and sports-grounds and extending their social welfare schemes. Homes for infants and children and vacation colonies were created, and the urban welfare authorities redoubled their efforts to care for the poor. The federal government created employment exchanges and instituted unemployment insurance and general social insurance. The poor received a legal right to financial assistance.

However, the general standard of living scarcely rose. Real wages climbed only slightly, while companies demanded an extended working day. This led to bitter confrontations with trade unions, which were determined to retain the standard eight-hour day under all circumstances. The abiding shortage of capital and mounting foreign debts made Germany increasingly vulnerable to international monetary flows and discouraged investment in German industry. In addition, the agricultural sector failed to share in the economic expansion after 1927. The German economy was still shaky and unable to offer much resistance to a world-wide depression. The apparent robustness and stability of the economy soon proved to be a cruel chimera, at the very latest by the time the Great Depression broke out.

The German republic suffered a serious loss on 28 February 1925 when Friedrich Ebert died in his fifty-fifth year. At a time when all the kings of Germany had failed, this son of the common folk proved himself royally,[20] as Theodor Heuss said, and 'accomplished an enormously difficult task as well as was humanly possible'.[21] But he won few friends among broad segments of the working class, and though he saved bourgeois society, the middle classes failed to rally *en masse* to the republican cause for which he stood.

In the ensuing election held on 26 April 1925, the middle classes elected as *Reichspräsident* Field Marshal Paul von Hindenburg—the victor of Tannenberg and chief of general staff during the war and now the most visible reminder of a heroic past. (That he had eventually lost the war seems to have been generally overlooked.) Hindenburg owed his election to his prestige and to the obstinacy of the Communists, who even after the first ballot insisted on their own candidate and refused to back the Centrist Chancellor Wilhelm Marx, the compromise candidate of the Centrists, Social Democrats and German Democrats. Though elected by the right-wing parties and personally faithful to the emperor, Hindenburg long upheld his oath to the Constitution of the republic and loyally discharged his duties—at least until his re-election in 1932. He never approved of the republic and his personal sympathies always lay with the right, but he seemed to increase the popularity of the republic, at least among the middle classes. Though a man of goodwill, the seventy-seven-year-old *Reichspräsident* was politically inexperienced and lacking in acumen, and he seemed neither physically nor mentally equal to his high office. Otto Braun, the prime minister of Prussia, commented with shock after his first meeting with Hindenburg on 'the obtuseness and completely apolitical outlook of this man', who, in Braun's view, was in desperate need of good political advisers. 'That good advice was not always given to him . . . became the great tragedy not only of Hindenburg but of the entire German people.'[22] Hindenburg's election marked a clear shift to the right in the German electorate and encouraged the resentments of the old ruling classes, which in Friedrich Meinecke's view did so much to poison the political atmosphere in Germany.[23]

Hindenburg's election as president and the hostility of much of the German public to Stresemann's policies of reconciliation with Germany's foreign enemies provided clear evidence that the system 'was fundamentally weaker than its supporters believed'.[24] Germany had begun to pursue an active foreign policy as early as 1922, and in signing the Treaty of Rapallo with the Soviet Union, finally succeeded in breaking out of her isolation. By this treaty the signatories affirmed their equality and renounced all claims arising from the period during and after the war. Stresemann followed this success by proposing a pact with Britain, France, Italy and Belgium. The German foregin minister realised that French needs for security would have to be met if the antagonism between France and Germany was to subside and if Germany was to regain her status as a great power.

In accordance with this thoroughly revisionist policy, Germany voluntarily recognised the western border imposed on her by the Treaty of Versailles. The inviolability of this border was guaranteed in a number of treaties signed in Locarno in October 1925 by Britain, Belgium, Poland and Czechoslovakia. The *Reich* further affirmed its acceptance of the permanent demilitarisation of the Rhineland. According to the treaties, all future disagreements would be settled by a court of arbitration. Paris sought to win similar German acceptance of her eastern border, but Stresemann refused, hoping to keep open the possibility that Germany might one day work out a peaceful revision of her eastern frontiers through negotiations with Poland.

The Franco-German rapprochement reached its climax in the conversations which Stresemann and the French foreign minister and former prime minister, Aristide Briand, held at Thoiry in September 1926. These statesmen discussed a complete settlement of the outstanding Franco-German issue, including intensive economic cooperation, a solution to the Saar question and more rapid French withdrawal from the Rhineland. However, this initiative had no concrete results, and the effects of Locarno itself were very slow to emerge. The French promptly evacuated the Cologne region on 1 February 1926, but did not withdraw from the remaining occupied territories until 1929 and 1930. This was not due to any lack of goodwill on the part of Briand, who was as fervent an advocate of reconciliation between the two peoples as Stresemann, but to resistance on the part of many Frenchmen who could not overcome their distrust of their eastern neighbour quite so swiftly. Meanwhile, Stresemann was consumed by mounting frustration, especially as he was increasingly subjected to violent attacks by the right-wing parties, who accused him of having further weakened the *Reich* by making concessions to the victors while gaining very little in return.

A direct consequence of Stresemann's Locarno policies was, however, Germany's admittance into the League of Nations, which took place shortly before the treaties were concluded. She was also accorded a permanent seat on the League Council. The high hopes which accompanied this event were evident in the speeches delivered by Stresemann and Briand. The former declared:

Germany enters today a circle of nations to which she is linked by many decades of unclouded friendship but which were also united against her in the last world war. It is an event of great historical import that Germany and these states now join together in the League of Nations in an abiding spirit of peaceful cooperation. This fact demonstrates more clearly than any words or programmes that the League can give a new direction to the political development of mankind. Human culture would be severely imperilled, especially in the present era, if the various peoples could not feel sure of an opportunity to fulfil their divine mission in peaceful, untroubled competition with one another.[25]

Briand replied:

The protracted series of painful and bloody conflicts which stain the pages of our history have come to an end; there is an end to war between us, an end to long mourning-veils. From now on there should be no more wars, no more forceful solutions. I know that differences of opinion continue to exist between our countries, but in future we should settle them before the courts as private persons do. Therefore I say: down with rifles, machine-guns and cannons! long live reconciliation, arbitration and peace![26]

In order to secure everlasting peace, Briand drew up a pact outlawing war, to be signed by France and the United States. The American secretary of state, Frank Billings Kellogg, extended it to a world-wide pact. On 27 August 1928 fifteen states signed the Kellogg Pact in Paris, solemnly declaring 'in the names of their respective peoples that they condemn recourse to war for the solution of international controversies, and renounce it as an instrument of national policy in their relations with one another'. They further pledged that 'the settlement or solution of all disputes or conflicts of whatever nature or of whatever origin they may be, which may arise among them, shall never be sought except by pacific means'.[27] The weakness of the Kellogg Pact was that it failed to provide for adequate sanctions against aggressors. It rested solely on the word of the signatory nations, that is on the abiding desire for peace among the peoples and governments of the world.

Stresemann's efforts to bridge the gulf between the peoples of Europe and to draw them closer together resulted in Germany recovering her position as a full-fledged member of the circle of nations. Berlin henceforth disposed of a forum where it could discuss among equals the still unresolved questions of disarmament, reparations and national minorities. Stresemann furthered the spirit of the Treaty of Rapallo and strengthened Germany's relations with the Soviet Union by means of trade, neutrality and friendship treaty signed in April 1926. However, all these successes on the international stage did not bring the republican government the internal credit it had hoped to reap. Stresemann's successes should have been universally acclaimed, but instead became the object of rancorous internal dispute.

After his fall as *Reichskanzler* in November 1923, Stresemann became foreign minister in the ensuing cabinets. From this position he dominated German foreign policy and ensured strong continuity. Continuity was sadly lacking, however, from Germany's domestic affairs, which were plagued by rapid changes in the government. The electoral system, dissension within the moderate centre and the divergent interests of the numerous parties made it impossible to form stable majorities after the collapse of the Weimar Coalition. In the period between February 1919 and January 1933 twenty-one different cabinets came to power. The moderate socialist and middle-class parties thereby lost an opportunity to focus their efforts on decreasing the influence of extremist elements. The fortunes of the extremists began to improve once again when the economy took a sharp turn for the worse and the hopes raised by Locarno and Germany's entry into the League of Nations found only gradual and partial fulfilment. The extremists soon waxed in strength and militancy, first foiling Stresemann's détente policies and eventually even crushing the republic.

Shortly before Stresemann's death, a committee of experts under the leadership of the American financier and government administrator Owen D. Young met in Paris to discuss German reparations. It rescheduled the annual payments to approximately 2,000 million marks over fifty-nine years, sparking a violent internal controversy within Germany. The German Nationals, the National Socialists and the 'Stahlhelm' (a union of former soldiers), launched a demagogic campaign against the Young Plan and the alleged 'enslavement' of the German people and arranged for a plebiscite to be held. When the plebiscite fell far short of the necessary one-third of all voters, the government agreed to the Young Plan. In so doing, the republic regained most of its financial and economic sovereignty since this plan did not include a system of mortgages to ensure payment. The immediate payments were also less onerous than Germany's previous obligations. The German government had been allowed for the first time to participate in the negotiations, and it was evident that further revisions in Germany's obligations might well be forthcoming. In addition, Stresemann achieved his most important political objective: the Allied withdrawal from the occupied areas of Rhineland. But Germans had now grown too impatient to appreciate the fruits of Stresemann's policies, which ripened too late to be of benefit to him. Just a few months before his death Stresemann commented to a British journalist:

I gave and gave and gave some more till finally my countrymen turned against me. If I had received a single concession after Locarno, I would have been able to win over my people. I still could, but you Englishmen gave nothing, and the only concessions you did make always came too late. . . . The future now lies in the hands of the young generation—the youth of Germany whom we could have won over to peace and the new Europe. If both have been lost—that is my tragedy and a great error on your part.[28]

The Great Depression and the Collapse of the Weimar Republic

In the very month of Stresemann's death—October 1929—the American stock market crashed, initiating a huge global financial crisis. An era of tremendous overproducton and speculation in the United States had drawn to a close. The Great War had made the United States the financial capital of the world, and Wall Street replaced London as the seat of the greatest stock market in the world. Payments on the war loans taken out by America's European allies filled her financial coffers to overflowing. This, combined with high tariffs to keep European imports at bay, generated a wave of prosperity that surpassed all expectations. Industrial investment soared, production raced ahead, and stock prices reached dizzying heights. Little attention was paid to the fact that American farmers were not participating fully in the prosperity and that agricultural exports were actually declining. Warnings that demand could not keep pace with supply were largely ignored. When the decline in demand spread throughout the economy and prices began to fall, an economic collapse ensued. Banks suspended payments, countless firms went bankrupt, unemployment soared and farmers were forced to sell their crops at a loss. Quickly the crisis spread to South America, Australia and Europe.

The German economy had already been severely demaged by inflation and had grown dependent on American capital after 1924. The first signs of an economic downturn were already visible in 1928. The credit and payment mechanism foreseen by the hotly disputed Young Plan no longer functioned. The recession of the winter of 1928–9 caused an abrupt increase in unemployment, which climbed to 3.5 million by February 1930. National income and demand declined substantially as a result. Production decreased even further, and tax receipts fell while demands on unemployment insurance shot upward. The resulting economic dislocation had a severe impact on the political situation, and a bitter dispute erupted over unemployment insurance. In the summer of 1928 this controversy led to the collapse of the Great Coalition, which Stresemann had done so much to create, between the Social Democrats, the German Democrats, the Centrists, the Bavarian People's Party and the German People's Party. The German People's Party demanded that unemployment benefits be reduced, the Social Democrats refused, and when both declined to compromise an open split developed in the coalition. Wracked by the opposing interests and views of its component parties, the Grand Coalition found itself unable to negotiate unanimous decisions as party loyalties proved stronger than the political exigencies of the times. Germans failed to come up with an adequate response to the key question posed in the *Reichstag* by the minister of finance, Hermann Dietrich: 'Are they a state or just a swarm of interest groups?'[29] Parliamentary government was paralysed, never to recover. The parties could 'no longer summon the strength or the will to achieve a compromise and to chart a steady, undoctrinaire course in the national interest over and above the competing concerns of the groups that supported them'.[30]

While the parties squabbled, there was an increase in the influence of those circles which believed that government affairs should be taken over for the duration of the economic crisis by an efficient cabinet relying on the emergency powers of the president and independent of Parliament. On 1 April 1930 Hindenburg appointed Heinrich Brüning chancellor, at the suggestion of General Kurt von

Schleicher. In his government declaration Brüning emphasised the special nature of his cabinet:

In accordance with the recommendations given to me by the president of the German *Reich*, the new cabinet is not bound to any coalition, though of course the political authority of this august house could not be overlooked in its formation. The cabinet has been formed with the intention of resolving as expeditiously as possible those problems widely deemed crucial to the survival of the *Reich*. This shall be our final attempt to resolve these problems with this *Reichstag*. . . . The government is willing and able to employ every constitutional means at its disposal in order to achieve its ends.[31]

Brüning had entered the Centre Party from the Christian trade-union movement, became a federal deputy in 1924 and developed a reputation as a financial expert. He was a conservative, energetic, pragmatic and highly intelligent man—who seemed frightfully indifferent to the sufferings of the people. He proceeded to deprive the *Reichstag* of many of its prerogatives in the belief that he could 'uphold the constitutional state even without democracy'.[32] In the autumn of 1931 he informed Hindenburg that he had 'come so far, even without infringing on the constitution, that the prerogatives of Parliament have been reduced to the level of the Bismarckian era'. Indeed, the 'head of state has acquired greater *de facto* power than the emperor ever held'.[33] Thus Brüning became 'the first chancellor in the dissolution of democracy in Germany'.[34]

He sought to restore healthy finances and a balanced budget to the federal, provincial and local levels of government by reducing prices, salaries and wages in keeping with the deflationary spiral and by radically cutting back imports while attempting to increase exports. When the *Reichstag* rejected a special tax, Brüning availed himself of article 48 of the Constitution in order to implement his programme by dint of an emergency decree. So the economic crisis became a political crisis as well.

When the *Reichstag* voted to repeal the emergency decree, Brüning appealed to Hindenburg to dissolve it and to order new elections—a mistake of the first order. Brüning hoped that decisive action on his part would rally the voters and persuade them to elect a conservative bourgeois majority which would support his policies. But this was not to be. What many had warned of, came to pass: the extremist parties shamelessly exploited the economic crisis for their own advantage and emerged victorious from the elections. The National Socialists, previously an insignificant rump of twelve deputies, elected 107 deputies to the new *Reichstag*. The Communists also scored large gains, advancing from fifty-four to seventy-seven seats. The government was flabbergasted. It would be unable to function if the Social Democrats did not reverse their policy and compromise their principles enough to keep Brüning in power.

Germany's foreign creditors grew nervous and increased the hitherto modest payments they had required on their loans. Unemployment and social distress worsened. In the end, a majority of the non-radical parties lent tacit support to Brüning's financial policies, but he proved unable to cope with the turmoil in the *Reichstag* provoked by the entry of large numbers of Nazis. Parliament was paralysed by a flood of right-wing bills and tumultuous confrontations between the Communists and National Socialists. These scenes were continued on the streets where Nazi supporters organised in the SA, (*Sturmabteilung*) and Communists enlisted in the *Rotfrontkämpferbund* fought pitched battles. While the bourgeois government tinkered, as if the economic crisis was merely a technical financial problem, rising numbers of Germans found themselves struggling for naked survival, for sufficient food for the next day and sufficient coal and wood for the next winter. When further foreign credits were withdrawn, the *Darmstädter Bank* became insolvent as did the *Nationalbank*, the first of the large banks. Panic-stricken mobs besieged other financial institutions, inducing all banks and stock exchanges to close their doors temporarily in July 1931. A sense of despair and hopelessness swept the land as the number of unemployed continued to climb from 4.9 million in January 1931 to over 6 million by December.

Still Brüning took no steps to mitigate the intense material deprivation. Quite to the contrary, he sought to regain control of the situation through further emergency decrees ordering tax increases, salary cuts, lower unemployment benefits and a reduction in public expenditure.

Brüning also sought to convince Germany's neighbours that it was wiser to make concessions now than to wait until the National Socialists or Communists had seized power. The American president, Herbert Hoover, was induced to propose a general moratorium on Germany's debts for the space of one year, a suggestion that was eventually adopted on 7 July 1931, despite French objections. However, Brüning failed in his larger aim of exploiting the economic crisis to achieve an extensive revision of the Treaty of Versailles. The former Allied powers rejected a complete settlement of the reparations problem, fewer restrictions on German armaments and an economic union between Germany and Austria, which found herself in equally dire financial straits.

But the Hoover moratorium alone did not suffice to take the wind out of the sails of the National Socialists. The middle-class centre and the right, the bulk of the business sector, many farmers and above all the youth with its 'craving for heroism'[35] felt increasingly alienated from the republic and swayed by Hitler's demagogic simplification of the problems besetting Germany. Hitler's gallery of scapegoats culiminated in the Jews and the alleged 'Jewification' of public life. In demonstrations across Germany embellished with military pomp and pageantry, Hitler spewed forth hateful tirades against the situation in Germany while appealing to national pride and the desire of the crowds for redemption from their penury. Hitler promised something for everyone: food for the jobless, low interest rates for farmers, protection against communism for the wealthy, rearmament for the army, strong profits and prostrate unions for industrialists, and a powerful new Germany for those who felt insult to their national pride.

In the autumn of 1931 the nationalist Opposition gathered in Bad Harzburg, where National Socialists, German Nationals, the *Stahlhelm*, the Pan-German League, the *Landbund* and various patriotic organisations united to form the 'Harzburg Front'. Its spokesmen were Adolf Hitler, Hjalmar Schacht, the former *Reichswährungskommissar* and president of the *Reichsbank*, and Alfred Hugenberg, the large industrialist and chairman of the German National People's Party who controlled Germany's largest media empire. Together these leaders proclaimed their determination to break with the prevailing political system. At about the same time, the vortex of political debate moved to party gatherings and street demonstrations. German cities were swept by scenes reminiscent of civil war, and by the end of the year the Social Democrats felt constrained to create their own combat unit in defence of the republic. And so the 'Iron Front' was formed on 16 December 1931 out of elements of the Social Democratic Party, labour unions, workers' sporting clubs, and the black, red, and gold *Reichsbanner*.

In May 1932 the Bishop of Regensburg, Michael Buchberger, wrote to Cardinal Michael Faulhaber in despair over the government's inactivity:

It is the middle of the summer and still virtually nothing has been done to revive the economy and create jobs. Abject poverty is everywhere, families are living on potatoes alone, the mood is almost desperate. If we have nothing but more of the same for another two months, Brüning will be finished. Some kind of revolution, from the right or the left, will be inescapable, and chaos and nirvana will result. Should not we bishops call upon the government to employ every means at its disposal to create jobs and generate earnings as quickly as possible? The tremendous strength of National Socialism lies in its ability to capture and exploit the reaction of the people towards the impotence of the federal government.[36]

The federal government condemned itself to impotence by disregarding the parties in the *Reichstag* and relying on the confidence of the president and his willingness to issue emergency decrees. When Hindenburg came up for re-election in the spring of 1932, the government threw its weight behind him and sought to win over his former opponents—the republican parties, the Social Democrats, the Centre and the German Democratic Party. This tactic was rendered unavoidable by the fact that much of the aristocracy and traditional nationalist groups had abandoned Hindenburg in favour of Hitler, who had also declared his candidacy. They were seconded in this choice by General von Seeckt and the former crown prince, among others. In the end, the eighty-four-year-old Hindenburg succeeded in defeating Hitler and Ernst Thälmann, the chairman of the Communist Party, though he required a second round and the help of the centrist and Social Democratic parties to do so.

In a final stab at decisive action, Brüning took up the struggle against the Nazis. On the advice of his minister of defence, Wilhelm Groener, he obtained an emergency decree 'in defence of state authority' that suppressed the National Socialist combat units of the SA and the SS—the so-called Protective Squad (*Schutzstaffel*). These units had greatly alarmed the government by encircling Berlin on the eve of the election.

Hugenberg and the nationalist press immediately raised a hue and cry, demanding that the black, red and gold *Reichsbanner* likewise be banned, though it—unlike the SA and SS—was thoroughly democratic and loyal to the republic. When Hindenburg supported this demand, General Groener resigned as minister of defence, though he retained his portfolio as minister of the interior, which he had held since October 1931. Groener's departure from the ministry of defence marked the withdrawal of a man who had done more than any other high army officer to serve the cause of the republic since its earliest days.

The National Socialists then emerged from several provincial elections as the strongest party in the *Landtag*, though they failed to win an absolute majority. Hindenburg thereupon withdrew his support for Brüning. Hindenburg had begun to lose confidence in his chancellor as early as the autumn of 1931, when it grew apparent that his own re-election as president would depend on the help of the Social Democrats. Brüning's fate was finally sealed when he decided to cease financial assistance for bankrupt junker estates and to auction them off instead in order to provide settlements for German farmers. By opposing the chancellor and shifting his own position further to the right, Hindenburg hoped to arrest the swing in the popular vote towards the extremist right-wing parties. Brüning was accordingly forced to retire, a discouraged and bitter man.

He had tried to extend his margin of manoeuvre further than political forces would allow. That he failed was due not only to the virtually hopeless structural and human snarl in Germany around 1930 but also to his own inability to play a stronger role in political life. His political potential was limited by this flaw in his nature—at a time when Germany was in an uproar, when millions of desperate people saw their only hope in Hitler's ascension to power.[37]

The policies of the German government during the following eight months only aggravated the social chaos and prepared the way for Hitler's appointment as *Reichskanzler* and for the Nazi triumph over the republic. The ageing president of the republic, Paul von Hindenburg, carried out his fateful swing to the right under the influence of his closest advisors, all hostile to democracy: his son and aide-de-camp, Oskar von Hindenburg; the opportunistic secretary of state Otto Meissner; Franz von Papen, the vain, conniving, intellectually shallow scion of the Catholic Westphalian aristocracy; and General von Schleicher, equally vain and untrustworthy, but a far superior political tactician. Hindenburg requested of Papen that he form a 'cabinet of national concentration' over and above the parties. This cabinet included Streicher, who had recommended to Hindenburg that Papen be appointed chancellor and who now assumed the portfolio of minister of defence.

Within Germany and without, the new government met with the utmost scepticism. However, the foreign policy pursued by Papen and the diplomat Konstantin von Neurath immediately proved most successful—thanks to be sure to the preliminary efforts of Stresemann and Brüning. At the Conference of Lausanne held in the summer of 1932 it was decided to terminate Germany's war reparations with a final payment of 3,000 million gold marks. In December 1932 the Geneva disarmament conference theoretically recognised Germany's claim, advanced by Brüning, to equality of armament.

But in internal affairs Papen was less successful, totally failing to win the cooperation of the Nazis. Indeed, bloody battles again erupted throughout the republic after the *Reichstag* was dissolved and the ban on Nazi storm-troopers was repealed as Schleicher's reward to Hitler for promising not to oppose the new government. Measures such as further cuts in unemployment insurance, pensions and wages and the introduction of a salt tax added to public dissatisfaction.

The federal government then declared a military state of emergency and took over the Prussian government previously controlled by Social Democrats. When faced with the Kapp putsch in 1920, the provincial government had summoned republican workers to its defence, but it no longer felt able to rely on this source of support. Hard hit by the ravages of unemployment, the workers were in no mood for a general strike. The Prussian ministers therefore yielded and allowed Papen to seize the Prussian *Reichskommissariat*. The deep intellectual and socio-economic crisis in Germany thus helped to seal the fate of Prussia, which terminated its long history—much maligned but often unjustly so—as a model democracy. The Social Democrat Otto Braun served as Prussian prime minister from 1920 till Papen's *coup* in 1932 and his party colleague Carl Severing served as minister of the interior from 1920 till 1926. Under their leadership Prussia embraced democracy while 'preserving many elements of the Prussian tradition such as moderation, diligence and a capacity for decisive action when necessary'.[38] Unfortunately, events were now to cut off this evolution and raze Prussia from the map.

Papen reaped the bitter fruits of these policies in the *Reichstag* elections of 31 July 1932. Thanks to a massive propaganda campaign, the National Socialists increased their vote to 37.4 per cent of the ballots cast and became the strongest party in the *Reichstag* with 230 seats. The majority that had agreed to tolerate the Brüning and Papen governments was lost, and henceforth the combined forces of the National Socialists and Communists were in a position to block all legislation. The Nazis demanded that they be allowed to form the government, but Hindenburg refused out of fear that 'a presidential cabinet headed by Herr Hitler inevitably develop into a party dictatorship likely gravely to exacerbate the social tensions among the German people'.[39]

Hindenburg's refusal to cooperate with the Nazis made them ferocious opponents of the government, whom no number of concessions could win over. Papen's counter-measures such as severe punishment for acts of political violence and terror either came too late or were negated by a no-confidence vote in the *Reichstag*—Papen's emergency decrees to stimulate the economy fell victim, for instance, to the latter fate. Papen failed to win the necessary army support for a *coup d'état* and the creation of an authoritarian state in which all parties, labour unions and employers' associations would be banned by emergency decree. When the *Reichstag*, newly elected in November, again refused to lend Papen its support, Hindenburg dismissed him and turned to Schleicher to form a government. This he did on 2 December 1932.

More perceptive and less rigid than Papen, the new chancellor first sought closer relation with the labour unions and the socialist wing of the Nazis, of which Georg Strasser was the most prominent spokesman. The chances of splitting the National Socialists seemed reasonably good after their defeat in the November elections. Lower voter turnout, a widespread feeling of apathy and resignation, disappointment over the failure of Hitler's negotiations with Hindenburg and fear of the extremism of the Nazis and their Führer resulted in 2 million fewer votes for the National Socialists and a decline to 33.1 per cent of the ballots cast. Strasser apparently feared that the Nazis might burn themselves out in bootless opposition and seemed willing to enter Schleicher's cabinet as vice-chancellor. However, Hitler moved swiftly to deprive Strasser of all his party functions, to overcome the resulting internal crisis and to emerge as the unquestioned leader of the Nazi movement.

Schleicher conducted further negotiations with the Christian and free unions, the centre parties and the Social Democrats, but all to no avail. The Social Democratic leadership even advised the unions not to engage in any further discussions with the chancellor. Schleicher thereupon proposed to dissolve the *Reichstag*, declare a state of emergency, ban the Nazi and Communist parties, and defer new elections for a period of six months. When Hindenburg refused, Schleicher submitted his resignation.

Papen in the meantime adopted a posture of unrelenting hostility to his successor and arranged through the Cologne banker Kurt von Schröder a rapprochement between Hugenberg's German Nationals, Hitler's National Socialists and the *Stahlhelm* under Franz Seldte. Together these leaders agreed to attempt to form a joint government under Hitler as chancellor and Papen as vice-chancellor. On 27 January Hindenburg had commented to two army generals: 'Surely, gentlemen, you don't believe that I am capable of making this Austrian corporal chancellor?'[40] Just three days later, at Papen's urging, Hindenburg asked Hitler to assume the office of chancellor. It was 30 January 1933.

Hugenberg and Papen, as it soon turned out, had completely underestimated Adolf Hitler. They believed that they had snared the rabble rouser and enmeshed him in a government in which only three National Socialists were present—Hitler himself as chancellor, the *Reichstag* deputy Wilhelm Frick as minister of the interior, and the former fighter pilot, SA leader and president of the *Reichstag* Hermann Goering, as minister without portfolio and commissar for air transport. Hugenberg and Papen were convinced that they would be able to control Hitler by conferring an official position upon him and surrounding him with German National and Conservative politicians. Only too late did they realise the depths of their illusion. Hitler was determined to use political power to implement the ideas outlined in *Mein Kampf* and innumerable speeches—ideas which Hugenberg and Papen considered a simple propaganda ploy. Ludendorff, though an enemy of the republic like Hugenberg and Papen, nevertheless sensed the depths of the catastrophe and dispatched an angry, prophetic letter to Hindenburg immediately upon hearing of Hitler's appointment:

By appointing Hitler as *Reichskanzler* you delivered our sacred German fatherland into the custody of one of the greatest demagogues of all times. I solemnly predict that this wretched man will be the ruin of the *Reich* and will bring down unspeakable sufferings on our nation. Coming generations will curse you in your grave for this misdeed.[41]

The appointment of this government sealed the fate of the Weimar Republic—even though the new government was only supported by the 33 per cent of the voters who had cast their ballot for the National Socialists and by the 7 per cent who had voted for the German Nationals. Without the sympathy and assistance of the victorious powers, the republic had proved unable in the end to withstand the stresses and strains of the lost war. The Allies' lack of sympathy burdened the fledgling republic from its earliest days with handicaps which even a firmly entrenched government heir to a long democratic tradition could scarcely have borne. How much less the German republic, which had to grow accustomed to the freedoms enunciated in her constitution! Politics in a multi-party state required a sense of responsibility and a willingness to compromise. Both were lacking in Germany. Habituated to an omnipresent and authoritarian government, the political parties and their supporters were not ready to act independently and tended to value order more than the freedom derived from a lost war. Outraged national pride and the social chaos issuing from inflation, unemployment and economic hardship distorted their view of reality and stoked a craving for the old ways. Overwhelmed by all their concerns, Germans attached ever less importance to democratic rights. Perplexed by the multiplicity of divergent interests in a modern industrial society, they failed to make use of their right to control developments through periodic elections and allowed the political system to wither. Finally even the democratic parties placed their own interests above those of the nation. In the end anti-democratic and megalomaniacal demagogues fought over the remaining spoils, using their power and the freedom they enjoyed under the Weimar Republic to destroy that freedom and to dismantle democratic government in Germany.

12

The Rise of Totalitarianism

1920:   Admiral Horthy elected regent of Hungary
1921:   Creation of the Irish Free State; Vladimir I. Lenin's New Economic Policy; Benito Mussolini assumes dictatorial powers in Italy
1923:   General Primo de Rivera forms a military dictatorship in Spain; proclamation of the Turkish republic
1924:   Death of Lenin
1926:   Joseph Pilsudski creates a dictatorship in Poland
1927:   Emergence of the Nanking government under Chiang Kai-shek
1929:   *Coup d'état* in Yugoslavia by King Alexander
1931–2: Creation of an independent Manchuria under a Japanese protectorate; formation of the Salazar government in Portugal; Franklin Delano Roosevelt is elected US president
1933:   Fascist dictatorship in Austria under Engelbert Dollfuss
1935:   A British-approved constitution for India takes effect
1936:   General John Metaxas becomes dictator of Greece
1939:   General Francisco Franco becomes dictator of Spain

The exaggerated nationalism whipped up by the First World War lingered elsewhere in Europe besides Germany during the following two decades. Other countries too discovered that the war and its immediate aftermath were only the first convulsion in a far lengthier crisis. The democratic state, as pioneered by the United States and the countries of Western Europe, seemed to be on the ascendant after the collapse of the great monarchies of Central and Eastern Europe. But in many countries democracy failed to strike deep and lasting roots. Numerous constitutions were adopted after 1919 based on the Enlightenment principles of the sovereignty of the people and the division of powers. Freedom was to be ensured by the multi-party system and constitutional guarantees of the equality of all citizens. Yet many countries lacked the necessary conditions in which these principles could flourish. In many cases the national interest was eclipsed by fierce internecine struggles between the political parties and interest groups. The people, the ultimate au-

265

thority in the democratic state, increasingly doubted the value of the democratic regimes under which they lived. They had grown habituated throughout the centuries to obeying orders and often lacked good political judgement, tolerance and a sense of responsibility. As modern economic life grew more complicated and concentrated, they were often tempted to surrender difficult decisions to the 'terrible simplifiers' of whom Jacob Burckhardt had warned.[1] The Great Depression, financial hardship and the fear of losing one's social status laid the groundwork for the triumph of fascist demagogues and their acolytes. These demagogues were often assisted in their work by frustrated nationalist ambitions and a craving for national power.

Tensions were further heightened by the fact that national self-determination as promoted by President Wilson, failed to bring about the expected era of peace. Many of the small nationalities previously submerged in the great empires of the Habsburgs, Romanovs and the Osmans achieved national independence, but the new states often included disgruntled minorities, especially in the border areas, and this provided a never-ending source of conflict.

Nationalist passions were soon aflame. The League of Nations was supposed to defend the rights of minority groups but was frustrated by the vehement insistence of many states on their own national sovereignty. Woodrow Wilson had originally advocated national self-determination as the means whereby the peoples of Europe could gain the freedom they required for progress and cultural advancement; but the nation-state came increasingly to be identified with the struggle for power and national expansion. Non-aggression pacts, arbitration agreements and promises of military assistance were soon overshadowed by a sense of malice and distrust, and good international relations became impossible.

The fledgling states of Europe failed to consolidate their new political and social order, and the old ruling classes were able to reassert their authority in many instances. Moreover, serious economic problems put the people and the political system under heavy pressure. Under circumstances such as these, movements demanding a return to authoritarian government gathered strength until finally democracy was overthrown in favour of fascism.

Not only in the Mediterranean countries of Italy, Spain, Greece and Portugal was pluralistic parliamentary democracy supplanted by dictatorial, totalitarian regimes but also in the Balkan states of Yugoslavia, Bulgaria, Hungary and Romania and in Poland, Austria and the Baltic countries. The Soviet Union had proclaimed the advent of a new and higher form of democracy after the October

Revolution, but under Joseph Stalin she too fell into pure dictatorship. The intense competition between the fascist and communist movements permeated much of Europe and poisoned the political atmosphere. Anti-marxism, anti-capitalism, anti-communism, anti-fascism, anti-Semitism and anarchism were some of the alluring slogans in a latent civil war that made it impossible to approach the burning issues of the day dispassionately and objectively.

Europe also failed to overcome its love of empire. The dominance of the white race had been shaken by the events of the war, but the old imperialism lived on in new forms. However, the self-confidence of the Asian and African peoples had been greatly strengthened by their contribution to the war effort in Europe. Politically awakened, they increasingly demanded the right to shape their own destiny in accordance with the honoured principle of national self-determination.

The peace treaty enlargened the French Empire by awarding Paris mandates over the Cameroons, Togo and Syria, and the French were determined to uphold absolute sovereignty over their realm. The British were prepared to yield, occasionally and grudgingly, to colonial demands, though in some instances only after serious conflict had erupted. Ireland achieved dominion status and full internal freedom in 1921, with the exception of the six counties of Protestant Ulster. One year later, Egypt was recognised as a sovereign and independent state, though the Suez Canal was long to remain under British occupation. As the economies of her other African colonies developed, Britain allowed the local chieftains to play a limited role in the administration. After the great sacrifices she had made in the world war, India demanded that she be treated like Ireland and granted full dominion status. London, however, was only prepared to grant a constitution providing for power sharing and limited self-government. This policy provoked a lengthy campaign of passive resistance led by the Indian lawyer and politician Mahatma Gandhi.

The collapse of the Ottoman Empire fired the hopes of the Arab peoples for full independence, but they too were soon disappointed. The British established local Hashimite rulers in Iraq and Trans-Jordan, which had been split off from Palestine, but preserved a strong imperial influence. Great Britain permitted Jewish immigration into Palestine, over which she had received a mandate after the war, but the opposition of the local Arab population produced conflicts which continue to this day. In Arabia itself Ibn Saud, the leader of the strict Muslim sect known as the Wahhabi, established and successfully extended his rule.

In the old Turkish heartland of Anatolia, Kemal Ataturk established a secular state based on the sovereignty of the nation and ensured its independence by adroitly playing off Britain against Russia. Persia likewise succeeded in fending off Russian and British interference.

In the Far East, Japan solidified her position as a great power. She assumed control over former German colonies in the region and extended her influence throughout the Pacific despite opposition from Britain and the United States. Though she resolved her disputes with the Soviet Union by means of a treaty signed in 1925, her fundamentally expansionist policy, as advocated primarily by the army and large industrial interests, did not change. Henceforth her attention would focus increasingly on China.

After Sun Yat-sen founded the Chinese republic, the old antagonism between north and south flared anew and the countryside was devastated by roving bands of mercenaries. After many years of military dictatorship, Chiang Kai-shek, the most successful leader of the Kuomintang, established a Nationalist Chinese government. It did not extend, however, to Outer Mongolia, which had become an autonomous people's republic. The soviet republics which had emerged in southern China after 1931 also escaped Nationalist control. The occupation of Manchuria by the Japanese and its subsequent transformation into the independent state of Manchukuo generated new tensions that culminated in 1937 in the Sino-Japanese War.

The United States emerged from the Great War as the world's greatest creditor, and she subsequently succeeded in taking over many of the foreign markets of the European nations. Turning her back on Wilson's foreign policy, the United States withdrew into isolationism in order to free herself of the European quagmire. A decade of unparalleled prosperity ensued, abruptly followed by the Great Depression, triggered by overproduction. After the election of the Democratic President Franklin Delano Roosevelt in 1932, the government began far-reaching intervention in the national economy and initiated the New Deal. Soon the US government too had taken on an autocratic tinge.

Washington's refusal to join the League of Nations deprived this organisation of one of its most important pillars. The United States began to cooperate more closely with Britain and together they sought to isolate Japan and to impede her expansion in an attempt to protect Anglo-Saxon interests. The United States also reinforced her influence in Central and South America, but her attempt to induce all the states of the Americas to adopt a common front in important questions was condemned to failure by a widespread fear of dollar imperialism. Anxious not to lose their independence, the countries of Latin America turned increasingly to the League of Nations and sought to intensify their economic relations with Europe.

While Japan emerged as a competitor of the capitalist West, the Soviet Union developed into a powerful ideological foe. After the Red Army, organised by Leo Trotsky, triumphed in the civil war, Lenin relaxed the pace of socialisation and introduced the New Economic Policy. This prompted a spurt in industrial and agricultural production. Lenin's successor, the Georgian Joseph Stalin, who had been the party's general secretary since 1921, broke with Trotsky's theory of permanent world revolution. He strove instead to build 'socialism in one country'[2] in order to prepare Russia to meet the great foreign challenges he expected. Industrialisation surged ahead, and the entire work force was coerced by the most ruthless of means to fulfil the state production plans. Heavy industry based on local raw materials arose in the Ural mountains and Siberia, and agriculture was collectivised. Under Stalin a totalitarian state emerged, combining Soviet communism with Great Russian nationalism and imperialism.

In foreign affairs Stalin strove to lead the Soviet Union out of her isolation by concluding neutrality pacts with Germany, Poland, France, Italy and the Little Entente of Yugoslavia, Romania and Czechoslovakia. The Soviet Union also entered the League of Nations. However, Stalin simultaneously lent support to the communist movements in France, Spain and China. By the time international frictions grew more heated after 1933, the Soviet Union was again a major military power which the Anglo-Saxon countries viewed as an even greater threat to their traditional freedoms than the fascist states.

To contemporaries caught up in the maelstrom of these political and ideological struggles, the preamble to the covenant of the League of Nations must have seemed terribly impractical and utopian. An egotistical lust for power and the fears and hatreds of the masses, aggravated by war and revolution, frustrated any resolution of long-standing conflicts and even threw up new problems. The charter of the League of Nations called upon the peoples of the world 'to promote international cooperation and to achieve international peace and security by the acceptance of obligations . . . and by the prescription of open, just and honourable relations'.[3] But many nations set out to extend their own power at the cost of weaker peoples. Wilson's crusade for a world of liberal democracy and international solidarity failed to lay the foundations of a new international order and was overwhelmed by the rise of totalitarian ideologies. Dreams of world revolution and the inherently expansionist tendencies of various nationalist and fascist movements left little room for national self-determination and set the stage for a new catastrophe which was to dwarf anything ever seen before.

13

From Hitler's Seizure of Power to the Outbreak of the Second World War

1933: Enabling Act; dissolution of the parties; concordat between the curia and the Reich; disarmament dispute and withdrawal from the League of Nations

1934: German–Polish Friendship Pact; Röhm crisis; Hindenburg's death; Hitler becomes chancellor and president

1935: Saar referendum; universal conscription; Anglo-German naval treaty; Nuremberg Laws

1935–6: Abyssinian War

1936: Occupation of the Rhineland; Rome–Berlin axis

1936–9: Spanish Civil War

1937: War breaks out between China and Japan

1938: *Anschluss* of Austria; Sudetenland crisis; 'Kristallnacht'

1939: Germany establishes a protectorate over Bohemia and Moravia; non-aggression pact with Russia; Second World War breaks out

In Germany the totalitarian tendencies of the industrial age were reinforced by the old ambition to achieve great power status. Many Germans 'were not content to be a people dependent on the mercy of the victorious powers'; they 'dreamed of the glory and grandeur of a new and larger Reich'.[1] The considerable success of the Weimar Republic in gradually restoring Germany's equality with the other nations of Europe was largely overlooked. Adolf Hitler assured Germans that he could succeed where the republic had failed, and was assisted in this by the nationalists who heaped scorn on liberal democracy and applauded the old values that had won Germans their national unity. These values were closely related to the Nazi concept of the *Volksgemeinschaft*, a socially and politically unified people led to new glory by a great leader.

Hitler's accession to power was therefore cause for rejoicing among the nationalist right. The conservative *Kreuz-Zeitung* commented the next day:

Is it not wonderful that from the midst the German people, crushed by the war and continually weakened thereafter by blind government policies, a new government has sprung with the former supreme commander [Hindenburg] at its head and the leader of a most passionate nationalist movement [Hitler] as its chancellor. .... It is the most nationalist government imaginable, and hence the government most urgently needed by a prostrated people, the strongest assurance of a great revival.[2]

The collapse of the monarchy had left a power vacuum, which widespread hostility to the republic had prevented it from filling. Suddenly this vacuum had ceased to exist. The prophecy of the poet Stefan George about the advent of 'the only man who can help, a man of action'[3] was seemingly fulfilled. But this man of action, as Thomas Mann pointed out in 1930, was one who 'had nothing in common with the traditional bourgeois world and its fundamental credo of freedom, justice, education, optimism and faith in progress', and who would subvert the bourgeois 'nationalism of the nineteenth century... moderated by strong cosmopolitan and humanitarian influences' and direct it against this same bourgeoisie.[4] In the end Hitler inflicted enormous death and destruction on the world and burdened himself and his chosen people with crimes without parallel in human history.

Hitler, the Man and the Politician

When Hitler commenced his political career he was 30 years old. His ancestors issued from the farmers and petty bourgeoisie of Lower and Upper Austria. His father, a government revenue officer, had six children in his third marriage, of whom Hitler was the fourth. His father's early death and frequent relocations of the family home had an unfavourable effect on the young Hitler. Though intelligent, he was always a mediocre student. At age 19 he went to Vienna and applied to the painting school of the Academy of Fine Arts. But his test drawings were judged unsatisfactory and he was rejected. When he tried to gain admission to the School of Architecture he was refused because he lacked a secondary school diploma. Nevertheless, Hitler persevered in Vienna till 1913. Without a profession or a goal in life, he eked out a scanty living by painting postcards and taking occasional jobs, after having consumed his orphan's allowance and a small legacy. He spent the nights in an asylum for homeless men and passed the days by going to the theatre, walking throughout the old imperial city and reading extensively, though without plan. In this way he acquired a demi-education which profoundly influenced all he thought and did for the rest of his life. Hitler himself wrote that these years in Vienna left such a lasting impression that 'I have had to learn little in addition; and I have had to alter nothing.'[5]

Here amidst the mixed population of the impoverished districts of Vienna were formed those hatreds and prejudices which would later become the scourge of Germany and Europe alike: Hitler's theory of a Germanic, and primarily German, master race destined to rule the world; his profound hatred of Jews, democracy, liberalism and humanism, indeed of all Western civilisation and of those social and intellectual circles from which it largely sprang; his admiration of naked power and contempt for the Christian religion; his fanatical *grossdeutsche* nationalism; and his scant regard for the individual.[6]

At the outbreak of the First World War Hitler volunteered for service in the Bavarian army, thus escaping the daily struggle for food, clothing and shelter. He served for four years on the western front, mostly as a messenger, was wounded twice and was awarded first- and second-class Iron Crosses. However, he was never promoted beyond the rank of corporal, supposedly for lack of leadership abilities. Near the end of the war his eyes were badly damaged in a gas attack, and it was while lying half blind in a military hospital that he heard the news of Germany's military collapse and the political revolution. He was consumed with a violent hatred for the 'November criminals' to whom he imputed full responsibility for the catastrophe, and he determined to take up the sword against them. In the autumn of 1919 Hitler joined the tiny German Workers' Party in Munich and made it the forum of his political views. He engineered a change in the party's name to the more attractive National Socialist German Workers' Party (Nationalsozialistische Deutsche Arbeiterpartei) and soon assumed the leadership. In this role he quickly discovered his extraordinary talents as a speaker and his ability 'to mobilise the collective subconcious'.[7] His boundless will to power and overestimation of his intellectual and political talents also surfaced in these years. Hitler was intoxicated by his sudden success, having previously wasted away his life in bitter frustration, vainly chasing after proud dreams, wary of other people and unable to make good friends. But he was persistent and determined, and convinced in his typically exaggerated way that he had been endowed by fate with a special personality. He recorded his decision to become the Führer in the first volume of his book, *Mein Kampf*, written in early 1923 while he was in prison. Shortly after his release from prison he took the first step towards the realisation of his ambitions when he helped to refound the NSDAP in 1925 after it had been banned everywhere in the Reich.

The Nazi political programme was based on Germany's military collapse in November 1918 and the calamities which thereafter befell the German people. Hitler proclaimed his intention to nullify the results of the war and of the revolution, to restore the nation to greatness and to eliminate all internal opposition to these designs by rooting out parliamentarianism. Nationalism and socialism would serve as the foundation for a comprehensive reordering of society and the state. Political parties would be abolished and the German people would be welded together in a strong racial community. Individualism, liberalism and democracy would be swept aside by the 'principle of untrammelled authority for the leader'.[8] In a speech delivered in October 1933 Hitler said:

National Socialism takes as the starting-point of its views and its decisions neither the individual nor humanity. It puts consciously into the central point of its whole thinking the *Volk*. This *Volk* is for it a blood-conditioned entity in which it sees the God-willed building-stone of human society. The individual is transitory, the *Volk* is permanent. If the liberal *Weltanschauung* in its deification of the single individual must lead to the destruction of the *Volk*, National Socialism, on the other hand, desires to safeguard the *Volk*, if necessary even at the expense of the individual. It is essential that the individual should slowly come to realize that his own ego is unimportant when compared with the existence of the whole people.[9]

This *Volk* would be freed of all divisive elements such as political parties, ideologies and religions and would be integrated into a tightly knit whole by a new, indigenous ethic and training. Thus it would be prepared, in Hitler's view, to become the mainstay of the Aryan or Nordic race and to play the leading political and cultural role in the world. Hitler considered himself singled out by fate to make this people the instrument of his own limitless will to power.

To Hitler ideas were nothing more than a means towards the ultimate goal of maximising his own might. They could therefore be adamantly denied if this later suited his purpose. Nevertheless, Hitler's policies were heavily influenced by certain fundamental concepts which never changed. The strongest of these was radical nationalism, recognisable from the very beginning and prominent in *Mein Kampf*. Hitler planned to unite as many of the German-speaking peoples of Europe as possible in a great German empire. To this 'Germanic state of the German nation', as Hitler called it,[10] would be subordinated the rights, freedom and dignity of the individual person, of social groups and of foreign peoples and countries. This brand of nationalism, which had sunk into mere megalomania and completely rejected any notion of international interdependence or cooperation, was an outgrowth of Hitler's racial theories. According to these theories, 'all occurrences in world history are only the expression of the races' instinct of self-preservation, in the good or bad sense'.[11] Adopting an extreme version of Social Darwinism, Hitler considered the struggle for survival to be the essence of history, the prime human mission on earth and the key to all progress. In this struggle the 'Aryan' race would emerge pre-eminent. ('Aryan' is a linguistic term meaning 'belonging to the Indo-Germanic group of languages'; it was inappropriately applied to a racial theory.)

All the human culture, all the results of art, science, and technology that we see before us today, are almost exclusively the creative product of the Aryan. This very fact admits of the not unfounded inference that he alone was the founder of all higher humanity, therefore representing the prototype of all that we understand by the word 'man'. . . . If we were to divide mankind into three groups, the founders of culture, the bearers of culture, the destroyers of culture, only the Aryan could be considered as the representative of the first group. From him originates the foundations and walls of all human creation.[12]

The Aryan race, in Hitler's view, rises above the egotism of the struggle for survival which permeates all nature and human history through his 'readiness to subordinate purely personal interests and hence through his 'ability to establish comprehensive communities'.[13] Within the Aryan race it is the Germanic peoples and, above all, the Germans themselves who have achieved particular eminence. It is their duty to create a solid nucleus of the Germanic race in Central Europe, to subjugate or even extirpate the 'lesser' peoples and races, and to rule thereafter as the master race.

Hitler's racial theories reached their greatest perversity in rabid anti-Semitism. He stated programmatically in *Mein Kampf*, 'The mightiest counterpart to the Aryan is represented by the Jew'[14] and 'Without the clearest knowledge of the racial problem and hence of the Jewish problem there will never be a resurrection of the German nation'.[15] Jews, in Hitler's view, were the enemy of all civilisation, the source of all evil and of all defeats and a foe of any ordered national life.[16] The outcome of this radical anti-Semitism was the gradual exclusion of Jews from German national life by means of measures that grew more and more horrifying.

Many of Hitler's ideas were rooted in the fervid nineteenth-century writings of the French diplomat Arthur Gobineau and his disciples. To the scapegoats fingered here, Hitler added bolshevism, which he held of course to be 'a product of Jewish thought' alongside 'British imperialism' and 'American plutocracy'.[17]

The historic task which Hitler ascribed to the German people was a direct outgrowth of his own nationalism, racial theories, anti-Semitism and anti-bolshevism. He wrote in *Mein Kampf*:

If the National Socialist movement really wants to be consecrated by history with a great mission for our nation, it must . . . without consideration of traditions and prejudices find the courage to gather our people and their strength for an advance along the road that will lead this people from its present restricted living space to a new land and soil, and hence also free it from the danger of vanishing from the earth or of serving others as a slave nation.[18]

In order to win new land and soil, no price was too high, no sacrifice too great, for 'Germany will either be a world power or there will be no Germany'.[19] In Hitler's view the struggle against the 'Diktat' of Versailles was only the starting-point of German expansionism, which would begin where it had ended six centuries earlier: 'We shall stop', Hitler announced, 'the endless German movement to the south and west, and direct our gaze toward the land in the east. At long last we break off the colonial and commercial policy of the prewar period and shift to the soil policy of the future.'[20] To this end, Hitler hoped to uncouple Poland and the successor states to the Austro-Hungarian Empire from their alliance with France and to conquer and permanently subjugate Russia in an effort to extend German 'Lebensraum'. Britain and Italy would view all this, Hitler believed, as willing allies or at least benevolent neutrals. These calculations were later the guiding spirit behind Hitler's foreign policy—a fantastic and totally apolitical adventure that had no chance of success once Britain and Poland refused to play out the roles which Hitler had assigned to them. But the pursuit of these dreams thrust Germany down the path to the Second World War and led the Führer in 1939 to take up the sword by which he himself would die in 1945.

In order to implement this ideology, Hitler needed to gain control of the state. His putsch of 1923, modelled on the example of the Italian fascists failed, netting him only a prison term. Hitler thereupon switched tactics and resolved to seek power through legal channels. However, he never tired of emphasising the anti-parliamentary nature of National Socialism, whose 'participation in a parliamentary institution can only imply activity for its destruction'.[21] Hitler's decision to pursue legal means also did not exclude the use of strong-arm tactics against political foes. Violence and ever more strident propaganda campaigns were measures intended to magnify the social chaos and create the impression in the public mind that only a leader prepared to go to any lengths would be able to save the situation and restore order.

After 1929 the Nazis began to score their first major successes with the middle classes, both urban and rural, who sympathised with Hitler's nationalist, anti-socialist, anti-capitalist and anti-Semitic rhetoric. At the same time the Nazis gained ground among the working classes. Hitler's claim to political power grew more and more serious until finally, as the leader of what had become the strongest single party in the *Reichstag*, Hitler achieved his goal in 1933 thanks to political intrigues pitting Papen against Schleicher.

Hitler had been ridiculed by his fellow soldiers for his wild, unbridled speeches; dismissed out of hand by other politicians as a fanatical rabble-rouser; and vastly underestimated by friend and foe alike. Now, with his nomination as chancellor, he had reached a position in which he could remodel Germany in his own image. Scarcely anyone, whether German or foreign, believed that this demagogue and political fanatic would long endure as the head of government. Very few thought in 1933 that Hitler really had the will to put his theoretical programme into terrible practice. How much greater was the shock when the reality of Hitlerian rule far outdid all that even his worst enemies had feared.

The Nazi State

After taking over as chancellor, Hitler set out with the utmost speed and determination to gather all the reins of power into his own hand. To this end he sought to gain control of the army, the police and the bureaucracy, usurp the legislative authority of the *Reichstag* and the *Reichspräsident*, eradicate the constitutional rights of the provinces, ban non-Nazi political and social organisations, and crush opposition from within his own party. First he sought a parliamentary majority in order to achieve this *Gleichschaltung* by pseudo-legal means. The *Reichstag* was dissolved on 1 February 1933 and new elections were set for 5 March. In order to ensure victory, the Nazis not only played skilfully on people's fears for the future of Germany but also arrested leftist politicians and limited freedom of assembly and of the press by means of legal emergency decrees approved by Hindenburg. When the *Reichstag* burnt early in the morning of the 28 February, the Nazis exploited the opportunity to issue the so-called 'Presidential Decree for the Protection of the People and the State',[22] which abrogated virtually all personal liberties 'until further notice'. The central government also assumed the power at this time to replace the provincial governments with *Reichskommissare*. This step marked the end of constitutional rule and the institution of a state of emergency. A rash of arrests, prohibitions, seizures and restrictions ensued, directed against all political opponents but primarily against the Communists.

Despite many acts of terror and a grandiose campaign emphasising nationalism and the dawn of a new era, the Nazis only garnered 43.9 per cent of the vote in the ensuing elections. They failed to achieve the great victory predicted by Joseph Goebbels, *Gauleiter* of Berlin, chief party propagandist and after early March 1933 minister of enlightenment and propaganda. In order to maintain a façade of legality, the National Socialists entered another coalition with the German National People's Party, which had won 8 per cent of the popular vote. Together these two parties could muster a slim majority.

The second key step in Hitler's consolidation of his power was the introduction in Parliament of the Enabling Act. This Act, which altered the Constitution and hence required a two-thirds majority of the *Reichstag*, conceded to the government full legislative authority over a period of four years. Hitler thus aimed to gain complete freedom of action. In a relatively moderate speech underlining the purity of his intentions, Hitler assured the *Reichstag* that he would

make use of this Act only in so far as necessary to carry out essential measures. The continued existence of both the *Reichstag* and the *Reichsrat* will not be called into question. The position and prerogatives of the *Reichspräsident* will remain unaffected. . . . The provinces will continue to exist, the rights of the Churches will not be diminished, their relationship with the state will not be changed.[23]

These concessions were aimed primarily at the Centre Party, which believed that its support for this Act would induce the National Socialists to look favourably on future Catholic requests. The Act passed with the support of the bourgeois parties and despite the opposition of the Social Democrats. It removed all the constraints which the Weimar Constitution had placed on the power of the state, extinguished parliamentary government in Germany and accorded Hitler, who had no intention of keeping his promises, a *carte blanche* for the implementation of his programme.

One week after the passage of the Enabling Act, the first Act was introduced to coordinate (*gleichschalten*) the provincial governments and their federal counterpart. According to this Act, provincial parliaments and local councils would be restructured to reflect the results of the Reichstag election of 5 March. A second Act, introduced on April 2, made all provincial governments subservient to the Reichsstatthalter, who had been installed in early March and who owed their allegiance to the Führer. Finally, all provincial parliaments were extinguished on 30 January 1934 and provincial governments became completely subservient to the federal government. For the first time in its long history, Germany had become a centralised unitary state.

The various political parties were also banned or forced to dissolve, and their property was seized. The labour unions were supplanted by the German Labour Front. This front comprised employers and employees, and all strikes or lock-outs were forbidden in order to ensure labour peace. All that remained was a 'single political party, the National Socialist German Workers' Party', which with its associated organisations became the sole source of political will in Germany and was proclaimed by the law of 1 December 1933, to be 'insolubly linked with the state'.[24]

This ended the Nazi revolution, according to Hitler, and the state would henceforth tread 'the firm path of evolution'.[25] 'Cross appointments in the party, state and bureaucracy became increasingly frequent and were the primary means of National Socialist domination.'[26] This was facilitated by the 'Act to Restore a Professional Civil Service' passed in April 1933. This Act required all civil servants to swear unqualified loyalty to the new state and thus made it possible to dismiss out of hand all political undesirables, Jews and bureaucrats with a different party affiliation.

By the end of the 1933 the democratic regime established by the Weimar Constitution had succumed to a one-party state which was fast becoming totalitarian. The cabinet, which had once believed it would be able to control Hitler, was reduced to political impotence, and old Hindenburg proved helpless in the face of the Nazi tide.

The spate of measures in Hitler's first year as chancellor was accompanied by countless acts of terror and violence. When Vice-Chancellor Papen criticised conditions in his Marburg speech of the spring of 1934, a serious crisis developed. Hitler felt pressured by political conservatives, who had not yet been totally silenced, and by SA opposition from within his own party. The SA had played an important role in Hitler's rise to power, but had not received its just deserts under the new regime and found itself largely excluded from power. It therefore insisted ever more stridently on a second revolution which would confer upon it a political status commensurate with its accomplishments on behalf of the Nazi Party. Its headstrong leader, the former army captain Ernst Röhm, hoped to absorb the Reichswehr into the SA and to take command over the resulting forces numbering in the millions. These designs were strongly opposed not only by the army generals but also by Röhm's rivals within the party, especially Göring, Goebbels and the leader of the SS, Heinrich Himmler. They encouraged Hitler to build up a new army with the help of the *Reichswehr* and to depose Röhm. On 30 June and 1 July 1934 Hitler had Röhm and the other leaders of the SA arrested and murdered by SS units on the unproven accusation that they were plotting a putsch. Hitler and his inner circle also took advantage of this opportunity to liquidate opponents outside the party. Jews, leading Opposition politicians and other undesirables were assassinated, whether on the left or the right, whether affiliated with conservatives, the centre parties or the labour movement. The hundreds of murders carried out on Hitler's orders were later legalised as an act of legitimate national self-defence, and Hitler declared before Parliament that he was the supreme judge of the German people. The *Reichswehr* and Himmler's SS felt that they had carried off a great victory; but the greatest victor was Hitler himself, who had liquidated an important rival while earning the gratitude and loyalty of the army.

One month after this brutal purge, President Hindenburg died. Hitler swiftly exploited this opportunity to complete the concentration of power in his own hands. By virtue of a law passed one day before Hindenburg's death on 1 August 1934, Hitler combined the functions of *Reichspräsident* and *Reichskanzler*. The army as well as judges and civil servants were required henceforth to swear an oath of allegiance to him. As the Führer and *Reichskanzler*, Hitler had succeeded in uniting all state and political authority in his own person and had 'coordinated' (*gleichgeschaltet*) all political and social institutions in Germany with the exceptions of the army and the church.

After Hindenburg's death Hitler became supreme commander of the army, which had not only proved loyal to the new regime but had even acted as Hitler's accomplice in the Röhm affair. Nevertheless, there was still some resistance to the National Socialists, especially among the older officers. Hitler was anxious to eliminate these elements from the army, and in 1938 he dismissed the minister of defence, General Werner von Blomberg, and the chief of the army command, General Werner von Fritsch, on the basis of innuendo and frivolous accusations. In their place he created an Army Supreme Command (*Oberkommando der Wehrmacht*) under his direct authority to which the three chiefs of the army sections and the general staff were required to report. Hitler thus consolidated his personal authority over the army as well.

The Führer apparently adopted a more cautious approach towards the churches. Though he never renounced his conviction that Christianity and National Socialism were fundamentally incompatible and fully intended to extirpate German Christianity in the end, Hitler sought at first to avoid an open confrontation for tactical reasons. He justified his attempts to throttle the Catholic political movement which had opposed the Nazis prior to 1933 by claiming he was merely 'de-confessionalising public life'.[27] An agreement was sought with the Vatican in order to make German Catholics more acceptant of the Nazis, to negate Catholicism as a political factor in Germany, and to consolidate the regime both internally and externally through the prestige that recognition by the Holy See would confer.

The Concordat with the Vatican was accordingly reached on 20 July 1933. It soon became apparent, however, that Hitler had not the slightest intention of honouring the sweeping concessions he had accorded the Catholic Church in the areas of parochial schools, church organisations, youth work and pastoral functions in exchange for its withdrawal from German political life. Once the pressing tasks of rearmament and reinforcement of Nazi power had been accomplished, Hitler resumed the open struggle with the Catholic Church, persecuting priests and Catholic opponents of the regime, instituting show trials and closing numerous monasteries and religious schools.

The Führer also introduced legislation to 'coordinate' the twenty-eight provincial Evangelical churches. This seemed to be an easier task in that the vast majority of German Protestants sympathised with National Socialism and the new government. The Protestant churches were also more vulnerable to Nazi ideology than the Catholic Church with its rigid hierarchy. The struggle for the soul of German Protestantism split the church after 1933 into a central 'Reichskirche' loyal to Hitler and a 'Confessional Church' that sought to maintain its intellectual and organisational independence. Led by such men as Martin Niemöller, a Berlin pastor and former U-boat captain, and Theophil Wurm, the Bishop of Württemberg, supporters of the 'Confessional Church' strongly opposed state measures. They protested against the eradication of the rule of law, epitomised by concentration camps and the Gestapo, against the muzzling of the press and the elimination of free speech. Even the arrest of many confessional pastors and other members of the congregation failed to break their resistance.

Though Hitler failed to 'coordinate' the Churches, they nevertheless did not pose much of a threat to the regime because most of their members either supported it or had resigned themselves to it.

In general, the *Gleichschaltung* proceeded much more quickly than even the National Socialists had hoped. After the Social Democratic and Communist leaders had either fled the country, been murdered or interned in concentration camps, Hitler set out to win over their followers to National Socialism, or at least to persuade them of the many advantages of his policies. He was greatly assisted in this by his success in sharply reducing the severe unemployment rate in Germany. The Nazis implemented the plans to reform and revitalise the German economy which had been drawn up before 1933, and many jobs were created for the 6 million unemployed. Brüning's policies of budgetary and monetary restraint were replaced by expansionist policies. Aided by a slight upswing in the economy, Hitler pushed vigorously ahead with many more measures to create jobs. By June 1933 the finance minister had already set aside a fund of approximately a thousand million marks to be invested by the *Reich*, the provinces and local districts in sewage and water pipes and the construction of roads, *autobahns*, bridges, canals, apartments, river control measures and party edifices. Money was also made available to private citizens to enlarge or renovate buildings. By the end of 1936 unemployment had been eliminated. The armaments industry also resumed its activity in the meantime, creating such a demand for labour that foreign workers had to be brought in. The transition from depression to moderate prosperity was accomplished without inflation and wages and prices remained stable. It is hardly surprising that a wave of confidence and faith in the future overtook the grey despair typical of the final years of the Weimar Republic.

Thanks to these accomplishments, the Nazi regime gained broad popular support and the social climate changed dramatically. There was no more talk of socialisation, as once demanded by the Strasser-wing of the party. Industrialists were styled *Wirtschaftsführer* (economic leaders) and were entrusted with the management of the firms. They were pressured, however, to improve working conditions for their *Gefolgschaft*, or 'follower', by the German Labour Front and special Nazi agents, or trustees known as *Treuhänder der Arbeit*, organised in January 1934 to oversee 'the preservation of labour peace'. Work places were made more attractive, toilets were installed, recreational facilities were built on company grounds and so on. The merging of industrialists and white- and blue-collar workers in the German Labour Front and a law requiring industries to organise company clubs were primarily cosmetic changes which did not alter the fundamentally capitalist economy. But the social climate was improved and belief in class warfare declined. All these measures were taken, according to the Nazis, 'for the common benefit of the people and the state', that is in order to consolidate the system and, as heavy industry and production goods capacity gradually expanded, in order to achieve Hitler's foreign goals.[28] On account of these foreign ambitions, the regime restricted the freedom of industrialists to do as they pleased and insisted on complete cooperation, but in return the industrialists were allowed free rein to manage their companies and to keep the profits. Economic clout could no longer be translated into political power, but few industrialists were so inclined in view of the vibrant state of economy.

Agriculture also benefited from the Nazi policy of economic self-sufficiency and transition to a war economy, and farmers were enjoined to produce as much as possible. However, agriculture too came under strict state controls. The type and extent of the crop and the amount of harvest to be delivered at a set price were all prescribed, so that in the end it was state revenues which rose, not the income of farmers. In order to maintain the size of individual farms, an Inherited Estates Act was passed on 29 September 1933. It decreed that all farms of 'from one *Ackernahrung* (land sufficient to support a family or 7.5 ha) to a maximum of 125 ha' could not be divided, sold or mortaged.[29] This prevented the accumulation of debt but also impeded raising capital in order to rationalise farm operations.

Rearmament, job creation and large-scale public works required the expenditure of vast sums of money which could not be raised by taxes and loans alone. Though exports were declining, increasing amounts of foreign exchange also had to be earned to pay for the imported raw materials required by the arms industry. Hjalmar Schacht managed to conjure up the necessary funds by means of the so-called 'Mefo-bills' guaranteed by the Reichsbank and on which payments were to begin in 1938. (Mefo = Metallforschung GmbH). (This was investment assistance in the form of hidden credits intended primarily for heavy industry. The term 'credit' was avoided so as not to arouse fears of inflation in the general population and 'bills' was used instead. These bills were guaranteed by the *Reichsbank* and could be exchanged for cash in German banks. Since Mefo-bills were guaranteed by the *Reichbank* the banks ran no risk and the bills could be held in place of cash. In this way, all available cash was brought into circulation, without necessitating an inflationary increase in the total number of bank notes.) The production of arms did not, however, generate the amount of revenue needed to pay back the loans. Since Hitler made no other funds available, these loans remained unredeemed, to be paid back by the conquered peoples after Hitler's 'final victory'.

The Nazis aimed to gain full mastery of every aspect of German life and were not content to control only the state. From the outset they endeavoured to bring all groups and organisations under the absolute power of the Führer and to bind them to the regime both materially and intellectually. To this end the Nazis fostered an array of mass organisations which encompassed and watched over every facet of life. 'There must be a will and that will must lead',[30] proclaimed the minister of the interior, Wilhelm Frick. The basis of the welter of organisations grouped around the Führer was the Nazi Party, pledged to blind allegiance. With its block and cell wardens, the party reached into every household and sought to control every manifestation of German life. 'The welding of the German people into a solid nation', as Frick put it, was overseen not only by the party but also by numerous other Nazi organisations comprising every age and occupation: youth organisations such as the Hitler Youth (*Deutsch Jungvolk*), the League of German Girls, the National Socialist Students' Association and the Labour Service; party affiliates such as the SA, the SS and the National Socialist Motor Transport Corps; Nazi professional organisations such as the German Labour Front, the Food Estate (*Reichsnährstand*), the Chamber of Culture, the League of University Professors, the League of Jurists, the Physicians' League and the Teachers' League; women's organisations such as the *Frauenschaft* and the *Deutsch Frauenwerk*; charitable institutions such as Social Welfare and Winter Aid; and finally the Nazi recreation association, 'Kraft durch Freude'.

Particular attention was paid to the management of cultural life. Intellectuals and artists were herded together in the Chamber of Culture with its subdivisions of the Press Association, the Authors' League, the Chamber of Music, the Chamber of Theatre and the Chamber of Film. Joseph Goebbels exercised strict censorship over these groups and quickly squelched any criticism or freedom of thought. Jewish artists and academics were excluded from the Chamber of Culture and thus barred from exercising their profession. All branches of modern science and modern art were condemned as degenerate or un-German and were banned. According to the Nazis, German cultural life was to be kept 'pure and free of all harmful and undesirable writings'.[31] Anything deemed 'un-German' was burnt in great public bonfires.[32] Celebrated names, the glory of German culture, appeared on the 'black list' of the Chamber of Culture: artists such as Ernst Barlach, Max Beckmann, Otto Dix, Erich Heckel, Ernst Ludwig Kirchner, Paul Klee, Käthe Kollwitz, Oskar Kokoschka, Franz Marc and Emil Nolde; writers such as Bert Brecht, Alfred Döblin, Franz Kafka, Heinrich Mann, Thomas Mann, Franz Werfel, Carl Zuckmayer and Stefan Zweig; composers such as Paul Hindemith and Arnold Schönberg; and many celebrated directors and architects. In their place the Nazis promoted artists and writers devoted to the heroic monumentalism and the racially conscious, so-called pure German art advocated by the regime . The universities fell under the mounting influence of professors loyal to the Nazi faith, and a stream of academics, many of them Jewish, left the country. Schools were instructed 'to nurture the political man' of Nazi ideology, that is a person 'who is rooted in his people in all he thinks and does, is ready to serve them and to sacrifice himself for them, and feels inextricably linked to the history and fate of his country'.[33]

The masses were dazzled by the propaganda on the radio and in newspapers and by the marching columns of *Volksgenossen*, who gathered on celebration days scattered throughout the year to pay hommage to National Socialism and the Führer. Many Germans succumbed to the dynamism of this brilliant leader, blind to the ruthless dictatorship being erected behind the 'grandeur and nobility' of spectacular party meetings. The concentration camps swelled with inmates who had been denounced by spies or functionaries as hostile or unreliable elements and whose names had appeared on the 'black lists' of the secret police or of the security service of the SS. Denied all semblance of justice, these people were delivered into the clutches of the SS and the police who punished them mercilessly for their alleged crimes against the '*Volksgemeinschaft*'. With unprecedented efficiency, the Nazis constructed a regime of fear and terror in which Jews in particular suffered the most outrageous horrors.

Defamed, deprived of their rights and expelled from the body politic, despoiled, brutally mistreated and finally massacred, the Jews were helpless in the grip of Hitler's fanatic hatred. The 'solution of the Jewish problem' began as early as 1 April 1933 with a boycott of all Jewish businesses and professional practices. A few days later the first Jewish functionaries were dismissed. On 15 April 1935 the Nuremberg Laws were promulgated, denying Jews all civil rights and forbidding them to marry Aryans or engage in extramarital sex with Aryans. The severest repression began on 9

November 1938 with a pogrom organised by Goebbels and known as the 'Kristallnacht'. Jewish places of business were plundered, virtually all synagogues were destroyed, ninety-one people of Jewish heritage were murdered and 26,000 were arrested and sent to concentration camps. All Jewish physicians, lawyers, businessmen and tradesmen were forbidden to practise their profession. Emergency laws were passed to prevent Jews from frequenting state schools, universities, cinemas, theatres, concerts, exhibitions and bathing facilities. Jews were also forbidden to purchase or own automobiles, telephones, newspapers, certain articles of clothing, jewellery and domestic animals. To the extent permitted by tight emigration laws, many Jews fled Germany, their homeland for generations. After 1 October 1941 even this escape was closed. The great settling of accounts, the 'final solution' announced by Göring as early as 1938, was about to begin. Almost all Jews who had not already been expelled, imprisoned or murdered were annihilated.

This crime against humanity, through which National Socialism disgraced both itself and generations of Germans to come, stemmed directly from Hitler's absurd racial theories and profound hatred of all Jewry. It was rendered possible, not least of all, by the weakened judicial system in the new Germany. The traditional principle of equality before the law was replaced by various National Socialist tenets, the most important of which was, 'Right is what serves the people.' In justifying the murders of 30 June 1934 Göring had announced on 12 July, 'We do not see the law as primary. That is and must remain the people.'[34] What best served the interests of the German people was decided by Hitler alone. His will became law and he, in his own words, became 'the supreme judge of the German people'.[35] No longer was legality the deciding factor, but the person involved. This fundamental inequality before the law contradicted all of Germany's written legal codes. After the introduction of special courts and the People's Court (*Volksgerichtshof*) in 1936, findings of guilt or innocence became a political question to be decided by the state and ultimately by Hitler himself. In a blunt declaration to the German Law Academy in October 1936, Heinrich Himmler stated:

We National Socialists set to work not without a sense of justice—which we bore within ourselves—but outside the law. From the beginning I was totally indifferent to whether our actions contravened some law. In the accomplishment of my duties I do what I can justify to my own conscience and what makes common sense in my work for the Führer and the German people. Foreigners ... spoke of course of lawlessness within the police and therefore within the state. They held everything to be lawless which did not conform to their own notions of law, but we in actual fact were laying the foundations of a new law based on the right to life of the German people.[36]

Hitler's Foreign Policy from 1933 to 1938

Hitler first elaborated his theory of the German people's right to life in *Mein Kampf*, as a justification for the agressive and expansionist foreign policy he intended to pursue. Four days after taking power, Hitler openly reaffirmed these intentions before an audience of army generals and confirmed them again on 5 November 1937. He stated that his primary goal was the abrogation of the Treaty of Versailles and that he therefore intended to reinforce the army and to introduce universal conscription. Once this aim had been achieved, Hitler informed the generals, the Nazis planned to conquer 'new *Lebensraum* in the east' and to secure these lands through 'relentless Germanisation'.[37] In this grand Nazi design, the strident demands for a peaceful revision of the Treaty of Versailles represented only the first step. Indeed, after this revision had been successfully accomplished, Hitler set about expanding Germany between 1937 and the outbreak of the war in 1939 into a *großdeutsche* national state. He then undertook a limited struggle for the dominance of Europe and finally, after June 1941, 'wild and senseless destruction to the bitter end. It all sprang from the same mind and the final stage was inherent in the first. Hitler never intended at any point to stop and content himself with what he had already accomplished.'[38]

The Führer owed the ease of his early victories to the political situation in Europe and the world in the 1930s and to the profound desire for peace in Britain and France. Torn over the attitude they should adopt towards the dictatorships of Hitler and Mussolini, the Western powers hoped to avoid conflict with Germany through a policy of appeasement. Hitler's aggressive policies were also eased by the Sino-Japanese conflict in the Far East; the intervention of Russia, the United States and Britain on the side of the Chinese under Chiang Kai-shek; the mounting nationalist resistance to British rule in India; the threat which this posed to Dutch colonies and French possessions in Indo-China; the Italian invasion of Abyssinia, and the Spanish Civil War.

Hitler adopted the clever ploy of basing his demands on the discarded Allied ideals of the First World War: disarmament and self-determination. He took every available opportunity to reiterate Germany's desire for peace and at the same time her demand that the 'Diktat' of Versailles be abrogated. This he finally accomplished through unilateral action and a *fait accompli*.

Hitler scored a considerable propaganda success in July 1933 when Germany signed the four-power agreement of understanding and cooperation which had been drawn up, largely at Mussolini's initiative, by Italy, France, Britain and Germany. Shortly thereafter he concluded the Concordat with the Vatican. The Führer then renewed the demand which previous chancellors had made the other great powers should have no more arms than Germany. When the other powers balked at reducing their military forces to Germany's level in order to effect equality, Hitler demanded that the limitations on German military strength be removed. France vehemently opposed this demand, and thereby eased the way for Hitler to do what he wished and repudiate the agreements which Stresemann and Brüning had signed. This gave him greater freedom to pursue his goals.

In October 1933 Germany withdrew from the Disarmament Conference and the League of Nations, complaining of discrimination. A deceptive plebiscite was then held to gain the approval of the German electorate for this step. At the same time, Hitler began secretly to rearm while evading the danger of German isolation by virtue of a series of bilateral treaties. In a stunning diplomatic reversal for both sides, Germany concluded a friendship and consultation pact with Poland on 26 January 1934. This treaty supposedly obviated any possibility of armed conflict for a period of ten years. Poland, deeply unsettled by the growing might of Germany, felt reassured, while Hitler secured his eastern flank and weakened the French security network in Eastern Europe. Paris responded with vigorous attempts to shore up the Little Entente between Czechoslovakia, Yugoslavia and Romania and to link it to the new Balkan Entente between Greece, Yugoslavia, Romania and Turkey. France also drew closer to the Soviet Union, which entered the League of Nations in September 1934, and they concluded a treaty of mutual assistance in May 1935. In addition, Paris and Rome signed a secret agreement in January 1935 according to which Italy would guarantee Austria's border with Germany in return for French concessions in Africa.

This series of successes for French diplomacy diminished Hitler's margin of manoeuvre in foreign affairs, but he regained his momentum through the recovery of the Saarland. In accordance with the Treaty of Versailles, a plebiscite was held in the Saar on 13 January 1935, and 91 per cent of the population voted to return to the Fatherland. The resulting wave of patriotic fervour in Germany,

British rearmament programme and a French decision to extend military service from eighteen months to two years all encouraged the Führer to announce officially on 9 March 1935 the creation of a German air force (though it already existed in fact) and to introduce universal military conscription on 16 March. This unilateral repudiation of the limitations placed on the German military by the Treaty of Versailles was accompanied by copious assurances of Germany's desire for peace. In May Hitler proposed before *Reichstag* a skein of bilateral non-aggression pacts and continued:

In relation to France, Germany has solemnly recognised and guaranteed the border as it stands after the Saar plebiscite. Disregarding past events, Germany has also concluded a pact with Poland banning the use of force—another most valuable contribution to the peace of Europe. We shall not only firmly adhere to this treaty but desire only to renew it in the future and thus to contribute to ever friendlier relations. All this we have done, even though it means, for instance, the renunciation of Alsace-Lorraine, a land for which we also waged two great wars. Yet we have done it, primarily in order to spare our own German people further bloodshed.[39]

Britain, France and Italy protested Germany's action and agreed in Stresa on 14 April 1935 to take collective action against any further unilateral steps on Germany's part. But Hitler's repudiation of the Treaty of Versailles called forth no concrete counter-measures, and so he was emboldened to carry on. On 18 June 1935 Germany concluded a naval treaty with Britain, ostensibly intended to forestall a naval arms race. By this action, London contravened the terms of the collective agreement it had just signed at Stresa and highlighted the confusion and carelessness of Western foreign policy. By agreeing to the treaty, the British signalled their acceptance of German rearmament as a *fait accompli* and encouraged Hitler in his belief that a wedge could be driven between Britain and the rest of Germany's foes. In fact, this treaty did mark the onset of a warming trend in Anglo-German relations, rendering Hitler's successes of the next three years all the more possible.

Britain's attitude and the shifting political climate that followed the Italian invasion of Abyssinia persuaded Hitler that the time was ripe for another step. Against all the advice of German military leaders and diplomats, troops were sent into the demilitarised Rhineland on 7 March 1936 and full German sovereignty was restored. At the same time Hitler repudiated the Treaty of Locarno, pointing to the Franco-Soviet alliance, which, he claimed, had already breached its terms. Again he repaired to the Reichstag to appear in the guise of a peace-loving statesman. Though fully prepared, he said, 'to fight for German equality', he was also ready to seek 'cooperation and mutual solicitude within Europe'.[40] Again the Western powers contended themselves with mere protests. The French government at first considered invading the Rhineland, but decided against this step when advised by the general staff that full mobilisation would be required and informed by Britain that she was not prepared for war. At the Nuremberg rally in September 1936, Hitler triumphantly announced a new four-year-plan aimed at economic self-sufficiency and further rearmament. The German army and economy, he said, should be 'ready for war and fit for action in four years time'.[41]

Hitler began to intervene together with Mussolini in the Spanish Civil War. At the same time the fascist leaders signed a treaty creating the Rome–Berlin axis, announced by Mussolini on 1 November 1936. By 25 November Germany had also concluded the anti-Comintern pact with Japan. One year later, Italy joined this pact directed against the Soviet Union.

Having gathered allies about him, Hitler was ready for a more aggressive policy in the east. On 5 November 1937 he informed the minister of war, the foreign minister and the supreme commanders of the army, the air force and the navy that the time had come for Germany to solve her 'Lebensraum' problem. This could only occur, according to later records of the meeting, 'by overcoming resistance and by the willing acceptance of risk.' The first goal was 'to crush Czechoslovakia and Austria simultaneously . . . in order to remove the threat to our flanks in case of any operations in the west'. The exact date of the German attack in the east would depend on the political events of the coming months and years, Hitler informed his audience, but he was determined to attack by 1943, or 1945 at the latest, because thereafter Germany would begin to lose her superiority in armaments.[42]

Two weeks later Lord Edward Halifax, the Keeper of the Great Seal and later foreign minister, appeared in Germany to speak with Hitler. According to the report of the foreign minister, Baron von Neurath, Halifax informed the Germans:

The British did not believe that the status quo had to be maintained under all circumstances. Among the questions in which changes would probably be made sooner or later were Danzig, Austria and Czechoslovakia. England was only interested in seeing that such changes were brought about by peaceful means.[43]

Hitler took these comments to mean that the British government would not seriously object if he were to alter Germany's borders to the east and the south-east. He accordingly changed his original timetable and resolved to occupy Austria immediately.

Austria had sought unification with the German *Reich* in 1918 and 1932. After the failure of the 1931 plan for a customs union, a bitter struggle erupted between the Social Democrats and the Catholic right reinforced by the *Heimwehr* of the minister of the interior, Ernst Rüdiger von Starhemberg. As a result, the government of Chancellor Engelbert Dollfuss grew increasingly dictatorial. Fierce opposition also came from the Austrian National Socialists backed by Germany. A putsch undertaken by the Nazis in Vienna on 25 July 1934 was defeated but not before Dollfuss had been murdered. Mussolini, at this time still adamantly opposed to the unification of Austria and Germany, moved Italian troops into the Brenner pass, and Hitler immediately denied any involvement in the Austrian conspiracy.

The tension between the German government and Dollfuss's successor as chancellor, the Christian Socialist Kurt von Schuschnigg, heightened as Schuschnigg strove to consolidate Austrian independence. Schuschnigg's foreign support withered as Britain proved increasingly indifferent and Italy drew closer to Germany. Eventually Schuschnigg was coerced in a meeting with Hitler in Berchtesgaden in February 1938 to cooperate with the German *Reich* in foreign policy and to accept some Austrian Nazis into his government. In order to reinforce Austria's national independence, Schuschnigg announced a referendum on 9 March in which Austrians would be asked if they wished to continue as a free, unified, independent, German-speaking, socialist, Christian state. But by this step the chancellor only hastened the delivery of Austria into the hands of the Nazis. A German ultimatum on 11 March demanded that Schuschnigg resign and be replaced by the National Socialist minister of the interior, Arthur von Seyss-Inquart. Seyss-Inquart was then instructed by Göring to seek the assistance of German troops in maintaining public order, allegedly endangered by socialist agitation. In the early morning of 12 March German troops marched into Austria and annexed her to the Reich without encountering any armed resistance and to the enthusiastic cheers of much of the population. Vienna became the provincial capital of the East Mark, and 99 per cent of the voters approved of unification with Germany in an ensuing referendum. Although the jubilation of most Austrians gave way in just a few years to bitter disappointment, the *Anschluss* seemed at the time to be the pinnacle of Hitler's achievements. The joyous reaction in Germany reflected the satisfaction Germans felt at the final creation of a *grossdeutsches Reich* embracing almost all German-speakers—a hope that had been quietly nurtured ever since the *kleindeutsch* settlement of 1866. Most could scarcely believe that the unification of Germany and Austria had been accomplished without provoking the intervention of the other European powers.

This easy victory spurred Hitler on in the summer of 1938 to pursue his next goal, the first step in the search for 'Lebensraum'. Three and a half million Sudeten Germans had been transferred to the new state of Czechoslovakia after the First World War and had been a source of conflict ever since. In a purported attempt to solve their problems, Hitler exerted pressure on the Prague government through the Sudeten German Party led by the former bank clerk and physical education teacher Konrad Henlein. When the Sudeten Germans were encouraged to exacerbate ethnic tensions by making exaggerated demands on the Prague government, Henlein responded enthusiastically, demanding in the eight Karlsbad Points full autonomy, complete freedom of expression for the 'German world-view' and reparations for the injustices suffered since 1919. The Prague government refused these demands and ordered partial mobilisation. War fever spread across Europe. Britain and France warned that a German attack on Czechoslovakia would have serious consequences and gave the impression that their prompt intervention had saved the peace. But Hitler rose to the challenge. He informed the *Wehrmacht*, 'It is my firm intention to crush Czechoslovakia in the near future through military action',[44] and issued orders to prepare for an invasion on 1 October.

Hitler's undisguised plans for invasion met with stiff resistance from the chief of staff of the army, General Ludwig Beck, and from the chief of naval staff, Vice-Admiral Günther Guse. Beck urged the government to do all it could 'to avert conflict with Czechoslovakia which can lead to a world war that would spell the end of Germany' and implored it 'to prevail upon the supreme commander of the army to reverse the war preparations which he has ordered'.[45] Beck then resigned rather than participate in the imminent disaster. His successor, General Franz Halder, planned a *coup d'état* together with the chief of military intelligence, Admiral Wilhelm Canaris, and opposition circles in the foreign office. Halder also informed the British government of his intentions and asked it to firmly oppose Hitler.

However, Halifax and the prime minister, Neville Chamberlain, were convinced that appeasement was the only way to save the peace. At the Nazi Party rally in Nuremberg on 12 September Hitler threatened to intervene in Czechoslovakia in order to protect the Sudenten Germans, and Henlein declaimed the slogan 'Home to Germany' ('Heim ins Reich'). Chamberlain hastened to Germany to advise Hitler that Britain was prepared to accept German annexation of the Sudetenland. The prime minister was encouraged in this direction by a report issued by Member of Parliament Lord Walter Runciman which confirmed the existence of discriminatory practices against minorities in Czechoslovakia and recommended the cession of the Sudetenland as a realistic solution. Britain persuaded France to support this course of action, and together they convinced Prague that it would have to accept the inevitable.

But even this did not obviate the danger of war. At a subsequent meeting with Chamberlain, Hitler demanded that the Sudetenland be transferred immediately to Germany and that Prague also cede the territories claimed by Poland and Hungary. The Czechs responded angrily to these demands and counted on Western support. War seemed inevitable. Britain asked Mussolini to intervene, and at the last minute a conference of the four great powers was arranged in Munich. Chamberlain, Daladier, Mussolini and Hitler drew up an agreement calling for the immediate evacuation of Sudetenland and its unification with Germany. Britain and France promised to guarantee Czechoslovakia's new borders, and both Germany and Italy declared their willingness to join in this guarantee once the problems of the Polish and Hungarian minorities had been settled.

Chamberlain and Hitler also issued an Anglo-German non-aggression and consultation agreement. Chamberlain was convinced that the results of the Munich Conference would vindicate the concessions to Hitler and the entire 'appeasement' policy, and upon his return to London he proclaimed that he had secured 'peace in our time'.[46] The British prime minister believed Hitler's assurances 'that once this question is solved Germany will pose no more territorial problems in Europe. ... As soon as Czechoslovakia solves her [minority] problems, peacefully and not through suppression',[47] Germany would raise no further claims on the Czechoslovak state.

Germans, and indeed most Europeans, felt greatly relieved that Britain and France had yielded to Hitler's demands. A lasting peace seemed at hand, and the fears of the German army generals appeared baseless. Hitler had achieved the century-old desire for a *grossdeutsches Reich* and far more. His position was unassailable. France's system of alliances was in total collapse, and like Britain, she was forced to accept the new political reality. The Western powers had been chased out of the eastern half of Europe and compelled to accept German pre-eminence on the Continent. Hitler could boast to his countrymen with much apparent justification:

I have restored to the *Reich* the provinces stolen from us in 1919; I have led back home millions of unhappy Germans who were torn from the Father-land; I have restored the thousand-year-old unity of German *Lebensraum*; and I have striven to do all this without shedding any blood and while sparing my people and others the horror of war.[48]

The Outbreak of the Second World War

Far from contenting himself with the consolidation of his gains, Hitler pushed ever forward in his plans for more living space. In so doing he deserted his previous policy and dropped the mask of the statesman whose greatest concern was for justice and peace. He finally felt strong enough to impose his first openly aggressive deed upon the German people and the world. While the Poles and Hungarians, encouraged by the Führer, clamoured for the annex-ation of those parts of Czechoslovakia inhabited by their linguistic fellows, Hitler occupied the Czech heartland and gave Slovakia its independence. Hitler's liquidation of the Czechslovak state revealed to the world the imperialist and geo-strategic nature of his policies. The Western heads of state were shocked to realise that they had bargained in good faith with a man who indulged in the most barefaced of lies and had no intention of keeping his word. Even Hitler's fellow fascist, Count Galeazzo Ciano, the Italian foreign minister and son-in-law of Benito Mussolini, recognised in the Führer a treacherous and unreliable partner with whom collabora-tion was impossible. German troops entered Prague on 15 March 1939, after Hitler had forced the government to surrender by threatening to destroy the capital through aerial bombardment. The transformation of the Czech segment of the country into the German protectorate of Bohemia-Moravia was a stunning breach of a solemn accord freely agreed to by the European powers. In the West the obvious bankruptcy of the policy of appeasement effected a sea-change in attitudes towards Hitler.

The British prime minister, Neville Chamberlain, felt personally betrayed and set out to shore up Western defences against renewed German aggression. In a speech in Birmingham on 17 March 1939 and shortly thereafter in the House of Commons, Chamberlain openly repudiated his appeasement policies and announced that Britain was now prepared, before she lost all influence in Europe, to guarantee Poland's borders. France joined in this declaration, and Romania, Greece and Turkey were given similar assurances.

Hitler found himself confronted with the possibility of general war if he engaged in further acts of violence. Yet he clung to his belief that the Western powers would not offer serious resistance and declared before an audience of army commanders, 'Our opponents are little worms. I saw them in Munich'.[49] Hitler was encouraged in his scorn for Britain and France by his dilettantish foreign minister, Joachim von Ribbentrop, a party member and former trade representative and ambassador in London who had replaced the conservative career diplomat Konstantin von Neurath in February 1938. Hitler hoped till the end that fear of war would once again cause Britain and France to back down when confronted with firm German action. But he was quite prepared to risk a great war as he directed his gaze towards Poland.

Immediately after the resolution of the Sudeten crisis in October 1938, the German government had entered into negotiations with Poland allegedly for the purpose of finding a 'comprehensive solution' to the tensions between them. Berlin demanded that the city of Danzig, inhabited largely by Germans, be reincorporated into the *Reich* and linked to the Fatherland by two extraterritorial corridors. In return, Hitler offered to recognise Polish economic rights in Danzig, create a free port in the city, guarantee the resulting borders and sign a non-aggression pact for a period of twenty-five years. In March 1939 Hitler presented his wishes again, this time in a more threatening tone. Still Poland rebuffed his advances, hoping to preserve her integrity by playing the Nazis off against their apparently implacable foes in Moscow. Emboldened by British guarantees of her borders, Poland ordered partial mobilisation on 23 March 1939. Warsaw had already informed Hitler through the Polish ambassador in Berlin that the German plans could lead only to war, and the mobilisation order confirmed the Führer's suspicion that the Poles would not submit as easily as Czechoslovakia had done. The *Wehrmacht* was therefore ordered to prepare an invasion. Resorting to his former tactics, Hitler publicly announced that all he sought was the return of Danzig and an extraterritorial motorway to East Prussia. But no European statesman believed him any more, and indeed Hitler declared before a group of army commanders that 'Danzig is not our ultimate goal. What we really want is to round off our *Lebensraum* in the east'.[50]

Hitler first attempted to counteract the anti-German alliance in Europe. After rescinding the German–Polish treaty of 1934 and the Anglo-German naval agreement of 1935, Hitler concluded non-aggression pacts with Denmark, Estonia and Latvia and a military agreement with Italy dubbed the 'Pact of Steel'. Then he even reached out to his ideological archenemy: the Soviet Union.

Since Germany could only be restrained with the help of Moscow, the Russians played a key role in the ensuing events. During the long Czechoslovakian crisis, Chamberlain had steadfastly ignored Soviet Union, though she was allied with France. Yet by the middle of April 1939 he was ready to propose to the Soviet Union that she participate in the defence of Eastern Europe by unilaterally guaranteeing the western borders of Poland and Romania. However, Stalin demanded that Britain's guarantees be extended to the Baltic states and that a comprehensive eastern alliance be drawn up detailing the obligations of the Soviet Union and the Western powers. At the insistence of France, the powers finally agreed on 24 July on a political alliance which would come into effect after the conclusion of a military pact. But the agreement collapsed when both the Romanians and Poles refused to allow the Russians free passage through their territory.

Hitler exploited this opportunity to conclude a pact of his own with the Soviet Union and thus to avoid a two-front war of the kind Germany had faced in the First World War. After secret preliminary negotiations about a German–Soviet trade deal, Ribbentrop was sent to Moscow on 23 August 1939, where he concluded, that same day, a trade and non-aggression pact.

The news of this pact caught the world by surprise—especially as Hitler had always viciously attacked the Bolsheviks and denounced them alongside Jews as a menace to the world. Stalin for his part had always bitterly condemned fascism and Nazi Germany. The astonishment was therefore all the greater when the Soviets made it possible for Hitler to invade Poland. At the time when the friendship pact was announced, no one in the West knew of the secret protocol which drew up German and Soviet spheres of interest in Eastern Europe, ascribing the Baltic countries to the Soviet realm, dividing Poland between the powers, and recognising Russian interests in Bessarabia. With this accord Hitler delivered all of Eastern Europe to bolshevism and accorded the Soviet Union the western border which she has regarded ever since as her due.

Though Warsaw, London and Paris were stunned by the news of the Nazi–Soviet pact, their policies did not change. Indeed, their determination to stand up to the Nazi menace was underlined by an Anglo-Polish mutual assistance pact signed on 25 August. Hitler had planned to invade Poland on 26 August, but delayed the attack when informed by Mussolini that Italy was not yet prepared for war. In the few days that remained, Hitler endeavoured once again to keep Britain out of the war by persuading her not to allow forthcoming events to explode into a general war. He apparently complied with British requests that he entered last-minute negotiations with the Poles, but this was merely a ploy designed to obscure his own responsibility for the war. Pressing ahead towards a violent solution, Hitler ordered the *Wehrmacht* to attack Poland on 31 August 1939.

In the early morning of the next day, German troops surged across the border without a declaration of war. Two days later Great Britain and France declared war on Germany. Hitler finally had the war he would have liked one year earlier. What he had cynically portrayed as a possibility in May 1939 was finally a reality. All bridges had been burnt; Germany could no longer escape unscathed. As Hitler said: 'It is no longer a question of right or wrong but of the survival or destruction of eighty million people.'[51]

In full knowledge of the perils of a second world war, Hitler invaded Poland and wittingly unleashed the war he had always foreseen as a means to realise his illusory dream of 'Lebensraum' for the German people. Only twenty years after the catastrophe of the First World War the world plunged into another great conflict— initiated by the Treaty of Versailles, which had excluded millions of Germans from their national state; allowed to develop by the weakness of the Western powers, who believed they could contain National Socialism through appeasement and encirclement; condoned by Stalin's blank cheque; and finally unleashed by Hitler's enormous hybris.

14

The Second World War and the Annihilation of the Third Reich

1939: Invasion of Poland; 'Phoney War' in the west; Russo-Finnish War
1940: Occupation of Denmark, Norway, Belgium, the Netherlands and France; Italy enters the war; Italy invades Greece
1941: Germany occupies the Balkans; invasion of the Soviet Union; the Atlantic Charter; Pearl Harbour and the entry into the war of the United States
1942: Turning-point in the submarine war; destruction of German cities commences; the Afrika Corps is defeated; Allied troops land in North Africa
1943: Casablanca Conference; Roosevelt demands unconditional surrender; Battle of Stalingrad; the Allies land in Sicily and Italy; Mussolini is overthrown; the Japanese are forced to retreat; Teheran Conference
1944: Allied forces land in Normandy; campaigns in France, Belgium and southern Holland; air attacks on Germany reach their climax; assassination attempt on Hitler; the Battle of the Bulge
1945: Allied armies push into Germany; Yalta Conference; the fall of Berlin; Hitler commits suicide; Germany capitulates; the first atomic bomb is dropped on Japan; Japan surrenders

The Course of the War until the Invasion of the Soviet Union

The German assault on Poland marked the beginning of another phase in Hitler's foreign policy in which he intended to reshape the world in the Nazi image, seize the 'Lebensraum' of which he had dreamed, permanently subjugate the conquered peoples and finally erect a world empire. 'Living space commensurate with the greatness of a nation is the basis of all power. One can do without for a while, but eventually a solution must be found, one way or

298

another',[1] Hitler told his generals in the early summer of 1939. Further success, he added, 'could not be achieved without the shedding of blood'. Germans 'had not elected Hitler to unleash a war' but rather 'to redeem them from the sufferings of the Great Depression. . . . Yet once he had achieved and consolidated power, he was essentially free to do as he wished'.[2] Though the establishment of a *grossdeutsches Reich* was welcomed by most Germans, Hitler's concept of 'Lebensraum' must have seemed anachronistic to most thoughtful people. It appeared to overlook the impact of the Industrial Revolution, which made national wealth and power less dependent on the extent of one's land, as during the feudal age, and more dependent on the sophistication of one's technology. Furthermore, as General Beck pointed out in 1937, 'the population of Europe has been so stabile for a thousand years and more . . . that substantial change cannot be brought about without an immense upheaval whose long-term consequences cannot be foreseen'.[3] But such an upheaval did not daunt Hitler; indeed, he welcomed it and was determined to provoke it despite all the advice of his military advisors. Still, he was well aware of the danger, and even his power-hungry cronies shuddered at the enormity of the risk they were running. When the announcement of the British declaration of war arrived in Berlin, Göring spontaneously declared, 'If we lose this war, may God have mercy on us.'[4]

The man in the street felt the same fear, and very few rejoiced at the outbreak of war. When conflict had threatened to erupt during the Sudeten crisis of 1938, the mood in Germany had been dark. The British ambassador, Sir Neville Henderson, reported from Berlin, 'The mood runs very much against a war',[5] and when Chamberlain and Daladier rushed to Munich in an attempt to save the peace they were spontaneously cheered by the crowds on the street. The fervour that had seized the nation at the outbreak of the First World War could not be rekindled, despite a Nazi campaign to stir up the public against the Poles, who were allegedly mistreating large numbers of Germans in West Prussia and Silesia. It was not only that Hitler had always emphasised his desire for peace; memories of the horrors of the First World War were still too fresh. Anxious and fearful, many hoped till the last moment that war could be avoided. 'They seemed like skittish animals in imminent danger' reported the Swedish industrialist Birger Dahlerus.[6] Yet as Henderson had predicted, they responded to the outbreak of war 'like sheep being led to the slaughter house', and marched off as ordered to carry out the commands of the Führer.

Though cruelly betrayed in their trust in Hitler and in his

supposed preoccupation with their welfare, Germans did what they saw as their duty, hermetically sealed off from the outside world, deprived of news from abroad, goaded by press and radio reports devised by Goebbels and intimidated by the omnipresent Gestapo. The German people tied their destinies, for better or worse, to a man who would eventually forsake them when they refused to undergo the self-liquidation he intended: 'If the German people is no longer strong and self-sacrificing enough to risk death for its continued existence', Hitler said late in the war, 'then let it die out and be extirpated by another, mightier power. I shall not shed any tears for the German people.'[7]

At first it seemed as if Hitler's decision to go to war would add a yet more glorious chapter to the Nazi record of victories. Poland, which relied on the support of the Western powers, was easily overrun in a matter of weeks. Along their western border and opposite East Prussia, Polish troops were thrown back by technically and tactically superior German forces supported by armoured divisions and the air force. Assistance from the Western powers failed to materialise, and the Poles were left alone to face both the Nazi onslaught and the ensuing Russian attack in the east. Driven away from Warsaw, the bulk of the Polish army was caught and obliterated in the bend in the Vistula River. The capital was devastated by aerial attack and the Polish government capitulated on 27 September 1939. One day later, Ribbentrop met with the Soviet foreign minister Vyacheslav Molotov and the partition of Poland was sealed. The eastern two-thirds were annexed by the Soviet Union, and the former German or Austrian areas of Poland, including the heavy industries in the west, were integrated into the *Reich* as the districts of West Prussia and Wartheland. The area around Cracow was placed under a German governor-general.

SS units under the command of Heinrich Himmler swept in behind the *Wehrmacht*. The Polish intelligentsia was severely persecuted, and Jews were shot on the spot or abducted to newly created ghettoes in Lodz and Warsaw. Meanwhile, the Soviet Union marched into Estonia, Latvia and Lithuania, and Stalin demanded that the Finns accept fortified Soviet bases on their territory. When Finland refused, the Soviets launched an attack on 30 November 1939. The Finns valiantly defended themselves in the ensuing winter war and received material assistance from the United States, Britain, France and even Italy, though Hitler offered no aid. The Soviet Union was expelled from the League of Nations and in the spring of 1940 Britain and France planned an expeditionary force to help the Finns. Stalin, afraid of losing his neutrality *vis-à-vis* the major powers, called a truce. By the Treaty of Moscow signed on 12 March 1940, Finland lost the Karelian Isthmus and parts of eastern Karelia and was required to give the Russians a lease on Hangö, which was needed for the defence of Leningrad.

After the Nazi victory over Poland, Hitler delivered a speech in the *Reichstag* offering Britain and France a peace treaty on the basis of the new status quo. This would have robbed the Western powers of virtually all influence over the balance of power on the Continent and they refused. Belgium, the Netherlands and Romania suggested peace settlements, but they were rejected by both Germany and Britain. At this point, Hitler decided upon his next offensive—not to the west as originally planned but to the north.

Britain and France had failed as yet to take an active part in the war. Inadequately equipped and without the slightest desire for war, the French took cover behind the Maginot Line they had constructed in 1930 and confined their warlike activities to occasional aerial sorties over nearby German border areas. The British dispatched what trained troops they had to France, stepped up their training programmes, and requested Australia and New Zealand to assist in the defence of the Suez Canal. At sea Britain sought to interdict the flow of supplies to Germany, but suffered heavy losses from a highly effective U-boat campaign. In order to tighten its blockade, the Royal Navy envisaged mining the Norwegian coastal waters and undertaking a military landing in Narvik; but Hitler pre-empted this plan by just a few hours when he launched a surprise assault on Denmark and Norway. Both countries were quickly overrun, ensuring the *Reich* of an uninterrupted flow of essential Swedish iron ore.

While German troops were still fighting the Norwegians and some British units which had managed to land, Hitler unleashed his great offensive in the west. Disregarding the neutrality of the Low Countries, the *Wehrmacht* pushed into Holland, Belgium and Luxembourg, compelling the Dutch army to surrender after Rotterdam had been flattened through aerial bombardment. British, Belgian and French divisions were driven back across the Meuse and the Somme as the Germans raced towards the Channel. After eighteen days of battle, Belgium capitulated. The British and French forces to the north withdrew to a pocket around Dunkirk, where they were quickly surrounded. They escaped annihilation, however, when Hitler refused to allow panzer divisions to join in the attack in the belief that these divisions should be kept fresh for the imminent final struggle for France. As a result, the British carried off 'the miracle of Dunkirk'. Every available ship or boat was sent across the Channel to rescue the core of Britain's professional army and to enable her to carry on the struggle. When the Germans finally entered Dunkirk on 4 June, only French units remained to be taken prisoner.

The southern flank of the German army launched its assault one day later. Within a space of fifteen days the Channel ports were seized, Orleans and Paris were occupied, and south-eastern France was conquered as far as the Swiss border. Then the German army simply rolled up the Maginot Line from behind. On 17 June the new French head of state, Marshal Philipp Pétain, sued for peace. His request had to be accepted not only by the Germans but also by the Italians, who had entered the war on 10 June. The peace treaty was signed on 22 June—in the same railway car in the same location in the woods of Compiègne where the German delegation had signed the armistice ending the First World War on 11 November 1918. The peace treaty was severe, delivering more than half of France including Paris, the north and the entire Atlantic coastline over to German occupation and administration. The French were required to shoulder the full cost of the occupation and to install in the unoccupied zone a government friendly to Germany. France also had to disband her army and demobilise all units of her fleet.

Pétain erected a strongly authoritarian regime in Vichy with the help of the royalist, anti-parliamentarian faction known as *Action française*. The civil rights of all citizens were severely curtailed, and Jews were denied the protection of the law. Pétain strove at first to maintain good relations with both London and Berlin, but was driven by his prime minister, Pierre Laval, to align himself more closely with the Germans. 'Free France' was represented by Charles de Gaulle, who fled to London, where he led a mounting resistance movement.

Within just a few months Hitler had risen to master of Europe. France had been defeated, Britain expelled from the Continent, and Norway, Denmark, the Netherlands, Belgium and Luxembourg occupied. Striding from victory to victory, Hitler took each of his victims by surprise and quickly overwhelmed it by dint of superior military strategy, modern weaponry (especially aircraft and tanks) and the application of a new form of warfare known as 'Blitzkrieg'. His self-esteem knew no bounds. To the great peril of Germany, he henceforth believed himself to be a far better military strategist than any professional soldier, especially since his reluctant and often apprehensive generals had never believed such success was possible.

Similar to his peace proposal after the fall of Poland, Hitler suggested after the fall of France that Britain now accept a truce. He added prophetically, 'I know full well that a continuation of the present struggle can only end in the utter destruction of one of the two warring parties'.[8] But Hitler's offer was refused by Winston Churchill, who had become British prime minister on 10 May 1940 and had assured the British people on this occasion that though he had nothing to offer but 'blood, toil, tears and sweat'[9] he would carry on the struggle to the end.

Hitler thereupon drew up plans for an invasion. But in just a few weeks time he was forced to abandon these plans when the German navy proved unable to land the bulk of twenty-five to forty divisions on British soil and the *Luftwaffe* failed to wipe out the Royal Air Force. The air war that began in early August 1940 inflicted heavy destruction on south-east England, London and the industries of the Midlands, but the *Luftwaffe* itself suffered such heavy losses at the hands of the Royal Air Force that the German army could not attempt a landing. Britain emerged from the 'Battle of Britain' with renewed vigour. Doubts about her will to continue the struggle were laid to rest, and the spirit of the resistance movements in Holland, Norway and France were raised. Confidence in British determination grew in the United States as well. In March 1941 President Roosevelt obtained authority through Lend-Lease legislation to provide war matériel to the government of any country whose defence the president considered essential to the defence of the United States.[10]

While the Battle of Britain raged, Italy detected a golden opportunity to attack the British in Egypt. Deprived of most of the glory of the victory over France because he had moved so late, Mussolini hope to record a great victory over the British Empire in North Africa. But his offensive failed and the British pushed the Italian army far back into Libya. Hitler quickly organised the German Afrika Corps under General Erwin Rommel, and it in turn drove the British back into Egypt.

Mussolini experienced even greater difficulty in Greece, which he attacked in April 1939 from bases in previously occupied Albania without former consultations with his friends in Berlin. As had been the case in North Africa, the Italian offensive bogged down after a very short time. Britain offered to assist the Greeks and landed troops in the spring of 1941. The Germans grew concerned that a British presence in the Balkans would threaten their positions in south-eastern Europe, and Hitler resolved to intervene. Yugoslavia, which had sought British assistance after overthrowing a pro-German government, was quickly conquered; the British were driven from the Balkans and the Greeks were forced to capitulate on

22 April. German troops occupied central Greece, the Peloponnesus and Crete. Romania, Hungary, Slovakia and Bulgaria joined the Axis of Germany, Italy and Japan in November 1940 or March 1941, and German ascendancy over the Balkans appeared secure.

The War Spreads

The entire continent was now occupied by German troops with the exceptions of Sweden, Switzerland, Italy, Hungary, Bulgaria and Spain. Hitler's victories had been won with stunning speed and an ease that far surpassed anything his contemporaries had imagined possible. But still the Führer dreamed of more living space. In his mind all these successes were small steps towards (or in the case of the Balkan campaign forced upon him by Mussolini, a distraction from) his main goal of expansion to the east. Hitler had considered plans for the invasion of the Soviet Union as early as the summer of 1940, and Franz Halder, the chief of the general staff at the time, made a note of some of Hitler's fundamental strategic considerations in late June 1940:

England's hope is Russia and America. If her faith in Russia dissolves, her faith in America will dissolve too for the defeat of Russia would immensely strengthen Japan's position in East Asia. If Russia is defeated, England's last hope will come crashing down and Germany will be left as the master of Europe and the Balkans.[11]

Like Napoleon before him, Hitler was convinced that Britain could not be brought to her knees so long as a strong military power still existed to the east. The Führer was no less persuaded that the Soviet Union, like his previous opponents, would quickly fall to German Blitzkrieg. He ruled out the advice of the navy that Germany join forces with Italy in order to strike against Britain in the Mediterranean—bringing Gibraltar, Malta, Alexandria and the Suez Canal into German hands—while simultaneously escalating the battle of the Atlantic in order to interdict the flow of supplies to Britain. Hitler seriously underestimated the industrial and military potential of the United States, as he underestimated that of the Soviet Union. Japan had joined the German–Italian pact on 27 September 1940, and Hitler considered her a formidable enough threat to dissuade the United States from entering the war against Germany. Accordingly, Hitler commanded the army in December 1940 to prepare 'to conquer the Soviet Union in a quick offensive before the struggle against England has drawn to a close'.[12]

The political friendship between Germany and the Soviet Union had already soured. During a visit to Berlin by the Russian foreign minister, Vyacheslav Molotov, in November 1940, Hitler had attempted to steer Soviet ambitions against Britain. The Führer made proposals concerning the division of the British Empire and encouraged the Russians to join the Axis. Molotov insisted instead on the elimination of sources of Russo-German discord in Europe and on the inclusion of Turkey, Bulgaria and Finland in the Soviet sphere of influence. Hitler had no intention, however, of conceding on these points, especially since the Germans had grown increasingly concerned about the expansion of Russian power in Finland, the Baltic states and along the Romanian border, even though Hitler himself had agreed to these advances or had quietly acceded to them. He guaranteed the borders of Lesser Romania, which had been compelled to cede Bessarabia and Bukovina to Russia, and to Stalin's great annoyance concluded a military alliance with Finland.

Nevertheless, the Germans were under no compulsion to attack the Soviet Union. Stalin did not pose the slightest threat to Germany after she had occupied the Balkans. Stalin punctiliously observed all delivery schedules of the raw materials he had promised, and by breaking off relations with Norway, Belgium, Yugoslavia and Greece, gave tacit recognition to Hitler's new order in Europe. The Führer attacked Russia not because of tensions between the two countries or even because of the continuing war against Britain; he attacked 'because Russia had always been designated on Hitler's internal map for German 'Lebensraum' and because the moment had arrived to execute the crowning glory in his plans for conquest'.[13]

The secret deployment of troops in the east, which turned Finland, Romania and Bulgaria into German bases, was supposed to be complete by 15 May 1941. As part of his strategic preparations, Hitler also concluded alliances with Hungary, Slovakia and Croatia, and in April 1941 intimated to Japan that conflict with the Soviet Union was possible. The Germans were therefore all the more astonished when Japan and the Soviet Union concluded a non-aggression pact shortly thereafter—a pact to which both powers were destined to adhere until after the German capitulation in 1945. Once the conquest of Greece and Crete was complete and the *Wehrmacht* was largely withdrawn, Hitler launched the great assault on the Soviet Union. On 22 June 1941 the Soviets were informed that Germany could no longer sit idly by while her eastern frontiers were allegedly menaced and German troops poured over the border.

Applying the well-proven strategy of the Polish and French

campaigns, three army groups attacked along a huge front stretching from Finland to the Caucasus. The Luftwaffe quickly took command of the skies, and German troops surrounded and broke through Russian defensive positions. In just a few weeks a vast expanse of territory was overrun, hundreds of thousands of dazed Russian soldiers were captured and huge stocks of war matériel were seized. The Germans hoped to advance as far as a line running from Leningrad and Moscow to the Lower Volga. This would have brought them the grain harvest of the Ukraine, the oil of the Caucasus and dominion over the Black Sea and the Baltic. But autumn mud and an early and very severe Russian winter beginning in mid-October held up the *Wehrmacht's* advance so that neither Moscow nor Leningrad could be taken. The bitter cold stalled the German trucks and panzers, and the troops, who were not equipped for winter warfare, suffered terribly. When the Red Army, which Hitler had already written off, mounted a surprise counter-offensive on 6 December, the German advance ground to a complete halt. Though the Russians punched gaping holes in the German front, Hitler denied all the requests of his generals that a full-scale retreat be ordered and instructed the army to hold its positions at any price.

A few weeks after the German invasion of the Soviet Union, Moscow and London signed an accord on 12 July 1941 which bound them not to accept a ceasefire or a peace treaty without the agreement of the other party. One month later, Roosevelt and Churchill met on board a warship to work out the political programme known as the Atlantic Charter. Taking up the ideas of Wilson and the 'Four Freedoms' based upon them which Roosevelt had affirmed before the American Congress on 6 January 1941, the charter proclaimed once again the ideal of the self-determination of peoples, rejected any conquests or territorial changes without the approval of the population involved and held up hope for a world free of fear and hardship.[14] On 11 September the president ordered American ships to open fire on any German U-boats they sighted and on 6 November he extended the Lend-Lease programme to include the Soviet Union. Convinced that only joint action could defeat the German dictator, Roosevelt was determined to oppose Hitler in any way he could, short of intervention in the war. The US Constitution and her traditional neutrality stopped him from taking this final step. This impediment was removed, however, on 7 December 1941, when the Japanese launched a surprise attack on the US fleet concentrated in Pearl Harbor. In this way the European war became a true world war. Hitler had urged the Japanese to attack the United States after his invasion of Russia turned out, contrary to all expectations, to be lengthy and gruelling. At Hitler's instigation, Germany and Italy jointly declared war on the United States, relieving Roosevelt of the political burden of taking this step. To her still undefeated foes of Britain and the Soviet Union, Germany had now added the world's mightiest power.

Nazi Terror and the Turning-Point in the War

America's entry into the war came at a time when Germany's capacities were already stretched to the limit. Although the United States was not yet prepared to play a major role in the struggle, even a man such as Hitler who invariably underestimated the Western democracies must have realised that the *Reich* could not hope to match the economic and military potential of this new opponent. Japan, moreover, showed no inclination to challenge the Soviet Union and confined her operations to China and the Pacific. Hitler's wartime alliance with the great power of the East was accordingly of no advantage to him. When the Soviet Union succeeded in repelling the Nazi advance on Moscow with the help of Siberian troops transferred from areas facing Japanese-controlled Manchuria, it became clear that Germany and Italy alone would have to fight the two-front war which Hitler had induced.

Russia's vast reserves of men and matériel came to the fore in the great counter-offensive of 6 December 1941. Struggling to defend their homeland and induced by German terror against the civilian population to fight till the last man had fallen, the Russians would inevitably win 'The Great Patriotic War' proclaimed by Stalin. By the end of the fateful year of 1941, Hitler himself sensed 'that no more victories could be won'.[15] None the less he carried on the struggle, hoping against hope that the Nazis would eventually win a war that had become a vast struggle of ideologies, unfurling a wave of destruction and annihilation which dwarfed anything ever seen before.

On 1 March 1942 Hitler denounced 'Jews, Free Masons and ideological foes in league with them' as 'the authors of the present war against the *Reich*'[16] and announced that a systematic crackdown was essential to the war effort. Ever loyal to his theories of race and the need for 'Lebensraum', Hitler ravaged the captured areas of Russia just as he had Poland. In many cases the peoples of the East originally hailed the German conquerors as liberators from Stalin's hated dictatorship, and the Führer could have won their enduring loyalty by confering self-government and autonomy on them in the name of 'freedom'. Instead, he unleashed his special units. Russian prisoners of war were regarded as Slavic *Untermenschen* and spared no horror in the realisation of Hitler's plans to Germanise the East and exploit its peoples in the interests of the master race. 'This in every way inferior people', said Erich Koch, the despotic *Reichskommissar* for the Ukraine, would live the life of helots, labouring for the Third *Reich* and 'supplying what Germany lacks'.[17] The *Wehrmacht* refused to implement the infamous instructions calling for summary execution of all captured political commissars, and the regular soldiers treated the civilian population humanely on the whole and took no part in the slaughter of Jews. But they did nothing to prevent the SS from carrying out Hitler's orders in a most brutal and systematic fashion. The persecuted civilian population turned against the invaders and sought desperately to evade capture, forced labour and deportation to Germany. They slipped into the forests and formed partisan units which attacked German soldiers behind the lines with mounting ferocity. Enmeshed in a hopeless struggle to hold the line against the advancing Red Army, the soldiers of the *Wehrmacht* soon faced incessant attack on all sides.

The SS, the police and Nazi bureaucracy competed with one another in procuring food and raw materials essential to the war effort and in deporting millions of Eastern civilians to work in the German arms industry. With its powerful military, police and economic capacities, the SS under Heinrich Himmler controlled the largest network. The SS also ran the Jewish ghettos, the numerous concentration camps which dotted Eastern Europe after the attack on Poland and the special extermination camps of Chelmno, Auschwitz, Belzec, Sobibor, Treblinka and Maidanek.

Before the outbreak of the war, Hitler publicly reaffirmed in a speech before the *Reichstag* a belief he had already expressed in *Mein Kampf*: the next war would result in the eradication of Judaism from Europe.[18] After the Polish campaign, countless pogroms were carried out in the occupied areas and Austrian and Bohemian Jews were deported to ghettos created in Lodz and Warsaw. In the autumn of 1941, the 'Final Solution', or systematic slaughter of all Jews, was begun. On 20 January 1942 representatives of the SS and the Berlin police as well as officials from various ministries attended the 'Wannsee Conference'. According to the minutes of this meeting, 'central control over the implementation of the final solution of the Jewish problem' was assigned to Himmler, the head of the SS and chief of the German police, 'without regard for geographic borders'.[19] Special units of the SS and the police were ordered to annihilate Jews and gypsies from the conquered territories of Eastern Europe. At the same time, Jews from prewar Germany, the Netherlands, Belgium, France, Norway, Hungary and the countries of south-eastern Europe were deported to the extermination camps in Poland. The horrors suffered by the millions of Jews handed over to Himmler and his henchmen for extermination in accordance with Hitler's wishes transcends all human imagination. It can be neither described nor comprehended:

Neither the suffering nor the numbers. The total figure could not be ascertained with certainty, but calculations vary between four and six million. But what does it matter whether it was four or six million men, women and children who were randomly herded together and driven into the demonic showers of Auschwitz and Maidanek. Darkness descends over the most abominable crime that man has ever committed against man.[20]

To the monstrous, factory-like slaughter in the extermination camps must be added the brutal mistreatment of inmates in the 'regular' concentration camps. Citizens of every nation in Europe met death through execution, starvation, sickness or suicide. Both extermination camps and concentration camps were usually linked to factories working for heavy industry or the SS. Here the inmates worked as slave labourers until they fell from exhaustion or were murdered in order to supply the material needs of their tormenters. These activities and the genocide of the Jews were kept secret from the German people and their full extent was not revealed till after the war.

While the SS engaged in horrendous crimes to the rear of the frontlines, the *Wehrmacht* renewed the offensive on the eastern front and in Africa. In May 1942 the German armies defeated the Russians near Kharkov, occupied the Crimea, crossed the Don and the Donets, and brought the entire Ukraine into German hands. From here they pushed south-eastwards and endeavoured, though in vain, to reach the oil-fields north and south of the Caucasus. At the same time, the Sixth Army under General Friedrich Paulus advanced into Stalingrad, which dominates the Lower Volga. But here it encountered strong Russian reserves and was surrounded. Hitler stubbornly forbade the Sixth Army to withdraw, though all attempts to relieve it failed. Slowly the German soldiers were ground down by the Russians in a desperate and bloody struggle. General Paulus was finally compelled to capitulate in late January 1943 with the remnants of what had once been a mighty army of 300,000 men.

In Africa too, the Germans first met with considerable success in the summer of 1942. The Africa Corps under Erwin Rommel conquered Tobruk and advanced into Egypt as far as El Alamein. But here the Germans were thrown back in a counter-offensive led by Field Marshal Bernard Montgomery. The crowning blows was dealt by the successful landing of American and British troops in Morocco and Algeria. Just three months after the catastrophe of Stalingrad, the last German and Italian units in Africa capitulated on 13 May 1943, ceding the entire southern coast of the Mediterranean Sea to the Allies.

Hard on the heels of their victory in Africa, the Allies prepared to invade Italy. Sicily was occupied in July 1943 and the mainland was taken under bombardment. Mussolini was then overthrown by dissatisfied party members, the king and the army, and was placed under arrest on 24 July. By 3 September the new Italian government under Marshal Pietro Badoglio had concluded an armistice with the Allies, leaving the *Wehrmacht* to defend the entire Italian front which at this time ran straight across the peninsula just north of Naples.

While the Allied armies were reversing the fortunes of war at Stalingrad and in North Africa, the Allied navies were seizing the initiative at sea. The reign of the German U-boats was broken early in 1943 through the use of radar, which enabled Allied ships and aeroplanes to locate German submarines with great efficiency. The losses were catastrophic and Germany's greatest sea weapon was largely nullified after mid-1943.

Meanwhile, the German air force was suffering heavy losses. While Hitler concentrated on the construction of short-range fighters and bombers designed to support his ground forces, the Allies built long-range bombers and fighters. They flew sortie after sortie, over western Germany primarily, by night at first and after 1943 by day as well. The German anti-aircraft guns were unable to staunch the assault and the civilian population was exposed to a rain of bombs. By war's end the British and American squadrons had reduced nearly all large German cities to rubble in an attempt to crush the spirit of the civilian population.

At the Casablanca Conference of January 1943 Roosevelt and Churchill agreed to assign the war in Europe priority over the war in the Pacific in view of the terrible losses which the Soviets were suffering and despite the Japanese threat to America. They also resolved to demand unconditional surrender from Germany and her allies. This formula was repeated soon afterwards in a meeting of Allied foreign ministers held in Moscow in October. Roosevelt and

Churchill subsequently met with Stalin for the first time at the Teheran Conference from 26 November to 3 December 1943 in an effort to coordinate the war effort in the East and West. Stalin strongly objected to Churchill's plan to push ahead into southern Europe, since this would have carried the Western powers into the Balkan areas of prime interest to Russia, and the Allied leaders eventually agreed to land British and American armies on the Atlantic coast instead.

The demand for unconditional surrender helped Hitler to justify continuance of the hopeless struggle. The lives and possessions of the German people were of no consequence to him in arriving at this decision. The 'National Socialist leadership' would go to any extremes, Goebbels declared in a speech announcing 'total war'[21] in the Berlin *Sportpalast* on 18 February 1943. The media and party rallies engaged in fanatic attempts to whip up a spirit of self-sacrifice, while the Nazis prepared to drag the entire nation into the vortex of their own annihilation. As glumly and passively as they endured the mounting devastation of the air war, the German people acquiesced to reduced rations, increased productivity, rising employment of women in the armaments industry, sharp cutbacks in the availability of consumer goods, the drafting of fifteen- and sixteen-year-old boys to man the flak batteries girdling the cities, and the call-up of all those in any way able to serve at the front. Criticism or expressions of war weariness or dissatisfaction were treated as traitorous attempts to sap the will to fight and were punished by death. Extreme caution, distrust of others and a fearful lack of human communication typified the hushed, oppressive atmosphere, though confidence in the Führer remained high on the whole. Spies and informers lurked everywhere: in the schools and universities, on the job, in the air-raid bunkers, and even within the bosom of the family. Bishop Clemens August von Galen had already denounced the ubiquitous terror in a sermon delivered on 13 July 1941:

German citizens are helpless and defenceless in the face of the sheer physical power of the Gestapo! . . . None of us can be certain—even the most loyal and conscientious citizen, completely innocent of all wrong-doing—that he will not be dragged from his home one day, deprived of all liberty and imprisoned in the cellars or concentration camps of the Gestapo.[22]

The fear and outward acceptance of the inevitable were supplemented by exhortations to endure and Goebbel's promises of new wonder weapons which would snatch final victory from the jaws of defeat. 'Work ten, twelve and if necessary fourteen or sixteen hours;

contribute all you have', Goebbels admonished the people.[23] A decree requiring all men and women to register for the purposes of national defence resulted after January 1943 in the induction of all men between the ages of sixteen and sixty-five and of all women between the ages of seventeen and forty-five. These draftees were either sent to the front or set to work in industry. The entire economy was trimmed for war production under the new armaments minister, Albert Speer. By coordinating every aspect of the economy, Speer's central planning staff achieved a huge leap in war production. Far more aeroplanes, tanks, trucks, ships, munitions and rockets rolled off the production lines than in the first years of the war. Transplanted from the cities to rural areas and even underground caves, the war industry continued to hum along at peak efficiency till early 1945.

Conspiracies Against Hitler

The anguish of the German people as the ferocity of the war intensified induced some courageous men and women to risk everything in their attempts to overthrow the Nazis. The first pockets of resistance sprang up before the war. Communists were cruelly persecuted after 30 January 1933, and many of those who escaped the wave of arrests following the burning of the *Reichstag* or did not emigrate succeeded in going underground, where they maintained a semblance of their former organisation. During the war, opposition groups united to form the *Rote Kapelle* (Red Chapel) under the leadership of Harro Schulze-Boysen and Arvid Harnack. They passed along information to the Soviets until they were discovered in August 1942.

Young Social Democrats, also subject to Nazi persecution, formed a resistance in which Theodor Haubach, Julius Leber, Wilhelm Leuschner, Carlo Mierendorff and Adolf Reichwein played a leading role.

Some Christian clergymen and parishioners, outraged by the reign of terror which Hitler unleashed across Germany, revolted against his inhuman ideology. Prominent personalities of both confessions—for instance the Evangelical theologican Dietrich Bonhoeffer and the bishops Michael von Faulhaber, Clemens August von Galen and Theophil Wurm—condemned the mass murder of the mentally ill, the handicapped, Jews and incurables. Pastor Martin Niemöller denounced the Nazis so unsparingly before his Berlin congregation that he himself was carted off to the Dachau concentration camp.

The first protests from within the *Wehrmacht* also arose fairly early and were given expression in the pointed resignation of General Beck in 1938. The internal resistance in Germany, however, did not become visible until February 1943, when Hans and Sophie Scholl, who had joined with other oppositional students, artists and academics in Munich in 1941, were caught distributing anti-Nazi leaflets. On 22 February 1943 they were condemned to death by the People's Court and executed. The Scholls had proclaimed their unwillingness to sacrifice their lives for the 'base lust for power of a party clique' and had demanded 'in the name of the German youth, that Hitler's state restore personal freedom, that most precious possession of the German people, of which we have been most ignobly deprived'.[24]

Many others also sought to overthrow the Nazi regime for many of the same reasons as well as fear for Germany's future: Carl Friedrich Goerdeler, the Lord Mayor of Leipzig till his retirement in 1937; Johannes Popitz, the Prussian minister of finance until July 1944; Ulrich von Hassell, the German ambassador in Rome until he was stripped of his post in 1938; and the Kreisau landowner Count Helmuth James von Moltke together with a group of friends from sharply contrasting political backgrounds. They all realised that effective measures could only be taken in collaboration with the army. Many prominent officers—such as Franz Halder, the former chief of army staff; Walther von Brauchitsch, the former commander in chief of the army who was dismissed in 1941; Admiral Wilhelm Canaris, the chief of intelligence in the war ministry, and Major-General Hans Oster—had dared to go to dangerous lengths in their opposition to Hitler as early as 1938. However, so long as the Führer was racking up one triumph after the other, no psychologically opportune moment ever arose to put their secret plans into action. As the situation on the Russian front grew more and more desperate, mounting awareness of likely defeat created a climate in which the officers could hope to succeed. An initial assassination attempt was undertaken by Major-General Hans Henning von Tresckow in 1943, but it failed. The conspirators were considerably strengthened when Erwin Rommel, the most popular army commander, and Colonel Schenk von Stauffenberg, the most dynamic of Hitler's opponents though he had been severely wounded in the war, were persuaded to play an active role. The moment to take action had finally arrived, especially as many of the generals' co-conspirators were already under arrest.

Though Hitler was sealed off from the outside world in his 'wolf's lair' near Rastenberg, East Prussia, Stauffenberg was able to gain access as chief of staff to the home army commander, and on 20 July 1944 he planted a bomb beside the Führer. But by a terrible stroke of misfortune the blast failed to have its desired effect. The plan to seize power, triggered by Stauffenberg's bomb, was put into effect in Paris by the military commander for France, General Karl Heinrich von Stülpnagel; but in Berlin and the other cities of the *Reich* the putsch collapsed on the news that Hitler was still alive. Beck and later Rommel committed suicide. Stauffenberg and a few other conspirators were shot. Hitler took his revenge on the remaining conspirators by means of the People's Court, whose cruel and cynical president, Roland Freisler, condemned 200 people to death and ensured their immediate execution. The full extent of the resistance among the old army élite, the administration and the labour movement is indicated by the 5000 further victims who were eventually executed in gaols and concentration camps right up to the final weeks of the war.

By the failure of the putsch, Hitler lived long enough to assume complete and utter responsibility for the final catastrophe. The truth would not again be obscured by another stab-in-the-back legend. The historical significance of the resistance movement lies in the fact that it managed to plan and carry out an assassination attempt even though little hope remained that the Allies would negotiate with the conspirators or that the final collapse could be averted. 'The assassination must be attempted, *coûte que coûte*', Tresckow had urged Stauffenberg from the eastern front. 'Even if it should fail, something must be done in Berlin. It is no longer solely a question of our immediate goals but of demonstrating to the world and to generations to come that the German resistance movement dared to take the ultimate step. Compared with this object, nothing else matters.'[25]

The Collapse of Nazi Germany

While the reign of terror within Germany was further intensifying in reaction to the failed assassination attempt of 20 July 1944, outside, the Allied ring of steel continued to tighten. On 5 July 1943 the *Wehrmacht* launched what turned out to be its final offensive on the eastern front in the central sector near Kursk. By the middle of the month the German advance had already been brought to a standstill and thereafter the initiative in all sectors stayed with the Soviets. In January 1944 the Germans lost the great struggle for Leningrad; in March they were driven from the Ukraine; in June they withdrew into Poland after their White Russian front collapsed. By August 1944 the *Wehrmacht* had been driven back to the positions from which it had launched its original invasion of Russia in 1941. When the Red Army finally initiated a great offensive in the Vistula region on 12 January 1945, Germany's allies in Finland and the Balkans had already concluded a truce so that the Russian troops in the east and south-east were free to join in the assault on the *Reich*.

In the south, American and British forces landed in Nettuno, south-west of Rome, on 22 January 1944. Fighting was heavy at first, but by May the Allies were advancing quickly and by early 1945 had reached the Po Valley. On 29 April the German forces were forced to capitulate.

In the west the strength of the German defences had been tested in August 1942 in an abortive landing at Dieppe undertaken primarily by Canadian troops. Finally, on 6 June 1944, the great assault on France began. A mighty Allied armada of 5000 ships and landing vehicles, 11,000 aeroplanes, strong paratroop units, two amphibious ports and an underwater fuel pipeline to England were marshalled to support the landing of 150,000 troops, 1500 tanks, thousands of vehicles and artillery pieces and immense quantities of supplies. The Germans had hastily constructed a defensive line, known as the Atlantic Wall, but it was still incomplete. Without depth and appreciable reserves, the Atlantic Wall afforded little protection against the overwhelming forces which landed in Normandy between Cherbourg and Caen. The Allies swiftly secured and extended their beachheads and soon built up such an advantage in men and matériel that no hope remained of throwing them back. By 29 July, 1.5 million superbly equipped soldiers were already on French soil under the American General Dwight D. Eisenhower and the British General Bernard Montgomery. As the pace of the Allied advance quickened after July, the French resistance became more active. The Resistance, supported by the British government and by the 'National Committee of the Free French' established in England by General Charles de Gaulle, increasingly harried the German occupiers after 1942 with military operations and acts of sabotage and assassination. As in the east so now in the west, German soldiers faced attack from all directions.

At the end of August 1944 the Allies crossed the Seine and the lower part of the Somme and marched into Paris, which the *Wehrmacht* had evacuated contrary to Hitler's orders. By September they reached the Meuse. After a second landing between Toulon and Cannes, American and French troops began pushing northwards towards Lyon in mid-August and conquered the city on 15 September. Hitler ordered a counter-offensive in the Ardennes on 16 December 1944, but after some initial success the Germans were inexorably driven back again.

While American and British forces rolled over northern France, Belgium, the Netherlands and on towards Aachen and the mountains of the Eifel, the Russians advanced on East Prussia. American and British troops, protected by complete air superiority, surged over the West Wall in early February 1945 and seized Cologne. On 7 March they crossed the Rhine at Remagen. In the east, the Russians overran northern Poland and Galicia, cut off East Prussia from the rest of Germany, pushed into Silesia and Pomerania and threatened to conquer Vienna.

Undaunted, Hitler ordered the last available reserves to be mobilised and the war continued. Nazi *Gauleiter* serving as 'defence commissars' zealously ensured maximum compliance with the Führer's orders. Beginning in September 1944 boys and old men were drafted into the *Volkssturm*, which had fallen under the command of Himmler, the chief of the Home Army, after 20 July 1944 and was trained and led by party members. Neither uniformed nor adequately equipped, the members of the *Volkssturm* were exhorted to throw themselves into the breach 'wherever the enemy seeks to tread on German soil'. 'The enemy desire to ravage Germany' would allegedly be broken and his passage barred 'until a peace treaty securing the future of Germany, of her allies and hence of all Europe can be arranged'.[26] Though spurred by propaganda and the swift retribution of summary courts 'to carry on the fight to the limits of your endurance',[27] most people sought simply to survive till the frightful war had passed. A flood of refugees, fleeing the brutality of the advancing Red Army, flowed out of eastern Germany and over the northern plain, magnifying the general misery and privation. Finally the fronts collapsed. The soldiers of the *Wehrmacht* still offered resistance only in order to save themselves or under the threats of crazed fanatics. All railway and motor vehicle traffic ground to a halt under a hail of Allied bombardment.

The myth was finally exploded that Hitler would come up with a last-minute strategy to reverse the Allied advance. The much-hailed wonder weapons—rockets and jet planes—failed to exert a decisive influence on the course of the war. Equally illusory was the hope that the Allied coalition would crumble as a result of the profound differences of opinion between Roosevelt, Churchill and Stalin which had arisen at Yalta in February 1945. All that remained was Hitler's resolve to drag not only the *Wehrmacht* but the entire

German people into the vortex of destruction. On 19 March he ordered the demolition of all 'military installations, all means of transportation or communication, all industrial plants or public utilities and all goods of any value within the *Reich* which the enemy may find useful for the continuation of the struggle now or in the forseeable future'.[28] He paid no heed to Albert Speer's vehement objections to 'carrying out acts of demolition that could threaten the survival of the German people',[29] and Speer was again reminded of what he had earlier heard Hitler say 'calmly and in full control of himself':[30]

If the war is lost, the people will be lost also. It is not necessary to worry about what the German people will need for elemental survival. . . . For the nation has proved to be the weaker, and the future belongs solely to the stronger eastern nation. In any case only those who are inferior will remain after this struggle, for the good have already been killed.[31]

However, Speer largely succeeded in preventing Hitler's final orders from being carried out.

Through all the confusion within the Nazi hierarchy, the internecine rivalries and attempts to influence him, Hitler had always maintained ultimate control;[32] but now he abandoned his responsibility, committing suicide on 30 April 1945. Two days earlier, Mussolini had been caught near the Swiss border by Italian partisans and shot to death. Goebbels too killed himself and his entire family. Himmler had already cast the Führer aside and attempted to negotiate with the Allies. With Berlin occupied by the Russians, and northern, western and southern Germany occupied by the Western powers, the Third *Reich* formally capitulated on 7 and 8 May 1945 in the midst of the slaughter and wanton destruction it had wrought. Fourteen days later Grand Admiral Karl Dönitz, whom Hitler had appointed his successor as '*Reichspräsident* and supreme commander of the army', was arrested. Germany ceased to exist as an independent nation, and all government functions were taken over by the Allies. At the outset of his political career Hitler had sworn that November 1918 must never be allowed to recur. This indeed became true, the Reich had ceased to exist.

Forty million people had died in Europe, including the Soviet Union. In Germany alone, 3 million soldiers had been killed, over 2 million people had been disabled, and more than half a million had perished in aerial bombardment. Of the 16 million German refugees driven from their homes in the east, over 4 million died or disappeared. To the toll of Hitler's twelve-year reign of terror in Germany must be added all the Jews, the gypsies, the Slavs, the 'unfit' and the political opponents whom he had massacred.

As the extent of Nazi crimes and horror became know, Germans wondered how all this had been possible. But 'no one who had lived through those twelve years in Germany had any right to be self-righteous now if he had not dared to hazard his life against such terror. Even Karl Jaspers said: We are all guilty, why did we not cry out in the streets over the injustice?'³³ In order to save themselves, many had seen only what they wished to see. They were silent about the rampant abuse of power first within Germany and then without. Indeed, many were extremely impressed by the power and glory which the Nazis had exuded at their height. But now nothing but ashes remained of the glory, of the hopes and dreams of the Third *Reich*. After years of illusion, the German people had to face a most bitter reality. They took their leave of Hitler, quickly and thoroughly, and sought to rediscover themselves amidst the wreckage wrought by their national hubris and irrational faith in the Führer.

Three months after the German surrender, Japan too capitulated. After stunning initial successes, the Japanese fleet suffered three stinging defeats in the Pacific as early as 1942. By 1943 Japan was completely on the defensive as the Americans hopped from one island to another, returning to the Philippines in late 1944. In the spring of 1945, units of the American fleet burst into the home waters, bombarding installations on the Japanese mainland and devastating cities through massive air attacks. Still the Japanese government spurned the surrender demand of the United States, Great Britain and the Soviet Union. Only after atomic bombs were dropped on Hiroshima and Nagasaki on 6 and 9 August did the emperor insist on immediate capitulation despite the remonstrations of his military commanders. The armistice ending the war was finally signed on 2 September 1945.

The most destructive war the world had ever seen had drawn to a close. The warring nations had thrown all they could muster into the struggle. Traditional values had gone up in smoke as German and Japanese ambition changed the face of the world. Now all power lay in the hands of the Allies. To them fell the task of restoring peace to the suffering nations and of determining the fate of the world.

15

The Postwar world

1945: Big Three conferences in Yalta and Potsdam; founding of the United Nations
1947: Peace treaties signed with Italy and the states of Eastern Europe; Truman Doctrine; announcement of the Marshall Plan; creation of the Federal Republic of India and of Pakistan
1948: Malayan Union; Ceylon and Burma gain their independence; foundation of the state of Israel
1949: North Atlantic Treaty Organisation; Mao Tse-Tung proclaims the People's Republic of China
1950: Creation of the United States of Indonesia; onset of the Korean War
1951: Conclusion of a peace treaty between Japan and the Western powers; European Coal and Steel Community
1954: The Algerian war commences; France withdraws from Vietnam; the United States supports South Vietnam
1955: Warsaw Pact
1956: Morocco and Tunisia become independent; Suez crisis
1957: European Economic Community (EEC)
1960: Cyprus and the Belgian Congo gain independence
1962: Algeria wins independence; Cuban missile crisis
1963: Civil war on Cyprus; rebellion in the Congo
1964: Malta gains independence

When the hour of unconditional surrender finally struck for Hitler's tyranny, amidst scenes of incredible devastation, Ludendorff's dire prediction of February 1933 had proved true. The *Reich* lay wasted and the German people were destitute.[1] The nations's political structure had been pulverised, the continuity of life had been ruptured, and the *Reich* had ceased to exist. Germany had twice endeavoured to become a world power and in so doing had fought against most of the world; now she collapsed into a state of national and political exhaustion, totally at the mercy of the victorious powers. Much of the country had been reduced to wrack and ruin—Hitler's final ambition after the devastation he had inflicted on the rest of Europe failed to bring the expected victory.

When the victory over Japan brought the Second World War to a close, the victorious powers faced the same problem as in 1918: how to guarantee the peace purchased at the price of a great war. After the First World War it was the victorious European powers who stood at the crux of world events and largely determined what would happen. But by 1945 the European powers had suffered such material and psychological damage that they were unable to recover the leadership role which had begun to slip away in 1918. An exhausted Europe fell back into the second rank of nations while two great superpowers emerged. Joined in an unnatural alliance by Hitler's war of aggression, the United States and the Soviet Union rushed to fill the power vacuum left by the war. But now that their joint victory over the Nazis had been achieved, the superpowers re-emphasised their conflicting political and ideological convictions and sought to reshape Europe and the rapidly shrinking world in their own dissimilar images.

The guiding principles of this restructured world were first enunciated by Roosevelt and Churchill in the Atlantic Charter of 1941. Roosevelt in particular was animated by many of the same political ideals as Wilson had been, and the Charter reaffirmed their belief that after peace had been restored all powers should respect the fundamental right of any people to self-determination. All nations should renounce territorial aggrandizement and seek economic cooperation so that all peoples might live free of fear and want. At the Casablanca Conference of 1943, Germany and her allies were expressly excluded from these principles and required to surrender unconditionally. However, Roosevelt, Churchill and Stalin agreed shortly thereafter in Teheran to strive to eliminate tyranny, enslavement and suppression from the face of the world. At Yalta the 'Big Three' reaffirmed their intention to base their solution to the political and economic problems of liberated Europe, apart from Germany, on democratic principles. Moreover, Stalin agreed to support Roosevelt's plan for a world-wide peace organisation called the United Nations which would work to ensure the security and prosperity of all nations of good-will. In this way, an enduring peace would be achieved.

The exhausted nations of Europe welcomed the creation of such an organisation in the hope that it would prove more effective than the League of Nations had been. The fifty-one founding members of the UN set out to draft a charter at their first meeting in San Francisco in April 1945. This charter was rooted in the principles enunciated by Roosevelt and Churchill for the preservation of peace and security, and it aimed to encourage the development of friendly relations between the nations and a means of surmounting the political, economic and social causes of war. The founding members endowed the new organisation with certain bodies. Like the League, the United Nations was intended not as a world government but as a forum where conflicts between the member states could be settled peacefully. Two key bodies were created: the General Assembly which meets annually and in which all members are considered equal; and the Security Council, consisting of five permanent members (the United States, the Soviet Union, China, Great Britain and France) and six elected members chosen for two-year terms. The General Assembly is entitled to discuss all questions pertaining to the Charter, to establish agencies and special organisations, to present recommendations to the Security Council and to suggest new member states. The Security Council is expected to provide leadership for the UN and to deal with dangers to the peace. In order to protect those nations with the greatest responsibility, the five permanent members of the Security Council were conceded a veto over all matters save procedural questions, which are decided by a simple majority. However, this veto power often impeded the work of the Security Council, and at times even throttled it. As a result, the General Assembly gained in importance and by November 1950 acquired the right to call emergency sessions, to recommend collective measures and to suggest military intervention in cases where lack of unanimity prevents the Security Council from taking steps to avert a threat to the peace.

The Charter members of the UN also established the Economic and Social Council with links to the International Monetary Fund (IMF) and the World Bank as well to special agencies as the World Health Organisation (WHO), the Food and Agricultural Association (FAO), the United Nations Relief and Rehabilitation Administration (UNRRA), the United Nations Educational, Scientific and Cultural Organisation (UNESCO) and the United Nations International Children's Emergency Fund (UNICEF). The UN also appointed trustees to administer territories which had not yet achieved full independence.

Responsibility for the administration of the UN as a whole was assigned to a permanent secretariat in New York under the secretary-general. As a result of the wave of international conflicts in the 1950s and 1960s, the general secretariat played a more political role, and secretaries-general came to function more as diplomats than as administrators.

The accomplishments of the UN have fallen far short of the idealistic hopes of its founders, especially its inability to restrain the nationalistic ambitions of its members or to deter many conflicts around the world. However, it has helped to allay many tensions, and its specialised agencies have accomplished a great deal in the economic, social and technical fields. World health has improved, illiteracy has been reduced, and irrigation projects and other technical improvements have been carried out in the developing countries. Though only fifty-one nations attended the founding convention of the UN in San Francisco in April 1945, membership had soared to 130 nations by 1971.

This growth in membership reflected a trend towards decolonialisation which began after the First World War and became an all-engulfing tide after the end of the Second World War. The colonial peoples, who had been urged by their European masters to help fight the tyranny of fascism, demanded their own right to self-determination once the great conflict was over. One after the other, they demanded independence and equality. Feeling that they had long been the victims of economic exploitation and socio-political suppression, they cultivated their own culture and religion and developed a strong sense of national identity which could only find redemption in the creation of independent states. As the old colonial empires shrank piece by piece, the number of independent states in the world leapt ahead.

Great Britain had already renounced her mandate over Iraq in 1930. After the Second World War she quickly granted independence between 1946 and 1948 to Transjordan and Palestine, India, Ceylon, Burma, and the territories of the Malay Peninsula, which united to form the Malayan Union. In 1955 the protectorate of Aden gained its independence and one year later Britain withdrew from the Sudan and the Suez Canal in Egypt. Ghana gained full independence in 1957, Singapore in 1959, Nigeria in 1960, Sierra Leone and Tanganyika in 1961, Uganda in 1962 and Kenya in 1963. The Mediterranean islands of Cyprus and Malta similarly acquired independence between 1960 and 1964. All these states remained at least nominal members of the British Commonwealth.

Shortly before the end of the Second World War, France granted Syria and Lebanon their independence. However, Paris determined to maintain Indo-China in its thrall and only withdrew after several years of battling the Communist Viet Minh and the great defeat of Dien Bien Phu. The truce of July 1954 resulted in the division of French Indo-China into Laos, Cambodia, South Vietnam and communist North Vietnam. Two years later, the French were forced to quit Morocco and Tunisia. In 1960 Togo, the French Cameroons, French Equatorial Africa, French West Africa and Madagascar became independent. Algeria gained her independence in 1962 but again only after a protracted war with France.

After attempting to control the vast expanses of Indonesia by force of arms, the Netherlands were forced in 1950 to concede independence to the 75 million inhabitants. Ten years later Italy lost Somaliland, the last of her foreign possessions, and the Congo became independent of Belgium.

By the end of the 1960s very little remained of the once proud European empires. However, many of the peoples who had just thrown off the yoke of colonialism found themselves embroiled in further conflicts generated by the instability of their new nations, intense nationalism, territorial rivalries and intractable economic problems. These problems impeded the creation of an effective international security system and afforded an opportunity for foreign intervention. The East–West ideological conflict deepened into a bitter confrontation, making it difficult for the new states to exist independently of the rival political blocks.

The East–West conflict moved into in East Asia very soon after the decolonisation process began. The communist movement sought to strengthen its political influence under the slogan 'Asia for Asians' and to undermine the position of the Western powers, notably Britain and the United States. Communism scored its greatest success in China, where Mao Tse-tung succeeded in driving Chiang Kai-shek from the mainland and establishing the People's Republic of China. While her struggle with the Soviet Union for the leadership of world communism intensified, China slowly established herself as the third superpower. Washington threw its support behind the Taiwanese government of Chiang Kai-shek and did not officially recognise the communist government of mainland China until 1978. In order to help erect a Western barrier against the expansion of communism in East Asia, Washington signed a peace treaty with Japan in 1951, in which Britain, France and other states joined. The Soviet Union on the other hand did not declare an official end to the war against Japan until 1956.

The reversal in the attitude of the United States and her Western Allies towards their former enemy stemmed for the most parts from events in Korea. After the defeat of Japan, Korea was occupied by the Russians north of the 38th Parallel and by the Americans south of this line. In 1945 the People's Republic of Korea was created in the Russian zone and in 1948 the Republic of Korea in the American area. When the Americans withdrew from their zone, the North

Koreans attacked in 1950. The United Nations offered the South Koreans military support, and an international though primarily American army intervened in the struggle. But Chinese intervention on the side of North Korea produced a military stalemate, and in 1953 a truce was arranged entrenching the division of the country. The first great armed conflict between East and West was thereby successfully contained and prevented from expanding into a world war.

The East–West rivalry was clearly apparent in many other world crises. After the Egyptian president, Gamal Abdel Nasser, expropriated their shares in the Suez Canal, Britain and France invaded Egypt, precipitating the 'Suez crisis'. Soon thereafter the stationing of Russian missiles in the People's Republic of Cuba prompted the 'Cuban missile crisis' which pushed the world to the brink of a third world war. It was avoided, it seemed, primarily due to the 'balance of terror' created by the nuclear capacities of both superpowers.

Europe also suffered from the Cold War between the United States and the Soviet Union. Peace treaties were signed with Germany's former allies in 1947, but they did nothing to alter the situation resulting from 'liberation' and occupation by the Red Army. The Baltic states, parts of Finland, eastern Poland and Bessarabia were absorbed into the Soviet Union. All the countries which the Red Army had overrun and occupied in the course of the war—Poland, Hungary, Romania, Bulgaria, Czechoslovakia and the eastern parts of Germany—remained under Russian domination. Moscow blocked all Western influence on internal policies within these countries, placed their governments in the hands of communist parties and gathered the emerging 'People's Democracies' into the Soviet orbit. This added up to a considerable increment in the power of the Soviet Union. Only the Yugoslav leader, Josip Tito, succeeded in keeping his communist government free of Russian tutelage. After several years of civil war, Greece too escaped Soviet hegemony. Nevertheless, the heart of Europe, vital to the maintenance of the political balance of power, had largely fallen under the domination of the Soviet Union, which quickly suppressed any hint of national independence.

The Western powers countered the extension of Soviet power through closer cooperation. Harry S. Truman, who had succeeded to the presidency of the United States upon Roosevelt's death in 1945, enunciated the 'Truman Doctrine' in a speech before both Houses of Congress on 12 March 1947, proclaiming the determination of the United States to 'assist free peoples to work out their own destinies in their own ways'.[2] At the same time Britain and

France concluded an alliance, known as the Brussels Treaty, against any German attack. When Belgium, Luxembourg and the Netherlands joined the alliance on 17 March 1948, it was extended to include any aggressor in Europe and thus took on a distinctly anti-Soviet aura. This tendency became even clearer when the North Atlantic Treaty Organisation was founded on 4 April 1949 by the parties to the Brussels Treaty joined by Denmark, Norway, Iceland, Italy, Portugal, Canada and the United States. The signatories agreed that armed aggression on any one of the members would be considered an attack on all and would be countered by joint resistance. This agreement was extended to include the zones which the parties occupied in Europe.

The unification of the Western world was not confined to military matters but proceeded apace in the economic sphere as well. Harry Truman believed that financial and economic assistance from the United States would best guarantee the development of 'orderly political processes'[3] on the basis of freedom and democracy. Secretary of State George C. Marshall accordingly announced in June 1947 the creation of a vast aid programme to provide the financial assistance which the devastated countries of Western Europe needed in order to put their economies back on their feet. At the same time, the government of the United States emphasised that it expected the peoples of Europe to come together in a joint effort to overcome their economic problems.

The first step in this direction was the creation of the Council of Europe. Its organs, a consultative assembly and a council of ministers, met in Strasbourg and coordinated political and economic cooperation among the member states. However, the Council of Europe is confined to this day to an advisory capacity. Of greater practical effect was the European Coal and Steel Community initiated by the French foreign minister, Robert Schuman. Created in 1952, it brought the entire coal and steel production of France, Italy, the Benelux countries and the Federal Republic of Germany under unified direction and eliminated competition in heavy industry in favour of cooperation. In 1957 these same countries formed the European Economic Community in an attempt to achieve gradual economic and monetary union and to regain at least some of the political and commercial heft which continental Europe had lost after 1945.

Meanwhile, the Eastern and Western political blocks entrenched themselves on each side of the demarcation line running from Lübeck to Trieste previously drawn by the triumphant and still friendly Allies. Bristling with weaponry, the superpowers waged the so-called Cold War, one of the chief sources of which was the struggle to control the economic might and political structure of Germany. On each side of the Iron Curtain, the recently vanquished Germans were admonished 'to support their respective master against that master's former friend and ally'.[4]

16

Germany from 1945 to 1949

1945: Annexation of the German territories east of the Oder–Neisse line by Poland or the Soviet Union; division of Germany into four occupation zones; Four Power status of Berlin; Potsdam Agreement between the United States, Great Britain and the Soviet Union; expulsion of Germans from the eastern territories; political parties re-established; the Nuremberg trials begin.

1946: Denazification; creation of the Socialist Unity Party in the Soviet zone.

1947: Creation of the United Economic Area (the Bizone); first and last conference of provincial prime ministers from all of Germany.

1948: London agreements; establishment of a central German authority in Frankfurt to manage the economy of the Western zone; creation of the German Economic Council in the Soviet Zone; the Allied Control Council ceases to function; currency reform in the Western zones; currency reform in the Eastern zone; the Soviet Union blockades Berlin; Berlin Airlift; the Western zones made eligible for economic aid from the Marshall Plan; creation of the Parliamentary Council

1949: Ratification of the Basic law by the provincial parliaments: formation of the Federal Republic of Germany (see Map 7).

The Occupation

Everything which transpired in Germany after 1945 had its origins in the war and the way in which it was waged. Outraged by the barbarian crimes of the Nazis, the Allies at first sought reparations, retribution and the liquidation of all German political authority. Reports of the atrocities committed in the East and in the extermination camps shocked world opinion which, unable to distinguish between the German people as a whole and those responsible for these horrors, embraced the Hitlerian thesis that all true Germans were devoted National Socialists. Unwilling to attempt to differentiate, the Western powers in particular were inclined to equate

'Hitlerism with Prussianism, the guilt of the Nazis with the guilt of the general staff' and claimed to trace in the development of 'German history from Frederick the Great to Hitler a continuous tendency towards violent imperialism'.[1]

With the intention of extirpating this proclivity once and for all, the victorious powers first considered depriving the Germans of all control over their own affairs and transforming the country into a political and economic vacuum. In this way, the Germans would be gradually reformed 'into at least a relatively peaceful and democratically-minded people'.[2] However, such plans proved utterly impracticable once the four unequal partners set about determining the concrete political consequences of Germany's defeat. Their sense of unity crumbled as the German threat was supplanted in the Western view by the rising menace of Soviet totalitarianism. Aided by the Siren song of Marxist ideology, Moscow had been busily transforming the economies, societies and political systems of entire nations, and in keeping with its governing ideology, was not about to tolerate any alternative social or political structures.

The Western Allies had already been confronted in Tehran and Yalta with Stalin's determination to retain what the Red Army had conquered. The Soviet dictator insisted that a considerable segment of eastern Germany must be ceded to the Soviet Union and Poland and that the Soviet Union would keep the Polish territory which Hitler had conceded to Stalin in the Molotov–Ribbentrop pact of 1939. Poland would be compensated in the west for these lost territories and her borders advanced to the Oder–Neisse line. At Russian insistence, the Big Three also agreed in Yalta in February 1945 to dismantle German industry and to distribute it among the states which had suffered most from German attack. Further material reparations would be appropriated from current production over a period of ten years. The Allies concurred that the principal German war criminals should be put on trial and that Germany should be divided up into a number of little states. The Soviets later opposed the latter scheme in the belief that if the administrative unity of Germany was maintained, the entire impoverished nation might be attracted into the Communist orbit. All three great powers were prepared to accept the expulsion of the German population from the annexed territories in the east. Churchill later sought to justify this step in his memoirs, saying: 'It must be remembered that we were in the midst of a fearful struggle with the mighty Nazi power. All the hazards of war lay around us, and all its passions of comradeship among Allies, of retribution upon the common foe, dominated our minds.'[3]

This cession of approximately one-quarter of the area of the German *Reich* was confirmed at the Potsdam Conference in July 1945 when the German territories east of the Oder–Neisse line were officially placed under Soviet or Polish administration. Though the Big Three agreed to postpone the final determination of Poland's western border till the final peace conference, the provisional arrangements created a *fait accompli* which could hardly be reversed, especially as the Allies had already agreed to the expulsion of the German population. Unlike the Western powers, Stalin did not conceive of Germany within her borders of 1937 but rather as whatever the war made of her. Therefore he considered that the Allied occupation rights did not apply to the annexed eastern territories. The remaining three-quarters of the old *Reich* was to remain a single legal entity, though divided into smaller occupation zones till the peace treaty was concluded, in accordance with the recommendations of the European Advisory Commission established in London on 14 January 1944. In the meantime, Germany would be fully demilitarised and democratised. The Big Three further agreed to allow the formation of political parties and provincial parliaments and to recreate a national state based on local districts. In the economic sphere, the Potsdam agreement provided for the dismantling of German syndicats and cartels under Allied supervision and the fostering of agriculture. The economic unity of Germany was to be maintained and the local population was to be treated uniformly across the various occupation zones.

Authority over all matters related to Germany as a whole was assigned to the Allied Control Council in early June 1945. On it sat the supreme commanders of the occupation forces who governed Germany in the name of the United States, Britain, France and the Soviet Union. The decisions of the Control Council were required to be unanimous. While sitting on the Control Council, the military governors also held supreme authority in their own zone and were responsible to their own government. Problems arose when the victorious powers began to pursue very different objectives in their own zones and could no longer reconcile their conflicting interests. The central administration envisaged by the Potsdam Agreement collapsed before it could even be constituted when the French scuttled plans to transfer responsibility for the administration to German secretaries of state named by the Allied Control Council and supervised by it. Emnity between the Allies grew as their professed intention of pursuing a unified policy proved impossible.

Germany's internal recovery was severely obstructed by the ideological conflicts among the four occupying powers and their contrasting security needs. France envisaged the Germany of the future as a loose federation of sovereign states. Similar to the time of the Congress of Vienna, the federal government would be endowed with very limited authority and the federal parliament would rest on an assembly of member states. The French military government accordingly resisted all attempts at centralisation and strongly de-centralised the administration of its own zone.

The British on the other hand strove to erect a federal state with a strong central government. In their own zone they created prov-inces, or *Länder*, administered by central offices with zone-wide responsibilities. The Americans also encouraged a federal state and soon formed provinces which dealt with joint concerns through a *Länderrat*, or council of provinces. The Soviets for their part imposed strict centralisation on their zone from the very beginning and created five new *Länder* administered by a central authority.

Though the Allies could not agree on the present and future structure of Germany, they were in perfect agreement on eradicat-ing the German past: punishment of the leading National Socialists, demilitarisation, denazification, democratisation, elimination of Prussia as a geographic entity and the dismantling of heavy indus-try. However, the means and the rigour with which they pursued these ends depended very much on the individual Allied power and on the evolution of relations between them. Thus Germany's fate came to depend on the interaction of the victorious Allied powers.

The Allies gradually settled comfortably into their respective occupation zones: the Russians in the east, the British in the north-west, the French in the south-west, the Americans in the south, and all four in the former capital of Berlin. No other Allied power had such a definitive and well-elaborated plan as the Soviet Union. By the end of May 1945 Moscow had already demanded that the United States vacate those areas of central Germany which had fallen to American arms but which the Yalta Agreement had ascribed to the Soviet zone. After the American troops withdrew from Saxony and part of Thuringia, the Russians handed over those sectors of Berlin which had been assigned to the Western powers.

Determined to establish firm control over its zone from the outset, the Soviet military government formed groups of exiled German communists in early May 1945 to act as the nucleus of the new 'anti-fascist and democratic order'. One group of ten set about forming a new administration under the leadership of Walter Ul-bricht, a former carpenter and communist *Reichstag* deputy who had been stripped of his German citizenship by Hitler in 1938 and had spent the war years in Moscow as a loyal acolyte of Joseph

Stalin. 'Unimpeded by theoretical considerations or personal feelings', Ulbricht always succeeded in 'implementing the directives he received from the Soviets with great skill and ruthlessness'.[4] From the beginning he dedicated himself to building up a communist system in the Soviet zone. A central administration was formed as swiftly as possible and staffed in such a way that the Sovietisation of the Russian zone by the Red Army and its German assistants was masked from the outside world. 'It must appear democratic, though we control it',[5] was the official word to the party faithful. To this end, Social Democrats, Centrists, Democrats and apolitical Germans with a demonstrable 'anti-fascist' record during the Hitler years were actively sought out and appointed as local mayors while the communists kept the key decisions such as personnel and education firmly in their own hands. Exiled German communists returning from the Soviet Union were placed in charge of the police, which was made independent of the local administrations.

The formation of central departments directly responsible to the Soviet Military Administration (SMA) was preceded by the establishment of anti-fascist, democratic political parties. At the behest of the SMA, the newly created Communist Party, Social Democratic Party, Christian Democratic Union and the Liberal Democratic Party immediately created a 'united front of democratic, anti-fascist parties'. Its purported goal, according to the founding declaration of the Communist Party, was the formation of an anti-fascist, democratic government in 'a parliamentary, democratic republic endowed with full democratic rights and freedoms for the people'.[6] The highest German authority was a committee on which each of the four official parties held five seats each. In addition, 'block committees' were created in all provinces, counties, cities and towns. These committees were supposed to carry out 'thorough democratisation' at the local level, and their decisions required the approval of all parties. This system made it impossible to outvote the German Communist Party working hand in glove with the SMA, and it paved the way for a revolution in the socio-economic structure of eastern Germany.

The first step in this direction was the land reform designed by the agriculture department of the SMA in August 1945 and introduced into the Russian provinces in September. All large rural holdings over 100 ha were expropriated without compensation, 'including all buildings, animate and inanimate property and other agricultural inventory'.[7]

Industrial reform followed in the autumn of 1945. All property belonging to the German *Reich* or Prussia, to the *Wehrmacht*, forbidden organisations, former National Socialists, war criminals or to 'people singled out by the Soviet military command on special lists or in other ways'[8] was either handed over to the provinces, counties and towns or converted into 'Soviet joint-stock companies' to pay war reparations. By the end of 1946, 45 per cent of the factories had become 'the property of the people'. All natural resources were taken over in the same fashion in 1947 and the banks followed in 1948. However, it was the denazification process which had the greatest impact on the lives of most people. Eighty per cent of the teachers and of other state employees were summarily dismissed and replaced by communists or anti-fascists. These generally younger replacements attended quick courses to prepare them for their positions before being sent out to help 'build a new kind of democracy' and anchor it as deeply as possible among the people.

Even in the Soviet zone, the German Communist Party had far fewer members than the Social Democrats. The Communists sought to secure their dominant position by merging the two parties, though this plan was stoutly resisted by the Social Democratic rank and file as well as by Kurt Schumacher, the old-time Social Democrat who had been imprisoned by the Nazis and had now become the party leader in the Western zones. Schumacher appealed to Otto Grotewohl, the chairman of the Social Democratic central committee in the Eastern zone, to resist Soviet and German communist pressure and either maintain his independence or, if necessary, dissolve the party. But Grotewohl bowed to Soviet pressure and agreed to an alliance with the communists. At a conference held in the Soviet zone on 21 and 22 April 1946, the Communist Party and the Social Democratic Party merged to form the Socialist Unity Party of Germany, though in a vote of Berlin Social Democrats, forbidden in the Eastern sector of the city, 82 per cent were opposed. In spite of massive interference in the elections, the new Socialist Unity Party failed to achieve an absolute majority in any provincial elections held in October 1946, though it did emerge as the strongest single party. Nevertheless, Moscow and its German accomplices forced a soviet system on the Eastern zone, paving the way for the division of Germany and the emergence of an Eastern state integrated into the Soviet bloc.

The central administrations of transportation, communications, fuel, commerce and consumer goods, agriculture and forests, finances, health, employment and social security, education and justice had been organised by the Soviets in such a way that they could be easily enlarged to form the all-German administrations envisaged by the Potsdam Agreement. The other occupying powers now sought to build up their own administrations along similar lines. They too established systems reflecting their own political beliefs and sought to entrench liberal democracy and the rule of law. They also strove to safeguard their own political and military security, starting with demilitarisation, denazification, democratisation and the dissolution of the great industrial cartels.

In the American zone, mandate governments were created as early as May 1945 to implement the necessary measures. Accorded limited powers, they were expected to rebuild the administration, revive economic life and carry out the orders of the Allies. In August the Americans allowed the formation of political parties at the local level and in September they remodelled the remnants of the old provincial structure to create the *Länder* of Bavaria, Württemberg-Baden, Gross-Hessen and finally Bremen, which lay in the British zone but was occupied by American troops. The first elections were held in January 1946 in rural areas and in June in the rest of the American zone. Provincial constituent assemblies were elected in the autumn of 1946. For the first time, provincial governments elected by universal, equal, free and secret ballot began to operate, and their decisions were generally accepted by the occupation authorities.

In order to restore some semblance of order in Germany and to catch up with the rapid pace of Soviet centralisation, General Lucius Clay, the military governor of the American zone, had summoned the provincial prime ministers in his zone to a meeting in Stuttgart on 17 October 1945. He enjoined them to coordinate the activities of all the provincial governments in the American zone and to meet periodically to discuss mutual difficulties. After the prime ministers had agreed on an organisational statute, the newly constituted provincial council met on 6 November 1945. It was expected to 'ensure a helpful level of uniformity in political, social, economic and cultural development and to organise government communications between the various occupation areas'.[9] The provincial prime ministers met once a month, and the decisions they took came into effect in the provinces after approval by the military government. The measures adopted by the provincial council strongly influenced the further political development of all of western Germany.

The British military government was primarily concerned at first with dismantling German industry as rapidly and effectively as possible and organising legitimate, democratic representation of the people. The British zone encompassed numerous distinct political entities—four regions, four provinces and a city state—and a central administration for the entire zone was swiftly created in 1945.

Managed by Germans, this central administration was organised according to function and was accountable to the military governor, Field Marshal Bernard Montgomery.

On 6 August 1945 the British approved the creation of free labour unions and political parties, and in February 1946 they created an advisory council with consultative powers only. Provincial elections were not held in the British zone until April 1947 after local administrative units had been rearranged in the late autumn of 1946 to create four provinces: Lower Saxony, Schleswig-Holstein, Nordrhein-Westfalen and the free city of Hamburg. The British zone encompassed Germany's industrial heartland in the Ruhr Valley, but it possessed the least arable land of all the zones, and the British were forced to provide large amounts of food drawn from their own reserves. This combined with the dissolution of the cartels and the dismantling of German industries posed enormous problems for the military administration and the British government.

In contrast to the British and the Americans who did not harbour any annexationist ambitions, the French strove above all to make their zone a French dependency. Ensconced in Baden-Baden, they maintained strict control over all facets of life and long scotched any attempts at inter-provincial cooperation within their zone. Speech and the press were subject to strict censorship, allegedly in order to root out all nationalist, fascist, militaristic and anti-democratic ideas. Even the terms 'German' or 'Germany' were discouraged and were not permitted in the official names of the political parties allowed after January 1946. Similar to the Soviets but unlike the Americans or British, the French lived off the agricultural produce of their own zone and pursued definite territorial aims. After the Saarland was occupied on 12 February 1946, Paris took immediate steps to separate it politically and economically from the rest of Germany. The Saarland was removed from the purview of the Allied Control Council and declared an independent state with its own constitution. In the rest of their zone, the French military government permitted only tiny administrative units, out of which the provinces of Baden, Württemberg-Hohenzollern and Rheinland-Pfalz gradually emerged by the end of 1947. Centralised though very weak 'assistance bureau' ensured the minimum necessary cooperation between the provinces.

In the cultural realm, the French outdid all the other occupation powers. Though eager to woo the German population, they pushed their generally rigorous occupation policy to extreme lengths and did all they could to promote the French language and civilisation in the schools and universities of their zone.

The Material and Spiritual Plight of Germans after 1945

In the midst of the political flux brought about by the collapse of the German state and the attempts of each Allied power to rebuild its own zone in its own way, the German people struggled through horrendous living conditions. Those who were not fleeing from the east generally lived amidst the rubble of ruined cities and towns. The physical devastation was mirrored in many cases by the intellectual void left by the collapse of the Nazi ideology. Inadequately nourished, with scarcely a roof over their heads, and often unaware of the fate that had befallen their family members, the people set about clearing mountains of debris from their cities and creating the first emergency shelters. Almost 5 million dwellings had been destroyed or damaged during the war. 'Men from 14 to 65, women from 15 to 50 . . . everyone was expected to work if he wished to obtain his daily ration.'[10] Refugees and expellees, returning soldiers and evacuated civilians all struggled along on foot or in carts or stock-cars to reach the bombed-out cities, though entry was often denied them unless they knew a trade in high demand.

The housing shortage was greatly aggravated by the 12 million people expelled by the Allies from their homes in the east and south-east. When they reached western Germany, they were generally without money or personal effects and barely managed to survive in emergency shelters in the countryside or in refugee camps erected in the primary provinces of first asylum, Schleswig-Holstein, Lower Saxony and Bavaria. Their professional and social integration into western Germany proved a difficult struggle over many years. In contrast to the Soviet zone, the land in western Germany had not been redistributed and was rarely for sale. Very few refugees who had lived on the land were therefore able to resume their former occupations. Refugee office workers and labourers also experienced great difficulty in establishing themselves and 'often scraped by barely above the survival level'.[11] Better opportunities awaited skilled workmen, professionals and civil servants. Former merchants and factory owners also re-established themselves relatively easily and were often able to take out loans on the basis of their former reputations.

The shortage of clothing, food and shoes which had first become noticeable towards the end of the war became life-threatening. Industrial production in 1946 reached only 33 per cent of its 1936 level. The supply of food dwindled and hunger became the foremost problem of occupied Germany. The rations available to the German population through official ration cards amounted to only 1000 to 1500 calories a day, though UN experts had established 2650 calories as the essential daily requirement. Immense queues formed before the shops, and with bread in very short supply the main staples became carrots, turnips and potatoes. Meat and sausage were rare while butter, vegetable oil and margarine were luxury items to be savoured in tiny amounts. American care-packages reached Germany very early and relieved the worst distress. Often the senders had lived in more straightened circumstances than the German recipients till the very end of the war. Young people were saved from the worst effects of hunger by child meals and school meals provided primarily by the Americans and the British.

The effects of hunger were compounded by the cold. In a letter to a friend, the writer Hans Erich Nossack portrayed the misery of the times:

I manage to hold out in the shop from eight o'clock till three. At three the transportation system starts to work again, but by then I am so frozen that I can barely walk, especially as I have only had two pieces of dry bread to eat. So reaching the U-Bahn is a struggle. My wife gives lessons in the morning and hurries at noon for about an hour to reach the feeding centre we rely on because we lack gas, electricity and cooking equipment—even though it costs most of our food coupons. With that, the most important matters have been taken care of. Around three o'clock my wife warms our food on the *Brennhexe*, which also takes a bit of the chill off the air. After eating, I always have work to do or wood to cut, etc. Between five and six, I try to sleep in order to draw a curtain over the day and make up for some of the missing calories. Later we drink a tea-like mixture and have another bite. If no visitors drop by, we sit and work facing one another under a 15-watt candle. At ten o'clock a siren screams out three times, at a quarter past ten, twice, and at half past, once. Then we have curfew. I usually stay up till about one o'clock, huddled in blankets before creeping, frozen, into bed.[12]

In order to survive, many people had to take bicycles or over-crowded trains to rural areas where they went on 'hamster tours' from farmhouse to farmhouse begging for food or trading the few objects of value which they had been able to save. Goods were exchanged on the black market—often plundered state property or merchandise stolen from the depots of the occupying forces—and fuel was 'organised'. People gathered wood in the forests or collected anything which could be traded for food. Cigarettes took the place of money, vast amounts of which were still in circulation but which only had value in combination with official coupons issued solely in emergencies. The attempts to scratch out a living were greatly complicated by the curfews imposed by the Allied powers and by the permits required to pass from one zone to another or from province to province.

Germans also felt the burden of a heavy moral cloud. The full extent of Nazi atrocities committed in the name of the German people against Jews and eastern peoples became widely known for the first time. Many at first could scarcely believe what they were told and felt a deep sense of shame when the evidence proved overwhelming.

Between November 1945 and October 1946 the leading National Socialists were tried for war crimes before an international military tribunal in Nuremberg. The resulting revelations were a source of deep dismay to the extent that they penetrated the struggle for personal survival. In spite of reservations about the legal validity of a trial in which the judge and prosecutor were identical, the German populace generally approved of all cases directed against individual war crimes, 'crimes against peace', and crimes against humanity such as murder, genocide, enslavement and persecution for political or religious reasons. All the Allied authorities and countries formerly occupied by the Germans held numerous further trials of major war criminals and leading Nazi functionaries. Most Germans accepted the sentences handed down as the inevitable consequence of past crimes.

On the other hand, the public rejected accusations of collective guilt according to which not only the National Socialist leadership but the entire German people were responsible for the war and the atrocities committed. The Allies' denazification programme, which aimed to free Germany 'from National Socialism and militarism', required every citizen over the age of eighteen to fill out a questionnaire, and it too was felt to be unjust and overly broad. Indeed, the Allied purge did prove to be ineffective and failed to achieve its stated goals. Though most leading Nazis were eliminated, many tainted experts and technocrats went unpunished because their skills were urgently needed. Many nominal, non-active members of the Nazi Party who were fully prepared to cooperate in the new order were so embittered and alienated that the Western Allies' prime objective, the restoration of democracy, was endangered. The Bishop of Württemberg, Theophil Wurm, wrote to British Christians in December 1945 to express his concern:

The Allied victory did not represent the triumph of pure good over pure evil. The military conquest and occupation of our country was accompanied by all the brutalities towards the civilian population of which the people of the Allied countries have quite rightly complained. What has since transpired in many of the zones in the name of denazification is also not likely to inspire an impression of superior justice and humanity. The numerous appeals to the German people to work their way out of misery sound like mockery wherever industry, including that which has nothing to do with armaments, is dismantled and or denied all raw materials.[13]

The churches played a major role in allaying the physical suffering and in ministering to the spiritual and intellectual needs of the people. They exhorted their overflowing congregations to exhibit courage and faith in God, and they addressed the question of moral guilt and repentence. On 19 October 1945 the Evangelical Council, meeting in Stuttgart, acknowledged 'with deep anguish that through us untold suffering has been visited on peoples and countries. . . . We accuse ourselves of not having professed our faith more courageously, prayed more truely, believed more joyously and loved more urgently. A new beginning shall now be made in our churches.'[14] The Catholic Reinhold Schneider, whose writings had been proscribed by the Nazis, showed his compatriots the path to a forthright and honourable admission of their misdeeds:

It should be our pride, so far as guilt is concerned, to confine our examination to ourselves and not to insist, for instance, that others were guilty too. This 'too' is a childish word. . . . It does not betoken a sense of honour, and this is what we are seeking. . . . In the life of a nation there can be times when contrition is the only appropriate response. It then becomes an historic achievement for a people.[15]

In the universities, too, professors who had not compromised themselves during the years of Nazi rule began to examine the past together with youths freshly returned from the horrors of war. Labouring under the most difficult of physical conditions due to lack of space and basic equipment and distrusted by the occupation authorities, professors and their students engaged in the painful process of rethinking and self-examination. In this way, they hoped to contribute to the renewal of cultural and intellectual life and to help overcome the social misery on all sides. The few who managed to gain admission to university seized the opportunity to catch up on all that German academia had missed during the long night of Nazi rule; they worked hard and were among the best students which German universities ever produced.[16]

The universities were allowed a great deal of leeway to renew themselves and to assist in reviving serious thought, truth and humanity. Radio, the press and the schools (when they reopened their doors somewhat later) were supervised more stringently, the degree depending on the Allied power in command. However, all the Allies were eager to ensure the success of re-education, denazification and democratisation.

After twelve years of intellectual isolation under the Nazis, German academics were eager for contact with the outside world. They appreciated the confidence others showed in them and relished the opportunity to read material which had long been withheld and to engage in free and open discussion. Never before in Germany had there been such a strong intellectual and moral impulse to rediscover oneself, to restore one's shattered life and to save 'a tolerable existence as a civilised people'.[17]

The Renewal of Political Life

These same aspirations underlay the reconstruction of political and social life. Labour unions and political parties had to be refounded and could not simply pick up where they had left off in 1933, especially since the Nazis had coordinated them, with the exception of Social Democrats. Moreover, the surviving politicians of the Weimar era, many of whom had suffered bitterly at the hands of the Nazis, realised that their former acrimonious rivalry had fatally weakened the democratic forces and had assisted the collapse of the republic.

Immediately after the Nazi defeat, political parties began to spring up spontaneously. The new Social Democratic Party (SDP) was particularly blessed with a pool of officials and members who had been active before 1933. The reconstruction of the party was led by Kurt Schumacher, who had been physically broken by twelve years in a Nazi concentration camp but was still blessed with a keen mind.

From the outset, Schumacher opposed attempts in the Soviet zone to combine the Social Democrats and Communists in a single party. Together with returning emigrants and the party leaders who had spent the war in exile in London under the direction of Erich Ollenhauer, Schumacher desired a united German Social Democratic party and not a Socialist Unity Party in tandem with the Communists. He advocated a free and democratic social order and found in Carlo Schmid, Adolf Arndt and Herbert Wehner men of varying origins and backgrounds who were able to keep the party intellectually open and attractive to broad strata of the population. Schumacher was personally untarnished by the Nazi years and became the chief spokesman of 'the other Germany' which had nothing in common with the Nazis and their collaborators. He claimed for his party the right to lead the new Germany and for all Germans the right to equality and self-determination.

At the first party convention in Hanover on 11 May 1946, the Social Democrats proclaimed their 'steadfast commitment to freedom and socialism. . . . There can be no socialism without democracy, intellectual freedom and freedom of speech, and there can be no socialism without humanity and respect for the individual.' So far as economic policies were concerned, the party hoped to rally 'all democratic forces' to the banner of socialism. Not only the political structure of Germany would be changed but the economic structure as well through the creation of 'a planned, socialist economy, shaped and moulded by all'. In this new economy, 'the interests of society as a whole' would determine 'the extent, type and distribution of production'.[18]

The Western occupation authorities frowned upon these economic aspirations, many of which were shared by the labour unions and some elements within ther CDU. In the summer of 1948 the Western powers blocked a Social Democratic attempt to socialise the coal industry in Nordrhein-Westfalen. Moreover, Social Democratic economic policies failed to find the popular support which the party had expected and the Social Democrats polled fewer votes than anticipated in the first provincial elections held in the three Western zones in 1946–47. After the election, the CDU and Free Democratic Party (FDP) joined forces to deny the Social Democratic candidate the post of economic director on the recently formed Frankfurt Economic Council. The Social Democrats thereupon decided to go into Opposition, where they remained for the following twenty years. The party established very high standards as the parliamentary Opposition and, in so doing, did the young German democracy a great service.

In the contrast to the Social Democrats, the Christian Democratic Union(CDU) was a brand new party. The CDU was originally founded in Berlin and the Rhineland, whence it quickly spread across the rest of Germany. Its members sprang primarily from the former Centre Party, though many had belonged to the prewar Liberal or Conservative parties. The founders of the CDU hoped to form a Christian people's party able to attract support among all social groups. They addressed their appeal to 'all forces eager to contribute to reconstruction who have an unshakable faith in the fine qualities of the German people and who are resolved to make Christianity and the high ideal of true democracy the cornerstones of renewal'.[19] The founders insisted upon an interconfessional alliance due to both to the bitter experiences of the Weimar Republic and to years of joint resistance by Catholic and Protestant Christians to the Nazi terror. Many former Centrist deputies believed that a uniquely Catholic party would be too weak to play a leading role in the new state; Protestants hoped to overcome their bisection into a liberal and conservative wing, a division which had diminished their influence in the Weimar Republic and kept them out of power.

To the strong middle-class element at the founding meetings of the CDU was added a Christian socialist component stemming from the former Christian trade unions. Both wings struggled from the outset to have the party adopt their economic and social programme. The new CDU was therefore a tangle of Christian socialist and capitalist, free-market strands which were ironed out in the compromise Ahlen Programme of 3 February 1947. According to this programme:

The German people will be endowed with an economic and social system which respects the rights and dignity of man, furthers the intellectual and material reconstruction of our society and secures internal and external peace. . . . The new economic system is predicated upon the belief that the era of unrestricted domination by private capital has come to an end. It is equally important, however, that private capitalism not be replaced by state capitalism, which would pose an even greater danger to the political and economic freedom of the individual.[20]

According to the Ahlen Programme, the large cartels would be broken up, the iron and mining industries would be socialised, and workers would be granted the right of co-determination. Konrad Adenauer, the CDU chairman in the British zone who increasingly emerged as the chief spokesman of the entire party, supported the Ahlen Programme all through the desperate winter in the Ruhr of 1946–7. However, from the summer of 1947 onwards, he was won over by the ideas of Ludwig Erhard, an economics professor and chairman of the Economic Council who advocated a socially responsible market economy. This type of system would attempt to combine state social policies with a market economy in order to provide fairness and balance. Adenauer was convinced that the United States would not support a socialist Germany and believed that Christian socialism was unrealistic and destructive of party unity. In the end, Erhard's beliefs carried the day as Adenauer rose to be president of the parliamentary council in 1948 and Chancellor of the Federal Republic in 1949. The Christian socialist wing of the CDU espoused Erhard's economic policies when their party began to close ranks in the face of the Social Democratic Opposition.

A separate party, the Christian Social Union (CSU), took shape in 1945 as part of the interconfessional Christian movement. Even earlier than the CDU, the CSU championed a free-market economy. The most outstanding of its founders was Joseph Müller, a former member of the German Resistance and a concentration camp inmate, who wished to create a democratic, centrally organised party with strong grass-root participation like the SPD. The party was constituted in Würzburg on 10 October 1945 but moved its headquarters to Munich in December. This party of prosperous farmers, merchants, tradesmen and small industrialists carried on many of the Catholic, federalist views of the old Bavarian People's Party, the strongest political force in Bavaria before 1933. Though predominantly Catholic, the CSU sought a political alliance of both confessions and became an independent though close partner of the CDU with which it formed a single bloc in the *Bundestag* after 1949.

The liberals first organised themselves in south-western Germany, then in Hessen and Nordrhein-Westfalen. They largely continued the traditions of the old south-western liberals and of the National Liberals, the relative strengths of which had varied from region to region. In Baden-Württemberg and Bavaria the old liberal tendency held the upper hand while National Liberalism, with its sensitivity to industrial interests, dominated in Hessen and Nordrhein-Westfalen. Both wings of the party were clearly middle-class. In December 1948 the various provincial and zonal associations united to form the Free Democratic Party. Theodor Heuss, a south German old Liberal and former *Reichstag* deputy was elected party chairman. His personal moral authority and charisma bound the FDP together more than any particular programme. In general, the Free Democrats emphasised individual initiative and the right to private property, while condemning both Marxist and nationalist socialism for paving the way to totalitarianism.[21] The Free Democrats shared the views of the CDU/CSU in regard to the economy and the political structure, but were closer to the SPD in questions of foreign policy, the legal system and cultural or educational policy.

The Communist Party of Germany (KPD) was given free rein in the Western zones to rebuild its organisation, often calling on members who had been persecuted by the Nazis. As in the east, the Communists drew up a relatively moderate programme and attempted to persuade the SPD to join them in a common front. However, this scheme fell through in the west because of the opposition of the Social Democrats and, increasingly, of the military governments. As society and politics evolved in western Germany under the leadership of the other parties, the KPD rapidly declined to a doctrinaire sect with little influence. When it was officially outlawed in 1956, the vast majority of western Germans had already thoroughly rejected it in view of events in the Soviet zone.

Other political associations were formed, some regional in nature and others appealing to special interest groups, but they remained very small. The trend to a three-party system was clear. Parties with nationalist or right-wing programmes also found little support after the inferno of the lost war.

The Formation of the Federal Republic of Germany

While the German political parties wrestled over their internal structure and sought to clarify their relationship with one another, the British and Americans sought to reorganise western Germany. The Americans were particularly eager for change because the reparations agreed to at the Potsdam Conference were hampering the economic recovery of all Western Europe and because they were forced to replace from their own reserves the industrial production knocked out by the war or by the dismantling of German factories. Washington sought to break the vicious circle by reducing the number of factories slated for dismantlement and considering ways to reorganise the German economy. It proposed a joint economic administration at the Paris conference of foreign ministers in June and July 1946, but this suggestion was blocked by France and the Soviet Union.

Great Britain and the United States thereupon resolve to proceed on their own. In August 1946 they agreed to merge their occupation zones in a unified economic area and summoned German experts to make the necessary arrangements. The administrative agreement drawn up by the German experts proposed the creation of central councils to administer the economy, finances, food and agriculture, the post office and transportation. The provincial ministers holding the corresponding portfolio would sit on the councils and each would be assigned five administrative offices. In accordance with the federal political structure favoured by the United States and the south German Provinces, the decisions of the councils and the offices could only be implemented if the provinces agreed to pass corresponding laws and regulations.

The German public first learned of this new phase in occupation policy in early September 1946 when the American secretary of state, James Franciş Byrnes, announced his government's intentions in Stuttgart:

We have learned, whether we like it or not, that we live in one world, from which world we cannot isolate ourselves. We have learned that peace and well-being are indivisible and that our peace and well-being cannot be purchased at the price of peace and the well-being of any other country. . . . Germany is part of Europe and recovery in Europe, and particularly in the states adjoining Germany, will be slow indeed if Germany and her great resources of iron and coal is turned into a poorhouse.[22]

Byrnes also indicated how the Americans hoped to proceed: 'We favor the economic unification of Germany. If complete reunification cannot be secured, we shall do everything in our power to secure the maximum possible unification.'[23] Byrnes emphasised however that the United States would welcome the participation of the French and Russian zones.

Germans in the Western zones saw Byrnes's speech as a sign of hope for a better future and supported the new course despite the block it struck at German unity. They hoped that it did not entail a final decision on the fate of the nation.

The extent of the rift between the Allied powers became apparent at the foreign ministers conference held in Moscow in April 1947. The Soviet Union held firmly to her demands for a unified German state, the Oder–Neisse boundary, Soviet participation in controlling the Ruhr area, the return of the Saarland and dissolution of the Bizone. On 5 June 1947 the Bavarian prime minister, Hans Ehard, convened a conference of provincial prime ministers attended by delegates from the eastern zone. However, the conference collapsed before it could really begin because of procedural wrangles and mutual mistrust.

The British and Americans forged ahead with their plans for a federative West Germany. The former bizonal administration was placed on a parliamentary footing and the United Economic Area was created. The administrative organs of this area—the Economic Council, the Executive Council and the Executive Directors—were responsible for taking all institutional, administrative and legislative measures essential to the survival of the German people. The most important of these institutions from a political standpoint was the Economic Council which was composed of fifty-two delegates elected by the *Landtage* and was supposed to act as the parliament of the United Economic Area. It held legislative powers and was empowered by the occupation authorities 'to direct the permissible economic reconstruction'.[24] However, the economy could not be rebuilt in a political vacuum and the deputies to this parliament (who joined to form parties) found themselves embroiled in political questions touching on all of Germany.

In the meantime, the Cold War intensified. The Truman Doctrine and the implementation of the Marshall Plan after the failure of the Moscow foreign ministers' conference manifested the determination of the Western Allies to stabilise their zones, integrate Germany into a reconstructed Europe and check communist expansion. In accordance with this policy, the United Economic Area was reorganized and expanded in February 1948 to form an embryonic state. The number of provincial deputies on the Economic Council was doubled and the Executive Council was replaced by a Provincial Council functioning as a second legislative body. The eight provinces in the American and British zones were represented on this council by two deputies each. The activities of the zonal administrations were coordinated by an Administrative Council, consisting of the directors of the zonal administrations and one head director. They were all elected by the Economic Council and confirmed by the military government. Though the Administrative Council was dependent on the occupying powers, it became in practice a virtual cabinet responsible to the Economic Council.

While the institutions of the 'United Economic Area' were still being reorganised, the United States and Great Britain allowed France to integrate the Saarland into her national economy in the hope that Paris would then permit the rest of the French zone to join the United Economic Area. Paris did prove willing at this point to contribute to the construction of a democratic West Germany within the community of free peoples.

When the three Western military governors set about drafting proposals for the unification of their zones, the Soviet military governor protested sharply and walked out of the Control Council, which ceased altogether to function as the supreme Allied authority. After protracted negotiations in London, the United States, Great Britain, France and the Benelux countries agreed on a fundamental policy towards Germany and in June 1948 they empowered the provincial prime ministers to convene a Constituent Assembly. The Western powers emphasised their desire 'to give the German people the opportunity to achieve on the basis of a free and democratic form of government the eventual re-establishment of German unity at present disrupted'.[25] Germany would cease to be governed by the military and the generals would be replaced by three high commissioners representing the interests of the occupying powers. The anticipated political, economic and legal unification of the three Western zones would deprive the Soviet Union of her veto rights over western Germany and exclude her from the International Ruhr Authority through which the six powers and West Germany would supervise heavy industry.

The rift between the Soviets and the Western Allies further widened on 20 June 1948 when a currency reform was carried out in western Germany and shortly thereafter in the Western sectors of Berlin. Without consulting the Germans, the Western Allies replaced the still legal but worthless *Reichsmark* with the new *Deutsche Mark* and converted all debts and holdings at a ratio of ten to one. Every inhabitant of the three Western zones was also accorded an immediate grant of 40 *Deutsche Mark* and a further 20 the following month. This reform, like the inflation of 1923, deprived the middle class of well-nigh all its savings while sparing the owners of stocks and real assets. It therefore failed to bring about the redistribution of wealth which many German politicians had hoped to see. On the other hand, the empty shops filled up overnight with previously horded goods and a wave of consumer demand, pent up for years, began to unfurl.

The Bank Deutscher Länder was founded to issue and manage the new currency. It was later renamed the Deutsche Bundesbank. After a few initial difficulties caused by rapidly rising prices, a balance was achieved quite swiftly between supply and demand. Government controls on the economy were therefore no longer essential, and Ludwig Erhard, the energetic new director of the economic administration, set out to cut away the tight economic regulations in accordance with his belief in the social market economy. The economic council approved the 'Post Currency Reform Economic Guidelines Bill' despite SPD opposition, and Erhard eliminated the entire system of rationing and controls, freed prices and liberalised the market, thereby maximising economic opportunity. Erhard was convinced that the resulting 'competition among producers for the favour of the consumer' would engender an economic order able to 'provide the greatest possible economic benefit and social justice for everyone'.[26] Full employment would be ensured, monopolies would be controlled to provide equality of opportunity, and the economic growth which Germany so urgently needed would be strongly encouraged. Erhard planned to maximise social justice, social progress and social security by increasing the gross national product on the one hand and, on the other, by taking state measures to correct strong inequities in the distribution of wealth and income. The Allies endorsed Erhard's plan to overcome the inequitable distribution of property through a scheme to share the burdens of the lost war.

The Soviet Union denounced the efforts of the Western powers to restore the economic unity of Germany as an infringment on the Potsdam Agreement and in her own zone she replaced the *Reichsmark* with an eastern *Deutsche Mark*. However, supply and demand were badly out of balance in eastern Germany because of the numerous factories being dismantled and the heavy reparations which the Russians were exacting on current production. As a result, the eastern mark rapidly lost value in comparison to its western rival. Which of the two new currencies would circulate in Berlin was totally unclear. The Western powers at first wished to allow both currencies, but the Soviet Union insisted that the eastern mark should be the only legal tender in all four sectors. The Allied Control Council had ceased to exist as a forum for negotiations, and the currency boundaries slowly hardened into firm political borders, reinforced by the far-reaching consequences of the London Agreement which drew Germany into the Atlantic Alliance.

Stalin resolved to drive the Western Allies out of Berlin, which lay in the middle of the Russian zone, and to take over the former capital in its entirety. On 20 June 1948 he blocked all land and water routes to the Western sectors of the city and halted all energy deliveries. But the Western powers refused to abandon their right to joint occupation of Berlin, as guaranteed by the Potsdam Agreement, and instituted an airlift in order to prevent the Soviets from starving the city into submission. Sufficient food and fuel were flown in to maintain over 2 million people till the blockade was finally lifted almost a year later on 4 May 1949. The action of the Western Allies was fully supported by Berliners, who refused to knuckle under to Russian pressure and willingly endured much hardship for the sake of freedom. Their fortitude, lent eloquent expression by the West Berlin mayor, Ernst Reuter, was not without strong emotional appeal in the international media. Yesterday's enemy became the ally of today, whose contribution to the struggle against Stalinist tyranny was greatly admired and who had to be defended if the Russian advance was to be stopped. The struggle for the freedom of West Berlin and the war in Korea provided the psychological foundations on which the new West German state was erected.

Before the Moscow conference in the spring of 1947, the United states had been content to postpone any final decision on Germany's future. Thereafter Washington decided to encourage the development of a separate western state in the context of its containment policy and was galvanised into action by the Berlin Blockade. Discarding all thought of a neutral, fully reunited Germany, the Americans aimed above all to deprive Stalin of the industrial potential of western Germany even if this meant the loss of the Soviet zone. In building up a separate western state, the Americans were anxious to secure the cooperation of German politicians, lest it appear that the new country was the product of another Western 'Diktat'. Still, most Germans viewed the rapid evolution of a western state with alarm. A majority of German politicians had welcomed the reform of the economic council and its associated institutions as a step towards relieving the depressed living conditions, but they shied away from all further measures tending to consolidate the division of their country.

On 1 July 1948 the three military governors called a meeting in Frankfurt. Here they handed over to the eleven provincial prime ministers proposals regarding the formation of a West German state and its relationship to the Western powers. These three 'Frankfurt Documents' called upon the provincial prime ministers to convene a constituent assembly by 1 September 1948 at which they would frame a constitution, suggest a restructuring of the *Länder* which had emerged after 1945 and agree on a German position towards a new Occupation Statute still to be drawn up by the military governors.

The Frankfurt Documents confronted the prime ministers with the thorny question of how to cooperate in the reorganisation of western Germany while avoiding any impression that they were creating a separate West German state which would likely encourage the Soviets to follow suit in the east. The first conference, to which the leaders of the various political parties were also invited, produced the so-called Koblenz Resolutions of 10 June 1948. In these resolutions the German politicians refused to convene a national assembly; however, they agreed to form a 'Parliamentary Council' which would draw up not a full-fledged constitution but a 'Basic Law' (*Grundgesetz*) to ensure uniform administration of the Western zones. When the Western powers insisted on a directly-elected national assembly and a constitution to be passed by this assembly and ratified by a popular referendum, the provincial prime ministers objected that both these objectives could only be achieved when full national sovereignty and freedom had been restored to all of Germany. A constitution on which only western Germans would be allowed to vote could not be considered a final constitution. At bottom, the German politicians did not wish to create a western entity with all the accoutrements of a full-fledged state.

The Germans were finally persuaded to seek a compromise with the military governors by Ernst Reuter's argument that the division of Germany was already a *fait accompli* and would not be interpreted as the outcome of anything which they did. After difficult negotiations with the military governors, a compromise solution was hammered out which emphasised the temporary nature of the emerging West German state. A Parliamentary Council was convened on 1 September 1948, but its members were elected by the *Landtage* and its decisions were ratified by the *Landtage* rather than by the people. 'The law which gave the political life of West Germany a legal framework based on individual human rights— during the transitional period till the unity of Germany was restored—was known simply as the 'Basic Law of the Federal Republic of Germany'.[27]

At the insistence of Bavaria, a constitutional convention assembled in Herrenchiemsee between 10 and 25 August 1948 in order to draft the Basic Law. On 1 September 1948 the Parliamentary Council was constituted in Bonn, consisting of sixty-five deputies elected by the *Landtage* and five representatives from West Berlin not entitled to vote. When the Council finished its work on 8 May 1949, four years after unconditional surrender, western Germany at least could look forward to the prospect of soon returning to the family of nations as an equal partner.

Reflecting the relative strength of the various political parties in the provincial parliaments twenty-seven of the sixty-five voting members of the Council were members of the CDU/CSU, a further twenty-seven members belonged to the SPD, five to the FDP and two each to the KPD, the German Party and the Centre. As its president the Parliamentary Council elected Konrad Adenauer, the former CDU leader in the provincial parliament of Nordrhein-Westfalen. His substitutes on the presidium were the Social Democrat Adolph Schönfelder and the Free Democrat Hermann Schäfer. Opinions were divided over the fundamental political philosophy on which the second German democracy be based. The classic liberal view, represented above all by Carlo Schmid, saw the essence of democracy in the separation of society and the state, the division of powers and a strong guarantee of human rights. The CDU, on the other hand, championed the view derived from natural law that the authority of the state resides in the people, which possesses unlimited authority within the bounds of ethics and natural law. The state is bound to respect the primacy of the people in its dealings with individuals and society as a whole. Despite these theoretical differences, the deputies were in fundamental agreement on the main issues and were able to arrive at mutually satisfactory solutions to practical problems. The constitution of the new political entity was rooted in the human rights essential to individual dignity and self-respect. The fundamental rights enunciated in the Basic Law did not need to be embodied in further legislation, as under the Weimar Constitution, but were directly applicable rights which the state and all its arms must observe. The Basic Law, it was emphasised, was a provisional measure intended to 'lend a new order to political life over a transitional period' until 'the entire German nation' could 'achieve liberty and unity through free self-determination'.[28]

The official name 'Deutsches Reich' was replaced in the West by 'Bundesrepublik Deutschland', in an allusion both to her federal political system and democratic, republican ideals. The federal system was desired by the occupying powers and supported by all members of the Parliamentary Council. However, differences of opinion arose over the exact distribution of powers to the federal and provincial governments. The SPD and FDP warned against exaggerated decentralisation and the dangers to national unity posed by particularist ambitions. The CDU/CSU on the other hand was prepared to give the *Länder* equality of status with the federal government. The military governors feared excessive centralism and the resulting disputes with them could not be resolved until April 1949.

When the Parliamentary Council finally completed its deliberations on 8 May 1949, the new state which emerged was a parliamentary democracy based on the rule of law. The government is fully responsible to the representatives of the people. The power to legislate is subject to the Basic Law, and the judiciary and the executive are bound by the legal system. The federal political structure accords the *Länder* the right to participate in the legislative and executive functions of the federal government and confers upon them sovereignty over certain realms such as education, church–state relations and internal administration.

The most important federal institution is the *Bundestag*. The deputies are chosen every four years through universal, equal and direct elections. As the embodiment of the nation's will, the *Bundestag* passes legislation, selects the chancellor and watches the government. Alongside the *Bundestag* is the *Bundesrat*, or Federal Council. It comprises representatives of the various provinces, the number of whom varies from three to five, depending on the total population of the province they represent. The *Bundesrat* may initiate legislation and has the right of objection to laws passed by the *Bundestag*.

The head of state is the *Bundespräsident*, or federal president. He represents the federal government internationally, concludes treaties with foreign powers, nominates candidates for the post of chancellor and appoints them if they are elected by the *Bundestag*. The federal president also has the power to appoint cabinet ministers, federal judges, senior civil servants and officers of the armed forces. He signs and promulgates federal laws. However, his instructions and commands are only valid when countersigned by the chancellor or the appropriate minister. In the Weimar Republic, the *Reichspräsident* was directly elected by the people and was thereby endowed with highest authority and legitimacy; in the *Bundesrepublik* on the other hand, the powers of the president are severely curtailed. Deprived of the authority granted to his predecessors by article 48 of the Weimar Constitution, the president cannot evolve into another *ersatz* emperor. He is elected for five years by the Federal Convention(*Bundesversammlung*), composed of *Bundestag* deputies and an equal number of deputies elected from the provincial parliaments.

The federal government includes the chancellor and his ministers. The greatest political authority is wielded by the chancellor, who is nominated by the president and elected by the *Bundestag*. He sets policy, suggests to the president which ministers should be appointed or dismissed, implements the laws passed by the *Bundestag* and is directly responsible to Parliament. He can only be dismissed from his post by a 'constructive vote of no-confidence', which requires a majority in the *Bundestag* to agree on a new chancellor at the same time that it dismisses the former chancellor. This provision is intended to prevent the kind of governmental paralysis which overtook the Weimar Republic in its final years. Besides discarding direct election of the president by the people, the Basic Law rejected such other features of the Weimar Constitution as referenda and plebiscites.

The Basic Law expressly ensures the independence of the judiciary and entrusts the administration of justice to autonomous judges subject only to the law. The constitutionality of laws is determined by the Federal Constitutional Court (*Bundesverfassungsgericht*), which is independent of all other institutions created by the Basic Law.

After the Basic Law was approved by the military governments on 12 May 1949, it was ratified by the *Landtage* and came into effect on 24 May. It is valid 'until the day a constitution is adopted which has been freely decided upon by the German people'.[29] Only then said Carlo Schmid, one of the fathers of the Basic Law, will 'the true constitution take shape as the work of all Germans, and nothing in this Basic Law will restrict the freedom of our people to design it as they see fit'.[31]

West Germans elected the first *Bundestag* on 14 August 1949. Shortly beforehand, the Soviet Union ended the Berlin crisis and urged a return to the previous four-power status, but offered no substantial concessions to the West at the Sixth Allied Foreign Ministers' Conference held in Paris between 23 May and 20 June. When Moscow proposed that an all-German Council of State be created, Marshall's successor as American secretary of state, Dean Acheson, responded that free elections must be held in the Eastern zone. With that he adopted a position which remained fundamental to all further East–West negotiations.

17

Germany after 1949

The German Question

The foundation of the Federal Republic provided the western

353

segment of Germany with the opportunity to manage its own
political, social, economic and cultural affairs. This did not mean
however that West Germans received full national sovereignty.
When the three Western powers approved the Basic Law, they
expressly reserved for themselves ultimate authority over foreign
affairs. Furthermore, the Occupation Statute, which was issued on
21 September 1949 in order to clarify and consolidate the Allied
position, accorded the Western powers the right to take over the
West German government at any time for security reasons or in
order to safeguard the democratic order. Moreover, the Western
powers had given their approval to the Basic Law, and it could not
be altered without their consent. Supreme authority continued to be
vested in the three Western powers and the civilian control agency,
the Allied High Commision, which they had formed.

The new German state saw as its immediate objectives the recovery of full national sovereignty and an end to the provisional nature
of the German state through reunification with the Soviet zone.
However, reunification could only be achieved in an international
context and was heavily influenced by the Cold War and the desire
of both East and West to reap maximum advantage from the
political reconstruction of Central Europe. The partition of Germany was sealed when the United States opted for a 'test of
strength'[1] with the Soviet Union, and Moscow realised that Germany could be neither Sovietised nor even neutralised and therefore
clung all the more tenaciously to the Eastern zone.

During the Berlin Blockade of 1948–9, the stage was set for
founding the German Democratic Republic, and a constitution was
drawn up. The new state was officially proclaimed on 7 October
1949 and thereafter two German states existed side by side.

Neither of these states had arisen primarily at the initiative of the
German people but rather at that of the occupying powers confronting one another in the Cold War. If they could not have all of
Germany, both sides wished to incorporate at least those areas
which they already occupied into their own sphere of influence in
order to enhance their own economic and military strength and
weaken their opponent. Each German state was firmly integrated
into its respective bloc, while the old questions of reparations and
denazification faded into the background. East and West alike were
anxious to gain maximum advantage in the Cold War by developing
the potential of their part of Germany—the human resources, raw
materials, industrial capacity and political weight— and by adding it
to their own bloc. Both German states soon became the most
obedient pupil and loyal ally of their respective superpower. In the

Federal Republic of Germany, no substantial Marxist or Communist party emerged to cast doubt on the pluralistic parliamentarism of the Western democracies; in the GDR opponents of the Stalinist regime were not allowed the slightest opportunity to voice their dissent. If the German states hoped to recover internal sovereignty, they had to demonstrate utter loyalty towards those who held ultimate power and could exercise it at any time. This premium on loyalty deprived Germans in both East and West of any real freedom of choice. While the Federal Republic became the front line of Western defence against the Soviet threat, the GDR cleaved as closely as possible to Soviet-style socialism and sought to outdo all other Soviet satellites in demonstrating her trustworthiness.

At first a certain parallelism existed in the structure of the two Germanies. Before the emergence of full-fledged states, provinces existed in both the Federal Republic and the GDR, and in both cases they provided the framework around which the new states were built. Although the provinces were officially recognised in the Constitution of the GDR, they were dissolved in 1952 as part of a sweeping reform and replaced by small administrative units known as *Bezirke* (districts). In West Germany, on the other hand, the federal structure originally introduced by the Western Allies continued to flourish. Prussia, the heart and soul of the old *kleindeutsches Reich*, had been disbanded at the Potsdam Conference, producing various remnants in both east and west which had no place in the traditional provincial structure. The Western occupation authorities therefore created new provinces, in some cases purely arbitrary and in others based on historical divisions. Though these provinces differed greatly in size, an overall balance was obtained, and the federal structure of West Germany was set on a solid foundation which has lasted to this day.

The federal structure of West Germany was established on roots going back to the Weimar Republic and the *Kaiserreich* and was intended by the German statesman and the Western Allies alike to form the basis of a future all-German state. However, this united Germany has yet to be established. The Soviet occupation authorities imposed on eastern Germany a legal and political order embodying their own ideology which frustrated the development of a democratic consensus in all parts of the country. Furthermore, Berlin has remained under the authority of the Allies ever since the war.

In the Federal Republic of Germany, the power of the central government is offset by the federal political system, the reduced authority which the Basic Law accords the *Bundespräsident*, the government's dependence on a majority in the *Bundestag* and the ability of the opposition to oversee government affairs. The electoral system has preserved this second German democracy from the myriad of fringe parties which were one of the chief reasons for the downfall of the Weimar Republic.

In contrast to the Weimar Constitution, which did not even mention political parties, the Basic Law of the Federal Republic expressly accords political parties the right to participate in the development of popular will.[2] At the same time, the authors of the Constitution required the parties to respect the basic democratic order and left it to the federal government to determine the manner in which elections would be carried out. The electoral system which was established is a mixture of first-past-the-post constituency voting and national representation by party lists. Some deputies are elected by lists while others are directly elected in their constituency. Only parties which poll more than 5 per cent of the nation-wide vote are allowed representation in the *Bundestag*. Citizens tended to concentrate their votes as a result, and eventually a three-party system emerged, ensuring a salutary degree of continuity. As the largest parties, the CDU/CSU and the SPD formed either the government or the opposition while the smaller third party, the FDP, usually acted as a coalition partner, moderating the policies of the larger parties.

The political system in the Federal Republic of Germany is stabilised, without being immobilised, by federalism; by the 5 per cent barrier for admission to the *Bundestag;* by the limitations on the authority of the *Bundespräsident;* by the ability of the chancellor to determine government policy; by the need for a constructive vote of non-confidence; and by the American-style Federal Constitutional Court (*Bundesverfassungsgericht*), which ensures the conformity of legislation with the Basic Law and protects the fundamental rights of the citizen. This political system offers a broad scope for democratic decision-making while the division of powers among the various organs and levels of government permits a balanced exercise of authority and reconciles centralism with regional differences.

The Adenauer Era

The first free elections to the German *Bundestag* were held on 14 August 1949. Since Parliament had yet to adopt the 5 per cent barrier to admission, eight parties gained representation. The

CDU/CSU polled most votes and formed a coalition government with the other parties to the right of the Social Democrats who became the Opposition. The Federal Convention (*Bundesversammlung*) convened on 12 September 1949 and in the second round elected Theodor Heuss, the chairman of the FDP, as the first *Bundespräsident*. His upright, liberal outlook and political prestige manifested the desire of the Federal Republic to implant herself firmly in the tradition of Germany's humanistic culture.

Three days later Konrad Adenauer of the CDU was elected the first chancellor of the Second German Republic by a plurality of a single vote. On 20 September 1949 Adenauer announced his desire to employ the 'relative freedom of the new state' in order to improve living conditions and to win back 'in cooperation with the Allied High Commision' Germany's right to freely determine her own foreign policy. To this end, Adenauer vigorously pursued a policy of European integration and sought 'to forge friendly relations including good personal relations with all nations but most especially with our neighbours: the Benelux countries, France, Italy, Britain and the Nordic countries'.[3] Adenauer took scarcely any notice of Germany's eastern neighbours but was most eager to lay to rest the historical feud between Germany and France. The German people largely adopted a sceptical, waiting attitude towards politics, concerning themselves primarily with the improvement of their immediate living conditions. The Marshall Plan and the currency reform relieved the worst of the suffering, though most cities still lay in ruin and industry was crippled. The misery was aggravated by high unemployment and appreciable inflation since the currency reform. The Korean War caused the price of raw materials to soar, increasing the deficit in the West German balance of payments and hampering industry which needed strong profits to finance reconstruction.

Ludwig Erhard, supported by Adenauer and the government parties, clung none the less to the social market economy and the course he had laid out. His stand was soon borne out by the economic upswing of 1951. What would later be termed the 'German economic miracle' began to take hold, though it was equally a miracle of hard work in which employers and employees joined hands to overcome the devastation of the war. In spite of the bombing, dismantlement and reparations, the basis of production in the various industrial sectors had been saved and Germany could adapt to the new technological standards. Modern equipment was acquired and production was rationalised even further. An enormous pent-up demand existed for consumer goods, and foreign orders were rising. Maximum production, strong sales and full employment seemed guaranteed for years to come. Soon West Germany not only paid off her foreign debts but became a creditor nation herself with one of the strongest, most stable currencies in Europe. The demand for labour grew so intense that it could only be satisfied by importing foreign workers.

This stunning economic success greatly facilitated political consolidation and development of the socially-responsive federal government envisaged by the authors of the Constitution.[4] Taking up a tradition honoured by the *Kaiserreich*, the Weimar Republic and, indeed, by the Nazis, the new German government introduced state social insurance. Even though most government assets had been wiped out by the war, health insurance, accident insurance, pension plan insurance, miners' insurance and unemployment insurance were all re-established. People who had been maimed or injured in the war and dependents of those who had been killed were given pensions, free medical treatment and secure employment. Those who had been held as prisoners-of-war were compensated. A particularly difficult problem was posed by the people who had fled their homes in the East or been expelled. Property which had survived the war intact was hit with a heavy one-time tax in order to help equalise the losses. This attempt to share the burden and ease the integration of the refugees into West Germany was an unparalleled initiative. By virtue of this measure, the state was able to offer those who had lost everything they owned in the war loans, low-interest payments and assistance in reconstructing their businesses. By the same token, people who had been persecuted by the Nazis for political, religious or racial reasons were also compensated.

Thanks to these initiatives plus rapid economic growth, the poorer elements in the population gradually overcame the worst of their penury, and the middle classes laid the foundations for the prosperity of the 1960s. However, great disparities in income remained and the basic structure of industry was little changed. The organised labour movement concentrated its demands on wealth redistribution and worker participation (*Mitbestimmung*) in the management of factories. In contrast to the Weimar Republic, employees were represented by only sixteen non-competing unions divided according to the industrial sector they represented. The unions' demands were taken up by the federal government and were partially achieved in cooperation with the opposition and the Confederation of German Trade Union (*Deutscher Gewerkschaftsbund*). Workers participation was introduced into the mining and iron and steel sectors, where firms of more than 1000 employees were required to ensure equal representation for management and employees on the supervisory council (*Aufsichtsrat*). The rest of West German industry has been governed since 1952 by the Works Constitution Act (*Betriebsverfassungsgesetz*), which requires all companies with at least five employees to create a works council with co-determination rights in regard to social-welfare issues and to the allotment of work and vacation time. Joint-stock companies are required to assign one-third of the seats on their supervisory councils to employee representatives. Autonomous collective bargaining, eliminated by the Third *Reich*, was again restored. This allows employers and employees to agree on wages and salaries free of state interference. The various unions bargain with the employer organisations through collective agreement commissions (*Tarif-kommissionen*). As a result of a pension reform adopted by the Adenauer government, pensions are automatically adjusted to reflect the wages negotiated by the collective agreement commissions.

One of the most difficult problems confronting the new state was the severe housing shortage in the wake of the war. In the bombed-out cities, people were often packed together in the most difficult of conditions. By 1950 approximately one-half of all West German families still sublet their dwellings. The state obviously had to intervene for the Federal Republic to claim that she truely adhered to a 'socially responsible market economy'. The first Housing Construction Act provided for the building of almost 2 million socially assisted apartments beginning in 1950. A second Housing Construction Act was passed in 1956 to continue the previous programme and to stimulate the construction of single-family housing as well.

The accumulation of savings was encouraged by offering premiums and later, when the reconstruction and consolidation phase had passed, by offering shares in privatised government property. This facilitated the accumulation of capital in private hands. Though the tension between capital and labour was not entirely eliminated by these measures, the Federal Republic's social welfare legislation and state subsidies safeguarded the social peace and won recognition for employees as equal partners in the development of the German economy.

The public gave Adenauer and the CDU much of the credit for West Germany's rapid economic recovery, her solid socio-political structure and the disciplined, democratic way in which competing interests had been reconciled. In contrast to the Weimar Republic, political parties remained mindful of their obligation to the nation as a whole. When elections were held to the second German

Bundestag in September 1953, 85.8 per cent of eligible voters cast a ballot, giving the CDU/CSU 45.2 per cent of the total. This was taken by the government as a demonstration of confidence and a strong mandate to continue both its internal policies and its foreign policy of Western integration.

Adenauer took his first steps in the latter direction only a few weeks after forming his first government, when he led the Federal Republic into the European Economic Council as a full-fledged member. In exchange for a promise to join the International Ruhr Authority and the Council of Europe, the High Commission allowed the German government to open consulates in foreign countries. Kurt Schumacher, the leader of the Opposition, warned that this step meant the abandonment of the Ruhr to foreign interests, and he opposed German entry into the Council of Europe as an associate member because the Saarland was accorded similar status. But Adenauer stuck to his policy of German concessions and tried to rally the West German and European public to his views. 'In the Europe of today', he said in early November 1949, 'ancestral enmities are fully outdated. I am therefore determined to make Franco-German relations the keystone of my policies. A *Bundeskanzler* must be both a good German and a good European.'[5]

Adenauer hoped to resolve the tensions over the Ruhr and the Saarland through European integration[6] and in fact achieved his first concrete success in this regard when Germany entered the Coal and Steel Community initiated by Robert Schuman. The Ruhr Statute was discarded and all Allied controls and limitations on Germany's heavy industry were lifted. The Federal Republic became an equal member in the European Coal and Steel Community alongside Belgium, France, Italy, Luxembourg and the Netherlands and by participating in this international organisation created the basis for a new relationship with France.

East–West tensions sharpened even more in the summer of 1950 as a result of the outbreak of the Korean War. The Western powers feared that a similar situation might arise in Germany and secured a promise from Adenauer to provide West German soldiers if a projected international European army was formed. Adenauer assured the Western powers of a German participation without holding any discussions inside the government or with the Opposition parties. He did not wish to forge a new German army but rather to raise 'forces . . . to be placed at the disposal of the entire democratic West. In this way he hoped to encourage the Western powers to drop their opposition to full national sovereignty for the Federal Republic, to guarantee West German security in the face of a rapidly rearming Soviet Union and to take the first steps towards a West European federation.'[7] Adenauer believed that by producing convincing evidence that West Germany could not be neutralised, he could compel the Soviet Union to alter her policies, thereby improving the chances of reunification. In this, he exemplified the idea that one should always seek to negotiate with the Russians from a 'position of strength'.

The opponents of this policy doubted that German unity could be restored through rearmament and decried a European defence community in which 'German legionnaires'[8] would be used to bolster the armies of the other European nations. Schumacher in particular considered measures such as this to be totally ineffectual in the event of a Soviet attack on Western Europe. He argued in a speech before the *Bundestag* on 19 March 1953:

A few German divisions in their midst would change nothing; an attack could only be deterred by the technical superiority of the Anglo-Saxon countries. The Social Democrats would only accept a German contribution to common defence if concrete military and political steps were taken indicating a clear desire in other nations for international solidarity with Germany.[9]

However, Parliament was unmoved both by this line of reasoning and the vehement protests of a majority of West German citizens, including many disillusioned former soldiers who opposed any further military operations (though they were often unfairly maligned on this score inside Germany and without). A majority in the *Bundestag* voted in favour of a European Defence Community, though the plan later fell through—not because of the strong German resistance but because of deep-rooted nationalism elsewhere in Europe, for instance in the French National Assembly, which firmly rebuffed a European army in August 1954.

While discussions were still underway about a European Defence Community and pursuant modifications to the relationship between the Federal Republic and the occupying powers, the Soviet Union addressed a note to the Western Allies on 10 March 1952 proposing 'immediate negotiations in regard to a peace treaty with Germany'. The treaty would be 'drawn up with the direct participation of Germany represented by an all-German government' and consideration would be given to ways in which 'an all-German government embodying the will of the German people can be formed with the least possible delay'.[10] Besides the peace treaty, Moscow included a number of proposals related to the restoration of German unity; the withdrawal of the occupying forces; guarantees of all democratic rights; the elimination of economic restrictions; permission to create an army, navy and air force for national self-defence; and a German commitment 'not to enter any coalition or alliance directed against any state whose military forces participated in the war against Germany'.[11] The Western Allies, fully supported by the West German government, responded that these proposals could only be accepted if free, all-German elections were first held under international supervision. Moscow's refusal was interpreted by the Western powers as proof that the Soviet proposals were merely intended to disrupt developments in the West. Two years later the Soviets renewed their offer, but again the Western Allies did not take it seriously. Adenauer for his part was unwilling to risk all his laborious efforts to regain Western confidence by insisting on negotiations with the Soviet Union, especially as he too was convinced that the neutralisation of Germany would inevitably encourage Soviet expansionism in Central Europe. It is very doubtful that Adenauer thereby turned his back on a genuine opportunity for reunification. The Opposition, however, decried Adenauer's insistence on tying the Federal Republic to the West as deeply injurious to the cause of German unity.

After the collapse of the European Defence Community, the West sought to reorganise its military alliance along national lines and to expand it to include the Federal Republic of Germany. At four conferences held in Paris between 21 and 23 October 1954, the United States, Canada, Great Britain, France and the Benelux countries agreed to renew the Brussels Pact by admitting Italy and the Federal Republic into a new alliance known as the Western European Union. At the same time, it was decided to admit the Federal Republic into NATO. Relations between the Federal Republic and the three occupying powers were also revised. The occupation came to an official end, and the problem of the Saarland was resolved by Europeanising it, returning full democratic rights to the population and recognising their right freely to determine their own future. All the members of NATO also guaranteed the security of the Federal Republic and West Berlin, recognised the Bonn government as the sole legal German government and reaffirmed that reunification and a peace treaty with all of Germany were fundamental priorities. The Eastern bloc sharply protested West German entry into NATO and suggested that free, all-German elections could be held in 1955 if the Paris agreements were not ratified. If the agreements were ratified, however, the Eastern nations threatened to conclude a friendship and mutual assistance treaty of their own, which would include the GDR. This threat came to pass on 14 May 1955 when the Warsaw Pact was signed.

With the coming into force of the Paris treaties on 5 May 1955, the West German government attained the main objective it had been pursuing since 1949: full sovereignty and equality within the Western alliance. The high commissioners were replaced by ambassadors, and the occupation troops became allied armies.

Four months later, Adenauer accepted an invitation to visit the Soviet Union. He obtained the liberation of the remaining 10,000 prisoners of war and agreed with the Soviets to establish diplomatic relations, but failed totally to advance the cause of reunification. Moscow announced that German unity was henceforth a matter for Germans to determine—but not at the expense of the German Democratic Republic, which the Soviet Union had recognised as a sovereign state on 25 March 1954.

So the German question remained open. Whether it could possibly have been resolved was never seriously explored. Both superpowers made it clear that the largest nation in Central Europe, with her strong economic and industrial potential, could not become a simple, neutral onlooker in the East–West struggle like Finland or Austria. The exchange of notes between the Soviets and the Western occupying powers indicated as early as 1952 that they all were interested first and foremost in securing their own sphere of influence. In spite of verbal commitments to German reunification, the occupying powers were equally determined to hold on to their own share, if necessary at the cost of division.

The Soviet resolve not to allow the overthrow of the Socialist Unity Party or East Germany's departure from the socialist camp was clearly demonstrated on 17 June 1953, three months after Stalin's death. There was widespread public dissatisfaction in the GDR with a system whose conformity to Moscow's wishes was enforced by a privileged strata of opportunists and functionaries, and this discontent erupted into spontaneous riots. But when the danger to the government became serious, the Soviets did not hesitate to send in tanks to restore peace and reinforce the communist government. The reality of the Soviet sphere found expression in Nikita Khrushchev's two-state theory, which called upon both East and West to reconcile themselves to the existence of two German states. After the Federal Republic had recovered full sovereignty, the Soviet Union launched a diplomatic offensive aimed at ending the Cold War, but even this did nothing to alter the division of Germany. The Russians hoped to encourage détente 'in view of the mounting need for political quietude in Europe, their own heavy arms expenditures and the desirability of increased East–West trade'[12]—but only a détente predicated on the acceptance of division and the political status quo.

For many of the same reasons, the West was increasingly inclined to call a halt to the Cold War during the presidencies of Dwight D. Eisenhower and John F. Kennedy. As time passed, a kind of 'peaceful coexistence' developed between the superpowers and their client states. Both sides tacitly agreed to respect the other's sphere of influence, as could be seen in 1956 during the popular uprisings in Hungary and Poland and in 1962 during the highly dangerous Cuban missile crisis.

The Federal Republic of Germany officially rejected Khrushchev's two-state theory and continued to consider herself the sole legitimate successor to the 'Deutsches Reich'. As a free people among other free peoples, West Germans not only refused to recognise the totalitarian state in the East but held any recognition of the GDR by a third power to be an unfriendly act. This so-called Hallstein doctrine, named after the secretary of state in the foreign office, long made it possible to isolate the GDR from most of the world. This was doubtless an impressive demonstration of the political and economic clout which the Second German Republic had acquired, but the German question came no closer to resolution. The Hallstein Doctrine also failed to hold up the détente process which the leaders of the United States, Britain, France and the Soviet Union all wished to further at their summit conference in Geneva in July 1955. Both camps hoped to thin out the armed forces facing each other in Europe and to make progress towards general arms control. Khrushchev again proposed the neutralisation of Germany, but the three Western leaders again refused.

That West German policy was not likely to result in reunification was made abundantly clear in the autumn of 1956 when the Soviet Union brutally suppressed a popular uprising in Hungary, providing convincing evidence of her determination to go to any lengths to protect her sphere of influence. The moral and political benefit which accrued to the West was immediately squandered when France and Britain intervened militarily in Egypt against the advice of the United States. Moscow's prestige recovered in the Eastern bloc and the chances of German reunification dimmed further. The Polish foreign minister, Adam Rapacki, proposed that Europe be transformed into a nuclear-free zone, and Walter Ulbricht suggested a confederation between the GDR and the Federal Republic, but the West responded coolly to both proposals; Konrad Adenauer advanced a plan which amounted to the neutralisation of the GDR, but the Russians rejected it. The Achilles' heel of the Rapacki plan was that it did not contain any overall agreement on security, and the suggestion of a German confederation was rejected because it assumed the existence of two equal states and thereby contradicted the policy of both the Federal Republic and her allies. The foreign ministers' conference of May 1959 again addressed the question of a final German peace treaty but again the stalemate could not be broken. Moscow clung to its two-state theory and Ulbricht's proposals for a German confederation, and rebuffed the peace plan of the American secretary of state, Christian A. Herter, who attempted to combine the re-establishment of German unity with an agreement on European security and free elections to an all-German constituent assembly.

From its inception, the East German state suffered continual population losses. By 1961 almost 3 million people had 'voted with their feet' and fled to the West by way of Berlin. This pointed up the internal weakness of the Ulbricht regime and was seen in the West as proof of its lack of legitimacy. As the years passed the stream of refugees into West Berlin swelled into a flood, severely damaging the GDR both politically and economically. In August 1961 the East German authorities took steps to halt the hemorrhage by constructing a great wall which sealed off the border to West Berlin. This attempt to consolidate the Soviet sphere of influence in Eastern Europe was endorsed by the Warsaw Pact and officially justified as an attempt to thwart 'subversion' and facilitate 'surveillance'.

To the bitter disappointment of the German people, the Western powers tolerated the construction of the wall because it occurred within the Soviet sphere of interest and did not affect the rights of the occupying powers in West Berlin so long as free access was maintained. Berliners looked on in helpless rage as the wall went up and the Americans, British and French did nothing but issue a joint note of protest against this infringement on the Four Power status of the entire city. The despondency was little relieved when Washington dispatched General Clay to Berlin to tighten the security arrangements for the free part of the city. However, the Western powers did guarantee that they would defend their rights in Berlin, freedom of access and Berlin's economic ties to the Federal Republic—by force if necessary.

The building of the wall marked the end of all illusions about the arrangement at which the superpowers had arrived. The mutual spheres of interest were clearly demarcated, and Khruschev's brand of peaceful coexistence descended over Germany as well. On 27 October 1961 at the Twenty-Second Congress of the Communist Party of the Soviet Union, he announced that a peace treaty with

Germany had lost all urgency.[13] The German question had reached a stand-off. The Opposition urged the government to take action, and the government exhorted the Allies, but all to no avail. Though Adenauer and his successor, Ludwig Erhard, were not yet ready for such a step, the West German government would clearly have to reconsider its claim to be the sole legitimate representative of the German people. New paths would have to be broached if the impasse was to be circumvented and new movement generated.

Though Adenauer failed to solve the German question (and probably could not possibly have solved it in view of Soviet aspirations), he did restore foreign confidence in the Federal Republic. Adenauer's dependability, in place of the old nationalist impetuosity, did much to foster rapid European integration. He played a major part in inspiring and shaping the Treaties of Rome, signed on 25 March 1957 by Belgium, France, Italy, Luxembourg, the Netherlands and the Federal Republic of Germany. The treaty crowned negotiations about a European Economic Community (EEC) and EURATOM to organise European cooperation in atomic research and the peaceful uses of atomic energy. The EEC treaty laid the foundations for a common market and for the coordination of the members' economic policies. The treaty also called for a customs union to encourage free movement of labour and free trade in goods among the countries of the EEC and a common agricultural policy. This economic union soon proved so successful that more and more countries applied for admission. In 1962, membership or associate membership was sought by Greece, Turkey, Spain and Ireland and by all the countries which had joined together in 1959 to form the European Free Trade Association (EFTA), namely, Britain, Norway, Sweden, Finland, Austria, Switzerland and Portugal. Seventeen African nations and Madagascar became associate members in 1963, and Nigeria followed suit in 1966. That same year, a further twenty-six nations took up diplomatic relations with the EEC. The beginnings of the 'political union' envisaged by the Treaty of Rome were delayed until December 1974, when the heads of government and of state convened in the Council of Europe and agreed that henceforth the European Parliament should be selected by direct elections. The first of these elections took place in June 1979.

The most astounding accomplishment of Adenauer's chancellorship was the Franco-German rapprochement which he had sought from the outset. What no one in France or Germany would have considered possible in 1945 came to pass remarkably quickly. Both peoples were ready to abjure their historic enmity and seek reconciliation despite their painful memories, and both governments attached supreme importance to close cooperation with one another within a framework of European agreements. This served to further strengthen the bonds between the French and German peoples.

The consolidation of the Federal Republic's international standing in the wake of West European integration was reflected in the expansion of relations with non-European nations as well. In 1961 the Federal Republic maintained embassies in sixty-two countries, legations in seven countries, a trade representation office in one country, and diplomatic representation or observers at the UN, the Council of Europe, NATO, the OECD, the EEC and EURATOM. The Goethe Institute, the German Academic Exchange Service, the German Institute for Foreign Relations, Inter Nationes and German schools abroad established a German cultural presence around the world. Cultural agreements governing artistic and scientific exchanges were signed beginning in 1953, releasing the Federal Republic from the intellectual isolation into which Germany had fallen after the Nazi seizure of power in 1933.

The Federal Republic maintained close contacts with many countries of the Third World, assisted in their development, sought to win their moral support and fostered an appreciation of the Federal Republic's special difficulties as a result of the division of Germany. In 1966 the Federal Republic participated in almost 3000 projects in ninety-three different countries. At this time, the bulk of West German aid flowed to India, Pakistan, Turkey, Greece, Syria, Afghanistan, Egypt, Spain, Chile and Brazil. The German Foundation for Developing Countries (*Deutsche Stiftung für Entwicklungsländer*) and other similar organisations supported the exchange and education of experts, organised meetings of leaders, and helped to train German experts for their work on foreign-aid projects.

As the legal successor to the German *Reich*, the Federal Republic recognised her particular responsibility to the state of Israel. She announced her intention to make amends at least for the material damages which the Jews had suffered at the hands of the Nazis and negotiations were opened with Israel and representatives of twenty-three Jewish organisations outside Israel. On 10 September 1952 the Federal Republic agreed to pay Israel 3000 million marks over a period of from twelve to fourteen years. These funds were intended to facilitate the acquisition of merchandise, the establishment of settlements and the integration of Jewish refugees in Israel. Another 450 million marks were made available to Jewish organisations for the support of needy Jews who had been mistreated by the Nazis. Bonn was resigned to the fact that such German–Israeli cooperation would be bitterly opposed by Israel's Arab neighbours, most of whom broke off relations with the Federal Republic in May 1965 when Bonn and Jerusalem first exchanged ambassadors.

The Grand Coalition

Konrad Adenauer had guided West German policy during three and a half parliaments ever since 1949. But setbacks in the German question and the emergence of serious internal difficulties led to his sudden retirement in mid-session, and on 17 October 1963 Ludwig Erhard was elected chancellor over Adenauer's opposition. But the popular and highly successful former economics minister never succeeded in creeping out from under the shadow of his illustrious predecessor and failed to come up with bold new initiatives in either domestic policy or foreign policy. He was finally forced to resign on 1 December 1966 after he failed to cut government expenses in line with a general economic recession.

Following Erhard's departure, a number of initiatives were undertaken. Now that relations with the West were on a firm footing, Bonn sought increased contacts with Eastern Europe. The SPD entered the government for the first time since the war, bringing with it a number of fresh ideas. The SPD had renounced its original socialist aspirations when it adopted the Godesberg Programme on 15 November 1959 and resolved to convert itself 'from the party of the working class into the party of all the people'. According to the Godesberg Programme:

The party seeks to bend the forces unleashed by the industrial revolution and the rise of technology to the service of freedom and justice for all. The social forces generated by capitalism fail to accomplish this foremost mission of our times. . . . The old forces are incapable of countering the brutal Communist challenge with a plan for a superior new order of political and personal freedom, self-determination, economic security and social justice.[14]

Like Adenauer and Erhard, the SPD realised that a solution to the German question was out of reach and announced that henceforth security considerations should take precedence over national re-unification. The SPD recognized the inevitability of the political status quo in Europe and affirmed her support for the European and Atlantic alliances of which the Federal Republic was a member. The party's new economic and social programme also reflected a shift towards the governing parties. Free enterprise was commended as were individual initiative and private ownership of the means of production so long as they did not stymie the development of a just social order.

These changes in the Social Democratic programme not only broadened the party's electoral appeal but made it a potential coalition partner for the middle-class parties. By the end of the Erhard era, the conservative government felt compelled to broaden its base of popular support in view of the economic recession, the electoral successes of the right-wing National Democratic Party and the political storm fomented by the debate over emergency laws.

The new chancellor, Kurt Georg Kiesinger, declared in December 1966 in his statement of government policy that the CDU, CSU and SPD had decided 'to form a joint government on the federal level'. Kiesinger continued:

This is doubtless a landmark in the history of the Federal Republic, an event to which our people attach many hopes and fears. Our hope is that this Grand Coalition, holding an enormous majority far in excess of two-thirds of the Bundestag, will manage to solve the difficult problems which it confronts, in particular will control the public deficit, provide cost-effective administration and ensure the growth of our economy and the stability of our currency.[15]

Germans looked with high hopes on the new coalition in which the Social Democrat Willy Brand held the portfolios of vice-chancellor and foreign minister. Grown accustomed to years of 'economic miracle', the public expected above all that the recession would be swiftly overcome, full employment would be restored and social benefits would be continued and expanded. The government was determined to make good use of its large majority in order to overcome the budget deficit of 3300 million marks and set the economy on the road to recovery.

Representatives of the government, academia, labour and business began to discuss 'concerted action' in February 1967. They all supported the social market economy but felt that the state should make better use of its capacity to manage that economy. A Stabilisation Act passed by the *Bundestag* on 14 June 1967 sparked an economic upswing by reducing taxes and encouraging investment. The growth rate of the gross national product rose from -0.2 per cent in early 1967 to 7.3 per cent in 1968 and 12.1 per cent in 1969. Unemployment declined precipitously and as profits rose so did wages, far outstripping the rise in consumer prices in 1968. The Federal Republic entered another boom, which helped to finance a host of projects undertaken in the wake of a fiscal reform which allowed the federal government to play a larger role in provincial programmes. Universities and university hospitals were expanded or newly built and the economy of the regions was improved.

The introduction of a medium-range financial plan made it easier for the federal government to manage its fiscal affairs. In order to raise additional funds, value-added tax was increased from 10 to 11 per cent, and a 3 per cent surcharge was added to individual and corporate taxes. At the same time, the state revised its social policy and tailored payments to the income of the recipients. Hourly-rated workers received the same right as salaried employees to be paid for up to six weeks in cases of sickness. An employment promotion scheme maximised occupational opportunities and gave the handicapped a legal right to occupational assistance. Education subsidies for individuals were also greatly expanded. Lower- and middle-income people were given increased incentives to save and appreciable improvements were made in burden equalisation and pensions for prisoners of war and dependants of the war dead.

Meeting the social and economic challenges proved to be less of a problem to the new government than the thorny issue of emergency laws inherited from the Erhard government. In the German Treaty of 1955, the three Western powers had reserved for themselves certain prerogatives related 'to the protection of the security of armed forces stationed in the Federal Republic'. According to the terms of this treaty, these prerogatives 'which are temporarily retained, shall lapse when the appropriate German authorities have obtained similar powers under German legislation enabling them to take effective action to protect the security of those forces, including the ability to deal with a serious disturbance of public security and order'.[16] The Federal Republic had long wished to nullify these remaining Allied prerogatives by passing an appropriate German law, but such a step required an amendment to the Basic Law and therefore a two-thirds majority of the *Bundestag*. After years of fruitless attempts to surmount this hurdle, the Grand Coalition provided a golden opportunity to press ahead.

Memories of the unfortunate experiences of the Weimar Republic were still fresh, however, and the emergency law debate aroused heated argument not only in the *Bundestag* but among the public at large. Numerous drafts were proposed and rejected under storms of controversy until finally the seventeenth amendment to the Basic Law was adopted on 30 May 1968. It set forth the procedure to be followed in case of armed conflict, internal emergencies, severe tensions or catastrophes. The public reaction was so intense because the government would have the right to abridge individual liberties in all these cases. The 'New Left' in particular was extremely hostile to the new law, arguing that its real aim was to limit democracy and civil rights under the pretext of annulling old prerogatives of the Allied powers.

The protest against the emergency laws was all the more impassioned in that the late 1960s was generally a period of social unrest, discontent with the state, and rebellion against tradition and the democratic principles anchored in the Basic Law by the generation which had grown up in the consumer society of the 1950s and 1960s. Inspired by the civil rights movement in the United States and the revolt against the war in Vietnam, the student protest movement gathered momentum in Europe in the mid-1960s, building on widespread dissatisfaction with many values of the older generation. The level of protest in the Federal Republic escalated abruptly when the Grand Coalition reduced the parliamentary opposition to a feeble rump and doubts arose as to the survival of a genuine democratic order.

Not only the state came under impassioned attack but all traditional authorities, parents, teachers and professors. Demands for social change grew ever more vehement and finally erupted into open violence. The leaders of the student movement came largely from middle-class backgrounds and established their power base in the Socialist German Student Union (*Sozialistischer Deutscher Studentenbund*) and the Socialist University Union (*Sozialistischer Hochschulbund*). They fired up many rather work-shy but enthusiastic followers 'with radical socialist arguments for catering to their taste for luxury'.[17] The students vehemently denounced the exploitation of the working class, though they received very little support from this quarter. Undeterred, they embraced the pure theory of permanent revolution, the elimination of social classes and the end of exploitation. The student radicals were eager to accept the benefits of a fundamentally materialist, industrial society, but they refused 'to direct their energy and sense of commitment towards improving and humanising this society and its institutions'; instead they placed their faith in 'the cult of violence'.[18] The state and its institutions resisted the 'extra-parliamentary' opposition and firmly opposed all activities contrary to the Basic Law.

Besides the economic and social challenges, Chancellor Kiesinger announced that his government hoped to address foreign-policy concerns. He stressed that the Federal Republic intended to remain utterly faithful to the alliances, security arrangements and peaceful policies she had previously espoused but wished at the same time to broach new economic, cultural and political paths in her relations with the East. The Hallstein Doctrine was modified and foreign policy was made more compatible with the actual situation. Other countries were allowed to recognise without fear of retaliation the *de facto* existence of two German states, though the Federal Republic herself did not go so far to recognise the GDR as a sovereign country. This approach paved the way for the assumption of diplomatic relations with Romania, Yugoslavia and all other states which had maintained diplomatic relations with East Germany. The momentum towards further rapprochement with the East was arrested, however, in the summer of 1968, when Warsaw Pact troops invaded Czechoslovakia, setting an abrupt and brutal end to the 'Prague Spring' of government reform. In the doctrine named after him, Leonid Ilyich Brezhnev declared that the Soviet Union would not permit any threat to the vital interests of socialism or any encroachment on the socialist community and made it clear that there would be no compromise.

Bonn sought an agreement among non-nuclear states barring the spread of nuclear weapons as well as a treaty with the Soviet Union, the GDR and other eastern neighbours proscribing the use of force in settling disputes. Both initiatives were rejected, however, by Moscow and East Berlin, which insisted that the Federal Republic must recognise the GDR as a sovereign state in accordance with international law before any negotiations could begin. Bonn refused this condition and inter-German relations returned to their deep freeze.

The Internal Development of the German Democratic Republic

The construction of the Berlin Wall marked a turning-point in the internal evolution of the GDR. Until then, the Socialist Unity Party had bent all its efforts towards gaining and consolidating political power. Once the new social and economic system was solidly entrenched, the party turned its attention towards increasing its efficiency. Long before the founding of the GDR, the Socialist Unity Party backed by the Soviet Military Administration had liquidated all other political possibilities by uniting under its leadership the other parties and the mass organisations in the National Front of Democratic Germany (since 1973 the National Front of the German Democratic Republic).

The heart of the National Front is the Antifascist Democratic Bloc founded in 1945 (known since 1949 as simply the Democratic Bloc). It comprises the Socialist Unity Party of Germany, the Christian Democratic Union, the German Liberal Democratic

Party, the Democratic German Farmers' Party, the German National Democratic Party, the Federation of Free German Unions, the Free German Youth, the Democratic German Women's League and the German Cultural League (since 1974 the Cultural League of the GDR). All these groups have representatives in the People's Chamber (*Volkskammer*) elected according to unitary lists with fixed apportionment. They all profess loyalty to the socialist state, recognise the paramountcy of the SED (Socialist Unity Party) and are structured in accordance with 'democratic centralism'. This is justified ideologically by the claim that a socialist society requires united, well-planned leadership by the working class and the party which represents it. However, this unity of purpose also requires the suppression of deviant groups or political opposition. Democratic centralism implies decision-making from the top down, election to the leading organs of state from membership in lower organs, the answerability of the leading organs to the electoral bodies, collective leadership, strict discipline within both the party and the state, minority subservience to the majority, binding decisions and finally unitary action. This organisational principle, allegedly practiced in particularly exemplary fashion within the ranks of the SED itself, was extended to society as a whole in order to 'ensure that all organs of state, collectives and associations in factories or other establishments, in cities or communes, make an effective contribution toward the realisation of unified state policy'.[19]

While the CDU and the German Liberal Democratic Party sprouted spontaneously in 1945 from roots extending back to the Weimar Republic, the German Democratic Farmers' Party and the German National Democratic Party were founded in 1948 as affiliates of the SED in an attempt to split support for the middle-class parties. After an early struggle over the coordination of the CDU and the Liberal Democrats in 1945–6, none of these four parties has played an important or independent role in the GDR. Their official role is to win over recalcitrant strata of the population to communism and the policies of the SED. In a similar vein, the mass organisations are expected to organise various strata of the population 'for active, conscious participation in the fulfilment of state and social goals' and to assist in 'developing the socialist consciousness of the working people, encouraging a sense of civic responsibility and fostering a willingness to contribute'.[20]

The largest of the mass organisations, the Federation of Free German Unions with over 9 million members, is supposed to forge 'a link between the central state leadership of the economy and the broad masses of workers' and train its 'members to participate consciously in the struggle to draw up, achieve and over-achieve the plans'.[21] Indeed, the foremost task of the Free German Unions is to ensure that each factory fulfils the quota assigned to it by the state economic plan. For the rest, the Free German Unions are confined to job training, supervision of accident protection and the distribution of vacation spots. The Federation of Free German Unions is also responsible for the social insurance of white- and blue-collar workers and of pensioners. However, it is decidedly not an instrument for advancing the interests of working people. The GDR proclaims itself to be the 'workers' and farmers' state' and as such does not recognise any legitimate labour struggle or any need for such tools of that struggle as strikes.

Responsibility for other social functions is delegated to various organisations controlled by the SED: the Free German Youth with over 2 million members from age 14 to 25, the Democratic Women's League comprising 1.4 million members and the Cultural League of the GDR comprising a half million members with a particular interest in cultural life. The Society for Sport and Technique provides paramilitary training and conditioning under the aegis of the Ministry of National Defence and prepares youths for service in the People's Army. The second largest association of all is the Society for German–Soviet Friendship with over 5 million members.

The SED controls not only the other political parties and social organisations, but the entire political system. The more than 2 million members of the SED are organised into approximately 75,000 cells, primarily in factories but also in residential districts. They receive their directions from over 250 city and county organisations. Above the county level are fifteen district directorates (*Bezirksleitungen*) and above them the Central Committee, elected by the 'highest organ' of the SED according to party statutes. At the present time, this Central Committee comprises 156 full members and fifty-one 'candidates' including all leading party functionaries. The permanent arms of the Central Committee are the Secretariat and the Politburo, which meet once a week under the chairmanship of the secretary-general. Together they form the centre of real political power. The Secretariat is the party executive which manages the state and its personnel. The Politburo is responsible for ideological and political policy. It makes all important political and organisational decisions and important political appointments. The political, economic and social directives of this body govern all activities of the state.

Until the early 1960s, the SED attempted to maintain direct control over every aspect of life through the party apparatus. However, as modern society grew more and more complicated—economically, technically, scientifically and socially—the party discovered that it was often no longer able to issue detailed instructions on how all problems were to be handled. A new, highly educated élite replaced the old party apparatchiks who had proved extremely loyal but lacked technical expertise. Excessive centralism gave way to a complicated system of parallel bureaucracies and a certain amount of decentralisation. This appreciably enhanced the effectiveness of the political system, while overall party control was maintained by installing the same people in the Politburo of the SED and the leading state institutions. These included the Council of State, responsible for diplomatic representation of the GDR, the issuing of election writs and the supervision of courts, public prosecutors' offices and parliamentary bodies; and the Ministerial Council, responsible for government business including such normal functions as foreign affairs, external and internal security and the management of state finances. In addition, the Ministerial Council oversees the entire centrally planned and led economic and social system. Numerous associated ministries and offices help it to carry out its functions.

One of the most important organs of the Ministerial Council is the State Planning Commission, which assumes responsibility for planning, directing and overseeing the entire economy of the GDR. The 'socialist system of production' was said to have triumphed after agriculture was collectivised and the economy was stabilised by blocking all possible escape routes to the West. Thereafter an era of 'post-revolutionary consolidation' began. The SED sought to provide effective leadership in this phase by embracing the 'technical revolution' and modernising its methods through the use of cybernetics and systems theory, computers, information theory and socio-economic forecasting.

Management reforms and material incentives were introduced to enhance productivity. The government hoped to reinforce the economic upswing through technological innovation and concentrated investment in key sectors and the encouragement of science. By the 1970s, however, the state reduced its attempts to mobilise the 'productive forces of science' as advocated by Walter Ulbricht. Adopting a more realistic stance under Erich Honecker, the SED attempted to fulfil social demands for consumer goods and to ensure domestic tranquillity. Deprived of any other choice, the GDR adapted to the political situation in Europe and settled as comfortably as possible into the existing system.

The construction of the Berlin Wall provided a convincing demonstration that German reunification would not occur in the near future and that the people of the GDR would simply have to cope with the far harsher lot which fate had visited upon them than upon the inhabitants of West Germany. The bulk of East Germans never identified with the state, as the SED would have liked, but their economic achievements and the rise of the GDR to the status of second greatest industrial power in Eastern Europe began to inspire a certain self-satisfaction. Pride in what East Germans had accomplished under vastly more difficult circumstances than West Germans, material incentives offered by the state, and recognition and promotions for those who contributed to fulfilling the party plan all began to have an effect. Experts were allowed greater leeway *vis-à-vis* party functionaries, and this too fostered an interest in high performance and professional success. The citizen's place in society was increasingly determined by professional competencies and not just political reliability. The opportunities for an East German to rise socially and enter the élite on the basis of qualifications and job performance broadened the social and political spectrum in the GDR while requisite professions of ideological faith dwindled towards a meaningless ritual.

The bulk of the population of the GDR is divided along professional and social lines—the intelligentsia in various fields, the workers, the collective farmers, the service professions and some people who are still active in the private economy. They take their direction from the political élites just under the Central Committee, the leading cadres and specialists, though they too are not entitled to take much initiative. Instead, all are expected to contribute to the 'highly developed socialist society' planned by the SED leadership. The central authorities determine in authoritarian fashion the sort of society this will be: the development of the forces of production; the organisation of the economy and professional opportunities; improvements in working conditions, living standards and social services; home construction; and the development of education, culture, health, sport and recreation. In case of conflict, protecting the political power of the SED leadership always takes precedence over the interests of the people.[22]

The population as a whole feels aloof from the government and is divided in its political views. It responds to the incessant regimentation and pressure to perform well in school and on the job with pragmatism and sly opportunism. 'The frailties of the system and its economic shortcomings, the influence of Western media, heightened demand for individual self-fulfilment but limited scope continually generate cynicism and resignation, political apathy and withdrawal into private life.'[23] Constant surveillance by the State Security Service and the rough treatment accorded political dissidents provoke anger and highlight the tensions in East German society. The family and to a certain extent the church provide a refuge from tightly controlled public life and the constant barrage of propaganda. They therefore assume extreme importance in the daily lives of the people.

During the consolidation phase beginning in the early 1960s, the SED largely refrained from the state terrorism of the 1950s and even loosened the reins of government at times. But it never allowed any doubts about its claim to absolute power. This attitude is manifested in the SED's unwillingness to submit to the rule of law and a division of powers as well as in its official ideology of collectivism and the 'socialisation of man'. This ideology allows the state to lock the individual into the system while socialising the means of production and planning the economy. The basic rights in the Constitution of the GDR are limited essentially to the right to participate in the system and thereby strengthen it. The political prerogatives of the citizenry are confined to the election of representatives by non-secret ballot to the lowest level of government. The plan for socialist reconstruction views workers, peasants and the middle classes not as the driving force but rather as the objects of a revolution carried out from above. All they are expected to contribute is political loyalty and mounting productivity.

The campaign to institute socialism and cement the ties to the Soviet Union and the 'socialist community of states' left little room for a flexible approach to the German problem. To be sure, the Constitution of 7 October 1949 was largely inspired by the Weimar Constitution, was still all-German in its fundamental assumptions and described all Germany as a 'unified tariff and commercial area surrounded by common tariff barriers'.[24] However, the GDR— like the Federal Republic—always assumed that it had laid the foundations on which the all-German state would be built. For this reason, the emergence of two German states was inevitable, and the GDR gradually abandoned her all-German pretensions in order to concentrate on building up a separate state.

As the contradiction between fact and theory grew more and more apparent, the GDR altered the Constitution in 1968 and openly proclaimed that she was the 'socialist state of the German nation' representing 'the political organisation of workers and peasants who are jointly engaged in implementing socialism under the leadership of the working class and its Marxist-Leninist party'.[25] While limiting the applicability of the Constitution to the GDR itself, the SED added that 'the German Democratic Republic and its citizens seek to overcome the division of Germany imposed on the German nation by the forces of imperialism. They seek gradual rapprochement between the two German states until their final reunification on the basis of democracy and socialism'.[26] However, the policy of ideological demarcation was increasingly emphasised in the ensuing years, and all mention of an enduring German nation to which both the GDR and the Federal Republic belonged was finally struck from the Constitution on 7 October 1974. According to the preamble of this revised version of the 1968 Constitution, the people of the GDR had exercised their right to national self-determination and had 'allied themselves eternally and irrevocably with the Union of Soviet Socialist Republics'. This 'close and fraternal alliance' was said to 'ensure further progress along the path of peace and socialism for the people of the German Democratic Republic' and the GDR was hailed as an 'integral part of the community of socialist states'.[27] Loyalty to this community henceforth supplanted in the official view loyalty to the all-German nation. Bonn may have continued to view the border with the GDR as an inner-German line marking the junction of the rump states making up the legal entity of Germany, but East Berlin considered it a normal international frontier separating two sovereign countries.

The Federal Republic after 1969

Early in 1969 the constellation of world powers began to shift, lending new impetus to internal politics in the Federal Republic. The United States finally freed herself from the quagmire of South-East Asia and began to seek 'a world balance of power among the three superpowers'[28] of the United States, the Soviet Union and China in a policy somewhat reminiscent of the European balance of power in the nineteenth century. Beginning with the Korean War and increasingly during the war in Vietnam, Washington had viewed China as a major threat and the development of friendlier relations with Peking necessarily affected the foreign policy of the Soviet Union. Under Brezhnev, the Kremlin altered its response to the American and West European offers of accommodation and in a declaration of Warsaw Pact states in March 1969 once again suggested a 'European security conference'. Though Moscow was still intent on excluding the United States from such a conference, it was favourably received by some segments of West European opinion, especially in the Federal Republic. The SPD and FDP announced their readiness to negotiate with the Soviets with a view to normalising Bonn's relations with the states of Eastern Europe and the GDR, which both these political parties now recognised as a sovereign state.

The CDU/CSU was willing to seek improved relations with Eastern Europe but limited its margin of manoeuvre by refusing to abjure the Federal Republic's claim to be the sole legitimate representative of the German people. This deprived the partners in the Grand Coalition of the fundamental accord they needed in order to develop an adequate foreign policy in the changed political climate of the times. Meanwhile, the FDP had altered its nationalist and moderately conservative policies in favour of a slight shift to the left, creating a new political situation. The Kiesinger government had succeeded in revamping social and economic policies and appreciably strengthening the economy while holding wages and prices stable; but it had failed to respond to the social demands of broad strata of the population. The SPD and the labour unions insisted ever more impatiently on extending co-determination rights in factories and on reforming social and cultural policies. Moreover, the lack of an effective parliamentary opposition under the Grand Coalition generated mounting social resistance to the entire political system. The stability of German democracy was threatened as the intellectual ambience grew ever more strident and intolerant. As the rifts deepened and society polarised, the Kiesinger–Brandt coalition was increasingly seen as a transitional government which would inevitably be replaced by a new political force.

Since the parties had originally agreed that the Grand Coalition would not be continued once its mandate had run out, the elections of September 1969 were awaited with great anticipation. Both large parties were convinced that they would win. The SPD was all the more confident because the FDP had agreed to cooperate with it during the election campaign and thereafter and had also helped in March 1969 to elect the SPD candidate for *Bundespräsident*, Gustav Heinemann. Heinemann had been a member of the Confessional Church during the Hitler years and had quit the CDU government in 1950 in protest against Adenauer's plans for rearmament.

The SPD–FDP coalition did win the election by a slim majority of twelve seats. The Social Democrat Willy Brandt became the new chancellor while the Free Democrat Walter Scheel became vice-chancellor and foreign minister. Many West Germans had looked upon the formation of the Grand Coalition with high hopes and now they expected even more domestic and foreign policy reforms from the new left-of-centre alliance. The government and its supporters proclaimed their intention to renew the Federal Republic through a policy of reform in continuity, inspiring young people in particular to eagerly anticipate the domestic reforms. The new government's policy of rapprochement with the East was also widely hailed, especially since this approach seemed to hold out the promise not only of a relaxation of tensions with the GDR but of East–West détente on a world-wide scale.

After the extra-parliamentarian opposition had largely spent its revolutionary force, pounding in vain against the firm foundations of West German democracy, the governing parties sought to moderate the internal climate and win over the restless youth by announcing an amnesty in May 1970. At the same time, the voting age was reduced from 21 to 18 and the age to stand for election from 25 to 21 in an effort to encourage a sense of participation among the youth—as well as gain new supporters for the governing parties. In addition, the government sought to increase its influence within the newly established citizen initiative groups (*Bürgerinitiativen*) which had sprung up in response to the public desire for increased political involvement. Politicians attempted to demonstrate their closeness to the average citizen, became leaders of some citizen initiative groups and hoped in this way to maintain control over a movement whose political influence was clearly mounting. Over a decade later, it finally entered Parliament in the guise of the Green Party.

The declared intent of the 'Small Coalition' to extend democracy was also apparent in its social legislation. The Works Constitution Acts (*Betriebsverfassungsgesetze*) passed in November 1971 extended the rights of the works council in social welfare, economic and personnel matters. It strengthened the position of individual workers by increasing their right to be informed and consulted about company affairs. However, union demands for increased representation on the supervisory councils were not satisfied.

In 1973 a federal–provincial commission presented an education report intended to promote equality of opportunity and to provide the individual with the greatest possible latitude to develop his talents regardless of social or regional background. A more complete array of educational opportunities was suggested in order to encourage all kinds of talent and to nurture their development. In addition, general and vocational education were placed on a more equal footing. The planned reforms stretched from the elementary level to primary school, secondary school, the universities and even adult education. As a result, primary schools, technical colleges, universities and technical universities were expanded or newly constructed at a huge cost in terms of personnel and equipment. Another reform was undertaken to adapt course content more closely to the increasingly complicated specialties demanded by the job market. Finally, a Federal Education Promotion Act provided social and financial assistance for students.

Numerous laws were passed to enhance the already extensive social security system. Health insurance was extended, accident insurance was enlarged to include children and students, professional rehabilitation for seriously injured workers was revised, pensions for war victims were increased, guaranteed pensions were adjusted to take the lowest income levels into account and a flexible age limit was instituted. An amendment to the Labour Promotion Act (*Arbeitsförderungsgesetz*) provided a winter indemnity to construction workers and three months of wages to the employees of firms which go bankrupt. Support payments for the unemployed were increased, and a standardised family allowance was introduced. Pregnancy leave was also extended. A second home-subsidy law raised the minimum income required to receive benefits and two tenant-protection laws passed in 1971 and 1974 protected tenants against excessive rents and arbitrary eviction. At the same time, the incentives were increased for employees to save and acquire property of their own.

The socialist–liberal coalition was also eager to reform the legal system in accordance with the changed social, economic and technological circumstances. Marriage and family law, sexual offence legislation and the penal code were all reformed. The sweeping reform plans of the new government also included re-zoning and changes in regional planning, which were carried out in cooperation with the provinces. In order to ensure a minimal quality of life, new areas had to be opened up to housing, the transportation and energy delivery system had to be extended, industrial plants created, the infrastructure built up, water quality improved, nearby recreational areas formed and the finite amount of land in the Federal Republic protected by encouraging greater restraint and environmental consciousness. An administrative reform created larger geographic units in order to increase efficiency. However, this spelt the end of many local communes which had evolved over centuries, and the reform proved very controversial. The government had hoped that re-zoning would strengthen its ties at the local level, but in most cases these ties were in fact weakened.

Most of these reforms required substantial increases in state expenditure, and when the economy began to deteriorate, the national debt soared. The rate of economic growth in the Federal

Republic began to decline as early as 1970 and tumbled in 1971 from 8.2 per cent to 2.7 per cent, which was below the level of inflation. When the price of oil began to rise precipitously in 1973, the entire world economy slowed. The growth rate of the West German gross national product fell to 0.5 per cent and then to -3.5 per cent in 1975. At the same time, the number of unemployed more than doubled, reaching 582,000 in 1974, while inflation rose to 7 per cent.

Though the government was alarmed, the German people lacked any sense of crisis, and the labour unions continued to demand and receive large wage increases. The federal and provincial debts kept rising, and the interest portion of government budgets swelled. Though the federal government had paid out only 2300 million marks in interest in 1970, that figure ballooned to 28,000 million marks in 1983. This surpassed government outlays for foreign aid, housing, education, science, administration and research and development.

Another serious problem which the SPD–FDP coalition had to confront was the wave of terrorism which swept the country beginning in the early 1970s. Taking their cue from the urban guerillas in South America, the 2 June Movement and the Red Army Faction under the leadership of the journalist Ulrike Meinhof and the student Andreas Baader endeavoured to bring about a revolution through violence and terror. They represented the German variant of an international phenomenon which shook the world during the 1972 Olympic Games in Munich when the PLO group Black September carried out an assassination attempt on Israeli athletes. The German terrorists bombed American and German government installations, kidnapped Peter Lorenz, the Berlin chairman of the CDU, and murdered Günter von Drenkmann, the president of the Berlin Court of Appeal, Siegfried Buback, the prosecutor-general, Jürgen Ponto, the chief spokesman for the Board of the Dresdner Bank, and Hanns Martin Schleyer, the president of the Employers' Association. Between May 1970 and November 1979 a total of thirty individuals lost their lives in terrorist attacks. A similar sense of shock and indignation was aroused by the highjacking of a Lufthansa aeroplane and the murder of its captain, Jürgen Schumann.

Faced with a rising tide of anxiety and fear, the state intensified the struggle against violent crime and tightened criminal sanctions against both the violent left-wing and violent right-wing extremists who began to emerge in the early 1980s. The federal and provincial governments resolved to resist terrorism with all available means and to exclude from government service those sympathisers who hoped to carry their revolutionary ideology into the bosom of the state by effecting a 'long march through the institutions' and becoming civil servants themselves. In January 1972, 'Principles Governing the Membership of Civil Servants in Extremist Organisations' were passed, requiring all candidates for government posts to demonstrate their loyalty to the Basic Law and refusing all those who were demonstrably hostile to the fundamental principles of West German society.

The CDU/CSU strongly supported the government's efforts to reinforce internal security, but it opposed many of the reformist designs of the left–liberal government as well as its foreign policy. Voter support for CDU/CSU increased in all the provincial elections between 1970 and 1972—in some cases substantially—while support for the SPD and FDP dwindled. The CDU/CSU leaders in Bonn took this as an indication of growing public dissatisfaction with the governing coalition and sought to lure some of the more conservative FDP deputies away from the government in order to undermine its majority in the *Bundestag* and overthrow it. When the first reading of the Eastern Treaties (*Ostverträge*) further aggravated the dissension in the government ranks, Rainer Barzel, the chairman of the CDU/CSU alliance in the *Bundestag*, drew up an alternate government, and on 27 April 1972 the CDU/CSU moved a no-confidence motion. It failed to pass by a margin of two votes. The Brandt–Scheel government remained in power, but the stalemate continued, and on 22 September 1972 the chancellor asked for Parliament to be dissolved. Interest ran high in the ensuing elections held on 19 November 1972 and voter participation reached 91.1 per cent of those eligible. The SPD–FDP coalition won the election with a solid majority in the *Bundestag* of forty-six seats. The left–liberal coalition resumed its reform course initiated in 1969, while the CDU/CSU resigned itself to a lengthy stay in opposition, and on 12 June 1973 selected Helmut Kohl as its new chairman.

The new SPD–FDP programme was necessarily more modest than the 1969 programme because of the economic woes which the Federal Republic had encountered. But Willy Brandt did not even see this modest agenda through. His personal assistant was unmasked as a spy for the GDR, and Brandt resigned on 6 May 1974. Helmut Schmidt, the finance minister in Brandt's second government and minister of defence in the first, was elected chancellor ten days later. His government colleagues were confident that this most energetic and self-assured of politicians would continue the path blazed by Brandt. Together with Hans-Dietrich Genscher of the FDP, the former minister of the interior and new vice-chancellor and foreign minister, Schmidt swiftly surmounted the crisis created by the espionage affair and Brandt's retirement. The prestige of the Federal Republic rose to new heights in the East and the West and the countries of the Third World.

Foreign policy was carried out in the climate of détente which the superpowers had been pursuing since the late 1960s. Both Brandt and Schmidt wished to take advantage of the opportunities created by this process and by 'change through accommodation'. Though convinced that the security of the Federal Republic could only be ensured within NATO and the EC and that détente could never eliminate the gulf between the democratic Western countries and the communist countries in the East, the SPD–FDP coalition hoped that rapprochement might at least bring about more normal relations in Central Europe. That such a policy would require official West German recognition of the political status quo in Europe was a bitter pill which responsible politicians had realised they would have to swallow as early as the end of the Adenauer era. It remained, however, for the Brandt government to draw the practical consequences of this realisation. First, the Federal Republic signed a treaty with the Soviet Union on 12 April 1970 binding both parties 'to recognise without reservation the territorial integrity of all the states of Europe in their present borders . . . and not to raise any territorial claims against any other state either now or in the future'.[29] Though a peaceful revision of these borders was not excluded, the partners considered 'today and in the future that the borders of all European states are inviolable, as they exist on the day this treaty is signed, including both the Oder–Neisse line forming the western boundary of the People's Republic of Poland and the border between the Federal Republic of Germany and the German Democratic Republic.'[30] On 7 December of the same year, the Federal Republic and Poland signed the Warsaw Treaty reaffirming 'the inviolability of the existing borders now and in the future', binding the parties 'to observe without reservation their mutual territorial integrity' and avowing 'that they have no territorial claims on one another and will not raise any such claims in the future'.[31] On 11 December 1973, the Treaty of Prague with Czechoslovakia confirmed that the Federal Republic and the Czechoslovakian Socialist Republic considered 'the Munich agreement of 29 September 1938 to be null and void'.[32] After Bonn had signed these treaties, nothing more stood in the way of a resumption of diplomatic relations with the communist states of Eastern Europe. The Hallstein Doctrine was totally nullified.

While the Federal Republic's Western allies welcomed the new

Ostpolitik, the parliamentary opposition warned against one-sided treaties which allegedly compromised West German security. The Eastern treaties were also hotly debated by the public at large. Some lauded the government for the courage it had shown in 'jettisoning most of the ballast, which has heretofore prevented it from cutting much of a swath in the West or any at all in the Communist East';[33] others emphasised the 'reality of totalitarian Soviet hegemony, the foreign policy of which rests mostly on sheer power'[34] and pointed to the Brezhnev Doctrine, the build-up of Soviet sea-power and Soviet policies in the Near East as 'powerful reasons' for their reservations. The United States, however, welcomed the German initiative, especially in view of the close proximity of her forces to Russian troops in Central Europe. After the end of the war in Vietnam, Washington had hoped to improve relations with the Soviet Union and China and had entered into negotiations with Moscow on limiting the numbers of missiles and submarines and removing antiballistic defensive systems. Washington also used the treaties which had been signed renouncing the use of force, to attempt to persuade the Soviet Union to guarantee the status of West Berlin and cease all threats against the city. In a Four Power agreement on Berlin signed in the old Control Council quarters on 3 September 1971, the Western powers succeeded in reaffirming their rights and responsibilities in Berlin, improving conditions for the population of West Berlin and strengthening the city's ties to the Federal Republic. Traffic along the transit routes to West Berlin was facilitated, the city was more closely integrated into the Federal Republic, though it did not become an integral part of West Germany, and travel and visitation between the two halves of the city were eased.

The Berlin Agreement reconfirmed joint Four Power responsibility for all of Germany, but ascribed inter-German relations to the sole authority of the two German states. On 21 December 1972, the Federal Republic and the GDR signed a Basic Treaty in which they pledged to respect one another's independence, not to alter the inner-German border by means of force, to develop 'normal good neighbourly relations on the basis of equality'[35] and to establish permanent missions in Bonn and East Berlin. Though the GDR wished to exchange ambassadors, Bonn refused, pointing to a Constitutional Court interpretation of the Basic Law which required that the GDR be considered an integral part of the legally still extant German *Reich* and not a foreign country. In the Basic Treaty, the Federal Republic therefore recognised the *de facto* existence of two German states but not their legal existence.

Though neither state was willing to change its views on a unified Germany, the Basic Treaty inaugurated a considerable improvement in inter-German cooperation and individual contacts across the border. The post and other means of communication were upgraded, travel and family reunification were facilitated, the number of border crossing points was increased, journalists were guaranteed freedom to carry out their task, non-commercial trade was expanded, and administrative contacts were strengthened. Though relations between the two German states suffered occasional setbacks, the policy of rapprochement considerably improved the living conditions of people on both sides of the border.

Better relations with the GDR also enhanced the international standing of the Federal Republic. By renouncing her claim to be the sole legitimate representative of the German people, the Federal Republic prepared the way for better relations between her Western allies and the communist countries of Eastern Europe. At the same time, Bonn increased its own freedom of action in the Balkans, the Near East, Africa and Asia. The Basic Treaty with the GDR also removed a major obstacle to détente and the normalisation of relations all across Europe. A Conference on Security and Cooperation in Europe (CSCE) was convened in 1973 and by 1975 produced a treaty guaranteeing the peace on the basis of universal acceptance of the European status quo. With this, the ultimate goal of SPD–FDP foreign policy had been accomplished: the normalisation of international relations in Europe.

The Federal Republic sought to advance the cause of peace in other ways as well: relations with the Third World were continually expanded; Bonn took part in organisations facilitating world trade and played a major role in extending the European Community and encouraging greater cooperation in Europe; the Federal Republic participated in the United Nations, which she entered in 1973 together with the GDR and supported arms control or disarmament negotiations. West German foreign policy revolves around ensuring the security of the Federal Republic. The Brandt and Schmidt governments and the 'Centrist Coalition' of the CDU/CSU and FDP in power since 1982 under Chancellor Helmut Kohl have all adamantly supported West German integration into the Atlantic Alliance and the democratic values on which it is based.

These democratic values have formed the universally acknowledged foundation of West German society ever since 1945, in spite of all political quarrels over practical policies. After the experiences of the Weimar Republic and the Nazi era, when unbridled fanaticism brought Bismarck's *Reich* to a fall amidst colossal pain and suffering, the fathers of the Basic Law were determined to entrench a new set of values in the Federal Republic. Thanks to the efforts of all West Germans, these values have struck root. To remain loyal to the fundamental democratic order while thrashing out all the socio-political quarrels which emerge constitutes an everlasting challenge which each new generation must meet.

Finally, the German question and the problem of reunification will likely 'remain unresolved for many years to come, for the fragile peace in Europe depends on recognition by all powers of the status quo in Germany. Her reunification, whether as a socialist or a democratic nation, would disrupt the East–West balance in Europe.'[36] The possibility, or from a national point of view, the danger cannot be excluded 'that the duration of this separation and the change in generations will lead to the formation of quasi-national attitudes in the two German states, separated by completely different, indeed diametrically opposed social systems, and that the memories of an all-German identity, though still strong in the older generation, now over 50, will gradually fade'.[37] German unity, forfeited as a consequence of the Third *Reich*, will continue to depend on developments on the world political stage.

References

1. Introduction

1. Leopold von Ranke, 'Geschichte und Politik', in Hans Hofmann (ed.), *Ausgewählte Aufsätze und Meisterschriften* (Stuttgart, 1942), p. 128.

2. Georg Wilhelm Friedrich Hegel, *Vorlesungen über die Philosophie der Weltgeschichte*, vol. i, first half: *Die Vernunft in der Geschichte* (1830) ed. Johannes Hoffmeister (Hamburg, 1970–5), p. 164.

3. Karl Marx and Friedrich Engels, *Ausgewählte Schriften in zwei Bänden* (Berlin, 1951), vol. i, p. 24.

4. Jakob and Wilhelm Grimm, *Deutsches Wörterbuch*, vol. iv, 1.2 (Leipzig, 1897), col. 3863.

5. Johan Huizinga, *Im Bann der Geschichte, Betrachtungen und Gestaltungen* (Amsterdam, 1942), p. 104.

6. Karl Georg Faber, *Theorie der Geschichtswissenschaft* (Munich, 1971), p. 35.

7. Golo Mann, *Deutsche Geschichte des 19. und 20. Jahrhunderts* (Stuttgart, Hamburg, Munich, 1966), p. 483. [Trans. as *Germany since 1789*, London, 1968.]

8. Jakob Burckhardt, *Weltgeschichtliche Betrachtungen* (Munich, 1949), p. 7.

9. Leopold von Ranke, *Geschichte der romanischen und germanischen Völker von 1949 vis 1515* (Leipzig, 1885³), p. vii.

10. Ahasver von Brandt, *Werkzeug des Historikers, Eine Einführung in die historischen Hilfswissenschaften* (Stuttgart, 1969–5), pp. 66 and 71.

11. Ernst Troeltsch, 'Uber Massstäbe zur Beurteilung Historischer Dinge' (Berliner Universitätschrift, 1916), in Heinz Quirin, *Einführung in das Studium der Mittelalterlichen Geschichte* (Brunswick, Berlin, Hamburg, 1950), p. 16.

12. Johannes Haller, *Die Epochen der deutschen Geschichte* (Stuttgart, 1951), p. 13.

13. E. H. Carr, *What is History?* (Harmondsworth, 1964), p. 26.

2. A Survey of German History To The Late Eighteenth Century

1. Friedrich Schiller, 'Der Graf von Habsburg', *Gesammelte Werke* (Lengerich, 1955), vol. iii, p. 551.

2. Francesco Petrarch, 'Über den päpstlichen Hof in Avignon', in Hans Hubschmid, (ed.) *Weltgeschichte* (Zurich, Stuttgart, 1968), vol. iii, p. 22.

3. Giovanni Pico della Mirandola, 'Über die Würde des Menschen', in Gottfried Guggenbühl (ed.), *Quellen zur Geschichte des Mittelalters* (Zurich, 1954), p. 286.

4. Ulrich von Hutten (in a letter from 1518) in Hans Hubschmid (ed.), *Weltgeschichte*, vol. iii, p. 16.

5. Martin Luther, 'An den christlichen Adel deutscher Nation von des christlichen Standes Besserung, 1520', in Otto Clemen (ed.), *Luthers Werke in Auswahl* (Bonn, 1912), vol. i, pp. 362–425; Martin Luther, 'Von der babylonischen Gefangenschaft der Kirche', in *Werke*, vol. i, pp. 426–512; Martin Luther, 'Von der Freiheit eines Christenmenschen', *Werke*, vol. ii, pp. 1–27.

6. Johann Georg Walch (ed.), *Martin Luther, Sämtliche Schriften*, vol. xxi, part 1: 'Luthers Briefe' (St Louis, 1903), pp. 1071f.

7. 'Die Zwölf Artikel der Bauernschaft in Schwaben, Februar 1515', in Hermann Barge *Der deutsche Bauernkrieg in zeitgenössischen Quellen*, part 1 (Leipzig, n.d.), pp. 138–46.

8. Martin Luther, 'Wider die räuberischen und mörderischen Rotten der Bauern, 1525', in *Werke*, vol. iii, p. 70.

9. A variation on Philipp Scheidemann's programmatic statement on 9 November 1918: 'Everything for the people, everything through the people', in Philipp Scheidemann, *Memoiren eines Sozialdemokraten* (Dresden, 1928), vol. ii, p. 311.

3. Germany and the French Revolution

1. Hugo Grotius, *De Jure Belli ac Pacis, Drei Bücher vom Recht des Krieges und des Friedens*, Modern German text and introduction by Walter Schätzel (Tübingen, 1950), p. 51.

2. Carlo Schmid, *Erinnerungen* (Berne, Munich, Vienna, 1979), p. 146.

3. John Locke, *Two Treatises of Government* (Cambridge, 1960), pp. 286f.

4. Montesquieu, On the Spirit of the Law (1745), German text from Walter Wulf (ed.), *Geschichtliche Quellenhefte* 6/7 (Frankfurt a. M., 1975⁵), pp. 58f.

5. Declaration of Independence of the United States of America.

6. Declaration of the Rights of Man and of the Citizen. English version in *France-Amérique 1776–1789–1917* (Paris, 1918).

7. Golo Mann, *Deutsche Geschichte*, p. 52 [See ch. 1 n. 7 for trans.]

8. 'Volk und Knecht und Überwinder / Sie gestehn zu jeder Zeit, Höchstes Glück der Erdenkinder / Sei nur die Persönlichkeit.' Johann Wolfgang von Goethe, *West-Östlicher Divan*, in *Goethes Werke* (Hamburg edition, 1964⁷), p. 71.

9. Immanuel Kant, *Kritik der reinen Vernunft*, in Walter Mönch, *Deutsche Kultur von der Aufklärung bis zur Gegenwart* (Munich, 1962), p. 77.

10. From the manifesto of the Duke of Brunswick (25 July 1792) in Walter Wulf (ed.), *Geschichtliche Quellenhefte* 6/7, pp. 85 f.

11. The levée en masse, an army law passed by the National Convention on 23 August 1793, in Paul Hartig (ed.), *Die Französische Revolution* (Stuttgart, n.d.), no. 42.

12. Volker Sellin, 'Von der aufgeklärten Monarchie zum bürokratischen Obrigkeitsstaat', in Wolfgang Böhme (ed.), *Preussen, eine Herausforderung*, Herrenalber Texte 32 (Karlsruhe, 1981), p. 48.

13. From an essay by Gneisenau in July 1807, in Fritz Lange (ed.), *Neidhart von Gneisenau, Schriften von und über Gneisenau* (Berlin, 1954), p. 295.

14. 'Stein on his politics, Petersburg, 20. Nov. 1812', in Walter Wulf (ed.), *Geschichtliche Quellenhefte* 6/7, pp. 111f.

15. Volker Sellin, 'Von der aufgeklärten Monarchie zum bürokratischen Obrigkeitsstaat', p. 48.

16. Circular from Stein to the members of the general directory on 24 November 1808, in Janko Musulin (ed.), *Proklamation der Freiheit* (Fischer 283, Frankfurt a. M., 1959), p. 93.

17. Johann Gottlieb Fichte, *Reden an die deutsche Nation*, in Gottfried Guggenbühl (ed.), *Quellen zur Geschichte der Neuzeit* (Zurich, 1954), p. 79.

18. Hans Herzfeld, *Die Moderne Welt* (Brunswick, 1964), vol. i, p. 62.

19. Ibid., p. 64.

20. 'Napoleon I. über den Krieg in Spanien', in Walter Wulf (ed.) *Geschichtliche Quellenhefte* 6/7, pp. 107f.

21. General York after the Convention of Tauroggen to the king (3 Jan. 1813), ibid., p. 113.

22. 'Hermann von Boyens Denkwürdigkeiten über König Friedrich Wilhelm III. zur Zeit der Erhebung, 1813', ibid., p. 114.

23. Frederick William IV, 'Aufruf an Mein Volk' of 17 March 1813, appeared on 20 March 1813 in the *Schlesische privilegierte Zeitung*, ibid., p. 115.

24. Letter from Theodor Körner to his father on 10 March 1813 in *Körners Werke* (Berlin, Leipzig, Vienna, Stuttgart, n.d.), pp. 497f.

25. From Fichte's 'Entwurf zu einer politischen Schrift' (Spring, 1813), in Walter Wulf (ed.), *Geschichtliche Quellenhefte* 6/7, p. 117.

26. Goethe speaking about Germany's future on 13 Dec. 1813, ibid., pp. 118f.

27. From Talleyrand's report to Louis XVIII on 5 Jan. 1815, in Duff Cooper, *Talleyrand* (Leipzig, 1935), p. 324.

28. Karl August Varnhagen von Ense, *Denkwürdigkeiten des eigenen Lebens*, part III (1843²), pp. 315–24.

29. See above n. 25.

30. See above n. 28.

31. From the *Deutsche Bundesakte* of 8 July 1815, in *Teubners Quellensammlung*, 'Vorwärts' volume, (Leipzig, 1927), pp. 48f.

4. The Restoration

1. From a letter from Metternich to Minister Berstett in Baden on 4 May 1820, in Tim Klein (ed.), *1848 – Der Vorkampf deutscher Einheit und Freiheit, Erinnerungen, Urkunden, Berichte, Briefe* (Ebenhausen, Munich, 1914), pp. 30f.

2. Golo Mann, *Deutsche Geschichte*, p. 134 [see Ch. 1 n. 7 for translation title].

3. Carl Ludwig von Haller, *Restauration der Staatswissenschaft* (rpt. of second edn, Winterthur, 1920, Aalen, 1964), pp. 473f.

4. From Article I of the Holy Alliance of 26 Sept. 1815, in Gottfried Guggenbühl (ed.), *Quellen zur Neuesten Geschichte*, pp. 127f.

5. Golo Mann, *Deutsche Geschichte*, p. 118.

6. Ibid., p. 119.

7. Johannes Gottlieb Fichte, 'Machiavell 1807', in *Nachgelassene Werke* III (1835), pp. 427f., in Eike Wolgast, 'Feste als Ausdruck nationaler und demokratischer Opposition, Karlsburgfest 1817 und Hambacher Fest 1832', *Burschenschaftliche Jahresgabe* (1984), p. 1.

8. Eike Wolgast, 'Feste', p. 2.

9. Adolf Laufs, 'Für Freiheit und Einheit: Das Nationalfest der Deutschen zu Hambach 1832', *Juristische Schulung* (1982), pp. 5, 326.

10. In Paul Wentcke und Wolfgang Klötzer (eds), *Deutscher Liberalismus im Vormärz, Heinrich von Gagern, Briefe und Reden 1815–1848* (Göttingen, 1959), p. 60.

11. Cited in Hugo Kühn (ed.), *Das Wartburgfest am 18. Oktober 1817* (Weimar, 1913), p. 74.

12. Cited ibid., p. 75.

13. Ernst Rudolf Huber, *Dokumente zur deutschen Verfassungsgeschichte* (Stuttgart, 1961), vol. i, pp. 90f.

14. From Stein's letter to Baron von Gagern on 24 Aug. 1820, in Hans Christoph Freiherr von Gagern, *Mein Anteil an der Politik*, vol. iv: *In der Einsamkeit. Die Briefe des Freiherrn vom Stein an den Freiherrn von Gagern 1813–1831* (Stuttgart, 1833), pp. 90f.

15. Dieter Langewiesche, 'Deutschland im Zeitalter der bürgerlichen Revolution', in Ploetz, *Deutsche Geschichte, Epochen und Daten* (Freiburg, Würzburg, 1979), p. 192.

16. Cited in Joseph Boesch, *Weltgeschichte* (Zurich, Stuttgart, 1966), vol. iv, p. 126.

17. From the message to Congress of 2 Dec. 1823 signed by President James Monroe and written by Secretary of State John Quincy Adams.

18. Louis Philippe's proclamation on 31 July 1830, in Walter Wulf (ed.), *Geschichtliche Quellenhefte* 8 (Frankfurt a. M., 1974[7]), p. 25.

19. From a speech by Siebenpfeiffer at the Hambacher Fest on 27 May 1832 in Tim Klein (ed.), *1848 – Der Vorkampf*, pp. 43f.

20. Friedrich Christoph Dahlmann, *Zur Verständigung* (Basle, 1838), pp. 85f.

21. List's petition to the Federal Diet on 14 April 1819, in Erwin v. Bekkerath, Karl Goeser and Friedrich Lenz (eds), *Friedrich List, Schriften, Reden, Briefe*, vol. i.1 (Berlin, 1932), pp. 492f.

22. Friedrich von Motz in a memorandum to Frederick William III in June 1829, in Willfried von Eisenhart Rothe and Anton Ritthaler (eds), *Vorgeschichte und Begründung des Deutschen Zollvereins 1815–1834, Akten der Staaten des Deutschen Bundes und der europäischen Mächte* (Berlin, 1934), vol. iii, p. 534.

23. Frederick William IV at the opening of the United Diet on 11 April 1847, in Tim Klein (ed.), *1848 – Der Vorkampf*, p. 91.

5. The Revolution of 1848

1. Cited in Gordon A. Craig, *Europe since 1815* (New York, Chicago, San Francisco, Toronto and London, 1966²), p. 139.

2. Cited in Theodor Schieder, 'Vom Deutschen Bund zum Deutschen Reich', in Bruno Gebhardt, *Handbuch der Deutschen Geschichte* (Stuttgart, 1960⁸), p. 123.

3. Ibid.

4. Georg Büchner, *Sämtliche Werke und Briefe* (Munich, 1980), p. 230.

5. In Paul Roth and Heinrich Merck (eds), *Quellensammlung zum deutschen öffentlichen Recht seit 1848* (Erlangen, 1850), vol. i, p. 55.

6. From a south German pamphlet, in Tim Klein (ed.), *1848 – Der Vorkampf*, pp. 115f.

7. From Struwe's motion before the pre-parliament on 2 April 1848, in Wilhelm Blos, *Die deutsche Revolution 1848–1849* (Stuttgart, 1892), p. 487.

8. From the chronicle of the Berlin revolution, in Tim Klein (ed.), *1848 – Der Vorkampf*, p. 161.

9. Edict of Frederick William IV on 21 March 1848, in Walter Wulf (ed.), *Geschichtliche Quellenhefte* 8 (7th edn Frankfurt a. M., 1974), p. 38.

10. Heinrich von Gagern when accepting the presidency on 23 May 1848, in Eduard Bernstein (ed.), *Dokumente des Sozialismus* (Berlin, 1902), vol. ii, p. 40.

11. From a speech by Heinrich von Gagern on 24 June 1848, in Theodor Schieder, *Vom Deutschen Bund zum Deutschen Reich*, p. 131.

12. The Kremser Declaration of 28 Nov. 1848, in Franz Wigard (ed.), *Stenographischer Bericht über die Verhandlungen der deutschen konstituierenden Nationalversammlung zu Frankfurt a. M.* (Frankfurt a. M., 1848/49), vol. vi, pp. 4551f.

13. Deputy Welcker's motion of 12 March 1849, ibid., vol. viii, p. 5666.

14. Frederick William IV about the imperial crown on 18 March 1848 in Walter Wulf (ed.), *Geschichtliche Quellenhefte* 8, p. 46.

15. Karl Schurz, *Lebenserinnerungen*, in Martin Stellmann (ed.), *Spiegel der Zeiten*, vol. iv: *Die Revolution und das 19. Jahrhundert* (Frankfurt a. M., Berlin, Bonn, 1958), p. 86.

16. French Foreign Minister Bastide to the French plenipotentiary in Berlin on 31 July 1848, in Hans Seifert (ed.), *Die Deutsche Frage 1848/49* (Stuttgart, n.d.), p. 33.

17. The Russian ambassador in Berlin to Russian Foreign Minister Nesselrode on 16 Feb. 1849 in Hans Seifert, *Die Deutsche Frage*, p. 32.

18. The French plenipotentiary in London, Drouyn de l'Huys, in a

personal note written in 1850, in Hans Seifert, *Die Deutsche Frage*, p. 34.
19. Golo Mann, *Deutsche Geschichte*, p. 250 [see Ch. 1 n.7 for translation title].
20. Ibid.

6. Industrialisation and the Social Question

1. Dieter Langewiesche, 'Deutschland im Zeitalter der bürgerlichen Revolution' in Ploetz, *Deutsche Geschichte*, p. 193.
2. Cf. Wilhelm Treue, Herbert Pönicke, Karl-Heinz Mannegold et al., *Quellen zur Geschichte der industriellen Revolution* (Göttingen, Berlin, Frankfurt, a. M., Zurich, 1966), pp. 11f.
3. Cited in Max Weber, 'Askese und Kapitalistischer Geist' in his *Gesammelte Aufsätze zur Religionssoziologie* (Tübingen, 1972), pp. 167ff.
4. Adam Smith, *An Inquiry into the Nature and Causes of the Wealth of Nations*, ed. R. H. Campbell (Oxford, 1976), vol. i, p. 374.
5. Ibid., p. 687.
6. Cited in Rudolf Braun, Wolfram Fischer et al., *Industrielle Revolution, wirtschaftliche Aspekte* (Cologne, 1972), p. 143.
7. Adam Smith, *The Wealth of Nations*, vol. i, p. 11.
8. Alexis de Tocqueville, *Oeuvres complètes* (Paris, 1865), vol. viii, pp. 365–9.
9. Cf. Friedrich Engels, *Die Lage der arbeitenden Klasse in England* (Barmen, 1845), pp. 137ff.
10. Philipp Andreas Nemnich, *Tagebuch einer der Kultur und Industrie gewidmeten Reise* (Tübingen, 1809), vol. i, p. 131.
11. *Eckermann's Gespräche mit Goethe* (12 March 1828), vol. ii, Fritz Bergemann (ed.) (Inseltaschenbuch, Frankfurt a. M., 1981), p. 641.
12. Golo Mann, *Deutsche Geschichte*, p. 252 [see Ch. 1 n.7 for translation title].
13. See above Chapter 3, Reform in Prussia and Austria.
14. Cited in Carl Jantke and Dietrich Hilger (eds), *Die Eigentumslosen. Der Deutsche Pauperismus und die Emanzipationskrise in Darstellungen und Deutungen der zeitgenössischen Literatur* (Freiburg, Munich, 1965), p. 379.
15. Friedrich List, *Das nationale System der politischen Ökonomie* (1841) Hans Volgt (ed.), (Munich, 1942), pp. 179f.
16. Friedrich List, 'Eisenbahnen und Kanäle, Dampfboote und Dampfwagentransport', in Carl von Rotteck and Carl Welcker (eds.), *Staatslexikon* (Altona, 1835), vol. iv, p. 650.
17. Friedrich Harkort on railways, in Wilhelm Treue, ibid., p. 69.
18. Werner Sombart, *Der moderne Kapitalismus* (Munich, 1927), vol. i, p. 12.
19. Johann Wolfgang v. Goethe, *Wilhelm Meisters Wanderjahre*, Book 3, Ch. 13, in *Goethes Werke* (Hamburg edition, 1964⁷), p. 429.
20. Cited in Carl Jantke and Dietrich Hilger (eds.), *Die Eigentumslosen*, p. 379.
21. Song of the Weavers in Peterswaldau and Langenbielau in *Deutsches*

Bürgerbuch für 1845 (rpt: Opladen, 1975), pp. 199f.

22. Cited in Walter Trog, *Die Nationale und die Industrielle Revolution* (Frankfurt a. M., n.d.), p. 48.

23. Jürgen Kuczinski, *Die Geschichte der Lage der Arbeiter in Deutschland von 1800 bis in die Gegenwart* (Berlin, 1947), vol. i, p. 61.

24. Bettina von Arnim, *Dieses Buch gehört dem König* (Berlin, 1852), vol. i, p. 536.

25. From the response of the mayor of Ratingen on 22 Aug. 1822 to a question from the Düsseldorf district magistrate about child labour in his district, in Wolfgang Köllmann, *Die Industrielle Revolution*, Kletts Arbeitshefte Nr. 4231 (Stuttgart, n.d.), p. 33.

26. Cited in Günter Brakelmann, *Die soziale Frage des 19. Jahrhunderts* (Witten, 1971[4]), pp. 27f.

27. Deputy Schuchard in the debate of 6 July 1837, in Wolfgang Köllmann, *Die Industrielle Revolution*, p. 32.

28. Friedrich Harkort, *Bemerkungen über die Hindernisse der Civilisation und Emancipation der unteren Klassen* (Elberfeld, 1844), p. 41.

29. Karl Marx and Friedrich Engels, 'Manifesto of the Communist Party 1848'. German text in *Ausgewählte Schriften in zwei Bänden*, vol. i (Berlin, 1951) pp. 23ff.

30. 1845 quotation from Benjamin Disraeli's novel *Sybil or the Two Nations* (London, 1927), p. 72.

31. Cited in Wilhelm Emmanuel von Ketteler, *Sämtliche Werke und Briefe*, vol. i,1, Erwin Iserloh (ed.) (Mainz, 1977), p. 19, n.5.

32. Wilhelm Emmanuel Ketteler, *Sämtliche Werke*, p. 18.

33. Ferdinand Lassalle, 'Offenes Antwortschreiben an das Zentralkomitee zur Berufung eines allgemeinen Deutschen Arbeiterkongresses zu Leipzig 1863' (Open Response to the Central Committee on the Convocation of a German Labour Congress in Leipzig in 1863) in Ernst Schraepler (ed.), *Quellen zur Geschichte der sozialen Frage in Deutschland*, vol. i: 1800–70 (Göttingen, 1955), pp. 184.

34. Lassalle on the state and the working class, 1862, in Walter Wulf (ed.), *Geschichtliche Quellenhefte* 9 (Frankfurt, Berlin, Munich, 1974[3]), p. 41.

35. From the programme of the worker education leagues, in *Pforzheimer Beobachter* 95 (1863).

36. From the founding declaration of the Pforzheim worker education league, in Franz Kistler, *Die wirtschaftlichen und sozialen Verhältnisse in Baden 1849–1870* (Freiburg, 1954), p. 233.

37. Marx and Engels, 'Manifesto of the Communist Party, 1848.'

7. Bismarck and German Unification

1. Cited in Golo Mann, *Deutsche Geschichte*, p. 253 [see Ch. 1 n.7 for translation title].

2. Prince William of Prussia in 1849, cited in Hellmut Diwald, *Geschichte der Deutschen* (Frankfurt, Berlin, Vienna, 1978), p. 340. By 'à la Gagern' is meant the attempt at national unification under the president of the Ger-

man National Assembly, Heinrich von Gagern.

3. Ibid.

4. Golo Mann, *Deutsche Geschichte*, p. 260.

5. The original of this letter has been lost. All that remains is a summary which Bismarck made for his father on 29 Sept. 1838 and which he also enclosed in a letter to his fiancée on 13 Feb. 1847. Otto von Bismarck to Countess Bismarck-Bohlen in *Otto von Bismarck in seinen Briefen, Reden Erinnerungen* (Munich, Leipzig, 1919), p. 38.

6. Otto von Bismarck to Gustav Scharlach, 9 Jan. 1845. Ibid., p. 55.

7. Letter from Bismarck to his wife on 3 May 1851, in Hans Rothfels (ed.), *Bismarck-Briefe* (Göttingen, 1955²), p. 146.

8. Bismarck's speech before the second chamber of the Prussian *Landtag* on 3 Dec. 1850, in Otto von Bismarck, *Dokumente der Staatsanschauung* (Berlin, n.d.), p. 108.

9. Bismarck on Austro-Prussian rivalry, cited in Walter Bussmann, *Das Zeitalter Bismarcks* (Frankfurt a.M. 1968⁴), p. 7.

10. Otto Fürst von Bismarck, *Gedanken und Erinnerungen* (Stuttgart, Berlin, 1911), vol. i, p. 179.

11. Walter Bussmann, *Das Zeitalter Bismarcks*, p. 25.

12. Comment of British foreign minister Clarendon, cited in Sieghard Rost, *Nationalstaaten und Weltmächte* (Frankfurt, Berlin, Bonn, n.d.), p. 3.

13. From Bismarck's March memorandum of 1858, 'Das kleine Buch des Herrn von Bismarck', cited in Walter Bussmann, *Das Zeitalter Bismarcks*, p. 40.

14. Golo Mann, *Deutsche Geschichte*, pp. 265f.

15. Ibid., p. 295.

16. Cited in Luigi Chiala (ed.), *Camillo Cavour, Briefe* (Leipzig, 1884), vol. ii, p. 156.

17. Letter written by Bismarck in St Petersburg on 5 May 1859 to General Gustav von Alvensleben, in Hans Rothfels (ed.), *Bismarck-Briefe*, p. 247.

18. Golo Mann, *Deutsche Geschichte*, pp. 301f.

19. Walter Bussmann, *Das Zeitalter Bismarcks*, p. 53.

20. Speech by Prince Regent William on 8 Nov. 1858, cited in Hellmut Diwald, *Geschichte der Deutschen*, p. 296.

21. Letter of Grand Duke Friedrich von Baden to Prince Regent William on 10 Nov. 1858, cited in Hellmut Diwald, *Geschichte der Deutschen*, p. 296.

22. Speech by Prince Regent William on 8 November 1858, cited in Diwald, *Geschichte der Deutschen*, p. 296.

23. Walter Bussmann, *Das Zeitalter Bismarcks*, p. 43.

24. Statement by Leopold von Gerlach in Dec. 1859, cited in Walter Bussmann, *Das Zeitalter Bismarcks*, p. 60.

25. Bismarck's letter to Roon on 15 July 1862, in *Bismarck in seinen Briefen, Reden, Erinnerungen*, p. 145.

26. Walter Bussmann, *Das Zeitalter Bismarcks*, p. 63.

27. Cited in Golo Mann, *Deutsche Geschichte*, p. 315.

28. Cited ibid., p. 303.

29. Cited in Walter Bussmann, *Das Zeitalter Bismarcks*, p. 64.

30. Bismarck before the budget commission on 30 Sept. 1862, in *Bismarck in seinen Briefen, Reden, Erinnerungen*, p. 153.

31. Cited in Walter Bussmann, *Das Zeitalter Bismarcks*, p. 67.

32. *Bismarck in seinen Briefen, Reden, Erinnerungen*, p. 149.

33. Cited in Robert von Keudell, *Fürst und Fürstin Bismarck, Erinnerungen aus den Jahren 1846 bis 1872* (Berlin, Stuttgart, 1901), p. 140.

34. Bismarck's letter to the Prussian ambassador in Paris, Count Goltz, on 24 Dec. 1863 in *Bismarck in seinen Briefen, Reden, Erinnerungen*, p. 173.

35. From the Prussian-Italian alliance of 8 April 1866, in Walter Wulf (ed.), *Geschichtliche Quellenhefte* 9, p. 47.

36. Otto von Bismarck, *Gedanken und Erinnerungen*, vol. ii, pp. 65f.

37. Rudolf von Ihring to the Austrian Julius Glaser on 1 May 1866, in *Rudolf von Ihring in Briefen an seine Freunde* (Leipzig, 1913), pp. 19f.

38. Rudolf von Ihring to Bernhard Windscheid on 19 Aug. 1866, ibid., pp. 206 f.

39. Hermann Baumgarten, *Selbstkritik des deutschen Liberalismus*, cited in Hellmut Diwald, *Geschichte der Deutschen*, p. 318.

40. August Bebel on the North German *Reichstag*, in Walter Wulf (ed.), *Geschichtliche Quellenhefte* 9, p. 56.

41. Otto von Bismarck, speech before the constituent *Reichstag* of the North German Confederation on 11 March 1867, in Lothar Gall, *Bismarck, Die grossen Reden* (Berlin, n.d.), p. 99.

42. Cited in Hellmut Diwald, *Geschichte der Deutschen*, p. 320.

43. Cf. Walter Bussmann, *Das Zeitalter Bismarcks*, p. 90.

44. Letter from Bismarck to the Prussian ambassador in Munich, 26 Feb. 1869, cited ibid., p. 101.

45. Cited ibid., p. 109.

46. From the memoirs of Karl Schurz, in Walter Wulf (ed.), *Geschichtliche Quellenhefte* 9, pp. 57 f.

47. Cited in Sieghard Rost, *Nationalstaaten und Weltmächte*, p. 61.

48. Cited ibid., p. 62.

49. Otto von Bismarck, *Gedanken und Erinnerungen*, vol. ii, p. 113.

50. Ibid.

51. Circular from Jules Favres to French diplomats, in Walter Wulf (ed.), *Geschichtliche Quellenhefte* 9, p. 62.

52. Lothar Gall, *Bismarck der Weisse Revolutionär* (Berlin, n.d.), pp. 438f.

53. Ibid.

54. Address of an assembly of Pforzheim citizens, in Diether Raff, *Zur Geschichte Pforzheims, Die Entwicklung von der Kleinstadt zur Mittelstadt* (Pforzheim, 1964), p. 58.

55. Heinrich von Sybel to Hermann Baumgarten on 27 Jan. 1871, in Julius Heyderhoff (ed.), *Die Sturmjahre der preussisch-deutschen Einigung 1859–1870* (Bonn, Leipzig, 1925), p. 494.

56. Carl Eckhard in the Baden *Landtag* (Dec. 1870), in Lothar Gall, *Der Liberalismus als regierende Partei: Das Grossherzogtum Baden zwischen Restauration und Reichsgründung* (Wiesbaden, 1968), p. 485.

8. The Empire Under Bismarck's Leadership

1. King William on his journey from Bad Ems to Berlin on 15 July 1871, cited in Hellmut Diwald, *Geschichte der Deutschen*, p. 30.

2. Gerhart Hauptmann, *Das Abenteuer meiner Jugend* (Gütersloh, 1954), pp. 110 f.

3. Cf. Johannes Hohlfeld, *Dokumente der Deutschen Politik und Geschichte von 1848 bis zur Gegenwart* (Berlin, n. d.), vol. i, nos. 57 and 83, pp. 198 ff.

4. Walter Bussmann, *Das Zeitalter Bismarcks*, p. 153.

5. From the *Syllabus complectens praecipuos nostrae aetatis errores*, in Gottfried Guggenbühl (ed.), *Quellen zur Geschichte der Neuesten Zeit* (Zurich, 1966⁴), pp. 216f.

6. Otto von Bismarck, *Gedanken und Erinnerungen*, vol. ii, p. 164.

7. From Count Arnim's edict of 26 May 1869, in Hans Rothfels (ed.), *Otto von Bismarck, Dokumente der Staatsanschauung* (Berlin, n.d.), p. 247.

8. Cited in Sieghard Rost, *Nationalstaaten und Weltmächte*, p. 88.

9. Cited in Erich Schmidt-Volkmar, *Der Kulturkampf in Deutschland, 1871–90* (Göttingen, 1962), p. 162.

10. 'I could not view the creation of this group as anything other than the mobilisation of the party against the state.' Otto von Bismarck in the Prussian *Landtag* on 30 Jan. 1872, in *Bismarck in seinen Briefen, Reden, Erinnerungen*, p. 275.

11. Bismarck to the tsar on 6 March 1874, cited in Erich Schmidt-Volkmar, *Der Kulturkampf in Deutschland, 1871–90* (Göttingen, 1896), p. 31.

12. Cited in Sieghard Rost, *Nationalstaaten und Weltmächte*, p. 92.

13. Bismarck in a speech before the upper house on 10 March 1873, in Hans Rothfels (ed.), *Otto von Bismarck, Dokumente der Staatsauffassung*, p. 256.

14. Otto von Bismarck, *Gedanken und Erinnerungen*, vol. ii, p. 155.

15. Cited in Karl Erich Born, 'Von der Reichsgründung bis zum ersten Weltkrieg', in Bruno Gebhardt, *Handbuch der Deutschen Geschichte*, vol. iii, p. 215.

16. Cited in Sieghard Rost, *Nationalstaaten und Weltmächte*, p. 93.

17. See above n. 13.

18. Otto von Bismarck in a programmatic speech before the *Reichstag* on 2 May 1879, cited in Walter Bussmann, *Das Zeitalter Bismarcks*, p. 192.

19. From an 1869 statement by Liebknecht directed against the Lassallians, cited in Joseph Boesch, *Weltgeschichte*, vol. 4 (Zurich-Stuttgart, 1966), p. 224.

20. Wolfgang Treue, *Deutsche Parteiprogramme 1861–1961* (Göttingen, 1961³), pp. 59f.

21. Cited in Walter Bussmann, *Das Zeitalter Bismarcks*, p. 179.

22. Harry Pross (ed.), *Die Zerstörung der deutschen Politik, Dokumente 1871–1933* (Frankfurt a.M., 1959), pp. 64ff.

23. Otto von Bismarck in a speech before the *Reichstag* on 9 Oct. 1878, in Hans Rothfels (ed.), *Bismarck, Dokumente der Staatsanschauung*, p. 384.

24. Otto von Bismarck in the autumn of 1871, in Lothar Gall, *Bismarck, die grossen Reden*, p. 209, and also to the foreign office counsellor, Lothar Buche, in late 1878 in Hans Rothfels (ed.), *Bismarck, Dokumente der Staatsanschauung*, p. 387.

25. Cited in Hellmut Diwald, *Geschichte der Deutschen*, p. 284.

26. Otto von Bismarck to the writer Moritz Busch on 26 June 1881, in *Bismarck und der Staat, Ausgewählte Dokumente* with an introduction by Hans Rothfels (Darmstadt, 1958), p. 359.

27. Otto von Bismarck in a speech before the *Reichstag* on 15 March 1884, in *Bismarck und der Staat*, p. 373.

28. Cited in W. F. Monypenny and George Earle Buckle, *The Life of Benjamin Disraeli Earl of Beaconsfield*, vol. v, 1868–76, pp. 133–4.

29. Otto von Bismarck in the *Reichstag* on 6 Feb. 1888, in Lothar Gall, *Bismarck, Die grossen Reden*, p. 339.

30. Cited in Sieghard Rost, *Nationalstaaten und Weltmächte*, p. 94.

31. Ibid.

32. Cited in Friedrich Curtius (ed.), *Denkwürdigkeiten des Fürsten Chlodwig zu Hohenlohe-Schillingsfürst* (Stuttgart, Leipzig, 1906), p. 118.

33. From the Kissinger Diktat of 15 June 1877, in Walter Wulf (ed.), *Geschichtliche Quellenhefte* 9, p. 75.

34. Three Emperors' League of 22 Oct. 1873, in Walter Wulf (ed.), *Geschichtliche Quellenhefte* 9, p. 71.

35. Otto von Bismarck in the *Reichstag* on 19 Feb. 1878, in Lothar Gall, *Bismarck, die grossen Reden*, pp. 140f.

36. Otto von Bismarck, *Gedanken und Erinnerungen*, vol ii, p. 261.

37. Otto von Bismarck in the *Reichstag* on 11 Jan. 1887, in Lothar Gall, *Bismarck, Die grossen Reden*, p. 279.

38. Cited in Sieghard Rost, *Nationalstaaten und Weltmächte*, p. 103.

39. Walter Bussmann, *Das Zeitalter Bismarcks*, p. 206.

40. Otto von Bismarck in the *Reichstag* on 11 Jan. 1887, in Lothar Gall, *Bismarck, Die grossen Reden*, p. 273.

41. Otto von Bismarck in the *Reichstag* on 11 Jan. 1887 and on 6 February 1888, ibid. pp. 282–357.

42. Otto von Bismarck in the *Reichstag* on 6 Feb 1888, ibid., p. 330.

43. Otto von Bismarck in the *Reichstag* on 6 Feb. 1888, ibid.

44. Bismarck on German colonial policies on 26 June 1884, in Walter Wulf (ed.), *Geschichtliche Quellenhefte* 9, p. 97.

45. Walter Bussmann, *Das Zeitalter Bismarcks*, pp. 235 f.

46. Crown Prince William on the occasion of Bismarck's seventy-third birthday on 1 April 1888, in: *Bismarck, Briefe, Reden, Erinnerungen*, p. 350.

47. From the so-called funeral pyre letter of court chaplain Adolf Stöcker to Baron Wilhelm von Hamerstein on 14 Aug. 1888 as published in *Vorwärts* in 1895, in *Bismarck, Briefe, Reden, Erinnerungen*, p. 350.

48. Cited in Walter Bussmann, *Das Zeitalter Bismarcks*, p. 236.

49. From Bismarck's departing request of 18 March 1890, in *Bismarck, Briefe, Reden, Erinnerungen*, p. 357.

50. Theodor Fontane to Georg Friedländer on 1 May 1890, in Kurt Schreinert (ed.), *Theodor Fontane, Briefe an Georg Friedländer* (Heidel-

berg, 1954), p. 125.

51. Friedrich Meinecke, *Erlebtes 1862–1901* (Leipzig, 1941), pp. 171ff.

52. The German chargé d'affaires in Paris on the French public reaction to Bismarck's dismissal, in Walter Wulf (ed.), *Geschichtliche Quellenhefte* 9, p. 110.

53. The German military attaché in Petersburg on the Russian reaction to Bismarck's dismissal, in Walter Wulf (ed.), *Geschichtliche Quellenhefte* 9, p. 112.

54. Cited in Sieghard Rost, *Nationalstaaten und Weltmächte*, pp. 107f.

55. Cited in Hellmut Diwald, *Geschichte der Deutschen*, p. 282.

56. *Punch*, London 29 March 1890.

57. Cited in Diwald, *Geschichte der Deutschen*, p. 282.

58. Ibid.

59. Hans Lothar von Schweinitz, *Denkwürdigkeiten II* (Berlin, 1927), p. 83.

60. Ludwig Bamberger, 'Zum Jahrestag der Entlassung Bismarcks 1891', *Gesammelte Schriften* (Berlin, 1897), vol. v, p. 340.

61. From Max Weber's inaugural lecture in Freiburg, in Lothar Gall (ed.), *Das Bismarck-Problem in der Geschichtsschreibung 1945* (Cologne, Berlin, 1971), p. 331.

62. Cited in Golo Mann, *Deutsche Geschichte*, p. 331 [see Ch.I n.7 for translation title].

9. Wilhelmine Germany

1. Cf. Fritz Sternberg, *Kapitalismus und Sozialismus vor dem Weltgericht* (Hamburg, 1951), p. 18.

2. Paul Lindenberg, *Im Weichbilde der deutschen Reichshauptstadt, Berliner Skizzen* (Berlin, 1887²), pp. 72f.

3. Adele Gerhard, *Die Familie Vanderhouten* (Berlin, 1909), p. 416.

4. Gustav Gundlach (ed.), *Die sozialen Rundschreiben Leos XIII und Pius XI*, in Jakob Schrieder (ed.), *Görres-Gesellschaft, Veröffentlichungen der Sektion für Sozial- und Wirtschaftswissenschaft*, Heft 3 (Paderborn, 1931).

5. Theodor Fontane to Georg Friedländer on 3 Oct. 1893, in Theodor Fontane, *Briefe*, pp. 235 f.

6. Now the Max-Planck-Gesellschaft.

7. Jeannot Emil Baron von Grotthuss, *Aus deutscher Dämmerung* (Stuttgart, 1909²), p. 10.

8. Friedrich Paulsen on the Nietzsche cult (1897) in *Zur Ethik und Politik, Gesammelte Vorträge und Aufsätze* (Berlin, n.d.), pp. 56f.

9. William II on 15 May 1890 before the East Prussian *Landtag*, in Johannes Penzler (ed.), *Wilhelm II, Die Reden in den Jahren 1888 bis 1905* (Leipzig, n.d.), vol. i, p. 114.

10. William II on 20 Feb. 1891 before the Brandenburg *Landtag*, ibid., p. 171.

11. Theodor Fontane to Georg Friedländer on 5 April 1897, in Fontane, *Briefe*, pp. 309 f.

12. Fritz Ernst, *Die Deutschen und ihre jüngste Geschichte* (Stuttgart,

1970), p. 26.

13. Cited in Hermann Baron von Eckardstein, *Lebenserinnerungen und politische Denkwürdigkeiten* (Leipzig, 1919), vol i, p. 218.

14. From Vollmar's Munich speech on 1 June. 1891, in Georg von Vollmar, *Über die nächsten Aufgaben der deutschen Sozialdemokratie, Zwei Reden*, (Munich, 1891), p. 5.

15. Cited in Otto Hammann, *Der Neue Kurs, Erinnerungen* (Berlin, 1918), p. 73.

16. Speech by William II on 6 September 1898, in *Wilhelm II, Reden*, vol. ii, pp. 111ff.

17. Karl Alexander von Müller (ed.), *Choldwig Fürst zu Hohenlohe-Schillingsfürst, Denkwürdigkeiten der Reichskanzlerzeit* (Stuttgart, 1931), p. 582.

18. Bassermann on 10 Nov. 1908 on the impact of the *Daily Telegraph* interview in the *Reichstag*, in *Reichstag, Stenographische Berichte*, XII Legislaturperiode, I. Session 1908, vol. 233, pp. 5374 C ff.

19. Privy Councillor Zimmermann to Kiderlen on 25 August 1909, in Ernst Jäckh (ed.), *Kiderlen-Wächter, Der Staatsmann und Mensch, Briefwechsel und Nachlass* (Stuttgart, 1924), vol. ii, p. 34.

20. Friedrich Stampfer, *Die vierzehn Jahre der ersten deutschen Republik* (Karlsbad, 1936), p. 7.

21. Friedrich Naumann in the National-Social Catechism of 1907, cited in Walter Bussmann, 'Deutsche Weltpolitik und unvollendeter Verfassungsstaat', in Ploetz, *Deutsche Geschichte*, p. 241.

22. Cf. Wolfgang J. Mommsen, *Imperialismustheorie* (Göttingen, 1980²), p. 7.

23. Ibid., p. 8.

24. Ibid., p. 9.

25. Particularly the classical writers on the theory of imperialism – Johan Atkins Hobson, Rudolf Hilferding, Joseph Alois Schumpeter and Vladimir Lenin – but Hans Ulrich Wehler as well. Mommsen emphasises that 'the imperialist expansion of the western industrial states has so far eluded convincing interpretation in the light of a single, unified theory in spite of many efforts'.

26. Cecil J. Rhodes, *The Last Will and Testament*, in Ludwig Zimmermann, *Der Imperialismus, Geistige, ethische und wirtschaftliche Zielsetzungen* (Stuttgart, n.d.), p. 9.

27. Jules Ferry, debate in the French Chamber of Deputies in July 1885, in Franz Ansprenger, *Politik im Schwarzen Afrika* (Cologne-Opladen, 1961), p. 453.

28. Feodor Mikhailovich Dostoevsky, *Tagebuch eines Schriftstellers* (Munich, 1923), vol. iv, pp. 474ff.

29. Bülow's speech before the *Reichstag* on 6 Dec. 1897, in *Reichstag, Stenographische Berichte*, IX. Legislaturperiode, V. Session 1897/98, 60 D.

30 S. E. Morison and H. S. Commager, *Das Werden der amerikanischen Republik, Geschichte der Vereinigten Staaten von ihren Anfängen bis zur Gegenwart* (Stuttgart, 1950), p. 360.

31. Cited in Gordon A. Craig, *Europe Since 1815*, p. 448.

32. Ibid., p. 451.

33. Alfred Thayer Mahan, 'The Interest of American Sea Power 1897', in Willard Thorp, *American Issues*, vol. i, *The Social Record* (Chicago, 1941), p. 906.

34. In Henry Steele Commager, *Documents of American History*, vol. ii: *Since 1898*, p. 33.

35. Cited in *Hans Lothar von Schweinitz, Denkwürdigkeiten des Botschafters* (Berlin, 1927), vol. ii, p. 404.

36. Alfred Count von Waldersee, *Denkwürdigkeiten*, p. 245.

37. Cited in Gordon A. Craig, *Europe Since 1815*, p. 491.

38. Article by Karl Marx in the *Herald Tribune* (1853), in Martin Stellman (ed.), *Die Neueste Zeit* (Frankfurt a.M., 1957), p. 31.

39. Comment of William II to Chancellor Bülow on the report of the ambassador to London, Count Metternich, on 16 July 1908, in *Grosse Politik*, vol. xxiv, pp. 104f.

40 Golo Mann, *Deutsche Geschichte*, p. 566 [see Ch. I n.7 for translation title].

41. Cited ibid., pp. 568f.

10. The First World War

1. Letter from Francis Joseph to William II on 5 July 1914, in Walter Wulf (ed.), *Geschichtliche Quellenhefte* 10 (Frankfurt a.M., 1974), p. 69.

2. Dispatch from Bethmann Hollweg to the German ambassador in Vienna on 6 July 1914, in Walter Wulf (ed.), *Geschichtliche Quellenhefte* 10, p. 70.

3. Viscount Grey of Fallodon, *Twenty-Five Years 1892–1916* (London, 1926), vol. ii, p. 20.

4. Karl Dietrich Erdmann, 'Die Zeit der Weltkriege', in Bruno Gebhardt, *Handbuch der deutschen Geschichte* (Stuttgart, 1959³), vol. iv, p. 23.

5. Carl Zuckmayer, *Als wär's ein Stück von mir* (Stuttgart, Hamburg, 1966), p. 211.

6. Cited in Golo Mann, *Deutsche Geschichte*, p. 591, [see Ch.I n.7 for translation title].

7. Tägl. Rundschau (ed.), *Kriegs-Rundschau, Zeitgenössische Zusammenstellung der für den Weltkrieg wichtigen Ereignisse, Urkunden, Kundgebungen, Schlacht- und Zeitungsberichte* (Berlin, 1914ff), vol. i, p. 29f.

8. From the shorthand report of the Kriegs-Rundschau, in *Kriegs-Rundschau*, p. 43. The original speech is preserved on a printing plate.

9. Haase's declaration before the *Reichstag* on 4 Aug. 1914, in *Reichstag, Stenographische Berichte* XIII. Legislaturperiode, II. Session 1914/16, vol. 306, 8 C.

10. SPD declaration, in *Der Volksfreund*, Karlsruhe, 1 Aug. 1914.

11. Cited in *Kriegs-Rundschau*, p. 113.

12. Comment by William II on an article in the *Frankfurter Zeitung* in December 1915, cited in Otto Hammann, *Bilder aus der letzten Kaiserzeit* (Berlin, 1922), pp. 128f.

13. Fritz Ernst, *Die Deutschen und ihre jüngste Geschichte*, p. 25.

14. Rudolf Hoffmann (ed.), *Der deutsche Soldat, Briefe aus dem Welt-*

krieg, Vermächtnis (1937), p. 445, cited in Fritz Ernst, *Die Deutschen und ihre jüngste Geschichte*, p. 38.

15. From William II's Easter message on 7 April 1917, in Walter Wulf (ed.), *Geschichtliche Quellenhefte* 10, p. 89.

16. From the peace resolution of the majority parties in the *Reichstag* on 19 July 1917, in Walter Wulf (ed.), *Geschichtliche Quellenhefte* 10, p. 90.

17. From the German note to the United States on 1 Feb. 1917 on the opening of unrestricted submarine warfare, in Walter Wulf (ed.), *Geschichtliche Quellenhefte* 10, p. 86.

18. Vladimir Ilyich Lenin, *Ausgewählte Werke* (Berlin, 1955), vol. ii, p. 8.

19. From a message from the German ambassador in Copenhagen to the imperial chancellor on 6 Dec. 1915, in Herbert Michaelis and Ernst Schraepler (eds.), *Ursachen und Folgen vom deutschen Zusammenbruch 1918 und 1945 bis zur staatlichen Neuordnung Deutschlands in der Gegenwart* (Berlin, 1959), vol. ii, document 270a.

20. Lev Davidovich Trotzky, *Über Lenin* (Moscow, 1924), p. 94.

21. Vladimir Ilyich Lenin, *Ausgewählte Werke*, vol. ii, p. 310.

22. From a report of the Sixth Army's post surveillance service on 4 Sept. 1918, in Herbert Michaelis and Ernst Schraepler (eds.), *Ursachen und Folgen*, vol. ii, document 356.

23. From Reinhardt's letter to his wife on 12 Oct. 1918, in Fritz Ernst, 'Aus dem Nachlass des Generals Walther Reinhardt', *Die Welt als Geschichte*, Jg.18 (Stuttgart, 1958), p. 42. Infantery general Walther Reinhardt was named Prussian minister of war on 4 Nov. 1918 and was the first chief of the army command in the Weimar Republic.

24. Diary note of Colonel i.G. Albrecht von Thaer on 1 Oct. 1918, in Albrecht von Thaer, *Generalstabsdienst an der Front und in der OHL* (Göttingen, 1958), pp. 233ff.

25. From the American president's message to Congress on 8 Jan. 1918, in Henry Steel Commager (ed.), *Documents of American History*, p. 253.

26. From the first note of the German government to President Wilson on 3/4 Oct. 1918, in Herbert Michaelis and Ernst Schraepler (eds.), *Ursachen und Folgen*, vol ii, document 400.

27. From the American president's note of 23 Oct. 1918, in Saul K. Padoves (ed.), *Wilson's Ideals* (Washington, 1942), p. 87.

28. See above n. 24.

29. Mathias Erzberger, *Erlebnisse im Weltkrieg* (Stuttgart, 1920), p. 336.

30. Fritz Ernst, *Die Deutschen und ihre jüngste Geschichte*, p. 48.

31. Ibid.

11. The Weimar Republic

1. Fritz Ernst, *Die Deutschen und ihre jüngste Geschichte*, p. 47.

2. Ernst Jünger, *Der Kampf als inneres Erlebnis, Sämtliche Werke* (Stuttgart, 1980), 2nd part, vol. vii, p. 73.

3. Fritz Ernst, *Die Deutschen und ihre jüngste Geschichte*, p. 50.

4. Eduard Bernstein, *Die deutsche Revolution* (Berlin, 1921), p. 198.

5. From the accord on the transitional economy between employer

groups and labour unions on 15 Nov. 1918, in Herbert Michaelis and Ernst Schraepler (eds.), *Ursachen und Folgen*, vol. iii, document 538.

6. From a declaration of the German National People's Party on 24 Nov. 1918, ibid., document 641.

7. From a speech by Majority Social Democrat Max Cohn during the conference of workers' and soldiers' soviets in Berlin on 19 Dec. 1918, in Johannes Hohlfeld (ed.), *Dokumente der Deutschen Politik und Geschichte von 1848 bis zur Gegenwart* (Berlin, n.d.), vol. ii, no. 177, pp. 423f.

8. From a declaration of the federal committee of the Centre party on 30 Dec. 1918, in Herbert Michaelis and Ernst Schraepler (eds.), *Ursachen und Folgen*, vol. iii, document 640.

9. From Ebert's inaugural speech as newly elected *Reichspräsident* on 11 Feb. 1919, cited in Waldemar Besson, *Friedrich Ebert*, (Göttingen, 1963), pp. 74f.

10. The German government on 11 Aug. 1919, in Johannes Hohlfeld, *Dokumente der deutschen Politik*, vol. iii, no. 10, pp. 60ff.

11. From Clemenceau's address to the German delegation on 7 May 1919 in Versailles before handing over the peace treaty, in Herbert Michaelis and Ernst Schraepler (eds.), *Ursachen und Folgen*, vol. iii, document 714.

12. From a speech by Scheidemann, cited in Ferdinand Friedensburg, *Die Weimarer Republik* (Berlin, 1946), p. 26.

13. Cited in Martin Stellmann, (ed.), *Die Neueste Zeit*, p. 65.

14. Wilhelm Hoegner, *Die verratene Republik, Geschichte der deutschen Gegenrevolution* (The Republic Betrayed, History of the German Counter-Revolution) (Munich, 1958), p. 52.

15. German government declaration of 26 Sept. 1923, in Johannes Hohlfeld, *Dokumente der deutschen Politik und Geschichte*, vol. iii, no. 22c, p. 131.

16. Cited in Arnold Harttung (ed.), *Gustav Stresemann Schriften* (Berlin, 1976), p. 375.

17. Fritz Ernst, *Die Deutschen und ihre jüngste Geschichte*, p. 73.

18. *Lord d'Abernon's Diary* (London, 1929), vol. ii, p. 290.

19. Ibid., p. 283.

20. Cited in Wilhelm Treue, *Deutsche Geschichte* (Stuttgart, 1978), p. 716.

21. Erich Eyck, *Geschichte der Weimarer Republic* (Erlenbach, Zurich, 1974⁴), p. 440.

22. Otto Braun, *Von Weimar zu Hitler* (Hamburg, 1949), p. 85.

23. Friedrich Meinecke, *Politische Schriften und Reden*, p. 365.

24. Fritz Ernst, *Die Deutschen und ihre jüngste Geschichte*, p. 75.

25. Cited in Henry Bernhard (ed.), *Gustav Stresemanns Vermächtnis, Der Nachlass in drei Bänden* (Berlin, 1932/33), vol. ii, p. 592.

26. Cited in Paul Schmidt, *Statist auf diplomatischer Bühne 1923–1945* (Bonn, 1954), p. 91.

27. The Kellog pact of 27 Aug. 1928, in Gottfried Guggenbühl, *Quellen zur Geschichte der Neuesten Zeit*, pp. 391f.

28. Cited in Werner Baron von Rheinbaben, *Kaiser, Kanzler, Präsidenten* (Mainz, 1968), pp. 243ff.

29. Cited in Erich Eyck, *Geschichte der Weimarer Republik* (Zurich,

1956), vol. ii, p. 339, n. 19a.

30. Karl Dietrich Erdmann, 'Die Zeit der Weltkriege' in Bruno Gebhardt, *Handbuch der deutschen Geschichte* (Stuttgart, 1959³), vol. iv, p. 166.

31. From Brüning's government declaration before the *Reichstag* on 1 April 1930, in Johannes Hohlfeld (ed.), *Dokumente der Deutschen Politik und Geschichte* (Berlin, n.d.), vol. iii, no. 88, p. 296.

32. Karl Dietrich Bracher, 'Brünings unpolitische Politik und die Auflösung der Weimarer Republik', *Vierteljahresschrift für Zeitgeschichte* 19 Jg. (1970), p. 122.

33. Heinrich Brüning, *Memoiren, 1918–1934* (Stuttgart, 1970), p. 387.

34. Karl Dietrich Bracher, 'Brünings unpolitische Politik und die Auflösung der Weimarer Republik', p. 122.

35. Fritz Ernst, *Die Deutschen und ihre jüngste Geschichte*, p. 87.

36. Records of Cardinal Faulhaber, vol. i, edited by Ludwig Volk (Mainz, 1975), in Rudolf Morsey, *Zur Entstehung, Authenzität und Kritik von Brünings Memoiren 1918–1924* (Opladen, 1975), p. 40.

37. Werner Conze, 'Brüning als Reichskanzler, Eine Zwischenbilanz', *Historische Zeitschrift* 214 (1972), p. 334.

38. Ulrich Scheuner, 'Preussen – ein Staat der Anstrengung und des Masses' (Prussia – A State of Effort and Moderation), in Wolfgang Böhme (ed.), *Preussen – eine Herausforderung*, Herrenhalber Texte 32 (Karlsruhe, 1981), p 25.

39. Report in the *Kölnische Zeitung* of 25 Nov. 1932 (morning edition no. 645), in Walther Hofer (ed.), *Der Nationalsozialismus, Dokumente 1933–1945* (Frankfurt a.M.), p. 25.

40. Cited in Theodor Eschenburg, *Die Rolle der Persönlichkeit in der Krise der Weimarer Republic*, p. 70.

41. Cited in Gerhart Binder, *Epoche der Entscheidungen* (Stuttgart, 1960⁵), p. 234.

12. The Rise of Totalitarianism

1. Cited in Walter Theimer, *Geschichte der politischen Ideen* (Munich, 1955), p. 384.

2. Joseph W. Stalin, *Fragen des Leninismus* (Berlin, 1951), p. 173.

3. From the Convenant of the League of Nations, in Gottfried Guggenbühl (ed.), *Quellen zur Geschichte der Neuzeit*, p. 377.

13. From Hitler's Seizure of Power to the Outbreak of the Second World War

1. Kurt Sontheimer, 'Der Nationalismus und seine Folgen', in *Deutschland, die geteilte Nation* (Heidelberg, 1983), p. 46.

2. *Kreuz-Zeitung* of 31 Jan. 1933, no. 31, in Werner Conze (ed.), *Der Nationalsozialismus, Quellen und Arbeitshefte* (Stuttgart, 1959), p. 52.

3. Stefan George, *Werke*, vol.1/2 (Munich, Düsseldorf, 1958), p. 418.

4. Thomas Mann, *Deutsche Ansprache, Ein Appell an die Vernunft* (A German Address and Appeal to Reason) (Berlin, 1930), pp. 13f.

5. Adolf Hitler, *Mein Kampf*, trans. Ralph Mannheim (Boston, 1943), p. 22

6. Walther Hofer (ed.), *Der Nationalsozialismus, Dokumente 1933–1945* (Frankfurt a.M., 1957), p. 11.

7. Sebastian Haffner, *Anmerkungen zu Hitler*, (Munich, 1978), p. 23.

8. From *Mein Kampf*, cited in Walther Hofer (ed.), *Deutsche Geschichte*, p. 35.

9. Cited in Alan Bullock, *Hitler: A Study in Tyranny* (London, 1952), p. 400.

10. Adolf Hitler, *Mein Kampf*, p. 255

11. Ibid., p. 296

12. Ibid., p. 290.

13. Ibid., p. 325

14. Ibid., p. 300.

15. Ibid., p. 339.

16. From a brochure on world-view education from the year 1944, in Walther Hofer (ed.), *Der Nationalsozialismus*, p. 731.

17. Ibid.

18. Adolf Hitler, *Mein Kampf*, pp. 645f.

19. Ibid., p. 654.

20. Ibid.

21. Ibid., p. 345.

22. Reprinted in Walther Hofer (ed.), *Der Nationalsozialismus*, pp. 53f.

23. Hitler's speech before the *Reichstag* on 21 March 1933 about the Enabling Act, in *Dokumente der deutschen Politik* (Berlin, 1935), vol. i, pp. 35f.

24. Paragraph 1 of the law forbidding the formation of new political parties, in *Reichsgesetzblatt*, Jg. 1933, Teil I, p. 479. Law on the Security of the Party and the State of 1 Dec. 1933, ibid., p. 1016.

25. Hitler before the *Reich* governors on 6 July 1933 on the end of the revolution, in Paul Meier-Benneckenstein (ed.), *Dokumente der deutschen Geschichte* (Berlin, 1935), vol. i, pp. 58f.

26. Volker Hentschel, 'Demokratie und totalitäre Herrschaft', in Ploetz, *Deutsche Geschichte*, p. 292.

27. From a 1935 speech by minister of the interior Wilhelm Frick, in Walther Hofer (ed.), *Der Nationalsozialismus*, p. 128.

28. From the law governing national labour of 20 Jan. 1934, in *Reichsgesetzblatt*, Jg. 1934, Teil I, pp. 45ff.

29. Inherited estates act of 29 Sept. 1933, in: *Reichsgesetzblatt*, Jg. 1933, Teil I, p. 685.

30. From a speech by minister Frick on 19 Nov. 1936, in Paul Meier-Benneckenstein (ed.), *Dokumente der Deutschen Politik* (Berlin, 1937), vol. iv, p. 201.

31. Directive from the president of the Authors' League on 25 April 1935, cited in Hildegard Brenner, *Die Kunstpolitik des Nationalsozialismus* (Reinbeck b. Hamburg, 1963), p. 194.

32. Ibid., pp. 186f.

33. From a speech by minister Frick at the provincial ministers conference on the new education on 9 May 1933, in Paul Meier-Benneckenstein (ed.), *Dokumente der Deutschen Politik*, vol. i, p. 301.

34. Göring on 12 July 1934 before lawyers and directors of public prosecutions, cited in Helmut Krausnick, 'Der 30. Juni 1934', supplement to the weekly newspaper *Das Parliament*, 30 June 1954, p. 317.

35. Hitler before the *Reichstag* on 13 July 1934, in Gerd Rühle (ed.), *Das Dritte Reich, Dokumentarische Darstellung des Aufbaues der Nation* (Berlin, n.d.), vol. ii, p. 245.

36. Cited in Hans Buchheim, Martin Broszat, Hans-Adolf Jacobsen, and Helmut Krausnick, *Anatomie des SS-Staates* (Olten, 1967), vol. i, p. 93.

37. Handwritten record by Lieutenant-General Liebmann of Hitler's speech before army and navy commanders on 3 Feb. 1933, in *Vierteljahreshefte Für Zeitgeschichte*, Jg. 2 (1954), p. 435.

38. Volker Hentschel, *Demokratie und totalitäre Herrschaft*, p. 295.

39. Hitler's speech before the *Reichstag* on 21 May 1935, in Paul Meier-Benneckenstein (ed.), *Dokumente der Deutschen Politik* (Berlin, 1937), vol. iii, p. 86.

40. Hitler's *Reichstag* speech on 7 March 1936, ibid., vol. iv, p. 112.

41. From Hitler's secret memorandum of Aug. 1936 on the aims of the four-year economic plan, in *Vierteljahreshefte für Zeitgeschichte*, Jg. 3 (1955), p. 20.

42. Transcript of the discussion in the *Reich* Chancellery on 5 Nov. 1937, in Walther Hofer (ed.), *Der Nationalsozialismus*, pp. 193ff.

43. Cited in Gordon A Craig, *Europe Since 1815*, p. 715.

44. Top secret military document of 30 May 1938, in Walther Hofer (ed.), *Der Nationalsozialismus*, p. 204.

45. Cited in Wolfgang Foerster, *Generaloberst Ludwig Beck, Sein Kampf gegen den Krieg* (Munich, 1953), pp. 118ff.

46. Cited in Karl Dietrich Erdmann, 'Die Zeit der Weltkriege' in Bruno Gebhardt, *Handbuch der Deutschen Geschichte* (Stuttgart, 1959³), vol. iv, p. 241.

47. From Hitler's speech in the Berlin sports palace on 26 Sep. 1938, in Walther Hofer (ed.), *Der Nationalsozialismus*, p. 207.

48. From Hitler's speech on 28 April 1939, in Sebastian Haffner, *Anmerkungen zu Hitler*, p. 44.

49. Cited in Hellmut Diwald, *Geschichte der Deutschen*, p. 138.

50. Hitler's declaration before the military leadership on 23 May 1939, in Walther Hofer (ed.), *Der Nationalsozialismus*, p. 227.

51. Hitler in May 1939, cited in Hellmut Diwald, *Geschichte der Deutschen*, p. 145.

14. The Second World War and the Annihilation of the Third Reich

1. Hitler's declaration before the military leadership on 23 May 1939, in Walther Hofer (ed.), *Der Nationalsozialismus*, p. 226.

2. Golo Mann, *Deutsche Geschichte*, p. 908 [see Ch. 1 n.7 for translation title].

3. Cited ibid., p. 898.

4. Cited in Paul Schmidt, *Statist auf diplomatischer Bühne, 1923–1945*, p. 474.

5. Cited in Golo Mann, *Deutsche Geschichte*, p. 896.

6. Birger Dahlerus, *Der letzte Versuch* (Munich, 1948), pp. 128f.

7. Comment by Hitler on 27 November 1941, in Sebastian Haffner, *Anmerkungen zu Hitler*, p. 198.

8. Hitler in his speech before the *Reichstag* on 19 July 1940, in Walther Hofer (ed.), *Der Nationalsozialismus*, p. 241.

9. Winston Churchill, *Reden 1938–1940* (Zurich, 1946), vol. ii, p. 320.

10. Lend-Lease law of 8 Feb. 1941, § 3, subparagraph 1, in H.E. Commager, *Documents of American History*.

11. From a discussion by the Führer on 31 July 1940, in Walther Hofer (ed.), *Der Nationalsozialismus*, p. 243.

12. Operation Barbarossa, Hitler's directives to the *Wehrmacht* on 18 Dec. 1940, ibid., p. 243.

13. Sebastian Haffner, *Anmerkungen zu Hitler*, p. 145.

14. *Grundlagen der Freiheit, Bedeutende Dokumente der Vereinigten Staaten von Amerika* (Bad Godesberg, n.d.), p. 38.

15. Hitler in late 1941, cited in Sebastian Haffner, *Anmerkungen zu Hitler*, p. 150.

16. Hitler's decree of 1 March 1942, in Walther Hofer (ed.), *Der Nationalsozialismus*, p. 248.

17. Erich Koch in a speech on 26 Aug. 1942, cited in Alexander Dallin, *Deutsche Herrschaft in Russland 1941–1945, Eine Studie über Besatzungspolitik* (Düsseldorf, 1958), p. 154.

18. Hitler's speech before the *Reichstag* on 30 Jan. 1939, in Walther Hofer (ed.), *Der Nationalsozialismus*, p. 277.

19. From the transcript of the Wannsee conference of 20 Jan. 1942, in Walther Hofer (ed.), *Der Nationalsozialismus*, p. 304.

20. Golo Mann, *Deutsche Geschichte*, p. 945.

21. Joseph Goebbels's announcement of total war in his speech from the Berlin Sports Palace on 18 Feb. 1943, in Walther Hofer (ed.), *Der Nationalsozialismus*, pp. 250ff.

22. Sermon delivered by Bishop Clemens August von Galen on 13 July 1941 on the arbitrary methods of the Gestapo, cited in Johann Neuhäusler, *Der Kampf des Nationalsozialismus gegen die katholische Kirche und der kirchliche Widerstand* (Munich, 1946²), part 2, pp. 177ff.

23. In his speech from the Berlin Sports Palace on 18 Feb. 1943 (see above n. 21).

24. From the last pamphlet of White Rose in Feb. 1943, in Inge Scholl, *Die weisse Rose* (Frankfurt a. M., 1953), pp. 151ff.

25. Cited in Golo Mann, *Deutsche Geschichte*, p. 952.

26. Hitler's decree of 25 Sept. 1944 on the creation of the *Volkssturm*, in Walther Hofer (ed.), *Der Nationalsozialismus*, pp. 252f.

27. From an order of the minister of justice on 15 Feb. 1945 concerning the creation of summary courts, ibid., p. 254.

28. Hitler's devastation order of 19 March 1945, ibid., pp. 259f.

29. Albert Speer, *Inside the Third Reich: Memoirs by Albert Speer*, trans.

R. and C. Winston (New York, 1970), p. 554.

30. According to the chief of the general staff Franz Halder, in Walther Hofer (ed.), *Der Nationalisozialismus*, p. 264.

31. Albert Speer, *Inside the Third Reich*, p. 557.

32. The controversy about the political structure created by the Nazis, which assumed particular importance in interpretations of the entire period between 1933 and 1945, has recently died down. See in this regard: Martin Broszat, 'Soziale Motivation und Führer-Bindung des Nationalsozialismus', *Vierteljahreshefte für Zeitgeschichte* (1970), pp. 392ff.; Hans Mommsen, 'Nationalsozialismus oder Hitlerismus?' in Michael Bosch (ed.), *Persönlichkeit und Struktur in der Geschichte* (Düsseldorf, 1977); Klaus Hildebrand, 'Nationalsozialismus ohne Hitler? Das Dritte Reich als Forschungsgegenstand der Geschichtswissenschaft', *Geschichte in Wissenschaft und Unterricht* (1980), pp. 289ff. and *GWU* (1981), pp. 200ff.; Eberhard Jäckel, *Hitlers Weltanschauung, Entwurf einer Herrschaft* (Stuttgart, 1981).

33. Cited in Fritz Ernst, *Die Deutschen und ihre jüngste Geschichte*, p. 122.

15. The Post-War World

1. See above Chapter 11, n. 40.

2. Speech by American President Harry S. Truman on 12 March 1947 in Henry Steele Commager (ed.), *Documents of American History* (1949), p. 721.

3. Ibid.

4. Peter Bollmann, Ulrich March and Traute Petersen, *Kleine Geschichte Europas* (Stuttgart, 1980), p. 167.

16. Germany from 1945 to 1949

1. Golo Mann, *Deutsche Geschichte* p. 939 [see Ch.1 n.7 for translation title].

2. Carlo Schmid, *Der Weg des deutschen Volkes nach 1945* (Berlin, 1967), p. 11.

3. Winston Churchill, *The Second World War*, 6 vols. (London, 1949), vol. V, p. 359.

4. Wolfgang Leonhard, *Die Revolution entlässt ihre Kinder* (Cologne, 1961), p. 336.

5. Ibid., p. 358.

6. Founding proclamation of the KPD on 11 June 1945, in Walrab von Buttlar, *Ziele und Zielkonflikte der sowjetischen Deutschlandpolitik 1945–1947* (Stuttgart, 1980), p. 134.

7. Land reform decree of Aug. 1945, in Hans Hartl and Werner Marx, *Fünfzig Jahre sowjetische Deutschlandpolitik* (Boppard, 1967), p. 195.

8. Order no. 124 of the SMA, 'On the Confiscation and Provisional Seizure of Certain Property Categories', cited in Hans Hartl and Werner

Marx, *Fünfzig Jahre sowjetische Deutschlandpolitik*, pp. 196f.

9. Charter of the *Länderrat* in the American Occupation Zone, § 2, in Theo Stammen (ed.), *Einigkeit und Recht und Freiheit, Westdeutsche Innenpolitik 1945–1955* (Munich, 1968), p. 53.

10. Wolfgang Trees et al., *Drei Jahre nach Null* (Düsseldorf, 1978), p. 89.

11. Peter Waldmann, 'Die Eingliederung der ostdeutschen Vertriebenen in die westdeutsche Gesellschaft' (The Integration of the East German Expellees into West German society) in Josef Becker et al., *Vorgeschichte der Bundersrepublik Deutschland* (Munich, 1979), pp. 179f.

12. Hans Erich Nossack in a letter of 30 Nov. 1945 to Hermann Kasack, in Bernhard Zeller, *Als der Krieg zu Ende war* (Munich, 1973), p. 91.

13. Cited in Generallandesarchiv Karlsruhe (ed.), *Der deutsche Südwesten zur Stunde Null* (Karlsruhe, 1975), p. 222.

14. Cited in Rudolph Hagen, *Die verpassten Chancen* (The Missed Opportunities) (Hamburg, 1979), p. 136.

15. Ibid.

16. Fritz Ernst, *Die Deutschen und ihre jüngste Geschichte*, p. 130.

17. Gerhard Ritter, *Europa und die deutsche Frage* (Munich, 1948), p. 200.

18. From the resolutions of the SPD party convention in Hanover on 11 May 1946, in Ossip K. Flechtheim (ed.), *Dokumente zur parteipolitischen Entwicklung in Deutschland seit 1945* (Berlin, 1963), vol. iii, pp. 17–20.

19. From the proclamation and party programme of the British zone CDU committee on 1 March 1946, ibid., vol. ii, p. 49.

20. From the CDU's Ahlen economic programme for Nordrhein-Westfalen of 3 Feb. 1947, ibid., pp. 53ff.

21. Cf. the FDP guidelines of 4 Feb. 1946, ibid., p. 274.

22. From the Stuttgart address of Secretary of State Byrnes on 6 Sept. 1946, in *Documents on Germany 1944–61* (Washington 1961, pp. 55 and 58f.)

23. Ibid.

24. 'Agreement on the Reorganisation of the Bizonal Economic Administration' of 29 May 1947, which was approved by the bizonal *Landtage* on 25 June 1947, in *Documents on Germany under Occupation 1945–1954*, selected and edited by Beate Ruhm von Oppen (Oxford, 1955), p. 228.

25. Cited in Wilhelm Cornides (ed.), *Europa Archiv, Zeitgeschichte, Zeitkritik, Verwaltung, Wirtschaftsaufbau* (Munich, 1946), p. 1349.

26. From the CDU's Düsseldorf principles of 15 July 1949, in Theo Stammen, ibid., pp. 94ff.

27. Carlo Schmid, *Der Weg des deutschen Volkes nach 1945*, p. 69.

28. From the preamble to the Basic Law, in: *Grundgesetz mit Deutschlandvertrag, Menschenrechtskonvention, Bundeswahlgesetz* (Munich, 1974[15]), p. 29.

29. Ibid., p. 80.

30. Carlo Schmid, *Der Weg des deutschen Volkes nach 1945*, p. 76.

17. Germany After 1949

1. Dean Acheson on United States policy towards Central Europe, in Hans Peter Schwarz, *Vom Reich zur Bundesrepublik* (Neuwied, 1966), p. 144.

2. See article 21 of the Basic Law in *Grundgesetz mit Deutschlandvertrag, Menschenrechtskonvention, Bundeswahlgesetz, Parteiengesetz*, p. 35.

3. First government declaration of Chancellor Konrad Adenauer before the German *Bundestag*, in *Verhandlungen des 1. Deutschen Bundestages*, 3rd session of 20 Sept. 1949, pp. 22–30.

4. Cf. article 20 of the Basic Law, n. 2.

5. Cited in *Die Zeit* 3 Nov. 1949.

6. Adenauer's interview with the *New York Times* on 7 March 1950.

7. Carlo Schmid, *Erinnerungen* (Berlin, Darmstadt, Vienna, 1979), p. 493.

8. Ibid., p. 500.

9. Ibid., pp. 501f.

10. From the Soviet government note to the governments of France, Great Britain and the United States on 10 March 1952, cited in Eberhard Jäckel, *Die deutsche Frage 1952–1956, Notenwechsel und Konferenzdokumente der vier Mächte* (Frankfurt a.M., 1957), p. 23.

11. Ibid., p. 24.

12. See p. 00

13. Herman Graml, 'Die Aussenpolitik', in Wolfgang Benz (ed.), *Die Bundesrepublik Deutschland* (Frankfurt a. M., 1983), vol. i, p. 364.

14. See Hans Hartl and Werner Marx, *Fünfzig Jahre sowjetische Deutschlandpolitik* (Boppard, 1967), p. 519.

15. From the Godesberg programme of 15 Nov. 1959, in *Grundsatzprogramm der Sozialdemokratischen Partei Deutschlands, beschlossen auf dem Ausserordentlichen Parteitag der Sozialdemokratischen Partei in Bad Godesberg vom 13.–15. November 1959*, party executive (ed.), (Bonn, 1959), p. 29.

16. Kurt Georg Kiesinger's government declaration of 13 Dec. 1966, in Bundesministerium für gesamtdeutsche Fragen (ed.), *Texte zur Deutschlandpolitik* (Bonn, Berlin, 1968ff.), vol. i, pp. 7f.

17. Article 5,2 of the Convention on Relations between the Three Western Powers and the Federal Republic (German Treaty) of 26 May 1952, in *Grundgesetz mit Deutschlandvertrag, Menschenrechtskonvention, Bundeswahlgesetz, Parteiengesetz*, p. 83.

18. René Ahlberg, *Ursachen der Revolte, Analyse des studentischen Protests* (Sources of Revolt, An Analysis of the Student Protest) (Stuttgart, 1972), p. 13.

19. Richard Löwenthal, *Der romantische Rückfall* (Stuttgart, 1970), p. 82.

20. Cited in *Wissenschaftlicher Kommunismus, Lehrbuch für das Marxistisch-leninistische Grundlagenstudium* (Scientific Communism, A Textbook of Basic Marxist-Leninist Studies) (East Berlin, 1979), pp. 444ff.

21. United States Senate, Committee on Foreign Relations, *Documents on Germany, 1944–1961* (Washington, 1961), p. 55.

22. Kunze, Töpfer, 'Die Gewerkschaften in unserer Gesellschaft', *Einheit, Zeitschrift für Theorie und Praxis des wissenschaftenlichen Sozialismus*, Jg.29 (East Berlin, 1974), p. 818.

23. Cf. Gerd Meyer, 'Die politische Elite der DDR', in Hans-Georg Wehling (ed.), *DDR* (Stuttgart, 1983), pp. 96f.

24. Ibid., p. 98.

25. Article 118 of the DDR constitution of 7 Oct. 1949, in Horst Hildebrandt (ed.), *Die deutschen Verfassungen des 19. und 20. Jahrhunderts* (Paderborn, Munich, Vienna, Zurich, 1982³), p. 225.

26. Article 1 of the DDR constitution of 9 April 1968, ibid., p. 235.

27. Article 8 of the DDR constitution of 9 April 1968, ibid., p. 239.

28. Article 6 of the DDR constitution of 7 Oct. 1974, ibid., p. 237.

29. Andreas Hillgruber, *Deutsche Geschichte 1945–1982* (Stuttgart, Berlin, Cologne, Mainz, 1983⁵), p. 105.

30. Treaty between the Federal Republic of Germany and the Soviet Union on 12 Aug. 1970, in Bundesministerium für gesamtdeutsche Fragen (ed.), *Texte zur Deutschlandpolitik*, vol. vi, pp. 93ff.

31. Ibid.

32. Ibid., pp. 258ff.

33. Ibid., Series II, vol. ii, pp. 210ff.

34. Quotation from *Der Spiegel* of 10 Aug. 1970.

35. Quotation from *Die Welt* of 13 Aug. 1970.

36. Treaty on the Basis of Relations between the Federal Republic of Germany and the German Democratic Republic, in Helmut Krause and Karlheinz Reif (eds.), *Die Welt seit 1945* (Munich, 1980), pp. 556f.

37. Andreas Hillgruber, 'Deutschland in der Weltpolitik des 19. und 20. Jahrhunderts, Rückschau und Ausblick', in Ploetz, *Deutsche Geschichte*, p. 348.

38. Ibid.

Select English-Language Bibliography

Note: This bibliography of recent books in English is intended to provide further reading for each period. It does not list titles cited in the references.

German-Speaking Countries up to the Eighteenth Century

ABEL, W., *Agricultural Fluctuations in Europe from the Thirteenth to the Twentieth Centuries*, London 1980.

ARNOLD, B. *German Knighthood 1050–1300*, Oxford 1985.

BARRACLOUGH, G. *The Origins of Modern Germany*, Oxford 1947.

BENECKE, G., *Security and Politics in Germany 1500–1750*, London 1974.

—, *Maximilian I: 1459–1519*, London 1982.

—, (ed.), *Germany in the Thirty Years' War*, London 1978.

—, and BAK, J. M. (eds), *Religion and Rural Revolt*, Manchester 1984.

BLICKLE, P., *The Revolution of 1525*, Baltimore, Md, 1982.

BRADY, J. A., Jr, *Turning Swiss: Cities and Empire 1450–1550*, Cambridge 1985.

BRECHT, M., *Martin Luther*, New York, 1985.

CARSTEN, F. L., *The Origins of Russia*, Oxford 1954.

—, *Princes and Parliaments in Germany from the Fifteenth to the Eighteenth Centuries*, Oxford 1959.

CHRISTENSEN, C. C., *Art and the Reformation in Germany*, Ohio University Press, 1979.

COHN, H., *The Government of the Rhine Palatinate in the Fifteenth Century*, Oxford 1965.

COWAN, A. F., *The Urban Patriciate: Lubeck and Venice 1580–1700*, Cologne-Vienna 1986.

DICKENS, A. G., *Martin Luther and the Reformation*, London 1967.

—, *The German Nation and Martin Luther*, London 1974.

DOLLINGER, P., *The German Hansa*, London 1970.

DU BOULAY, F. R. H., *Germany in the Later Middle Ages*, Cambridge 1983.

EVANS, R. J. W., *Rudolf II and his World: A Study in Intellectual History 1576–1612*, Oxford 1984.

FUHRMANN, H., *Germany in the High Middle Ages. c.1050–1200*, Cambridge 1986.

GREYERTZ, K. von. (ed.), *Religion and Social Protest: Three Studies in Early Modern Germany*, London 1984.

HEER, F., *The Holy Roman Empire*, London 1967.

HOFFMEISTER, G. (ed.), *The Renaissance and Reformation in Germany*, New York 1977.

HOLBORN, H., *A History of Modern Germany*. vols. i: *The Reformation*, New York 1959 and ii: *1648–1840*, New York 1965.

HUBATSCH, W., *Studies in Medieval and Modern German History*, New York 1985.

KIRCHNER, H., *Luther and the Peasants' War*, Philadelphia, Pa, 1972.

KOURI, E. T. and SCOTT, T. (eds), *Politics and Society in Reformation Europe*, London 1987.

KRIEDTE, P. *Peasants, Landlords and Merchant Capitalists*, Leamington Spa 1983.

LEUSCHNER, J., *Germany in the Later Middle Ages*, Amsterdam, 1980.

LORTZ, J., *The Reformation in Germany*, London 1968.

MOELLER, B., *Imperial Cities and the Reformation*, Philadelphia, Pa 1972.

OVERFIELD, J. H., *Humanism and Scholasticism in Late Medieval Germany*, Princeton, NJ, 1984.

PANOVSKY, E., *The Life and Art of Albrecht Dürer*, Princeton, NJ, 1955.

PARKER, G., *The Thirty Years' War*, London 1984.

SABEAN, D. W., *Power in the Blood: Popular Culture and Village Discourse in Early Modern Germany*, Cambridge 1984.

SCRIBNER, R. W., *For the Sake of Simple Folk: Popular Propaganda for the German Reformation*, Cambridge 1981.

—, and BENECKE, G., *The German Peasant War of 1525: New Viewpoints*, London 1979.

STRAUSS, G. (ed.), *Pre-Reformation Germany*, London 1972.

TRACY, J. D. (ed.), *Luther and the Modern State*, Kirksville, Miss., 1986.

WHALEY, J., *Religious Toleration and Social Change in Hamburg 1529–1819*, Cambridge 1985.

The Eighteenth Century

BAUMANN, T., *North German Opera in the Age of Goethe*, Cambridge 1985.

BLANNING, T. C. W., *The French Revolution in Germany: Occupation and Resistance in the Rhineland 1792–1802*, Oxford 1983.

CRAIG, G. A., *The Politics of the Prussian Army 1640–1945*, Oxford 1955.

HOOVER, A. J., *The Gospel of Nationalism: German Patriotic Preaching from Napoleon to Versailles*, Stuttgart 1986.

INGRAO, C. W., *The Hessian Mercenary State: Ideas, Institutions and Reform under Frederick III*, Cambridge 1987.

KOSELLECK, R., *Critique and Crisis*, Oxford 1987.

RAEFF, M., *The Well-Ordered Police State: Social and Institutional Change through Law in the Germanies and Russia, 1600–1800*, New Haven, Conn. 1983.

ROSENBERG, H., *Bureaucracy, Aristocracy and Autocracy: The Prussian Experience 1660–1815*, Cambridge, Mass. 1958.

VAN CLEVE, J. W., *The Merchant in German Literature of the Enlightenment*, Chapel Hill, NC 1986.

The Nineteenth Century

Textbooks

BERGHAHN, V. R., *Modern Germany: Society, Economy and Politics in the Twentieth Century*, 2nd edn Cambridge 1988.

CARR, W., *A History of Germany 1815–1985*, London 1986.

CRAIG, G. A., *Germany 1866–1945*, Oxford 1978.

—, *The Germans*, New York 1982.

DAHRENDORF, R., *Democracy and Society in Germany*, London 1968.

HOLBORN, H., *A History of Modern Germany*, vol. iii, *1840–1945*, London 1969.

MANN, G., *Germany since 1789*, London 1968.

RAMM, A., *Germany 1789–1919*, London 1967.

SAGARRA, E., *A Social History of Germany*, London 1977.

The Revolutions of 1848–9

EYCK, F., *The Frankfurt Parliament*, London 1968.

—, (ed.), *The Revolutions of 1848–49*, London 1972.

NAMIER, L., *The Revolution of the Intellectuals*, London 1944.

NOYES, P. H., *Organisation and Revolution*, Princeton 1966.

STADELMANN, R., *Social and Political History of the German 1848 Revolution*, Ohio U. P. 1975.

VALENTIN, V., *1848*, London 1940.

Industrialisation and Society

BADE, K. (ed.), *Population, Labour and Migration in Nineteenth- and Twentieth-Century Germany*, Leamington Spa 1987.

BLACKALL, E. A., *The Novels of the German Romantics*, Ithaca, NY 1983.

BOSSENBROOK, W., *The German Mind*, Detroit 1961.

CLAPHAM, J. H., *The Economic Development of France and Germany 1815–1914*, Cambridge 1936.

EVANS, R. J., *Death in Hamburg*, Oxford 1987.

FOUT, J. C. (ed.), *German Women in the Nineteenth Century*, New York 1984.

FRANZOI, B., *At the very least she pays the Rent: Women and German Industrialisation 1871–1914*, Westport, Conn. 1985.

FREVERT, U., *Women in German History: From Bourgeois Emancipation to Sexual Liberation*, Oxford 1988.

GILLIS, J. R., *The Prussian Bureaucracy in Crisis 1840–1860*, Stanford, Calif. 1971.

GRAY, M. W., *Prussia in Transition: Society and Politics under the Stein Reform Ministry of 1808*, Philadelphia, Pa 1986.

HAGEN, W. W., *Germans, Poles and Jews: The Nationality Conflict in the Prussian East 1772–1914*, Chicago, Ill. 1980.

HENDERSON, W. O., *The Zollverein*, London 1959.
—, *The Rise of German Industrial Power*, London 1975.
—, *The State and the Industrial Revolution in Prussia 1740–1870*, Liverpool 1958.
JOERES, R. E. B. and MAYNES, M. J. (eds), *German Women in the Eighteenth and Nineteenth Centuries: A Social and Literary History*, Bloomington, Ind. 1986.
KITCHEN, M., *The Political Economy of Germany*, London 1978.
KOHN, H., *The Mind of Germany*, London 1962.
LAMBI, I. N., *Free Trade and Protection in Germany*, Wiesbaden 1963.
MCCLELLAN, D., *State, Society and Universities in Germany 1700–1914*, Cambridge 1980.
MAYNES, M. J., *Schooling for the People: Comparative Local Studies of Schooling History in France and Germany 1750–1850*, New York 1985.
ROBERTS, J. S., *Drink, Temperance and the Working Class in Nineteenth-Century Germany*, London 1984.
SCHLEUNES, K. A., *Politics and Pedagogy: Schooling in Prussia and Bavaria 1750–1900* Oxford 1989.
SNELL, J. L. *The Democratic Movement in Germany 1789–1914*, Chapel Hill, NC 1976.
WALKER, M., *German Home Towns*, Ithaca, NY 1971.
WUNDERLICH, F., *Farm Labor in Germany 1810–1945*, Princeton, NJ 1961.

Bismarck and German Unification

ANDERSON, E. N., *Social and Political Conflict in Prussia*, New York 1968.
BÖHME, H. (ed.), *The Foundation of the German Empire*, Oxford 1971.
EYCK, E., *Bismarck and the German Empire*, London 1968.
GALL, L., *Bismarck*, London 1987.
HAMEROW, T. S., *Restoration, Revolution, Reaction*, Princeton, NJ 1958.
—, *The Social Foundations of German Unification*, 2 vols, Princeton, NJ 1969–72.
—, (ed.), *The Age of Bismarck*, New York 1972.
HARRIS, J. F., *Eduard Lasher 1829–1884*, Lanham, Md 1984.
HOPE, N., *The Alternative to German Unification*, Wiesbaden 1973.
KENT, G. O., *Bismarck and his Times*, Southern Ill. U. P. 1978.
PFLANZE, O., *Bismarck and the Development of Germany*, Princeton, NJ 1963.
—, (ed.), *The Unification of Germany*, Hinsdale, Ill. 1968.
STEEFEL, G., *Bismarck, the Hohenzollern Candidacy and the Origins of the Franco-Russian War of 1870*, Cambridge, Mass. 1962.
STERN, F., *Gold and Iron*, London 1977.
TAYLOR, A. J. P., *Bismarck*, London 1955.
WALLER, B., *Bismarck at the Crossroads*, London 1974.
ZUCKER, S., *Ludwig Bamberger*, Pittsburgh, Penn. 1975.

Imperial Germany 1871–1914

Industry and agriculture

BARKIN, K. D., *The Controversy over German Industrialization 1890–1902*, Chicago 1970.
BRUCK, W. F., *Social and Economic History of Germany 1888–1938*, Oxford 1938.
BRY, G., *Wages in Germany 1871–1945*, Princeton 1960.
CECIL, L., *Albert Ballin*, Princeton 1969.
DESAI, A. V., *Real Wages in Germany 1871–1913*, Oxford 1968.
EVANS, R. J. (ed.), *The German Peasantry*, London 1985.
STOLPER, G., *The German Economy from 1870 to the Present*, London 1967.
VEBLEN, T., *Imperial Germany and the Industrial Revolution*, London 1915.
WEHLER, H.-U., *The German Empire*, Leamington Spa 1985.

State and society in Imperial Germany

ALBISETTI, J. C., *Secondary School Reform in Imperial Germany*, Princeton 1983.
(ANGEL-) VOLKOV, S., *The Rise of Popular Antimodernism in Germany*, Princeton 1978.
BLACKBOURN, D., *Class, Religion and Local Politics in Wilhelmine Germany*, New Haven 1980.
CECIL, L., *The German Diplomatic Service*, Princeton 1976.
CREW, D., *Town in the Ruhr*, New York 1979.
DEMETER, K., *The German Officer Corps*, London 1965.
ELEY, G., and Blackbourn, D., *The Peculiarities of German History*, Oxford 1985.
EVANS, R. J. (ed.), *Society and Politics in Wilhelmine Germany*, London 1978.
GELLATELY, R., *The Politics of Economic Despair*, London 1974.
GUTTSMAN, W. L., *The German Social Democratic Party 1875–1933*, London 1981.
HERWIG, H., *The German Naval Officer Corps*, Oxford 1973.
IGGERS, G. G. (ed.), *The Social History of Politics*, Leamington Spa 1986.
—, *Students, Society and Politics in Imperial Germany*, Princeton 1982.
RINGER, F. K., *The Decline of the German Mandarins*, Cambridge, Mass. 1969.
RITTER, G. A., *Social Welfare in Germany and Britain*, Leamington Spa 1986.
SPREE, R., *Health and Social Class in Imperial Germany*, New York and Leamington Spa 1988.
WITT, P.-C. (ed.), *Wealth and Taxation in Central Europe*, Leamington Spa and New York 1987.

Parliamentary and extra-parliamentary politics

CHICKERING, R., *Imperial Germany and a World Without War*, Princeton,

NJ 1975.

—, *We Men Who Feel Most German*, London 1984.

ELEY, G., *Reshaping the German Right*, New Haven, Conn. 1980.

—, *From Unification to Naziam*, London 1985.

EPSTEIN, K., *Matthias Erzberger and the Dilemma of German Democracy*, Princeton, NJ 1959.

EVANS, E. L., *The German Center Party*, Carbondale, Ill. 1981.

LEVY, R. S., *The Downfall of the Anti-Semitic Political Parties in Imperial Germany*, New Haven, Conn. 1975.

MOSSE, G. L., *The Nationalization of the Masses*, New York 1975.

NICHOLS, J. A., *Germany After Bismarck*, Cambridge, Mass. 1958.

PECK, A., *Radicals and Reactionaries*, New York 1979.

PULZER, P. J., *The Rise of Political Antisemitism in Germany and Austria*, New York 1964.

RÖHL, J. C. G., *Germany Without Bismarck*, London 1967.

SPERBER, J., *Popular Catholicism in 19th-Century Germany*, Princeton, NJ 1984.

SUVAL, S., *Electoral Politics in Wilhelmine Germany*, Chapel Hill, NC 1985.

TIRRELL, S. R., *German Agrarian Politics After Bismarck's Fall*, New York 1971.

ZEENDER, J. K., *The German Center Party 1890–1906*, Philadelphia, Pa 1976.

Social Democracy

EVANS, R. J. (ed.), *The German Working Class*, London 1982.

FLETCHER, R., *Revisionism and Empire*, London 1984.

GAY, P., *The Dilemma of Democratic Socialism*, New York 1962.

GUTTSMAN, W. L., *The German Social Democratic Party 1875–1933*, London 1981.

HALL, A., *Scandal, Sensation and Social Democracy*, Cambridge 1977.

LIDTKE, V., *The Alternative Culture*, Oxford 1985.

—, *The Outlawed Party*, Princeton, NJ 1965.

MOSES, J. A., *German Trade Unionism from Bismarck to Hitler*, 2 vols., London 1981.

ROTH, G., *The Social Democrats of Imperial Germany*, Totowa NJ 1961.

SCHORSKE, C. E., *German Social Democracy, 1905–1917*, New York 1972.

Women, family and youth

BECKER, H., *German Youth. Bond or Free*, London 1946.

EVANS, R. J., *The Feminist Movement in Germany 1894–1933*, London 1976.

EVANS, R. J., and LEE, W. R. (eds), *The German Family*, London 1980.

HACKETT, A. K., *The Politics of Feminism in Wilhelmine Germany, 1890–1918*, New York 1979.

LAQUEUR, W., *Young Germany*, New York 1962.

QUAETERT, J. H., *Reluctant Feminists in German Social Democracy*,

Princeton NJ. 1979.
STACHURA, P. D., *The German Youth Movement, 1900–1945*, London 1981.

Cultural life

ALLEN, A. T., *Satire and Society in Wilhelmine Germany*, Louisville 1985.
GRAY, R., *The German Tradition in Literature*, Cambridge 1965.
PASCAL, R., *From Naturalism to Expressionism*, New York 1973.
SACKETT, R. E., *Popular Entertainment*, Cambridge, Mass. 1982.

Foreign Policy

ANDERSON, P. R., *The Background to Anti-English Feeling in Germany 1890–1902*, Washington, DC 1939.
BALFOUR, M., *The Kaiser and His Times*, London 1964.
BERGHAHN, V. R., *Germany and the Approach of War in 1914*, London 1973.
CROTHERS, G. D., *The German Elections of 1907*, New York 1967.
DEHIO, L., *Germany and World Politics in the 20th Century*, New York 1959.
FISCHER, F., *War of Illusions*, London 1975.
GEISS, I., *German Foreign Policy 1871–1914*, London 1976.
HECKART, B., *From Bassermann to Bebel*, New Haven, Conn. 1974.
HULL, I. V., *The Kaiser and his Entourage*, Cambridge 1982.
JARAUSCH, K., *The Enigmatic Chancellor*, New Haven, Conn. 1973.
KEHR, E., *Battleship Building and Party Politics in Germany*, Chicago, Ill. 1973.
KEHR, E., *Economic Interest, Militarism and Foreign Policy*, Berkeley, Calif. 1977.
KENNEDY, P. M., *The Rise of the Anglo-German Antagonism*, London 1980.
LAMBI, I., *The Navy and German Power Politics 1862–1914*, London 1984.
McCLELLAN, D., *The German Historians and England*, Cambridge 1971.
RÖHL, J., and Sombart, N. (eds.), *Kaiser Wilhelm II*, Cambridge 1982.

War and Revolution, 1914–1918

The beginning of the First World War

CLARKE, I. F., *Voices Prophesying War*, London 1970.
FARRAR JR, L. L., *The Short-War Illusion*, Santa Barbara, Calif. 1973.
FISCHER, F., *War of Illusions*, London 1975.
KENNEDY, P. M., (ed.), *The War Plans of the Great Powers 1880–1914*, London 1979.
KITCHEN, M., *A Military History of Germany*, London 1975.
RITTER, G., *The Sword and the Sceptre*, London 1973.

The strains of total war

ARMESON, R. B., *Total War and Compulsory Labor*, The Hague 1964.
BERGHAHN, V. R., and KITCHEN, M. (eds.), *Germany in the Age of Total War*, London 1981.
FELDMAN, G. D., *Army, Industry and Labor in Germany 1914–1918*, Princeton, NJ 1966.
MENDELSSOHN-BARTHOLDY, A., *The War and Germany Society*, New York 1971.

Reaction, Reform and Revolutionary Ferment

CARSTEN, F. L., *War Against War*, London 1982.
FISCHER, F., *Germany's War Aims in the First World War*, London 1969.
GATZKE, H., *Germany's Drive to the West*, Baltimore, Md. 1950.
GOODSPEED, D. J., *Ludendorff*, London 1966.
HORN, D. (ed.), *War, Mutiny and Revolution in the German Navy. The World War I Diary of Seaman Richard Stumpf*, New Brunswick, NJ 1967.
KITCHEN, M., *The Silent Dictatorship*, London 1976.
KOCKA, J., *Facing Total War*, Leamington Spa 1984.
MEYER, H. C., *Mitteleuropa in German Thought and Action*, The Hague 1955.
WHEELER-BENNETT, J., *Brest Litovsk. The Forgotten Peace*, London 1938.

The Revolutions of 1918/19

BERLAU, A. J., *German Social Democracy 1914–1921*, New York 1949.
BURDICK, C. B., and LUTZ, R. H., *The Political Institutions of the German Revolution*, Stanford, Calif. 1968.
CARSTEN, F. L., *Reichswehr and Politics* Oxford 1966.
—, *Revolution in Central Europe*, London 1972.
COMFORT, R. A., *The Politics of Labor in Hamburg 1918–1924*, Princeton, NJ 1962.
HORN, D., *The German Naval Mutinies of World War I*, New Brunswick, NJ 1969.
MISHARK, J. W., *The Road to Revolution*, Detroit, Mich. 1967.
MITCHELL, A., *Revolution in Bavaria*, Princeton, NJ 1965.
MORGAN, D. W., *The Socialist Left and the German Revolution*, Ithaca, NY 1975.
ROSENBERG, A., *A History of the German Republic*, London 1936.
RÜRUP, R., 'Problems of the German Revolution', *Journal of Contemporary History*, 1968, 109–26.
RYDER, A. J., *The German Revolution of 1918*, Cambridge 1967.
WALDMAN, E., *The Spartacist Uprising*, Marquette 1958.

The Weimar Republic, 1918–1933

Economic Dislocation and Counter-Revolution

ANGRESS, S., *The Stillborn Revolution: The Communist Bid for Power in*

Germany 1921–1923, Princeton, NJ 1963.

BRESCIANO-TURRONI, C., *The Economics of Inflation*, London 1937.

CORNEBISE, A. E., *The Weimar Republic in Crisis: Cuno's Germany and The Ruhr Occupation*, Washington, DC 1977.

—, *Iron and Steel in the German Inflation*, Princeton, NJ 1977.

FELIX, D., *Walter Rathenau and the Weimar Republic: The Politics of Reparations*, Baltimore, Md. 1971.

FERGUSSON, A., *When Money Dies*, London 1975.

GORDON, H. J., *The Reichswehr and the German Republic*, Princeton, NJ 1957.

—, *Hitler and the Beer Hall Putsch*, Princeton, NJ 1972.

GRAHAM, F., *Exchange, Prices and Production in Hyperinflation Germany*, Princeton NJ 1930.

HOLTFRERICH, C. L., *The German Inflation 1914–1923*, Berlin 1985.

LAURSEN, K., and PEDERSEN, J., *The German Inflation 1918–1923*, Amsterdam 1964.

MOELLER, R. G., *German Peasants and Conservative Agrarian Politics 1914–1924*, Chapel Hill, NC 1985.

NICHOLLS, A. J., *Weimar and the Rise of Hitler*, London 1968.

RINGER, F. K. (ed.), *The German Inflation of 1923*, New York 1969.

RUPIEPER, H.-J., *The Cuno Government and Reparations*, The Hague 1979.

SCHMIDT, R. J., *Versailles and the Ruhr*, London 1968.

WAITE, R. G. L., *Vanguard of Nazism*, Cambridge, Mass. 1952.

WHEELER-BENNETT, J., *The Wreck of Reparations*, London 1933.

Intellectual and Cultural Activity

BULLIVANT, K. (ed.), *Culture and Society in the Weimar Republic*, Manchester 1978.

DEAK, I., *Weimar Germany's Leftwing Intellectuals*, Stanford, Calif. 1968.

GAY, P., *Weimar Culture*, New York 1968.

HERF, J., *Reactionary Modernism*, Cambridge 1984.

KLEMPERER, K. von, *Germany's New Conservatism*, Princeton, NJ 1957.

LAQUEUR, W., *Weimar: A Cultural History*, New York 1975.

MANVELL, R., and FRAENKEL, H., *The German Cinema*, London 1971.

MOSSE, G. L., *The Crisis of German Ideology*, New York 1964.

PATTERSON, M., *The Revolution in German Theatre 1900–1933*, London 1981.

STERN, F., *The Politics of Cultural Despair*, New York 1961.

TAYLOR, R., *Literature and Society in Germany 1918–1945*, Brighton 1980.

Party Politics

DORPALEN, A., *Hindenburg and the Weimar Republic*, Princeton, NJ 1964.

ESCHENBURG, T., et al., *Road to Dictatorship*, London 1970.

EYCK, E., *A History of the Weimar Republic*, 2 vols., London 1962.

FISCHER, R., *Stalin and German Communism*, Cambridge, Mass. 1948.

FOWKES, B., *Communism in Germany Under the Weimar Republic*, London 1984.

GRATWOHL, R. P., *Stresemann and the DNVP*, Lawrence, Ka. 1980.

HERTZMAN, L., *DNVP*, Lincoln, Nebr. 1963.
HUNT, R. N., *German Social Democracy 1918–1933*, New Haven, Conn. 1964.
NICHOLLS, A. J., and MATTHIAS, E. (eds.), *German Democracy and the Triumph of Hitler*, London 1971.
WHEELER-BENNETT, J., *The Wooden Titan*, London 1936.

Weimar Foreign Policy

BRETTON, H. L., *Stresemann and the Revision of Versailles*, Stanford, Calif. 1953.
DAWSON, P., *Germany's Industrial Revival*, London 1938.
DYCK, H. L., *Weimar Germany and Soviet Russia*, London 1966.
FREUND, G., *The Unholy Alliance 1918–1926*, London 1957.
GATZKE, H., *Stresemann and the Rearmament of Germany*, Baltimore, Md 1954.
JACOBSON, J., *Locarno Diplomacy*, Princeton, NJ 1971.
LAQUEUR, W., *Russia and Germany*, London 1965.
LEE, M., and MICHALKA, W., *German Foreign Policy 1917–1933*, Leamington Spa 1987.
POST JR, G., *The Civil-Military Fabric of Weimar Foreign Policy*, Princeton, NJ 1973.
STEHLIN, S. A., *Weimar and the Vatican 1918–1933*, Princeton, NJ 1983.
TURNER, H. A., *Stresemann and the Politics of the Weimar Republic*, Princeton, NJ 1963.

Economic Tensions and the Rise of the Nazis

ABRAHAM, D., *The Collapse of the Weimar Republic*, New York 1981.
BESSEL, R., *Political Violence and the Rise of Nazism*, New Haven, Conn. 1984.
CHILDERS, T., *The Nazi Voter*, Chapel Hill, NC 1984.
—, and FEUCHTWANGER, E. J. (eds.), *Social Change and Political Development in Weimar Germany*, London 1981.
EVANS, R. J., and GEARY, D. (eds), *The German Unemployed 1918–1936*, London 1986.
FARQUHARSON, J. E., *The Plough and the Swastika*, London 1976.
FEST, J., *Hitler*, London 1974.
FISCHER, C., *Stormtroopers*, London 1983.
FROMM, E., *The Working Class in Weimar Germany*, Leamington Spa 1984.
HAMILTON, R. F., *Who Voted for Hitler?* Princeton, NJ 1981.
KATER, M. H., *The Nazi Party*, Cambridge, Mass. 1983.
KELE, M. H., *Nazis and Workers*, Chapel Hill, NC 1972.
LEBOVICS, H., *Social Conservatism and the Middle Classes in Germany*, Princeton, NJ 1969.
NOAKES, J., *The Nazi Party in Lower Saxony*, Oxford 1971.
NYOMARKAY, J., *Charisma and Factionalism in the Nazi Party*, Minneapolis, Minn. 1967.
ORLOW, D., *The History of the Nazi Party*, 2 vols., Newton Abbot 1973.
PATCH, W. L., *Christian Trade Unions in the Weimar Republic*, New

Haven, Conn. 1985.

PRIDHAM, G., *Hitler's Rise to Power*, London 1973.

SOHN-RETHEL, A., *Economy and Class Structure of German Fascism*, London 1978.

SPEIER, H., *German White-Collar Workers and the Rise of Hitler*, New Haven, Conn. 1986.

STACHURA, P. D. (ed.), *Unemployment and the Great Depression in Weimar Germany*, London 1986.

TURNER, H. A., *German Big Business and the Rise of Hitler*, Oxford 1985.

From Brüning to Hitler

BENNETT, F. W., *Germany and the Diplomacy of the Financial Crisis*, Cambridge, Mass. 1962.

BROSZAT, M., *Hitler and the Collapse of Weimar Germany*, Leamington Spa and New York 1987.

DIEHL, J. M., *Paramilitary Politics in Weimar Germany*, Bloomington, Ind. 1977.

EKSTEINS, M., *The Limits of Reason*, London 1975.

HALPERIN, S. W., *Germany Tried Democracy*, London 1946.

JAMES, H., *The Reichsbank and Public Finance in Germany 1924–1933*, Frankfurt 1985.

—, *The German Slump*, Oxford 1986.

The Third Reich, 1933–1945

The Face of the Nazi Dictatorship

ALLEN, W. S., *The Nazi Seizure of Power*, Chicago, Ill. 1965.

AYCOBERRY, P., *The Nazi Question*, London 1979.

BEYERCHEN, A. D., *Scientists Under Hitler*, New Haven, Conn. 1977.

BLEUEL, H. P., *Sex and Society in Nazi Germany*, Philadelphia, Pa 1973.

BRIDENTHAL, R., et al. (eds), *When Biology Became Destiny*, New York 1984.

CONWAY, J. S., *The Nazi Persecution of the Churches*, London 1968.

FEST, J., *The Face of the Third Reich*, London 1970.

GILES, G. J., *Students and National Socialism in Germany*, Princeton, NJ 1986.

GRUNBERGER, R., *A Social History of the Third Reich*, London 1974.

HELMREICH, E. C., *The German Churches under Hitler*, Detroit, Mich. 1979.

HIDEN, J., and FARQUHARSON, J., *Explaining Hitler's Germany*, London 1983.

HILDEBRAND, K., *The Third Reich*, London 1984.

KERSHAW, I., *The Nazi Dictatorship*, London 1985.

KOCH, H. J., *The Hitler Youth*, London 1975.

LEWY, G., *The German Catholic Church and Nazi Germany*, London 1964.

MOSSE, G. L., *Nazi Culture*, New York 1966.

NOAKES, J. (ed.), *Government, Party and the People in Nazi Germany*, Exeter 1980.

POIS, R. A., *National Socialism and the Religion of Nature*, London 1986.

RHODES, A., *The Vatican in the Age of the Dictators*, London 1973.
RITCHIE, J. M., *German Literature under National Socialism*, London 1983.
RUPP, L., *Mobilizing Women for War*, Princeton, NJ 1978.
SCHOENBAUM, D., *Hitler's Social Revolution*, London 1967.
STACHURA, P. D., *The German Youth Movement 1900–1945*, London 1981.
STEINBERG, M. S., *Sabres and Brownshirts*, Chicago Ill. 1977.
STEPHENSON, J., *Women in Nazi Society*, London 1975.
WALKER, L. D., *Hitler Youth and Catholic Youth, 1933– 1936*, New York 1979.
WEBER, R. G. S., *The German Student Corps in the Third Reich*, London 1986.
WELCH, D., *Nazi Propaganda*, London 1983.
WRIGHT, J. R. C., *Above Parties*, Oxford 1974.
ZAHN, G., *German Catholics and Hitler's Wars*, London 1962.

Economic Conditions and Mobilisation for War

BORKIN, J., *The Crime and Punishment of I. G. Farben*, London 1979.
DEIST, W., *The Wehrmacht and German Rearmament*, London 1981.
FARQUHARSON, J. E., *The Plough and the Swastika*, London 1976.
KLEIN, B. H., *Germany's Economic Preparations for War*, Cambridge, Mass. 1959.
O'NEILL, R., *The German Army and the Nazi Party*, London 1966.
OVERY, R., *The Nazi Economic Recovery, 1932–1938*, London 1982.
SCHWEITZER, A., *Big Business in the Third Reich*, New York 1972.
TURNER, H. A. (ed.), *Nazism and the Third Reich*, New York 1972.
WHEELER-BENNETT, J., *The Nemesis of Power*, London 1953.

Nazi foreign policy and Hitler

BINION, R., *Hitler among the Germans*, New York 1976.
BRACHER, K. D., *The German Dictatorship*, New York 1970.
BROSZAT, M., *Hitler's State*, London 1981.
BULLOCK, A., *Hitler*, New York 1964.
CARR, W., *Arms, Autarky and Aggression*, London 1972.
—, *Hitler*, London 1978.
COMPTON, J. V., *The Swastika and the Eagle*, Boston 1967.
FEST, J., *Hitler*, London 1974.
FRAENKEL, E., *The Dual State*, New York 1969.
HILDEBRAND, K., *The Foreign Policy of the Third Reich*, London 1973.
HIRSCHFELD, G., and KETTENACKER, L. (eds.), *The 'Führer State'*, Stuttgart 1980.
HITLER, A., *Mein Kampf*, London 1969.
JÄCKEL, E., *Hitler's Weltanschauung*, Middletown, Conn. 1972.
KOEHL, R., *The Black Corps*, Middletown, Conn. 1983.
LEACH, B., *German Strategy Against Russia*, Oxford 1973.
NEUMANN, F., *Behemoth*, New York 1966.
PETERSON, E. N., *The Limits of Hitler's Power*, Princeton, NJ 1969.
RICH, N., *Hitler's War Aims*, 2 vols., New York 1973.
SCHMOKEL, W. W., *Dream of Empire*, New Haven, Conn. 1964.

STACHURA, P. D., *The Shaping of the Nazi State*, London 1978.
STOAKES, G., *Hitler and the Quest for World Dominion*, Leamington Spa and New York 1987.
STONE, N., *Hitler*, London 1980.
TREVOR-ROPER, H. R. (ed.), *Hitler's Table Talk*, London 1953.
WAITE, R. G. L., *The Psychopathic God*, New York 1977.
WEINBERG, G. L., *The Foreign Policy of Hitler's Germany*, Chicago 1970.

Occupation, Exploitation and Extermination

ARENDT, H., *Eichmann in Jerusalem*, New York 1963.
BARTOV, O., *The Eastern Front, 1941–1945*, London 1986.
BAUM, R. C., *The Holocaust and the German Elite*, London 1982.
DALLIN, A., *German Rule in Russia, 1941–1945*, London 1957.
DAWIDOWICZ, L. S., *The War Against the Jews, 1939–1945*, Harmondsworth 1976.
FLEMING, G., *Hitler and the Final Solution*, Stanford, Calif. 1984.
GORDON, S., *Hitler, Germans and the 'Jewish Question'*, Princeton, NJ 1984.
GROSS, J. T., *Polish Society under German Occupation*, Princeton, NJ 1979.
HILBERG, R., *The Destruction of the European Jews*, London 1961.
HIRSCHFELD, G., *Nazi Rule and Dutch Collaboration*, Oxford and New York 1988.
HÖHNE, H., *The Order of the Death's Head*, London 1969.
HOMZE, E. L., *Foreign Labour in Nazi Germany*, Princeton, NJ 1967.
KOGON, E., *The Theory and Practice of Hell*, London 1950.
KRAUSNICK, H., *et al.*, *Anatomy of the SS State*, London 1968.
LAQUEUR, W., *The Terrible Secret*, London 1980.
MASSING, P., *Rehearsal for Destruction*, New York 1967.
MILWARD, A., *The New Order and the French Economy*, Oxford 1970.
—, *The Fascist Economy of Norway*, Oxford 1972.
MOSSE, G. L., *Germans and Jews*, London 1971.
REITLINGER, G., *The Final Solution*, London 1953.
—, *The SS*, New York 1957.
—, *The House Built on Sand*, New York 1960.
STONE , N., *Hitler*, London 1980.
SCHLEUNES, K., *The Twisted Road to Auschwitz*, Champaign-Urbana, Ill. 1970.
SCHULTE, T., *The German Army and Nazi Policies in Occupied Russia*, Oxford 1988.
SERENY, G., *Into That Darkness*, London 1974.
STEINER, J. M., *Power Politics and Social Change*, The Hague 1976.
TRUNK, I., *Judenrat*, New York 1977.
WARMBRUNN, W., *The Dutch under German Occupation*, Stanford, Calif. 1963.

The Final Years

BAIRD, J. W., *The Mythical World of Nazi War Propaganda*, Minneapolis, Minn. 1974.

BALFOUR, M., *Propaganda in War*, London 1979.
BRAMSTED, E. K., *Goebbels and National Socialist Propaganda*, London 1965.
DEUTSCH, H. C., *The Conspiracy against Hitler in the Twilight War*, London 1968.
GRAML, H., *et al.*, *The German Resistance to Hitler*, London 1970.
HALE, O. J., *Captive Press in the Third Reich*, Princeton, NJ 1964.
MILWARD, A. S., *The German Economy at War*, London 1965.
PRITTIE, T., *Germans Against Hitler*, London 1964.
RITTER, G., *The German Resistance*, London 1958.
SPEER, A., *Inside the Third Reich*, London 1970.
ZEMAN, Z. A. B., *Nazi Propaganda*, London 1973.

Occupation and division 1945–1960

The Western Zones

BALABKINS, N., *Germany under Direct Controls*, New Brunswick, NJ 1964.
BALFOUR, M., *Four-Power Control in Germany and Austria*, London 1956.
CLAY, L. D., *Decision in Germany*, London 1950.
EDINGER, L. J., *Kurt Schumacher*, Stanford, Calif. 1965.
Farquharson, J., *The Western Allies and the Politics of Food*, Leamington Spa 1985.
FITZGIBBON, C., *Denazification*, London 1969.
GIMBEL, J., *The American Occupation of Germany*, Stanford, Calif. 1968.
—, *The Origins of the Marshall Plan*, Stanford 1976.
KENNEDY, E., *After the Holocaust*, London 1981.
PETERSON, E. N., *The American Occupation of Germany*, Detroit, Mich. 1977.
PRONAY, V., and WILSON, K. (eds), *The Political Re-education of Germany and Her Allies after World War II*, London 1985.
SPOTTS, F., *Churches and Politics in Germany*, Middletown, Conn. 1973.
ZAYAS, A. de, *Nemesis at Potsdam*, New York 1975.
ZINK, H., *The United States in Germany*, Westpoint, Conn. 1957.

The Soviet Zone and East Germany

BARING, A., *Uprising in East Germany*, Ithaca, NY 1972.
CHILDS, D., *East Germany*, London 1969.
KRISCH, H., *German Politics under Soviet Occupation*, New York 1974.
LEONHARD, W., *Child of the Revolution*, London 1956.
NETTL, J. P., *The Eastern Zone and Soviet Policy in Germany, 1945–1950*, Oxford 1951.
SANFORD, G. W., *From Hitler to Ulbricht*, Princeton, NJ 1983.
STERN, C., *Ulbricht*, London 1965.

The Shaping of the Federal Republic

ADENAUER, K., *Memoirs*, London 1966.

BALFOUR, M., *West Germany*, London 1968.
BERGHAHN, V. R., *The Americanisation of West German Industry 1945–1973*, Leamington Spa 1986.
BRAUNTHAL, G., *The Federation of German Industry in Politics*, Ithaca, NY 1965.
CHILDS, D., *From Schumacher to Brandt*, Oxford 1966.
CULLINGFORD, E. C. M., *Trade Unions in West Germany*, London 1973.
GOLAY, J. F., *Founding the Federal Republic of Germany*, Chicago, Ill. 1958.
GRAF, W. D., *The German Left Since 1945*, Cambridge 1976.
GROSSER, A., *The Federal Republic of Germany*, New York 1964.
HARTMANN, H., *Authority and Organization in German Management*, Princeton, NJ 1959.
HEIDENHEIMER, A., *Adenauer and the CDU*, The Hague 1960.
LOEWENBERG, G., *Parliament in the German Political System*, Ithaca, NY 1967.
MERKL, P. H., *The Origins of the West German Republic*, Oxford 1963.
PRIDHAM, G., *Christian Democracy in Western Germany*, London 1977.
PRITTIE, T., *Adenauer*, London 1972.
SPIRO, H. J., *The Politics of German Codetermination*, Cambridge, Mass. 1958.
STAHL, W. (ed.), *The Politics of Postwar Germany*, New York 1963.
TAUBER, K. P., *Beyond Eagle and Swastika*, 2 vols., Middletown, Conn. 1967.
THAYER, C. W., *The Unquiet Germans*, New York 1957.
TILFORD, R. B., and PREECE, R. J., *Federal Germany*, London 1969.
WALLICH, H. C., *Mainsprings of the German Revival*, New Haven, Conn. 1955.
WIGHTON, C., *Adenauer. Democratic Dictator*, London 1963.

Foreign Policy and Rearmament

BÖLLING, K., *Republic in Suspense*, New York 1964.
HANRIEDER, W. F., *West German Foreign Policy 1949–1963*, Stanford, Calif. 1967.
—, *The Stable Crisis*, New York 1970.
KELLEHER, C. M., *Germany and the Politics of Nuclear Weapons*, New York 1975.
KNORR, K. (ed.), *Nato and U.S. Security*, New York 1959.
PATERSON, W. E., *The SPD and European Integration*, Lexington, Mass. 1974.
SMITH, J. E., *The Defense of Berlin*, Baltimore, Md 1963.
SPEIER, H., *German Rearmament and Atomic Warfare*, Evanston Ill. 1957.
WINDSOR, P., *City on Leave*, London 1963.
—, *German Reunification*, London 1969.

West Germany since the 1960s

West Germany and the International System

CALLEO, D., *The German Problem Reconsidered*, Cambridge 1979.

COONEY, J. A., *et al.* (eds), *The Federal Republic of Germany and the United States*, Boulder, Col. 1984.

CRAWLEY, A., *The Rise of Western Germany*, London 1973.

GRIFFITH, W. F., *The Ostpolitik of the Federal Republic of Germany*, Cambridge, Mass. 1978.

GROSSER, A., *Germany in Our Time*, London 1971.

HANRIEDER, W. F. (ed.), *West German Foreign Policy*, Boulder, Col. 1980.

Hartrich, *The Fourth and Richest Reich*, London 1980.

KEITHLY, D. M., *Breakthrough in the Ostpolitik*, Godstone 1986.

KRIPPENDORFF, E., and RITTBERGER, V., *The Foreign Policy of West Germany*, Beverly Hills, Calif. 1980.

MORGAN, R., *The United States and West Germany 1945–1973*, London 1974.

—, *West Germany's Foreign Policy Agenda*, Beverly Hills, Calif. 1978.

SMITH, E. O., *The West German Economy*, New York 1983.

TILFORD, R. (ed.), *The Ostpolitik and Political Change in Germany*, Farnborough 1975.

VOGL, F., *German Business After the Economic Miracle*, London 1973.

West German Politics Since the 1960s

BAKER, K. L., *et al.* (eds), *Germany Transformed*, Cambridge, Mass. 1981.

BECKER, J., *Hitler's Children*, London 1977.

BEYME, K. von, and Kaase, M. (eds.), *Elections and Parties*, London 1978.

BEYME, K. von, and SCHMIDT, M. G. (eds.), *Policy and Politics in the Federal Republic of Germany*, Aldershot 1985.

BURKETT, T., *Parties and Elections in West Germany*, London 1975.

CHALMERS, D., *The Social Democratic Party of Germany*, New Haven 1974.

CHILD'S D., and JOHNSON, J., *West Germany*, London 1981.

CONRADT, D. P., *The German Polity*, New York 1978.

DAHRENDORF, R., *Democracy and Society in Germany*, London 1968.

DÖRING, H., and SMITH, G. (eds), *Party Government and Political Culture in West Germany*, London 1982.

DYSON, K., *Party, State and Bureaucracy in Western Germany*, Beverly Hills Calif. 1977.

EDINGER, L. J., *Politics in Western Germany*, Boston, Mass. 1977.

GOLDMAN, G., *The German Political System*, New York 1974.

GRAF, W. D., *The German Left Since 1945*, London 1974.

JOHNSON, N., *Government in the Federal Republic of Germany*, Oxford 1973.

KOLINSKY, E., *Parties, Opposition and Society in West Germany*, London 1984.

LOEWENBERG, G., *Parliament in the German Political System*, Ithaca, NY 1966.

NAGLE, J. D., *The National Democratic Party*, Berkeley Calif. 1970.

NEVEN-DUMONT, J., *After Hitler*, London 1969.

PAPADAKIS, E., *The Green Movement in West Germany*, London 1984.

PATERSON, W. E., and SMITH, G. (eds.), *The West German Model*, London 1981.

PRIDHAM, G., *Christian Democracy in Western Germany*, London 1977.

SCHWEIGLER, G., *National Consciousness in Divided Germany*, Beverly Hills, Calif. 1975.

SMITH, G., *Democracy in Western Germany*, London 1979.

SONTHEIMER, K., *Government and Politics in West Germany*, London 1972.

TILFORD, R., and PREECE, R. J. (eds.), *Federal Germany*, London 1969.

WALLACH, H. G. P., and ROMOSER, G. K., *West German Politics in the Mid-Eighties*, New York 1985.

Culture and Society in East and West Germany

BULLIVANT, K., *Realism Today*, Leamington Spa 1987.

BURDICK, C., *et al.* (eds.), *Contemporary Germany*, Boulder, Col. 1984.

DEMETZ, P., *Postwar German Literature*, New York 1972.

GACHNANG, J., *New German Painting*, Milan 1982.

HEARNDEN, A., *Education in Two Germanies*, Oxford 1974.

HINTON-THOMAS, R., and BULLIVANT, K., *Literature in Upheaval*, New York 1975.

HUEBNER, T., *The Literature of East Germany*, New York 1970.

HUETTICH, H. G., *Theater in a Planned Society*, Chapel Hill 1978.

KREJCI, J., *Social Structure in Divided Germany*, London 1976.

PARKES, K. S., *Writers and Politics in West Germany*, London 1986.

SANFORD, J., *The Mass Media of the German-speaking Countries*, London 1976.

—, *The New German Cinema*, London 1980.

SEBALD, W. G. (ed.), *A Radical Stage: Theatre in Germany in the 1970s and 1980s*, Oxford 1988.

WILD, T. (ed.), *Urban and Rural Change in West Germany*, London 1983.

Annotated Name Index

Dual Alliance with Bismarck in 1879.

Antonelli, Giacomo 137
1806–1876, Italian theologian. Secretary of state to Pope Pius IX. His reactionary stance helped to prolong the *Kulturkampf*.

Arndt, Adolf 339
b. 1904, German politician and jurist. Member of the *Bundestag* (SPD). Joined the party executive in 1956 and became chairman of the *Bundestag* committee on constitutional law. The 'star jurist' of the SPD. In 1963 senator for arts and sciences in Berlin.

Arndt, Ernst Moritz 60, 67
1769–1860, German poet and writer of political tracts and songs. Member of the *Burschenschaft*. Sat in the German National Assembly 1848–9. Participated in the Wars of Liberation.

Arnim, Achim von 38
1781–1831, German Romantic writer. Collected *Volkslieder* 1806–8. Together with Clemens Brentano published *Des Knaben Wunderhorn*, the first comprehensive collection of old and new German *Volkslieder*.

Arnim, Bettina von 101
née Brentano, 1785–1859, German poetess. Advocated political and intellectual emancipation.

Arnim, Harry von, Count von in 1870 151, 161
1824–81, German diplomat. Ambassador to Lisbon in 1862, to Munich and Rome in 1864, and to Paris in 1872. Supported the monarchist cause in France. Recalled in 1874. Condemned to prison for misappropriation of government documents. Fled to Switzerland and published severe criticisms of Bismarck in 1876. Condemned in absentia to five years in prison for treason.

Arnim, Otto von 131
1813–1903, Bismarck's brother-in-law.

Augustenburg, Friedrich Duke von 132
1829–80. Became Friedrich VIII, duke of Schleswig-Holstein-Sonderburg-Augustenburg. After the death of Frederick VII of Denmark, claimed in 1863 to inherit Schleswig-Holstein. Had himself proclaimed Duke of Schleswig-Holstein, but was brushed aside and forced to abjure this claim by Bismarck who wished to annex the duchies to Prussia.

Augustinus, Aurelius 22
354–430, saint and foremost scholar of the ancient Latin church.

Baader, Andreas 382
1944–77, German terrorist. Sentenced to three years in prison in 1968 for setting a department store on fire. Member of the Red Army faction. Committed suicide in prison.

Babeuf, François Noël 105
1760–97, French Jacobine. Wanted to form a 'communist' state with 'national sharing of goods and jobs'. Executed after a conspiracy to overthrow the bourgeois government was uncovered.

Bach, Johann Sebastian 37
1685–1750, German musician and composer. Became organist in Arnstadt in 1703 and in Mühlhausen in 1707. In 1708 became organist and concert master at the ducal court in Weimar. Very prolific. His compositions

represent one of the greatest expressions of western civilisation.

Badoglio, Pietro 310
1871–1956, Italian marshal. Chief of the general staff during the Ethiopian campaign of 1936. Overthrew Mussolini in July 1943, took over the government and capitulated to the Allies.

Bamberger, Ludwig 123, 176
1823–1899, German economist and politician. Became a National Liberal deputy in the *Reichstag* in 1871 and a Liberal deputy in 1881. Advised Bismarck on currency reform. Championed free trade and opposed Bismarck's tariff and colonial policies.

Barlach, Ernst 285
1870–1938, German sculptor, graphic artist and poet.

Barzel, Rainer Candidus 383
b. 1924, German politician. Entered the *Bundestag* in 1957. Minister of all-German affairs 1962–3, vice-chairman of the CDU/CSU parliamentary group 1963–4 and chairman 1964–73. Chairman of the federal CDU 1971–3. Minister of inter-German relations 1982–3. President of the *Bundestag* 1983–4.

Bassermann, Friedrich, Daniel 73, 192.
1811–55, German politician. Member of the second chamber in Baden. Confidant of the revolutionary government in Frankfurt a. M. Member of the Pre-parliament and the National Assembly.

Bastide, Jules 82
1800–79, French politician. Participated in the Paris revolution of 1832. Condemned to death, fled to London, was pardoned in 1834 and returned. Became foreign minister for a short time during the revolution of 1848. Opponent of

Napoleon III.

Baumgarten, Hermann 135, 144
1825–93, German historian and professor in Karlsruhe. Advocated a *kleindeutsch* Prussian state.

Baxter, Richard 88
1615–91, English theologian and writer of morally uplifting works. Championed a mild form of Puritanism (Baxterism).

Bebel, August 137, 157, 211, 214
1840–1913, German Social Democratic politician and publicist. Master turner. Entered the labour movement in 1861. With the exception of 1881–3, sat in the *Reichstag* from 1867 till his death. Helped to found the SPD in 1869 and soon became its leader. Sentenced with Liebknecht in 1872 for plotting treason and in 1886 for membership in an outlawed society. Lived in Berlin after the socialist law was repealed.

Beck, Ludwig 292, 299, 313
1880–1944, German general. Became chief of the army general staff in 1935. Resigned in 1938 out of opposition to Hitler's plans for war. Leader of the military resistance in Germany. Committed suicide on 20 July 1944.

Becker, Nikolaus 68
1809–45, German poet. Wrote the so-called Song of the Rhine in 1840 ('Sie sollen ihn nicht haben . . .').

Beckmann, Max 285
1884–1950, German painter and graphic artist. Became a professor at the Frankfurt Academy of Art in 1916. Emigrated to the Netherlands and then to the USA in 1947. Expressionist.

Beethoven, Ludwig van 38
1770–1827, German composer.

Paid Mozart a short visit in Vienna in 1787 and took up residence there in 1792. Studied under Haydn and Salieri among others. First appeared in public as a pianist in 1795. Began to go deaf and became completely so in 1818. After Haydn and Mozart, the third and last of the great Viennese classical composers.

Bell, Johannes 241
1868–1949, German politician and lawyer. Entered the Prussian Chamber of Deputies in 1908 and was a Centrist deputy in the *Reichstag* from 1912 to 1923. Became colonial minister in 1919 until the dissolution of this ministry in November 1919. Minister of transport 1919–20. Signed the Treaty of Versailles together with foreign minister Hermann Müller. In 1926 became minister of justice and minister of the occupied regions.

Benedetti, Vincent Count 140–1
1817–1900, French diplomat. Ambassador in Berlin 1864–70. Mediated the Austro-Prussian peace after the battle of Königgratz. In 1870 delivered the French demands in regard to the Spanish throne, thereby triggering Bismarck's Ems dispatch.

Benedict XV 223
1851–1922. Nunciature secretary in 1883 and entered the curia in 1887. Became pope in 1914. Named archbishop of Bologna in 1907 and cardinal in 1914; became pope in 1914. Attempted, without success, to bring about peace in 1917 with his note 'to the leaders of the warring nations'.

Benz, Carl Friedrich 180
1844–1929, German engineer. Built the first operable automobile with an internal combustion engine in 1885–6. Founded the firm of Benz & Co. in Mannheim in 1883. Amalgamated with the Mercedes works in Cannstatt in 1926 to form Daimler-Benz.

Bernstein, Eduard 196, 234
1850–1932, German politician. Co-authored the Gotha programme in 1875. Grew estranged from orthodox Marxism and became the theoretical champion of revisionism. Was a *Reichstag* deputy (with short interludes) from 1902 to 1928.

Berstett, Wilhelm Baron von 57
1769–1837, Baden statesman. Represented Baden in the *Bundestag* after 1816. He and von Berckheim led it out of the Confederation of the Rhine in response to Metternich. Became minister of foreign affairs in 1818 and was prime minister of Baden from 1820 to 1830.

Bethmann Hollweg, Theobald von 191–2, 210, 214, 218, 222
1856–1921, German politician. Became president of the province of Brandenburg in 1899, Prussian minister of the interior in 1905, secretary of internal affairs in 1907, and *Reichskanzler* and Prussian prime minister in 1909. Resigned in 1917 in response to the ultimatum of Emperor William II.

Bismarck, Herbert Count von, Prince von in 1898 173
1849–1904, German diplomat. Became secretary of the foreign office in 1886 and was Prussian minister of state from 1888 to 1890. Son of the chancellor.

Bismarck, Otto von, Count in 1865, Prince in 1890, Duke of Lauenburg in 1890 104, 114–18, 120, 122–3, 126–43, 145–77, 183, 187, 189, 192, 198, 201–3, 238, 386.
1815–98, Prussian envoy to the

Founded a locomotive works in Berlin in 1837.

Boulanger, Georges 167
1837–91, French general and politican. Minister of war 1886–8. A chauvinist and the main proponent of revenge against Germany. The party which supported him called itself the Boulange, and its members were Boulangistes.

Boulton, Matthew 89
1728–1809, English industrialist. Colleague of James Watt whose machines he helped to develop for industrial applications.

Boyen, Hermann von 46
1771–1848, Prussian general. Collaborated with Scharnhorst on the Prussian army reform. Bülow's chief of staff during the wars of liberation. Minister of war 1814–19 and again 1840–7. Under him general conscription was introduced in 1814 and the *Landwehr* ordinance in 1815.

Brandt, Willy 369, 379, 383–4, 386
originally Herbert Ernst Karl Frahm, b. 1913. German politician (SPD). Joined the Social Democrats and the SAP in 1931. Emigrated to Norway in 1933. Deprived of German citizenship in 1938 and became a Norwegian citizen. Fled to Sweden in 1940. Returned to Germany in 1945 as a correspondent for Scandinavian newspapers. Recovered his German citizenship and renewed his SPD membership in 1947. Sat in the *Bundestag* from 1949 to 1957 and then again after 1969. Entered the Berlin Chamber of Deputies in 1950 and was its chairman 1955–7. Mayor of Berlin 1957–66. Became chairman of the SPD in 1964. Foreign minister and vice-chancellor during the grand coalition 1966–9 and

chancellor 1969–74. Chairman of the Socialist International after 1976 and of the north-south commission 1977–80.

Brauchitsch, Walther von 313
1881–1948, German field marshal. Became an artillery inspector in the German *Reichswehr* in 1932, commander of *Wehrkreis* I, Königsberg/Prussia in 1933, and commander-in-chief of the army in 1938. Demanded that he be relieved of his duties several times after the outbreak of the Second World War and was finally dismissed in 1941 on account of his alleged responsibility for the failure of the winter campaign in Russia.

Braun, Otto 250, 261
1872–1955, German politician. Prime minister of the Prussian coalition government (SPD, DDP, Centrists and DVP) 1920–32. SPD candidate for *Reichspräsident* in 1925. Was dismissed by Chancellor Papen from his position as *Reichskommissar* for Prussia in July 1932 on the basis of Article 48 of the Weimar constitution.

Brecht, Bertolt 285
actually Eugen Berthold Friedrich Brecht, 1898–1956. German writer and theatre director. Lived in Berlin from 1924 till he emigrated in 1933. Returned to East Berlin in 1948 where he founded the Berliner Ensemble with his wife Helene Weigel. Brecht is recognised as one of the most important and influential writers of the twentieth century for his partly realistic, partly satiric and grotesque stories, lyric, poetry and ballads, but most of all for his work as a dramatist and theoretical writer.

II to become *Reichskanzler* and Prussian prime minister in 1900. Dismissed in 1909.

Bullock, William 98
1813–67, American inventor. Invented the rotary press in 1860.

Bunsen, Christian Karl Josias Baron von 80
1790–1860, Prussian diplomat and academic. Envoy to Rome, Bern and London. Secretary-general of the Archaeological Institute in Rome. Mediated between Prussia and England in religious and cultural questions.

Bunsen, Robert Wilhelm 98
1811–99, German chemist. Professor in Marburg and Heidelberg. Developed spectral analysis together with Kirchhoff.

Burckhardt, Jacob 266
1818–97, Swiss cultural and art historian. Originally studied theology, then history and art history with Ranke and Kugler in Berlin and Bonn. Professor in Zurich and Basel 1855–93. His pessimistic cultural criticism was very influential, especially on Nietzsche.

Byrnes, James Francis 344
1879–1972, American politician. Supreme Court judge 1941–2, secretary of state 1945–7, governor of South Carolina 1951–5. Advocated reconciliation with Germany.

Byron, George Gordon Lord 116
1758–1824, English poet. Famous for his description of travels in the countries of the Mediterranean and Asia Minor and for his Romantic verse epics from the orient.

Cabet, Etienne 105
1788–1856, French publicist and utopian socialist.

Calvin, John 26, 88
actually Jean Cauvin, 1509–64, Franco-Swiss reformer. After humanist, theological and legal studies, converted to Protestantism. Moved to Geneva in 1541. Reorganised the church along stricter lines and introduced new ecclesiastical ordinances.

Canaris, Wilhelm 292, 313
1887–1945, German admiral. Head of military intelligence in the *Wehrmacht* office of the war ministry in 1935. Head of the foreign intelligence office in 1938. Participated in the resistance to Hitler, was dismissed in 1944 and executed in 1945.

Caprivi, Georg Leo von, Count von in 1891 188–91, 202
1831–99, German general and statesman. Succeeded Bismarck as chancellor 1890–4 and as Prussian prime minister 1890–2.

Carnot, Lazar Nicolas, Count in 1815 40
1753–1823, French statesman and minister of war. Organised the army ('levée en masse') in 1793. Member of the Directory. Minister of war 1800–15, minister of the interior in 1815. Exiled after the Bourbons returned.

Castlereagh, Robert Stewart, Viscount, Marquis of Londonderry 52
1769–1822, English statesman. Played a key role in the Act of Union between Ireland and the United Kingdom. Determined England's anti-Napoleonic policies. Foreign minister 1812–22 and represented England at the Congress of Vienna. Opposed the annexationist ambitions of Prussia and Russia and sought to preserve the European balance of power.

Cavour, Camillo Count Benso di C.
121–2, 135
1810–61, Italian statesman and champion of Italian unity. Founded the newspaper *Il Risorgimento* (1847) which lent the nationalist movement its name. Was the first minister of the Kingdom of Sardinia after 1852.

Chamberlain, Arthur Neville
292–4, 296, 299
1869–1940, English statesman. Conservative MP after 1918. Minister of health 1923–31, party leader 1930–40, chancellor of the exchequer 1931–7. Prime minister 1937–40.

Chamberlain, Joseph 203
1836–1914, English politician. Mayor of Birmingham 1873–6. Entered the House of Commons in 1876 and played a leading role in the reorganisation of the Liberal Party. President of the board of trade in Gladstone's ministry and secretary of state for the colonies 1895–1903, in Salisbury's ministry. His policy of tightening commerical and political bonds within the Empire precipitated the Boer War (1899–1902). Retired in 1903.

Charlemagne 7, 8, 9
742–814. Became king of the Franks in 768 and Roman emperor in 800. King of the Lombards as well, after taking over the Italian kingdom in 774.

Charles I 228
1887–1922. Emperor of Austria and king of Hungary (as Charles IV) in 1916–18. The calculated leak by the French government of the peace feelers he had extended resulted in his political humiliation in 1917. After popular demonstrations demanding the restructuring of his realm in 1918,

Charles renounced his right to rule. Expelled from Austria. After two vain attempts to recover the throne in Hungary was banned to Madeira in 1921.

Charles IV 17
1316–78. Became German king and king of Bohemia in 1346. Crowned emperor in 1355 and king of Arles in 1365. Issued in the Golden Bull a written constitution for the empire. Founded the university of Prague in 1348.

Charles V 24, 27–8
1500–58. Became Charles I, king of Spain in 1516. Emperor of the Holy Roman Empire from 1519 to 1556. In 1521 ceded the German patrimonial lands to his brother, Ferdinand I, despite his belief in a universal empire. Abdicated in 1556.

Charles X, Philippe, Count of Artois
62
1757–1836. French king 1824–30. Reactionary internal policies. By the July ordinances, triggered the revolution of 1830 which resulted in his overthrowal.

Charles, archduke 47
1771–1847, Austrian archduke and military commander. Great success in the third coalition war. Reformed the Austrian army when serving as president of the council of war and minister of war. Was relieved of his command in 1809 after the defeat of Wagram.

Chiang Kai-shek, 268, 287, 323
1887–1975, nationalist Chinese leader. Educated 1906–11 in Chinese and Japanese military academies. Worked with Sun Yat-sen in 1911, studied in Moscow in 1923. Became director of the military academy in Whampoa in 1924 and leader of the

Kuomintang in 1925 after the death of Sun Yat-sen. Broke with the communists. Captured Peking in 1928. Halted the civil war in 1937 because of the outbreak of the Sino-Japanese war. Resumed the civil war in 1947 and was forced to flee to Taiwan in 1949 when Mao conquered the mainland.

Churchill, Winston 219, 303, 310, 316, 320–1, 328
1874–1965, English statesman. Entered the House of Commons in 1900 as a Conservative. Became a Liberal in 1905 and then crossed the floor again in 1925. A member of the government 1906–29 with only short interludes. Without political office 1929–39. British prime minister 1940–45 and symbol of the war effort. Re-elected prime minister in 1951. Resigned in April 1955 for reasons of health. Won the Nobel Prize for literature in 1953.

Ciano, Galeazzo Conte C. di Cortellazzo 294
1903–44, Italian politician. Participated in the march on Rome in October 1922. Became minister of the press and propaganda in 1935 and a member of the fascist great council. Foreign minister 1936–43. Opposed German policies leading to war. Condemned to death in 1944 by one of Mussolini's special courts and shot.

Clay, Lucius 333, 365
1897–1978, American general. Eisenhower's deputy in 1945 and military governor of Germany 1947–9. Organised the air lift during the Soviet blockade of Berlin. President Kennedy's special ambassador to Berlin in 1961.

Clemenceau, Georges 222, 239–40
1841–1929, French politician. Entered the National Assembly in 1871. Opposed the peace treaty with Germany. President of the Paris city council in 1875. Prime minister 1906–9 and again in 1917. He hoped at the Paris peace conference to annex the German territories west of the Rhine and to weaken Germany militarily. Defeated in the presidential election of 1920 and retired from politics.

Clovis I 7
ca. 465–511. King of the Salian Franks in 482. Founder of the Frankish kingdom.

Columbus, Christopher 17
1443–1506, Genoese seafarer in the service of Spain. In an attempt to reach India, landed in San Salvador on 12 October 1492. Continued his voyage to Cuba and Haiti. Undertook three more voyages (1493–6, 1498–1500, 1502–4) during which he discovered the northern coast of South America and the eastern coast of Central America.

Conrad I 8, 9
d. 918. Became duke of the Franks in 906 and German king in 911.

Conrad II 10
ca. 990–1039. Became German king in 1024. Crowned emperor in 1027 and acquired the kingdom of Burgundy in 1033.

Conrad III 11
1093 or 1094–1152. German anti-king to Lothar von Supplinburg 1127–35 and his successor in 1138.

Conrad IV 11
1228–1254. Elected German king in 1237. Ruled after 1250.

Copernicus, Nicolaus 21
1473–1543, German astronomer. After studying in Cracow and Italy, became a canon in Frauenburg. Created the Copernican (heliocentric) system though this was not generally accepted in place of the geocentric Ptolemaic system until after Galileo and Kepler had completed their work.

Corinth, Lovis 186
1858–1925, German painter and graphic artist. After studying at the Königsberg Academy and in Munich, Antwerp and Paris, became a leading member of the secessionist movement in Munich and then in Berlin. Sought to reconcile art for art's sake with vital realism. After 1912 his style became free and highly intellectual.

Cuno, Wilhelm 244
1876–1933, German economist and politician. Joined the imperial treasury office in 1907 as an administrator. Took part in the peace negotiations of 1918–19 as an economic expert. Became chancellor in 1922. Responded to the occupation of the Ruhr with passive resistance which in the end ruined Germany's finances and her currency. Defeated in 1923 in a no-confidence vote.

D'Abernon, Edgar Vincent, Viscount D. in 1926 247–8
1857–1941, English politician and diplomat. Conservative MP in 1899–1906. Ambassador to Berlin in 1920–6 and a major influence on Stresemann's rapprochement policies.

Dahlerus, Birger 299
1891–1957, Swedish industrialist. Attempted to mediate between the German and British governments on the eve of the Second World War.

Dahlmann, Friedrich Christoph 65, 72
1785–1860, German historian and politician. Professor in Kiel, Göttingen and Bonn. Member of the Frankfurt parliament in 1848. Advocated the unification of Germany under Prussian leadership.

Daimler, Gottlieb 180
1834–1900, German engineer. Invented the first high-speed gasoline engine in 1883. Built an automobile in 1886 at the same time as Carl Benz and founded the Daimler Motor Co. in Cannstatt in 1890.

Daladier, Edouard 293, 299
1884–1970, French politician. Became a radical socialist deputy in 1919. Held portfolios in several ministries between 1924 and 1937. Prime minister 1938–40 and signed the Munich agreement. Arrested by the Vichy regime in 1940 and held in Germany 1943–5. Re-elected to parliament 1946–58.

Dawes, Charles Gates 248
1865–1951, American politician and financial expert, lawyer and banker. Head of supply procurement for the American expeditionary force in France in the First World War. Director of the Budget in Washington 1921–2. Chaired the committee of experts which worked out the Dawes Plan in 1923. Was awarded the Nobel Peace Prize in 1925 jointly with Joseph Austin Chamberlain. Vice-president 1925–6, then ambassador to London till 1932.

de Gaulle, Charles 302, 315
1890–1970, French general and statesman. After the French defeat of 1940, organised the resis-

tance from London. Headed the provisional government 1944–6. Returned to power in 1958 after the revolt in Algeria. Introduced a new constitution providing for a presidential system with a strong executive and plebiscites. Ended the Algerian war by conceding independence. Together with Adenauer sought Franco-German reconciliation.

Delcassé, Théophile 204, 207
1852–1923, French politician. Elected to the Chamber of Deputies in 1889 as a radical socialist. Became undersecretary for the colonies in 1893. Secretary of the colonies 1894–5 and foreign minister 1898–1905. Resigned in the wake of the first Moroccan crisis. Minister of the navy 1911–13, ambassador to Petersburg 1913–14 and once again foreign minister in 1915. Resigned when the attack on the Dardanelles failed.

Déroulède, Paul 167
1846–1914, French writer and politician. Founded the chauvinist *Ligue des patriotes* and a follower of Boulanger. Also known for his patriotic poems and his dramas.

Dietrich, Hermann Robert 255
1879–1954, German jurist and politician. Mayor of Kehl 1908–14 and of Konstanz 1914–18. Sat in the Baden *Landtag* in 1911–19 as a National Liberal then a Democrat. Foreign minister of Baden 1918–20. Cofounder and member of the executive of the DDP. Sat in the Weimar National Assembly and the *Reichstag* from 1919 to 1933. Minister of food 1928–30, then minister of economics or finance in the Brüning government.

Vice-chancellor 1930–2. Directed the Bizonal committee for food and agriculture 1946–7.

Disraeli, Benjamin, Earl of Beaconsfield in 1876 160, 194–6

1804–81, English statesman and novelist. First a writer, then a Tory member of the House of Commons after 1837. Became party leader in 1869. Opposed Peel in the tariff question. Prime minister in 1868 and again 1874–80. Acquired a majority of the Suez Canal shares for Britain in 1875 and had Queen Victoria proclaimed Empress of India in 1876. Opposed Russia's plans for the Balkans in the Russo-Turkish war and at the Berlin Congress. Considered to be the originator of Britain's imperial policy.

Dix, Otto 285
1891–1969, German painter. Became a professor in Dresden in 1927. Was dismissed in 1933 and persecuted as a 'degenerate'artist.

Döblin, Alfred 285
1878–1957, German writer and physician. Played a major role in establishing the contemporary German novel.

Dönitz, Karl 317
1891–1980, grand admiral of the German navy. Became commander of the U-boat fleet in 1936, and supreme commander of the navy in 1943. Named in Hitler's will as his successor and in early May 1945 formed the last Nazi government in Flensburg-Mürwik. Deposed and arrested on 23 May 1945 by the Allied supreme command. Sentenced in the Nuremberg trials.

Dollfuss, Engelbert 291
1892–1934, Austrian politician.

Goethe's friend and assistant after 1823.

Eckhard, Carl Maria Joseph 144
1822–1910, German politician, jurist, banker. Studied law and politics in Freiburg and Heidelberg. Dismissed from the public service in 1849 for his participation in the revolution. Deputy in and later vice-president of the second chamber of the Baden Diet. Helped found the Baden National-Liberal Party which he led 1863–72. Member of the *Reichstag* 1871–4. Co-founded the Rhenish Credit Bank in Mannheim in 1870. Vice-chairman of the BASF board in Ludwigshafen 1873–97 and chairman 1903–7.

Edward VII of England 188
1841–1910. Became king of Great Britain and Ireland and emperor of India in 1901. Favoured the formation of the *entente cordiale* with France.

Ehard, Hans 344
1887–1980, German politician (CSU) and jurist. Minister of justice in 1945 in the Schäffer cabinet. Prime minister of Bavaria 1946–54 and 1960–2. CDU chairman 1949–55. President of the *Landtag* 1954–60.

Eisenhower, Dwight David 315, 364
1890–1969, American general and politician. Thirty-fourth president of the United States (1953–61). Became supreme commander of the American forces in 1942. Led the Normandy invasion in June 1944. Supreme commander of the American occupational forces in Germany and member of the Allied Control Council from July till November 1945.

Eisner, Kurt 243
1867–1919, German politician. One of the leaders of the Independent Social Democrats in Munich during the First World War. Imprisoned in January 1918 for active participation in the munitions workers' strike. Released in October. As chairman of the workers', soldiers' and peasants' soviet, proclaimed on 7 November 1918 the formation of the 'free state of Bavaria' and became its prime minister. Failed to master the crisis and suffered a devastating defeat in the elections to the *Landtag*. Murdered by the radical right.

Elizabeth I of England
1533–1603. Became queen in 1558. Restored Anglicanism as the official religion. Pursued a clever policy towards Catholics. Had Mary Stuart of Scotland executed in 1587. During her reign England established herself as a great power by defeating the Spanish armada. Discovery and conquest of Virginia.

Engels, Friedrich 102, 104–6, 108–9
1820–95, German politician and theorist of socialism. Studied Hegel's dialectics and philosophy of history in Berlin 1841–2. Member of the Communist League. Worked closely with Marx beginning in 1844 and broke with the followers of Hegel. Co-publisher with Marx of the 'Communist Manifesto' in 1848. Took part in the Palatine revolt and when it failed fled to England where he supported Marx.

Erhard, Ludwig 341, 346, 357, 366, 368, 370
1897–1977, German politician (CDU). Assistant in and then head of the institute for economic analysis from 1928 to 1942. Hon-

ourary professor in Munich in 1947. Became economic director of the Bizone in 1948 and entered the *Bundestag* in 1949. Finance minister 1949–63 and vice-chancellor 1957–63. Chancellor 1963–6. Father of the 'economic miracle'.

Erzberger, Matthias 222, 231, 243
1875–1921, German politician. Centrist deputy in the *Reichstag* after 1903. During the First World War Erzberger evolved from being an advocate of an annexationist peace to a conciliatory peace. Became secretary of state without portfolio in October 1918. Signed the armistice as the leader of the German delegation. Minister of finance 1919–20. Created a unified financial administration in the *Reich*. Became a target of radical right-wing agitation and was assassinated.

Faber, Karl Georg 2
b. 1925, German historian. In 1953 became an adviser to the federal institute for geography and space studies and in 1967 professor of recent and contemporary history in Saarbrücken.

Faulhaber, Michael, von in *1917* 258, 312
1869–1952, German Catholic theologian. Became a priest in 1892. Professor of Old Testament studies in Strasbourg 1903–10. Bishop of Speyer 1911–17. Chaplain general to the Bavarian army in the First World War. Became archbishop of Munich and Freising in 1917 and a cardinal in 1921.

Favre, Jules 142
1809–1890, French statesman. Outstanding representative of the moderate republicans. Had a

strong influence on the transition to the third republic. As foreign minister handled the peace negotiations of 1871.

Ferdinand II 29
1578–1637. Emperor of the Holy Roman Empire. Strong proponent of the counter-reformation.

Ferry, Jules 170, 194, 197
1832–93, French politician. Member of the National Assembly. As minister of education pushed anticlerical education legislation through the assembly. Was prime minister 1880–1 and 1883–5 and successfully expanded the French empire.

Fichte, Johann Gottlieb 51
1762–1814, German philosopher. Professor in Jena and Erlangen. Professor at the university of Berlin in 1810 and its first freely elected vice-chancellor. Raised the dialectical method of thesis-antithesis-synthesis to a fundamental principle of philosophic thought.

Fliedner, Theodor 103
1800–64, German Evangelical theologian. Pastor in Kaiserswerth 1822–49 where he founded numerous nurses' training centres.

Foch, Ferdinand 231
1851–1929, French marshal. Chief of the Allied armies in France in 1918. Foch's offensive in July 1918 brought about the decisive breakthrough in the war in the west. Led the French armistice delegation in 1918.

Fontane, Theodor 173, 183, 186–7
1819–98, German writer and theatre critic. A pharmacist and then a journalist. Influential theatre critic for the *Vossische Zeitung* till 1889. His novels are both literary masterpieces and

cultural and sociological sources.

Francis II 42

1768–1835, German emperor from 1792 to 1806. Created the Austrian empire in 1804 out of the hereditary Habsburg lands. Abdicated as German emperor in 1806 under pressure from Napoleon and styled himself Francis I, emperor of Austria.

Francis Ferdinand 214

1863–1914, archduke of Austria. Heir apparent to the throne of Francis Joseph I. Became inspector-general of the armed forces in 1913. Assassinated in Sarajevo on 28 June 1914 by the Serbian nationalist Princip.

Francis Joseph I 130, 175, 214, 222

1830–1916. Became emperor of Austria in 1848 and ruled at first as an absolute monarch. Crushed revolts in Italy and Hungary. Lost Lombardy in 1859 in a war with Sardinia. After the defeats of 1866, was forced to withdraw from Venetia and to accept the Prussian annexation of Schleswig-Holstein. Became king of Hungary through the Austro-Hungarian settlement of 1867.

Francke, August Hermann 37

1663–1727, German Evangelical theologian and pedagogue. Studied in Erfurt, Kiel and Leipzig. Professor of Greek and Oriental languages after 1692 and of exegesis after 1698 in Halle. Pastor in the neighbouring town of Glaucha. Spread Lutheranism beyond the borders of Europe.

Franco, Francisco

1892–1975, Spanish general and statesman. Commanded the Spanish foreign legion in 1922. Became chief of staff in 1934. Led a military revolt in Spanish Morocco in 1936 which triggered the Spanish civil war. Triumphed in 1939 with assistance from Germany and Italy. Created a fascist, pro-clerical government. Became head of state in 1936.

Frank, Hans

1900–46, Nazi politician and lawyer. Became Bavarian minister of justice in 1933 and a federal minister in 1934. Although responsible for the legal system and president of the German Law Academy, had no influence over Hitler's legislation. Became governor-general of Poland in 1939. Was condemned in 1946 by the international military tribunal in Nuremberg and executed.

Frederick I, Barbarossa 14

1122 or ca. 1125–90, duke of Swabia. Elected German king in 1152. Crowned emperor by Hadrian IV in 1155. Led the third crusade in 1189.

Frederick I of Baden 124

1826–1907. Became regent in 1852 and grand duke in 1856. Advocated liberal policies and championed national unity under Prussian leadership. Forced to fight against Prussia in 1866 by the mood of his people and by Baden's geographic location. After being defeated, was a warm supporter of Bismarck.

Frederick II 13, 17

1194–1250. Became king of Sicily in 1198 under papal domination. In the struggles for the German throne he was supported by Pope Innocent III against Otto IV and was elected king in 1212. Crowned emperor in 1220. Became king of Jerusalem in 1228 during the fifth crusade. Excommunicated by Pope Gregory IX in 1239 and deposed by Innocent

IV in 1245 at the Council of Lyon.

Frederick II of Prussia, the 'Great' 31, 46

1712–86. Became king in 1740. Ruled as an enlightened despot. Established Prussia as a great power.

Frederick III 171

1831–88. Became German emperor and Prussian king in 1888. As crown prince fell foul of his father and especially Bismarck. Took over the government in 1888 when extremely ill. His death ended the political hopes of the liberals.

Frederick VII 131

1808–63. King of Denmark after 1848. His attempt to annex Schleswig led to war with the German Confederation.

Frederick William I of Prussia

1688–1740. Became king in 1713. Laid the foundations for Prussia's rise to great power status.

Frederick William III of Prussia 49, 60

1770–1840. Became king in 1797. At first maintained Prussian neutrality towards France and managed to enlarge Prussia in 1803 and 1805. Entered the war against Napoleon I in 1806 and was forced to sign the humiliating Peace of Tilsit in 1807.

Frederick William IV of Prussia 66–7, 75, 76, 79–82, 101, 113, 116, 124

1795–1861. Became king in 1840. Refused the United Diet of 1847 periodicity and a constitution, but was forced to make concessions after the outbreak of the revolution of 1848. Refused in 1849 to accept the position of hereditary emperor offered by the National Assembly. Abdicated in 1858.

Frederick William, the Great Elector 31

1620–88. Became elector of Brandenburg in 1640. Transformed Brandenburg into a unitary, absolutist state.

Freisler, Roland 314

1893–1945, Nazi judge. Took part in the First World War and was captured by the Russians. Became a Bolshevik commissar in the Ukraine in 1920 and a member of the Nazi party in 1925. As president of the People's Court after 1942, was one of the most radical upholders of Nazi justice. Employed the justice system for political terror, especially in the trials of those who had participated in the plot to kill Hitler on 20 July 1944.

Freud, Sigmund 184

1856–1939, Austrian psychiatrist and neurologist. Became a professor in Vienna in 1902. Emigrated to England in 1938. Founded the science of psychoanalysis.

Frick, Wilhelm 263, 284

1877–1946, Nazi politician. Worked in the offices of the Munich police 1919–23. Took part in the Hitler putsch in 1923. Entered the *Reichstag* in 1924 where he led the Nazi parliamentary group. Minister of the interior in Thuringia in 1930–1 and *Reich* minister of the interior 1933–43. Protector of Bohemia and Moravia 1943–5. Condemned to death at the Nuremberg trials and executed.

Friedeburg, Hans-Georg von

1895–1945, German grand admiral. Became second admiral of the U-boat fleet in 1941, commanding admiral in 1943 and succeeded Dönitz in 1945 as supreme commander of the navy. On Dönitz's instructions, signed the partial capitulation before Montgomery on 4 May 1945 and co-signed the full capitulation of the German *Wehrmacht* on 7 May 1945 in Reims and on 9 May 1945 in Berlin-Karlshorst. Committed suicide on 15 May 1945.

Fritsch, Werner Baron von 280
1880–1939, German general. Supreme commander of the army 1935–8. Oversaw the expansion of the army under Hitler. Resisted the Führer's risky, expansionist policies and was dismissed in February 1938 after an intrigue organised with Hitler's approval. Was freed in a subsequent court-martial and placed in charge of an artillery regiment.

Fritsche, Hans
1900–53, German journalist. Member of the German National People's Party 1923–33. Editor for the Telegraphen-Union news agency 1924–33. Joined the Nazis in 1933. Head of the news service in the press section of the ministry of propaganda 1933–42 and head of the government press division after 1938. Plenipotentiary for the political supervision of broadcasting in Greater Germany and at the same time a leading radio commentator 1942–5. In 1946 accused of war crimes by the Nuremberg tribunal but found not guilty.

Fröbel, Julius 127
Pseudonym of Carl Junius, 1805–1893, German politician and writer. Lecturer in mineralogy in Zurich after 1833. Was a member of the extreme left at the Frankfurt National Assembly.

Condemned to death in Vienna, but pardoned. Travelled in the United States and became German consul in Smyrna in 1873.

Fugger 21
Augsburg commercial and banking family, ca. 1459–1598.

Funk, Walther
1890–1960, Nazi politician, financial journalist. In 1933 became government press chief and secretary of state in the ministry of propaganda. Simultaneously president of the *Reichsbank* after 1939. Was responsible in this capacity for the economic and financial war effort. Condemned to life imprisonment in 1946 by the Nuremberg tribunal, but released in 1957 on account of illness.

Gagern, Heinrich Baron von 59, 77, 111
1799–1880, German liberal politician. Studied law in Heidelberg. Co-founder of the *Burschenschaft*. Joined the Hessen civil service in 1821. Dismissed in 1833 on account of his liberal views. Became head of the Hessen government in 1848 and first president of the Frankfurt National Assembly. Encouraged the election of the Austrian archduke Johann as *Reichsverweser* and of Frederick William IV as emperor. When Frederick William declined, Gagern resigned from the National Assembly. Was Hessen's envoy to Vienna in 1864–72.

Galen, Clemens August Count von 311–12
1878–1946, German Catholic theologian. Became bishop of Münster in 1933 and a cardinal in 1946. Opposed Nazi racial and ecclesiastical policies in widely

disseminated articles and sermons.

Gama, Vasco da, *count in 1503* 17
1469–1524, Portuguese seafarer. Dispatched by King Manuel of Portugal in 1497 to discover a sea passage to India. Sailed around the Cape of Good Hope and reached western India in 1498. Established settlements in eastern Africa during his second voyage in 1502. Appointed viceroy of India in 1524.

Gambetta, Léon 142
actually Napoléon G., 1838–82, French statesman. Parisian lawyer and leader of the republican party. Proclaimed the republic on 4 September 1870. Minister of the interior in the provisional government. Became president of the chamber in 1877, government leader 1881–2.

Gandhi, Mahatma 267
actually Mohandas Karamchand G., 1869–1948, leader of the Indian independence movement. Led South African Indians 1893–1914. In India, led the passive resistance movement against British rule. Arrested several times and carried on a hunger strike in prison as a form of political protest. Achieved Indian independence in 1947 but refused all political offices. His attempt to persuade Hindus and Mohammedans to work together failed.

Garibaldi, Guiseppe 122, 135
1807–82, hero of Italian independence. Led Italian rebels against Austria in 1848 and defended the Roman Republic in 1849 against French troops. Became president of the Italian National Assembly in 1857. In 1860 led the 'March of Garibaldi's Thousand' to Marsala in order to free Sicily from Genoa

and thereby hastened the process of Italian reunification. Member of the Italian parliament.

Gauss, Carl Friedrich 97
1777–1855, German mathematician, astronomer and physicist. Professor and director of the observatory in Göttingen after 1807.

Genscher, Hans-Dietrich 383
b. 1927, German politician (FDP), lawyer. After 1945 a member of the LDPD in the Soviet zone. Went to the Federal Republic in 1952. Entered the *Bundestag* in 1965 (FDP). Became deputy party chairman in 1968. Minister of the interior 1969–74 and foreign minister thereafter. Chairman of the FDP 1974–84.

George V 152
1819–78. Last king of Hanover (1851–66). Strongly anti-liberal. When he supported Austria in the Austro-Prussian war of 1866, he was deposed, his domains were annexed and his property was confiscated. Spent his years in exile primarily in Vienna and Paris.

George, Stefan 272
1868–1933, German poet. After studying philosophy and art history, travelled throughout Europe. In 1892, founded the *Blätter für die Kunst*, the chief organ of the George circle.

Gerlach, Leopold von 116, 125
1790–1861, Prussian general. Became adjutant to Prince William of Prussia in 1826. Personal friend of Frederick William IV. Intellectual leader of the 'camarilla' based on Christianity and the estate system. Opposed German unity and strongly supported the reaction.

Goethe, Johann Wolfgang, von after 1782 37, 38, 51, 62, 94, 99 1749–1832, German writer and poet. Spent boyhood in Frankfurt, studied in Leipzig 1765–8 and in Strasbourg in 1770. At the court of Duke Karl August von Weimar from 1775 till his death. The foremost representative of two literary eras, *Sturm und Drang* and German Classicism. Highly admired by many of the Romantics and the educated nineteenth-century bourgeoisie.

Gotthelf, Jeremias 95, 99 Pseudonym of Albert Bitzius, 1797–1854. Swiss writer and reformed pastor. Deeply suspicious of modern civilisation and urban life. Saw peasant life as the culture created by God.

Gramont, Antoine Alfred Agénor Duc de, Prince de Bidache 140 1819–80, French politician. A Bonapartist after 1848. Foreign minister in the Ollivier cabinet of 1870. Sought a war with Germany after 1866. Retired in 1870.

Grey, Edward, Viscount G. of Fallodon after 1916 215 1862–1933, English statesman. Entered the House of Commons in 1885 as a Liberal. Foreign secretary 1905–16. Sought to allay the tensions between the great powers. Resigned in protest against Lloyd George's policies in 1916.

Grimm, Jacob 38 1785–1863, German philologist. Founded Germanic philology. Librarian and professor in Göttingen and Berlin. Deputy in the Frankfurt National Assembly in 1848. Together with his brother Wilhelm published the *Kinder- und Hausmärchen* (1812ff.) and *Deutsche Sagen* (1816–

18). Began work in 1838 on his *Deutsches Wörterbuch* (1852–61). In his *German Grammar* (1819–37) and *History of the German language* (1848) he outlined the principles which had governed the development of the German language.

Grimm, Wilhelm 38 1786–1859, German philologist. Librarian in Kassel and professor in Göttingen. Collaborated closely with his brother Jacob and published many literary works.

Groener, Wilhelm 259 1867–1939, German general and minister. Succeeded Ludendorff on 26 October 1918 as quartermaster in chief. After 9 November 1918 organised the retreat and demobilisation of the army. At Hindenburg's bidding, aligned himself with Ebert in order to ward off a soviet system of government. Minister of defence 1928–32 and minister of the interior 1931–2 in Brüning's second cabinet.

Gromyko, Andrei Andreievich b. 1909, Soviet politician, agronomist. Joined the Communist Party in 1931 and the foreign service in 1939. Ambassador to the United States 1943–6. Sat on the UN security council 1946–8 and served as ambassador to Great Britain 1952–3. Appointed deputy foreign minister in 1946. First deputy foreign minister 1949–57 and foreign minister 1957–85. Entered the Central Committee in 1956 and the Politburo in 1973. Became first deputy prime minister in 1983 and head of state in 1985. Resigned 1988.

Grotewohl, Otto 332 1894–1964, German politician.

Joined the SPD in 1920 and sat in the *Reichstag* 1925–33. As Social Democratic chairman in the Soviet zone, yielded to Communist pressure in 1946 and agreed to a merger of these parties in the SED, whose co-chairman he became. Prime minister of the GDR in 1949 and deputy chairman of the Council of State in 1960.

Grotius, Hugo 33
actually Huig de Groot, 1583–1645, Dutch academic and statesman, senior government official, jurist. Opposed Prince Maurice of Orange and was sentenced to life imprisonment in 1619. Fled to Paris in 1621 where he was Swedish envoy 1635–45. One of the founders of international law. Set the stage for the Enlightenment.

Guse, Günther 292
1896–1953, German admiral. Head of the navy command in 1935, chief of the sea warfare staff 1937–8 and then inspector of navy intelligence till 1940. Named commanding admiral of the Baltic fleet in 1940 and chief of the navy high command in the east in 1943. Granted temporary leave of absence that same year and then returned to active service. Died in 1953 as a Soviet POW.

Gustav II, Adolf of Sweden 29
1594–1632, became king in 1611. Intervened in the Thirty Years War in 1630, saving the hard-pressed Protestant princes.

Gutenberg, Johann 21
actually Johann Gensfleisch zum Gutenberg, between 1394 and 1399–1468, German printer, inventor of the printing press. Lived in Strasbourg 1434–44, leaving documentary evidence of membership in the goldsmith guild. In Mainz in 1448. Entered the service of the archbishop of Mainz in 1465.

Haase, Hugo 217
1863–1919, German politician. Entered the *Reichstag* in 1897 as an SPD deputy. Co-chaired the party after 1911 with Ebert. Encouraged the SPD in vain in 1914 to refuse to vote for war credits. Became chief spokesman of the radical pacifist wing in late 1915. Co-founder of the Independent Social Democrats in 1917. Haase and Ebert became co-chairmen of the Council of People's Representatives on 10 November 1918. Haase resigned on 29 December 1918 with the other Independent Social Democrats. Died from the effects of an assassination attempt.

Händel, Georg Friedrich 37
1685–1759, German composer and organist. Apprenticed at the Hamburg opera 1703–6 and then went to Italy. Became Kapellmeister for the elector of Hanover in 1710. Went to London in 1712 and became artistic director of the Royal Academy of Music in 1719.

Haldane, Richard Burdon, Viscount H. of Cloan after 1911 211
1856–1928, English politician. Head of the war office in 1905. Undertook a fruitless mission to Berlin in 1912 in an attempt to reach agreement on naval building. Lord chancellor in 1912 and 1924.

Halder, Franz 292, 304, 313,
1884–1974, German general. Became chief of army staff in August 1938. Established contacts with the German resistance be-

cause of his opposition to Hitler's risky foreign policy. Disagreed with Hitler on strategic priorities in the Russian campaign. Arrested after 20 July 1944 and held in a concentration camp till the end of the war.

Halifax, Edward Wood, Lord Irwin in 1925, Viscount H. in 1934, Earl of H. in 1944 290, 292

1881–1959, English politician. Lord privy seal and leader of the House of Lords. Foreign secretary 1938–40. Approved the Munich agreement and also advocated an Anglo-French guarantee for Poland. Ambassador to Washington 1941–6.

Haller, Carl Ludwig von 57

1768–1854, Swiss political writer. Entered the service of Austria after establishment of the Helvetic Republic. Professor of constitutional law and Swiss history at the Bern academy. After the old constitution was restored in 1814, became a member of the Great Council in Bern till 1820. Joined the French foreign ministry in 1825. Returned to Switzerland after the July revolution. Member of the Great Council of Solothurn 1834–7.

Hallstein, Walter 364

1901–82, German jurist and politician. Professor in Rostock 1930–41, in Frankfurt a.M. 1941–8 and in Georgetown in 1948. Headed UNESCO commission of the Federal Republic in 1949. In 1950 Adenauer appointed him to lead the German negotiators of the Schuman plan and named him secretary of state in the chancellor's office. Moved later to the Foreign Office. President of the EEC commission in 1958 and of the European movement in 1968. Entered

the *Bundestag* in 1969.

Halske, Johann Georg 85

1814–90, German industrialist, originally a mechanic. In 1847 co-founded the Siemens & Halske telegraph company.

Hansemann, Adolf von 170

1827–1903, German banker of the Bismarck era.

Hardenberg, Karl August Baron von, Prince von in 1814 44, 46

1750–1822, Prussian statesman. A Hanoverian civil servant till 1782, then president of Duke Karl W. F. von Braunschweig's *Klosterrat*. Minister of the margrave of Ansbach-Bayreuth in 1790 and Prussian minister in 1791. Dismissed in 1806 at Napoleon's behest, and reappointed in 1807. Prussian chancellor in 1810. Carried on Stein's reforms. Represented Prussia (together with W. v. Humboldt) at the Congress of Vienna.

Harkort, Friedrich 96–7, 102, 104

1793–1880, German industrialist and politician. Interested in social problems and popular education. Liberal attitudes. Founded a centre-left political party. Later member of the Liberal Party.

Harnack, Arvid 312

1901–42, German political economist. Visited Russia in 1932 and was a convinced communist. Joined the currency division of the *Reich* ministry of economics in 1933. Entered the Nazi party in 1937. Supplied the Soviet embassy in Berlin and also Moscow with valuable military and political information. Discovered in 1941 by the *Wehrmacht* radio detection service. Arrested in 1942 and executed by the National Socialists.

in the colonial department of the Foreign Office 1901–6, then director of the Anatolian Railway Co. in Constantinople. Member of the *Deutsche Bank* board of directors 1908–15. Member of the *Reichsbank* central committee. Became secretary of state in the Treasury department in 1915 and directed financial policy. Appointed vice-chancellor and director of the department of the interior in 1916. A German diplomat in Moscow in 1918. Led the DNVP in the *Reichstag* 1920–4. Toppled Erzberger in 1920.

Helmholtz, Hermann Ludwig Ferdinand, von after 1882 98
1821–94, German physicist and physiologist. In 1849 became professor of physiology in Königsberg, then in Bonn and Heidelberg. In 1870 professor of theoretical physics in Berlin. Became president of the newly founded National Institute of Physics and Technology in 1888.

Henderson, Sir Neville Meyrik 299
1882–1942, English diplomat. Envoy to Belgrade 1929–35. Ambassador to Buenos Aires 1935–7 and to Berlin 1937–9.

Henlein, Konrad 292–3
1898–1945, Sudeten German politician. In October 1933 founded the Sudeten German *Heimatfront* which under the name Sudetan German Party advocated autonomy and received a majority of the votes in the parliamentary elections of May 1935. After the Munich agreement, became *Reichskommissar* for the Sudetenland. In 1939 became a *Gauleiter* and *Reichsstatthalter*. Condemned to death in 1945 and executed.

Henry I 9
876–936, Became Duke of Saxony in 912, German king in 919.

Henry II, Saint 10
973–1024, Became German king in 1002 and emperor of the Holy Roman empire in 1014.

Henry III 11
1017–56, Elected German king in 1026 and ruled after 1039. Crowned emperor in 1046.

Henry IV 11
1050–1106, Elected German king in 1053. His mother Agnes of Poitou was regent from 1056 to 1066. Quarrelled with Pope Gregory VII over lay investiture and was excommunicated. Threatened with dethronement, he undertook a penitential pilgrimage to Canossa in 1077. Absolved by the church. Triumphed over the rival claimants to the throne, Rudolf von Schwaben and Hermann von Salm. Excommunicated again in 1080. Crowned emperor by Clement III, the anti-pope whom he had appointed. Quarrelled with his youngest son, Henry (V).

Henry V 11
1081–1125. Became German king in 1106. Refused to renounce right to invest bishops and abbots. Arrested Pope Paschal II in order to coerce him into crowning Henry emperor in 1111. Ended the quarrel over investiture in 1122 and concluded the Concordat of Worms of 1125.

Henry VI 11
1165–97, Elected German king in 1169. Ruled after 1190. Crowned emperor in 1191.

Henschel, Carl Anton 97
1780–1861, German engineer and manufacturer. In 1803 superin-

tendent of building in Hesse-Kassel. Entered the family firm in Kassel in 1817 and built the first locomotive in 1848.

Herder, Johann, Gottfried, von in 1802 37, 38
1744–1803, German writer and philosopher. Studied theology in Königsberg. In 1776 became superintendent and court chaplain in Weimar.

Herter, Christian Archibald 365
1895–1966, American politician. Entered the foreign service in 1916 and became a Republican member of the House of Representatives in 1943–53. Governor of Massachusetts 1953–7. In 1956 became undersecretary of state under J. F. Dulles. Secretary of State 1959–61. Advocated a flexible approach to the Soviet Union.

Hertling, Georg Baron von, Count von in 1914 218
1843–1919, German Catholic philosopher and politician. Centrist *Reichstag* deputy 1875–90 and 1896–1912. Became party chairman in 1909. Prime minister of Bavaria 1912–17 and supporter of Bethmann Hollweg. In November 1917 became *Reichskanzler* and Prussian prime minister. Resigned in late September 1918.

Hess, Moses 105
1812–75, German socialist. Cofounded the *Rheinische Zeitung* in 1841. Became its editor and Parisian correspondent in 1842. Active in the German communist movement in Brussels and Paris in 1845–8.

Hess, Rudolf
1894–1987, Nazi politician. Flight lieutenant in the First World War.

Joined the National Socialists in 1920. Participated in the Hitler putsch in 1923. Became Hitler's deputy in 1933 as party leader and *Reichsminister*. Flew to Scotland in May 1941 in the hope of inducing Great Britain to enter peace negotiations with Germany and join in an attack on the Soviet Union. Interned in England in 1941–5. In 1946 sentenced by the International Military Tribunal in Nuremberg to life imprisonment. Last prisoner left in the Allied war criminal prison in Spandau.

Heuss, Theodor 250, 342, 357
1884–1963, German politician. After working as a journalist, became a DDP *Reichstag* deputy in 1924–33 and a lecturer at the political institute in Berlin. In 1946 helped to found the FDP and became the minister of culture in Württemberg-Baden. As a member of the Parliamentary Council played a leading role in framing the Basic Law. President of the Federal Republic 1949–59.

Hilferding, Rudolf 247
1877–1941, Austro-German social scientist, politician, publicist and physician. In 1904–23 co-published *Marx-Studien*. *Vorwärts* editor 1907–16. As a pacifist, he joined the Independent Social Democrats and ran its chief organ, *Die Freiheit*. Returned to the SPD in 1922 and joined the Party executive. Minister of finance in 1923 and 1928–9. Member of the *Reichstag* 1924–33. Emigrated to France in 1938. Died in the hands of the Gestapo after attempted suicide.

Himmler, Heinrich 280, 286, 299, 308–9, 316–17,
1900–45, Nazi politician. Took part in the Hitler putsch in 1923. Head of the SS in 1929 and Mu-

nich police chief in 1933. In June 1936 became head of all the police in his capacity as secretary of state in the ministry of the interior. Was put in charge in 1939 of resettlement and forced Germanisation in eastern and southeastern Europe. Organised the final solution of the Jewish question. In 1943 became minister of the interior and in 1944 supreme commander of the home army and head of army procurement. Organised the *Volkssturm* in early 1945. After attempting to open peace negotiations with the Allies in April 1945, was stripped of all his offices and expelled from the Nazi party. Committed suicide in British detention.

Hindemith, Paul 285
1895–1963, German composer. Prominent musical theoretician and teacher. Considered a pioneer of modernism. Abandoned major and minor tonality and reordered the twelve chromatic notes.

Hindenburg, Oskar von
1883–1960, German officer. Adjutant and adviser to his father, Paul v. Hindenburg. His career ended in 1934 with the death of his father.

Hindenburg, Paul von 218–19, 222, 224, 229, 231, 250–1, 255–6, 259–63, 279–80
1847–1934, German general and politician. In 1915 field marshal and supreme commander in the east. In 1916 chief of the army general staff. Took over the army supreme command. In 1918 organised demobilisation in the west. Elected *Reichspräsident* in 1925 and re-elected in 1932.

Hitler, Adolf 246, 258, 259, 261–3, 271–320, 328, 330–1,

1889–1945, German dictator, leader of the National Socialist German Workers' Party. Became chancellor in 1933 and was Führer and chancellor from 1934 to 1945.

Hobbes, Thomas
1588–1679, English philosopher. Lived in exile in Paris 1640–51. Applied the mechanistic, scientific method to political science.

Hoffmann (von Fallersleben), August Heinrich 68
1798–1874, German lyric poet and Germanist. Appointed a professor in Breslau in 1830 but was dismissed in 1842 on account of his National-Liberal views. Rehabilitated in 1848. In 1860 became the librarian of Duke von Ratibor zu Corvey. Wrote the *Deutschlandlied* (German national anthem).

Hohenlohe-Schillingsfürst, Chlodwig Prince zu, in 1840 Prince von Ratibor and Corvey 162, 189–90
1819–1901, German diplomat and politician. Bavarian prime minister and foreign minister 1866–70. Ambassador to Paris in 1874. Governor of Alsace-Lorraine in 1885. Chancellor and Prussian prime minister 1894–1900.

Holstein, Friedrich von 131–2, 202–5, 207
1837–1909, German diplomat, jurist. Attaché in St Petersburg, Rio de Janeiro, London and Washington 1861–8. After serving as second secretary in the Parisian embassy (1871–6), was recalled to the Foreign Office in Berlin where he became a close adviser to Bismarck. Participated after 1885 in attempts to oust Bismarck. Principal foreign policy adviser to Caprivi and Bülow after 1890.

Honecker, Erich 375
b. 1912, German politician. Roofer. Member of the communist children's movement, the young Spartacus league and the red youth pioneers 1922–26. Became secretary of the communist youth movement in Saar region in 1931. Joined the KPD in 1929. Arrested in 1935 and sentenced in 1937 to ten years imprisonment. Rejoined the KPD in 1945 and became youth secretary of the Free German Youth in the Soviet occupation zone. First chairman of the Free German Youth 1946–55. Joined the central committee of the SED in 1946 and became a deputy in the *Volkskammer* of the GDR in 1949. Secretary of the security commission of the SED central committee in 1956. Member of the politburo in 1958. Chairman of the national defence council in 1971. Became first secretary of the central committee and successor to Walter Ulbricht. Entered the Council of State of the GDR in 1971 and became its chairman in 1976.

Hoover, Herbert Clark 257
1874–1964, thirty-first president of the United States (1929–33). Mining engineer, Headed the commission for relief in Belgium 1915–19 and the US food administration 1917–19. Organised a European aid programme in 1918. Secretary of commerce 1921–8. As a Republican, elected president in 1928. Defeated in 1932 by F. D. Roosevelt. Chairman of the commission on organisation of the executive branch of government 1947–9 and 1953–5.

Horthy, Niklos 265
1868–1957, Hungarian statesman and admiral. Formed a national army in opposition to the soviet republic. Elected regent of Hungary in 1920 by the National Assembly. Forced to step down in 1944 and lived thereafter in Portugal.

Hugenberg, Alfred 258–9, 263
1865–1951, leading German businessman and politician. Helped to found the Pan-German League in 1891. Chairman of the Krupp board of directors 1909–18. Built up his own company after 1916 (daily newspapers, news agencies, advertising firms and film companies). A DNVP deputy in 1919 and party chairman in 1928. Opposed the Brüning government. Became minister of economics and food under Hitler. Resigned in June 1933.

Huizinga, Johan 2
1872–1945, Dutch historian. Professor in Gröningen and Leiden. During the Second World War imprisoned for a time by the Germans. Proponent of an aristocratic culture rooted in the middle class and an astute critic of modern mass society.

Humboldt, Wilhelm Baron von 47
1767–1835, Prussian academic and statesman. Studied law in Frankfurt/Oder and Göttingen. Envoy to Rome in 1801–8. Became director of culture and education in the ministry of the interior in 1809. Envoy to Austria in 1810. Represented Prussia at the Congress of Vienna. Member of the German territorial commission in Frankfurt a. M. in 1816 and envoy to London in 1817. Minister of estate and communal affairs in 1819. Forced to resign in 1819 because of his opposition to the Karlsbad Decrees.

Hutten, Ulrich von 20–1
1488–1523, German humanist and publicist. Knight of the Holy

Roman Empire. Studied at various universities including Erfurt. Crowned poet laureate in 1517 by Emperor Maximilian I. Proponent of the reformation.

Ibn-Saud, Abdul-Aziz 267
1880–1953, founded the kingdom of Saudi Arabia and became its king in 1926. Grew up in exile in Kuwait. Reconquered Riyadh in 1902 and extended his rule throughout Arabia. Named Wali by the Turks in 1914. Sultan in 1922.

Isabella II 140
1830–1904. Became queen of Spain in 1833, first under the guardianship of her mother and then under the regency of Espartero 1841–3. Repeated revolts during her reign. After the revolution of Cadiz, fled into exile in France in 1868 and abdicated in 1870 in favour of her son Alfonso XII.

Jahn, Friedrich Ludwig 38, 62, 67
1778–1852, German educator. Teacher in Berlin. Opened the first gymnastics field near Berlin in 1811 and initiated the gymnastics movement in Germany. Helped found the *Burschenschaften* and the German *Bund*. Arrested and imprisoned in 1819 for demagogery. Under police surveillance 1825–40. Member of the Frankfurt National Assembly 1848–9.

James I of England 1
1566–1625. Became king of Scotland in 1567 and king of England and Scotland in 1603.

Jaspers, Karl 318
1883–1969, German philosopher. First a psychiatrist at the University of Heidelberg and then professor of psychology in 1916 and professor of philosophy in 1921. Forbidden to teach from 1937 to 1945. Professor of philosophy in Heidelberg in 1945 and in Basle after 1948. Foremost proponent of the philosophy of existentialism.

Jefferson, Thomas 35
1743–1826, third president of the United States. Member of the Virginia colonial legislature in 1769. Member of the continental congress in 1775–6. Drafted the Declaration of Independence of 4 July 1776. Governor of Virginia 1779–81, envoy to Paris in 1785–9, vice-president in 1797. Elected president in 1801 and 1805.

Jérôme Bonaparte 43
1784–1860, brother of Napoleon I. King of Westphalia 1807–13. Fought in Russia in 1812 and at Waterloo in 1815. After 1816 lived in Austria, Italy and Switzerland as the Prince de Montfort.

Jode, Alfred
1890–1946, German general. Distinguished himself during World War I and thereafter as a general staff officer. As chief of the army command, advised Hitler after 1939 in all strategic and operational matters. Signed the capitulation of the German *Wehrmacht* in Reims on 7 May 1945 at the behest of Dönitz. In 1946 sentenced to death by the International Military Tribunal in Nuremberg and executed.

Joffre, Joseph Jacques Césaire 218
1852–1931, French marshal. Chief of the general staff in 1911. As supreme commander on the north and northeastern front, stopped the German advance in the Battle

of the Marne in September 1914. Became supreme commander of all French troops in 1915. Relieved of his duties in 1916 for lack of further victories.

Johann 77
1782–1859, Austrian archduke. As army commander met with little success in the wars against France. Played a major role in the Tyrolian rebellion of 1809. Elected German *Reichsverweser* in 1848 by the Frankfurt National Assembly.

Jünger, Ernst 233
b. 1895, German writer. Literary proponent of a conservative revolution.

Kafka, Franz 285
1883–1924, Austrian writer. Studied law in Prague 1901–6. Insurance company employee 1908–17. First signs of tuberculosis in 1917. Moved to Berlin in 1923. Returned to Prague in March 1924 because of worsening health. His writings represent an early German counterpart to French surrealism.

Kahr, Gustav, knighted in 1911 246
1862–1934, German politician. President of Upper Bavaria in 1917–24. Became commissar of state in 1923. Put down the Hitler putsch in 1923 with the help of the police and the army. President of the supreme Bavarian administrative court 1924–7. Shot by the Nazis during the Röhm affair.

Kant, Immanuel 32, 37, 38
1724–1804, German philosopher from a Pietist Protestant background. Professor of logic and metaphysics in Königsberg 1770–97. In the *Critique of Pure Reason*,

published in 1781, Kant developed his philosophy of transcendental idealism.

Kapp, Wolfgang 242
1858–1922, German politician. General manager of the agricultural credit bank *Ostpreussische Landschaft*. Founded the German Fatherland Party in 1917. Attempted a putsch in March 1920 and died in custody.

Karl Wilhelm Ferdinand von Braunschweig, Duke 40
1735–1806, Prussian general. Supreme commander of the allied armies in France in 1792 and of the Prussian army in 1806.

Keitel, Wilhelm
1882–1946, German field marshal. Headed the army organisation department 1929–34 and the *Wehrmacht* office of the ministry of defence after 1935. Head of the newly created army supreme command in 1938. In charge of the truce negotiations in Compiègne in 1940. By offering his resignation, attempted to dissuade Hitler from attacking the Soviet Union. His influence on military planning and military campaigns progressively diminished as the war continued, but believing in Hitler's 'genius' he passed along the Führer's commands. Condemned to death by the International Military Tribunal in Nuremberg and executed in 1946.

Kellogg, Frank Billings 252
1856–1937, American jurist and politician. Republican senator from Minnesota 1917–23. Ambassador to London in 1924. As secretary of state 1925–9, sought to impose United States hegemony on Latin America. Won the Nobel Peace Prize in 1929 for the war renunciation pact (Kel-

logg Pact) which he initiated.

Kemal Atatürk 268
pseudonym of Mustafa Kemal
Pasha, 1880–1938, Turkish states-
man. Took part in the Young
Turkish revolution of 1908–9.
Commanding general in the First
World War. In 1919 led the na-
tionalist movement against the
Allied and Greek occupation.
Elected chairman of the Great
National Assembly in 1920. Drove
the Greeks from Asia Minor in
1921. Became the first president of
the Turkish Republic in 1923.
Following the European model,
made Turkey a modern state.

Kennedy, John Fitzgerald 364
1917–1963, thirty-fifth president
of the United States. Democratic
member of the House of Representatives 1947–53. Senator from
Massachusetts in 1953–61. Elected
president in 1960 in a close victory
over Richard Nixon. Assassinated
in 1963.

Kerensky, Alexander Feodorovich
225
1881–1970, Russian politician.
After the February revolution of
1917 became minister of justice in
the provisional government and
minister of war. Prime minister in
July 1917. Fled during the October revolution. Lived thereafter
in exile and went to the United
States in 1940.

*Ketteler, Wilhelm Emanuel Baron
von* 102–3
1811–77, German Catholic theologian and jurist. Deputy in the
Frankfurt National Assembly
1848–9. Entered the *Reichstag* in
1871 as a Centrist deputy. Became bishop of Mainz in 1850
and founded the Fulda bishops'
conference in 1867. Encouraged
Catholic political influence.

Keudell, Robert von 139
1824–1903, German politician
and diplomat. Confidant of Bismarck. Envoy to Constantinople
in 1872 and to Rome in 1873.
Ambassador to Rome 1876–87.
Conservative member of the
Reichstag 1871–2 and 1890–3.
Prussian deputy 1888–93.

Khrushchev, Nikita 363–6
1894–1971, Soviet politician.
Party secretary in Moscow
1931–7. Member of the central
committee of the communist
party 1935–66. During the Second World War, organised partisan resistance in the Ukraine.
Secretary of the central committee 1949–53. First secretary of the
central committee 1959–64 and
chairman of the council of ministers of the USSR (prime minister) in 1958–64. Initiated the
de-Stalinisation process (20th
party congress in February 1956).
Dismissed from all these functions in October 1964.

Kiderlen-Wächter, Alfred von 208
1852–1912, German diplomat.
Secretary of state in the foreign
office in 1910. Opposed the naval
programme.

Kiesinger, Kurt Georg 369, 371, 379
1904–88, German politician (CDU).
Technical employee in the radio
department of the foreign office
1940–45. In 1948 became the provincial director of the CDU in
Württemberg-Hohenzollern.
Joined the CDU executive committee in 1950. Member of the
Bundestag from 1949 to 1980 (save
1958–69). Prime minister of
Baden-Württemberg 1958–66.
Chancellor of the grand coalition
1966–9. Federal chairman of the
CDU 1967–71.

Kirchhoff, Gustav Robert 98
1824–87, German physicist. Professor in Breslau, Heidelberg and Berlin. Worked with Bunsen on spectral analysis.

Kirchner, Ernst Ludwig 285
1880–1939, German painter and graphic artist. Helped to found *Die Brücke.*

Klee, Paul 285
1879–1940, German painter and graphic artist of Swiss origin. Influential teacher and theoretician in the *Bauhaus.* Professor at the Düsseldorf academy 1931–3. After his dismissal, moved to Bern.

Klopstock, Friedrich Gottlieb 37
1724–1803, German poet. Paved way for *Empfindsamkeit, Sturm und Drang* and intensely personal modern literature.

Koch, Erich 308
1896–1986, Nazi politician. Moved from the *Freikorps* to the Nazi party in 1920. Became an East Prussian *Gauleiter* in 1928 and entered the *Reichstag* in 1930. Supreme president of East Prussia in 1933, As commissar for the Ukraine in 1941–4 responsible for the brutal exploitation of the civilian population. Condemned to death in Poland in 1959, but not executed.

Köhl, Hermann 249
1888–1813, early German flyer. After the First World War, a postal flyer, later chief of night flight for Lufthansa. In 1928 flew across the North Atlantic for the first time from east to west in a single-engine Junkers W 33.

Körner, Theodor 49
1791–1813, German poet. Celebrated patriot from the time of the wars of liberation. Killed serving as an officer in the Lützow free corps.

Kohl, Helmut 383, 386
b. 1930, German politician (CDU). Entered the provincial legislature of Rheinland-Pfalz in 1959. Chairman of the CDU parliamentary group 1963–9 and of the provincial party 1966–73. Prime minister of Rheinland-Pfalz 1969–76. Deputy chairman of the federal CDU 1969–73. Took over as chairman in 1973. CDU/CSU candidate for chancellor in 1976 and chairman of the CDU/CSU parliamentary group. Became chancellor in 1982.

Kokoschka, Oskar 285
1886–1980, Austrian expressionist painter and dramatist. Professor at the Dresden academy of art 1918–24. Emigrated to Prague in 1934 and to London in 1938.

Kollwitz, Käthe 285
1867–1945, German graphic artist and sculptor. Moved to Berlin in 1891. Professor 1918–33. Prominent expressionist graphic artist whose works express sympathy for the proletariat and its problems.

Kolping, Adolf 103
1813–66, German Catholic theologian. First a shoemaker journeyman, then became a priest in 1845. Founded a Catholic journeyman's association in Cologne in 1849, the basis of the later Kolping foundation.

Kornilov, Lavr Georgeievich 225
1870–1918, Russian general. As supreme commander of the Russian army, organised and led the Kornilov putsch from August to September 1917. Putsch was put down by the Bolsheviks. After the October revolution, commanded

the volunter white army.

Koser, Reinhold 174
1852–1914, Prussian historian. Director of the *Preussisches u. Geheimes Staatsarchiv* after 1896.

Kossuth, Lajos 75
1802–94, Hungarian politician. Led the independence movement of 1848–9. Elected regent after the Habsburgs were deposed in 1849. After the revolt was crushed, resigned and fled abroad. Led the Hungarian exiles.

Kosygin, Alexei Nikolayevich
1904–80, Soviet politician and textile engineer. Joined the communist party in 1927 and sat on the central committee in 1940–64. Named deputy chairman of the council of people's commissars in 1940. Prime minister of the RSFSR 1943–6. Finance minister in 1948, then minister of light industry till 1953. Chief of the economic planning council 1959–60. Member of the politburo 1948–52 and again after 1960. Succeeded Khrushchev in 1964 as chairman of the council of ministers.

Kotzebue, August von 59
1761–1819, German dramatist. Served Russian interests 1781–90. Later dramatist in Vienna and director of the German theatre in St Petersburg. An adversary of Goethe, the Romantics and Napoleon I. Ridiculed the liberal ideas of the *Burschenschaften*. Murdered by the student Karl Ludwig Sand.

Krupp, Alfred 97, 104
1812–1887, German industrialist. Expanded his father's firm to include the production of railway equipment and munitions.

Krupp, Friedrich 97
1787–1826, German industrialist. In 1811 founded a factory in Essen for the production of cast steel.

Kühlmann, Richard von 227
1873–1948, German diplomat. Diplomatic counsellor in London 1900–14. Envoy to the Hague in 1915. Ambassador to Constantinople in 1916. Secretary of state in the foreign office 1917–18.

Lamartine, Alphonse de 71
1790–1869, French poet and diplomat. Entered the Académie française in 1830. Foreign minister of the provisional government in 1848. Considered to be the great French Romantic poet.

Lassalle, Ferdinand 104–5, 123, 127, 157
1825–64, German Social Democratic politician and publicist. Studied philosophy and philology in Breslau and Berlin. Became familiar with Blanc's theories in Paris in 1845. Advocated a socialist, democratic kingdom. In 1863 founded the General Association of German Workers, the embryo of the Social Democratic movement.

Laval, Pierre 302
1883–1945, French politician, lawyer. Became a deputy in 1914. Was a socialist till 1919, then without a party. A senator in 1927–40. Repeatedly a minister 1925–31. In 1931 prime minister and minister of the interior in a centre-right cabinet. Foreign minister and prime minister 1934–6. Became deputy prime minster of the Vichy government in 1940. Dismissed and arrested in December 1940. Named prime minister again in April 1942 as a result of German pressure. Fled in 1945 from exile in Sigmaringen to Spain. Deported to Austria and extra-

dited to France by the United States. Sentenced to death and executed.

Leber, Julius 312
1891–1945, German politician. SPD *Reichstag* deputy 1924–33. In a concentration camp 1933–7. Thereafter joined the German resistance and was involved in the preparations for the attempted putsch of 20 July 1944. Arrested on 5 July 1944, sentenced to death by the People's Court and executed.

Legien, Carl 180, 235
1861–1920, German labour union leader. Helped to found the General Commission of Free German Trade Unions in 1890 and served as its chairman till 1919. SPD deputy in the *Reichstag* 1893–8 and 1903–18. After 1918 advocated cooperation with factory owners. In 1919 co-founded and became chairman of the General Association of German Trade Unions. Initiated the successful general strike in response to the Kapp putsch in March 1920.

Léhar, Franz 186
1870–1948, Hungarian operetta composer. Military bandmaster. Contributed to the revival of classical Vienesse operetta.

Leiningen, Prince Karl zu 77
1804–56, German liberal politician. Member of the first chambers of Bavaria, Hessen-Darmstadt and Baden. Became president of the upper chamber of the Bavarian parliament in 1843. After 1847 supported German unification through a constitutional Prussian state. In 1848 became president of the first imperial ministry in Frankfurt a. M.

Lenin, Vladimir Ilyich (after 1901 the political alias of V.I. Ulyanov)

225–7, 236, 269
1870–1924, Russian revolutionary statesman. Connected to the revolutionary movement in Russia after 1887. In 1895 founded the 'Union for the Liberation of the Working Class'. Arrested for revolutionary propaganda and exiled to Siberia. Emigrated in 1900 to Munich, London and Geneva. Became Bolshevik leader in 1903. Participated in the attempted Russian revolution of 1905. Emigrated again, ending up in Zurich. Published *Pravda* beginning in 1912. Returned to Russia in late March 1917. After the October revolution, chairman of the council of people's commissars and proponent of the Treaty of Brest-Litovsk. Oversaw the establishment of the Soviet system against internal and external opposition.

Leo, XIII 154
1810–1903. Appointed cardinal in 1853, pope in 1878. Advocated ending the *Kulturkampf*. Extended the ecclesiastical hierarchy by creating 248 new bishoprics. In 1881 opened the Vatican archives to academic research. Established a biblical commission.

Leopold II 170
1835–1909, king of Belgium in 1865. One of the first to recognise the economic benefits of exploiting the Congo which he had founded and whose sovereign he became in 1885.

Leopold Prince von Hohenzollern-Sigmaringen 140–1
1835–1905. His candidacy, supported by Bismarck, for the Spanish throne prompted the Franco-Prussian War of 1870–1.

Lesseps, Ferdinand Marie Vicomte de 196

1805–94, French diplomat and engineer. Originated and built the Suez Canal (1859–69). Began construction of the Panama Canal in 1879, but became entangled in the bankruptcy of the Panama Company and was sentenced to five years in prison. Later rehabilitated.

Lessing, Gotthold Ephraim 37
1729–81, German dramatist and critic. Studied theology, philology and medicine. Lived in Berlin after 1748 as an independent writer. Became a dramatic producer in Hamburg in 1767 and librarian to a Wolfenbüttel prince in 1770.

Leuschner, Wilhelm 312
1890–1944, German politician. Entered the Hessen *Landtag* in 1924 as an SPD deputy. German Trade Union Association district secretary in Hessen 1926–8. Hessen minister of the interior 1928–32. Member of the German Trade Union Association executive 1932–3. Concentration camp inmate 1933–4. Connections to the Kreisau circle. Condemned to death in September 1944 by the People's Court and executed.

Liebermann, Max 186
1847–1935, German painter and graphic artist, leading impressionist in Germany.

Liebig, Justus, von in 1845 98–9
1803–73, German chemist. Professor in Giessen and Munich. Initiated laboratory instruction in German universities and introduced artificial fertilizers.

Liebknecht, Karl 157, 234, 236, 243
1871–1919, German socialist. Entered the Prussian Chamber of Deputies in 1908 as an SPD deputy and the *Reichstag* in 1912. Denounced the SPD's common front policy during the First World War and voted against war credits. Excluded from the SPD parliamentary group in 1916. After a pacifist manifestation in Berlin in 1916, found guilty of treason and sentenced to four years in prison. Proclaimed the 'free socialist republic' on 9 November 1918. Murdered, together with Rosa Luxemburg, by Free Corps officers in 1919.

Liebknecht, Wilhelm 157
1826–1900, German politician. Participated in the revolution of 1848–9. Emigrated to Switzerland and London. Befriended Marx and Engels. After returning to Germany, entered the *Reichstag* together with Bebel in 1867 as the first deputies of a left-wing party. In 1869 helped to found the Socialist Workers' Party of Germany (renamed SPD in 1890).

Lilienthal, Otto 180
1848–96, German aeroplane constructor. Built and tested the first gliders capable of carrying a man in Berlin 1891–6.

List, Friedrich 65–6, 96, 99
1789–1846, German political economist. Professor in Tübingen. In 1819 helped to found the German Industry and Trade Union. Condemned to prison in 1822 for advocating democratic reforms. Emigrated to the United States and returned to Germany as an American consul. Championed a unified German tariff, the building of railways and protective tariffs.

Livingstone, David 197
1813–73, English missionary and explorer. Became a missionary in southern Africa in 1841. Discovered Ngami Lake in 1849, Victoria Falls on the Zambezi in 1855, was the first white man to cross

southern Africa from west to east and explored the entire course of the Zambezi till 1864.

Lloyd George, David, in 1945 Earl Lloyd George of Dwyfor 208, 222
1863–1945, British statesman. Entered the House of Commons in 1890 as a Radical-Liberal. Chancellor of the exchequer 1908–15. Minister of munitions in 1915 and secretary of state for war in 1916. Became prime minister in late 1915. Signed the Treaty of Versailles together with Wilson and Clemenceau. Thereafter advocated moderate treatment of Germany in order to forstall total economic collapse and the rise of Bolshevism. Resigned as head of government in 1922. Became Liberal party chairman in 1926. Resigned from this office in 1941.

Locke, John 34
1632–1704, English philosopher. Studied medicine, theology and philosophy. Member of the civil service for a time. Exponent of English empiricism and, in political theory, of the sovereignty of the people, monarchical executive power and representative democracy.

Löbe, Paul 241
1875–1967, German writer, editor and politician. Leading Silesian Social Democrat. Repeatedly president of the *Reichstag* during the Weimar Republic. Arrested in 1933 and 1944. Member of the Bundestag 1949–53.

Lorenz, Peter 382
1922–88, German politican (CDU). Chairman of the Berlin CDU. Abducted on 27 February 1974 by the '2 June Movement' and released again on 5 March.

Louis XVI of France 62
1754–93. King 1774–92. Summoned the Estates General in 1789 and thereby initiated the events leading to the French Revolution. Attempted to flee in 1791. The monarchy was abolished in 1792, and Louis was arrested, tried, and executed in 1793.

Louis XVIII, Count of Provence 62
1755–1824, brother of Louis XVI. Fled abroad in 1791. Returned to Paris in 1814 as king. Fled again to Ghent during the 'Hundred Days' of Napoleon and returned to Paris in 1815.

Louis Philippe of France 63, 70, 92
1773–1850. Became duke of Chartres in 1785, and as Louis XIX, 'king of the French' in 1830–48. At first supported the French Revolution, but went to Austria in 1793 and lived in exile as duke of Orléans. As king, was first inclined to liberalism then grew increasingly anti-democratic. Overthrown in 1848, fled to England where he lived as the duke of Neuilly.

Loyola, Ignatius of 27
actually Inigo Lopez de Recalde, 1491–1556, Spanish officer and founder of a religious order. Turned to religion after being wounded near Pamplona. Undertook a pilgrimmage to Jerusalem in 1523, then resolved to become a priest. Ordained as a priest in 1537 and elected the first general of the Jesuit order he had founded. One of the most prominent representatives of the Catholic reform and counterreformation.

Lucius, Robert Baron von Bellhausen 172
1835–1914, Prussian politician. Entered the *Reichstag* in 1870

(*Freikonservativ*). Prussian minister of agriculture 1879–90.

Ludendorff, Erich 218–19, 221–2, 224, 227–31, 246, 319
1865–1937, German general. Head of the deployment section on the general staff 1908–12. After conquering the fortress of Liège, was made chief of the general staff under Hindenburg. Orchestrated the successful defensive campaign in East Prussia. As first quartermaster-general formed, together with Hindenburg, the third supreme army command in late August 1916. Dismissed on 26 October 1918. Participated in the Hitler putsch of 1923. Failed in 1925 to win election as *Reichspräsident*. Founded the Tannenberg League in 1926 and waged a publicity campaign against 'super-governmental forces' (Free Masons, Jews, Jesuits, Marxists) whom he blamed for the German defeat in the First World War.

Lüderitz, Franz Adolf 169
1834–86, wealthy German merchant. In 1883 purchased the port of Angra Pequena and coastal territory in southwest Africa and had it placed under the protection of the German *Reich* in 1884. This formed the nucleus of the later colony of German Southwest Africa.

Ludwig II of Bavaria 143
1845–86, king in 1864. Patron of Richard Wagner. His anthropophobia and large debts led in 1886 to the installation of his uncle Luitpold as regent; Ludwig was interned in Castle Berg on Lake Starnberg, where he drowned shortly thereafter.

Luther, Hans 247
1879–1962, German jurist and politician. Secretary of the German Conference of Cities 1913–18. Mayor of Essen 1918–22. Minister of food in 1922, minister of finance 1923–5 and chancellor 1925–6. President of the *Reichsbank* 1930–3. Ambassador to the United States in 1933–37. After 1945, Luther became an adviser on political and economic reconstruction. Chairman of a committee on the restructuring of the Federal Republic in 1953 and president of the 'League for German Expatriates' beginning in 1958.

Luther, Martin 22–6
1483–1546, German reformer. Studied in Erfurt 1501–5. Magister. After 1505 Augustinian monk in Erfurt. Studied theology in Erfurt and Wittenberg. Ordained a priest in 1507. Travelled to Rome in 1510. Received a doctorate in 1512. Professor of Holy Writ in Wittenberg. The Heidelberg disputation and interview with Cajetan, the papal legate. Leipzig disputation in 1519. Threatened with excommunication in 1520 and excommunicated in 1521. Was summoned by Charles V to the Worms *Reichstag* of 1521, but refused to recant. Banned by the Empire in the Edict of Worms. Granted asylum on the Wartburg by Frederick III of Saxony. Translated the New Testament into German.

Luxemburg, Rosa 234, 236, 243
1871–1919, Polish socialist. Founding member in 1893 of the internationalist 'Social Democracy of the Kingdom of Poland'. Settled in Berlin in 1898 and joined the SPD. Opposed revisionism and participated in the Russian Revolution of 1905. After 1907 taught political economy in the SPD party school in Berlin. Sen-

tenced to one year in prison in 1914 for anti-military remarks. Helped found the Spartacus League. In preventive custody 1916–18. Played a major role in the founding of the German Communist Party on 30 December 1918. After the failed January uprising in Berlin (which she opposed), was murdered together with Liebknecht by Free Corps officers.

MacMahon, Patrice Maurice, Marquis of, Duke of Magenta in 1859 141

1808–93, French marshal. Participated in the Crimean War and in a successful campaign against the Kabyles. Governor-general of Algeria 1864–70. Wounded and taken prisoner in the Franco-Prussian War. Suppressed the Paris Commune in 1871. President 1873–9.

Maffei, Joseph Anton von 97

1790–1870, German entrepreneur. Took over his father's tobacco factory in 1815. Encouraged by List, resolved to build a locomotive in 1836. Began to build steamships in 1847.

Magellan, Ferdinand de 17

ca.1480–1521, Portuguese seafarer in the service of Portugal and then Spain. Received five ships from Charles V in which he set out in 1519 to find a western passage to the Moluccas. Reached the Mariana islands and the Philippines in 1521.

Mahler, Gustav 186

1860–1911, Austrian composer and conductor. Educated in Vienna. Conducted in Kassel, Leipzig, Budapest, Hamburg and elsewhere. Became conductor of the Vienna *Hofoper* in 1897 and soon thereafter its director. Guest conductor at the Metropolitan Opera in 1907 and director of the Philharmonic Society in New York.

Mann, Golo 2

b. 1909, German historian and publicist. History professor at Olivet College, Michigan 1942–3 and at Claremont Men's College, California 1947–64. Thereafter professor of political science at the Stuttgart *Technische Hochschule*.

Mann, Heinrich 285

1871–1950, German writer. Studied in Berlin and Munich. In 1930 elected president of the writers' section of the Prussian Academy of Arts. Emigrated to Czechoslovakia in 1933, then to France. In 1940 fled to Spain, then to California. In 1949 first winner of the National Prize of the GDR.

Mann, Thomas 186, 272, 285

1875–1955, German writer. In 1933 emigrated to Switzerland and was deprived of his German citizenship. Went to the United States in 1939 and returned to Switzerland after the war. Championed a cosmopolitan, humanist, democratic outlook. Won the Nobel Prize in 1929.

Mao Tse-Tung 323

1893–1976, Chinese politician. After studying at the college of education became a library assistant in Peking in 1918 and joined Marxist circles. In 1919 became a lecturer at the Hunan college of education and helped in preparations for the founding of the Chinese Communist Party. In 1921 led the party organisation in Hunan. Entered the central committee and the politburo in 1923.

After the Communist victory in the civil war, proclaimed the People's Republic of China in 1949. Was appointed chairman of the central soviet of the People's Republic and in 1954 elected president of the People's Republic of China.

Marc, Franz 285

1880–1916, German painter and graphic artist. During frequent travels, came in contact with avant-garde French artists. Helped to found *Der blaue Reiter* in 1911. Killed at Verdun in 1916 in the First World War.

Maria Theresa 31

1717–80. Archduchess of Austria, after 1740 Queen of Bohemia and Hungary and German Empress. Upheld her right to the throne against Prussia in the first and second Silesian wars and in the war of Austrian succession.

Marshall, George Catlett 325, 352

1880–1959, American general and politician. Chief of army staff in the First World War. In 1939–45 chief of staff of the United States armed forces. Sought in vain through a special commission in China to orchestrate a compromise between Chiang Kai-shek and the communists. As secretary of state 1947–9, pursued a policy of containment built on economic as well as military assistance. Secretary of defence 1951–2. Awarded the Nobel Peace Prize in 1953.

Marx, Karl Heinrich 65, 102, 104–6, 108–9, 127, 210

1818–1883, German socialist philosopher, founder of Marxism and dialectical materialism. Studied jurisprudence and philosophy in Bonn. Editor-in-chief of the liberal *Rheinische Zeitung* 1842–3.

Collaborated with Friedrich Engels. Wrote the Communist Manifesto in 1848. Lived in exile in Paris and London. Played a leading role in the first Communist International founded in 1864.

Marx, Wilhelm 250

1863–1946, German jurist and politician. Member of the Prussian Chamber of Deputies 1899–1918 and of the *Reichstag* 1910–18 and 1920–32. Member of the Weimar National Assembly in 1919 and of the Prussian provincial assembly. Centrist parliamentary group leader in 1912–23 and party leader in 1922–8. Chancellor in 1923–5. Thereafter prime minister of Prussia. Defeated by Hindenburg in 1925 in the elections for *Reichspräsident*. Minister of justice in 1926 and once again chancellor in 1926–8.

Max von Baden, Prince 229–30, 234

1867–1929, succeeded to the Baden throne due to the childlessness of Archduke Friedrich II. Advocated a conciliatory peace during the First World War. On 3 October 1918 named chancellor of the first coalition cabinet of the German Empire. Negotiated with President Wilson on the basis of the latter's 'fourteen points'. Announced on his own initiative the abdication of William II on 9 November 1918.

Maximilian I 17

1459–1519, German emperor in 1493. Created the Imperial Chamber of the Holy Roman Empire at the Worms *Reichstag*. Proclaimed the 'eternal land peace'. Dürer's patron.

Mayer, Julius Robert 98

1814–78, German physician and

physicist. Established the law of the preservation of energy.

Mehmed Ali Pasha 67
pseudonym of Karl Detroit, 1827–78, Turkish general of German origin. Arrived in Constantinople in 1843 as a cabin-boy. Became an officer in 1853. Led an army corps in Bosnia in 1875–7. Supreme commander of the Turkish army in Bulgaria during the Russo-Turkish war. Killed in 1878 by Albanian rebels.

Meinecke, Friedrich 174, 251
1862–1954, German historian. Professor in Strasbourg, Freiburg and Berlin. Opposed annexationist war aims during the First World War. Rejected National Socialism and was dismissed in 1935 from his position as editor of the *Historische Zeitschrift*.

Meinhof, Ulrike 382
1934–76, German journalist. Became a terrorist and lived underground after 1970. Arrested in 1972. Committed suicide in 1976.

Meissner, Otto 260
1880–1953, German diplomat. In 1919 councillor in the chancery of the *Reichspräsident* and in 1920 chief of the chancery. After 1923 secretary of state under Ebert, Hindenburg and Hitler.

Mendel, Gregor Johann 98
1822–84, Austrian geneticist. Secondary school teacher, then Augustinian abbot in Brünn.

Menzel, Adolph von 186
1815–1905, German painter and graphic artist. Became famous for his pen-and-ink illustrations on wood of Kugler's *Geschichte Friedrichs d. Grossen*. As a painter, he anticipated impressionism.

Metaxas, Joannis
1871–1941, Greek general and politician. Chief of staff 1915–17. Supported King Constantine I's neutrality policies. In exile 1917–20 and again in 1923 after failed military putsches. Minister 1928–36. Encouraged the return of King George II. Prime minister in 1936. Became head of government for life in 1938. Rejected the Italian ultimatum of October 1940 and came to symbolise the Greek resistance.

Metternich, Klemens Wenzel Nepomuk Lothar, Count von, Prince von in 1813 47, 51, 55, 57, 59, 70, 74, 76, 114
1773–1859, Austrian statesman. Envoy to Dresden 1801–3 and to Berlin 1803–5. Ambassador to Paris 1806–9. Foreign minister in 1809. Brought about Austria's entry into the Prusso-Russian alliance against Napoleon. Presided over the Congress of Vienna in 1814. Concluded the Holy Alliance in 1815. Became chancellor in 1821 and chairman of the ministerial conference on internal affairs in 1826. Member of the Privy Conference of State in 1835. Fled to England in 1848. Returned to Vienna in 1851.

Meyendorff, Peter Baron 82
1796–1863, Russian diplomat of German origin. Participated in 1812–13 in the campaigns against Napoleon. Envoy to Stuttgart in 1832 and to Berlin in 1839. Became ambassador to Vienna in 1850, where he attempted to mediate between Prussia and Austria. Recalled in 1854.

Michaelis, Georg 218
1857–1936, German politician. Undersecretary of state in the Prussian ministry of finance in

1909. Chief of the grain office in 1915. Prussian commissar of state for the distribution of food in February 1917. Bethmann Hollweg's successor in 1917 as chancellor and Prussian prime minister. Dismissed on 1 November 1917. President in chief of Pomerania in 1918. Thereafter influential in the German Evangelical Revival Movement.

Mierendorff, Carlo 312
1897–1943, German politician. After involvement in the labour movement became an SPD *Reichstag* deputy in 1930. In a concentration camp 1933–8. After his release, joined the Kreisau circle. Killed in an aerial attack on Leipzig.

Molotov, Vyacheslav Mikhailovich 299, 305
(pseudonym after 1906 of V. M. Skryabin), 1890–1986, Soviet politician. Co-founder and editor-in-chief of *Pravda* (1912). Member of the revolutionary military committee in 1917–18. Close collaborator of Stalin. Chairman of the council of people's commissars 1926–41. Foreign minister 1939–49 and 1953–6.

Moltke, Helmuth von, Count von in 1870 150
1800–91, Prussian field marshal. Chief of the army general staff 1858–88. Directed operations in the war against Austria (1866) and in the Franco-Prussian war (1870/71). Entered the Prussian House of Lords in 1872. Eminent military writer.

Moltke, Helmuth von 216
1848–1916, German general. Quartermaster-general in 1903. Chief of the general staff in 1906. Resigned in 1914 after the German setback in the battle of the

Marne. Chief of the deputy general staff in Berlin in 1915.

Moltke, Helmuth James Count von 313
1907–45, German jurist. Opposed National Socialism and founded the Kreisau circle. Arrested in January 1944. Condemned to death and executed in January 1945.

Monroe, James 61, 200
1758–1831, fifth president of the United States (1817–25). Democrat. Governor of Virginia 1799–1802 and 1810. In 1803 concluded the Louisiana purchase in Paris. Secretary of state in 1811. Secretary of war in 1814. Acquired Florida from Spain in 1819. Proclaimed the Monroe doctrine in 1823.

Montesquieu, Charles de Secondat Baron de la Brède et de Montesquieu 34
1689–1755, French political philosopher and writer. President of the Bordeau senate 1716–26. Travelled through several European countries studying political conditions. Originated the political theory of the separation of powers.

Montgomery, Bernard Law, Viscount M. of Alamein in 1946 310, 315, 334
1887–1976, British field marshal. Supreme commander of the eighth army in the Second World War. In 1943 supreme commander of the British invasion. Commander of the British occupation zone in Germany in 1945–8 and member of the Allied Control Council in Berlin. Deputy supreme commander of NATO forces in 1951–8.

Morse, Samuel 97
1791–1872, American inventor

and portrait painter. Co-founder and first director of the National Academy of Design in New York. Invented the electromagnetic telegraph and developed Morse code. In 1844 established the first telegraph between Washington D.C. and Baltimore.

Motz, Friedrich von 66
1775–1830, Prussian statesman. Tax receiver in the Kingdom of Westphalia 1803–13. President in chief of the province of Saxony 1821–5. As minister of finance, reformed the financial administration and concluded a tariff agreement with Hesse-Darmstadt in 1828.

Mozart, Wolfgang Amadeus 38
1756–91, Austrian composer. Concert master of the archbishop's orchestra in Salzburg after 1769. Three journeys to Italy in 1769–73. Archbishop's organist 1779–80. Lived in Vienna after 1780 as an independent musician. Stands in the tradition of Viennese classicism between Haydn and Beethoven and had the greatest range of any composer.

Müller, Hermann 241, 342
1876–1931, German politician. Joined the SPD in 1893 and entered the party executive in 1906. *Reichstag* deputy 1916–18 and 1920–31. Member in 1918 of the Berlin executive council of the workers' and soldiers' soviets. Chairman of the party and its parliamentary group 1919–27. Foreign minister 1919–20. Together with Bell signed the Treaty of Versailles. Chancellor in 1920 and 1928–30.

Müller, Joseph 342
1898–1979, German jurist and politician. Before 1933 in the Ba-varian People's Party, then legal adviser to church institutions. In 1939 entered the intelligence unit of the army supreme command. In 1939–40 explored through the Vatican the possibility of a conciliatory peace with England on behalf of the Beck/Canaris/Oster group. Arrested in 1943. Helped found the CSU in 1945. Provincial chairman 1945–9. Bavarian minister of justice 1947–9 and deputy prime minister. Minister of justice again 1950–2.

Münzer, Thomas 24
ca. 1489–1525, German theologian, Augustinian monk. An early supporter of Martin Luther. In 1523 founded the League of Faithful and Divine Will with the goal of creating a divine, socialist state. Intellectual leader of the peasant army which was annihilated near Frankenhausen. Captured in 1525 and executed.

Mussolini, Benito 246, 287, 290–1, 293–4, 296, 302, 310, 317
1883–1945, Italian politician. Elementary school teacher in 1901. Joined the Socialist Party. Became editor-in-chief of the party newspaper *Avanti* in 1912. Had a major influence on the ideological direction of the party, which expelled him however when he advocated Italian entry into the war. In November 1914 founded the daily newspaper *Il Popolo d'Italia*. Took part in the war 1915–17. In March 1919 founded the *Fasci di Combattimento* which he transformed into the National Fascist Party in November 1921. After the march on Rome in 1922, eliminated his political opponents and changed the constitutional system. Fascist *Duce* and head of government.

Conciliatory policy towards the church. Abyssinian war in 1935. Intervened in the Spanish civil war in 1936 and entered the Second World War in 1940. Military setbacks. Opposition from within the fascist party. Deposed and arrested on the instructions of Victor Emanuel III. Freed in 1943 by German paratroopers. Created the 'Republica Sociale Italiana' in northern Italy. Shot on 28 April 1945 by Italian partisans while fleeing into Switzerland.

Nachtigal, Gustav 169
1834–85, German explorer of Africa, military doctor. In Algeria and Tunis after 1863. Brought Togo, the Cameroons and German Southwest Africa under German sovereignty.

Napoleon I 41–54, 88, 92, 94, 95
Originally Napoleone Buonaparte, later Napoleon Bonaparte, 1769–1821, emperor of the French. Lieutenant in 1785, general in 1793. Suppressed the royalist uprising in 1795. Became supreme French commander in Italy in 1796 and in Egypt 1798–9. Premature return to Paris in 1799. Coup d'état on 18 Brumaire (9 Nov. 1799). First consul for ten years, elected for life by plebiscite in 1802. Crowned emreror of the French in 1804 and king of Italy in 1805. Deposed in 1814. Given the island of Elba for his principality. After returning from Elba, the hundred days of renewed Napoleonic rule. Permanently exiled to St Helena in 1815.

Napoleon III 71, 93–5, 117–23, 133–5, 138–41
actually Charles Louis Napoleon Bonaparte, 1808–73, emperor of

the French. President of the republic in 1848 after a coup d'état. Confirmed in office for ten years in 1851 and finally named emperor in a popular referendum. Captured and deposed in the Franco-Prussian war of 1870–1.

Nasser, Gamal Abdel 324
1918–70, Egyptian officer and politician. Distinguished himself as a colonel in 1948 in the first Arab-Israeli war. Participated in founding the Committee of Free Officers which overthrew King Faruk I in July 1952. Member of the Revolutionary Council. Supreme commander of the armed forces. In 1953 deputy prime minister and minister of the interior. President of Egypt in 1954–61. Leading spokesman of the non-aligned movement alongside Nehru and Tito.

Naumann, Friedrich 181
1860–1919, German politician and Evangelical theologian. Sought to win over the working class to Christian socialism and collaboration with the state. Repeatedly a member of the *Reichstag* between 1907 and 1918. Chairman of the Democratic Party and a member of the National Assembly in Weimar in 1919.

Neurath, Konstantin Baron von 250, 290, 295
1873–1956, German diplomat. Envoy to Copenhagen in 1919. Ambassador to Rome in 1921 and to London in 1930. Foreign minister 1932–8. *Reichsprotektor* in Bohemia and Moravia in 1939–43. Sentenced in 1946 by the Nuremberg tribunal to fifteen years imprisonment. Released in 1954.

Nicholas I, Pavlovich 118
1796–1855, tsar of Russia in 1825. Suppressed the Decembrist up-

rising and created an autocratic regime. Successful wars against Persia and Turkey. Made Poland a Russian province after the uprising of 1830–1. In 1849 helped Austria to crush the revolution in Hungary. Waged the Crimean War.

Nicholas II, Alexandrovich 224
1868–1918, tsar of Russia in 1894. Was compelled by the revolution of 1905 to agree to a constitution, which he partly rescinded in 1907. Decided to go to war in 1914 to preserve Russian influence in the Balkans. Assumed personal command of the armed forces in 1915. Abdicated after the February revolution in response to popular pressure (15 March 1917), was arrested and exiled to Siberia. In July 1918 was murdered by the Bolsheviks together with his family in Ekaterinburg.

Nicholas II 11
ca. 980–1061, pope in 1058. Triumphed over Benedict X in Rome in 1059. Strengthened the influence of the College of Cardinals over papal elections (papal election decree of 1059).

Niebuhr, Barthold Georg 38, 44
1776–1831, German historian and diplomat. Served the Danish and Prussian states till 1810. Professor in Berlin 1810–12. Prussian envoy to the Holy See 1816–32, then professor in Bonn.

Niemöller, Martin 281, 312
1892–1984, German Evangelical theologian. U-boat commander during the First World War. Studied theology after the war. Managing director of the Home Missions in Westfalia 1924–30. Pastor in Berlin-Dahlem in 1931. Member of the Confessional church during the Third *Reich.* Arrested in 1937, sent to the concentration camp in Sachsenhausen and then to Dachau in 1941. President of the Evangelical church in Hessen and Nassau in 1947–64. Staunch pacifist.

Nietzsche, Friedrich Wilhelm 184–5
1844–1900, German philosopher. Professor of classical philology in Basle 1869–79. Lived in various areas of Switzerland and Italy after 1879 because of progressive nerve disease. Radical critic of all values. Greatly influenced existentialism and twentieth-century *Lebensphilosophie.* Aphoristic style gives broad scope to interpretations of his thought.

Nolde, Emil 285
actually Emil Hansen, 1867–1956, German painter and graphic artist. Member of *Die Brücke.* Defamed in 1933 as a degenerate artist. Forbidden to paint in 1941.

Noske, Gustav 236
1868–1946, German politician. Entered the *Reichstag* in 1906. Federal government agent and governor of Kiel in 1918. Member of the Council of People's Representatives and placed in charge of military affairs. Suppressed a series of leftist uprisings in various areas (January to March 1919) and was denounced as a 'traitor to the working class'. Resigned after the Kapp putsch in response to pressure from his own party (SPD). President in chief of the Hanover region in 1920–33. Strong opponent of National Socialism. Arrested after 20 July 1944.

Nossack, Hans Erich 336
b. 1901, German writer. Studied law and philosophy till 1922. Forbidden to publish in 1933.

Lost all his manuscripts in 1943. Independent writer after 1956. Guest lecturer in poetics at the university of Frankfurt a. M. in 1957. Awarded the Georg-Büchner prize in 1961.

Ollenhauer, Erich 339
1901–63, German politician (SPD). Joined the *Sozialistische Arbeiterjugend* in 1916 and became its chairman in 1928. After 1933, member of the SPD executive in exile in Prague, Paris and London. Returned to Germany in 1946. Deputy party chairman of the western zone SPD. Entered the *Bundestag* in 1949 and became deputy chairman of the SPD parliamentary group. As leader of the party and of the parliamentary opposition, continued Schumacher's policies after his death and also advocated the transformation of the SPD into a party with broad appeal to all strata of the population. Vicepresident of the Socialist International in 1951 and president in 1963.

Oster, Hans 313
1887–1945, German general. Joined the intelligence unit in the ministry of defence in 1933. From 1935 to 1943 led the central office of military intelligence and was chief of the foreign intelligence office under Admiral Canaris. Strong opponent of Hitler's regime. By virtue of his access to information, became the organisational centre of army resistance to Hitler. In the winter of 1939–40 kept the Dutch, Danes and Norwegians informed about the continually shifting dates on which their countries were to be attacked. Arrested after 20 July 1944 and murdered in the Flossenbürg concentration camp on 9 April 1945.

Otto I, the Great 9, 10
912–73. Elected German king in 936 and crowned emperor in 962.

Otto II 9
955–83. Elected German king in 961, ruled after 973. Joint emperor with his father Otto I after 967.

Otto III 9
980–1002. Became German king in 983 under the guardianship of his mother Theophanu and then under his grandmother Adelheid till 995. Crowned emperor in 996.

Otto, Nikolaus August
1832–1891, German engineer and inventor. Worked after 1862 on developing a gas engine. Founded a gas engine factory in 1864 and in 1876 invented the Otto carburrettor engine.

Papen, Franz von 260–3, 277, 279
1879–1969, German politician. Joined the Centre Party in 1918. Sat in the Prussian *Landtag* 1920–8 and 1930–2. Chancellor in June 1932. Resigned in December 1932. Vice-chancellor in Hitler's cabinet. Placed under house arrest in 1934. Thereafter German envoy to Vienna. Ambassador to Ankara 1938–44.

Paulsen, Friedrich 185
1846–1908, German philosopher and pedagogue. Professor in Berlin after 1878. Advocated the ethic of modern humanism.

Paulus, Friedrich 309
1890–1957, German field marshal. After helping to build up the German tank force, became lieutenant-general and quartermaster-in-chief of the army general staff in 1940. In January 1942

was given supreme command over the sixth army, which he sacrificed at Hitler's command. A Russian prisoner-of-war with the remnants of the sixth army till 1953. Member of the National Committee of Free Germany. Settled in the GDR in 1953.

Pestalozzi, Johann Heinrich 46
1746–1827, Swiss pedagogue. Foremost originator of modern pedagogy. Founded and directed various educational institutions.

Pétain, Henri Philippe 302
1856–1951, French marshal and chief of state. After proving himself as a military commander ('the saviour of Verdun'), was made commander-in-chief of the French forces in May 1917. Inspector-general of the army 1922–32. Minister of war in 1934. Ambassador to Spain in 1939. Became prime minister in June 1940 after the Reynaud government resigned. Concluded the peace treaty with Germany and Italy on 22 June 1940. Vichy chief of state, endowed with plenipotentiary powers by the National Assembly. Some cooperation with Hitler. In April 1945 Pétain was tried before the French supreme court and in August 1945 was condemned to death for treason. His sentence was commuted by de Gaulle to life imprisonment and banishment to the island of Yeu.

Peter I, the Great 30
1672–1725, Russian tsar in 1682, at first under a regent. In 1697 visited western Europe incognito. Reformed Russia after the western model and established modern Russia as a great power.

Peters, Karl 170
1856–1918, German colonial

politician. In 1884 founded the Society for German Colonisation. By means of treaties acquired the nucleus of what later became German East Africa, which was taken under German sovereignty in 1885. In 1887 concluded a leasing deal with Zanzibar and in 1889–90 a protective agreement with Uganda. Cofounder of the Pan-German League.

Petrarch, Francesco 19–20
1304–74, Italian writer. Studied in Italy and at the papal court in Avignon, France. Crowned poet laureate in Rome in 1341.

Pfitzner, Hans 186
1869–1949, German composer. Worked as a conductor and teacher in Berlin and Munich 1908–18. City director of music and opera in Strasbourg. At the Prussian Academy of Arts in Berlin in 1920–9 and then at the Academy of Music in Munich till 1934.

Philip II of Spain 28
1527–98, king after 1555. Waged war against France 1556–9, against Turkey in 1571 and against the rebellious Netherlands in 1567. Strife with England led to the destruction of the Spanish armada in 1588. As the Catholic champion, Philip was the dominant figure in the counter-reformation.

Pilsudski, Josef
1867–1935, Polish politician. Leader of the Polish Socialist Party after 1894. Advocated Polish political autonomy and founded a military liberation organisation. In 1916 led an abortive uprising in Russian-occupied Poland. Imprisoned in 1917 in the fortress of Magdeburg. Re-

turned to Warsaw in 1918. Took control of the state and the army. After military conflict with Russia in 1920, withdrew temporarily from political life. In May 1926 formed an authoritarian regime with the help of the army. Sought to protect Poland by concluding non-aggression pacts with the Soviet Union and Germany.

Pius VII 60

1742–1823. Became pope in 1800. Concluded a concordat with France in 1801. Crowned Napoleon I in Paris in 1804. Rome was occupied by French troops in 1808 and in 1809 the papal states were joined to France and Pius was taken captive. Returned to Rome in 1814. The papal states were restored in 1815.

Pius IX 70, 154

1792–1878. Became pope in 1846. Very popular at first because of his liberal reforms and support for the Italian unification movement, but after an uprising in Rome was forced to flee to Gaeta. Rome was incorporated into the Kingdom of Italy in 1870. Promulgated the dogma of papal infallibility. His resistance to modern ideas isolated the church.

Poincaré, Raymond 244, 248

1860–1934, French statesman. Prime minister and foreign minister 1912–13. Sought alliances with Russia and England. President of the republic 1913–20. As chairman of the reparations commission in 1920 insisted on a strict interpretation of the Treaty of Versailles. Sabotaged the world economic conference convened in Genoa by Lloyd George to settle German reparations payments. Initiated the occupation of the Ruhr and encouraged separatism

in the Rhineland. Became prime minister for the third time in 1926. Retired in 1929 for reasons of health.

Polo, Marco 200

1254–1324, Venetian explorer. Went to northern China with his father and uncle in 1271 and remained in the service of the ruler of Mongolia from 1275 to 1292. Governor of Kiang-nan province. Returned to Europe in 1292. His description of his travels greatly influenced the knowledge of geography in the fourteenth and fifteenth centuries.

Ponto, Jürgen 382

1923–77, German banker. Spokesman for the board of the Dresdner Bank. Murdered by the Red Army faction.

Popitz, Johannes 313

1884–1945, German politician. Secretary of state in the finance ministry 1925–9. Prussian minister of finance 1933–44. When the Second World War began, took up ties to the resistance movement around Beck and Goerdeler. Arrested on 20 July 1944. Executed in 1945.

Posadowsky-Wehner, Arthur Count von, Baron von Postelwitz 190–1

1845–1932, German politician. Secretary of state after 1893 and simultaneously vice-chancellor and Prussian minister of state in 1897–1907. Member of the *Reichstag* 1912–18. German National member of the National Assembly in 1919 and of the Prussian *Landtag* 1928–32.

Primo de Riviera y Orbaneja, Miguel Marqués de Estella

1870–1930, Spanish general and dictator. Captain-general of Catalonia in 1922. Together with Alfonso XIII carried out a putsch in 1923 against the parliamentary government. Created a military dictatorship in 1925. Dismissed by the king in 1930 in response to public pressure.

Puttkamer, Johanna von 116
1824–1894, became Otto von Bismarck's wife in 1847.

Radek, Karl 236
actually K. Sobelsohn, 1885–1939, Soviet politician. Became acquainted with Lenin and the Bolshevik leaders in Switzerland in 1904. In Warsaw during the revolution of 1905. Moved to Germany in 1907 and worked as a journalist for the SPD. Collaborated with the Bolshevik central committee in Russia in 1917. Sent to Germany in late 1918 and represented the Russian Communist Party at the founding of the Communist Party of Germany. In March elected *in absentio* to the central committee of the Russian Communist Party. Returned to Russia in 1920. Deprived of all his positions in 1924 as a Trotskyite and expelled from the party in 1927. After capitulating to Stalin, was readmitted in 1929 and worked as a journalist. Was arrested in 1936 and sentenced in a show trial to ten years imprisonment.

Raeder, Erich Hermann Albert
1876–1960, German grand admiral. Served in the imperial German navy 1894–1918. After the war, was summoned to the central office of the navy department. Inspector of naval education in 1922. Commander of light naval forces on the North Sea in 1924 and chief of Baltic operations in 1925. Chief of the navy command in 1928. Supreme commander of the German navy 1935–43. Disagreed with Hitler on the question of large surface ships and compelled to cede naval supreme command to Dönitz. Sentenced to life imprisonment by the Nuremberg Tribunal in 1946. Released prematurely in 1955 for reasons of health.

Raleigh, Sir Walter 1
ca. 1552–1618, English seafarer. Favourite of Queen Elizabeth I. In 1585 founded the first British settlements in North America. Accused of treason under James I and held in the Tower of London 1603–16. Undertook an expedition to Guiana in 1617 and was executed when it failed.

Ranke, Leopold, von in 1865 38
1795–1886, German historian. Professor in Berlin after 1825. In 1859 became chairman of the Historical Commission of the Academy of Sciences in Munich. Founded the modern study of history.

Rapacki, Adam 364
1909–70, Polish politician. After studying economics, found employment at the Warsaw Institute of Economic Research. German prisoner-of-war 1933–45. Entered the Polish Socialist Party in 1945. Played a leading role in 1948 in the unification of the Socialist Party and the Communist Workers' Party. Member of the central committee 1948–68. Minister of shipbuilding 1949–50 and of universities 1950–6. Foreign minister 1956–68.

Rathenau, Walther 220, 243
1867–1922, German industrialist and politician. Joined the board of the Allgemeine Elektrizitäts-Gesellschaft (AEG) in 1899. In 1914–15, head of the depart-

ment of raw materials essential to
the war effort in the war ministry.
Economic adviser to the federal
government after 1918. Member
of the socialisation commission in
1920. Minister of reconstruction
in 1921. Foreign minister in 1922.
Participated in the reparations
conference of Genoa and concluded the Treaty of Rapallo.
Diffamed by nationalist and
anti-Semitic circles for attempting to fulfil the terms of the
Treaty of Versailles. Murdered
on 22 June 1922 by a secret
right-wing organisation.

Reger, Max 186
1873–1916, German composer.
University music director in
Leipzig after 1907. Considered an
intermediary between late romanticism and modernism.

Reichwein, Adolf 312
1898–1944, German pedagogue.
In 1930–3 professor of history
and citizenship studies at the pe-
dagogical university in Halle.
Was dismissed for opposing
National Socialism. Became a
village teacher in 1933. Member
of the Kreisau circle in 1942–4.
Arrested on 5 July 1944. Condemned to death after 20 July and
executed.

Reinhardt, Walther 228
1872–1930, German general.
Chief of general staff of the
Württemberg army corps in the
First World War. Last Prussian
minister of war in 1919. In October 1919 named first chief of
the reorganised army command.
Forced to resign in 1920 after the
Kapp putsch, against which he
had wanted to deploy the *Reichswehr.*

Reuter, Ernst 347
1889–1953, German politician.

Joined the SPD as a young man.
After 1918 helped to build up the
KPD's Berlin organisation. Secretary-general of the KPD in 1921.
Expelled from the party in 1922
and returned to the SPD. Head of
the Berlin transportation department 1926–31. Mayor of Magdeburg 1931–3. Sat in the *Reichstag*
1932–3. Imprisoned in a concentration camp 1933–5. A government adviser and professor in
Turkey in 1935–46. Again head
of the Berlin transportation department in 1946. Elected mayor
of Berlin in 1947, but prevented
from taking office till 1948 by a
Soviet veto. Governing Mayor of
Berlin in 1950–3. In 1948–9 led
the resistance against the Berlin
blockade.

Rhodes, Cecil 194, 197
1853–1902, English politician.
Gained great wealth and political
influence through the acquisition
of diamond fields. Became a
member of parliament in Cape
Colony in 1881. In 1885 orchestrated the British occupation of
Bechuanaland, and then the acquisition of what later became
Rhodesia by the British South
Africa Company founded in
1889. Prime minister of Cape
Colony after 1890. Encircled the
Boer Transvaal Republic. Resigned in 1896.

Ribbentrop, Joachim von 294, 296,
299
1893–1946, Nazi politician. Joined
the National Socialists in 1932
and became Hitler's chief adviser
on foreign policy. Concluded the
Anglo-German naval agreement
of 1935 as ambassador with special responsibilities. Ambassador
to London 1936–8. Foreign minister and SS-*Obergruppenführer*

1938–45. Condemned to death by the Nuremberg Tribunal and executed.

Ricardo, David 90, 106
1772–1823, English economist. Successful banker. Became an MP in 1819. Developed Adam Smith's classical economic theories. A leading proponent of free trade.

Rödiger, Georg Ludwig Julius Konrad 59
1794–1866, German *Burschenschaftler.* Student in Heidelberg 1814–16, in Worms 1816–17 and then in Jena till 1819. Took part in the *Wartburgfest* in 1817. Graduated in philosophy in 1819. Arrested in Berlin for participation in a revolutionary movement. Released in 1820 and expelled from Prussia. Appointed to a position as a secondary school teacher in Frankfurt in 1824.

Röhm, Ernst 280
1887–1934, Nazi politician. Company commander and general staff officer in the First World War. Formed a Free Corps in 1919 and joined the German Workers' Party (later National Socialist German Worker's Party). Resigned from the army in 1923. Organised the SA. Participated in the Hitler putsch. Nazi member of the *Reichstag* 1924–5. After friction with Hitler, became a military adviser in Bolivia 1928–30. Recalled by Hitler. SA chief of staff in 1931. Bavarian minister of state and federal minister without portfolio in 1933. In 1933–4 restructured and armed the SA as a militia force and rival to the army. Murdered on Hitler's orders on 1 July 1934.

Rössler, Constantin 123
1820–96, German political writer. Became a publicist for the Prussian government in 1860. Director of the official literary office in 1877. Legation counsellor in the Foreign Office in 1892–4.

Rommel, Erwin 303, 310, 313–14
1891–1944, German field marshal. In 1935 lieutenant-colonel and liaison officer on the staff of the *Reich* youth leader. Commander of a panzer division in 1940. Took over command of the Afrika corps in Libya in 1941. In 1942 field marshal and commander of the German-Italian panzer army in northern Africa. Commander-in-chief of army group B in Italy and then in northern France in 1943–44. Connections with the German resistance movement after the spring of 1944. When these came to light after 20 July, was forced by Hitler to commit suicide on 14 October 1944.

Roon, Albrecht von, Count von in 1871 125–6, 128
1803–79, Prussian general. Minister of war in 1859–73. Prime minister for a short period in 1873. Friend of Bismarck.

Roosevelt, Franklin Delano 268, 302, 307, 310, 316, 320–1, 324
1882–1945, thirty-second president of the United States (1933–45). Lawyer. Democratic senator in 1910. Assistant secretary of the navy in 1913. Governor of New York in 1924. Elected president in 1932. Re-elected in 1936, 1940 and 1944. Relinquished eastern Europe to Stalin in the Second World War.

Roosevelt, Theodore 200
1858–1919, twenty-sixth president of the United States

(1901–9). Jurist. As the champion of American expansionism in the office of the assistant secretary of the navy (1897–8), encouraged the war against Spain. Governor of New York in 1899–1900. Republican vice-president under McKinley in 1901. After McKinley's assassination, took over as president in 1901 and was re-elected in 1904.

Rosenberg, Alfred
1893–1946, Nazi ideologue, architect. Joined the National Socialists in 1921. Editor of the *Völkische Beobachter* in 1923 and alongside Goebbels the chief Nazi propagandist. In 1930 wrote *The Myth of the Twentieth Century*. As *Reichsleiter*, became head of the Nazi Foreign Office in 1933 and supervisor of Nazi ideological education in 1934. Minister of the occupied eastern territories in 1941–5, but failed to persuade Hitler and the *Reichskommissare* officially subordinate to him to favour the non Great-Russian national groups. In 1946 was condemned to death by the Nuremberg Tribunal for 'sowing racial hatred' and executed.

Rousseau, Jean-Jacques 37, 38
1712–78, French Swiss writer and cultural philosopher. Connected with the *encyclopédistes* in Paris after 1742. Was forced to leave France in 1766 and spent several years in Switzerland and England. Returned to Paris in 1770. Highly influential on the French Revolution, democratic demands and educational theory.

Rouvier, Maurice 207
1842–1911, French jurist and politician. Lawyer. Deputy of the moderate left 1871–1903. Senator 1903–11. Often a minister. Prime minister 1887–1905/6. Carried out the separation of church and state in 1905.

Runciman, Walter, Viscount R. of Doxford in 1937 293
1870–1949, English politician. Liberal or National Liberal member of parliament 1899–1937. Often a minister. In 1938 mediated between the Czechoslovak government and the Sudeten German Party (Runciman mission). The British posture in concluding the Munich accord was based on his report.

Salazar, Antonio de Oliveira
1889–1970, Portuguese politician. Professor of economics and public finance in 1917. Helped to found the Catholic Party. Deputy in 1921. Finance minister after a military coup in 1926. Prime minister 1932–68. Issued a corporatist constitution in 1933. Assisted Franco in the Spanish civil war 1936–9.

Salisbury, Robert Arthur Talbot Gascoyne-Cecil, Marquess of 168
1830–1903, English statesman. Secretary of state for India in 1866 and 1874–8. Foreign secretary 1870–80. Took over the Tory leadership in 1871. Prime minister 1885–92 and 1895–1902 and almost always foreign secretary as well till 1900. Advocated a strong imperial and colonial policy in Africa. Sought a compromise with France in the Fashoda crisis of 1898.

Sand, Karl Ludwig 59
1795–1820, German theology student. A fervent supporter of the *Burschenschaft* movement, he stabbed August von Kotzebue to death on 23 March 1819, prompt-

ing the issue of the Karlsbad Decrees. Executed in 1820.

Sauckel, Fritz
1894–1946, Nazi politician.
Gauleiter in Thuringia in 1927.
Prime minister and minister of
the interior 1932–3, *Reichsstatthalter* of Thuringia and Brunswick 1933–45. Plenipotentiary
for labour in 1942 and responsible for the mass deportation of
foreign workers to Germany.
Condemned by the Nuremberg
Tribunal in 1946 and executed.

Savigny, Friedrich Carl von 38
1779–1861, German jurist. Professor of civil law 1810–42. Prussian minister of justice 1842–8.
Originated the historical school
of jurisprudence.

Schacht, Hjalmar 247, 258, 283
1877–1970. German banker. Director of the National Bank in
1916. Joined the DDP in 1918.
Currency commissioner in 1923.
Introduced the *Rentenmark*.
President of the *Reichsbank*
1924–30 and 1933–9. Simultaneously minister of finance in
1934–7. Connections to Hitler
after 1930. Schacht's financial
policies formed the basis of the
Nazi job creation and rearmament programmes. Dismissed in
1937 after a disagreement with
Hitler. Contacts with the German resistance movement towards the end of the war. Held in a
concentration camp 1944–5.
Found not guilty by the Nuremberg Tribunal.

Schäfer, Hermann 349
1892–1966, German politician,
DDP then FDP after 1945. Deputy chairman of the Hamburg
FDP in 1946 and deputy chairman of the British zone FDP in
1947. Member of the Parliamen-

tary Council in 1948–9. Member
of the *Bundestag* 1949–53, chairman of the FDP parliamentary
group and *Bundestag* president.

*Scharnhorst, Gerhard Johann David,
von in 1804* 44, 46
1755–1813, Prussian general.
Head of the war department
1807–10. Chief of general staff in
1810. Carried out the Prussian
army reform. Set the stage for the
uprising against Napoleon. Blü-
cher's chief of staff in 1813.

Scheel, Walter 379
b. 1919, German politician.
Joined the FDP in 1946. Member
of the Nordrhein-Westfalen
Landtag 1950–3 and of the *Bundestag* 1953–74. Minister of economic cooperation 1961–6. Vice-
president of the *Bundestag*
1967–9. Party chairman 1968–74.
Foreign minister in 1969 and
alongside Willy Brandt the main
advocate of the new *Ostpolitik*.
Federal president 1974–9.

Scheidemann, Philipp 230, 234, 237,
241, 256,
1865–1939, German politician.
SPD *Reichstag* deputy 1903–18.
Member of the party executive
after 1911 and parliamentary
group chairman after 1913. Advocated a conciliatory peace.
Member of the Council of People's Representatives 1918–19
and of the Weimar National Assembly 1919–20. Prime minister
in February 1919. Resigned in
June 1919 in protest against the
Treaty of Versailles. *Reichstag*
deputy again 1920–33. Emigrated
after the Nazis seized power.

*Schiller, Johann Christoph Fried-
rich, von in 1802* 37, 116, 124
1759–1805, German writer. Grew
up in Marbach. Studied law, then
medicine 1773–80. Military doc-

tor 1780–82, then fled to Mannheim. Dramatist in Mannheim 1783–4. In 1785 accepted the invitation of his friend Körner to Leipzig and Dresden. Settled in Weimar in 1787 and in 1789 became a professor of history in Jena. Settled permanently in Weimar in 1799. Alongside Goethe the most important dramatist of Sturm und Drang German classicism. In his theoretical and aesthetic writings, the most influential representative of German idealism.

Schirach, Baldur von
1907–74, Nazi politician. Leader of the Nazi student league in 1927. *Reichsjugendführer* in 1931 and *Jugendführer des Deutschen Reiches* in 1933. Built up the state youth organisation (Hitler youth). In 1940–5 *Gauleiter* and *Reichsstatthalter* in Vienna. Condemned by the Nuremberg Tribunal in 1946 to 20 years in prison.

Schlegel, August Wilhelm, von in 1815
1767–1845, German writer and literary critic. Worked on Schiller's publications till 1797. Published *Athenäum* in 1798–1800. Lectured in Berlin 1801–4. Secretary and travel companion of Mme de Stäel 1804–17. After 1818 professor of art and literary history in Bonn.

Schlegel, Friedrich, von in 1815
1772–1829, German writer and critic. In Jena in 1796 and 1801. In Berlin 1797–1801. Co-publisher of *Athenäum*. Studied Sanscrit and ancient Persian in Paris 1802–4. Converted to Catholicism in 1808. Entered the literary, propagandistic and diplomatic service of the Austrian government in 1809. Legation

counsellor at the Frankfurt *Bundestag* 1815–18.

Schleicher, Kurt von 260, 262, 277
1882–1934, German general and politician. Political specialist on Groener's staff 1918–19 and then in the general army offices of General von Seeckt. In 1926 chief of the newly formed *Wehrmacht* section of the ministry of defence. In 1929 head of the ministry bureau under minister of defence Groener. In June 1932 minister of defence in Papen's cabinet, whom he replaced as chancellor in early December. Dismissed by Hindenburg at the end of January 1933. Murdered in the 'Röhm putsch' on 30 June 1934.

Schleiermacher, Friedrich Daniel Ernst 38, 60
1768–1834, German Protestant theologian and philosopher. Pastor at the Berlin Charité in 1796. Professor in Halle 1804–6. Helped to found the university of Berlin.

Schleyer, Hanns-Martin 382
1915–77, German industrialist. Member of the board of Daimler Benz AG. President of the Federation of German Employers' Associations in 1973 and of the German Industry Association in 1977. Kidnapped on 5 September 1977 by terrorists and discovered murdered on 18 October 1977.

Schlieffen, Alfred Count von 215
1833–1913, German field marshal. Took part in the wars of 1866 and 1870–1 as a Prussian general staff officer. Chief of the army general staff 1891–1905. Very successful at training general staff officers. The operations plan that he devised and which was named after him was only

posed the unification of the SPD and KPD. SPD chairman in 1946. Entered the *Bundestag* in 1949.

Schuman, Robert 325, 360
1886–1963, French politician. First a German citizen then, after the restitution of Alsace-Lorraine, a French citizen. A lawyer in 1912. A French deputy 1919–40. For a short period in 1940, undersecretary of state for Alsace-Lorraine. Deported to Germany in 1940, fled in 1942 and joined the French resistance. In 1944 helped to form the Mouvement Républicain Populaire, deputy of both constituent assemblies in 1945–6 and of the National Assembly in 1946–62. Minister of finance in 1946 and 1947, prime minister in 1947–8, foreign minister 1948–52, and minister of justice 1955–6. President of the European movement in 1955. First president of the European parliament in 1958–60, then its honorary president.

Schumann, Jürgen 382
1944–77, German airliner captain. Joined Lufthansa in 1967. Killed in 1977 in his airliner which had been commandeered by Arab terrorists.

Schurz, Carl 71, 81, 139
1829–1906, American politician and journalist of German background. Participated in the 1849 insurrection in Baden and the Palatinate. Emigrated to the United States in 1852. Joined the Republican Party and supported Lincoln in the election campaign. American envoy to Madrid 1861–2. Took part in the Civil War, ending as a Northern general. Senator from Missouri 1869–75. Helped to found the Liberal Republican Party in 1872.

Secretary of the Interior 1877–81.

Schuschnigg, Kurt von 291
1897–1977, Austrian politician, lawyer. Christian-Social representative on the National Council 1927–33. Minister of justice 1932–4 and also of education after 1933. Succeeded Dollfuss as chancellor in July 1934. Temporarily minister of education, minister of defence and foreign minister as well. Resigned in 1938 after the German invasion. Was arrested. Held in a concentration camp in 1941–5. Professor in St Louis, USA 1948–67. Returned to Austria in 1968.

Shuvalov, Paul Count 173
1830–1908, Russian general. Participated in the Crimean War and the war against Turkey 1877–8. Ambassador to Berlin 1885–94. Governor-general of Warsaw 1895–97.

Schwann, Theodor 98
1810–82, German anatomist and physiologist. Professor in Louvain and Liège.

Schwarzenburg, Felix Prince 79, 112, 113, 115
1800–52, Austrian statesman. Joined the diplomatic service in 1824. Became a lieutenant-general in 1848 and, after helping to put down the October insurrection in Vienna, prime minister. As a proponent of autocratic centralism, imposed a unitary constitution on Austria and dissolved the *Reichstag* by force of arms. Sought in vain to have the entire Habsburg realm admitted into the German Confederation. Compelled Prussia to accept the Olmütz agreement in 1850.

Schweinitz, Hans Lothar von 176
1822–1901, Prussian general.

Ambassador to Vienna 1869–76, then to St Petersburg till 1892.

Seeckt, Hans von 242, 259
1866–1936, German general. General staff officer in the First World War. Head of the newly created general army offices in 1919. Chief of army command in 1920. As the commander-in-chief of the military, Seeckt 'created' the new German army and prevented its integration into the Republic. Was dismissed in 1926. Member of the *Reichstag* (DVP) 1930–2. Helped to form the Harzburg Front. Military adviser to Chiang Kai-shek 1933 and 1934–5.

Seldte, Franz 262
1882–1947, German manufacturer and politician. In 1918 founded the *Stahlhelm* which was integrated into the SA in 1933. Opposed the Weimar Republic, fulfilment of the Treaty of Versailles and reconciliation with the West. *Reichskommissar* for the Labour Service 1933–4. Minister of labour 1933–45.

Severing, Carl 261
1875–1952, German politician. SPD deputy in the *Reichstag* 1907–11 and 1920–33. Member of the National Assembly 1919–20. Prussian minister of the interior 1920–6 and 1930–2. Federal minister of the interior 1928–30. Arrested for a short period in 1933. After the Second World War, was elected to the provincial parliament of Nordrhein-Westfalen.

Seyss-Inquart, Arthur 291
1892–1946, Austrian politician. Linked to the Austrian Nazis after 1931 and joined the party in 1938. Member of the council of state in 1937. At Hitler's insistence, named Austrian minister of

security and of the interior in February 1938. Became Austrian chancellor in March 1938. Paved the way for the German invasion and the *Anschluss* of Austria. *Reichstatthalter* for the East Mark 1938–9. Minister without portfolio 1939–45. As *Reichskommissar* for the occupied Netherlands in 1940–5, responsible for the exploitation of the Dutch economy and workforce, for various suppressive measures and for the deportation of Jews. Condemned to death by the Nuremberg tribunal in 1946.

Siebenpfeiffer, Philipp Jakob 64
1789–1845, German political writer and jurist. In 1815 administered the city of Landau on behalf of Austria. Joined the Bavarian civil service in 1816. Attempts to publish liberal newspapers blocked by censorship. Author of the Hambach Festival proclamation. Condemned to prison, fled to Alsace and then to Switzerland. After 1834, professor extraordinarius in Berne.

Siemens, Werner, von in 1888 97–8
1816–92, Prussian officer, industrialist. Established the science of electrotechnics. With Halske, founded the Siemens & Halske telegraph company in 1847. Invented the electric generator in 1866.

Simson, Eduard, von in 1888 80, 144
1810–99, German jurist and politician. Member of the Frankfurt National Assembly in 1848. Became its president in December 1848. As a member of the hereditary emperor group, led the deputation which offered the emperor's crown to Frederick William IV. Member of the Prussian Chamber of Deputies

1858–67. National-Liberal member of the *Reichstag* 1867–77. President of the imperial court in Leipzig 1867–91.

Smith, Adam 88–90, 99
1723–90, Scottish political economist and moral philosopher. Professor of moral philosophy in Glasgow 1752–63. Founded classical economics. Chief proponent of early liberalism.

Speer, Albert 317
1905–81, German architect and Nazi politician. Joined the National Socialists in 1931. Superintendent of construction in Berlin in 1937. Minister of arms and munitions in 1942. Inspector-general of German roads, water and energy. Condemned in 1946 to twenty years imprisonment.

Spinoza, Baruch de 116
1632–77, Dutch philosopher of Jewish Portuguese heritage. Excommunicated by the Jewish community in 1656. Advocated a utilitarian concept of the state, founded rational biblical criticism and encouraged religious tolerance. His undogmatic, immanent criticism of religion influenced Lessing, Herder, Goethe and German idealism.

Stadion, Johann Philipp, Count von S.-Warthausen 47
1763–1824, Austrian statesman. As envoy to London, Berlin and Petersburg, encouraged the formation of a great coalition against Napoleon. Foreign minister 1805–9. His plan for a general German uprising against Napoleon failed. Replaced by Metternich. Minister of finance after 1816.

Stalin, Joseph (Iosif Vissarionovich)

267, 269, 296–7, 299, 305, 307, 311, 316, 320, 328–9, 331, 347–8 (originally Dzhugashvili), 1879–1953, Soviet dictator. Entered a seminary for orthodox priests in Tiflis in 1894. Expelled in 1899 for spreading Marxist ideas. Joined the Russian Social Democratic Party. Contacts with Lenin after 1905. Repeatedly exiled between 1907 and 1917. Joined the central committee of the Russian Communist Party and the *Pravda* editorial staff. In March 1917 returned to Petrograd from Siberia. Political commissar in the civil war and commissar of nationalities. In 1919 member of the organisational and political bureau. General-secretary in 1922. Greatly intensified industrialisation and the ruthless collectivisation of agriculture beginning in 1928. Liquidated all real and supposed opponents in the party, the army and the state after 1935. Adopted a clearly expansionist foreign policy. After the German attack on the Soviet Union, became chairman of the defence committee. Purposeful negotiating strategy at the wartime conferences with the western powers. Set the stage for the expansion of the Russian sphere of influence after 1945. Became Soviet chief of state in 1953.

Stanley, Henry Morton, Sir in 1899 197
actually John Rowlands, 1841–1904, English explorer. Became a correspondent for the *New York Herald* in 1867 and searched for Livingstone at its behest in 1869–71; found him in 1871. Explored the Congo basin 1879–84.

Starhemberg, Ernst Rüdiger Prince von 291

1899–1956, Austrian politician. Active after 1918 in self-defence and Free Corps units. Participated in the Hitler putsch in 1923. Joined the Austrian *Heimwehren* in 1927 and became their leader in 1930. Vice-chancellor 1934–6, succeeded Dollfuss, after his murder, as leader of the Patriotic Front. Advocated close association with Mussolini and resistance to Nazi Germany. Emigrated in 1937.

Stauffenberg, Claus Count Schenk von 313–14

1907–44, German officer. Chief of staff of a panzer division in Africa in January 1943. Severely wounded. In July 1944 chief of staff to the commander of the Home Army. In the summer of 1943 joined the resistance circle around Goerdeler, Beck and Witzleben. In order to remove Hitler, developed a detailed plan for an assassination and a putsch. This plan called for Stauffenberg both to carry out the assassination and to lead the uprising in Berlin. When the assassination attempt failed on 20 July 1944, Stauffenberg was arrested, condemned and immediately shot.

Stein, Karl Baron vom 44, 45, 46, 49, 60

1757–1831, German statesman. Joined the Prussian civil service in 1780. Supervised mining in Prussia's western provinces after 1784. President of all chambers of the Rhine-Westphalian provinces in 1796. Minister of finance, trade and economics in 1804. Initiated reforms in 1807–8, which he was prevented from completing by the intervention of Napoleon I. Dismissed in 1808. Became adviser to Tsar Alexander I in 1812.

Participated in the Congress of Vienna.

Stephan, Heinrich, von in 1885 149

1831–97, German politician. Organised the German postal service. Became director of postal services in the North German Confederation in 1870. Invented the post card, introduced the telephone, integrated the telegraph into the postal service, unified postal regulations and charges and in 1874 organised the world postal union.

Stephenson, George 92

1781–1848, American inventor. Invented the steam locomotive in 1814.

Stinnes, Hugo 235

1870–1924, German industrialist. One of the leading representatives of the coal and steel industry. DVP deputy in the *Reichstag* 1920–3. During the inflation, built the Stinnes concern into the largest company in Germany.

Stoecker, Adolf 172

1835–1909, German Protestant theologian and politician. Court and cathedral chaplain in Berlin 1874–89. Head of the Berlin city mission. Founded the Christian-Social Workers' Party in 1878. Anti-semite. Member of the Prussian Chamber of Deputies in 1879–98 and of the *Reichstag* 1881–93 and 1898–1908. Helped to found the Evangelical-Social Congress in 1890.

Strasser, Georg 262

1892–1934, Nazi politician. Joined the party in 1921. Participated in the Hitler putsch. *Reichstag* deputy in 1924–32. Took an anti-capitalist line. Increasingly Hitler's rival within the party. Became head of the

Nazi national organisation in 1932, but resigned demonstratively from all party positions in December. Murdered by the SS in 1934.

Strauss, Johann 186
1825–99, Austrian composer. Celebrated as the 'walz king' during his tours of Russia and the United States. Began to compose operettas in 1871. Originator of the Viennese operetta.

Strauss, Richard 186
1864–1949, German composer. Conducted in Munich, Weimar and Vienna.

Streicher, Julius
1885–1946, Nazi politician and elementary school teacher. Leader in 1919–22 of the German Socialist Party, which he merged into the National Socialists in 1922. Participated in the Hitler putsch of 1923. Nazi *Gauleiter* in Franconia 1924–40. Brutal and unscrupulous anti-semitic propagandist, main instigator of the anti-semitic pogroms. Condemned to death by the Nuremberg Tribunal in 1946 and executed.

Stresemann, Gustav 245–8, 251–4, 260, 288
1878–1929, German politician. National-Liberal deputy in the *Reichstag* 1907–12 and 1914–18. Advocated annexationist war aims during the First World War. Opposed Bethmann Hollweg and helped to topple him. Opposed the peace resolution of the *Reichstag* majority in July 1917. Helped to found the DVP in December 1918 and became its chairman. Chancellor from August to November 1923. Thereafter foreign minister in various cabinets till his death.

Struve, Gustav von 74
1805–70, Baden politician. Together with Hecker led the Offenburg Assembly in 1847. Played a leading role in the Baden insurrection of 1849. Fled to the United States and fought on the Northern side in the civil war.

Stülpnagel, Karl Heinrich von 314
1886–1944, German general. Quartermaster-general of the army general staff in 1938–40, then chairman of the Franco-German truce commission till December 1940. Served in Paris as military commander for France between February 1942 and July 1944. Leading member of the military resistance to Hitler and leader of the actions in Paris against the SS on 20 July 1944. Condemned to death by the People's Court and executed.

Stumpff, Hans Jürgen
1889–1968, German general. Head of the *Luftwaffe* personnel office in 1933–6. *Luftwaffe* chief of staff 1937–9. In 1940–3 commander of Air Fleet 1 in the West and then of Air Fleet 5 in Norway and Finland. Commander of the *Reich* Air Fleet in 1944–5. Co-signed the German capitulation in Berlin-Karlshorst.

Sun Yat-sen 268
1866–1925, actually Sun Wen, Chinese politician. Attended a mission school in Honolulu from 1879, became a Christian, and studied medicine in China 1886–92. Founded the League for the Renewal of China in 1894. Spent sixteen years in exile after a failed uprising in 1895. After the revolution of 1911 and the overthrow of the emperor, became president of the new Republic of China. His 'Second Revolution' failed in

1913. In Japan 1913–17. In 1917 and 1921 head of a counter-government in Canton, that was expelled in 1922. Returned to Canton in 1923. Accepted the Soviet offer of an alliance. Transformed the Kuomintang into a cadre party and created its army.

Sybel, Heinrich von 144
1817–95, German historian. Professor in Bonn, Marburg and Munich. Member of the Prussian Chamber of Deputies 1862–4 and opponent of Bismarck. National-Liberal deputy in the *Reichstag* in 1867. Member of the Chamber of Deputies in 1874–80. Director of the state archives in Berlin after 1875. Founded the *Historische Zeitung* in 1859.

Talleyrand, Charles Maurice de, after 1817 Duke de T. Prince de Benevent (1806–15) 52–3
1754–1838, French statesman. Bishop of Autun 1788–91. As a member of the estates general in 1789, advocated the expropriation of church property. In 1792, first diplomatic mission on behalf of the revolutionary French government. Expelled from France in 1794 for alleged contacts with the deposed king. Foreign minister 1797–1807. Opposed Napoleon's policy of conquest. At the Congress of Vienna orchestrated equal treatment for France as a great power. Resigned in 1815. Ambassador to London 1830–4.

Thälmann, Ernst 259
1886–1944, German politician. Transport labourer. Joined the SPD in 1903. In the First World War a member of the Independent Social Democrats, then the Communist Party. Entered the *Reichstag* in 1924. KPD chairman in 1925 and a candidate for *Reichspräsident* in 1925 and 1932. Arrested by the Nazis in January 1933 and shot in 1944 in the concentration camp of Buchenwald.

Thaer, Albrecht Daniel 99
1752–1828, German agronomist. Professor in Berlin. Founded in 1806 the first institute of higher agricultural studies. Founded the systematic science of agriculture.

Thiers, Adolphe 138, 142
1797–1877, French statesman and historian. Deputy in 1830. Repeatedly a minister 1832–5. Prime minister and foreign minister in 1836 and 1840. A conservative Republican after the February revolution of 1848. Exiled after Napoleon III's coup d'état in 1852. A deputy again in 1863. Led the opposition to Napoleon III's policies. Became president of the Republic in 1871. Clashed with the monarchistic majority in parliament and resigned in 1873.

Tieck, Ludwig
1773–1853, German writer. Studied in Halle and Göttingen, then became a writer. In 1794 began to retell the tales of the old German *Volksbücher* in his *Volksmärchen* and *Romantische Dichtungen*. In 1799 joined the early Romantic circle in Jena. Brought Spanish literature to the attention of the Romantics and explored medieval literature. Theatre adviser in Dresden 1819–42, then privy councillor in Berlin. Considered to be the most prolific and versatile of the early Romantics.

Tirpitz, Alfred, von in 1900 204, 210, 222
1849–1930, German admiral. Secretary of state in the navy de-

partment 1897–1916. Grand admiral in 1911. Initiated a systematic programme to build up the German navy and encouraged public support through the German Navy League which he had helped to found in 1898. Resigned in March 1916. DNVP *Reichstag* deputy 1924–8.

Tito, Josip 324
1892–1980, actually Broz. Yugoslav marshal and politician. Mechanic. Joined the Social Democrats in 1910. As a soldier in the Austro-Hungarian army, was captured by the Russians in 1915. Joined the Red Army in 1917 and the Yugoslav Communist Party in 1920. Secretary of the metal workers' union in 1927. Repeatedly arrested. Emigrated in 1934. Became a member in 1934 of the Yugoslav Communist Party central committee and politburo. Participated in the Spanish civil war 1936–8. Secretary-general of the Yugoslav Communist party in 1937. Organised the Yugoslav resistance to the German and Italian occupation after 1940. President of the Antifascist Council of National Liberation in 1943. Prime minister and minister of defence in 1945. Minister of state in 1953. After clashing with Stalin, deviated from Stalinism and pursued a Yugoslav path to socialism. A prominent spokesman of the non-aligned movement.

Tocqueville, Charles Alexis Henri Clérel Count de 90
1805–59, French historian, political theorist and politician. Member of the National Assembly in 1848. Foreign minister in 1849. One of the greatest political analysts of his day.

Treitschke, Heinrich von 128, 135, 170
1834–96, German historian and politician. Professor in Freiburg, Kiel, Heidelberg and Berlin after 1874. National Liberal deputy in the *Reichstag* 1871–84. Published the *Preussische Jahrbücher* 1866–89.

Tresckow, Henning von 313–14
1901–44, German general. Opposed the Nazi regime after 1938. On the general staff of the centre army group in 1941 and in 1944 chief of staff of the second army on the eastern front where he gathered a circle of like-minded officers. The assassination attempt on Hitler in which he was involved did not succeed. Committed suicide after 20 July 1944.

Troeltsch, Ernst 184
1865–1923, German Protestant theologian and philosopher of history. Professor in Bonn, Heidelberg and Berlin after 1914. In 1919–21 secretary of state for Evangelical affairs in the Prussian ministry of culture.

Trotsky, Leon Davidovich 225, 227, 269
(Cover name for Lev D. Bronstein), 1879–1940, Russian revolutionary politician. Took part in several attempts to overthrow the monarchy after 1897 and was exiled to Siberia. Fled abroad in 1902. Joined the Mensheviks in 1903 and opposed Lenin with his theory of 'permanent revolution'. Played a major role in the revolution of 1905. Was arrested and once more fled abroad. Returned to Russia after the February revolution. Joined the Bolsheviks. Chairman of the Military Revolutionary Committee formed on 9 October 1917. As foreign min-

ister led the Russian delegation to the peace negotiations in Brest-Litovsk. Commissar of war in 1918. Major contribution to the Bolshevik victory in the civil war. In the struggle to succeed Lenin, was defeated by the unscrupulous Stalin. Emigrated in 1929. Was murdered in Mexico in 1940 by an agent of the Soviet secret police.

Truman, Harry Spencer 324–5
1884–1972, thirty-third president of the United States. Judge. Democratic senator from Missouri in 1935. Roosevelt's vice-president in 1945. Became president after Roosevelt's death in 1945. Re-elected in 1948.

Ulbricht, Walther 365, 375
1893–1973, German politician. Cabinet-maker. Soldier 1915–18. Joined the SPD in 1912 and the KPD in 1919. Party secretary in Thuringia in 1921. Elected to the KPD central office in 1923. Went to Moscow in 1924. Returned to Germany in 1925. *Reichstag* deputy 1928–33. Emigrated to France in 1933 and to the Soviet Union in 1938. Returned to Germany after the war. Deputy chairman of the SED 1946–50. Member of the politburo after 1949. Secretary-general after 1950–3, then first secretary of the SED. First deputy chairman of the Council of Ministers in 1949–60. Chairman of the newly created Council of State and of the National Defence Council in 1960. Retired in 1971.

Urban II 13
1042–99, cardinal bishop of Ostia in ca. 1080. Pope in 1088. Continued the work of Gregory VII. Called for a crusade at the synods

of Piacenza and Clermont which he convened.

Varnhagen von Ense, Karl August 84
1785–1858, German writer. As a literary critic, supported *Junges Deutschland*.

Victor Emanuel II 121–2
1820–78, king of Sardinia 1849–61, king of Italy after 1861. The sole Italian ruler after 1848 to remain faithful to the liberal constitution. Gave Cavour a free hand in the unification of Italy. After Cavour's death, his popularity was a major factor in consolidating the kingdom of Italy.

Victoria of England 196
1819–1901, queen of Great Britain in 1837. Empress of India in 1876. Grandmother of William II.

Virchow, Rudolf 153
1821–1902, German pathologist. Founded cellular pathology. Professor in Berlin in 1856. Member of the Prussian Chamber of Deputies in 1862 and of the *Reichstag* 1880–93.

Vollmar, Georg Heinrich von 188
1850–1922, German politician. Member of the Bavarian Chamber of Deputies in 1893–1918 and of the *Reichstag* 1881–1918. Leader of the reformist wing of the SPD.

Voltaire 33, 116
1694–1778, actually François Marie Arouet, French philosopher and writer. In exile in England 1726–29. Member of the Académie française after 1746. Guest of Frederick the Great in Berlin 1750–3. Foremost representative of the French enlightenment.

Wagner, Richard 186
1813–85, German composer. Grew up in Leipzig. Kapellmeister in Magdeburg, Königsberg and Riga after 1834. Court Kapellmeister in Dresden in 1841. Fled to Switzerland in 1849. Summoned to Munich in 1864 by King Ludwig II of Bavaria. In Bayreuth after 1871. Foremost composer of German romantic opera. Saw opera as universal art. The production of his operas has become a great festival which every year draws many admirers to the Bayreuth theatre.

Waldersee, Alfred Count von 202
1832–1904, Prussian field marshal. Moltke's deputy in 1882. Chief of the general staff in 1888. His penchant for political involvement and his connections brought him into conflict with Bismarck. Supreme commander of the European contingent during the Boxer Rebellion of 1900–1.

Wallenstein, Albrecht Eusebius Wenzel von 29
1583–1634, duke of Friedland in 1625, duke of Mecklenburg and prince of Sagan in 1627. Military commander during the Thirty Years War. Served the Habsburgs and used his own estates as the basis of supply for his armies. In 1626 defeated Ernst II von Mansfeld and in 1627 drove Christian IV of Denmark from the mainland. The emperor did not pursue Wallenstein's far-reaching plans to create an absolute monarchy in the Holy Roman Empire. His dismissal in 1630 was engineered by the Spanish, the Jesuits and Maximilian of Bavaria. Was again appointed commander-in-chief of the emperor's forces in 1631.

In 1632 fought the battle of Lützen against King Gustav Adolf of Sweden, who died in the battle. His negotiations with Sweden, Brandenburg and Saxony on the creation of a third party and his refusal in 1633 to defend Bavaria and the Danube led to his dismissal. Accused of treason and abandoned by his army, he was murdered in 1634 by the Irish captain Devereux in the pay of the emperor.

Washington, George 36
1732–99, American general and first president of the United States (1789–97). Attended the continental congress in Philadelphia in 1774. Became commander-in-chief of the American forces in 1775. Presided over the constitutional convention in 1787. Unanimously elected president in 1789.

Watt, James 87, 89
1736–1819, English engineer. In 1765 invented the first useful low-pressure steam engine.

Weber, Max 113, 176
1864–1920, German social scientist and thinker. One of the originators of modern sociology. Professor of commercial and German law in Berlin in 1893. Professor of political economy in Freiburg, Heidelberg and Munich after 1894.

Weber, Wilhelm Eduard 97, 216
1804–91, German physicist. Professor in Leipzig and Göttingen. Together with Gauss constructed the first electromagnetic telegraph.

Wehner, Herbert 339
b. 1906, German politician. Joined the KPD in 1927. In 1929 became secretary of the Revolutionary

Union Opposition. Deputy secretary of the Saxony KPD in 1930. Member of the *Landtag* and deputy chairman of the parliamentary group. Emigrated to Moscow in 1937 and then to Sweden. Broke with the Communists in 1942. Joined the SPD in 1946 after returning to Germany. Entered the *Bundestag* in 1949. Chairman of the *Bundestag* committee on all-German affairs in 1949–66. Deputy party chairman in 1958–73. Minister of all-German affairs in 1966–9. Chairman of the SPD parliamentary group in 1969–83.

Weitling, Wilhelm 105
1808–71, German socialist. After living in Paris as a journeyman tailor, joined socialist circles. Joined the League of the Just in 1836. Participated in Blanqui's attempted revolution of 1839. Lived in New York after 1849.

Welcker, Karl Theodor 79
1790–1869, German politician and professor of constitutional law in Kiel, Heidelberg, Bonn and Freiburg. Together with Rotteck led the liberal opposition in the Baden chamber after 1831. Published the liberal *Staatslexikon*.

Welser 21
Old patrician Augsburg family. Founded large commercial enterprises (ca. 1500–61).

Werfel, Franz 285
1890–1945, Austrian writer. Expressionist lyric poet and dramatist. After publication of his first poems, became a publisher's reader in Leipzig 1912–14. Fought in the First World War 1915–17, then lived in Vienna as an independent writer. In 1938 emigrated to the United States by way of France, Spain and Portugal.

Werner, Anton von 186
1843–1915, German painter. Director of the Berlin Academy of Art in 1875.

Wichern, Johann Hinrich 103
1808–81, German Protestant theologian. Founded the *Rauhes Haus* in Hamburg in 1833. At the Wittenberg church conference of 1848 initiated the Home Missions. Senior consistorial councillor in Berlin in 1856. Foremost Protestant social reformer of the nineteenth century.

William I 81, 103, 111–12, 124–7, 130, 134, 140–1, 143–4, 163, 168–9.
1797–1888, German emperor and king of Prussia. Became first in line to the Prussian throne when his brother Frederick William IV, was crowned king. Fled to England in 1848 after an unsuccessful attempt to put down the revolution. After the revolt in Baden and the Palatinate was suppressed in 1849, became military governor of the Rhineland and Westphalia. Regent in 1858. King of Prussia in 1861. President of the North German Confederation 1867–71. Emperor 1871–88.

William II 171–5, 184 186–91, 204, 206–8, 210, 214–17, 221–2, 230
1859–1941, German emperor and king of Prussia (1888–1918).

Wilson, Thomas Woodrow 223, 229–30, 239, 266, 269, 320
1865–1924, twenty-eighth president of the United States (1913–21). Democrat. Professor of history and political economy at Princeton in 1890–1910. Governor of New Jersey in 1910–13. Nobel Peace Prize in 1919.

thedral of Zurich after 1518. First theological publication against the obligation to fast in 1522. The first and second Zurich disputations on his sixty-seven theses in 1523. Beginning of the Zurich reform. Mounting controversy with Luther after 1525 over transsubstantiation.

Subject Index

(Germany, England, France, Italy, Austria, Prussia, Russia and the
United States are not listed individually.)

497